SUPREME POWER

ALSO BY JEFF SHESOL

Mutual Contempt:
Lyndon Johnson, Robert Kennedy,
and the Feud that
Defined a Decade

SUPREME POWER

FRANKLIN ROOSEVELT vs. THE SUPREME COURT

Jeff Shesol

W. W. NORTON & COMPANY New York London

Printed in the United States of America
First Edition

For information about permission to reproduce
selections from this book, write to Permissions,
W. W. Norton & Company, Inc.,
500 Fifth Avenue, New York, NY 10110

For information about special discounts for bulk
purchases, please contact W. W. Norton Special Sales
at specialsales@wwnorton.com or 800-233-4830

Manufacturing by RR Donnelley, Harrisonburg
Book design by Dana Sloan
Production manager: Devon Zahn

Library of Congress Cataloging-in-Publication Data

Shesol, Jeff.
Supreme power : Franklin Roosevelt vs. the
Supreme Court / Jeff Shesol. — 1st ed.
p. cm.
Includes bibliographical references and index.
ISBN 978-0-393-06474-2 (hardcover)
1. United States. Supreme Court—History—20th century.
2. Political questions and judicial power—United States—
History—20th century. 3. United States—Politics and
government—20th century. 4. Roosevelt, Franklin D.
(Franklin Delano), 1882–1945—Political and social views.
I. Title.
KF8742.S495 2010
347.73'2609—dc22

2009046365

W. W. Norton & Company, Inc.
500 Fifth Avenue, New York, N.Y. 10110
www.wwnorton.com

W. W. Norton & Company Ltd.
Castle House, 75/76 Wells Street, London W1T 3QT

1 2 3 4 5 6 7 8 9 0

To Rebecca

The Fathers of the Constitution studied nothing more than to secure the complete independence of the judiciary. The President was not permitted to remove the judges, nor Congress to diminish their salaries. One thing only was either forgotten or deemed undesirable, because highly inconvenient, to determine,—the number of judges in the Supreme court. Here was a weak point, a joint in the court's armour through which a weapon might some day penetrate.

—JAMES BRYCE,
The American Commonwealth (1889)

CONTENTS

SUPREME POWER

INTRODUCTION

THE COCKTAILS WERE typically strong, and tonight they felt like fortification.

The president himself had mixed the drinks, a custom he fulfilled with a practiced carelessness. But on this night—February 2, 1937—neither his tranquil air nor his potent drinks did much to dispel the unease among his aides, who gathered in his small private study, upstairs at the White House.

Franklin Roosevelt raised a glass to the Supreme Court—the Court as it was, and the Court as he hoped it would be soon. "The time for action," Roosevelt told the group, had come; their confrontation with the Court could no longer be postponed. "Unpleasant as it is, I think we have to face it." These advisers, for thirty-six more hours, were the only men in America who could know precisely what this meant—which accounted for their sense of foreboding.

A journalist once called Roosevelt "apparently the least worried man in the country"; tonight, he was the least worried man in the room. He mimicked the morose expressions of his aides, who were not at all looking forward to the evening ahead, an annual dinner to honor the Supreme Court justices. Yet the president was clearly relishing the fact that, at that very moment, seven of the Court's "Nine Old Men" were arriving downstairs in the East Room, along with other protagonists in the national drama about to unfold.

Two weeks into his second term, Franklin Roosevelt stood at the pinnacle of power. He was the prevailing force, the predominant fact of American life. He had won, in November 1936, the biggest landslide in the nation's history: a staggering 61 percent of the popular vote and nearly the entirety of the electoral college. His new and massive coalition—liberals, labor, women, and minorities—gave him a mandate not simply to continue as president but to add expansively to the achievements of his first term. The nation was now closer to one-party rule than it had been since Reconstruction. During his first term, Roosevelt had enjoyed a comfortable—and mostly compliant—majority on Capitol Hill. Now, at the start of his second, the imbalance of power was even more pronounced. In February 1937, the Senate contained seventy-six Democrats; the opposition, such as it was, totaled twenty, most but not all of them Republicans.

In Roosevelt's view, the landslide enabled him—at long last—to take on his most powerful, most implacable opponent, which he saw as the biggest impediment to social and economic progress in America: the United States Supreme Court.

By the time of Roosevelt's second inaugural, in January 1937, the Supreme Court—in a series of devastating rulings—had left much of the New Deal in ruins. The centerpiece of Roosevelt's first-term agenda was the National Recovery Administration (NRA), known by its symbol, the Blue Eagle, which appeared everywhere from shop windows to the costumes of chorus girls. On "Black Monday," May 27, 1935, the Court struck it down—repudiating, by a stunning 9–0 vote, not just the program but its entire system of minimum wages, maximum hours, and workers' rights. Next to fall was the pillar of the New Deal's farm policy: the Agricultural Adjustment Act (AAA). Then the Guffey Coal Act. Then a state minimum-wage law. No Supreme Court in history had ever struck down so many laws so quickly. Between 1933 and 1936, the Court overturned acts of Congress at ten times the traditional rate. To accomplish this, justices disinterred long neglected doctrines and breathed new life into obscure clauses of the Constitution. The Court was creating "new doctrine now faster than I can absorb it," complained Justice Harlan Fiske Stone, whose increasingly angry dissents made him a hero to New Dealers.

It was not just the number of adverse opinions but their stridency, their sweeping nature, that created an atmosphere of crisis in Washington. By 1937, the Court's majority had made amply clear that the very notion of the New Deal—its use of governmental power to relieve the suffering caused by the Great Depression and to create a new and more just social and economic order—was an affront to the Constitution, whether that power was exercised by the federal government or the states. The Court, Roosevelt complained to the press, had established a "'no-man's-land' where no government—state or federal—can function." Social Security, soon to face the Court's scrutiny, seemed certain to fall, as did the National Labor Relations Act, as did just about everything of significance that Congress had passed or Roosevelt was likely to propose.

If reform was now impossible, so was recovery. Harold Ickes, Roosevelt's Secretary of the Interior, thought that the president faced a very clear choice: curtail the Court or submit to "judicial tyranny."

Roosevelt did not suppose that his triumph at the polls had in any way chastened the Court; the old maxim that "the Court follows the election returns" could not possibly apply to an institution that had been flouting, so consistently and flagrantly, the popular will. Indeed, the four or five most conservative justices, with every opinion they wrote against the New Deal, seemed almost to invite public outrage, to welcome it. The November landslide meant little to them. To Roosevelt, though, it meant the strength to strike back—and quickly.

By the night of the Judiciary Dinner, all the pieces were in place. The plot had taken years to conceive. Its chief architect was the attorney general, Homer Cummings, who, at the president's insistence, carried out his work covertly. No one—not Roosevelt's "Brain Trust," not his cabinet—was to know of the plan until the last possible moment.

The plan was this: to pack the Court.

Roosevelt would subdue the Court's conservatives by outnumbering them. In an audacious gambit, he would ask Congress to enlarge the Court's membership to fifteen—adding, essentially overnight, up to six liberals to the bench. He would obscure this, his true goal, in trumped-up concerns about judicial performance, claiming that the "nine old men in kimonos" (as Will Rogers called them) were slow, infirm, and overwhelmed by their work.

Indeed, the Hughes Court, in 1937, was the oldest in history. The average age of its members was seventy-one; five of the nine were seventy-four or older. The superannuation of the justices had been a public concern even before two newspaper columnists, in a brutal best-seller called *The Nine Old Men*, described them as "aloof from all reality, meting out a law as inflexible as the massive blocks of marble that surround them in their mausoleum of justice."

In January 1937, the president began to inform several top advisers about his plan. All were astounded; some were distraught. One senior counselor reacted with "extreme political fear and shock," confessing to a colleague he was "scared to death." What terrified him was precisely what delighted Roosevelt: the artfulness, the deviousness, of making the case against the Court one of infirmity rather than ideology. When the cloak came off—as the president's men expected it would—Roosevelt's motives would stand exposed and his integrity, they feared, would be in tatters.

They fretted, directed a pointed question or two toward the president, but could see it was pointless. He was committed. Roosevelt might take some time in reaching a decision, but once he had reached it, he did not tend to question it. Plus, he was a man who loved surprises, and he was about to spring a big one.

The Judiciary Dinner was not the right moment to drop the bombshell, but FDR greatly enjoyed the fact that he had one to drop. As a confidant recalled, the president joked that he was having a tough time deciding "whether to take only one cocktail before dinner and have it be a very amiable affair, or to have a mimeographed copy" of the Court-packing plan "laid beside the plate of each justice and then take three cocktails to fortify himself against their reactions."

The first lady, Eleanor, joined the president in the study, gently reproving him for the frayed state of his dinner suit. FDR was then wheeled out of the room, into the elevator, and onward to the East Room, where his guests—nearly ninety tonight, about what one expected for a state dinner—were assembling into a receiving line.

The Judiciary Dinner had been, for more than half a century, one of the final events of the winter social season at the White House. Even under the dynamic Roosevelts (in contrast to the Hoovers or Coolidges or, really, any first couple since the preceding Roosevelts), these "official entertainments," as one observer put it, were "too stiff to be amusing and too little pompous to be impressive." State dinners—with their bland, rote formality, with their decorative ferns and palms arranged much as they had been when Chester A. Arthur was president—were, inevitably, devoid of excitement. Particularly when the guests were Supreme Court justices. On the theory that old men have delicate stomachs, Henrietta Nesbitt, the Roosevelts' housekeeper, served only the mildest fare: consommé, filet of sole, green peas, and ice cream.

Tonight, however, there was a charge in the air. The first to greet the president was the Chief Justice, Charles Evans Hughes—gracious, even warm, despite years of strife between the Court and the White House. Hughes, as ever, was a commanding presence. His brow was stern but his eyes were lively; his grand white mustache and regal beard defined, for many, the very idea of a Chief Justice. This was his second stint on the Supreme Court: in 1916, after six years as an associate justice, he had stepped down to run for president, and very nearly beat Woodrow Wilson, the incumbent. Herbert Hoover put Hughes back on the bench in 1930, this time as chief. He was a natural in the role. "To see him preside," said Felix Frankfurter, who later joined Hughes on the Court, "was like watching Toscanini lead an orchestra."

Yet by 1937, the Hughes Court was at war—not only with Roosevelt but with itself. The unanimity of Black Monday had masked deep personal and philosophical divisions; most of the rulings against the New Deal were 5–4 or 6–3 splits, falling along generally predictable—and seemingly indelible—lines. Hughes found himself caught in the middle, tacking left and then shifting right, trying to achieve a balance between the Court's liberals, who largely shared Roosevelt's idea of a "living" Constitution, and the Court's conservatives, who staunchly, bitterly rejected it.

Standing in the East Room on the night of the dinner, Hughes betrayed none of this. Neither did his brethren, who trailed him in the receiving line. There was Pierce Butler, a Harding appointee, seventy years old but showing no quietude of age or experience: Butler was a bully, a pugilist, a man who had lifted himself out of poverty and disdained those who could not manage the same. There was Benjamin Cardozo, a soft but forceful voice for liberalism. Cardozo had the most delicate temperament of any justice and seemed almost wounded by the contentiousness of his colleagues; the Court felt to him like a prison.

And there was Owen Roberts—affable but unknowable, and, more often than not, the Court's deciding vote.

They and the other justices—all but one—were cordial to Roosevelt. Only James McReynolds, sour-faced and aloof, reflected the true state of relations within the Court and between the judicial and executive branches. McReynolds, the president's fiercest critic on the Court, was known to have vowed "never [to] resign as long as that crippled son-of-a-bitch is in the White House." This was the first presidential dinner invitation that McReynolds had accepted in four years, and he had done so only to appease some of the other justices.

The third branch, the Congress, was represented by the chairmen of the Judiciary Committees, House and Senate. Idaho Senator William Borah, the old Republican, was here as well. Only one night before, in a nationwide radio address, Borah had denounced those on "the political side of the government" who attacked the integrity of the Court. He feared an all-out assault on the independence of the judiciary—a razing of the last remaining barrier to "bureaucratic control over everything that touches our daily living." Borah urged the nation to steel itself for a fight. "Experience," he warned, "teaches that it is difficult to set constitutional bounds to the action of a political party enjoying great political power."

And now, as the guests assembled in the East Room, Chief Justice Hughes strode across the room to shake hands with Borah. "Great speech," Hughes told him, within earshot of a dozen people. He said it was bold, statesmanlike. To others, the speech sounded like a preemptive strike. Against what, exactly, was unclear. The existence of a presidential plan to curb the Court had been widely rumored in recent weeks. Details of the proposal, some of them accurate, were filtering out to men like Borah—who would, presumably, have much to say about its success or failure.

Still, only a handful of the dinner guests—namely, the advisers who had joined the president for cocktails beforehand—knew the exact shape and timing of Roosevelt's message to Congress on the judiciary. Attorney General Cummings slid next to Sam Rosenman, FDR's counselor and speechwriter, and whispered, "I wish this message were over and delivered . . . I feel too much like a conspirator." Rosenman eyed

Cummings, whose tall frame was furtively bent, and told him he looked the part. "I wish it were over, too," Rosenman confided.

Roosevelt, though, was savoring the moment. After dinner, while the women—in keeping with tradition—retired to the Blue Room and Green Room, the men drew closer to the president or clustered elsewhere in the hall, in separate knots of conversation, holding cigars and cups of coffee. Roosevelt was laughing, bantering, jabbing his cigarette holder for emphasis, even more expansive than usual—a man utterly at ease with himself, his audience, and his secret.

His guests joined in his laughter: Hughes, the other justices, members of Congress—even Roosevelt's aides, who knew that this dinner, for some time to come, would mark the last moment of peace these men would know together.

Chapter One

COMPLETE CONTROL

THE CROWD BEGAN to cluster at the corner of Hoffman and Bolton, near the entrance to the Armory, in the late afternoon—a quiet, orderly crowd, more women than men. To fortify themselves for the wait, many carried thermos bottles of hot coffee and picnic boxes neatly packed with sandwiches. Some brought supper as well; even now, hours before the speech, there was no guarantee of a seat inside the hall.

The candidate himself was not yet in Baltimore, but was on his way. His train, the Roosevelt Special, was speeding northward through Virginia after a swing through the Southeast. The Baltimore speech, billed as one of the biggest of the entire 1932 campaign, was to be one of the last: the November election was little more than a week away. Governor Roosevelt worked on his address all the way to Baltimore, breaking only when the train pulled into Mount Royal Station shortly after 6 p.m. and local Democrats stepped on board to join him for a perfunctory dinner.

The Armory, by now, was filled to capacity, and probably beyond that—18,000 people were packed onto the floor, in the galleries, the aisles, every corner of the hall. Another 2,000 huddled outside under amplifiers. The crowd cheered gamely, then grew restless, as state officials took turns at the podium assailing President Hoover. By the time

Senator Millard Tydings stepped to the microphone, the audience had started to murmur in protest. They wanted FDR.

And then, moments later, they had him. Hitting Tydings mid-sentence, the band thundered into "Anchors Aweigh"; a roar greeted Roosevelt. Horns and whistles sounded in shrill blasts and a flurry of newspaper confetti filled the hall. FDR clutched the arm of his son James, and ascended a wooden ramp to the platform. He let the demonstration roll for a few minutes, then began his broadside.

"I am waging a war in this campaign," he declared, "a frontal attack against the 'Four Horsemen' of the present Republican leadership—the horsemen of Destruction. Delay. Deceit. Despair." The administration, he said, was in the grip of a failed doctrine, one "so unsound, so inimical to true progress, that it has left behind in its trail everywhere economic paralysis, industrial chaos, poverty and suffering." His voice hoarse, his tone severe, Roosevelt marched through a bill of particulars, every charge drawing wild shouts from the crowd. Standing beside a Democratic donkey made of yellow chrysanthemums, he assailed Hoover and the GOP: their downplaying of the Depression and indifference to human suffering; their "dizzy" mixed messages on Prohibition; protectionist policies that had stifled exports; and a federal budget that, as it slid deeper into deficit, slighted the Americans who most needed relief.

"Let's see who is responsible for that failure," Roosevelt continued. "After March 4, 1929"—Hoover's Inauguration Day—"the Republican Party was in complete control of all branches of the federal government." And here, for the only time that night, he departed from his carefully prepared text, to itemize each branch: "the Executive, the Senate, the House of Representatives and, I might add for good measure, to make it complete, the Supreme Court as well."

Again, there were cheers, but nothing like the bedlam—the shrieking, whistling, and hat-waving—that greeted Roosevelt's suggestion that Prohibition should be relaxed. The biggest line of the speech was this: "And now, a word as to beer." The *New York Times* cited this comment, but made no mention of Roosevelt's statement about the Court. *The Washington Post*, though, shouted its significance from the front page: "Roosevelt Says G.O.P. Has Had Supreme Court Control Since 1929."

Hoover and his men could scarcely contain themselves. Roosevelt's remark was, they felt, the answer to a fervent prayer. For months now, Republican operatives had been following FDR from state to state, from rally to rally, in the hopes that somewhere along the way, out of indiscipline, overconfidence, or sheer exhaustion, he would slip and say something they could portray as radical. They trailed him to the Pacific Coast—no luck. They followed him south—again, nothing. By the time Roosevelt reached Baltimore, Republicans had begun to mutter to reporters that FDR must have some very shrewd managers; left to his own devices, they were certain, the wild-eyed Roosevelt would have revealed himself by now.

Here, then, in the eleventh hour of the campaign, was the long sought opportunity. Republicans seized it with relish. From GOP campaign headquarters at the Waldorf-Astoria in New York, from the wood-paneled suites of Wall Street law firms, came a cry of righteous indignation. The Roosevelt "slur" brought coordinated confessions of "shock," "amazement," and "outrage" from Republican governors, congressmen, and leading members of the bar. "There never has been and never can be any politics in our Supreme Court," said Silas Strawn, a Republican finance chairman and the former head of the American Bar Association. "The Supreme Court is above and beyond politics," said a renowned New York attorney. "Any candidate should be condemned for dragging the Supreme Court into partisan politics in this way," said another. James M. Beck, a Republican congressman who had served as solicitor general, declared that FDR's off-the-cuff comment "saps the foundation of government. . . . Roosevelt's speeches for some time have led me to the conclusion he is a demagogue. Now," Beck said, "I'm certain of it."

Robert Mainzer, another leading corporate lawyer, sent a telegram imploring Calvin Coolidge to denounce FDR. (Coolidge declined.) By dragging the Supreme Court "into the political arena," Mainzer wrote the former president, FDR's statement was "arousing the most intense feeling against Roosevelt."

Of course, the Republican old guard, men like Mainzer, had already been known to hold an intense feeling against Roosevelt. And the trumped-up controversy over the Supreme Court won them few, if any, new converts. Except for the reliably conservative *Washington Post*, which demanded that the governor "immediately . . . withdraw" his "insult to the Court," the other arbiters of opinion shrugged it off. The *Baltimore Sun* tweaked the "defenders of the Hoover faith" for their "exaggerated anxiety." The *New York Times* conceded that FDR's comment was "needless and foolish"—only because "it lent itself to . . . violent perversion" by "eager Republicans," whose "sense of outrage," the editors concluded, "is highly artificial and will have not the slightest effect upon the Presidential campaign."

Hoover, though, was not ready to concede the point. In Indianapolis, three days after FDR's speech, the president slashed at Roosevelt before a wildly cheering crowd, calling him a "chameleon on Scotch plaid" for switching positions on the tariff. Hoover's speech, like Roosevelt's in Baltimore, was an extended ramble across the issue landscape, from railroad rate regulation to home ownership. Hoover did not mention the Court until the end, when he paused to carefully repeat Roosevelt's remark, word for word. The charge of judicial partisanship, Hoover said, was "atrocious." Then, his voice rising with emotion, the president directed his audience to Roosevelt's "deeper implication": "Does he expect the Supreme Court to be subservient to him and his party? Does that statement express his intention, by his appointments or otherwise, to attempt to reduce that tribunal to an instrument of party policy and political action for sustaining such doctrines as he may bring with him?"

This, Hoover declared, was the defining issue of the campaign: "whether we shall go on in fidelity to the American traditions or whether we shall turn to innovations, the spirit of which is disclosed to us by many sinister revelations and veiled promises. My friends, I wish to make my position clear," he concluded, as if his position were not clear enough: "I propose to go on in faith and loyalty to the traditions of our race."

Over the coming days, the controversy, such as it was, slipped from the front page into the mid-section of the newspapers, before disappearing altogether. Still, Roosevelt was not taking any chances. His campaign managers, while confident about the approaching election, had been "startled," one said, by Roosevelt's comments in Baltimore. Calling the Supreme Court "Republican" was simply not the sort of thing one did publicly, let alone in the final stretch of a campaign. Roosevelt's "advisers do not want him to stir up any hornet nests," the

Baltimore Sun reported. To "guard against last-minute slips," they preferred to have him "retire into seclusion." That, of course, was impossible, so Roosevelt from that point forward would appear at rallies, whip up the party faithful, and deliver sanitized speeches that said nothing new and little of substance.

He had, however, no regrets. "What I said last night about the judiciary is true," Roosevelt told Senator James Byrnes of South Carolina the day after the Baltimore address, "and whatever is in a man's heart is apt to come to his tongue—I shall not make any explanations or apology for it!"

The Court issue—and, indeed, the Hoover campaign—had come to naught. On November 8, Franklin Roosevelt won forty-two states and a popular-vote margin of nearly 18 points. It was a stunning repudiation of Republican rule, if not quite, however, the end for the Hoover administration, which remained in place for another four months—a gloomy, uncertain, and seemingly interminable period that would last until Roosevelt was constitutionally permitted to assume power on March 4, 1933. An interregnum of this length—a requirement in the early days of the republic, when men and the machinery of government moved more slowly—seemed an undue, even a dangerous, indulgence during a time of economic emergency. The Twentieth Amendment to the Constitution, the so-called Lame Duck Amendment, which would cut the wait in half, had been almost fully ratified by the time of FDR's election. This was too late to hasten his inauguration, but its impending approval ensured that Franklin Roosevelt, in the winter of 1932–33, was the last president-elect to be stuck so long in suspended animation.

Meanwhile, the Depression continued to exact its heavy human toll. Three years after the stock market crash, the sense of trauma had not abated, and conditions continued their downward spiral toward chaos and disintegration. "Nobody is actually starving," Hoover had insisted during the campaign. "The hoboes, for example, are better fed than they had ever been." If so, the same could not be said of the millions of Americans who lived as scavengers: chasing vegetable trucks in the hopes that a stray ear of corn or head of lettuce might fall off; loitering in alleys behind hotels, waiting for pails of refuse to be placed outside; scouring pastures for dandelions, wild onions, and weeds that, until recently, had been left to cattle. On the eve of the election, more than 20 percent of the students in New York City schools were malnourished; in mining country, the number often exceeded 90 percent, as starving children drowsed or sat glassy-eyed at their desks. That is, where the schools were still open. Across America, state and local governments lacked the funds to maintain the schools or pay the teachers. In Arkansas, more than three hundred schools spent ten or eleven months a year with their doors locked.

More than 12 million people, a quarter of the labor force, were unemployed. Thousands of immigrants, finding America something less than a land of opportunity, returned to their countries of origin. Or they went elsewhere: in 1931, more than 100,000 Americans applied for jobs in the Soviet Union. For Americans lucky enough to keep their jobs, hours were fewer and wages lower. Incomes were down even more sharply in rural America, where prices for farm products, low for years, had finally collapsed, fueling foreclosures, delinquencies on farm debts, and increasing unrest. By one estimate, a quarter of the land in Mississippi was put up for auction. To keep warm, families burned the corn they raised; it was cheaper than selling the corn to buy coal. The banking system was in a state of collapse: institutions of all kinds were failing at an alarming rate, with some avoiding failure only by locking their doors. Whether this was the bottom, or just the beginning, was entirely unclear. It was little wonder that Roosevelt, in his speech in Baltimore, had invoked the Four Horsemen of the Apocalypse.

But for the time being, his election had changed nothing. Until March, the nation would continue to be led by an administration that was philosophically opposed to "taking the federal government into the relief business." And so Franklin Roosevelt faded from view. There was little he could do as the nation sank deeper into the Depression. He met with his advisers and made plans to address the banking crisis; refused Hoover's bizarre insistence that he endorse Republican economic policies; and, incongruously, took a fishing cruise to the Bahamas on a private yacht. Roosevelt also selected his cabinet. The men who had worked to get him elected, particularly those who had been with him before his nomination at the Chicago convention, lined up to receive their due; but FDR declared himself against distributing cabinet appointments as rewards for past service.

This was disappointing news for Homer Cummings.

Cummings, a Connecticut Democrat, was a member of the group known informally as FRBC: For Roosevelt Before Chicago. In a sense, Cummings was for Roosevelt more than fifteen years before Chicago. In 1916, the two men had worked together to reelect Woodrow Wilson. After the campaign, Cummings, a leading member of the Democratic National Committee, wrote to FDR in the hopes that the young Assistant Secretary of the Navy, a dozen years his junior, would inscribe a photograph of himself. Roosevelt gladly obliged, asking Cummings to return the favor, and looking forward to "future campaigns and victories together."

That seemed a safe bet. Roosevelt and Cummings were on upward trajectories that seemed certain to intersect again. They came from the same region, the largely Republican Northeast, where, despite their party affiliation, each had won political office at a young age: Roosevelt, at twenty-eight, as a state senator from Dutchess County, New York; Cummings, at thirty, as mayor of Stamford, Connecticut. Though Cummings lacked FDR's effortless charm—most did—he won admirers by his hard work and his eloquence. One observer, having seen Cummings on the stump, described him as "forceful . . . suave and subtle, yet stingingly sarcastic at times. . . . He spoke not as a mere wordster, but as one having the confidence of a cause which inspired and emboldened him." Cummings was even more effective in the courtroom. In 1924, as a county prosecutor, he defied public opinion by fighting to acquit a vagrant wrongly accused of murdering a well-known parish priest. Cummings's dramatic performance brought him national acclaim. More than twenty years later, when a movie (*Boomerang*) celebrated the case, Cummings might well have been cast as himself: his cool, deliberate manner, his confidence and clarity, his gold-trimmed pince-nez, clipped on the bridge of his slightly hawkish nose—all seemed straight from central casting.

Higher office eluded him, but he refused to recede. At the 1920 Democratic Convention in San Francisco, Cummings delivered an impassioned keynote address that won him not only praise but the votes of twenty-seven delegates for president. He was not, however, a serious contender. The presidential nomination went to the honorable if unexceptional James M. Cox, the governor of Ohio, while the second seat on what one Democrat called that "hopeless ticket" went to Franklin Roosevelt. When FDR accepted the nomination in a front-porch ceremony in Hyde Park, Cummings delivered warm introductory remarks. Roosevelt never forgot either of these speeches; out of an excess of either gratitude or generosity, he talked about them for years.

Twelve years later, in 1932, Cummings was back in the business of promoting FDR, this time for the presidency. Using his powers of persuasion, and calling in every outstanding political debt, Cummings brought many members of Congress on board. Before long, newspapers reported that Cummings was running the campaign. He was not—that job was shared between FDR's closest aide, Louis Howe, and the DNC's James Farley, who was bitterly certain the stories had been planted by Cummings. Regardless, Cummings was entrusted with the role of floor manager at the Chicago convention. Here he was mostly effective, but, at times, he pushed too hard. His high-handed refusal to cut a deal for half of Connecticut's votes cost FDR all the delegates of Cummings's home state—a terrific embarrassment. "Cummings is an outstanding lawyer," a member of the DNC reported to Roosevelt. "He has plenty of courage. But . . . he lacks the sixth sense which invariably distinguishes the successful political leader."

"The spirit that died with Wilson lives again!" Cummings wrote Roosevelt at the time of his election. "May the good God be with you in your great task." Cummings, now, had his own great task: to become U.S. attorney general. He lobbied intently for the job—making the rounds, calling in chits, and insisting in his diary that other men, not his own ambitions, were driving him to do it. He wrote that Joseph E. Davies, a former Wilson adviser, was "exceedingly anxious that I should be Attorney General," adding, "I asked him if he did not think anyone was foolish to want to be Attorney General. [Davies] said, of course, it is perfectly idiotic in view of what the Attorney General is going to be up against."

It was already clear that the central challenge for the next attorney general would be to help Roosevelt avoid a collision with the conservative majority of the Supreme Court. With this in mind, Senator-elect William McAdoo of California, one of Cummings's key promoters, raised "the possibility of changing the law with regard to the Supreme Court so as to get the antiquated judges off the bench," as Cummings noted in his diary. Over lunch in mid-January, McAdoo asked his opinion whether it would be constitutional to relegate justices aged seventy or seventy-two to emeritus status on the Court, with no more than one of them permitted at any given time to hear cases. McAdoo said he would be "glad to introduce such a bill" if Cummings would draft one.

"He said he had talked to Governor Roosevelt about it and the latter liked the idea," Cummings noted. "McAdoo said that this would get rid of some of the 'old fossils.' " McAdoo regretted the idea of forcing Louis D. Brandeis, the great liberal justice, off the bench—but then, Brandeis "was pretty well along in years already and so it would not so much matter."

On February 3, 1933, FDR called Cummings to offer him a position as Governor-General of the Philippines. "My goodness," Cummings replied, "that is a hell of a ways away." Roosevelt laughed. "I am not trying to get you out of sight," he insisted. The post was, in its way, a prestigious one—William Howard Taft had been the first to hold it—but it was of course a crushing disappointment to Cummings. A new era was dawning in Washington, and the Philippines were exceedingly far from the action.

As attorney general, FDR had selected Thomas Walsh of Montana—a gruff and powerful presence in the Senate, an authority on the Constitution, and a relentless investigator. He was also, at seventy-three, a newlywed. A week before the inauguration, Walsh flew to Havana to marry a wealthy Cuban widow, twenty years his junior. On their return to Washington, they stopped for dinner in Daytona Beach. Walsh felt a stabbing pain in his abdomen. He dismissed it as indigestion and drank a bit of soda to settle his stomach. That night, a doctor told him his blood pressure was alarmingly high and that he should remain in Florida. Walsh refused; it was unthinkable, he said, that he should miss the inaugural. (He also had big plans, as he had announced to the press, to spend the first two months of the Roosevelt administration on an extended honeymoon, "show[ing] my wife the beauties of Montana.") The next morning, Senator and Mrs. Walsh boarded an Atlantic Coast Line train for Washington. By the time it pulled into Union Station that evening, under a steady rain, Walsh was dead. He would be buried in his wedding suit.

Roosevelt huddled with his aides in the Mayflower Hotel. He confessed to one associate that he could not think of a single, reasonable replacement for Walsh—not, at least, while he was distracted by the inauguration and the banking crisis. He said he might leave the position open until he had time to think about it. "Well," interrupted Missy LeHand, his influential secretary, "perhaps Homer Cummings would make a good appointment." She may not have been the first to mention Cummings's name; rumors of his selection were already circulating. But LeHand's offhand comment seemed, in an instant, to settle the matter, and Cummings was called to the Mayflower.

The hotel, when he arrived, was so choked with job-seekers and hangers-on that it was hard for Cummings to reach the suite. When he did, Roosevelt got quickly to the point. Cummings was to be attorney general—"for a few weeks," after which he would go, as planned, to the Philippines. With that, the president-elect and his acting attorney general got right to work. They talked for the next two hours, covering many pressing issues, among them whether it was constitutional for Roosevelt to declare, as he intended, a bank "holiday"—to close the nation's banks as a means of preventing their collapse. Two days later, Cummings skipped most of the inaugural parade to spend the afternoon among his law books, happily considering the question.

Time magazine thought the appointment a fine one—"as a stopgap." Cummings was "a good lawyer if not a great one." He would, *Time* assumed, soon find himself on a slow boat to the Philippines just "as soon as President Roosevelt finds someone nearer the Walsh calibre."

The inaugural platform, on the East Front of the U.S. Capitol, was draped in bunting, the only bit of brightness on a leaden and wintry afternoon. Wind scattered a gray mist over the crowd. On the rostrum, in a billowing black robe and with a white beard that looked, to many, like that of Zeus or Jehovah, stood the Chief Justice of the United States, Charles Evans Hughes. He faced Franklin Roosevelt, who, with right hand raised and left hand placed firmly on a massive, seventeenth-century Dutch Bible, followed Hughes through the oath of office. The new president pledged to "preserve, protect, and defend the Constitution of the United States. So help me God."

From their vantage point on the platform, FDR and Hughes could see—over the heads of the spectators and across First Street—the site of the new Supreme Court Building. It was not much more than a hole in the ground. An old tavern that had served, during the Civil War, as the Capital Prison and, after that, as the home of the National Women's Party, had been recently razed to make room for the architect Cass Gilbert's grand (or grandiose) vision in marble, alternately described in the press as a temple or a mausoleum. For the next two years, at least, the Supreme Court was to remain on the second floor of the Capitol, in a room still called the Old Senate Chamber, which the Court had occupied since 1860. The space was too small to offer individual chambers for the nine justices. Except for oral arguments and weekly conferences, the men worked at home.

On that inaugural afternoon, if not for Hughes's actual presence on the platform, the Supreme Court might have been forgotten entirely. Still, Hughes was only a bit player that day, and his Court was an afterthought. The nation now had a new president, a new Congress, the promise of a New Deal—and yet the same old Court, made up of the same old men, placed there by presidents past. The mostly vacant lot across the street from the Capitol, the huge cavity in the earth, almost suggested that the Court itself had been closed for business and torn down, along with nearly every other vestige of the old order.

In this moment of common purpose, the Supreme Court stood apart. What Alexander Hamilton had once described as the "least dangerous branch" of government now appeared the least essential. The Court represented tradition at a time when many Americans demanded a clean break. It imposed restraints against action when action was needed; it offered safeguards against executive and legislative overreach when the problem, many Americans agreed, was not an excess of governmental power, but a lack of it—or, at least, a lack of will to use it. The imperative now was change, not continuity; resolve, not reflection; motion, not circumspection. The Supreme Court seemed, at best, an irrelevance, at worst, an impediment.

In March 1933, the cry was not "justice" but "relief." What was at stake was not simply the eventual return of prosperity. It was the survival of democracy. Could representative government, with its checks and balances, with its suspicion and fragmentation of power, respond quickly and effectively to mass hunger, unemployment, desperation, and rage? And if not, could such a system endure much longer? The experience of Germany, Italy, and Japan suggested it could not. Economic dislocation in each country begat political dissolution; all three had succumbed to fascism. A few Americans, on the left and right margins of the nation's political life, voiced interest in a dictatorship of one kind or another, whether by the proletariat or by an all-powerful executive, an American *Führer*. But even those at the center of the spectrum, sensible people like Alfred Landon, the Republican governor of Kansas, thought it might take a little bit of dictatorship to save democracy: "Even the iron hand of a national dictator," said Landon at the time, "is in preference to a paralytic stroke." *Barron's*, the business paper, posited that "a mild species of dictatorship will help us over the roughest spots in the road ahead." Al Smith, who had preceded FDR both as governor of New York and the Democratic nominee for president, asked: "What does a democracy do in a war? It becomes a tyrant, a despot, a real monarch." He said this approvingly.

Suddenly, nothing seemed to matter but one man. "People are looking to you almost as they look to God," one citizen wrote the new president. Roosevelt's power was manifest from his first moments in office. By the clarity of his words, his voice, and his purpose, he transformed the national mood even before he had left the inaugural podium. Roosevelt was like a light in the darkness; and over the next three months—the Hundred Days—that darkness began to lift. He managed to convey, all at once, a profound self-directedness and yet an open-mindedness; a steely resolve and yet a sense of joy, even delight in his work; a clear-eyed pragmatism and, at the same time, a romantic belief that anything was possible if the American people put their minds to it. In FDR, none of these traits seemed to contradict; he embodied each paradox comfortably, just as he projected strength and vigor despite his paralysis. His personality was his power, and he wielded it expertly.

No president had attempted—or accomplished—so much so quickly. The Hundred Days were astonishingly productive. Roosevelt shaped fifteen major laws and propelled them through a Congress controlled fully by Democrats for the first time since 1916. By the time the session ended in June—an "extraordinary session," as Roosevelt rightly called it—an exhausted Congress had enacted emergency banking legislation; a national relief system and a national agricultural policy; securities regulation; a massive public works program; a system of voluntary, but enforceable, industrywide codes to raise wages, limit working hours, improve labor conditions, and to permit collective bargaining. Roosevelt had also created the Civilian Conservation Corps (CCC); abandoned the gold standard; provided mortgage relief for farmers and other homeowners; and more. Drawing deeply on the ideas of Wilson's New Freedom, Theodore Roosevelt's New Nationalism, and the work of other reformers, and seizing proposals that had long been shelved, FDR asked his aides to revive them, reconcile them, and expand them. He and his Brain Trust improvised the rest. At an early press conference, FDR compared himself to a quarterback who has a "general plan" of the game, who knows what the next play will be, but "cannot tell you what the play after the next play is going to be" until he sees if the last one worked. The New Deal that emerged was an amalgam of overlapping and at times competing approaches, all proceeding from one basic premise: that government had an obligation to provide for the welfare of its citizens.

The New Deal was, in many ways, less radical than it appeared, and the same could be said of the new president. Roosevelt was not looking to destroy capitalism, as some feared; he was trying to save it. "To preserve," he said later, "we had to reform." This was his instinct: to *restore*, *secure*, *stabilize*, *save*. These were the words he used to describe the New Deal, and they flowed naturally from a man who had been raised in privilege and steeped in tradition, a country gentleman who believed deeply in the virtues of work, the nobility of the land, and the ideals of the nation's founders. Roosevelt was conservative in the true sense of the word: he believed that the past should inform the present and future, and sought to maintain what was best in America—the profit system included. Frances Perkins, his Secretary of Labor, observed that "Roosevelt took the status quo in our economic system . . . for granted. . . . He was content with it. He felt that it ought to be humane, fair, and honest, and that adjustments ought to be made so that the people would not suffer from poverty and neglect, and so that all would share." John Maynard Keynes, the British economist, praised FDR for operating "within the framework of the existing system." Roosevelt resisted calls—some emitting from Wall Street itself—to nationalize the banking industry. Indeed, in every sector, he left many established, entrenched interests untouched. He viewed them—for a time, anyway—as essential partners in this new national enterprise.

To those who saw something alien and un-American in the New Deal, Roosevelt insisted that no "strange values" informed his agenda; rather, he said, he was "finding the way again to old, but somewhat forgotten, ideals." Though some of his methods might be new, his "objectives were as permanent and as old as human nature itself." When Roosevelt spoke this way, he did so deliberately, and a bit defensively. But it was consistent with his mission as he perceived it: reform, not revolution; indeed, reform as the last, best means to forestall revolution.

Still, there could be no understating the magnitude of what Roosevelt accomplished during the Hundred Days, or the transformative effect it had on the shape and scale and indeed the entire orientation of the federal government; on the powers of the presidency; on the compact between government and the people; on the economy; and on the feel and fabric of American life. During the 1932 campaign, in a speech at the Commonwealth Club in San Francisco, Roosevelt had argued that the exercise of individual liberty depended on some degree of protection from the ravages of the marketplace, and that the task of twentieth-century government was "to assist in the development of an economic declaration of rights, an economic consitutional order" with an emphasis on security. Thus, however conservative the essential aims of the New Deal, and whatever intellectual debts it owed to the past, the Hundred Days marked the turning of a page—the advent of something fundamentally new. Roosevelt himself did not contest this. Indeed, he relished it. At the end of the congressional session, at a signing ceremony in the Oval Office, he declared that "more history is being made today than in [any] one day of our national life." A senator added: "During all time."

Democracy worked: that was the verdict of the first Hundred Days.

After only three months in office, Roosevelt had renewed the nation's faith in representative government. In his inaugural address, FDR had raised the possibility of asking Congress for "broad Executive power to wage a war against the emergency, as great as the power that would be given to me if we were in fact invaded by a foreign foe." This had not proved necessary. A benign brand of dictatorship (if there could be such a thing) had not been required. Roosevelt had shown that the presidency, with the right man in the office, could be a force for progress, and that the chronically slow-grinding machinery of government could be shifted into high gear without a radical alteration of the balance of power. "Our Constitution," Roosevelt contended, "is so simple and practical that it is possible always to meet extraordinary needs by changes in emphasis and arrangement without loss of essential form." By June, many believed he had proven the point.

Not all, of course, were convinced. Henry Ashurst, an Arizona senator who, like nearly all of his Democratic colleagues, had backed the New Deal right down the line, worried in his diary that, "behind the façade of fear and need," Congress had just made "experiments on a grand scale and temporarily transmuted our way of life from individualism into regimented state socialism. . . . For aught we know, this Congress may have done what Russia did by her bloody revolution." James M. Beck scoffed at House colleagues who cited the "emergency" as a reason for overriding their doubts and backing the New Deal. To do so, he said, meant "there is no Constitution. It means its death." Beck tended toward extremes. Still, the fact that a New Deal supporter like Ashurst expressed similar concerns reflected the extent to which notions of "constitutionality," across the political spectrum, were rooted in long-held beliefs in free markets, property rights, state sovereignty, and limited government. Though few expressed it openly at the start of the Roosevelt Administration, the New Deal struck many Americans not simply as wrongheaded policy or reckless experimentation, but as a transgression of time-honored ideals. To these critics or quietly concerned citizens, the new president—however noble his aims might be—was governing outside the system.

Clearly, during those frenzied first months, questions about the constitutionality of the New Deal had not been settled—only deferred. While FDR had shown that a democracy could act quickly and decisively, he had not firmly established that it could do so within the confines of the Constitution.

Neither Roosevelt nor the Congress nor the American people had the last word on that. The last word belonged to the justices of the Supreme Court. Their judgment would be rendered in time—not immediately, but in time. For now, the Court was out of session and mostly out of mind. By the time of Roosevelt's triumphal bill-signing in mid-June, most of the nine justices had already escaped the Washington heat, making their seasonal migration to cooler climes. Few Americans took note of their absence; just as few would mark their return to Washington at the start of the new term in October. With all that had happened in a mere hundred days, with all that had already changed and was sure to change soon, the comings and goings of nine old men seemed largely beside the point.

Chapter Two

STORM CENTER

IF THE SUPREME COURT in 1933 was the quietest place in the nation's capital, Charles Evans Hughes may well have savored the silence. After what it had taken to win confirmation as Chief Justice, Hughes, surely, had no great ambition for making headlines.

It had only been three years since Hughes had undergone a searing battle over his nomination—the fiercest such fight in more than a century. "Mr. Hughes was the bull's eye," observed *Time* in 1930, though the real target was the Supreme Court itself: its growing power and, according to the Court's critics, its rightward lurch. Throughout the 1920s, and with increasing vehemence over the latter half of the decade, the Supreme Court had defended the interests of corporations, the rights of property, and "liberty of contract" against encroachments by government—particularly against states' attempts to regulate business on behalf of public health, welfare, or morality. Chief Justice William Howard Taft and his conservative brethren—imbued with a sense that they were saving civilization from Bolsheviks, collectivists, and other sundry radicals—voided state and federal legislation at a record rate. In what the dean of Harvard Law School called a "carnival of unconstitutionality," the Court erased more laws from the books between 1921 and 1930 than it had in the first hundred years of its existence.

By the time President Hoover nominated Hughes to replace the dying Taft, in February 1930, a storm was gathering. An incongruous collection of the aggrieved—liberals, Progressives, and southern states' rights conservatives—"rumbled and roared with pent-up . . . resentment" against the Court, as *Time* observed. They took issue with particular rulings, but also, more fundamentally, with federal judges' apparent tendency to usurp powers that belonged to legislators, and to render decisions that were, as the columnist Walter Lippmann put it, "out of harmony with the needs and the interests and ideals" of the vast majority of the American people. This had been true even before the stock market crashed, taking so many lives and fortunes along with it; but the complaints against the Court gained force when the economy descended into depression.

Even so, Hughes had expected—and had been assured by Hoover—that his confirmation would be automatic. This was not unreasonable. It would have been hard to create a better nominee for Chief Justice than Charles Evans Hughes. His qualifications were, by any objective standard, in any era, unparalleled. Hughes had served as governor of New York, U.S. Secretary of State, and very nearly, if not for the reservations of a few thousand Californian voters, president of the United States. More to the point, he had previously served on the Supreme Court: between 1910 and 1916 he had distinguished himself as an associate justice, before resigning his seat to run against Wilson.

By 1930, Hughes was very possibly the greatest lawyer in the United States—the most sought after and celebrated, in any event. Hughes spoke, thought, argued, and acted at all times with precision; he was like a perfectly honed instrument, created for the courtroom. So persuasive was Hughes that when he presented arguments before the New York Court of Appeals, its chief judge, Benjamin Cardozo, refused to reach any results for at least twenty-four hours—sufficient time, Cardozo hoped, to shake free of the spell that Hughes had just cast.

That said, Hughes was not a showman—not one of those courtroom caricatures who strut, all bombast and bluff, before judge and jury. On the contrary: he was crisp, intense, efficient. He prevailed not by the force of his personality but of his intellect. As a child in Newark, New Jersey, he had displayed a natural brilliance and an unnatural degree of self-discipline that propelled him, by the age of eleven, through the entirety of the high school curriculum; his parents, after moving the family to Brooklyn, then schooled him mostly at home, steeping him in the classics and, especially, the scriptures, before sending him, at fourteen, to Madison (later Colgate) University and then, at sixteen, to Brown University. At Columbia Law School, Hughes was first in his class; on the New York bar exam, which he took in 1884, his score was the highest ever awarded. Hughes had a prodigious, photographic memory. He was reported to read—and fully absorb—several hundred pages an hour. He could dictate a speech from start to finish and deliver it hours later, almost word for word, without reference to his notes. "His is the best mind in Washington; to this everyone agrees," wrote an observer in the 1920s (adding that this might not be excessive praise, as Washington was not exactly overstocked with great minds).

He also—and this could not be discounted—looked the part. By the 1930s, the downward sweep of Hughes's white mustache, terminating at either end in a sharp point, and his Van Dyke beard, thrusting forward like a spade, had long since fallen out of style, as Hughes was likely aware: he looked like a figure who had stepped out of history to speak to the ages. It is possible that no man had ever looked more like a Chief Justice than Charles Evans Hughes. In the view of many of his contemporaries, no man had ever looked (or sounded) more like God Almighty. Hughes radiated a kind of moral authority, a stern, superior mien that exuded judgment: "one just did not drool or needlessly talk if Hughes was around," recalled Felix Frankfurter of Harvard Law School.

He had this effect on everyone, it seemed. Theodore Roosevelt called Hughes the "bearded iceberg," and over the decades there were countless variations on this theme: "Chilly Charlie" and worse. Beneath the frost, though, was fire—something "volcanic in his . . . nature," his grandson recalled. Hughes was often plagued by self-doubt, sudden shifts of mood, and bleeding ulcers; his intense work habits sent him frequently to the edge of nervous exhaustion. And despite his cool, detached appearance, he burned with moral fervor. Hughes made his name as an investigator, exposing greed and fraud in New York's gas and insurance industries. In those days his beard was red, and it gave him, in the eyes of some, a radical air; cartoons portrayed him as a bespectacled tornado. When he revealed, with relish, the campaign contributions that insurance companies had made to the GOP, Republican bosses condemned him for "ripping the party wide open." In 1907, public acclaim carried him into the statehouse in Albany, where, as the "fighting Governor," he wore stiff, high collars and looked down, literally, on the corruption and compromise (this, too, was a vice) he saw around him. Like many progressives, he regarded himself as somehow above politics. He treated members of his party—with their hunger for "honest graft," patronage, and other petty inducements—as below contempt, and refused to cut deals with the Republican machine. For the most part, by appealing directly to the people, he succeeded regardless.

Over the decades, Hughes's sanctimony was leavened by a certain skepticism, a recognition that the world did not yield so easily to reason or moral suasion. His loss to Wilson in 1916 made this clear. Hughes's outlook was also tempered by tragedy: in 1920, his twenty-eight-year-old daughter, Helen, died of pneumonia. After that, he lost some of his air of invulnerability and began—to a small degree—to let the world in. He grew more capable of expressing the wit, charm, and even playfulness that his family and few close friends had seen. Some Washington correspondents began to write about "the new Hughes": the open, engaging Secretary of State in the Harding administration, the delightful raconteur at dinner parties ("His stories were of the 'that reminds me' variety," *The New Yorker* observed, "but he told them well"). Still, there were limits. "That new warmth, recently detected . . . ," joked a journalist who had known Hughes for years, "is like the light ray of a star which has needed a million years to reach the earth; it was always there but it required a long time to get across."

His guiding philosophy, like his personality, was something of a paradox. The irony of his selection by Hoover—and anointment by Taft (literally from his deathbed) as a "solid" conservative—was that as associate justice he had been consistently, at times even courageously, liberal. By the time Hughes left the Court in 1916, he had frequently aligned himself with Oliver Wendell Holmes, Jr., and Louis Brandeis in defending civil rights and civil liberties, and in affirming minimum wages for women, maximum hours of work for women and children, and workmen's compensation laws. On the bench, as in the statehouse, Hughes showed the pragmatic streak of many early progressive reformers.

But by 1930, Hughes's liberalism seemed consigned to the distant past. Hoover wanted a man devoid of "liberal tendencies," and

Hughes—by then a defender of railroad magnates and insurance companies, of oil and chemical and mining concerns—seemed to promise "a conservatism less cheerful than Mr. Taft's," as *Time* predicted, but no less reliable. In the view of *The New Republic*, Hughes's service in the Harding cabinet, in addition to his corporate law practice, "subjected him to continued reactionary influence." Many years later, Hughes's apologists were to insist that his liberalism, like his personal charm, had really been there all along, just below the surface. They argued that during the decades of Republican rule, he had never joined his party's prostration at the altar of American commerce, placing his faith, instead, in the socially redeeming acts of charitable groups. But there was little on the record to suggest this. At the time of his nomination as Chief Justice, it would have been hard to contradict the verdict of *Time*: that "the pure white flame of Liberalism had burned out in him to a sultry ash of Conservatism. . . . His mind had captured his heart."

This made for an ugly confirmation fight. Senator George Norris, a progressive Republican from Nebraska, claimed that "no man in public life exemplifies the influence of powerful combinations in the political and financial world as does Mr. Hughes." More than a decade after leaving the bench, Hughes was being made to answer for virtually everything the Court had done in his absence. Progressive senators of both parties took to the floor and, with surprising ferocity, assailed the Court as a political body, made up of politically minded men. "The Supreme Court is not only determining legal questions but it is likewise determining the great economic questions," complained Burton Wheeler, a Montana Democrat. That charge, at the time, was startling enough; but one went further still, calling the Court an "economic dictator." Another senator warned that if conservative justices continued to defy the people's will, "there is no human power in America that can keep the Supreme Court from becoming a political issue, nationwide, in the not far-distant future." And a few, more menacingly, threatened to limit the Court's powers by constitutional amendment.

Their aim was not really to derail Hughes's nomination but instead to chasten him in the hope that he would moderate his decisions. These senators also wanted to alert the public to what they saw as the Court's persistent conservative bias. In this sense, the debate was groundbreaking—and, for the public, edifying. For more than a century, there had been periodic eruptions against Supreme Court rulings; populists, progressives, and labor unions pressed frequently for judicial reforms, some of them quite radical (and none of them successful). But justices had never been so openly portrayed—on the floor of the Senate, no less—as lawmakers, ruling by the dictates of their own predilections. Scholars like Felix Frankfurter saw the debate as something close to a great awakening. "Let us face the fact," he wrote at the time, "that Justices of the Supreme Court *are* molders of policy, rather than impersonal vehicles of revealed truth."

The clamor did not subside with Hughes's confirmation (by a vote of 52–26). Three months later, the Senate, still roiling, refused Hoover's selection to fill the seat left vacant by the death of Justice Edward T. Sanford—the first such rejection in thirty years. The nomination of John J. Parker, a federal judge in North Carolina, failed, ostensibly because he had ruled against the civil rights of black Americans and against the interests of labor. But this vote, like the Hughes upheaval, had less to do with the nominee himself than with the decades-long battle between "human rights" and "property rights," and with the Court's defense of the latter. In June 1930, the Senate, having finally exhausted itself—if not the subject—approved Hoover's second choice: Owen J. Roberts, a well-respected corporate lawyer from Philadelphia. In the mid-1920s, Roberts had won acclaim as the conscientious prosecutor of Harding administration officials during the Teapot Dome scandals. On this basis and little else, liberals embraced him as one of their own and, for the time being, moved on to other issues.

"As you well know, you are returning to slavery." Thus did Justice James McReynolds, who had sat alongside Hughes during his previous tenure, welcome him back.

Four of the eight current justices had served with Hughes before, and all were pleased to see him return. Yet this bonhomie masked deep divisions. McReynolds's black humor better captured the mood. Hughes entered a Court long split over social and economic questions and, more fundamentally, over the role of the judiciary in a democratic system.

The principal weapon in these internecine wars was a single phrase in the Fourteenth Amendment denying states the power to "deprive any person of life, liberty, or property, without due process of law." At the time the amendment was adopted, in 1868, the due process clause struck Congress and the courts as unambiguous. The word "process" made plain its concern with the procedures by which a government acted: how laws were enacted, how fairly they were enforced. The Fifth Amendment, part of the Bill of Rights, had placed the same constraint on federal power; now it was being applied to the states, with the aim of protecting newly freed slaves against oppression.

It was not long, however, before railroad lawyers, monopolists, and conservative thinkers like Thomas M. Cooley, a prominent Michigan judge and law professor, were arguing—before increasingly receptive state and federal judges—that the guarantee of due process shielded individuals and corporations against the legislative restrictions of property rights. Reflecting this influence and the sympathies of the elites, which were solidly behind the railroads and other new and massive corporations, courts in the 1880s began to scrutinize the substance of legislation, especially in the economic realm. Judges created standards by which to assess whether a challenged regulation was "just" and "reasonable" rather than "arbitrary" or "oppressive."

This, as it emerged, was the doctrine of "substantive due process." The Supreme Court was slower to embrace it than state courts, but by the end of the nineteenth century took it up in earnest. Over the next three decades, if not with perfect consistency, it struck down an unprecedented number of state regulations on this basis. Between 1920 and 1926, the Court voided more social and economic legislation on due process grounds than it had in the preceding half century. Judges had other tools to safeguard property rights, among them the contracts and commerce clauses of Article I of the Constitution and the takings clause of the Fifth Amendment. But it was only a slight exaggeration to suggest, as one legal scholar did in the 1930s, that substantive due process was "the hub around which the whole Constitution now revolves."

The spear was the Constitution's, but the battle was the Lord's: as radical and reform movements sprang up to combat the injustices of the industrial era, conservative judges saw themselves as fighting a holy war against what the historian Charles Beard called the "oncoming hosts of communism and anarchy." The liberties they defended were, in the admiring words of the English jurist Henry Maine, a "bulwark of American individualism against democratic impatience and socialistic fantasy."

Justice Holmes, who deplored moral certitude in any sphere, most of all the law, led the counterreaction on the Court. In a 1921 dissent, he scoffed at the "delusive exactness" of the majority's application of the due process clause, adding,

> There is nothing that I more deprecate than the use of the Fourteenth Amendment beyond the absolute compulsion of its words to prevent the making of social experiments that an important part of the community desires, in the insulated chambers afforded by the several states, even though the experiments may seem futile or even noxious to me and to those whose judgment I most respect.

Clearly, the issue, as Holmes saw it, far transcended the Fourteenth Amendment. He and other justices, most significantly John Marshall Harlan and Louis Brandeis, believed that legislatures were empowered by the Constitution to make policy without undue judicial interference. "If there be doubt as to the validity of the statute," Harlan wrote in his impassioned dissent in *Lochner v. New York* (1905), the most notorious of all substantive due process decisions, "that doubt must . . . be resolved in favor of its validity, and the courts must keep their hands off."

By 1930, when Hughes returned to the bench, the Court's internal argument was as fierce as it had ever been. During the previous decade, Chief Justice Taft, outwardly genial but increasingly combative, had only widened the breach. So had stalwart conservatives such as George Sutherland, who contended that the judge's role was not to defer to the legislature but to stand "as a shield" for "the individual against the unjust demands of society," even if that meant "disregard[ing] the wishes and sentiments of a majority of the people."

This, more than any particular matter of constitutional law, was the chief dispute between the Court's two wings, and the dividing line between its conservatives, the so-called Four Horsemen (Sutherland,

Pierce Butler, James McReynolds, Willis Van Devanter), and its liberals (Brandeis, Holmes, Harlan Fiske Stone). The cleavage in the Court, while certainly not consistent in every case, was fundamental. It meant that in a very real sense, the Court, in 1930, had no center at all.

If any man had the persuasive power, tact, and shrewdness to lead the Court to common ground, it was Charles Evans Hughes. But it was far less clear whether common ground existed, even in theory. Could one justice's ardent belief in judicial restraint possibly be reconciled with another's assertion of judicial supremacy? Could these differences even be finessed, on a case-by-case basis, to avoid an endless string of 5–4 decisions in which a single justice determined the outcome? And where, in the end, did Hughes himself stand? Would he, as chief, be a force of cohesion, or would he—despite the Depression, and in the face of growing popular agitation against the Court—hold the line, consolidating the conservative victories of the 1920s?

The president who appointed Hughes and the senators who opposed him all thought they knew the answer—and all, it soon appeared, had been wildly wrong. The Supreme Court term of 1930–31 was not one of the most dramatic. But by the time the Court recessed in June, ending Hughes's first full term as Chief Justice, everything, it seemed, had changed. In a single term, Hughes had confounded his critics, emboldened the forces of social and economic reform, and, many observers agreed, ushered in a new era in constitutional interpretation—one that was only getting started, to be sure, but its direction was clear to all.

"Liberals Have It," declared *Time*. The *Literary Digest* hailed "The Supreme Court's Shift to Liberalism"; *Current History*, and just about everybody else, saw the "Supreme Court in a New Phase." It was the triumph—and, given his ordeal in the Senate, the vindication—of Charles Evans Hughes. Fifteen years in the embrace of the Republican old guard had apparently done nothing to diminish his liberal impulses. Hughes, at long last, was reunited with Holmes and Brandeis—but now these three, joined by Harlan Fiske Stone and Owen Roberts, had become a five-man majority. *The New Republic*, exultant, claimed that the four conservative justices had been "abruptly dethroned" and were now left to "fulminate in bitter but futile dissent. . . . The years of invalidating state legislation designed to achieve an economic democracy, of glorifying property rights at the expense of human rights through a narrow constitutional interpretation, are over."

Many scholars agreed. One law review concluded that Hughes and Roberts had "carried the day for pragmatism and liberal tolerance." Edward Corwin, a professor at Princeton, said that under Hughes, the Court had quickly "recovered an important segment of lost territory." Corwin was heartened not only by particular decisions, but by the new majority's embrace of the idea that law could be a tool to remedy, rather than perpetuate, the harshest realities of American life. Constitutional interpretation, Corwin said, was now "more flexible, more free" from outworn dogmas than it had been in a generation. Still, he cautioned that the present majority was "narrow and precarious."

And then, just as quickly, the pendulum swung back. By 1932, the liberal resurgence of the previous term felt like a distant memory—and a painful one for those who, in their euphoria, had proclaimed the end of judicial orthodoxy. "The prediction so freely made last spring that a new era in the history of our Court was dawning seems not to be fully realized," Stone wrote to a friend. Suddenly, surprisingly, Hughes and Roberts looked a lot like the conservatives they replaced. "I am puzzled by them," a law professor wrote Stone. The justice was, too: seeing intelligent men like Hughes and Roberts on the other side of the divide left Stone, increasingly, to question his own views and seek reassurance from Brandeis and Holmes.

Indeed, despite initial impressions, the early Hughes Court could not be said to mark much of a shift from Taft's tenure. The majority showed the same suspicion of state economic regulations, striking them down in several cases on grounds of due process, equal protection, or a narrow interpretation of the commerce clause. The Depression—or, more specifically, the governmental response to it—had created new constitutional uncertainties, and the Court majority, in response, seemed to be walking the line between laissez-faire and the emerging welfare state.

In early 1932, when the ailing, eighty-nine-year-old Holmes was eased off the bench, President Hoover replaced him with, by most accounts, the most distinguished liberal jurist in America: Benjamin Cardozo of New York. That Hoover chose to do so reflected three things: that, in an election year, he hoped to avoid another bloody fight with his party's progressives; that his friend, Justice Stone, had pressed him hard to pick Cardozo; and, not least, that the appointment would not alter the balance of power on the Court. The conservative majority looked solid again, and Cardozo would simply be taking Holmes's place in an embattled minority of three.

The schism could be (and often was) overstated. During the 1930 to 1932 terms, the nine justices were in complete agreement—that is, unanimous—85 percent of the time on questions of state and federal economic power. Still, the remaining 15 percent was bitterly contentious. It was also fraught with consequence—especially for Franklin Roosevelt, if he was to have any hope of delivering the New Deal he had promised during his campaign for president.

"The Supreme Court is above and beyond politics"—this was the retort of a leading member of the New York bar in 1932, when Roosevelt had charged that Republicans controlled the Court. The lawyer's comment reflected a widely held (and much cherished) view of the judiciary as a sort of secular priesthood: on entering, it was believed, the judge renounced all preexisting prejudices; he was purified, or sanctified, by the black robe he donned.

Some of the justices encouraged this view. Taft had called the Court a "sacred shrine," and Hughes, at the laying of the cornerstone of the new Court building in 1932, declared that "the Republic endures and this is the symbol of its faith." (When the building opened a few years later, he extended the metaphor: "these altars," he wrote a friend, "are now established in a magnificent temple, with every convenience not only for the priests but for those who bring their sacrifices and petitions.") To the mainstream press, the justices were "black-robed gods," perched far above the fray. Their remoteness, their formal pronouncements, their severe public face—all enhanced the Court's authority at a time when other institutions were crumbling. In 1929, just after the stock market crash, the *New York Times* described the nine men as "justice incarnate. They know it, and so do the spectators. And the spectators like it. In a day when cathedrals are little more than examples of architecture, when legislatures, state and national, hold little inspiration . . . , the Supreme Court is a great comfort to the imagination. Here at least it is still possible to feel the majesty of law."

And the absence of partisanship. "The Supreme Court of the United States is made up of men who have resigned themselves to a life of judicial piety," intoned a prominent newspaper columnist. "Theirs is not to forward the fortunes of any party. . . . Theirs is only to preserve the immutable principles of American jurisprudence as it has come to them through centuries upon centuries of ethics and morality."

Of course, a judge might retain an idle interest in politics, just as he might follow the pennant race in baseball, but it had no conceivable effect on his official duty. In 1922, when progressives charged that George Sutherland, former senator from Utah and present Supreme Court nominee, was a Republican partisan, the *New York Times* stated archly: "In their private hours certain dignified old gentlemen may or may not talk a little politics over a game of bridge; but their partisanship is unrevealed to the public and has probably been greatly tempered by time."

This view—so assiduously promoted over the decades by those who, for their own reasons, portrayed Supreme Court justices as oracles of received wisdom rather than thinking, feeling, fallible men—had always been either overly sentimental or willfully naive. But it was rarely less accurate than during the 1932 presidential race. The contest, to begin with, took place in a time of national crisis. The two candidates represented dramatically different philosophies and constituencies. And the nine gentlemen of the Supreme Court, no less than any other Americans, and probably more than most, took a powerful interest in the unfolding campaign. Of course, they took care to express their preferences only among family and trusted friends; but there is no question that those preferences were strongly felt.

Brandeis—who had always dabbled in public affairs, more or less discreetly, from the bench—frequently discussed the campaign in letters to his close associate, Frankfurter. "Roosevelt's nomination is a comfort," Brandeis wrote in July 1932, from his vacation home on Cape Cod. As the campaign progressed, he informed Frankfurter, with satisfaction, that "all our Washington friends believe H.H. is doomed." Stone, who had served in the Coolidge administration alongside

Hoover, was more conflicted. Stone was fond of him personally, and was a member of the "Medicine Ball Cabinet," an unofficial group of Hoover advisers who tossed a six-pound ball around the South Lawn of the White House early in the morning. Stone had little enthusiasm for what FDR called "bold, persistent experimentation"—or for FDR himself, whom Stone dismissed as "an utterly impossible man for President." At the same time, Stone privately acknowledged the need for a change in national direction. "The truth of the business," he wrote to Frankfurter in September, "is that we are in a sad state politically, as well as economically, and if, as a result of the approaching election, the air is cleared somewhat, it will be a very fortunate thing."

The conservative justices conceded that the nation was in crisis. But a Roosevelt victory, they believed, would cause a collapse. Willis Van Devanter, who long ago had served as a Republican Party official, complained to a friend that FDR was "making empty and impossible promises." To his sister, Van Devanter wrote that Roosevelt was "a dreamer" and "far from stable," but that the Depression "blinds people to everything that is said excepting the call for a change. . . . I am praying that Roosevelt and his demagogic cohorts will not succeed." So were Van Devanter's like-minded colleagues. "Mr. Justice Sutherland thinks the result is in doubt but that Roosevelt has a slight advantage," Van Devanter confided to a friend. Sutherland "is not a pro-Hoover man but thinks Roosevelt quite unfitted and unsafe for the presidency. Mr. Justice [Pierce] Butler thinks Roosevelt will pretty certainly be elected but that for the good of the country. . . . Mr. Hoover should be reelected. Of course," he added, "I quote them only in confidence."

Van Devanter followed every major speech by the candidates; handicapped the race, region by region and state by state; and eagerly sought reports from party operatives. He did so because, after more than twenty years on the Court, he remained a fierce partisan, and because, more important, he—like millions of Americans—believed that the fate of the nation hung on the election results. He did not regard political developments with the bemused detachment once imagined by the *New York Times*. None of the justices did. Few justices, if any, ever had.

• • •

The fact of Roosevelt's victory did not surprise the justices, though its scale certainly did. "I was not expecting that [Hoover] would be so overwhelmingly defeated," reflected Van Devanter, who had expected the president to carry a dozen states; Hoover won only half that number. Stone greeted the result with ambivalence: "the campaign agony is over," he wrote to his sons. And while he hoped the results might have a chastening effect on Republicans—who had failed, in Stone's view, to remain "alive to realities"—he did not have great expectations for the future. "I cannot see in Roosevelt and his entourage any improvement over Hoover," he concluded.

Brandeis, of course, felt differently. "The job has been thoroughly done," he wrote to Frankfurter the day after the election. "Now comes FDR's real task. He must think out his policy & put it over Congress as W[oodrow] W[ilson] did, and he must begin the work of educating the Country as soon as possible." Brandeis himself was eager to assist: at the end of November, he traveled to Warm Springs, Georgia, for a face-to-face conversation with the president-elect. Though it lasted no more than twenty minutes and FDR "did most of the talking," Brandeis reported to Frankfurter that the meeting was "satisfactory." Roosevelt, he added, "seems well versed about the fundamental facts of the situation. Declared his administration must be liberal and that [he] expected to lose part of his conservative supporters—I told him 'I hope so.' That he must realign . . . part of the forces in each party."

Brandeis was one of only two justices—the other was Cardozo—who could have felt at ease in the new political order. Cardozo did not, like Brandeis, entangle himself in the affairs of the other branches, but both men had long been friendly with FDR, and both supported the New Deal—if not its emerging particulars (about which Brandeis, with his long-standing objection to the centralization of power, held grave doubts), then its broader objectives.

That made them a distinct minority on the Supreme Court of 1933. Most, if not all, of the other justices suddenly looked like relics of another era, another century even. Van Devanter, who as a child had watched Lincoln's funeral procession; Sutherland, who was born in England before either Disraeli or Gladstone had become prime minister; Hughes, who as a college student had no running water or central lighting in his dormitory, kept a closetful of coal there to heat his room, and was given a servant called a "slave"—these were nineteenth-century men. The pieties of their youth were now condemned as, at best, outmoded, or, at worst, a fraud; their jurisprudence seemed, to many, fundamentally at odds with reality. A generational and cultural chasm separated them from the young men—boys, almost—known as Frankfurter's "Happy Hot Dogs," who rushed out of Harvard and other law schools in 1933 infused with the idea that the Constitution was neither sacrosanct nor immutable, but a pliable instrument of social progress.

Nearly two decades had passed since Louis Brandeis posed the question whether popular discontent with the law was "due, in large measure, to the fact that [it] had not kept pace with the rapid development of our political, economic and social ideals." To New Dealers—Roosevelt foremost among them—this was an article of faith. In 1926, in a speech at Milton Academy, he had joked about conservatives' yearning for a world that no longer existed. "My old neighbor on the Hudson River, Rip Van Winkle, went soundly asleep," Roosevelt told the students, "and seemed annoyed, on waking up many years later, to find that the world was very different. Rip has many successors today. . . . They have not been physically asleep, but they have come to view the world with eyes of the past. They have pictured a world and a life which they have known and have liked; they have put a little halo around it and said, 'This is mine by heritage and choice—I will protect it and oppose any change.' " Roosevelt argued that legal doctrine, like religious dogma, had fallen dangerously out of step with the times. But he was an optimist. "Christianity," he said, "is great enough and broad enough to throw off the control of dead hands and to march forward in step with the progress of mankind. So also with law—from time to time it seems a hopeless drag on progress; but in the end it proves sufficiently elastic to catch up."

Two of the Court's conservatives were less concerned with catching up than getting out.

During the summer of 1932, even before Roosevelt was elected, Willis Van Devanter had "rather definitely" resolved to retire. He was seventy-three—after Brandeis, the oldest of the "Nine Old Men"—and was feeling the infirmities of age. He had suffered a stroke several years earlier, "which bears heavily upon him," Brandeis observed, though his work in conference was unimpaired. Van Devanter's letters spoke of senescence and decay—the decline of ailing relatives, the deaths of friends, detailed arrangements for the estates of deceased family members. He had been on the Court longer than any of his colleagues. All of the men he had served alongside as a young judge in Wyoming "are now gone," Van Devanter lamented in a letter to a friend. All of his colleagues from the Eighth Circuit Court of Appeals: "gone." Of all the justices who had been on the Supreme Court when Van Devanter joined in 1910, only he and Hughes survived. The rest: "gone."

To look at Van Devanter in 1932—this small, severe, and quiet man—it was hard to imagine that, in his youth, he had gone hunting with Buffalo Bill. Van Devanter was in fact a cultivated man, born in Indiana to a prosperous family—old Dutch stock that had arrived in New Amsterdam in 1662 and, quite unlike their countrymen, the Roosevelts, drifted westward over the generations. In 1884, at the age of twenty-five, after practicing law for a few years, Van Devanter migrated further still, to Cheyenne, in the Wyoming Territory, as yet untamed and largely undeveloped.

Van Devanter rose rapidly in state politics (statehood came in 1890). At age thirty he was appointed chief justice of the Wyoming Supreme Court, resigning a year later to represent the great cattle companies and the Union Pacific Railroad, at a time when both were under near-constant federal investigation for fraud. During the 1896 presidential campaign, he traveled the state on horseback, stumping for William McKinley and against William Jennings Bryan. His reward was a position in the Department of the Interior, with domain over public lands and Indian affairs. Theodore Roosevelt, impressed by his quiet competence and apparent progressivism, named him a federal judge; President Taft, several years later, appointed him to the Supreme Court. Democrats like Bryan protested violently—and futilely—that Van Devanter was beholden to the railroads, an impression he did little to curb as an associate justice.

Van Devanter's vote was rarely in doubt: he "lined up always with the conservatives and voted almost always in favor of big business," noted the *New York Times*. Still, his clarity and persistence gave him an influence in the justices' weekly conferences that few outside the room perceived, in part because Van Devanter wrote so few opinions—only one a year by the 1931 term. His "pen paralysis" was so acute that, more than once, the chief had to take a case back from him, gently offering to relieve his burden as the end of a term approached.

Van Devanter was ready to shed his burdensome job for good when Congress, in a fit of fiscal discipline during the summer of 1932, slashed the pensions of retired federal judges in half. For Holmes, who had just left the Court, this meant a reduction in annual pay to $10,000. His colleagues and friends were deeply aggrieved. It looked like a slap, and to what end? It saved the Treasury virtually nothing. Congress, in any event, had probably not intended the pay cut to apply to Supreme Court justices, but the comptroller general determined otherwise. At Brandeis's instigation, Frankfurter urged the Senate to amend the appropriations act at once. Senators were sympathetic—but too busy, they shrugged, to restore the pension any time soon.

"CONFIDENTIAL!!," began a letter from Stone to Frankfurter. "You will be interested to know that I think I have started something going which will result in a restoration of Mr. Justice Holmes' retirement allowance" and the pension for all justices. Frankfurter rejoiced. Holmes, he replied, did not need the money, but "the country's honor" was at stake—this and more. "Of course," Frankfurter added, "there are the wider implications which you have so effectively had in mind. You have again done the state service."

The winking reference, as both understood, implied that not one, but two, of the Court's conservatives—Van Devanter and Sutherland—were inclined to retire. Their eagerness to go was not, within the Court, much of a secret. But the pension cut had upset their plans. "I do not like the idea of losing half of my salary," Van Devanter complained. Neither did Sutherland, aged seventy, who had missed half of the 1927 term due to illness and spent part of 1932 in similarly poor shape. "When the Court convened in the fall," Van Devanter wrote his sister in January 1933, Sutherland "seemed to have fully recovered but he has been slipping back some and he indicated to me today that he was anxious that the changes made in the bill pending in the Senate should be approved and enacted into law."

That spring, Congress restored the pension in full. Frankfurter excitedly told FDR that "before long, you are likely to have two vacancies to be filled," and named the two men in question. Roosevelt was pleased—and professed to be surprised, though rumors to that effect had been circulating. "But when is McReynolds going to retire?" he asked. While hardly the Court's most influential conservative, McReynolds was certainly its most outspoken. "Isn't he going to resign?" Frankfurter doubted it.

As it turned out, however, no justice was going to resign any time soon. The pay cut, Hughes later recalled, "was notice to all the Justices that they could no longer rely upon the congressional promise." If Congress had cut the allowance once, it might well do so again. "There is no assurance" otherwise, Van Devanter wrote his sister, adding, "no one knows how long the depression will last." For the time being, he and Sutherland would stay put.

And so the prospect, the mere specter, of a renewed cut of $10,000 cost Roosevelt the opportunity to appoint two new justices at the start of his term. The replacement of Van Devanter and Sutherland with liberal justices would have given the new president a solid majority. The chance to transform the Court was lost for now. Roosevelt would have to reckon with the Court as it was—a Court that, as a columnist predicted, was unlikely to "change in personnel except as death may do so."

Chapter Three

SHORTCUTS

"HAVE I A legal right to do this?" Roosevelt asked a group of senators in the Oval Office. He was talking about his plan to devalue the dollar. "Mr. President," replied Thomas Gore of Oklahoma, who opposed the idea, "you could go on the street right now, knock down an old man, drag him into the White House, and take his clothes. You could sell them second-hand. It would be just about as legal as what you are planning to do. But that doesn't matter. You can do it anyway." Roosevelt roared his approval, and, indeed, did it anyway.

He was not always so cavalier. He had gone to some lengths to ensure that his executive order declaring a bank holiday—closing all the nation's banks to protect them from runs and ruin—rested on solid constitutional grounds. And when the Senate, in an attempt to reduce unemployment, passed a bill to limit the workweek to thirty hours, Roosevelt opposed it in part because he believed it to be unconstitutional. Still, his exchange with Gore was telling. In shaping the recovery program, the Constitution was a concern—but not an overriding one. Far more pressing was the question of how quickly a given bill could be drafted, passed, and made effective.

The first phase of the New Deal unfolded not in an orderly procession of new laws but in a rush—a scramble. FDR, a senator observed, "sent Congress so many messages that we grew dizzy. Before we could analyze one message . . . swiftly upon that message would come another and yet another . . . until Senators and Representatives became whirling dervishes. . . . We ground out laws so fast that we had no time to offer even a respectful gesture toward grammar, syntax, and philology." Homer Cummings put it similarly. "I went about with my pockets bulging with half-baked proclamations and undigested legislation, all requiring attention, study, and formulation," he wrote in his diary in April. "It was a period of rapid-fire opinions, all of which had to be oral and immediate. I probably made some mistakes. I do not know yet what they were but it would be strange if they did not exist. However, the times were hectic and the need was great. . . . The result," he added with pride, "was that nothing was stalled because of any inaction on the part of the Attorney General." That was how the president wanted it. "Homer is a great fellow," Roosevelt said to a cabinet member. "He can always find a way to do things."

In this environment, even a quick fix to a piece of legislation was often not deemed quick enough. That spring, the administration readied a series of reforms to cheapen the U.S. currency, mainly to relieve the burden of debt carried by millions of Americans, but also to prevent Congress from taking more extreme inflationary measures. Incredibly, despite the sweeping nature of the reforms, no one asked the Justice Department for an opinion. The attorney general, taking this in stride, offered his anyway: that parts of the legislation "ran afoul" of a decades-old Supreme Court precedent. Still, he was confident things could easily be set right. With FDR's blessing, he altered the wording of a crucial clause or two; but it was too late. "The matter had progressed so far . . . ," Cummings reflected, "that apparently the changes were not made."

The farm recovery plan, or Agricultural Adjustment Act (AAA), was drafted and passed in the same manner—that is, in haste, without any serious consideration of its constitutionality, despite its novel tax provisions. This was all too typical of the early New Deal. Even its centerpiece reform—the National Recovery Administration—became, in effect, a grand constitutional gamble. As conceived, the NRA was a vast, complex system of "industrial self-government," its aim to promote cooperation between management and labor, bring down prices, set minimum wages and maximum hours, and establish the right of workers to bargain collectively. To accomplish this, the National Industrial Recovery Act empowered businesses to draft codes of fair competition that, when approved by Roosevelt, would acquire the force of law.

This delegation of congressional authority to the president (specifically, the power to turn a code into a law) was unprecedented. It was also unconstitutional—at least in the view of Charles Wyzanski, a young Labor Department lawyer who had helped draft the bill. Wyzanski wrote his mentor Felix Frankfurter that the president's codemaking authority went "so far beyond the bounds of constitutionality that it would be useless" to defend it in court. He further feared the Recovery Act exceeded the power of Congress to regulate interstate commerce. Jerome Frank, another Frankfurter man in the administration, found it "shocking" that not a single constitutional lawyer had been asked to review the codemaking apparatus. The bill, Frank said, could have been squared with well-established constitutional doctrine, but no one had bothered.

Wyzanski urged Frankfurter to intervene—which he did to little effect, his long friendship with FDR notwithstanding. His concerns were brushed aside in the hurry to enact the bill. Another train had left the station. "The whole project is very ambitious," Cummings soon acknowledged, "and if not properly handled, or if conducted in a headlong manner, may lead to serious trouble." By this, though, he meant the operation of the agency, not its legal underpinnings. He did not seem to share the concerns of Wyzanski and Frank. Few did. The prevailing view within the administration was best expressed by a lawyer at the new agency: "Its constitutionality," he said, "is unassailable."

On this, as on most matters, Roosevelt was guided by a serene, supreme self-confidence. He had faith—naive and self-justifying, perhaps, but deeply felt—that if his instincts told him to do something, it almost certainly was constitutional. Robert H. Jackson, who had known FDR as a state senator and later served as a Supreme Court justice, observed that "the president had a tendency to think in terms of right and wrong, instead of terms of legal and illegal. Because he thought that his motives were always good for the things that he wanted to do, he found difficulty in thinking that there could be legal limitations on them." If it was necessary, it was right; if it was right, it was legal. Thus were his actions consistent with the Constitution.

This was more a matter of temperament than training (or a lack thereof). Though he was loath to describe himself as such, Roosevelt was, in fact, a lawyer. After graduating from Harvard College, he had attended Columbia Law School, where he was, at best, an indifferent student. During his first year, he failed contracts and one other course, though he received B's in other subjects. He took make-up exams that fall to stay with his class and passed them easily. Still, he continued to find the whole business boring, at times stifling. Most of his professors took a traditional view of the law and Constitution—an approach heavy on abstractions, formulas, and fine doctrinal shadings that struck Roosevelt as irrelevancies.

In 1907, when he passed the bar, he saw no reason to return to school and left without receiving a degree. Though this practice was hardly uncommon, he took a perverse pride in it, as if it revealed just how little he cared. More than a quarter century later, as governor of New York, he was invited to address a dinner of the law school's alumni. Nicholas Murray Butler, Columbia's president at the time, gently teased, "You will never be able to call yourself an intellectual until you come back to Columbia and pass your law exam." Tossing his head back, Roosevelt roared. "That," he laughed, "just shows how unimportant the law really is."

He did, however, practice law for a few years. In 1907 he began work as a clerk at the Wall Street firm of Carter, Ledyard & Milburn, which represented the American Tobacco Company and Standard Oil of New Jersey; FDR, though, was too young to have anything to do with clients like these. Instead he ran errands, which he greatly preferred to writing briefs or doing research in the law library. His fellow clerks generally liked him, even if some groused that he left them with the hard work, took long lunches, and dressed a bit too impeccably. In a year's time Roosevelt was promoted to managing clerk and sent to defend clients in small claims cases in the squalid municipal court on Rivington Street, on the Lower East Side. "I don't think he liked . . . legal work," Eleanor Roosevelt recalled, "but he enjoyed the contacts that it brought him with people. . . . He learned a good deal that he never had an opportunity to know anything about before . . . the conditions of people's lives." Decades later, FDR himself observed that "my Municipal Court work laid the foundation for politics better than any other factor in my life."

Though he was good with clients and largely successful in court, he failed to make a positive impression on the firm's partners, one of whom told FDR's mother, Sara, that her son would never amount to anything in the law. This did not trouble Roosevelt. He was well aware that the firm offered a man of his station a path to greater wealth, leisure, and social standing, and that passion for the law was not a prerequisite for success. Still, he had no interest in it. His ambitions lay elsewhere. He was already telling a fellow clerk that he expected to follow his distant cousin Theodore as assistant secretary of the Navy, governor of New York, and president of the United States.

"While he began [his professional] life as a lawyer . . . ," Robert Jackson later wrote, "his mental processes were not those of a lawyer, for legal education is really schooling in a way of thought. He did not really like the judicial process with its slow movement, its concern with detail, its insistence on primary evidence, its deliberation. He wanted short cuts." Indeed, in the early 1920s, when Roosevelt briefly returned to the profession, his approach to the law alienated some of his partners. "He's a nice fellow . . . ," one of them said, shrugging, to Frances Perkins, "but we can never make a lawyer of him. . . . He comes to conclusions. He hasn't got the patience to work things out." Not in a legal brief or a courtroom, perhaps, but Roosevelt had dedicated himself to a life in the political arena, and deplored the general lack of public-mindedness in the bar. In speeches, he lectured lawyers to take a less refined and more pragmatic view of their societal responsibilities, and to apply their talents to "get at the causes of the epidemics in our midst."

As president, Roosevelt displayed this same pragmatism, impatience with legalistic reasoning, and confidence that the law, properly applied, could be a tool, an implement, a means to advance the public interest. He believed in a Constitution that, as Chief Justice Edward Douglass White said in 1914, was not "a barrier to progress" but was, instead, "the broad highway through which alone true progress may be enjoyed"—a quotation that Roosevelt was fond of repeating. Or, as he himself put it, in more prosaic terms: the "Constitution has proved itself the most marvelously elastic compilation of rules of government ever written."

Roosevelt was hardly alone in this view. The idea of an "elastic" (or "organic" or "living") Constitution had long been gaining adherents in law schools and progressive circles. "Society . . . ," Woodrow Wilson wrote in 1912, "must obey the laws of life, not of mechanics; it must develop. All that progressives ask . . . is permission—in an era when 'development,' 'evolution,' is the scientific word—to interpret the Constitution according to the Darwinian principle; all they ask is recognition of the fact that a nation is a living thing and not a machine." It was the influence of Darwin, clearly, that accounted for the abundance of biological metaphors. The founders, wrote an editorialist for the *New York Times* in 1900, "put together a skeleton, covered only with sufficient elastic tissue to give it action." The Constitution they drafted "is not a fossil or a mummy." On the Supreme Court, Holmes was the principal spokesman for the idea that, as he wrote, "the provisions of the Constitution are not mathematical formulas . . . they are organic living institutions."

The shift was more than semantic. The nation's founders—steeped in the Enlightenment, intellectually indebted to Newtonian science—had seen the Constitution as a machine, a well-calibrated instrument. "Natural law," invariable as gravity, dictated common law; legal reasoning was formalistic and deductive. The facts of a case pointed to certain rules or precedents, and the judge's job was simply to declare which rule governed. Notions like these soon fell out of intellectual fashion, but made a resurgence toward the end of the nineteenth century, when they were conjoined with doctrines of more recent vintage (such as substantive due process) and put to use in nullifying the income tax, overturning a ban on child labor, narrowing the scope of the antitrust laws, and more. The defenders of the Constitution-as-mechanism had, as a rule, a greater stake in the established economic order and, not coincidentally, in judicial doctrines that perpetuated it. One's choice of metaphor said much about one's politics.

This period of judicial assertiveness was also, not coincidentally, the high-water mark of judges' timeless insistence that they did not make law; the more aggressive they grew in overruling legislatures, the more they assumed a posture of humility and passivity. The law, they said, was a science, and the Constitution was just what it said it was, in plain language. A judge merely followed its dictates—certainly not those of his conscience or even his judgment. They maintained, as Chief Justice John Marshall once proclaimed, that "courts are the mere instruments of the law, and can will nothing."

In his landmark study, *The Common Law* (1881), Holmes dismissed this as an elaborate pose. The formal logic of the law, he argued, was at best an illusion, at worst a mask for what actually determined the outcome of cases: "the felt necessities of the time, the prevalent moral and political theories, intuitions of public policy, avowed or unconscious, even the prejudices which judges share with their fellow men." Holmes did not lament this. Rather, he felt that it was time for judges to admit and embrace it. Under his influence, many did, including Brandeis and Cardozo, both of whom believed that judges should consider the likely social impact of their decisions. Only in this way, they said, could judges know whether justice was, in fact, being done.

The apostles of "organic law" subscribed to the modern notion that human beings—not immutable natural laws, as laissez-faire economists and politicians and judges insisted—were the primary agents of change in the world. In the late 1920s, in an influential book called *The Living Constitution*, a Columbia law professor named Howard Lee McBain argued that the Constitution had not been "handed down on Mount Sinai by the Lord God of Hosts." Instead, it had been written by men and was always in the process of being interpreted—and reinterpreted—by men. "Judges are men," McBain declared, with a touch of defiance. If this obvious fact needed stating at all—defiantly, no less—it was due to the fierce resilience of what Felix Frankfurter called the "theological tradition" of jurisprudence. Its high priests did not deny that judges were, in fact, human beings. What they did dispute was that the human element—whether prejudice, doubt, fear, or favor—played a role in judicial decisions.

Yet by the 1930s it was getting harder for anyone to insist that constitutional terms like "liberty" and "property" and "due process of law" had some kind of intrinsic meaning—let alone one that compelled judges to decide, far more often than not, in favor of capital over labor, private interest over public, the individual over the community. Decades of thundering dissents by Holmes and Brandeis had done much damage to this proposition. So had the attacks of "legal realists" like Jerome Frank of Yale, who derided judges' incantation of "magical phrases" to create the appearance of consistency, clarity, and impartiality in decisions where none existed. Cardozo's *Nature of the Judicial Process* (1921), one of the source texts of the new movement, stressed the ambiguity of some of the most frequently invoked provisions of the Constitution—for example, the due process clause. "Here," Cardozo pointed out, "is a concept of the greatest generality. . . . Liberty is not defined. Its limits are not mapped and charted. How shall they be known? Does liberty mean the same thing for successive generations?"

The judge's role, as Cardozo defined it, was to respect precedent but to imbue enduring principles with new relevance, always serving the public good. Like Cardozo, most realists were deep believers in democratic government. Their assault on abstraction and formalism in law was, in part, an attempt to redeem the promise of self-government, by empowering communities (local, state, and national) to correct injustices through social welfare legislation and by valuing facts above legalistic abstractions. But over time it became apparent that the realists' rejection of the idea of a higher law—and thus their denial that any objective basis or absolute moral standard existed to guide judicial decisions—called into question whether America's really could be a government of laws, or merely of men.

The latter notion terrified traditionalists like James M. Beck. What the realists saw as simple, incontrovertible facts, conservatives saw as cunning, barely cloaked arguments for "personal government"—in other words, dictatorship. In Beck's view, the day that judges—or, for that matter, presidents—were free to determine for themselves what the Constitution provided, the Constitution was dead. During the Hundred Days, in the climate of crisis and national unity, few other than Beck gave voice to such concerns; but he did so with fervor, and no doubt spoke for others. When the House of Representatives (briefly) debated the Agricultural Adjustment Act, Congressman Beck erupted that the Constitution made perfectly plain that the federal government had no power to regulate agriculture. Those who suggested otherwise, he said, were using democratic institutions to subvert democracy. "Chancellor

Hitler," he concluded, "is at least frank about it. We pay the Constitution lip service, but the result is the same."

Hard as it was for Beck to believe, Franklin Roosevelt harbored no dictatorial ambitions. "Personal government" was not his goal. He did, however, conceive of government in highly personal terms—in the sense that strong relationships might overcome the natural tendency of any one branch to regard the other two with suspicion. Checks and balances, by design, slowed down—sometimes to a halt—the gears of governance. What the framers put in place was a system of mutual frustration; what Roosevelt sought was a process of cooperation, collaboration. In that spirit, he saw no reason why the Supreme Court should not become a partner in his efforts. This, he told his aides, was how things had worked in New York. As governor, he said, he had consulted freely and frequently with the state's highest court. There is no clear evidence that he ever did so. What he might have been remembering was that the New York Court of Appeals had backed him on certain important questions, namely, his legal battle with the legislature over control of the state budget. Regardless, Roosevelt looked back at his years in Albany as an idyllic time of cross-branch collaboration. He expressed this feeling to Justice Cardozo, who had served on the Court of Appeals until shortly before FDR was elected president. "As I have told you," he wrote to Cardozo on the eve of the inauguration, "I hope that I can have at least in part the same type of delightful relations with the Supreme Court which I had with the Court of Appeals."

This was not a vague or idle ambition. In Robert Jackson's view, FDR hoped to consult with the Supreme Court on remedies for the Depression. This idea, offensive as it was to the constitutional separation of powers, did not strike FDR as in any way improper. "Roosevelt didn't see as clearly the line of distinction between executive and judicial power as some people did," Jackson recalled. Neither did he feel as bound by past practice—though American history held one notable example of a president looking to the Court for counsel. In 1793, George Washington, striving to keep the country out of the European war, sought the Supreme Court's advice on a range of complex questions, including the powers of the federal government and the obligations imposed by treaties between the United States and France. In a letter to the justices, Secretary of State Thomas Jefferson explained that President Washington "would be much relieved if he found himself free to refer questions of this description" to the Court, whose expertise "would secure us against errors dangerous to the peace of the United States." Chief Justice John Jay, in a delicately worded reply, offered his regrets.

Chief Justice Hughes, 140 years later, was similarly cool to the suggestion—which FDR had passed along through associates. Though Hughes, at the time of the inaugural, had expressed pleasure at "being associated with you in our great American enterprise," no one who knew Hughes would have seen this as anything more than a pleasantry. Of the other justices, only Brandeis discussed policy matters with the president, but he carefully refrained from discussing cases or constitutional questions. Mostly, to keep a certain distance, Brandeis used Frankfurter as a conduit. The Harvard professor offered to perform a similar service for Harlan Fiske Stone, another old friend. "As things come up from time to time which you think should reach [FDR's] ears," he wrote, "you ought to feel free to communicate them." Stone did, on occasion, pass along thoughts on personnel (but nothing more).

If anyone was ideally suited to this role, it was Felix Frankfurter. His relationships at the highest levels of government were so extensive, and his influence so pervasive, that some of his friends said that a Supreme Court appointment, when it inevitably came, would be a step down. Descended from a line of rabbis three centuries long, Frankfurter, by 1933, seemed to regard the whole of official Washington as his congregation. "He will deny it if you ask him," the *New York Times* observed. Frankfurter worked hard to stay out of the spotlight, shunning interviews and public speeches in favor of the telephone, lengthy handwritten letters, telegrams, and stealthy visits to the White House, the homes of Supreme Court justices, and the offices of his "boys"—young men like Tom Corcoran and Ben Cohen whom he had placed in strategic positions throughout the administration. Quietly but energetically, the bantam, birdlike professor offered counsel on matters of politics, policy, and law. He bounced into rooms, laughing and chattering, speaking rapidly in a voice that bore traces of Vienna, from which he had emigrated in 1894 at age twelve.

Frankfurter's covert role earned him comparisons to everyone from Machiavelli to Iago, Svengali, Rasputin, Richelieu, and Jiminy Cricket—"the chirping little Keeper of the Conscience," as *The New Yorker* described him. FDR, in this analogy, was Pinocchio, the cricket's "big, happy-go-lucky, venturesome friend and master." Frankfurter had known Roosevelt well for more than two decades—a friendship formed in the checkerboard halls of the State, War, and Navy Building, where, on the eve of the First World War, both men had served in the Wilson Administration. As the years passed, FDR called on him with growing frequency. Amid an endless stream of needless flattery, Frankfurter offered the president advice on New Deal policies and, increasingly, shared his thoughts on the predilections and personalities of the Supreme Court justices—who, in turn, sought his insights into that often perplexing man in the White House.

This back-channel communication was in no way at odds with Frankfurter's belief in the independence of the judiciary. On the contrary: the division of governmental power into three branches, Frankfurter once said, was not a "technical legal doctrine. . . . Functions have been allowed to courts as to which Congress itself might have legislated; matters have been drawn from courts and vested in the Executive. . . . Enforcement of a rigid conception of separation of powers would make modern government impossible."

What Roosevelt really needed, more than the justices' advice, was their assent: he needed them to uphold the New Deal when its programs were inevitably challenged in court. In 1933, in that remarkable moment of common purpose, it was fair to assume that the justices, no less than anyone else, wanted to do their part. Judges were human beings; surely they could not be indifferent to suffering on such a scale. Some lower court judges were not: the District of Columbia Supreme Court, in an early, favorable ruling on the NRA, cited an old maxim that the "safety of the people is the supreme law," adding that, during an emergency, "all laws should be read . . . in light of the law of necessity."

There were also signs that some U.S. Supreme Court justices might be taking "judicial notice" of what Brandeis once called "an emergency more serious than war." Just weeks after Roosevelt took office, the Court, in a surprisingly relaxed interpretation of federal anti-trust laws, permitted more than a hundred coal companies to pool output and merge sales operations. Hughes, writing for the majority, emphasized the public purpose served by such a business combination—to "aid in relieving a depressed industry" and eliminate the "evils" of slash-and-burn competition. A few months later, in a commencement address at Deerfield Academy, Hughes again appeared to signal sympathy with the broader objectives of the New Deal. Sounding a bit like the reform-minded governor of a quarter century earlier—and not unlike FDR himself—the Chief Justice relegated pure, unmitigated individualism to the past. "We cannot save ourselves," he declared, "unless we save society. No one can go it alone."

All this suggested that the Supreme Court, as *Time* observed, was "not unresponsive to the shifting economic thought of the nation. . . . New ideas, like cosmic rays, have a way of penetrating its ancient wall of detachment." The recent past seemed to bear this out. When, in previous decades, the tide of reform had surged, the Court had tried to slow it but did not attempt to reverse it altogether. By 1933, in the view of most scholars, the Court—despite its conservatism in recent decades—had sufficient precedents to sustain just about anything Roosevelt might conceivably propose.

Historically, the Court—whether out of judicial restraint, deference to public opinion, or an instinct for self-preservation—had most often chosen the path of least resistance, and now appeared likely to do so again. In the Supreme Court term ending in June 1933, the majority upheld state regulations in a number of areas, from farm equipment to gas rates, that it might once have placed outside the reach of government. The decisions concerned state, not federal, power, but were welcome news for the administration. "In dealing with given cases," Homer Cummings told a gathering of the American Bar Association, "I am confident that the Courts, in the words of Mr. Justice Holmes, will consider them 'in the light of our whole experience, and not merely by what was said a hundred years ago.' " During the first half of 1933, that confidence was widely shared.

• • •

"Take the New Deal to Court!" demanded *The New Republic* that fall. If the Supreme Court, as it appeared, shared in the spirit of national purpose, then the time to press for a verdict was now, before that spirit ebbed. It was widely assumed that New Deal lawyers would quickly seek test cases to establish the constitutionality of innovative new laws lest those laws be flouted without fear. This proactive approach to litigation, as practiced by previous administrations, entailed searching out and prosecuting the most unsympathetic offenders; crafting airtight cases that presented the constitutional issues in the most favorable light; and pressing for expedited hearings.

But by late 1933, none of this had been done—an uncharacteristically passive posture for an activist administration. With each passing month, the administration's failure to move quickly into the courtroom became more and more of an embarrassment, casting a shadow over the New Deal and encouraging violators and critics. An impression spread—through the press, the government, and the business community—that such hesitancy revealed a lack of confidence. It was an "open secret in Washington," *The New Republic* observed, "that the legal defenses of the New Deal are in a bad way." Others (Stone included) complained that the Department of Justice was shockingly short on legal talent. Cummings, after twenty-five years on the Democratic National Committee, had at least as many political debts to repay as he now had jobs to dispense. "Whenever a deserving Democrat has turned up who could not be unloaded anywhere else, Homer Cummings has obliged," reported Drew Pearson and Robert Allen, who wrote a widely read newspaper column. They added that the appointment of J. Crawford Biggs as solicitor general—the principal official who argues cases before the Supreme Court—was a favor to a senator and a cabinet member and had filled New Dealers with "much . . . disgust."

To a certain extent, the administration was simply distracted. After the first Hundred Days came the second, and the third; and with the nation still mired in the Depression, passing new recovery measures still took precedence over testing them in court. There was also a tactical argument for foot-dragging: administration officials assumed that after a while, the results of the NRA and AAA would speak for themselves more persuasively than any legal brief. The programs, it was hoped, would be legitimated by their own success—or, at least, entrenched enough that any justice would think twice about overturning them and inviting widespread upheaval, outrage, even panic.

In other words, the official approach to litigation was to avoid it as long as possible. When an NRA case made it onto the Supreme Court's calendar, Cummings moved to have it postponed. The justices, to his relief, obliged. "Our good fortune still holds in the Supreme Court," he scribbled in a note to Roosevelt. Felix Frankfurter, who shared their belief that the New Deal was constitutional, also shared their reluctance to test the proposition. "Why are you so anxious for a decision," he asked an insistent law student, "until you are sure of getting the right one?" As an exceedingly close observer of the Court, Frankfurter saw no indication of a fundamental shift. "Supreme Court decisions . . . may unmake us," he cautioned a fellow advocate of minimum-wage legislation—which, in recent decades, had been overturned more than once by the Court. "It seems to me foolish beyond words to be cavalier about them and to be hopeful that a changed Court or changing times will make for a very liberal outlook on the part of the Court, and more particularly does it seem foolish to me beyond measure to build on expectations of a *bouleversement* from the majority of the nine. I can assure you that there is no right to any such hope under the leadership of Hughes, let alone the others."

Even so, the delays were costly. Unresolved concerns about the constitutionality of the National Recovery Act, in particular, had a corrosive effect on the agency's operations. General Hugh Johnson, its administrator, was in many ways the least inhibited man in Washington: binging, alternately, on work and alcohol; throwing fits and pursuing vendettas; and ever waging some relentless campaign. Yet for all his brash confidence, Johnson felt himself a paper tiger. He nurtured deep doubts about the basic provisions of the Recovery Act. For the NRA's codes to be effective, the government needed power, obviously, to enforce them. Foreseeing this, Johnson had demanded and received "a rigorous licensing power"—in effect, the ability to shut down any company that failed to comply. But even before the act had passed, Johnson had already concluded that this authority lacked a constitutional basis—just as Charles Wyzanski had complained to Frankfurter.

From the start, then, the NRA was something of a bluff. Lacking authority he himself could believe in, Johnson saw that the act was "absolutely unenforceable without a strong surge of public opinion behind it." He threw himself, full-bodied, into generating that surge—hoping, in effect, to intimidate businesses into complying with the codes. In this way, what had begun as an instrument of industrial-governmental cooperation became, under Johnson's command, a mass movement. "Those who are not with us are against us," he declared. The NRA was more than a government program. It was equal parts spiritual revival, political campaign, and wartime mobilization. It spawned songs, public meetings, parades—including the biggest march in the history of New York, nearly 2 million people pouring down, or standing along, Fifth Avenue. The NRA's logo, the fearsome Blue Eagle, and its motto, "We Do Our Part," were, for a time, almost as ubiquitous as the flag and "In God We Trust." They graced any product or the front window of any business that complied with a code. The eagle flew atop the masthead of the *New York Times* and most other papers; it alighted on the ad pages of popular magazines. In October 1933, a reader of the *Saturday Evening Post*, for example, would find, in the span of a few pages, NRA-approved advertisements for Duofold "health underwear," Mennen menthol-iced lather shave, and Shuron Firmflex shock absorber mountings for rimless eyeglasses. Each, clearly, was doing its part.

All the while, Roosevelt was approving codes at breakneck speed, hoping that by the time the NRA faced its day in court, the judges would be presented with a fait accompli. It was a gamble, but it was really the only option. And for a time it seemed to be working well. Industries, one by one, fell into line. By September 1933, the president was signing several codes a week; before the year's end, the rate was two a day. Still, it was apparent to some observers that all this activity was a sign not of prowess but of weakness: "one of the deepest weaknesses of the administration," *The New Republic* judged in November. This echoed Johnson's, and by now Roosevelt's, own worries about the NRA's future.

In Roosevelt's circle, the blithe assuredness—or cockiness—of spring had given way, by the fall, to a growing unease. The administration began to steel itself for a fight not just in the Supreme Court but throughout the entire federal judiciary. On November 8, 1933,

Cummings handed the president an extensive report on "the political alignments now existing in our Federal Courts." The memo proceeded—district by district, judge by judge, beginning with the Supreme Court and descending, by degrees, all the way down to police courts, courts of claims, of customs and patent appeals—to demonstrate just how fully the deck was stacked against the New Deal. "I am sure you will find [this] exceedingly interesting," Cummings concluded. "You will note that of 266 Judges listed, only 28% are Democrats."

On the campaign trail, Roosevelt had charged Republicans with "control" of the Supreme Court bench. That had been easy to quantify: seven justices were Republicans, two were Democrats. But now, thanks to the work of his attorney general, Roosevelt could see just how far that control extended, and just how difficult it was going to be for the New Deal to get a fair trial.

Not all New Dealers were alarmed. Many doubted that the Supreme Court would dare cross the president—or the public. FDR's popularity was high; the economic emergency was still acute; and popular enthusiasm for the NRA, while hardly spontaneous or self-sustaining, suggested that Americans stood solidly behind reform. In *The Nation*, a law professor derided the Court as "powerless" to do anything but ratify the New Deal. "The revolution is here," he proclaimed. "A revolution in the Supreme Court is bound to follow as a matter of course." And if it did not? The professor added ominously that "no one would be surprised if Congress and the President should utilize the power, which they always have in reserve, of 'packing' the court—that is to say, of appointing additional justices to secure a favorable majority. . . . The court has been packed before . . . and it can be packed again."

Indeed, the number of justices was not sacrosanct. The Constitution, in fact, says nothing on the subject. The size of the Supreme Court bench is determined by Congress and can be changed, as Woodrow Wilson once wrote, "whenever the legislative will so pleases." The British historian and legal scholar James Bryce, in his classic study of U.S. political institutions, *The American Commonwealth* (1888), observed that the founding fathers had either "forgotten or deemed [it] undesirable" to determine the number of justices, perhaps because a growing nation might, before long, need more judges, from the lowest courts to the very highest. Yet this invited abuse. "Here," wrote Bryce, "was a weak point, a joint in the court's armour through which a weapon might some day penetrate."

In 1789, Congress set the Court's membership at six, directly tying the number of justices to the number of federal circuit courts. In 1801, Congress severed that link. The number of justices fell to five. Over the next seven decades, Congress would expand and contract the Court with some frequency—sometimes in response to the Court's jurisdiction, but more often such concerns were a pretext for a power struggle between the president and Congress. James Madison, James Monroe, John Quincy Adams, and Andrew Jackson all tried to convince Congress that the Supreme Court needed more judges; all failed, due to the refusal of Congress to grant these presidents the chance to make appointments. Only in 1837, on the last day of Jackson's term, did Congress raise the count to nine, and then, in 1863, to ten to secure the Court's support for Abraham Lincoln's war policies.

Up and down the number went, as presidents and Congress battled for control. In 1866, when Andrew Johnson nominated his attorney general to fill a vacant seat on the Court, Congress promptly eliminated the seat—and, for good measure, another as well, pending the next retirement. That same year, Republicans erupted in violent condemnation of the Court's decision in the *Milligan* case, which called into question the military occupation of the South and sparked fears that the Court would overturn the whole legal framework of Reconstruction. In that event, *Harper's Weekly* declared, "let the Supreme Court be swamped by a thorough reorganization and increased number of Judges. . . . The remodeling of the Court may truly be called an extreme measure, to be adopted only in most extraordinary cases, as that which would arise if the . . . Judges should deliberately undertake to nullify the will of the majority of the people of the United States." The idea won little support in the Congress, where members of both parties denounced it as a "desperate and disgraceful" attempt to "pack" the Court.

Yet it loomed, as ever, as a threat—just as Bryce had foreseen. "This method," he wrote, looking back at the controversy, "is plainly susceptible of further and possibly dangerous application." If Congress and the president—so often at odds with one another—found themselves united in opposition to the Supreme Court, then what, Bryce asked, could stop them from packing it?

> Not the mechanism of government. . . . Not the conscience of the legislature and the President, for heated combatants seldom shrink from justifying the means by the end. Nothing but the fear of the people, whose broad good sense and attachment to the great principles of the Constitution may generally be relied on to condemn such a perversion of its forms. . . . To the people we come sooner or later: it is upon their wisdom and self-restraint that the stability of the most cunningly devised scheme of government will in the last resort depend.

By 1933, the threat seemed remote. In the interest of judicial efficiency, Congress had restored two seats to the Court in 1869, raising the number of justices to nine. And there it stood. By the time Franklin Roosevelt became president, the number had been fixed for nearly sixty-five years. It remained subject, as ever, to the wishes of Congress, but few Americans could possibly have remembered a time when there were any more or less than nine men in robes.

In April, a precinct committeeman from Illinois wrote FDR with an idea. Resistance to the New Deal, the man wrote, was rising, and might soon "force us to take short cuts. If the Supreme Court's membership could be increased to twelve, without too much trouble, perhaps the Constitution would be found to be quite elastic." Roosevelt had Louis Howe, his closest adviser, respond to the letter, offering thanks for the official's "kindness in sending the suggestion." Still, nothing indicates that Roosevelt took the idea seriously. Though the *Literary Digest* attributed rumors of Court-packing plans to "the intimate Presidential circle," the diaries of Cummings, Ickes, and other advisers reveal no thinking along these lines. The columnist Mark Sullivan was almost certainly correct in declaring that "such suggestions are very distant from reflecting the President's mind."

Chapter Four

THE DYING OF THE LIGHT

"THIS AFTERNOON MOTHER and I go, with the other Justices and their wives, to be received by the President and Mrs. Roosevelt," Harlan Fiske Stone wrote his two sons shortly after the inauguration. He added, with a wink: "I am not sure but what the pillars of the Constitution will fall. Some of my brethren seem to think so."

During the first year of the Roosevelt presidency, as New Deal programs began their slow passage through the judicial system, there was little for the justices to do but wait, attend to other business, and watch—with varying degrees of enthusiasm or dismay—as the new president transformed the national landscape. Willis Van Devanter's reaction was typical of the Court's conservatives. For a brief moment, he looked favorably on the bank closings, describing himself as "much pleased" with Roosevelt's action. "The financial situation appears to be well in hand," Van Devanter wrote his sister just after the inauguration, adding, "the President has been taking a courageous course." Within a few weeks, however, his doubts resurfaced. "Some of the subsequent measures do not look so good," he told a friend. "My fear is that we are going to pile up an indebtedness which cannot be paid for a century and that we are drifting towards things which are wholly impracticable."

James McReynolds was downright alarmist. While conceding, in a letter to his brother, that "the new President has gotten some apparently worthwhile things accomplished," he hastened to add that Roosevelt's "farm relief plan looks simply crazy & if put into law nobody can tell what will happen. I hope Congress will show some good sense. And the fact that Roosevelt has proposed such a thing is evidence of his mental infirmity—& lack of stability." This was a frequent charge by McReynolds. "I think the head is utterly incompetent," he wrote his brother. "So have been the people who should have led the way. They have been imbeciles!" The United States, he added ominously, was headed for another crash.

Brandeis looked more favorably on the New Deal. This was to be expected. Few Americans had worked as long, or strenuously, or effectively for social reform and social justice as Louis D. Brandeis. In the years before 1916, when Wilson made him the first Jewish member of the Supreme Court, Brandeis made his fortune practicing commercial law in Boston and then made his name as "the people's lawyer"—battling injustice and corruption, often forgoing his fee, and insisting, with increasing force and persuasiveness, that empirical, socioeconomic data, not just legal formulas, should help guide judges' decisions. In 1908, in the case of *Muller v. Oregon*, Brandeis went before the Supreme Court to argue on behalf of a state law that limited working hours for women in factories and laundries. Brandeis not only won a 9–0 decision—no small feat, for the Court of the period had been mostly intolerant toward reform—but also created an enduring model for defending reform measures in court. His brief in the case—the "Brandeis brief," as it became known—dedicated two pages to legal precedent and more than a hundred pages to evidence (medical reports, psychological studies, and more) of the devastating effects of long working hours on the "health, safety, morals and general welfare of women." Oregon's law, Brandeis insisted, could only be judged against this background. "Until his famous argument . . . ," *The New Republic* noted in 1916, "social legislation was argued before our courts practically *in vacuo*, as an abstract question unrelated to a world of factories and labor and trade unions and steel trusts."

By 1933, Brandeis stood above reproach. He had long ago quieted the critics of his nomination—who had charged, among other things, that as a zealous advocate, he lacked the "judicial temperament." His legal philosophy now seemed ascendant, as social and economic facts were increasingly admitted into courtrooms; he had predicted much of what befell the country in 1929; his disciples populated the new administration; and his advice was eagerly sought, and frequently heeded, by the president himself. To the lawyers who staffed the New Deal, Brandeis was a hero, moral exemplar, and more. On meeting the justice, one young man concluded that "this was about the closest I was ever going to get to meeting God in person." Even someone as hard-boiled as Ickes had to admit, after his first audience with Brandeis, feeling "as if I were sitting at the feet of one of the fine old prophets." Brandeis's mane of gray hair invited the comparison. So did his righteous tone. Many, FDR included, called him "Old Isaiah." Others noted his likeness to Lincoln (whom his uncle had helped nominate in 1860): the deep-set, sensitive eyes, the lanky, slightly burdened figure, the air of grace and hard-won wisdom.

Still, from the beginning, Brandeis was uneasy about important aspects of the New Deal. While seeing "promise in many specific undertakings," as he wrote Frankfurter, he often referred to Roosevelt's reforms as *Kunststucke*: "clever tricks." As early as the summer of 1933 he had decided that "things are not going well here." The NRA in particular was having "troubles galore." Several months later, he saw "evidence . . . that the *Kunststucke* (including both NRA and AAA) are having the effect of retarding recovery."

The New Deal had run headlong into the obsession of Brandeis's life: "bigness." Above all, Brandeis placed his faith in the individual, the family farmer, the small businessman, the local community—all of which, he believed, faced annihilation in an era of industrial combination. He did not, like Theodore Roosevelt, accept bigness as an inevitability of the machine age. While the New Nationalists had hoped to tame and control the forces of consolidation, Brandeis—who helped shape Wilson's New Freedom—demanded instead that monopolies be crushed and competition restored. "Power," he said, "must always feel the check of power." He saw unbounded authority of any kind—private or public; business or labor; legislative, judicial, or presidential—as anathema to individual liberty. Hence his abhorrence of the NRA. Not only did it concentrate power in the hands of the president, but it waived certain anti-trust laws and allowed—even required—corporations to collude in the drafting of codes.

Bigness, Brandeis warned a member of Roosevelt's Brain Trust, was always badness. "It was a terrible thing to vest absolute power in one man," he lamented to Frankfurter. FDR's feeling of "infallibility," he believed, was a grave danger, with the price to be paid in failed experiments, lost opportunities, and the emboldening of "reactionaries." To his daughter, Brandeis wrote that "if the Lord had intended things to be big, he would have made man bigger—in brains and character."

"You are, I am sure, aware that [Stone] has genuine sympathies on the essential issues of the day," Frankfurter informed Roosevelt shortly after the inauguration. "He is one of the really dependable liberals on the Court."

This was true—though it did not make him a New Dealer. Son of a Chesterfield, New Hampshire, farmer, and looking rather like one himself—broad-shouldered, wide-browed, and square-chinned; plainly dressed, despite his wealth and station, in a New England "sugarloaf" hat—Harlan Fiske Stone was moderate in style, outlook, and temperament. Nearly a decade after his Amherst College acquaintance, Calvin Coolidge, had appointed him to the Court—following many years as the dean of Columbia Law School and a short stint as attorney general—Stone remained a loyal Yankee Republican. His perspective on economic policy was fairly orthodox. It differed little from that of Hoover, whom he considered a dear friend. Fundamentally, Stone was an individualist who believed that the existing social order was sound—not in need of much modification, least of all by do-gooders and dreamers.

All of this had placed him—at first—in the company of the Court's conservatives. When Stone arrived on the Court in 1925, Chief Justice Taft invited him to his home on Sunday afternoons with the other conservatives. For a time, Stone also lined up with them in the majority. Before long, though, Stone found himself deeply, often bitterly, at odds with his conservative colleagues over basic questions of law, and he joined Holmes and Brandeis in dissent. Like them, he had a natural skepticism and a loathing of dogma. Like them, he reacted angrily to the insistence that the Constitution's meaning was static, perfectly apparent, and easy to apply. Stone also deplored the majority's willingness to override state legislatures when they passed social and economic reforms; he believed, above all, in judicial restraint.

Even so, one of his clerks later wondered whether Stone might have stuck with the conservatives had they been "abler and more attractive men." McReynolds, trying clumsily to draw Stone back into the fold, once demanded that he get out of the "fog" and "Stop, Look, and Listen," lest he "unconsciously aid" the liberals. At its core, however, this was not a problem of personalities. It was a clash of worldviews—and Stone's was changing. The Depression had shaken his faith in untrammeled individualism. "Mere material gain to the individual may not in itself be the social good it once was conceived to be," he reflected. Business leaders, Stone had come to believe, were the true "enemies of capitalism"; they had badly betrayed the public trust. "Perhaps the most astonishing manifestation of our times is the blindness of those who have the big stake in our present system to its evils," he wrote Frankfurter. He even took it upon himself to educate his old friend Hoover. "The issues," Stone implored the former president, "cannot be settled by an appeal to the eighteenth-century philosophy of individualism in the abstract, for that philosophy cannot be completely adapted to the twentieth-century state."

Again, this did not make him a New Dealer. He remained wary of the type—a category that included the president himself. "I certainly wish him well," Stone wrote his sons early in the Hundred Days, but he soon came to deplore the expansion of presidential power; the hasty resort to "drastic" and untested measures; the broad and vague mandates given to new agencies; and the apparent abdication of Congress and the GOP. Dispirited by the New Deal, relegated by Hughes—whose imperiousness infuriated him—to writing mostly inconsequential opinions, Stone sank into what one of his clerks considered a "genuine depression." He considered quitting the Court and going into private practice. "I miss the old crowd," he wrote Hoover in March. Events were moving so quickly, he added, that it seemed decades, not a mere two months, had passed since the inauguration. "Most of the party have left town by now and the Stones remain, hanging like the last leaves on the tree."

The medicine ball he used to toss with Hoover on the White House lawn now sat on his desk, the sad relic of another era.

But Stone was resilient. By the fall, he had reconciled himself to living under the new regime. His social calendar was full, and with the coming end of Prohibition, he could again indulge his passion for wines, reserving many bottles ahead of repeal to restock his once ample cellar. More important, after the Court's long quiet season, Stone was about to reckon with the nation's most pressing questions. "We live from day to day on political and governmental excitement over gold seizures, N.R.A., etc.," he wrote his sons at the start of the term, adding—with a characteristically muted but real sense of excitement—that "some of these matters, I imagine, will ultimately get to our Court."

That fall, the Supreme Court heard what Stone identified as "the first of the 'New Deal' cases argued before us." It was in fact a Minnesota state law, not a New Deal measure, that came before the Court, but the Minnesota statute was similar in spirit and purpose to important elements of Roosevelt's agenda. The case, born of desperation in the farm belt, concerned the epidemic of foreclosures. In April 1933, prompted in no small part by a mob of several thousand farmers, the Minnesota legislature had passed a "mortgage moratorium," allowing cash-strapped homeowners to seek relief in court. John Blaisdell was one of them. A judge awarded him a two-year extension in the term of his mortgage at a greatly reduced monthly payment. Blaisdell's lender, the Home Building & Loan Association, sued, claiming that the moratorium violated Article I, Section 10, clause 1 of the U.S. Constitution, which forbids states from "impairing the obligation of contracts." When Minnesota's highest court ruled for Blaisdell, Home Building & Loan appealed to the U.S. Supreme Court.

As an associate justice, Hughes had gone farther than any of his colleagues in defending a state's right to override contracts in the public interest. Those cases, however, concerned public contracts—railways, for example, or telephone lines—not private contracts like the one John Blaisdell had with Home Building & Loan. This gave liberals a measure of hope in this case, but not much confidence. *Harper's Monthly*, reviewing Hughes's record as Chief Justice, concluded that "he cannot . . . be counted on in the present crisis to support the revolutionary aspects of the New Deal. He is noted neither for realistic perception nor for extraordinary vision."

After the *Blaisdell* decision, however, he would be credited with both. On January 8, 1934, joined by Brandeis, Cardozo, Roberts, and Stone, Hughes affirmed the decision of the Minnesota Supreme Court in ringing tones: the moratorium stood. The Chief Justice spoke of "the necessity of finding ground for a rational compromise between individual rights and public welfare." As governor of New York, almost thirty years earlier, he had said the same thing many times; but it was no longer just an exhortation—now it was a mandate. "The question," he continued, drawing heavily on language provided by Cardozo, "is no longer merely that of one party to a contract as against another, but of the use of reasonable means to safeguard the economic structure upon which the good of all depends. It is no answer to say that this public need was not apprehended a century ago, or to insist that what the provision of the Constitution meant to the vision of that day it must mean to the vision of our time."

Hughes described the Constitution as a flexible, adaptable instrument. He conceded that some of its provisions were highly specific, giving judges unmistakable instructions. But other sections—such as the contracts clause—were no more than "a broad outline," which meant that "construction is essential to fill in the details." Therefore—and this was the crux of his argument—the clause might be read one way (restrictively) in normal times, but another way (more loosely) in a moment of great urgency. And this, clearly, was such a moment. "While emergency does not create power," Hughes said, in the most frequently quoted passage of his opinion, "emergency may furnish the occasion for the exercise of power." In other words, the Depression did not give the state new powers; rather, it gave lawmakers recourse to powers they always held in reserve. Or, as Hughes had put it in the 1920s, a "legislature may meet public emergencies by action that ordinarily would go beyond its constitutional authority. . . . Unusual and urgent conditions may justify temporary expedients." This helps explains why, in his *Blaisdell* opinion, Hughes took pains to emphasize the "temporary and conditional" nature of the Minnesota law, which was set to expire in two years.

Hughes concluded with a preemptive shot at the dissenters. "We find no warrant for the conclusion that the [Contracts] clause has been warped," he declared. Quite the contrary: the Court's majority "sought to prevent the perversion of the clause through its use as an instrument to throttle the capacity of the states to protect their fundamental interests. This development," he added, again echoing Cardozo, "is a growth from the seeds which the fathers planted."

George Sutherland wrote the dissent. Pale, slender, and soft-spoken, and looking, in the view of some observers, more like a French teacher than a judge, Sutherland was a quiet force on the Court of the twenties and thirties. He was generally gracious toward his colleagues, tolerant of opposing views, and, at the same time, utterly immovable. "The sweetness of disposition makes Sutherland all the more effective," noted the columnists Drew Pearson and Robert Allen. "Sutherland can wrap the poison in a pill of sweet and sonorous pontification."

Born in England in 1862, Sutherland was raised from infancy in the Utah Territory, where he imbibed the Mormon notion that the Constitution was divinely inspired and that, as Brigham Young had prophesied, the document's fate would someday hang "upon a single thread." Though not himself a Mormon, Sutherland held fast to this article of faith as he rose through the ranks of the Republican Party. As a U.S. senator, he backed, for a time, the agenda of Theodore Roosevelt, but soon lost patience with reformers—denouncing them, in his quiet but fervent way, as "an amiable band of insurgent soothsayers, who have been going up and down the land indulging in cabalistic utterances" and "careening after novel and untried things." Neither the public interest nor the Constitution were well served, in Sutherland's view, by "doubtful experiment" or "a mania for regulating people." James Bryce, the British historian, described Sutherland as the "living voice of the Constitution"—but if so, it was a confining Constitution, a set of limitations. On the Court, where President Harding placed him in 1922, Sutherland set about defending the Constitution against all manner of encroachments, and assumed the intellectual leadership of the conservative majority.

Now, after a decade of predominance, Sutherland did not go meekly into the minority. Uncharacteristically, his dissent in *Blaisdell* was full of scorn, sarcasm, and a sense of imminent doom. The mortgage moratorium, he began, was bad enough, but "trivial" in comparison to the damage done by the majority opinion: "Serious and dangerous inroads upon the limitations of the Constitution . . . are almost certain to ensue." He likened the majority to a group of "bewildered travelers lost in a wood," wandering in a circle while thinking it was a straight line. He rejected, even mocked, Hughes's claim that "emergency may furnish the occasion for the exercise of power." The Constitution, for Sutherland, had a consistent—not contingent—meaning. "It does not mean one thing at one time and an entirely different thing at another time," he wrote, adding pointedly, "if the provisions of the Constitution be not upheld when they pinch as well as when they comfort, they may as well be abandoned."

This should have been sufficient. Sutherland's dissent was devastating—"one of the great opinions in American constitutional law," Brandeis told him (while declining, of course, to join him). Sutherland had answered all Hughes's arguments but one: that an economic emergency existed. He could have conceded this—or simply ignored it. After all, by his own reasoning, the point was moot, with no bearing on how the contracts clause should be interpreted. But Sutherland, it seemed, could no longer contain himself. He went on to deny what for most Americans had become the central, inescapable reality of their lives.

The Depression, wrote Sutherland, was "nothing new. From the beginning of our existence as a nation, periods of depression, of industrial failure, of financial distress, of unpaid and unpayable indebtedness, have alternated with years of plenty." Nothing about the Depression was new—except that Americans like John Blaisdell and the lawmakers who abetted him had forgotten "the vital lesson that expenditure beyond income begets poverty, that public or private extravagance" ends only in ruin. Sutherland was nostalgic for a time when "indiscretion or imprudence was not to be relieved by legislation," when the strict enforcement of contracts taught people to live thriftily and to repay their debts through "self-denial and painful effort."

Extravagance, indiscretion, imprudence: here was the verdict of Justice Sutherland on the unemployed, on the farmers whose homes had been seized and sold, on the millions in the breadlines. And here, in typically harsh terms, was the enduring influence of Herbert Spencer, the late nineteenth-century English philosopher whose work, in the Gilded Age America of Sutherland's youth, was often placed on equal standing with that of Plato and Aristotle. "Survival of the fittest"—originally Spencer's phrase, not Darwin's—served as a mission statement not only for laissez-faire capitalism and indifferent government, but also for the constitutional doctrines that made America safe for liberty, property, and "rugged" individualism.

Sutherland and the Court's conservatives believed, throughout their long lives, in what Spencer called the "mercy of severity." As Spencer wrote in *Social Statics*, his seminal work, in 1851: "The forces at work exterminate such sections of mankind as stand in the way, with the same sternness that they exterminate beasts of prey and herds of useless ruminants." This process of "purification" could not—and must not—be impeded by the state. "The ultimate result of shielding men from the effects of folly," Spencer said, "is to fill the world with fools." Or, as he elaborated in *Social Statics*:

> Pervading all Nature we may see at work a stern discipline, which is a little cruel that it may be very kind. . . . The poverty of the incapable, the distresses that come upon the imprudent, the starvation of the idle, and those shoulderings aside of the weak by the strong, which leave so many "in shallows and in miseries," are the decrees of a large, far-seeing benevolence. . . .
>
> The process *must* be undergone, and the sufferings *must* be endured. No power on Earth, no cunningly-devised laws of statesmen, no world-rectifying schemes of the humane, no communist panaceas, no reforms that men ever did broach or ever will broach, can diminish them one jot.

George Sutherland, more than three quarters of a century later, saw the Depression—and reforms like Minnesota's, and, it was safe to assume, the entire New Deal—through this same prism.

"A red-letter day," Homer Cummings exclaimed. He called the president that evening and found him "exceedingly gratified and happy." Cummings told him confidently that "the Liberal forces are in majority control of the Court, at least so far as Emergency Legislation is concerned." Many agreed. On the basis of the *Blaisdell* decision, Henry T. Rainey, Speaker of the House, predicted that the Court would "sustain every [NRA] code thus far enacted or hereafter enacted to get the country out of the depression." The editors of the *New York Times* believed that not only the NRA but the entirety of the New Deal was likely to be upheld by a Court majority that saw the Constitution "as a living and flexible organism."

Others thought this premature. Congressman James Beck, no friend of the New Deal, thundered that "the alphabetical excrescences of our already swollen Federal bureaucracy should not take too much encouragement" from *Blaisdell*, because it concerned state, not federal power. *Collier's* magazine, noting this fact, took the long view. "There is bound to be a long conflict," the editors predicted; the conservatives were sure to be heard from again. Yet *Collier's* was certain that in the end, the New Deal would prevail. "Congress, backed by public opinion, has always in reserve the power to override the Supreme Court," the editors explained. "The method is simple. More judges can be created. Of course the creation of new judges chosen to change the ruling opinions of the court would be a desperate remedy. The prestige of the court would suffer. Still the power exists and if the provocation were great enough it could be used."

Two months later, on March 5, 1934, the same five justices took another step away from provoking Congress or the president. They were led, this time, by Owen Roberts. The case, *Nebbia v. New York*, was similar to *Blaisdell* in that it concerned state regulation of economic activity: in this instance, the price of milk. The dairy industry, like the rest of the agricultural sector, was in crisis. In Wisconsin, dairy farmers had dumped milk in the streets rather than sell it for less than the cost of production. The New York legislature, unnerved by the threat of collapse and disorder, had created a control board to set a reasonable price per quart—nine cents, it turned out. New York fined Leo Nebbia, a Rochester grocer, five dollars for violating the law. He had done it intentionally, as a test of his "liberty," and appealed the case all the way to the U.S. Supreme Court.

"Neither property rights nor contract rights are absolute," declared Justice Roberts, flatly and, it seemed, impatiently. His disenchantment with tired clichés and outdated dogma was plain—namely, with the Court's frequent invocation, over the past half century, of the Fourteenth Amendment guarantee that no state shall "deprive any person of life, liberty, or property, without due process of law." This was one of the principal means by which the Court denied states the power to regulate the economy—except in those cases where the Court deemed a business to be "affected with a public interest." Did milk meet that standard? Roberts wrote that it did not—"in the accepted sense of the phrase." The dairy industry was not a public utility. Having conceded this, Roberts then widened the definition of "public interest" to the point of obliterating it.

Despite the long list of precedents that Roberts cited, this was largely new territory—for the Court and for the justice himself. He and Hughes had upheld price-fixing legislation before; both took the view that the due process clause prohibited price controls only when the policy was arbitrary, discriminatory, or capricious. In this sense, *Nebbia* was more a reaffirmation than a doctrinal revolution. Still, Roberts's abandonment of the restrictive "public interest" test—only two years after joining the majority in affirming it—was momentous. He was said to have paced the floor of his home late into the night before deciding to throw in his lot with the liberals. This he did—in ringing terms. "It is clear," Roberts wrote for the majority, "that there is no closed class or category of businesses affected with a public interest." The Constitution, he added pointedly, "does not secure to any one liberty to conduct his business in such fashion as to inflict injury upon the public at large."

Arthur Krock, the influential columnist for the *New York Times*, noted just how grim the justices looked on the day of the decision, as if they had reached "an ominous fork in the road" and could no longer march together as one. (When they ever had, Krock did not say.) *Blaisdell* and *Nebbia*, wrote Krock, revealed Hughes and Roberts as ardent liberals, and exposed "a grave and deep chasm" in the Court. McReynolds's dissent in the New York case—punctuated throughout with exclamation marks—made that especially clear. According to the conservative minority, Leo Nebbia's right to set his own price for milk was fundamental. "Facile disregard of the Constitution . . . ," McReynolds charged, "will inevitably lead to its destruction. Then, all rights will be subject to the caprice of the hour; government by stable laws will pass." The result, he concluded, quoting a Civil War–era case, was "anarchy or despotism."

For the second time in a matter of weeks, liberals were overjoyed by a decision. Many hailed *Nebbia* as even more important than *Blaisdell*—because Roberts's opinion did not rest on the crutch of temporary, "emergency" powers. Laissez-faire, crowed Princeton's Edward Corwin, a leading liberal scholar, was "in full retreat." He judged it "not at all unlikely" that the Court would uphold the NRA as a valid use of the congressional power to regulate commerce. "At least it has already blazed a fairly feasible trail to such a consummation," he wrote in a 1934 book titled—tellingly—*The Twilight of the Supreme Court*. "A new era has dawned," declared the *New York World-Telegram*. New Deal critics did not disagree. An old friend of Van Devanter wrote him that the majority opinion in *Nebbia* "leaves a trail a mile wide to drive anything through"—any policy, no matter how radical.

There were still a few skeptics. Stone perceived *Nebbia* as no more than a partial victory. For all the boldness of Roberts's language, Stone saw the opinion as fragile, conditional. Just as Hughes, in *Blaisdell*, had placed emphasis on the economic emergency—which presumably would pass—Roberts stopped short of creating sweeping new doctrine. Instead, he suggested that the Court would consider future regulations on a case-by-case basis. Both justices had marked out a path for a possible retreat.

"Has the Supreme Court abdicated?" asked Alpheus Thomas Mason, a political scientist. He doubted it. Mason noted that the Court, not too long ago, had upheld "equally radical measures"—laws protecting tenants from eviction, laws prescribing the hours and wages of employees of interstate carriers—precedents that, he pointed out, failed to "embarrass the Court later on" when it abandoned them. Also, as a number of observers had pointed out, *Blaisdell* and *Nebbia* said not a word between them about the powers of the federal government, which the Court tended to see as a different matter entirely.

If this was indeed the "twilight" of the Supreme Court, as liberals like Corwin hoped, the vehemence of Sutherland's and McReynolds's dissents showed that the conservatives were not slipping quietly into the darkness. Soon, the justices would hear their first true New Deal case, and—it was still safe to assume—the four hard-liners would have some say in the result.

Chapter Five

HEAVY BOMBARDMENT

THE DINNER GUESTS, four or five hundred of them—all men, "Big Men," it was said—filed into the Willard Hotel in Washington for the spring gathering of the Gridiron Club. Its roster represented the upper echelons of government, business, and the press. The club, such as it was, existed mostly for the purpose of throwing these dinners twice a year. Each dinner was an expansive revue of skits, songs, and speeches. There were two rules: everything said (or sung) would remain off the record, and "ladies are always present." Not physically—but gentlemen were expected to comport themselves as if their wives and daughters were actually in the room. All jokes were to be in good taste.

Tonight—April 14, 1934—the skits were "wonderfully clever, full of good humor and set forth the fallacies of the present policies in a telling way." Such was the view of Justice Van Devanter, who sat on the dais between General Douglas MacArthur, the Army chief of staff, and Senator David Reed of Pennsylvania, and dined on Terrapin à la Maryland, Mousse of Smithfield Ham in Aspic, and other courses, followed by vanilla ice cream, fancy cakes, and Pancho Arango cigars. The president of the United States, always the guest of honor, sat at the center of the high table. The spring dinner had been delayed a week because FDR had taken ill while fishing off the coast of Florida. But tonight, as he tossed his head back and roared at the jokes, including those at his expense, it was clear he was well and in his usual high spirits.

The evening's entertainment, as Van Devanter noted, was a mostly-in-good-fun fusillade against the New Deal. A typical skit portrayed a group of squawking penguins (played by reporters) offering rote praises to their benevolent penguin dictator, whom they called the Quarterback. ("The lesson in this skit," Van Devanter wrote his sister, taking it all rather seriously, "was that the changes which are under way lead only to utter dependence and ruin.") In a similar vein, Senator Reed stiffly sang, to the tune of "America the Beautiful," a lament at the passing of his favorite ship, *The Constitution*:

Farewell, farewell, O shattered hulk
And battered stern and prow;
In youth you well protected us,
We'll sing your requiem now.
Look! Faltering there her threadbare sail
Against the horizon shrunk;
She founders in the New Deal gale!
The Constitution*'s—sunk!*

This, for Reed, was a warm-up. The club had selected him to speak for the opposition. He glanced nervously at his typewritten remarks. Reed, a well-starched Republican, was not known as an orator. Still, he got off to a reasonable start, acknowledging FDR "from across the party wall" and saying a few words about the Depression—mainly, the need to find remedies that would not leave "lasting scars." Then, without a hint of a smile, Reed eased into the humorous portion of his speech. He noted that Washington was a city of monuments: Pierre L'Enfant, in sketching his plan for the capital, had created public squares and circles to be graced with statues of famous men—so many such spaces that America did not have enough famous men to fill them. Reed suggested, therefore, that statues be made of "infamous" men—for example, those whose fertile minds had conceived of the NRA; of dollar devaluation, which, Reed said, had destroyed the credit system at home; or of withdrawal from the gold standard, which had destroyed America's credit abroad.

Returning to his seat—to prolonged applause—Reed was greeted by a delighted Willis Van Devanter. The justice leaned toward him. "Are you wanting the President to answer your speech?" he asked. Reed said that he was. They knew that the president, by tradition, would get the last word. Reed and Van Devanter looked down the high table and watched as a group of aides and cabinet officers huddled around FDR, whispering to him as he scribbled changes in the margins of his draft.

A few moments later, Roosevelt was helped to his feet, received an enthusiastic welcome, and then, as one journalist recalled, "murdered the senator." Roosevelt's tone was calm, his humor unforced (and mostly unscripted). He began by agreeing with Senator Reed: yes, he said, Washington was indeed a beautiful place; the glories of American history were well represented by the city's monuments. Roosevelt recalled his early years in the capital—a time of leisurely Sunday strolls through town and frequent stops to admire the statues. He remembered a few that the senator, it appeared, had forgotten.

There was the Lincoln Memorial, honoring the first president to devalue the dollar, a man who not only saved the union but conducted a great "social revolution." There was the great white obelisk of the Washington Monument, honoring a man who had said to hell with the Continental Congress and ran the army and the nation as he saw fit. Across from the White House, Roosevelt continued, stood the likeness of a man atop a reared-up horse—Andrew Jackson, who defied the constitutionalists by destroying the Bank of the United States. Finally, there was the memorial to John Paul Jones and its inscription: "I have not yet begun to fight!"

Then, more gravely, Roosevelt addressed the critics of the New Deal. "They do not know what the Constitution is. . . . They do not know or realize that the Constitution has changed with the times. Let me illustrate my meaning," he said—appropriating, without acknowledgment, Reed's other metaphor. "In our early maritime history we constructed a great ship and called it *The Constitution*. We put in it the best timbers which could be found, and we constructed it according to the best plans and experience of that period. . . . We sent it forth to do battle. It was crowned with success and achieved wonderful victories. We came to revere it and even to have an affection for it. We still [do] . . . because of what it accomplished in its day. But no one," said Roosevelt, "would be fool enough now to send it out to fight even a tugboat. It has been superseded entirely by what has happened and been learned in the meantime. So with the Constitution of the United States. We revere it and have an affection for it because of the principles which it reflects." But as times change, he concluded, the Constitution, too, must change.

Van Devanter, who sat sourly throughout, found the speech "ingenious" but ominous. A few nights later, at a small dinner celebrating his seventy-fifth birthday, Van Devanter, joined by McReynolds, Pierce Butler, and a handful of other aging conservative judges, expressed shock that in the days since the Gridiron Dinner, no one had said a single word about FDR's peroration on the Constitution; no one seemed to appreciate its significance. This realization cast a pall over the birthday dinner. As a cold and steady rain fell outside, compounding their gloom, the men talked of little but their fears for the future. Their views, Van Devanter recalled in a letter to his sister, ranged from "utter hopelessness" to a faith, however fragile, that someday—if it was not too late already—the nation would regain its "common sense."

The judges were not the only ones feeling embattled. That spring, President Roosevelt wrote Felix Frankfurter that "we have been under very heavy bombardment." Opposition forces, he said, were coming together—"show[ing] their teeth" and "shrieking to high heaven." Republicans "are denouncing me as a murderer, and the old-line press harps increasingly on state socialism and demands the return to the good old days." Even so, Roosevelt was confident that the economy would rebound and Congress would pass most of his program. "This major offensive on the part of the enemy will fail," he assured Frankfurter. "I am not afraid of the big bad wolf."

The offensive was really only getting started. However haltingly, the economy was growing—joblessness was down and prices, industrial production, and national income were up—and bankers and businessmen, energized by the improving climate, expressed outrage at every new regulation. They began to press, for the first time in a determined way, against the New Deal. "The honeymoon is over," Justice Stone wrote Hoover, "and we may witness the beginning of real political discussions."

But what began, in 1934, were not political discussions but rather, as *Time* described them, "private fulminations and public carpings against the New Deal" as a routine part of the workday. "As soon as the businessman sees a slight improvement," said Senator Tom Connally, a Texas Democrat, "he keeps shouting 'the government must get out of business.' Businessmen do nothing but belly-ache." The era of business-government cooperation, much heralded by the Brain Trust and embodied by the NRA, continued, in the limited sense that the codes remained on the books—like a marriage still valid in the eyes of the state, even though mutual affection had given way to suspicion and bitter recriminations.

Though the Depression was hardly over, the spirit of shared sacrifice it had engendered among business leaders—the belief that the emergency justified grand experiments—was expiring. The New Deal cut against most businessmen's basic belief in markets as self-correcting and in an economy that operated according to natural laws—helped along, of course, by the occasional benevolent intervention of men like themselves. The New Deal, they said, was not causing the recovery, it was slowing the recovery by interfering with the laws of supply and demand, and by stifling individual initiative. The government, as they saw it, was picking winners (newly aggressive labor unions) and losers (management); running a deficit; creating uncertainty by changing the rules of the market; and replacing the practical wisdom of entrepreneurs with the grandiose schemes of bureaucrats and Brain Trusters—"bright-eyed madm[e]n," as *Nation's Business* called them.

"It is perfectly apparent," said New York's Bertrand Snell, the House Republican leader—who, before his election to Congress, owned a power plant and ran a cheese manufacturing company—"that the main objective of this 'new deal' administration is to punish those who have earned and saved money, to redistribute wealth by taking it from those who have been thrifty and passing it to those who have been and still are shiftless." The critique, at its most extreme—and this is where it naturally slid, toward the extreme—portrayed the New Deal as totalitarian. One heard this in speeches at the chamber of commerce, at shareholders' meetings, and at gatherings of Kiwanis, Lions, Eagles, and Elks; one read it in company circulars and GOP press releases. The attack was amplified—in apocalyptic terms—by spokesmen like Ogden Mills, Secretary of the Treasury under Hoover. Mills decried

Roosevelt's creation of "an all-powerful central government . . . to control and direct the lives and destinies of all." As in Germany, Italy, and the USSR, supreme power was "lodged in the hands of a single fallible being." This was a war—a holy war—for freedom and the survival of democracy in America.

To others, the charge seemed almost comically overheated. Donald Richberg, second in command at the NRA, diagnosed it as "post-depression psychosis." Indeed, the vitriol flowed from deep reservoirs of fear, resentment, and fury; it could not be answered by an earnest appeal to the facts. The Depression had dealt business leaders a triple blow: first, the market and the economy had crashed; second, the captains of industry and finance had been held accountable; and third, Roosevelt had come to their rescue. Wall Street was far angrier about all this than Main Street, for high finance had taken the brunt of the blame. New securities laws, moreover, sent a very plain message that bankers could no longer be taken at their word or trusted to govern their own affairs. This, to Wall Street, was the unkindest cut. Just a few years earlier, bankers had been second to no one in prestige and self-regard. But the world they knew had been turned on its head. Wealth, once considered a sign of virtue, now suggested a lack thereof. Their rage at Roosevelt became all-consuming. It spread like a toxin throughout the business community.

Roosevelt, in response, began to express his own irritation. The New Deal, after all, was his plan to save capitalism, not supplant it. He was not naive; he had known too many businessmen to imagine that the Depression had awakened them to the public interest or convinced them to place it above profits. Yet he had believed, for a time, that the crash had chastened businessmen sufficiently that they would go along with the government, particularly when it was trying to make their companies more productive and profitable. Roosevelt was taking heat from liberals for the big-business orientation of the New Deal, for siding frequently with industry against the claims of labor and consumers. He found it galling, therefore, that those same companies would attach sinister labels—*fascism*, *communism*, *regimentation*—to programs that were helping them.

In the summer of 1934, Roosevelt began to answer his critics in earnest. He used his first fireside chat of the year, on June 28, to renew his case for the New Deal, assess the state of the recovery, and ask Americans a "simple question: Have you as an individual paid too high a price for these gains? Plausible self-seekers and theoretical die-hards will tell you of the loss of individual liberty. . . . Have you lost any of your rights or liberty or constitutional freedom of action and choice?" Roosevelt urged Americans to take a look at their Bill of Rights to confirm that they had not "suffered the impairment of a single jot of these great assurances." The programs of the New Deal, he said, were expressions of America's deepest values and traditions. As for the "Doubting Thomases," they simply "fear progress." In a speech a few weeks later, he added, more sharply, that some businessmen would be glad to revive the "law of the tooth and the claw": the old days of stock manipulation, secret deals, rampant fraud, and frequent panics. "The people of the United States," he declared, "will not restore that ancient order." Privately, he was even more scornful. "The fundamental trouble with this whole Stock Exchange Crowd," he wrote a member of his Brain Trust, "is their complete lack of elementary education. I do not mean lack of college diplomas, etc., but just inability to understand the country or the public or their obligations to their fellow man. Perhaps you can help them to acquire a kindergarten knowledge of these subjects."

Roosevelt was popular enough—and the signs of recovery manifest enough—to withstand the attacks of a disorganized and still discredited enemy. "We're far stronger than ever," boasted Thomas Corcoran and Benjamin Cohen, a pair of young and increasingly influential New Dealers, in a letter to their mentor, Felix Frankfurter, in April 1934. "Politically the Skipper still stands tremendously high and has the fundamental faith of the generally inarticulate mass." Still, the two men acknowledged what they called "a real seriousness in the home situation. . . . The initial impulse of the election of two years ago and the super-prestige of its sweep have been largely spent," they told Frankfurter.

The principal trouble was the National Recovery Administration. Two years after its creation, its leaders claimed great accomplishments: the NRA had returned 3 million people to work; abolished child labor;

established the minimum wage as a standard measure; strengthened workers' right to collective bargaining; and, remarkably, achieved all this through voluntary agreements. But this was only one side of the story. Almost from its inception the NRA had been a headache for anyone associated with it: shopkeepers, labor unions, big businesses, the administration. "Administrative mistakes," noted Corcoran and Cohen, were plaguing the program. They reported that "the inevitable impossibility" of managing the NRA, a problem that Brandeis privately "foretold over a year ago, [was] now yawning open for even the public to see."

Bad management, though, was the least of it. The NRA was tilted—in its structure, its mandate, its operation—in favor of big business. Code authorities—invested, by the Recovery Act, with the power to draft agreements on wages, hours, and prices—were so thoroughly dominated by the largest trade associations that the representatives of labor and consumers were often shut out entirely. The laxity (or utter lack) of governmental oversight and the haste of the code approval process almost ensured that big business used its authority to maximize profits, not wages. These were problems of design, not merely implementation. And as General Hugh Johnson, NRA's administrator, had warned at the outset, the government was essentially powerless to enforce the codes as written. Codes were flouted just as soon as they were signed. The Blue Eagle was not so fearsome after all.

Except, perhaps, to small-business owners. Small businesses, in truth, were frequently more exploitative than big ones: in the backroom of the little laundry or cobbler down the block, sweatshop conditions all too often prevailed. But New Deal critics were looking for martyrs—victims of a dictatorial, tyrannical government—and small-scale proprietors fit the bill nicely, particularly those whose stores had been raided, books seized, windows shuttered, and employees laid off for the length of an investigation and trial, and often for good. Senator Gerald Nye, a North Dakota Republican, denounced the Blue Eagle as "a bird of prey upon the masses." Hugh Johnson felt powerless to counter this impression. He regretted that the codes had ever been extended to barbers, seamstresses, and the like, and regretted further that the NRA was obliged to enforce those codes as best it could. In this way the NRA, weak as it was, gained a reputation as an oppressive force, dictating to the little shop on the corner precisely when and how often its cashier was allowed to take a cigarette break.

Labor strife was another problem. The Recovery Act, by endorsing the right to organize, touched off an unprecedented drive for unionization. Within days of the bill's passage, the United Mine Workers launched a membership campaign that swelled its ranks from 100,000 to more than 400,000 by the summer of 1934. Membership in the International Ladies Garment Workers Union grew fivefold between the start of 1933 and the middle of 1934. All this met, predictably enough, with massive resistance by employers. Many created "company unions," controlled by management, and leaned hard on employees to join.

Workers appealed to the NRA—to little avail. When the administration failed to crack down on employers, union leaders grew increasingly frustrated and bellicose, attacking Homer Cummings for giving them "the shabbiest treatment accorded to any set of people in recent years" and for "badly bungl[ing]" the only injunction suit the Department of Justice had bothered to pursue. The Secretary of Labor, Frances Perkins, warned unions against expecting "the millennium on a silver platter." But workers were asking for little more than what had been promised. The situation continued to disintegrate. To handle labor disputes, General Johnson set up a National Labor Board, which was soon revealed as impotent in the face of strikes and work stoppages—more than 1,800 in 1934—large and small, many of them violent.

It was all unraveling so quickly. "The NRA was headed hell-bent for a bust," recalled George Creel, a progressive journalist. "Going back to Washington was like a journey into bedlam, for all touch with the sane and simple had been lost. Each visit found scores of new agencies, boards, and commissions, headed by campus experts and . . . theorists; and the spread of the bureaucratic mania had the sweep of a pestilence."

Even before the worst had hit, President Roosevelt showed a certain ambivalence about his creation. On March 5, 1934, he addressed a conference of code authorities—some 5,000 businessmen—and spoke of the NRA as a "great test to find out how the business leaders in all groups of industry can develop capacity to operate for the general welfare." They were succeeding, he declared. "Self-regulation" was working—"without violation of the constitutional or the parliamentary system" of government. Roosevelt asserted that "the great bulk of complaint or criticism of the Recovery Act does not go to the Act itself or to its basic principles, but rather to the details of mere method." His audience, presumably, knew better.

"*You* have set up representative government in industry," he said, sounding as if he were offering praise, when in fact he was transferring blame. "*You* are carrying it on. . . . *You* on code authorities are your industrial brother's keeper." Ben Cohen, reviewing a book about the NRA, took a similar tack: "If the business features of the codes are defective," he wrote, "it is largely the responsibility of business itself. The deficiencies of the codes are . . . not the deficiencies of the New Deal." This was a distinction without a difference. The administration and Congress had created the NRA. With the president's blessing, Johnson had transformed it into something just short of a crusade. Industry groups were drafting the codes, but Roosevelt was signing them into law. It would be hard, perhaps impossible, to separate himself from the consequences.

From the beginning, Roosevelt had seen the NRA "purely as an emergency agency," as Perkins recalled. It was set to expire or be reauthorized by Congress—in June 1935. Thus in late 1934, NRA officials began drafting amendments to correct its constitutional and other defects. But hostility toward the NRA—from the left and the right—had grown so overpowering that members of Congress took no real interest in remedial legislation. Some added that it was pointless to tinker with the NRA before the Supreme Court had decided its fate.

Despite the troubles of the NRA and the public's increasing ambivalence about the New Deal in general, Roosevelt himself remained enormously popular. The Republican Party, meanwhile, was discouraged, intimidated by FDR, and at war with itself, as progressives and conservatives vied for control. The party had no clear national leader. Neither did it have an identifiable platform, beyond its positions on Roosevelt (against), the New Deal (against), commercial enterprise (for), and the Constitution (for). GOP chairman Henry P. Fletcher kicked off the campaign for the fall mid-term elections by comparing Roosevelt to Hitler and accusing him of trying to "emasculate" the Constitution. James Farley, the Democratic Party chairman and U.S. Postmaster General, retorted that the Republicans "have no issue . . . so they leap for the constitutional issue, about which they can be as vague as they wish." FDR laughed that Republicans were so desperate for a rallying cry that they were going to "come out in favor of the Ten Commandments . . . [and] sweep the country."

All this left him optimistic about the elections. Still, a sort of grim exhaustion had set in. Harold Ickes noted how tired he appeared, how he seemed to lack the "carefree spirit which has been so characteristic of him." Roosevelt was showing the strain not only of the conservative assault, but of the tug-of-war among his advisers over the pace of reform. Raymond Moley, who had been with Roosevelt since Albany, urged a "breathing spell." This, he said, would allow business to adjust and enable the administration to consolidate gains, build support, and think a bit more clearly about the future. The president's more liberal aides objected strongly. To delay, they said, was to invite unrest, even revolution; four years into the Depression, millions of starving and suffering Americans could hardly be expected to wait patiently for jobs, security, and sustenance. Roosevelt saw the merits of both approaches. But with each successive attack on proposals he regarded as moral, practical, and essential, he drifted a little further to the left. What he sought in November was not simply an affirmation of past performance. He wanted a mandate to go farther, to be bolder.

The November results were staggering. TIDE SWEEPS NATION, read the headline in the *New York Times*, which called the election "the most overwhelming victory in the history of American politics"—a landslide not just for the Democratic Party but for FDR, who was not even on the ballot, and for the New Deal. Roosevelt's triumph obliterated a truism of American politics—that in off-year elections, the president's party inevitably lost seats in Congress. In 1934, voters gave Democrats three quarters of the Senate—the widest margin ever in that chamber—as well as nine more seats in the House and thirty-nine governorships. In so doing, said the *New York Times*, they "literally destroyed the right wing of the Republican party" and "invested the President with the greatest power that has ever been given to a Chief Executive." Most observers agreed. "One often hears Roosevelt spoken of as 'dictator,'" noted one newspaper. "He has now won the powers of a dictator without giving them the name. Now," the editors added approvingly, "he has the liberty of acting." So said the *Berliner Tageblatt*, a Nazi Party organ.

In mid-November, Roosevelt traveled to Tupelo, Mississippi, to herald the successes of the Tennessee Valley Authority, which, he said, was bringing not only electrical power but hope and opportunity to the American South. His underlying message, however, was that "opposition is fading . . . fading in the light" of improved conditions across the nation. This progress, he added, "is not coming from Washington. It is coming from you. You are not being federalized." What this meant, he said, was an end to "the kind of rugged individualism that allows an individual to do this, that or the other thing that will hurt his neighbors. He is forbidden to do that from now on."

Frankfurter, in a typically gushing note to FDR, asked whether his intended audience was actually the Supreme Court. "Mr. Justice Holmes had a favorite remark," Frankfurter recalled, "when, as a naughty boy, he used to put some stinger in an opinion. With a mischievous twinkle in his eye he would say such and such a phrase or sentence was 'calculated to give the brethren pain.' I think Holmes would have recognized a mischievous twinkle or so in your speech at Tupelo."

After a tumultuous year—a year of some progress, no doubt, but also of unrest, scattered violence, and vituperation; a year in which, as Roosevelt recalled with amusement, critics compared him not only to Hitler but to Cesare Borgia and Judas—FDR could look ahead with renewed confidence. Over Thanksgiving, Rexford Tugwell, a member of the Brain Trust, joined him for a respite in Warm Springs, where they went swimming, driving, and picnicking with friends. Tugwell was struck by the president's "dogged determination to work out dreams in practice. He is convinced," Tugwell wrote in his diary, "that he has to transform the country physically and morally in his time and do it without a great change in government structure or in domestic processes." Tugwell added: "Maybe he can."

Maybe. After the election it did seem, for a moment, that anything was possible—even, perhaps, the redemption of the NRA. Roosevelt told Tugwell that the administration and Congress would soon get to work on fixing the act. Until then, he said, his strategy was to keep things as quiet as possible.

Chapter Six

THE GOLDEN RULING

"WILL THE SUPREME Court follow the election returns?"

That question, posed by many in November 1934, echoed the words of Mr. Dooley—the well-loved, if fictional, Irish pub owner of a turn-of-the-century newspaper column. But was it true? Did the justices follow the returns? Soon the Hughes Court would say.

The New Deal was already on trial across the nation—and faring badly. Federal judges were blasting the New Deal from the bench, delivering long speeches that had little to do with the law and everything to do with ideology. The dockets of lower courts, reported *Time*, were "sagging" with challenges to the New Deal, especially the NRA, in what the magazine called a "gigantic tortoise race of litigation." By late 1934, several of these cases had completed their slow path to the Supreme Court: tests of the NRA, the AAA, monetary policy, a pension scheme for railway workers, and a federal moratorium, not unlike Minnesota's, on farm foreclosures. The administration's strategy of delay had run its course. The Court's judgment, whatever it might be, was going to come swiftly in a cascade of decisions.

Some observers questioned whether the Court's leniency toward economic experiments by the states said anything about its view of federal legislation. But concerns like this failed to dampen the optimism, even the giddiness, that prevailed in administration circles after the mid-term elections. The American people had endorsed the New

Deal, and now, it appeared, the Supreme Court was about to ratify their vote and to give the president's program, at long last, a clean bill of constitutional health.

Within the Department of Justice—now housed in its newly built, Art Deco–inflected headquarters on Pennsylvania Avenue, nearly halfway between the White House and the Capitol—there was little to indicate that a big test, let alone a series of them, was coming, or that the fate of the New Deal hung in the balance. Here and there in the cavernous building, down this corridor or that, one might find a small team of lawyers working intensely, even anxiously, on Supreme Court briefs; but the general mood, from the top man down, was one of unconcern. When the Court convened in October 1934, Homer Cummings sent a quick note to Solicitor General J. Crawford Biggs to inquire about any New Deal cases now pending. "I would like to have a little outline about these cases," Cummings instructed, "and the manner in which they are to be handled." The first case, Biggs replied, concerned "hot oil."

It was a gangster's term. Oil was "hot" when produced or shipped illegally, and America was awash in it when Roosevelt took office. Overproduction was rampant; every newly discovered field (the oil industry not being known for self-restraint) sent prices further downward, to such an extent that in 1933, a barrel of Texas crude cost a dime—the price of a can of Campbell's Vegetable Soup. Oil-producing states, having imposed strict limits on production, found themselves outmatched by bootleggers. There were just too many pipelines and tank cars to keep watch on them all. In 1933, in a little noticed section of the Recovery Act, Congress authorized the president to do what the states could not. Section 9(c) of the act was a broad grant of power: FDR could do essentially whatever he deemed necessary in order to stanch the flow of hot oil. Thereafter, in a series of industry codes and executive orders, Roosevelt criminalized the transport of hot oil and made overproduction a federal offense.

Soon, preceded by a volley of press releases, federal agents took to the East Texas fields waving badges and summonses, and trailed by a contingent of wire service photographers. Cummings reported to Roosevelt on the "encouraging results": violators were being hauled into district court and the torrent of illegal oil had slowed to a trickle. He provided, for Roosevelt's review, newspaper clippings with pictures of his agents. Their authority, however, was already in dispute. A pair of small-scale Texas producers, Panama Refining and Amazon Petroleum, asserted their constitutional right to pump as they pleased—at least within limits prescribed by the state, not the federal government. The companies charged that the hot oil ban (which they had violated flagrantly and often) exceeded the authority of Congress to regulate interstate commerce and delegate legislative power to the president. Following the trial and appeal, the Supreme Court agreed to hear oral arguments in mid-December 1934.

In preparing their brief, government lawyers received an unpleasant shock. One of the regulations being challenged in the case—a regulation the agents had been vigorously enforcing—did not, in fact, exist. A diligent lawyer, checking his citations, simply could not find it on the books. The code, it turned out, had been drafted, approved by the president, and then—well, it was unclear exactly what had happened after that, but it appeared that a stenographer or perhaps a typesetter had failed to put the code in print.

It was an inauspicious beginning to the defense of the New Deal. And though the Justice Department had informed the Court of the oversight (and sheepishly corrected the order), the justices, during oral argument, were disinclined to let the issue drop. They asked the oil companies' attorney whether he had actually *seen* the code that landed his clients in jail for several days. He replied that the only copy he had ever seen was "in the hip pocket of an agent sent down to Texas from Washington."

"It is a rather extraordinary situation," Justice Stone observed in a letter to his brother. "Executive orders, purporting to have the force of law, violation of which was a crime, not being published or authenticated in any way so that those charged with criminal offenses could tell whether or not their acts were prohibited. Strange doings!" Brandeis, perhaps more than the others, was troubled by this. It was Brandeis, after all, who once said, famously, that "sunlight is the best disinfectant," and "Old Isaiah" saw no sunlight here. Instead, he saw a government acting without transparency or care—issuing orders and codes at the rate of several a day and not even bothering to publish them all.

His chief concern, though, came as more of a surprise to administration lawyers: the delegation of power by Congress to the president. In a 195-page brief, the government had dispensed with the issue in only three pages, for a perfectly good reason—the Court had not once, in its entire history, cited the improper delegation of power as a reason to overturn an act of Congress. The Court had repeatedly reaffirmed the principle that the legislature could not transfer to others its power to make a law, but that standard had proved loose enough to accommodate the rise, in the first part of the twentieth century, of administrative and regulatory bodies like the Interstate Commerce Commission. As far back as 1916, Elihu Root, president of the American Bar Association, had declared that "the old doctrine prohibiting the delegation of legislative power has virtually retired from the field and given up the fight."

Now it appeared to have some fight left in it. During the oral argument, Brandeis seemed horrified by the president's authority to criminalize certain behavior without first making findings of fact. In other words, the law allowed FDR to act without justifying action; Section 9(c) failed to provide an explicit standard to determine when the president was, or was not, empowered to cut off a shipment of hot oil. Paul Freund, a former Brandeis clerk who worked in the Solicitor General's office, reported to Frankfurter that "several of the others—Van D. most vigorously—were evidently with [Brandeis] on this. The hearing was really concerned with the fundamentals of representative and responsible government, not with the ills of the oil industry."

The decision came on January 7, 1935. When the Court convened at noon, Chief Justice Hughes almost seemed to be stalling: after ten other opinions were presented, the Court broke for lunch, in a departure from routine procedure (and Hughes, it was noted, was not a man to depart from procedure). Only later did it become clear that he had been waiting for the stock market to close. The Court's ruling in *Panama Refining Co. v. Ryan*, though it concerned a single industry, carried major, if uncertain, implications for the entire economy; it might be best to let the markets sleep on it.

All but one justice, it turned out, were with Brandeis. The eight-man majority, in an opinion written and now read aloud by Hughes, overturned the hot oil provision of the Recovery Act. "There are limits of delegation which there is no constitutional authority to transcend," Hughes thundered from the bench, gesturing emphatically, conveying disapproval. "We think that Section 9(c) goes beyond those limits. . . . The Congress has declared no policy, has established no standard, has laid down no rule. . . . If Section 9(c) were held valid, it would be idle to pretend that anything would be left of limitations upon the power of the Congress to delegate its lawmaking function."

Cardozo, the lone dissenter, gently mocked the notion that Congress left the president "to roam at will among all the possible subjects of interstate commerce, picking and choosing as he pleases." The Recovery Act itself, he said, had provided a sufficient standard. Like the majority, he believed the delegation of legislative power was not unbounded, but Cardozo had "no fear that the nation will drift from its ancient moorings as the result of the narrow delegation of power permitted by this section. What can be done under cover of that permission is closely and clearly circumscribed."

"The Supreme Court went Republican," declared the humorist Will Rogers. Perhaps not, but the decision—especially its near unanimity—reconfigured, in an instant, the political landscape. Only two months after the November election, it destroyed the sense of FDR's invulnerability and breathed new life into a moribund opposition. Though the ruling's direct impact on the operation of the New Deal was limited—and easily mitigated by a new act of Congress—it dealt the first serious setback to the Roosevelt juggernaut. The Court, crowed the Republican *New York Herald Tribune*, had thrown "this revolutionary nonsense into the Potomac where it belongs." The fiercely conservative *Chicago Daily Tribune* hailed the justices, particularly the "handsome" and "distinguished" Hughes, for "put[ting] the brakes on the development of a dictatorship in the United States."

The administration was inclined—publicly, at least—to shrug off the decision. Roosevelt himself set the tone, cheerily suggesting at a press conference that the opinion provided helpful advice on ways to improve the New Deal. Senior officials told reporters that the hot oil law had been badly drafted; with a little more care, they said, similar mistakes could be easily avoided. The opinion, they pointed out, said nothing about the Recovery Act as a whole. Donald Richberg, who had recently taken the helm of the NRA from Hugh Johnson, saw "no reason to feel disturbed," because the Court "has not, even by implication, cast a doubt upon the validity" of the NRA. Senator Robert Wagner of New York actually insisted that because the justices had declined to overturn the entire NRA, they had in fact endorsed it.

But the official bravado failed to mask the sense of shock in administration circles. "The anxiety . . . was profound," recalled Robert Jackson, who was serving at that time as a Treasury Department official. The Court had made clear there were limits to delegation—but left little clue where those limits might lie. This would mean more guesswork on Capitol Hill; the defects in legislation would be hard to identify or to fix. Even more worrisome, to many in the administration, was the loss of the votes of Brandeis and Stone—not to mention those of Hughes and Roberts. Some of Roosevelt's supporters predicted the end not only of the NRA but the AAA and, for that matter, the rest of his domestic agenda. "There was less delegation to the President in Section 9(c) than in almost any other New Deal legislation," *The Nation* observed. "If all these acts must go down, our economic structure might go with them."

Hence the muttering in Congress and throughout the government about stripping certain powers from the Court, perhaps by amending the Constitution. A radical remedy, no doubt; but if *The Nation* was right, it might be Roosevelt's only recourse. Court-packing now seemed out of the question. The 8–1 decision in *Panama Refining* had put an end to any casual talk about packing the Court. To reverse the ruling, Roosevelt would have to add eight justices. Even "the wildest New Dealer," assumed the *Chicago Daily Tribune*, "is not ready to go that far."

A few nights after the decision, Harold Ickes attended a small "stag dinner" at the Danish ambassador's home. Justices Roberts and Stone were also there. "I like both of these men very much," Ickes wrote in his diary. "They are friendly and human, and, especially with Mr. Justice Roberts, there was a little joshing back and forth about the decision in the oil case. He assured me that he is entirely sympathetic with what we are trying to do in the oil matter and that he hoped we would pass a statute that would enable us to carry out our policy." (Indeed, the administration and Congress did exactly that.)

The justices were less favorably inclined toward the administration's policy on gold—the next New Deal case on the Court's docket, and one with far greater implications than *Panama Refining*.

FDR, ever since his first day in office, had been tightening the government's grip on the gold supply. This was part of a complex, interlocking set of policies designed to create inflation—to drive the value of the dollar down and send prices up, enabling farmers and others to make a living again. Gold was brought under federal control by degrees, by a succession of laws and executive orders that, among other things, banned the hoarding and export of gold; made it illegal to hold, buy, sell, or trade gold without a license; and abandoned the gold standard. In June 1933, the government took another important—and unusually aggressive—step by voiding any clause in any contract, private or public, that guaranteed payment in gold.

The "gold clause"—rarely noticed, only occasionally invoked—was part of every government bond and nearly all corporate bonds. It was a standard feature of mortgage agreements and other contracts. For creditors, it offered protection against inflation or congressional tinkering with the currency. But for millions of Americans in debt—and the government itself—that clause was a ticking time bomb. The gold value of the dollar, before Roosevelt reduced it, was $1.69. This meant that a bank, for example, could suddenly require a farmer to make mortgage payments in gold coin—transforming a $10,000 mortgage into one worth $16,900, raising the farmer's debt burden by nearly 70 percent. Or, to take another example, not at all theoretical, the bearer of a $1,000 Liberty Bond could walk into the Federal Reserve Bank and demand $1,690 in gold coins. To Roosevelt and his advisers, the situation was intolerable. Gold obligations in the United States equaled about $100 billion, an amount twenty-five times greater than the nation's total gold reserves. The solvency of the federal government itself was at stake.

Still, Roosevelt's policy had many detractors, and some of them were members of the Supreme Court. "The action on the gold clause is terrifying in its implications," Brandeis wrote to Frankfurter. "The deliberate repudiation by the Government of its own solemn obligations . . . [is] alarming." Stone was so appalled by the administration's action that he vowed never to buy a government bond again. Even Cardozo, the New Deal's strongest supporter on the Court, was troubled by what he saw as unfairness to creditors. And yet, as Cardozo wrote to a friend about the case, "the difficulty is that most people fancy it to be the business of a court to condemn as 'unconstitutional' everything that is unfair. Nothing of the kind! There is room for a lot of immorality within the confines of the Constitution and of constitutional law."

Was the cancellation of the gold clauses constitutional? Moral? Advisable as a matter of policy? Of these three questions, courts were supposed to concern themselves only with the first; but the strands, clearly, were going to be difficult to disentangle in the cases that reached the Court in January 1935. All the litigants invoked "moral considerations [that] transcend the literal terms" of the law, in the words of one government lawyer. Still, the central, constitutional issue facing the Court was one it had addressed many times before, most recently in *Blaisdell*: whether a contract was so sacrosanct that it should override the public interest, even—in this instance—at the cost of sending individuals, businesses large and small, and the U.S. Treasury itself into bankruptcy.

Arguments began on January 8, the day after the hot oil decision, and continued for three days. Attorney General Cummings himself took the lead. (His confidence in Solicitor General Biggs, who typically argued Supreme Court cases, was on the wane after *Panama Refining* and other stumbling performances.) Cummings had worked so hard in preparing for the gold cases, he told Missy LeHand, FDR's assistant, that he had begun "to feel a bit like King Midas." He arrived at the courtroom in customary dress: cutaway coat, striped trousers, derby hat, and spats—complemented, for good luck, by gold cuff links, a gift from the president.

As opposing counsel made their statements, Cummings sat serenely in his morning coat, chewing small bits of paper (this was a habit). When his moment came, he did not leap so much as glide into action. It was a spellbinding performance—one reporter called it a "stump speech"—and the audience, including the justices, sat silent and rapt.

(This was not due entirely to the power of his oratory: tradition dictated that when an attorney general made an argument, he was not to be interrupted.) Cummings began by describing, in dramatic detail, the "stupendous catastrophe" that would follow if the Court ruled against the government. The collapse, he suggested, would "stagger the imagination. It would not be a case of 'back to the Constitution.' It would be a case of 'back to chaos.' "

The basic conflict in the cases, as Cummings portrayed it, was between the "supposed sanctity and inviolability of contractual obligations" and the nation's "power of self-preservation." Coining money, controlling the currency—these, he said, were the powers of a sovereign nation, expressly granted by the Constitution, but rendered meaningless by the gold clauses. "So obsessed are our opponents by the idea of sanctity of contracts," Cummings charged, "that they are even prepared to assert their validity when they pre-empt the federal field. To me this seems a monstrous doctrine." If the government had failed to act as it did, it would have forfeited its ability to adjust the gold content of the dollar, thus "delivering the destiny of America into private hands" and rendering the United States "a cripple among the nations of the earth."

Cummings, at this point, ceded the podium to his able, if ineloquent, associates, who then spent many difficult hours fielding the questions that the justices might have preferred to direct at the attorney general, had protocol not prevented them. The four conservatives' hostility was clear in every comment. This was hardly a surprise. The real question was how the others were leaning, and no one could tell. Even so, after three days of oral arguments, Cummings predicted victory—by a slim margin.

President Roosevelt suggested a new motto for the Cummings clan: "All is not gold that glitters." But he did not share in his attorney general's confidence. Indeed, the president was rattled by what he had been told about the justices' questions. On the evening of January 10, only hours after the argument had ended, he expressed his deep concern to Robert Jackson. What if we lose? the president asked. What can be done to protect the country from chaos? Jackson recalled that FDR "was quite determined that he just could not accept an adverse decision." Yet Roosevelt did not make clear—for he was not quite sure—what he meant by that. Remedial legislation? Court-packing? No option was off the table. Not even, as Jackson put it, "outright defiance."

Jackson mentioned an article that he, along with many New Dealers, had just read in *Political Science Quarterly*. Sidney Ratner, a Columbia professor, reexamined the old contention that Ulysses S. Grant had packed the Court to get it to reverse its decision in the first Legal Tender case, *Hepburn v. Griswold* (1870), in which the justices ruled paper money to be unconstitutional. "Strikingly parallel," Ratner believed, to the gold clause cases. Ratner argued that Grant had, in effect, packed the Court, filling two seats—one vacant, the other newly created by Congress—with men he knew would overturn the ruling (which they did, in short order). And what, Ratner asked, was wrong with that? Grant had done it, after all, to save the Court from itself—from the "lamentable weaknesses" of some of its justices.

Earlier that day, Roosevelt had suggested the same thing to Harold Ickes. There were, of course, no vacancies on the Court, so this meant creating them—and filling them with liberals. "I told him that that is precisely what ought to be done," Ickes recalled. "It wouldn't be the first time that the Supreme Court had been increased in size to meet a temporary emergency and it certainly would be justified in this case." This, Ickes told Roosevelt, was the price the Court must pay for defying the popular will. At the cabinet meeting the next afternoon, Cummings joined the rising chorus, saying that if the Court went against the government, the number of justices should be increased at once.

The Court-packing discussion ended there. No plans were drafted, memos written, or meetings held. Still, the idea appeared in the press, attributed, once again, to nameless presidential advisers. By 1935, this was becoming almost standard practice. Any time an important New Deal case was pending, newspapers reported (based on leaks, rumors, or just plain surmise) that Roosevelt, if displeased by the decision, might pack the Court. White House officials never denied it. Whether to test the waters, to intimidate the Court, or simply to blow off steam, they indulged in a good deal of this sort of talk. Others did, too. The editors of *The Nation* refused to rule out packing the Court, "though this strikes us as a repugnant idea."

There was, in any event, more than one way to curb a court. The White House and its allies readied a range of constitutional amendments. One aimed to reassert congressional power over the currency. Most, however, went well beyond the issue at hand—going so far, in one case, as to forbid any lower court from ruling on the constitutionality of an act of Congress. Another amendment, drawn up by Senator Edward Costigan of Colorado, would empower Congress to regulate wages, hours, labor conditions, and industrial production levels, and would prevent the Supreme Court from voiding such laws on the grounds of due process. Roosevelt asked Tom Corcoran and Jack Scott, an NRA lawyer, to look into this. Around the same time, FDR told Senator George W. Norris that he was warming to an idea Norris and others had been pushing since the early 1920s: an amendment requiring a vote of at least two-thirds of the Court's membership to overturn an act of Congress. Some New Dealers wanted to make this retroactive.

Henry Wallace, the Secretary of Agriculture, took an even more radical line: in an article in *Collier's*, he urged the creation of a four-person council "closely attached to the presidency" and invested with the authority to propose changes to the Constitution. The public would vote on these amendments directly; the Supreme Court would be barred from reviewing them.

All this, no doubt, offered some measure of psychological satisfaction. But none of it offered an immediate, practical solution to the problem of a bankrupt government. With this in mind, officials drafted legislation to "cover all contingencies." For example, if the Court required the Treasury to pay bonds in gold, the government could then tax the profits at a rate of 60 percent—resulting in no net gain for the bondholder, and no loss for the Treasury. Or, as Robert Jackson advised FDR, Congress could prohibit citizens from suing the government for damages.

As this flurry of paper—draft proclamations, resolutions, amendments—began to litter desks at the White House, Treasury, and Justice Department, Roosevelt considered how to take the campaign, literally, to the streets. On January 14, over lunch with Cummings and Henry Morgenthau, the Secretary of the Treasury, FDR asked how they could get the man in the taxicab, as he put it, to care about the case and support some kind of action against the Court. The president had an idea and pressed it hard on Morgenthau: what if the Treasury, quietly and purposefully, were to startle the bond and foreign exchange markets into going wobbly? The sense of crisis, Roosevelt said, would prompt average citizens to say, "For God's sake, Mr. President, do something about it." And "if I do," Roosevelt concluded, "everybody in the country will heave a sigh of relief and say thank God."

Morgenthau was aghast. As Cummings joined in, agreeing with Roosevelt, "I argued harder and more intensely than I have ever before in my life," Morgenthau said later. He appealed to the president's conscience and common sense. The markets, he said, might not recover for many months; and what would become of public trust in the Treasury? Morgenthau added sharply that he did not presume to advise Cummings on legal matters and did not need Cummings to advise him on financial matters. "Mr. President," he said, pointing his finger at Roosevelt, "don't ask me to do this."

"Henry," FDR replied, "you have simply given this thing snap-judgment. Think it over."

In the morning, they spoke by telephone. FDR's gentle tone suggested that he himself had reconsidered. That evening, he confirmed it. At a dinner at the vice president's home, Roosevelt and Morgenthau sat on either side of Mrs. Garner. The president leaned behind her back and said, "Well, Henry, I am glad to see that you are smiling again." This, Morgenthau understood, signaled retreat. "You know," FDR said to Mrs. Garner, "Henry was very serious for an hour yesterday . . . I was arguing with him about the gold case and in arguing I often take the side of the opposition in order to bring out the various points, but of course I didn't believe in those arguments." Had the president really been playing devil's advocate? Or had he just changed his mind? Morgenthau was unclear. Either way, he was relieved. If the president had ordered him to destabilize the markets, Morgenthau had been prepared to refuse—and resign.

Weeks passed without a ruling on gold. On Saturday, February 2, in order "to avoid an unnecessary crowding of the Court room" the following Monday—the day of the week that decisions were usually announced—the Chief Justice issued an unprecedented statement that "the Court is not ready." A week later, he did it again. By now the uncertainty had begun to wear on the public, the markets, and the administration, which Ickes described as "jittery." Roosevelt met repeatedly with Cummings—huddling after cabinet meetings, talking over long lunches at the White House, debating which of many paths to take.

Roosevelt leaned, increasingly, toward "outright defiance"—Robert Jackson's phrase. On February 9, after the Court had postponed its decision a second time, Roosevelt called Cummings and Donald Richberg to the White House and dictated a speech—"for use if needed," Cummings scribbled at the top of his copy. The draft had all the hallmarks of Roosevelt's best speeches: the calm, conversational, but determined tone; the recitation of essential facts; the rendering of the stakes in real world terms; and a call to action that, by the time Roosevelt had finished speaking, seemed the only conceivable response to the problem.

Yet this was unlike any speech that Roosevelt had ever given. It was a declaration of independence, of sorts, from the system of checks and balances. "I do not seek to enter into any controversy with the distinguished members of the Supreme Court of the United States who participated in this . . . decision," the president planned to say.

> They have decided these cases in accordance with the letter of the law as they saw it. It is nevertheless my duty to protect the people of the United States to the best of my ability. To carry through the decision of the Court to its logical and inescapable end will so endanger the people of this Nation that I am compelled to look beyond the letter of the law to the spirit of the original contracts.
>
> I want every individual or corporation, public or private, to pay back substantially what they borrowed. That would seem to be a decision more in accordance with the Golden Rule, with the precepts of the Scriptures and the dictates of common sense.

The Court, in other words, might have the last word on the Constitution; but Roosevelt was beholden to a higher law.

The draft, over the coming days, made the rounds among a small circle of officials, accumulating small revisions but not changing much in substance. Its measured tone, its air of utter reasonableness, fooled no one. The speech was incendiary. After reading it aloud to Henry Morgenthau, Roosevelt added that Joseph P. Kennedy, chairman of the Securities and Exchange Commission, "thinks the statement is so strong they will burn the Supreme Court in effigy."

Pearson's, a small Washington printing plant, received the gold clause opinions in pieces. For important cases, this was standard procedure. Cutting opinions into sections ensured that no typesetter had more than a few lines. Pearson's, in this fashion, had safeguarded the Supreme Court's secrecy for many years, and had never once leaked the outcome of a case. The precautions seemed especially well justified now, with the stakes of the gold cases so high, and with speculation so intense. "Capital Tense," read a headline in the *New York Times*. For more than a month, the paper observed, the uncertainty had "cast a shadow over the government deeper than any since the banking crisis of 1933."

On February 16, 1935, the Supreme Court was silent; the first Saturday in three weeks that the Chief Justice had not issued another delay. Cummings promptly canceled a trip to Florida and went back to work on emergency plans. "We are all reasonably confident, however, of the outcome," he wrote in his diary that night, "and these measures were taken out of abundant caution." By Monday morning, February 18, the anticipation was almost unbearable. In the hours before the Court convened at noon, the corridors outside the courtroom grew thick with spectators; Capitol police had to clear a path for the nine men to reach their chambers. The wives of the justices and of cabinet members took their seats. Senators and labor leaders who arrived a moment too late fought for space in the doorway or against the back wall.

At 12 p.m. the justices filed into the room, and at 12:01, Hughes began to read the majority opinions. He seemed to speak more loudly than usual; there was more drama, or perhaps it was tension, in his voice. He summarized the two decisions, both of them 5–4, both in favor of the government. The opinion in the private bond case, *Norman v. Baltimore & Ohio Railroad Co.*, followed Hughes's reasoning in the Minnesota mortgage case of a year ago. Here, again, Hughes saw limits to the liberty of contract. "When contracts deal with a subject matter which lies within the control of the Congress," he said, "they have a congenital infirmity." It was the prerogative of Congress to regulate the currency. "If the gold clauses now before us interfere with the policy of the Congress in the exercise of that authority"—and he judged that they did—"they cannot stand." Before he moved on to the second case, he wanted to make something clear: "We are not concerned with consequences." Meaning, the Court had reached its decision without respect to the threat of economic collapse.

His tone grew more vehement. Hughes had already announced that the government won the Liberty Bond case, *Perry v. United States*, but it did not seem that way as he read the opinion. Every sentence sounded like a rebuke. "There is a clear distinction," he said curtly, between this case and *Norman*. "The bond now before us is an obligation of the United States." And the nation, no less than an individual, was bound by its word. To support the administration's policy here, he said, would be to say that "the Congress can disregard the obligations of the government at its discretion, and that . . . the credit of the United States is an illusory pledge. We do not so read the Constitution."

Having lectured the government on the limits of constitutionality and public morality, having drawn this bright, inviolable line, Hughes then announced that it did not apply in this case. The plaintiff, he declared, had suffered no damages. Hughes concluded neatly: "He is not entitled to be enriched."

The last word that day belonged to James McReynolds.

McReynolds had a personality far larger than his contributions to the law. A reporter who covered the Court described him as "the most colorful" of the conservatives, a "tempestuous old buzzard . . . just completely uninhibited." "He spoke his mind freely and somewhat bluntly—as children do," recalled one of the few men in Washington who called him a friend. Tall, gaunt, and usually dour, McReynolds lived alone—still a bachelor in his late sixties—and worked alone in his apartment, but for the company of a single, miserable law clerk, who was forbidden even to receive a telephone call. If McReynolds was capable of charm or civility, it appeared limited to his interactions with debutantes at gatherings of polite society. "McReynolds," recalled

Frankfurter, "was a hater." Indeed, he refused to talk to the two Jewish justices, Brandeis and Cardozo, or to sit beside them; having campaigned against the latter's appointment—reportedly urging Hoover not "to afflict the Court with another Jew"—McReynolds read the newspaper during Cardozo's induction ceremony, rustling the pages for greater effect.

Unlike his conservative brethren, McReynolds had not pulled himself up by the bootstraps. The son of a plantation owner and physician, he had gone to civilized schools (Vanderbilt, University of Virginia Law School) and chosen civilized professions (law and real estate), settling in Nashville. In 1896, he ran for Congress as a pro-gold, anti-Bryan Democrat and lost. Political patrons pulled him up to Washington, where, as Woodrow Wilson's attorney general, he led efforts to bust the trusts—winning a reputation as a fighting liberal but so antagonizing everyone around him that when Wilson named him as associate justice, in 1914, the natural conclusion was that the president had "kicked him upstairs." (It seems more likely that Wilson chose his fellow southerner and Virginia alumnus without much reflection; either way, "true Wilsonians," as one recalled, were in "anguish" at the nomination, and Wilson himself was known to regret it.)

From the bench, McReynolds would interrupt lawyers with caustic questions, many of them inaudible; but on decision days, he often delivered bitter and extended harangues. In his high-pitched voice, which carried the lilt of his Kentucky roots, he yelped and drawled for emphasis, making few gestures save a finger leveled at an offending lawyer. His jurisprudence, once "turbulent and uncertain," as *The New Republic* had seen it, had by 1935 settled into a reflexive, and contemptuous, conservatism. McReynolds described the Depression as a "temporary inconvenience"—one that the American people could overcome by waking up "to their obligations, rather than their so-called rights." He was a dependable voice for "a government of specified and limited powers" and an implacable opponent of the New Deal. "If Roosevelt doesn't ruin the country," he said to a friend, "it will be because it can't be ruined."

It was not a surprise, then, to find McReynolds in the minority in the gold clause cases. He abhorred Roosevelt's monetary policy. "We would have been much better off if the old [gold] standard had been maintained," McReynolds wrote to his brother. "And it could have been. Brains at the top none too good!" He added that the cases "have given me a lot of bother. I did not want to write the dissent & tried to escape." Having failed at that, he cribbed most of the arguments from a memo George Sutherland had supplied him—strong stuff, if fairly rote.

On decision day, as Hughes read the majority opinion, McReynolds gave little indication that he was even paying attention—leaning back in his high leather chair, head on the cushion, his eyes half-closed and fixed on the ceiling. By the time he leaned forward to deliver his dissent, many of the spectators—clearly depleted after an hour and a half of Hughes—had already begun to seep out of the courtroom. But when McReynolds started speaking, they froze and then crowded back in; as he continued, some of them gasped.

Beginning calmly, his arms resting on the table, McReynolds quickly gained force and velocity. His face was red; his voice seethed with indignation. "It is impossible," he said, "to overestimate the result of what has been done this day. The Constitution as many of us have understood it, the Constitution that has meant so much is gone." This was wholly off the cuff; none of it appeared in his written opinion, which he gave not a glance. "The guarantees which men and women heretofore have supposed protected them against arbitrary action, have been swept away. The powers of Congress have been enlarged to such an extent that no man can foresee their limitations." He was reluctant, he said, to speak about such things. "God knows I wish I didn't have to. But there are some responsibilities attaching to a man on this bench to reveal . . . , in all its nakedness, just what has been done. . . . Here we have a monetary system, the extent—I almost said the wickedness—of which is almost beyond comprehension." If Congress and the president can "sweep away" the gold clauses "with a word," he declared, "this is Nero in his worst form."

The speech was "the last roar of an old lion," one observer said. McReynolds confided to his brother that the performance "took a good deal out of me. . . . Whether wise or no may be a question. But I wanted to attract some attention to the true situation. To that end it seems to have succeeded." Of course, the apparent truth of the situation varied according to one's politics. To *The Nation*, the bitterness of the dissent served mainly "as a disquieting reminder of how easily the die might have fallen the other way," and as a powerful reminder that before long, something drastic would have to be done to strip the Court of its right to overturn acts of Congress.

"The President is gratified by the decision of the Supreme Court."

That terse statement did nothing to capture the mood of exhilaration in the White House. Roosevelt had been on tenterhooks since the morning. Just before noon, as the moment approached, a small group of aides gathered in the Cabinet Room. Roosevelt joined them a few minutes later, prompted by a news ticker that said Hughes had begun speaking. Officials from the Treasury and the Securities and Exchange Commission were stationed in the Supreme Court marshal's office, with a line open to the SEC's chairman, Joseph P. Kennedy, who was empowered to shut down the stock market if things came to that. Kennedy had set up a telephone relay: when, at 12:07 p.m., the good news on the first case came in from the Court, he placed a call to Roosevelt in the Cabinet Room. Two minutes later, Kennedy conveyed the results in the second case. Roosevelt joked that his only regret was that he didn't get to deliver his speech.

But he did so, that afternoon—in private, anyway, for a handful of appreciative aides. The attorney general was one of them. When Cummings arrived at the White House shortly after the decisions were announced, Roosevelt was having lunch with Morgenthau and Cordell Hull, the Secretary of State. "Everybody was smiling," Cummings recalled. He and Roosevelt congratulated each other. Cummings said he hadn't felt this cheerful since the day FDR had been elected. After lunch, the president insisted on reading a portion of the radio address. "It produced a humorous effect which he enjoyed and so did all the rest of us," Cummings wrote in his diary. "I think we all felt enormously relieved." They debated whether to go ahead and prohibit citizens from suing for damages, but decided to let the matter rest for a while. Roosevelt then took a swim in the White House pool, and declared he was going to Hyde Park to sleep for four days.

He commemorated his victory in a memo to Kennedy: "It seems to me," Roosevelt wrote, "that the Supreme Court has at last definitely put human values ahead of the 'pound of flesh' called for by a contract." He repeated his playful lament: "The Nation will never know what a great treat it missed in not hearing the marvelous radio address the 'Pres' had prepared for delivery . . . if the cases had gone the other way." He quoted his favorite section, the one about the Golden Rule. "What a tragedy," he concluded, "that posterity has been deprived of this and similar gems!"

Later that week, a few of those gems appeared on the front page of the *New York Times*. Someone—possibly the president himself—had shown highlights of the draft to Arthur Krock. Had the address been delivered, Krock wrote, "it would have marked the most sensational and historic episode in the constitutional history of the United States since Andrew Jackson said of a Supreme Court ruling: 'John Marshall has made this decision; now let him enforce it.'" Roosevelt's draft, Krock added portentously, might "still be in existence. . . . It may be that, before the New Deal has been completed, another situation will arise which will bring the President to the radio to make, in revised form, the speech he has now laid aside." Raymond Moley, after hearing Roosevelt recite a portion of it, suggested the same thing: save the speech, Mr. President, because you'll need it when the Supreme Court declares the NRA unconstitutional.

The *New York Times* called it a "golden ruling," and Roosevelt agreed. Yet "in spite of our rejoicing," he wrote to Angus MacLean, the assistant solicitor general, "I shudder at the closeness of five to four decisions in these important matters!" It was not lost on FDR that Hughes, in upholding the government's policy, had made clear how much the justices deplored it. (On this, the Court was unanimous.) The government had won the Liberty Bond case on, in effect, a technicality; what Cummings described as the "curious language" of the opinion was hardly a firm, constitutional foundation for future action.

The decisions had been handed down, but the fundamental questions—judicial and political—remained unresolved. The Chief Justice, by having it both ways, had created all kinds of confusion. "A great diversity of impressions seems to prevail," Cummings noted in his diary. To Stone, who wrote a concurrence, Hughes's *Perry* opinion "seemed to face both ways." Wall Street bankers, too, saw a "straddle."

Henry M. Hart, Jr., of Harvard Law School believed that "few more baffling pronouncements" had ever been issued by the Court, adding that the *Perry* opinion was just as confusing on the hundredth reading as on the first.

In the words of a former Supreme Court clerk, Hughes, as a general matter, "followed the command of a simple, forthright logic only so far as it illuminated the road he wished to follow." In the gold clause decisions, Hughes's path was more sinuous than usual. Still, along the way, he had accomplished much. He had averted a potential collapse of the U.S. economy; he had reaffirmed, again within certain bounds, the ability of government to act in the public interest; and, not least, he had avoided a clash among the branches of government, a political bloodletting that the nation, still weakened by the Depression, could ill afford.

Chapter Seven

THE LAST THIN LINE

"PEOPLE CAN'T EAT the Constitution," said Senator William Borah, the Idaho Republican, by way of explaining his party's defeat in the 1934 mid-term elections. Republicans had run against Roosevelt on a platform of individualism, enterprise, and love of country and the Constitution, and had lost so badly that the GOP seemed on the edge of extinction. Republicans' reverence for the Constitution, while heartfelt, had struck many voters as trumped up and cynical, and served to underscore the party's lack of answers to enduring economic problems. Americans in 1934 wanted a program, not pieties.

Undeterred, a group of conservatives from both parties—prodded and funded by some of the nation's leading businessmen—formed a new organization with a mission "to defend and uphold the Constitution," to ensure governmental respect for property rights, and to "combat radical trends." They called their group the American Liberty League. It was in many ways the brainchild of John Jacob Raskob, a senior executive at DuPont and General Motors who had been chairman of the Democratic National Committee. In early 1934, Raskob wrote to an associate about his plans to "induce" big companies to "organize to protect society from the suffering which it is bound to endure if we allow communistic elements to lead the people to believe that all business men are crooks . . . and that no one should be allowed to get rich."

The American people, it could safely be assumed, were unlikely to respond to a call to let the rich get richer. Thus Captain William H. Stayton, another founder, said that the new group could not achieve its goals without first creating "a moral or an emotional issue." Stayton saw no issue that "could command more support or evoke more enthusiasm among our people than the simple issue of the 'Constitution.'" Still, it would take work. "Public ignorance concerning [the Constitution] is dense and inexcusable," Stayton said, "but, nevertheless, there is a mighty—though vague—affection for it. The people, I believe, need merely to be led and instructed, and this affection will become almost worship and can be converted into an irresistible movement. . . . I think our first appeal should be to the effect that the Constitution is perfect. . . . We seek to rescue it from those who misunderstand it, misuse and mistreat it."

This rescue mission had, in fact, been underway for at least a decade and a half. In the immediate wake of the First World War, some of the patriotic societies that had helped lead the fight for preparedness and intervention rededicated themselves to promoting "the meaning and value of our Constitution," as the National Security League put it, and to the defense of "our national legislatures from dangerous proletarians." The virulent wartime strain of patriotism lost little of its potency as fears of socialism, Bolshevism, and various other isms resulted in a Red Scare in 1919 and, through the 1920s, in an energetic embrace of "constitutionalism" and "true Americanism" as "the best and only effective antidote against . . . alien cults." The recent arrival of millions of immigrants was another, related source of anxiety, and groups like the Sentinels of the Republic pressured state governments to require that the Constitution be taught in public and private schools.

Thus began a sustained campaign to "save our form of government," as James M. Beck described it. In 1919, the patriotic societies had succeeded in establishing September 17—the date the Constitutional Convention had adjourned in 1787—as a national holiday known as Constitution Day, an occasion for solemn invocations of the founders' wisdom as well as for oratorical contests, pageantry, parades, and military exercises. A few years later this became part of an extended celebration called Constitution Week. Its unsubtle slogan: "Cherish the Constitution lest we perish." In 1924, the document itself, recently disinterred from its steel vault, was put on display at the Library of Congress alongside the Declaration of Independence in, as it was officially termed, a "Shrine." Government officials believed that this inspiring sight would strengthen Americans' resolve in the struggle against Bolshevism.

These efforts had flagged in the late 1920s, as the nation plunged into the Depression and as the leaders of these pressure groups, the pillars of commerce and conservative thought, lost a large measure of their moral authority. But the advent of the New Deal gave their concerns a new urgency. This time, it appeared, the barbarians were not at the gates, they were actually inside the White House. The Liberty League, therefore, tapped into a well-established tradition of conservative calls to arms. It drew not only its inspiration but its structure, membership, and list of benefactors from these groups, as well as a more recent incarnation: the Association Against the Prohibition Amendment (AAPA), established by businessmen who saw alcohol taxes as essential to easing the burden on other industries. In 1933, as repeal became imminent, AAPA leaders shifted their animus to the New Deal: to the threat it posed, in numerous ways, to the ideals, privileges, and prerogatives these men had long cherished.

The League was also heir to the "Stop Roosevelt" movement of the Chicago convention of 1932. It was no coincidence that the League's founding membership was composed almost entirely of Democrats who had opposed FDR's nomination and favored that of Al Smith, despite the latter's loss to Hoover in 1928. Smith, who had preceded Roosevelt as governor of New York, nursed a vicious grudge against FDR, citing, loudly, a long list of grievances. He resented FDR for ignoring his advice and for using Albany as a launching pad to the presidency. He also somehow believed that his very public carping should not disqualify him to serve in Roosevelt's cabinet, and was further angered in 1933 when no offer was forthcoming. Smith's bitterness consumed him. Once a man of the people, he moved into an office in the newly built Empire State Building (the construction of which had been financed by Raskob), smoked cigars, and seethed. He joined the League as a founding member.

Throughout 1934, the American Liberty League filled its coffers and its top ranks. The latter soon included John W. Davis, a prominent conservative lawyer and the Democratic nominee in 1924; Irénée du Pont, of the Delaware conglomerate, who deplored the New Deal's "continual gnawing at the vitals of the Constitution"; E. F. Hutton, chairman of the board of General Foods; and a few prominent Republicans. Atop the organizational chart sat a Kansas City lawyer named Jouett Shouse, handpicked by Raskob to serve as president. It was not the first time Raskob had installed him to run an organization. Only five years earlier, Shouse—who, in previous incarnations, had been a newspaper reporter, race-horse breeder, banker, lawyer, member of Congress, and assistant Secretary of the Treasury under Wilson—had been given the reins of a deeply divided Democratic Party and charged with the task of rebuilding it after the electoral disasters of 1920, 1924, and 1928.

"I want my fellow Democrats everywhere to forget past differences, to get together . . . , to present a solid front," Shouse said at the time of his appointment in 1929. And while he did not succeed in repairing the breach—this was beyond the talents of any individual—he did infuse the party with energy and purpose. Under Shouse's direction, and with ample financial backing from Raskob, Pierre du Pont, and the financier Bernard Baruch, the Democrats, according to *Time*, unleashed "one of the most sustained and effective political barrages ever known in the U.S." and, in the 1930 midterm elections, made great progress toward regaining control of Congress. Shouse, the very model of what *Time* called a "Midwestern business-and-sporting man"—affable in spirit, athletic in build, straight briar pipe between his teeth as he broke into an easy grin—began to be described as "the focal figure of the Democratic party," its kingmaker for 1932. Yet Shouse—along with Raskob, the du Ponts, and their allies—chose wrong that year. Their ardent backing of Al Smith, and their vehement, almost irrational loathing of FDR, seemed to spell their end in Democratic politics. And so, by 1934, the man who had urged Democrats to get together was prepared to do everything in his power to split the party and bring down its popular president.

Victim of a press leak, the League launched prematurely in the summer of 1934 before its leaders had a chance to recruit, as they had intended, some well-known moderates. They had even hoped their group would be known by the egalitarian acronym "ALL"—but the cognitive dissonance of a group purporting to speak for all Americans while being bankrolled by the du Ponts might explain why the press, after the first day's coverage, refused to oblige.

The very structure of the League gave the game away: it dedicated separate divisions to the rights of homeowners, savings depositors, life insurance policy holders, bondholders, and stockholders, but had not so much as a subcommittee dedicated to, say, the freedom of speech. Though Shouse did his best to set an elevated, broad-minded tone—at least at the outset—his vision of the Constitution, as critics promptly pointed out, was heavy on property rights and light on other liberties. From the start, as Arthur Krock observed, the League "was set down in the public mind as a conservative group, inimical to the President and his policies . . . and created for the sole purpose of bringing back the Old Deal and its evils, including the placement of private property over everything else."

The League's directors did little to counter the impression. In August 1934, Alfred P. Sloan, the president of General Motors, disembarked the German liner *Europa* after three weeks' vacation in the South of France. There on the dock, a contingent of reporters asked him whether it was true that he had joined the fledgling League. Sloan said yes, indeed he had, and gave the group his blessing. (He had already given his money.) Then he changed the subject, taking the opportunity to attack recent proposals to limit workers' hours. "Of course I believe in more leisure for workers," said Sloan, whose company had been merciless in pushing assembly-line workers past the point of exhaustion. But first, he said, "we should earn our leisure."

It was easy to paint the League—as Harold Ickes did—as a coalition of "disgruntled politicians" as well as "industrialists, constitutional lawyers, and captains of finance who drove our good ship onto the rocks." Senator Elmer Thomas of Oklahoma called its leaders "gold dollar men." In December 1934, a Gridiron skit portrayed them in top hats, raising money to save the Constitution; as the Shouse character opened the morning mail, a cash register rang. "If anybody's in favor of saving the Constitution," he said, "it's a sure sign he's got at least a million dollars."

Roosevelt himself gleefully jumped in. At a press conference, he joked—to roars of approval from the correspondents—that a friend had told him the League had two of the Ten Commandments covered:

"Love thy God and forget thy neighbor." FDR added, to more laughter, that "God," to the League, clearly meant "property." He said that he had lain in bed that morning reading the financial pages, and when he saw that Wall Street considered the League "an answer to a prayer," he had laughed for ten minutes.

The League was easily ridiculed, but could not be so easily dismissed. Its leaders, despite having fallen largely out of public favor, still commanded a certain respect; and the group's core message, while somewhat out of vogue, still appealed to Americans who felt at odds with the New Deal—with its centralization of control, its redistribution of wealth and power, its supposed repudiation of values (thrift, industry, individualism) that they angrily refused to see as outworn. These Americans felt increasingly like an embattled minority—which in fact they were—outcasts and aliens in their own land, making a last, brave stand for the "faith of our fathers." The League gave them hope and it gave them a voice. In their gratitude, they sent it a rush of donations—an "avalanche," Shouse called it—many as small as a single dollar, demonstrating a popular appeal that extended well beyond Wall Street.

"Who is going to be the other party now?" asked *Time* after the 1934 election. It was not at all inconceivable—indeed, it was widely believed—that the Liberty League would soon replace the Republican Party. Many predicted that Republican progressives would become Democrats, leaving conservatives of both parties to gather under the banner of the League. Democratic liberals certainly hoped so. Ickes, an old Bull Mooser who had bolted the GOP alongside Theodore Roosevelt, welcomed the existence of the Liberty League. "That's fine!" he told reporters. "I've been hoping ever since 1912 that we'd have political parties divided on real issues. . . . I'd like to see all the progressives together and all the conservatives together." FDR did, too. Imagine, he often told his aides, what the Democratic Party can accomplish once the "reactionaries" are removed from its ranks.

Embracing its role as conservative standard-bearer, the American Liberty League roared into the political arena in January 1935. One week after the Supreme Court's hot oil decision, the League began to issue what its leaders called "constructive criticism": first, an expression of concern about the federal deficit; next, a fairly restrained denunciation of the NRA. Then, week after week, the attacks increased in frequency and pitch, until the League, by spring, was waging an all-out assault on the New Deal.

Across the landscape they roamed, strafing everything in sight: an emergency work relief bill, in Shouse's words, marked the "most revolutionary" delegation of power to the president in history and spelled the end of democracy in America; bonus payments to World War veterans, he predicted, would cause the monetary system to collapse; a bill to create an independent labor relations board was "obnoxious" and should, in any event, await the Supreme Court rule on collective bargaining; Social Security legislation was unnecessary and "too hasty"; an effort to help tenant farmers and other agricultural workers to buy farms, a program that the advocates of property rights might have been expected to salute, amounted to a "Russianization" of agriculture and would create "a government-sustained peasantry." The attack spread inevitably from means to motives. Roosevelt, the League charged, was concealing a darker purpose: to trigger a complete economic collapse and then, in the resulting vacuum, to assert total control.

In this account of apocalyptic struggle, all that protected the nation from totalitarianism was the institution that Shouse described as the "last thin line": the U.S. Supreme Court. If the League was going to succeed in "saving the Constitution," it would have to enlist not just the Supreme Court but the entire federal judiciary in its crusade. Drawing on its considerable network of supporters in the nation's leading law firms, the League prepared to carry its assault on the New Deal into the courtrooms.

For Franklin Roosevelt, with the GOP largely vanquished and the Liberty League still finding its feet, the real political trouble was on the left, where many held the view that the New Deal had not gone far enough. Left-wing critics, slower to emerge than those on the right, made up for lost time in 1935, crowding the national center stage in a colorful and seemingly infinite variety, and airing countless, mostly disconnected grievances. Some pressed for radical reforms; others, farther out on the fringes, equated capitalism with fascism; still others, testing their volume, simply made noise.

Credible leaders emerged across the nation. In Wisconsin, Bob and

Phil La Follette, heirs to the insurgent Republicanism of their father, Robert, founded a new Progressive Party. In California, Upton Sinclair, the great muckraker of the Theodore Roosevelt era, started a movement to end poverty and inspired a new generation of Californian radicals. In Minnesota, Governor Floyd Olson, a Farmer-Laborite, preached what he called "the gospel of government and collective ownership of the means of production" and openly pondered a run for president in 1936. Single-issue movements flourished, particularly that of Dr. Francis E. Townsend, the sixty-eight-year-old former country doctor whose plan for a guaranteed old age pension inspired such fanatical devotion that Townsend openly mused about doing "a little dictating to the president."

The most formidable figures on the left were a duo of demagogues: Huey Long, the senator and virtual dictator of Louisiana, and proponent of a popular plan to "Share Our Wealth"; and Father Charles Coughlin, the fiery "radio priest" and apostle of inflation. They were the only left-wing leaders who actively worried President Roosevelt in early 1935. Both, in fact, were building massive, enthusiastic national movements that could be converted, it appeared, into a third party. A Democratic Party poll that spring revealed that in a three-way race for president against FDR and an unnamed Republican, Long had the support of nearly 11 percent of the electorate—not yet enough to tip the balance against Roosevelt, but this was without a single day of campaigning by the electrifying Long.

In the Senate, a motley collection of aging radicals, progressives, and mavericks grew increasingly restive. Men like Burton Wheeler of Montana, George W. Norris of Nebraska, and Hiram Johnson of California were, in obvious respects, natural supporters of the New Deal. For them, as for FDR, the New Nationalism and New Freedom were a formative influence. From his first days in office, Roosevelt had sought their ideas and relied on their votes. But they were a balky group, and disinclined to fall neatly into line behind FDR (or anyone else). Though they tended to vote together, they were not a cohesive bloc so much as a band of heretics, an alignment of loners, each convinced of his own moral and intellectual superiority. "Prima donnas," scoffed Rex Tugwell, who knew them well. "F.D.R. needed the progressives," Tugwell reflected. "He was one of them; but he could not, now that he was President, be their leader. He had to head the Democratic party," which included southern conservatives, northern city bosses, and ethnic, working-class voters—groups that these mostly western agrarians saw as greedily self-interested and unduly rewarded by FDR.

Almost from the start, these progressives had been unhappy with the New Deal. They were unsettled by its grand ambition to establish a new economic order and, no less, by its methods: its frenetic improvisation, accommodation of big business, and apparent indifference to two of the progressives' long-standing bêtes noires, trusts and political machines. They also feared its centralization of power. "We have too precious a heritage of freedom and democracy to entrust it to fascism, communism or any other -ism that implies centralization of too much power in the hands of any one individual," Wheeler declared in 1935. That included New Dealism, which in the view of many progressives had been far too tolerant of industrial combinations and placed far too much authority in the Oval Office.

The need for a rapprochement was growing. On the evening of May 14, Roosevelt invited a handful of Senate progressives—along with Felix Frankfurter, Harold Ickes, and Henry Wallace, the Secretary of Agriculture—to the White House for a long overdue airing of grievances. The senators did most of the talking. They urged the president to seize the reins, stop appeasing big business and southern conservatives, and push his agenda to completion. This, they told him, was the only effective answer to Long and Coughlin. Just before midnight, the senators left the White House convinced, as Bob La Follette told Frankfurter, that FDR was "going to go into the stride of his old aggressive leadership."

And yet he did not. As his advisers split into opposing camps—one favoring short-term recovery measures and renewed collaboration with business; the other eager for systemic reform and confrontation—Roosevelt drifted uncertainly between the two. Despite his healthy tan, the product of a fishing trip to the Bahamas, FDR appeared "tired, harassed and supersensitive" to observers—the toll, *Time* presumed, of the "growing confusion among plain citizens as to the direction of the New Deal program, [and] growing doubt as to whether the President himself knew where it was leading."

Though Roosevelt remained popular, and though the economy continued to improve, the overall picture was bleak. Across the country, labor was in what seemed a perpetual state of upheaval; the number of unemployed, though declining, was shockingly high, nearly one fifth of the workforce; and the output of the Hundred Days, especially the NRA, seemed to have exhausted itself, with little new to replace it. In Congress, what remained of the Roosevelt agenda had been bottled up in committee by an accidental alliance of liberal and conservative critics. In the courts, where his allies were few in number, nearly four hundred challenges to New Deal laws were pending. And there, looming above it all, was the specter of the Supreme Court, shadowing every step Roosevelt had taken or might hope to take, just as soon as he determined which way he was heading.

On May 6, 1935, the Court issued its first major ruling since the gold clause decisions. The case concerned the nation's railway workers. The Depression—and the growth of other means of transportation, from the roadways to the skies—had dealt such a serious blow to the railroads that the industry shed half of its labor force between 1920 and 1933, a decline of 1 million employees. Well-established lines went under; tens of thousands of miles of track were shut down by bankruptcy or simply abandoned; engines rusted in weed-choked railyards. Even workers who hung onto their jobs—older workers, mostly, due to a strict seniority system—lived on the edge of privation. Their pensions, when they finally retired after decades of backbreaking work, were nonexistent, or virtually so.

In 1934, responding to these conditions and to pressure from the railway workers' unions, Congress cobbled together a compulsory national pension system in the last, frantic days of the session. Workers were required to contribute one third of the pension fund, the railroads two thirds. Roosevelt was dissatisfied with several features of the bill: it was, he said publicly, "crudely drawn." In the end, though, he could not bring himself to veto the Railroad Retirement Act. Instead, as he signed it, he urged Congress to fix it just as soon as possible.

But the railroad companies—more than 130 of them, acting together—moved more quickly than Congress and filed suit before a single payment had been made into the fund. They saw the act as unconstitutional on two counts: it took their property without due process of law; and, by including in its sweep the 200,000 employees whose jobs did not take them across state lines, it exceeded the power of Congress to regulate interstate commerce. In October 1934, the Supreme Court of the District of Columbia endorsed both of these arguments and shut down the pension fund. The administration appealed to the U.S. Supreme Court, which heard arguments the following March, 1935. The government's argument, Cummings assured FDR, was handled in "brilliant fashion," but Cummings was concerned enough about the outcome that he had taken pains to include the railway brotherhoods in the brief-writing process—"to avoid heartburns and recriminations" in the event that the government lost the case.

This it did, in dramatic fashion. The Court was again divided 5 to 4, no less bitterly than before. But the alignment was new, startling, and, for New Dealers, menacing: this time, Roberts had split from Hughes and joined the conservatives.

Railroad Retirement Board v. Alton Railroad Co. was the first major opinion Roberts had written since *Nebbia*, more than a year earlier, and he seemed to relish the return to center stage. Before the assembled crowd, he read his opinion with unusual intensity. Actually, he did not read it so much as perform it: Roberts, who had an uncanny memory, only rarely glanced at the paper in front of him. His voice, cold and precise, cut through the small courtroom; he folded his arms across his black robe and then, leaning forward for emphasis, put them down on the desk, looking straight at the spectators on the semicircular benches. He never stumbled or paused. More often than not, as a government lawyer recalled, Roberts's performances were "little works of art," and this was one of his best.

It was certainly his most strident. Roberts, a former railroad lawyer, sounded at times as if he were arguing the case as counsel for the carriers, not deciding it as an impartial judge. He ridiculed the Railroad Retirement Act—on constitutional grounds, as a matter of sound business principles, even as a matter of public morality. It was, he said, an affront to common sense. It existed "solely in the interest of the employee . . . purely for social ends," with no regard at all for the businesses involved. Roberts took particular offense at the "theory" that pensions improved morale and, therefore, job performance. If this was morale, Roberts said, his voice heavy with sarcasm, then "the surest way to destroy it in any privately owned business is to substitute legislative largess for private bounty and . . . transmute loyalty to employer into gratitude to the Legislature."

This was not all. Even if a "cheerful" worker were a more efficient one, he said, it hardly followed that "the fostering of a contented mind on the part of an employee" had anything to do with interstate commerce. For if it did, then there was "no limit to the field of so-called regulation": Congress could order a business to provide, say, free medical care for employees, or school for their children, or clothes, or housing, or food, or, he added, reaching the crescendo of this *reductio ad absurdum*, "a hundred other matters" that might, in some fashion be thought to "relieve the employee of mental strain and worry."

Ultimately, the act ran aground on the due process clause of the Fifth Amendment. Had Roberts left it at that—had he disposed of the case on the narrowest terms possible, in keeping with the Court's unwritten rule of self-restraint—Congress might have been able to comply with the decision by revising the law. Yet Roberts went further, rejecting the very idea of a relationship between retirement security and interstate commerce—in any industry. He had issued, in effect, a preemptive veto of similar legislation.

Hughes had written the dissent, and read it from the bench with vehemence and a touch of irritation. "The gravest aspect of the decision," he began, "is that it does not rest simply upon a condemnation of particular features of the Railroad Retirement Act," but "raise[s] a barrier against all legislative action of this nature." And that, he declared, "is a conclusion of such serious and far-reaching importance that it overshadows all other questions raised by the act. . . . The conclusion thus reached is a departure from sound principles, and places an unwarranted limitation upon the Commerce Clause."

At Cardozo's suggestion, Hughes drew an analogy between retirement plans and workmen's compensation laws—for the Court had frequently sustained the latter. "I perceive no constitutional ground upon which the one can be upheld and the other condemned," Hughes said. "The fundamental consideration which supports this type of legislation is that industry should take care of its human wastage, whether that is due to accident or age. That view cannot be dismissed as arbitrary or capricious. It is a reasoned conviction based upon abundant experience." The commerce clause, Hughes concluded, did not require that Congress be perfect or wise, simply that it be permitted to govern.

In its cold and authoritative logic, in its barely contained fury, Hughes's dissent was a tour de force—"the boldest, frankest, indeed, the greatest opinion of his career," in the view of Yale Law School's Thurman Arnold. As a dissent, its effect, of course, was limited; it served mainly to underscore how extreme the majority's position was. After reading the majority opinion, Felix Frankfurter wrote to Justice Stone, "I am prepared to believe that there are no limits to wrong-headedness. It is really shocking." Stone agreed: it was, he replied, "the worst performance of the Court" since its notorious *Lochner* decision, thirty years before, and was likely to plague the Court just as long. The Railroad Retirement Act "was not a very good bill," Stone wrote his sons, "but it seems to me that constitutionalism has gone mad when it assumes to forbid the federal government from establishing such a system."

The sense of outrage—less at the immediate result than its long-term implications—was widely shared. So, too, was a feeling of foreboding. In an unsigned editorial in *The New Republic*, Frankfurter and his fellow Harvard Law professor, Henry Hart, warned that the majority's wanton, almost defiant disregard of the realities faced by railroad workers "reinforced, as nothing else could, the doubts of those who question the capacity of Court and Constitution to satisfy the needs of our national life." Arnold, in *The Nation*, wrote that "the menace of the Supreme Court will continue to hang like an ominous cloud over all legal attempts to solve the social problems that are crowding upon us." The front page of the *New York Times* put it succinctly: "SOCIAL PROGRAM IN PERIL."

Roosevelt agreed. The *Alton* decision, he said to his advisers, was "rotten"—one of the worst in American history. In the Senate, his lieutenants scrambled to protect pending bills, starting with the largest pension plan ever conceived: Social Security. Joseph Robinson of Arkansas, the Senate majority leader, declared a bit hastily that the bill would have to be redrafted; others, including Roosevelt himself, deemed it safe because lawmakers, with the Court very much in mind, had rested the bill on the government's taxing power rather than the commerce power. Thurman Arnold took little comfort in this. Roberts's hostility was so "ingrained," he argued, that the justice "may find a way to dispose even of acts which are based on the taxing power."

The NRA, Roosevelt said privately, was now doomed. And that, most likely, was just the beginning. Cummings warned him that *Alton* was "a forecast of what we may expect with reference to almost any form of social legislation the Congress may enact. . . . This is a terrific handicap," he added, "and brings up again, rather acutely, matters we have previously discussed, including a proposed Constitutional amendment." A few months earlier, anticipating an adverse decision on gold, Cummings had drafted an amendment requiring a vote of at least seven of the justices in order to nullify an act of Congress. It had gone nowhere. FDR had been more interested in offsetting a possible bad decision than in limiting the powers of the Supreme Court. Now, however, that sense of restraint was fast fading—and not simply on Roosevelt's part.

Within twenty-four hours of the *Alton* decision, the *New York Times* described a "growing movement" of law professors, practitioners, and, not least, "men of nearly all philosophical tendencies in the capital" in favor of some kind of permanent solution. Recent rulings were generating such anxiety in the country, the *Times* reported, that these and other leaders "have begun to scan the horizons for some radical venture" that would recalibrate the balance of power among the branches of government. William Green of the American Federation of Labor (AF of L) declared himself in favor of any such amendment. Leaders of the railway brotherhoods lined up quickly behind a bill to impose a 7-vote requirement—though this was a statute, not an amendment, which meant the Court could strike it down.

"There seems to be no way out of a constitutional amendment," Rex Tugwell noted in his diary on May 9, 1935. He was not at all concerned by this; indeed, he welcomed it, especially the prospect of taking the issue to the country, as he told Roosevelt at lunch that day on the porch of the White House. "It seems to me that a better campaign issue could not be devised," Tugwell said, not least because it promised to "separate the sheeps [*sic*] from the goats," driving conservative Democrats, at long last, out of the party.

The ground had shifted: what had only recently seemed radical, almost unthinkable, was coming to seem reasonable, even inevitable. Whether by act of Congress, amendment to the Constitution, or some other means, the Court would have to be curbed. Cummings, on May 11, addressed a memo to the assistant solicitor general, Angus MacLean:

> Has any study been made in this office of the question of the right of the Congress, by legislation, to limit the terms and conditions upon which the Supreme Court can pass on constitutional questions? I have seen several memoranda from time to time spelling out a theory by which this result could be achieved without a constitutional amendment. My recollection is that our files will somewhere disclose briefs on the theory that the Supreme Court has no right to pass on constitutional questions at all. . . .
>
> I think it would be well to have this pretty thoroughly covered, but in addition to this it would be well to cover the subject I first above mentioned; namely, the question of legislation which would not cut off the right of the Supreme Court to pass on constitutional questions, but which would limit it somewhere with a view to avoiding 5 to 4 decisions.

In this relaxed, almost offhand manner, Cummings kicked off what he was soon to call "a project of great importance."

On Sunday, May 12, six days after the Supreme Court's ruling on railroad pensions, Harry Hopkins, administrator of the federal relief program, joined Harold Ickes and a few others for lunch with Justice Roberts and his wife, Elizabeth. "Roberts is pleasant, [and] tells good stories," Hopkins wrote in his diary that day, "but his social philosophy comes from Andy Mellon"—the Pittsburgh banker and industrialist who had served FDR's three Republican predecessors as a tax-cutting Secretary of the Treasury, and was now being prosecuted for tax evasion. "Pretty dismal to think of Roberts on the Supreme Court for twenty years more," added Hopkins.

And yet: wasn't this the same justice who, a little more than a year earlier, had cheered liberals with his emphatic declaration, in the New York milk case, that the Constitution did not entitle businesses to "inflict injury upon the public at large"—prompting one newspaper to proclaim, "a new era has dawned"? In the space of fourteen months, he had not only swung from one side to the other; he had swung from one extreme to the other.

Who was Owen Roberts?

If Roberts was an enigma, he did not look the part. There was nothing opaque about him, no air of mystery. He was neither cryptic nor closed nor self-contradictory; if anything, he was straightforward, almost bland. He was affable, though—more comfortable in his own skin, it appeared, than most of his fellow justices were in theirs, more likely to slip out of his chambers and strike up conversations in the corridor with acquaintances, pages, reporters. From his home in Georgetown, he rode the streetcar to work more often than not; anyone who failed to match this tall, hale, broad-shouldered passenger with the stiff Harris & Ewing portrait that occasionally appeared in the paper might have thought him on his way to a meeting at the chamber of commerce.

Yet he confounded nearly all who tried to understand him. Most observers did not begin to know how to characterize him. Roberts, on any given day, in any given newspaper, might be described as conservative or liberal or "semi-liberal." He was either "New Dealish" or against the New Deal, urbane or rugged, worldly or living in a "mental darkroom." Often, correspondents simply shrugged their shoulders and called him unpredictable, "the question mark of the Court," a man "on the borderline." Only one thing seemed clear: "As Justice Roberts goes, so goes the Supreme Court," as the *Wall Street Journal* observed. His deciding vote made him, in a very real sense, a rival to Roosevelt as the most powerful man in America.

The justice who now controlled the Court did not, in his youth, intend to become a lawyer at all, because he did not believe that lawyers were honest men. Before long, he found he was made for the law. The son of a Philadelphia hardware merchant, Roberts attended the University of Pennsylvania—first as an undergraduate, then as a law student. His record there was so brilliant that in 1898, after conferring his law degree, the school immediately hired him as a lecturer, and soon a professor of property law. He was also a practitioner of the first order—a master of concision, with a powerful mind, an uncanny memory, and a relentless sense of self-discipline. He was never one to wander, falter, or speculate; he had an unerring instinct for the right precedent or fact that would yield the right result for his client.

Over the next three decades Roberts shuttled back and forth between private practice and public service, excelling in both. As a prosecutor during the First World War, he litigated espionage cases, revealing himself, as one newspaper put it, as "vigorous, shrewd and tenacious." Returning to the law firm he founded, he represented insurance companies, railroads, and the like, and was rewarded with ample retainers, seats on corporate boards, and an income of $150,000 a year. In 1924, Senator George Wharton Pepper—one of Roberts's law school mentors and most attentive patrons—pressed President Coolidge to appoint Roberts as one of the two lead prosecutors in the Teapot Dome cases. Roberts's work sent Albert B. Fall, Harding's disgraced Secretary of the Interior, to prison for bribery—an impressive performance, and one that won Roberts acclaim far beyond his hometown.

Philadelphia, in the 1920s, still wore the label "Victorian"—not altogether unhappily. Despite occasional advances by reformers, despite successive waves of immigration, the city remained, in many respects, defiantly nineteenth century in character. *Harper's*, on the eve of the First World War, observed that "the one thing unforgivable in Philadelphia is to be new, to be different from what has been." Roberts thrived in this climate. Though he had not been born to privilege, he settled comfortably into the city's Republican elite. The stately town house on Delancey Street; the sprawling, 700-acre estate ("Bryncoed," Welsh for "Wooded Top of the Hill") in Chester County, west of Valley Forge; the prominence at the bar and in the city's social and civic life—all this suited a man who had made himself, by his natural brilliance and relentlessness, into a pillar of Philadelphia society.

He articulated its values perfectly. In 1923, speaking at the Waldorf-Astoria in New York, at a dinner given by the American Bankers' Association, Roberts assailed the Senate Judiciary Committee for investigating oil companies—an effort he dismissed as "propaganda" for nationalization of the industry. "Are we prepared to revise our ideas of government?" Roberts asked.

> Are we prepared to go into a frank state of socialism in this country with all that it means in the suppression of ambition, in the deterrence of industry, in the holding back of men who want to arrange their affairs for their good and the economic good, then for the good of us all—are we to go into a state of socialism, or are you men and men like you . . . prepared to get out, take off your coats and root for good old-fashioned Anglo-Saxon individualism?

The audience cheered; these men, it was clear, were prepared. Roused by their response, Roberts attacked the government for asserting control over everything in its reach. "Everywhere you turn," he added, "judicial and semi-judicial administrative commissions, investigating bodies, inspectors of every known variety are found. The result is that the business man in American today feels that he is doing business with a minion of government looking over his shoulder with an upraised arm and a threatening scowl." Such vehemence—in the era of Harding and Mellon, of laissez-faire, of tax cuts, of the slackening of controls and general loosening of oversight—was hard to account for, but it was real, and forcefully expressed by Owen J. Roberts.

These views, in the twenties, were freely expressed by men of means; but by 1930, when President Hoover nominated Roberts for a seat on the Supreme Court, the Depression had called them into serious question. Hence the muttering by Senate progressives about Roberts's "corporation frame of mind." Yet their heart was not in it; having exhausted themselves in successive fights against the nominations of Hughes and John J. Parker, they quickly consented to Roberts, taking heart in his reputation for probity. So, too, did much of the liberal press: the *Philadelphia Record* predicted that "as a learned, high-minded and constructive lawyer of liberal convictions, Mr. Roberts . . . will do much to strengthen public confidence in the Supreme Court." *Outlook* expected "to find Justice Roberts not infrequently siding with Holmes, Stone, and Brandeis," and the *Chicago Daily News* assumed that "on problems of law his views will be both sound and progressive."

Other commentators were sure that the opposite was true. Edward Corwin said that even in the context of the Philadelphia bar, Roberts was considered a conservative. Perhaps the most sensible view, given all the confusion, was expressed by the *Baltimore Sun*: "Neither the liberals nor the conservatives can be absolutely certain in which direction his mind will move."

Over the next five years, that debate continued—even within the Court itself. Stone, at the time of Roberts's nomination, had written his sons that Roberts "is a hard worker, has a good mind, and has had a wide range of experience. I should expect him to deal in the liberal way with important constitutional problems, because he has the type of mind that would take in all aspects of a problem." But within a year Stone had grown increasingly concerned about Roberts's rightward drift. Each new term brought further confirmation. In 1934, Stone strongly dissented when Roberts—on the basis of a highly literal reading of the Constitution—stripped the Federal Trade Commission of its power to regulate industrial mergers. That same year, when Roberts won liberal accolades for his opinion in *Nebbia*, Stone, in a letter to a Columbia Law School professor, dismissed Roberts's public interest doctrine as "not a novel one."

But this was not the popular impression. Few of these cases aroused much attention; and Roberts, for that matter, emitted enough mixed signals during his first years on the Court to keep parties guessing which way he really leaned. Then *Nebbia*, as far as most in the press were concerned, settled the matter: Roberts, it was clear, was a liberal. Only a few, like Frankfurter, remained unconvinced. "Really, really—Roberts ought not to have been with the obscurantists," he complained to Stone in January 1935, when Roberts lined up with the four conservatives (and Hughes with the three liberals) in a Seventh Amendment case. But no one else appeared to notice: the 5–4 decision, announced the same day as the hot oil ruling, did not even merit a mention in the *New York Times*.

Hence the shock, dismay—and, in conservative circles, the unexpected delight—created by Roberts's opinion in the railway pensions case. A friend of Van Devanter, writing to congratulate him on the result, said that "I was particularly delighted to note that the majority opinion was written by Justice Roberts"—a sign that he "has definitely aligned himself" with the conservatives. This now seemed beyond dispute. A dozen years after addressing the American Bankers' Association, Owen Roberts, at long last, had revealed himself as precisely the same man who had given that speech. He had taken off his coat, put on his judicial robes, and was rooting for good, old-fashioned, Anglo-Saxon individualism.

For liberals, the *Alton* decision was a crushing blow. But not all had lost hope. "Justice Roberts is a young man," Brandeis told a friend. "He'll learn."

Chapter Eight

BLACK MONDAY

IN MARCH 1935, Daniel Oren Hastings, a Republican senator from Delaware, stood on the floor of the Senate and challenged "anybody" to say a good word for the National Recovery Administration. No one bothered. The pall of silence in the chamber was only one of many signs that the NRA, having been granted, in effect, a stay of execution by the Supreme Court in its hot oil decision in January, was dying regardless. That spring, Donald Richberg, the agency's chairman, gave a "pep talk" to 1,500 NRA employees who felt increasingly that they needed to find other employment. Richberg's cheerleading was undercut by the fact that he himself had already announced he would quit in July; other leading officials too were jumping ship.

The Recovery Act, passed in 1933 as an emergency measure, was due either to expire or to be reauthorized by Congress in June 1935. Its fate was very much in question. Postmortems were already being issued. In a widely publicized study, economists at the Brookings Institution called the NRA an exercise in counterproductivity: by stimulating prices more than wages, it had impaired rather than improved purchasing power and, the authors wrote, "on the whole, retarded recovery." Then they broadened their indictment: "Not only did the program fail to work out as planned, but the plan itself was in our judgment a mistaken one." Richberg, outraged by the report—which landed on his desk and in the papers just as Congress was considering the NRA's future—called it "political propaganda," but this was unpersuasive. Brookings was well known for its non-partisanship.

The NRA was not entirely devoid of support, either from business or labor. In May, more than a thousand businessmen, fearing the return of cutthroat competition (and, perhaps even more acutely, the return of enforcement of the anti-trust laws) if the codes were to lapse, came to Washington to press Congress for two more years. At the same time, William Green of the AF of L, to the approving roars of a rally of 18,000 clothing workers, threatened a general strike if the act were not extended. But even ardent New Dealers had pretty well given up on the agency. Most believed it was beholden, utterly and by design, to big business. Roosevelt himself appeared ambivalent. Though he dutifully asked Congress to extend the act for another two years, he resisted calls from virtually all quarters to radically overhaul it and asked, instead, for minor revisions. Raymond Moley called this a "throwing-up of the presidential hands." The Senate, sensing this weakness of commitment, passed a resolution to extend the Recovery Act for a mere nine months, writing in an explicit exemption for intrastate businesses—so narrowing the scope of the act that senators might as well have killed it outright. Many promised a filibuster if the House extended the act further.

The NRA was waging a war for its existence on several fronts, and losing on each. In the courts, the act was under continual siege. Between December 1933 and May 1935, federal district court judges sustained the act in nine out of the nineteen tests of its constitutionality, nearly a 50 percent success rate; but there was cold comfort in this. The federal bench, as the U.S. attorney general had reported in 1933, was dominated by Republicans; and since that time, ten of the fourteen Republican judges who had decided NRA cases ruled against the government. The four who defied their party affiliation and upheld the NRA were progressive, Bull Moose Republicans—who were few in number. (Four of the five Democratic judges sustained the NRA, the lone exception being a states' rights southerner.)

Most of these cases concerned small-scale proprietors: gas station operators, dry cleaners, and the like. Code compliance was in fact far worse among small businesses, where sweatshop conditions had often prevailed before 1933; but in the view of many Americans, evils on such an infinitesimal scale hardly merited the attention of, let alone prosecution by, a massive federal bureaucracy. Small-business code violators—many of them well intentioned but desperate; others, quite ruthless and desperate—had been made by the press, the GOP and the Liberty League into the principal martyrs of the New Deal. Thus even a government victory in the Supreme Court, if that were possible, would have the makings of a public relations fiasco: one imagined the White House cheering its legal triumph as, say, a tailor was handcuffed and hauled off to prison for giving his seamstress shorter cigarette breaks than the code permitted.

Such was the pool of potential test cases on which the NRA's survival depended. It was little wonder that some of Roosevelt's advisers, Frankfurter chief among them, still counseled delay. They hoped to postpone the Supreme Court's review of the NRA until the fall, by which time the old law would have expired and a new and better replacement would, presumably, be in force. Roosevelt, however, appeared to agree with the NRA's critics in Congress: until the Court had marked the boundaries of acceptable federal action, it was pointless to craft a new Recovery Act or expend much energy in repairing the old one. Employers were not going to obey it, prosecutors were not going to enforce it, and Congress was not going to pass it without the sanction of at least five of the nine justices. In this unlikely sense, the Court had become the NRA's only hope for redemption. The NRA was dead unless the Court decided to revive it.

For Roosevelt, this was a time of acute discomfort and indecision. He stalled—not so much as a matter of strategy but because there seemed to be no good options and no way around the Supreme Court. Frances Perkins told Roosevelt that in case the NRA expired, she had drafted federal legislation to regulate wages and hours. He replied, half-jokingly, "You're pretty unconstitutional, aren't you? Are you trying to say that the Constitution doesn't matter between friends, the way Theodore [Roosevelt] did? You know," he continued, "I have been in office for two years and haven't had an appointment for the Supreme Court. That is most unusual, I am told. What that Court needs is some Roosevelt appointments. Then we might get a good decision out of them."

• • •

It was unlikely, however, that one appointment, or even two, could save the NRA. In January, the hot oil case had been decided by an 8–1 margin, sending New Deal lawyers into a spiral of self-doubt and second-guessing. To make matters worse, only three days before the decision had come down, the government, caving in to the continuing pressure, had filed an appeal in another NRA case, this one concerning the Lumber Code. William Elbert Belcher, a lumber mill owner in soft-pine country—Bibb County, Alabama—had gone to trial for paying his laborers too little, working them too hard, and firing all who complained. In the fall of 1934, a federal district court judge in Birmingham declared the NRA unconstitutional on all three grounds claimed by Belcher: first, that the act constituted an unlawful delegation of legislative power; second, that Belcher's wage and hour violations had no direct bearing on interstate commerce; and third, that the Lumber Code, which Belcher had not signed, denied his right to due process. The government appealed directly to the Supreme Court, which agreed to hear arguments in the case.

At this point, an argument of another kind consumed the government lawyers, who spent the next two months debating whether to withdraw the appeal and hope for a better test case. Some of this was simple skittishness after *Panama Refining*. But *Belcher* had problems all its own, as the NRA's Don Richberg made startlingly clear. "I have not defended the provisions of the Lumber Code," he declared at a Senate hearing. "It was one of our early codes, in which some unfortunate experiments were undertaken." Richberg had reluctantly agreed to go forward with the case only when district attorneys sent word that if it were dismissed, they would halt all pending prosecutions. In February 1935, when Cummings mentioned *Belcher* at a cabinet meeting, it was obvious "the President was not particularly enthusiastic about going on with the case." Neither was Stanley Reed, the incoming solicitor general, who urged abandonment. So did Frankfurter. NRA lawyers, however, dug in their heels, and Cummings wavered.

G. Stanleigh Arnold, a special assistant to the attorney general, made a strong, eleventh-hour pitch to Cummings to continue with the case. While admitting that dismissal would, on a personal level, give him "great relief," Arnold argued that "a withdrawal at this time will have consequences only a little less disastrous than a complete defeat." As Arnold saw it, abandoning the case would delight the NRA's critics and elicit a howl of protest from labor. It also meant that the government would face "a formidable array of lower court decisions against us by the time we again reach the Supreme Court." Further delay, Arnold concluded, was disastrous: "I don't see how it is possible to continue half-code and half-chaos . . . with any fairness or dignity."

His plea was rejected. On March 25, with oral arguments less than three weeks away, the Justice Department asked the Court to dismiss the case—which it did, promptly. The consequences, as Arnold had foreseen, were severe: by dumping *Belcher*, the government triggered an epidemic of code violations, broke the spirit of the already dejected NRA staff, and put the administration in the untenable position of asking for the extension of a law it appeared unwilling to defend in court. "The White House," reported *Time*, the right-leaning weekly, "was afraid to go to bat." The Liberty League, the National Association of Manufacturers, and their allies in the press and Congress denounced—while reveling in—the administration's decision. Huey Long felt no need to contain his glee: "I knew the NRA was unconstitutional and they knew it, but they're trying to keep it alive. . . . This Alabama man who defied every part of it was allowed to tell 'em where to go."

Steel, coal, automobiles, textiles: these were massive industries, national in scope, each employing many thousands of Americans, each of great import to the flow of commerce and the health of the economy. Any would have provided worthy grounds on which to stage what might be the last legal defense of the NRA. But as the *Belcher* debacle had shown, the government's failure to seek the right sort of test cases meant that it had to choose from the cases at hand. Now there was really only one option left. It was in this way that the fate of the NRA came to rest on a kosher poultry plant in Brooklyn.

There were in fact few industries, large or small, that warranted regulation more than the kosher poultry trade: though the word "kosher" suggested a certain purity, and implied strict, rabbinical supervision, the industry was ridden with vile, contaminated facilities, wretched working conditions, and corruption. Many tons of diseased chickens were sold at a discount to the butchers and retailers who, in the predawn hours, placed their orders at the slaughterhouse and saw the birds killed according to Jewish ritual (however loosely observed), before selling the tainted poultry to unknowing customers.

The four Schechter brothers ran the two largest live poultry plants in Brooklyn. In 1934, they were convicted on nineteen counts of violating the NRA's Live Poultry Code: among other offenses, they had filed false reports and sold contaminated chickens. And, like W. E. Belcher and so many other small-business owners, they had paid employees less and worked them longer than the code allowed. The U.S. Court of Appeals for the Second Circuit, which sat in New York, upheld all but the last of these convictions. The court drew an important distinction between the chickens, which were part of the stream of interstate commerce (many having been raised outside New York) and therefore subject to regulation by Congress, and the employees, who were not; their wages and hours, the court said, were purely a local concern.

On balance, Richberg regarded this as "a strong favorable decision from the federal court of highest authority next to the Supreme Court." The *Schechter* case had the additional virtue of being the only NRA case available for appeal to the Supreme Court before June. Richberg, feeling continual heat from code officials, persuaded Cummings and Reed to press ahead. On April 3, he wired Roosevelt, who was on a week-long fishing trip, and urged immediate action on *Schechter*: "Otherwise," Richberg warned, "present discouragement will gradually destroy industrial recovery program." Roosevelt wrote on his copy of the radiogram that, while he was still in the Caribbean, Richberg should talk to Cummings about it.

The message touched off a brief but intense argument by wire. Frankfurter, who considered the case a suicide mission, had his protégé, Tom Corcoran, wire the president on the boat and urge him to resist Richberg's advice: "F.F. suggests most impolitic and dangerous to yield . . . because fundamental situation on court not changed. Further suggests you wire Cummings not to take hasty action." Roosevelt cabled Cummings to that effect, but it was too late; Cummings had already appealed. ("I believe to this day that the President's message was deliberately held up" by Cummings, Corcoran claimed a few years later.) The government and the Schechters both petitioned for *certiorari* on the points each had lost in the circuit court, and the Supreme Court immediately agreed to hear the case.

"I assume that you have been kept well informed with regard to kosher poultry," a Justice Department official wrote to Frankfurter two weeks later. "None of us are particularly happy over the situation—to put it mildly. The case has been set down for argument on May 2. We're galloping to the guillotine."

It was Richberg who had pushed the hardest for the appeal, and who best understood the workings of the NRA. For these reasons, Cummings asked him—"with perhaps a touch of gentle malice," Richberg said later—to join Solicitor General Reed in arguing the case. Richberg and Reed were an unfortunate tandem: during the two-day argument, Reed stuck to the legal particulars and stumbled from the start, while Richberg, speaking in aphorisms ("it is regimentation," he said, "which brings order out of chaos") at a high emotional pitch, fared little better with the skeptical justices. McReynolds, after asking a typically sarcastic, incredulous set of questions, piled up the briefs, snapped a rubber band loudly around them, dropped the stack even more loudly on the floor, leaned back in his chair, and closed his eyes.

Representing the Schechters was an even more unlikely pair of attorneys: Joseph Heller of Brooklyn, and Frederick H. Wood, a partner at the Wall Street firm of Cravath, deGersdorff, Swaine & Wood, who was, not incidentally, a member of the Liberty League. Indeed, it was at the League's prompting—along with that of the Iron and Steel Institute, a trade association that violently opposed the NRA—that Wood leapt in at the last minute to aid Heller. ("Impressive altruism," noted *The Nation* dryly.) In the courtroom, however, Heller did not seem to need the help; the justices laughed heartily as Heller ridiculed the most byzantine provisions of the Live Poultry Code, his thick accent enhancing his intended comic effect. It was left to Wood to intone, predictably (but effectively), that if the commerce clause applied here, it applied everywhere, and soon Congress would find itself "in charge of all human activity."

• • •

The justices made quick work of the case. Scarcely three weeks passed between the oral argument and the day of decision. By noon on May 27, 1935—"Black Monday," as it soon became known—the courtroom was filled to capacity. Outside in the hallway, an overflow crowd, denied a chance to see the proceedings, strained at the barriers, refusing to disperse. Richberg, on the way to his seat, flashed a taut grin to a friend. "I feel as though I were waiting for a jury to come in—guilty or not guilty," he said. Tension showed in nearly every face—except, incredibly, those of the nine justices, who appeared not only relaxed but cheerful as they filed in and took their seats.

First there was a bit of throat-clearing: Pierce Butler read an opinion in a life insurance case. Spectators, who had come to witness history as it happened, shifted in their seats. Then, in a cascade, came three decisions: each one unanimous; each, in its own, distinct way, a rebuke to Franklin Roosevelt and a blow to the New Deal.

Sutherland's opinion, in *Humphrey's Executor v. United States*, held that Roosevelt had flagrantly exceeded his constitutional powers by firing, in 1933, a disruptive Republican member of the Federal Trade Commission. Next, Brandeis did away with the Frazier-Lemke Farm Mortgage Moratorium Act, calling it an unconstitutional confiscation of private property without compensation. This was not a New Deal measure; it had been driven to passage by Huey Long and was, in Roosevelt's estimation, so "loosely worded" that it "require[d] amendment"; but like the Railroad Retirement Act he had signed it regardless, and now he shared in the disrepute.

When the Chief Justice began to read the opinion in *Schechter*, there was a sharp, audible intake of breath by the crowd. Richberg stiffened; his face went pale. He had no time to recover: it was over as soon as it began. After the first few sentences of the 9–0 opinion, a reporter scribbled Richberg a note on a scrap of paper: "Can there be a new Recovery Act?" Richberg handed back his reply: a question mark.

Hughes, shifting back and forth in his chair, occasionally stroking his Jovian beard, grew more animated as he spoke. His performance had a hypnotic effect. The spectators were still and mostly silent—but for an occasional murmur and a young man's shout of "Hot dog!"—as the chief methodically laid waste to the NRA. He ruled it unconstitutional on two grounds: first, that the president's codemaking authority was so ill defined as to be "virtually unfettered," and was therefore an illegal delegation of power by Congress; and second, that neither the employees of Schechter Poultry, nor its chickens, were engaged in interstate commerce.

"The poultry," Hughes said, might have originated outside New York, but "had come to a permanent rest within the state" and were thus a local concern. So, too, were the wages and hours of employees, which had no direct bearing on the flow of commerce among the states. The distinction between "direct" and "indirect" effects, Hughes added, was "a fundamental one, essential to the maintenance of our constitutional system." What he meant was that the line between direct and indirect effects was the line between federal and state authority over commerce. Without that distinction, Hughes said, "there would be virtually no limit to the federal power, and for all practical purposes we should have a completely centralized government." This had been Wood's contention. "It is not the province of the Court to consider the economic advantages or disadvantages of such a centralized system," Hughes averred. "It is sufficient to say that the Federal Constitution does not provide for it."

Hughes did not invent the doctrine of direct versus indirect effects. Rather, he revived it after four decades of disuse and disrepute. Since the turn of the century, the Court had taken a mostly permissive view of federal regulation of any economic activity that had the potential, however indirectly, to impede the flow of interstate commerce. That came to an abrupt, unforeseen, and seemingly decisive end in *Schechter*. This was all the more surprising because the Court had not been required to address the question at all. Having overturned the NRA on the grounds of its excessive delegation of power—"delegation running riot," as Cardozo put it—the justices could have left it at that, in keeping with the Court's tradition of deciding cases on the narrowest ground possible. Instead, as Robert Jackson recalled with some bitterness, "the Court, having thus killed the NRA, proceeded to deal its corpse a second blow."

Hughes's resort to a largely discredited doctrine—Edward Corwin called this a "miraculous evocation of the one-time dead"—prompted two of his colleagues to separate themselves, somewhat, from the majority opinion: Cardozo, joined by Stone, drafted a concurrence. While acknowledging that a distinction existed between national and local economic activity, they cautioned that "what is near and what is distant may at times be uncertain." Cardozo also said that "the law is not indifferent to considerations of degree"—implying that indirect effects, in some other case, might be so great as to merit federal regulation.

Stone had long distrusted the formula as rigid and detached from reality. "I hope . . . you noted," he later wrote Harvard's Thomas Reed Powell, "that two members of the Court did not join in proclaiming the distinction between direct and indirect effects upon Commerce to be the universal touchstone of Constitutionality." Though Stone would not miss the NRA, he confided in Powell that "I can take no comfort" in *Schechter*—for "I am as aware as anyone that the power to deal with industry, which has now become national . . . , should reside somewhere." Now it existed in a sort of limbo.

Donald Richberg, who had walked into the courtroom that day with a nervous smile on his face, now slumped in his seat. When Hughes's long lecture was through, the chairman of the NRA—an agency that, in practical effect, no longer existed—slunk dejectedly out of the courtroom. "The decision was rather sweeping," Richberg muttered to reporters, and then he was gone, off to the White House to see FDR. Out the door burst another spectator. No one knew his name, but his feelings were clear. "The revolution," he shouted, "is over!" And then he, too, was gone.

As the rest of the crowd filtered out, a messenger made his way to Tom Corcoran and Ben Cohen and summoned them to the anteroom of the clerk's office. There they found Brandeis. The old justice—his long arms in the air while a page removed his black robe—looked to Corcoran like an avenging angel of destruction. Brandeis was agitated, short of breath, but exultant.

"You have heard," he gasped, "our three decisions. They change everything." Make sure Felix is in Washington by morning, Brandeis told them; he needs to explain the situation to FDR. "The President," Brandeis said, in the most damning judgment delivered that day, "has been living in a fool's paradise."

Corcoran expressed concern that the Court's holding on interstate commerce would imperil some of the bills now making their way through the Congress. Brandeis was unmoved. "I am not familiar with the various pieces of legislation," he replied, "but I should not be surprised if everything would have to be redrafted. . . . Everything that you have been doing must be changed" in light of the Court's unanimous decisions. "I want you to go back and tell the President that we're not going to let this government centralize everything," Brandeis told the two men. "It's come to an end."

"You mean it was unanimous against us?"

The president had been meeting with Robert Jackson and other Treasury officials when Richberg called with the news. "Where was Old Isaiah?" Roosevelt asked. "What about Ben Cardozo?" FDR was stunned—if not by the decision, then by the defection of the Court's liberals. Jackson, not insincerely, suggested that the Court had done Roosevelt a great service, that it had spared him the greater indignity of having the Congress refuse to renew the NRA. Roosevelt appeared to agree.

For most of that Monday, he seemed to be taking it all rather well. Eleanor Roosevelt told a friend she was dreading dinner with her husband that night; she was sure he would be deeply upset; incredibly, though, she found him even more carefree than usual. This mood, however, did not last for long. After dinner, on the phone with Hugh Johnson, the former head of the NRA, the president said bitterly that the justices would not have dared knock down the program in its earliest days; but now that the public had turned against it, they saw they could do as they pleased. He said he would not have minded if the Court had ruled that the act was badly drafted and needed revision. Instead, the Court killed the whole program and struck at him personally—accusing him, as he saw it, of seeking dictatorial powers.

Later that evening, Roosevelt told Missy LeHand to meet him in the office in twenty minutes' time; after wrapping up a short meeting, he had some work he wanted to do. LeHand, who understood Roosevelt's rhythms better than anyone, believed that she had at least half an hour; the president had never been in a meeting that failed to run long. After thirty minutes had passed, however, a butler burst into her office and said, "The President is waiting." She knew this meant trouble. Indeed,

FDR was furious. He did not, in fact, have any work to do; what he needed, desperately, was diversion. To get his mind off the Supreme Court, LeHand launched into the latest political gossip. She also got out the president's stamp collection—his favorite pastime—on which he now worked, alone, until midnight.

"Today," Homer Cummings wrote that night, "was a bad day for the Government." He had received word of the decisions while eating lunch in his office. He put down his ham sandwich and began a hurried series of meetings that lasted late into the evening. *Schechter*, he believed, "is an ultra-States rights decision and turns the clock back a great many years, or attempts to do so. A good many people are saying that either the Supreme Court was wrong, or the Constitution was wrong; and this," he observed, "has revived talk about Constitutional amendments, or other methods" of preventing the Court from thwarting the will of the people. "This opinion," Cummings concluded, "in the long run, will not stand, as the people have a way of carrying out their purposes."

"The Constitution," announced the *Wall Street Journal*, "has survived the depression."

The morning papers howled with the news. Most, in their eagerness, had already removed the NRA Blue Eagle that, for the past two years, had flown, by mandate, on their mastheads; the *Chicago Herald & Examiner* replaced it with an American flag. This as much as any headline reflected the newspapers' overwhelmingly favorable reaction to the Court's decisions—a "smashing three-fold blow," as *The Washington Post* put it, against "haphazard, personal, planless government, cavalier and contemptuous in its attitude toward the fundamental law." The arch conservative *Chicago Daily Tribune* proclaimed that the Court had ended Roosevelt's reign of terror—in which the "little man" had been cowed, even imprisoned, for exercising his God-given liberties. "It does not matter that the persons in the American government were not terrorists . . . ," observed the editors; New Dealers "enacted and enforced laws that made terrorism unescapable."

In Washington, D.C., outside the town house of Justice Butler, someone took a piece of chalk and scrawled, in large, childlike letters, a single word on the sidewalk: NUTS. It was hard to know how many Americans shared this view. The White House, tallying telegrams from across the country, insisted that nine out of ten urged the revival of the NRA, but this was hardly what statisticians would call a "significant sample." There were, as yet, no truly reliable barometers of popular opinion. George Gallup, at the leading edge of a new "science," had only just begun to conduct polls, and while politicians and the press paid close attention to the results, no one knew how fully to trust them. Even so, it seemed beyond doubt that most Americans had lost faith in the NRA and marked its passing with a shrug. "On the whole," observed the *New York Times*, "the country took it all very quietly."

This was not true of labor unions. Leaders like Sidney Hillman of the Amalgamated Clothing Workers of America were roused to a new militancy. "We won't listen to the Supreme Court," he shouted at a rally. Hillman and thousands of dressmakers marched through the garment district of New York City, chanting songs that ridiculed the Supreme Court. To the tune of "Three Blind Mice," the marchers, mostly women, sang:

Nine old men, nine old men
Hear what they say, hear what they say
"The Constitution does not permit
A shorter week and more pay for it"
The bosses were right whatever they did
Said nine blind men.

David Dubinsky, president of the International Ladies Garment Workers Union, struck a similarly defiant tone: "The Supreme Court, which places property rights above human interests, to whom the dry-as-dust terms of the Constitution, written more than 150 years ago, are more precious than the lives and the needs of millions of workers, could nullify the NRA . . . but it cannot take away the economic power of the workers." Dubinsky was not as confident as he sounded. He and other union leaders knew that with the NRA out, and the fate of pending labor legislation now very much in doubt, their only remaining weapon might be the strike.

On Wall Street, meanwhile, there were reports of "rejoicing," and across the nation many small-business owners subscribed to the same views that F. L. Evans, proprietor of Evans & Son ("Kokomo's Largest Wall Paper Store"), expressed in a letter to FDR:

> Well my Dear Sir they gave you rope and you hung yourself, as I knew you would. You tried to tell me when I could open my doors and when to lock them[,] what I could sell for, and what I should pay in wages, as to my profits you didn't give a —, yet I must pay the taxes you insolently piled upon me. The Supreme Court sat down on you. You and your professor communistic satelites [sic] did your utmost to make Russia out of this U.S., you and yours have and still are catering to the tramps, bums, the riff raff, and trashy illiterates of this Country.

But many businessmen, large and small, had a mixed reaction to *Schechter*. Their sense of relief at the elimination of the NRA was commingled with anxiety about the near-term effects. In large-scale, heavily unionized industries, the codes appeared to hold up fairly well—most likely due to management's fear of provoking strikes and mob violence. But in most sectors, the early signs were troubling. Within weeks of the decision, the Bureau of Labor Statistics found serious backsliding in every state of the union. Working hours were extended; wages were slashed. Some manufacturers actually took back previous wage hikes by deducting them from workers' paychecks. In the coal industry, wage negotiations broke down overnight. "Draw your own conclusions," snapped the AF of L's William Green to reporters. Child labor increased sharply, as children younger than sixteen left school in large numbers to work sixty-hour weeks. And though construction companies generally stuck with the codes, the Bureau of Labor Statistics reported that across the South, "common labor (negroes)" were systematically "being 'put back in their place' "—their wages cut, in some cases, to 10 cents an hour, less than a third of the average rate in the region.

Prices—no longer set by code agreements—dropped immediately and sharply on items like cigarettes, liquor, books, and medicines. Price wars resumed, prompting some small-business owners—the same grocers, druggists, and tobacconists who had so loathed the codes—to complain to the White House about the return of "predatory price-cutting" and "cutthroat competition." Groups ranging from the National Association of Manufacturers to the National Paint, Varnish and Lacquer Association called hasty meetings and urged their members to salvage the best features of their respective codes. "We are a funny people," observed Will Rogers. "Business men have howled from every luncheon table the evils of the whole NRA. . . . Now the same men are rushing back to the banquet tables and unoccupied microphones and shouting, 'Wages must be maintained,' 'Cut-throat competition must be curbed,' 'Child labor is wrong.' . . . You just can't please some people."

Congress watched it all in apparent indifference. In part, this was due to members' distaste for the NRA. Indeed, when the news of the *Schechter* decision reached the chamber, not a single senator rose to criticize the Court. But the silence was also a sign of confusion. Congressional leaders were unsure just how much authority they had left over the economy. A Justice Department official, assessing the damage, concluded that the Court's failure to provide any "iron-clad criteria" for the exercise of the commerce power created a vast realm of uncertainty. Donald Richberg called it a "twilight zone" in which it was unclear who, if anyone, had the power to govern.

Senate leaders promptly issued a freeze on labor regulations of any kind. And this, it appeared, was only the start of the shutdown. "Hardly a single major act, either enacted or projected . . . might not in some way be affected by the NRA decision," noted the *New York Times*. The "big push" that the White House had planned for the remainder of the congressional session—a $4 billion work relief program; a bill to reform public utilities; a bill to increase jobs by limiting the workweek to thirty hours; legislation to enlarge the authority of the AAA—was stopped in its tracks.

Not all of this, however, was done in earnestness. Conservative Democrats who had never liked the New Deal but had been afraid to oppose it seized on *Schechter* as a pretext to stall the president's agenda. As Senator Hiram Johnson wrote to his son, the NRA decision had left many of the southern, states' rights Democrats who ran Congress "as gleeful as the standpat Republicans. . . . Every rat seems to have come out of his hole and is making faces at the White House. . . . They are all in the open now." Gleeful indeed, Republicans abandoned all restraint. On May 28, House leaders had to adjourn early to stop Republicans from spending the entire day praising the Court and attacking the

New Deal; the move prompted a near riot on the House floor, with the Speaker rapping so hard for order that it seemed to some he would break the gavel.

"It has been an awful headache . . . ," Roosevelt told Frances Perkins. This was his postmortem on the NRA. "We have got the best out of it anyhow. Industry got a shot in the arm. Everything has started up." He was hopeful that industry would, for the most part, abide by the codes, but he showed no interest in reviving the program. He said his legal advisers were "pretty certain that the whole process is unconstitutional and that we have to restudy and revise our whole program. . . . So let's give the NRA a certain amount of time to liquidate. Have a history of it written, and then it will be over."

Beyond this, Roosevelt had not determined what to do. He was still taking in information, soliciting opinions, and conferring with a procession of visitors—labor, business, and congressional leaders, members of the cabinet and Brain Trust—in what must have felt like one unending meeting, lasting days and leading nowhere. Much of this concerned potential legislative substitutes for the NRA. But among his closest advisers, talk turned to the problem of the Supreme Court itself. "I tell you, Mr. President," Cummings complained, "they mean to destroy us." He saw no point in salvaging the NRA. "Mr. President," he barked, pounding his fist in his hand, "this is all over. You can't do anything of that kind any more. They have set their face against us. We will have to find a way to get rid of the present membership of the Supreme Court."

"We have to meet this issue," declared Harold Ickes, "or abandon any effort to better the social and economic conditions of the people." Roosevelt seemed inclined to agree. On May 29, Rex Tugwell visited the president and found him "all steamed up," talking at length about a great crisis that had to be met head-on. "I suppose you and I are rather dumb," Roosevelt said, "because all the smart people think that what we should do is compromise and temporize with the situation, but I am inclined to fight." Tugwell, not for the first time, urged a constitutional amendment to curb the Court. The president gave the impression that he agreed and was preparing to take the issue to the country.

Roosevelt did not drop any hints at that afternoon's press conference—his first since Black Monday. Two hundred correspondents pressed into the Oval Office to see whether FDR looked in any way shaken by the Court's decision. He did not. "I wrote a story that you have not lost your old smile," said a reporter. "You bet I haven't," Roosevelt replied. "It is working overtime." The room erupted in knowing laughter. Roosevelt had little to say about the NRA; "the real spot news," he said, was not happening in Washington, but elsewhere in the country, where the effects of the decision were not yet clear. He said he believed that 90 percent of cotton textile companies, for example, "want to play the game on the level. But what happens . . . ," the president wondered, "if ten percent of them go out and hit below the belt?" His implication was clear: trusting in the best intentions of business was not likely to maintain prices and labor conditions.

As the conference concluded, a reporter asked whether Roosevelt had spoken to anyone about limiting the powers of the Supreme Court. "No," he said flatly, then reconsidered. "I suppose that we have had about fifty different suggestions. They go all the way from abolishing the Supreme Court to abolishing the Congress, and I think abolishing the president. That is so as to make it complete." Again, the correspondents laughed. Roosevelt, indeed, had not lost his old smile, even if it was just for show.

Privately, he seethed. He continued to weigh alternatives to the NRA—every day brought a new suggestion from his aides—but with the Court seemingly dead set against the New Deal, and against him personally, the exercise seemed almost pointless. The real lesson of Black Monday, as FDR and his advisers perceived it, was that the Court would stop at nothing to curb Franklin Roosevelt. The clinching evidence was not *Schechter*, but another of the unanimous decisions delivered that day. In the tumult over the NRA, *Humphrey's Executor v. United States* had almost completely escaped the attention of the press—but not of the president. "That damn little case," recalled Robert Jackson, "made Roosevelt madder at the Court than any other decision. . . . [He] thought they went out of their way to spite him personally."

The case concerned William E. Humphrey, a former commissioner of the Federal Trade Commission (FTC), the agency charged by Woodrow Wilson with busting trusts and protecting consumers. During the 1920s, Humphrey, a Republican appointee, had done more than anyone to turn the once independent agency into a tool of corporate interests. In 1933, Roosevelt removed him from his post after a month of trying, gingerly if a bit clumsily, to induce Humphrey—well known for his belligerence—to resign, and after checking with constitutional scholars to be sure that he had the authority to do so. Humphrey replied that he was not going anywhere. Indeed, he continued to show up at his office until his former colleagues, increasingly desperate, barred him from entering the doors of the commission.

Unlike *Schechter*, this was a case that Roosevelt had expected to win. Stanley Reed, the solicitor general, went even further: *Humphrey*, he said, "couldn't be lost." Only seven years earlier, in *Myers v. United States*, a 6–3 majority of the Supreme Court had said emphatically that officials appointed by a president could be removed by a president—a power without limit, Taft had declared. In ruling against Roosevelt in *Humphrey*, the Court could have allowed him to save face by acknowledging that he had relied, in good faith, on *Myers*. It could also have conceded it was reconsidering that decision. Instead, Sutherland's opinion implied that Roosevelt had flagrantly disregarded "plain" dictates of the Constitution.

Sutherland neatly dispensed with *Myers* by holding that Humphrey, as an FTC member (unlike Frank S. Myers, a postmaster), occupied "no place in the executive department"; the FTC, a creation of Congress, exercised "quasi-legislative or quasi-judicial," not quasi-executive, powers. All this placed Humphrey beyond Roosevelt's reach. Sutherland's opinion was so dismissive of conflicting precedents, so laden with moral judgment, and, in the end, so full of certitude about matters that, in actual fact, had been hotly debated since the founding of the republic, it was no wonder that Roosevelt concluded the Court was not only trying to curtail him but to humiliate him as well.

"They cannot tell the Executive how to manage the country," Rex Tugwell complained. Again he urged Roosevelt to press for a constitutional amendment to give the federal government greater control over commerce. "Draw the issue rather clearly now," Tugwell advised. That, he said, "would settle this question, once [and] for all."

Even without Roosevelt's encouragement, the idea had gained momentum literally overnight. Arthur Krock reported that within twenty-four hours of the NRA ruling, "the throwback force of the interstate commerce passage of the opinion began to be realized, and today talk is everywhere of a constitutional amendment to rewrite that clause to conform to modern industrial conditions." Proposals, some new, some familiar, came in a rush—so many that on May 30, the *New York Times* printed a guide for its readers' reference. There were amendments to permit Congress to regulate wages, hours, labor conditions, and industrial production levels; to require at least a two-thirds vote of the Court's members in order to overturn a federal law; to expand the list of industries "affected with a public interest"; to mandate that the justices deliver advisory opinions on pending legislation; to remove social and economic policy from the Court's jurisdiction; and more. The proposals came from constitutional scholars, politicians, practitioners, union leaders, and small businessmen. "Respectfully suggest you urge Congress pass constitutional amendment setting up regulation of minimum wages and hours," C. I. Kahn, vice president of the International Handkerchief Manufacturing Co., wired the president, in one of many such submissions.

A group of four House members, seeking wholesale changes to the national charter, called for a new constitutional convention. On the whole, however, congressional leaders were cool to the prospect of amending the Constitution. "Not in the cards," said Senator Pat Harrison of Mississippi. "We would not get anywhere with that. That would take too long." It was true: no amendment could offer immediate relief. But this was a cloak for his real concern. Like many of his fellow southern Democrats, Harrison feared that any amendment would strengthen the federal government and thereby weaken—or end—the sovereignty of the states.

For this and other reasons, Felix Frankfurter worried that the amendment issue, if not handled deftly, would play into the hands of the Liberty League. On May 29, in a letter to Roosevelt "on the issue of the Supreme Court vs. the President," Frankfurter warned that "a general attack on the Court . . . would give opponents a chance to play on vague fears of a leap in the dark and upon the traditionalist loyalties the Court is still able to inspire."

While agreeing that an amendment was necessary, Frankfurter counseled delay. He argued that given time, the conservative justices would overplay their hand; "popular grievances" would build. And that, he wrote,

> is why I think it so fortunate that the Administration has pending before Congress measures like the Social Security bill, the Holding Company bill, the Wagner bill, the Guffey bill. Go on with these. Put *them* up to the Supreme Court. Let the Court strike down any or all of them next winter or spring, especially by a divided Court. *Then* propose a Constitutional amendment giving the national Government adequate power to cope with national economic and industrial problems. That will give you an overwhelming issue of a positive character arising at [the right] psychological time for the '36 campaign, instead of [the] mere negative issue of being "agin" the Court which, rising now, may not be able to sustain its freshness and dramatic appeal until election time.

The president—for the time being, at least—agreed. In *Schechter*, a unanimous Court had killed an unpopular program, a poor basis for a campaign. The time was not right. That did not mean, however, that the president was "going to lie down and take this," as a frustrated Tugwell believed. Franklin Roosevelt did not take anything lying down. Two days after his initial press conference, in which he had said virtually nothing, FDR called reporters back into the Oval Office for another one. And this time, he would have plenty to say.

Chapter Nine

OPENING GUN

ON MAY 31, 1935, as the president dressed for his news conference, his press secretary, Steve Early, ran through potential questions and made conversation. Early mentioned that he had driven to work that morning with his brother-in-law, a journalist named George Holmes. "George says that those boys up there"—on the Court—"think that this is still the horse-and-buggy age," Early said. Roosevelt showed no reaction. He slipped on the coat of his dark gray suit and invited Felix and Marion Frankfurter, who were staying at the White House, to join him for the conference. The professor, having been widely, and only somewhat fairly, blamed for the long delay in taking the NRA to court, preferred to stay behind the scenes; his wife, however, came along, as did Eleanor Roosevelt. The president gestured to an aide that he was ready to be wheeled into the Oval Office.

He took his place behind the desk at 11 a.m. On one side he placed a stack of twenty or so yellow telegrams; on the other, an open copy of the *Schechter* opinion. As the press filed in he wore a puckish grin, suggesting something out of the ordinary. Steve Early appeared tense. Charles Michelson, publicity director of the Democratic National Committee, entered and looked bored. After about ten minutes—the conference was late in starting—the group was joined by Joseph Robinson, the Senate majority leader, who placidly puffed on a cigar. The first lady sat nearby, smiling perfunctorily and knitting a blue sock. When her husband finally started speaking, her smile froze and faded; she put her needles in her lap and watched him attentively.

Roosevelt began as he almost always did: with a question for his questioners. "What is the news?" he asked pleasantly, fitting a cigarette into his six-inch holder. "That's what we want," responded a reporter. The room was at capacity: correspondents pressed up against the desk, the walls, each other. Those in the back stood on tiptoes for the duration. "Do you care to comment any on the NRA?" asked one. "Well, Steve, if you insist," Roosevelt replied. "That's an awful thing to put up to a fellow at this hour of the morning, just out of bed. Suppose we make this background and take some time because it is an awful big subject to cover."

He lifted the first telegram from the stack on his desk. They were all from businessmen, he said; he had selected them himself. "I have been a good deal impressed by—what shall I call it?—the rather pathetic appeals that I have had from all around the country to do something," he said. Roosevelt began to read them, one after another, letting most speak for themselves but following others with brief interpretations. "In other words," he said, after reading one from a small retailer who pleaded for protection from cutthroat competition, "'Mr. President, please save me.'" He went on in this fashion. Nearly all the telegrams urged the revival of the NRA; but one, "from a rather prominent lawyer in Atlanta who is also in business," proposed removing the Court's jurisdiction over interstate commerce. "That is another angle—another suggestion," Roosevelt said blithely, and moved on without further comment. Several minutes later, he wrapped up this part of his presentation with a second telegram calling for limits on the Court's power. "And so forth and so on," added Roosevelt, implying that he had many more in this vein.

He turned now to *Schechter* itself. "The implications of this decision," he said, "are much more important than almost certainly any decision of my lifetime or yours, more important than any decision probably since the *Dred Scott* case, because they bring the country as a whole up against a very practical question. That is in spite of what one gentleman said in the paper this morning, that I resented the decision. Nobody," he said, "resents a Supreme Court decision. You can deplore a Supreme Court decision, and you can point out the effect of it."

Which is what he did—point out its effects—for the remainder of his press conference. It was a remarkable performance. For nearly an hour and a half, Roosevelt spoke without notes, without interruption, slowing only occasionally to replace the cigarette in his ivory holder. Never had a president talked so directly, so extensively, or with such ease and fluency about the Constitution—its interpretation, its evolving meaning. His tone was calm and firm. His smile, which rarely left his face, failed to conceal his seriousness or, on occasion, his irritation. Only once, though, did he truly betray the tension he must have felt: raising his arm to emphasize a point, he saw that it was trembling slightly, and placed it back on the arm of his chair.

Like a tenth justice delivering a dissent, he dissected the opinion. He quickly dismissed its argument against delegation before moving on to what really troubled him. The Court, he said, had revived the narrow, nineteenth-century definition of interstate commerce as limited to goods in transit. Since that era, Roosevelt continued, "the whole tendency . . . has been to view the interstate commerce clause in the light of present-day civilization. The country was in the horse-and-buggy age when that clause was written," he said—perhaps remembering the phrase of George Holmes, or that he himself had said the same thing from time to time. But communities, he added, were no longer self-supporting. Conditions in any one state affected conditions in any—or every—other "We are interdependent—we are tied in together. And the hope has been that we could, through a period of years, interpret the interstate commerce clause of the Constitution in the light of these new things."

He was warming to his theme. The decision, said Roosevelt, "does bring us up rather squarely . . . to the big issue and how we are going to solve it. The big issue is this: does this decision mean that the United States government has no control over any national economic problem?" Yes, he said, this was exactly what it meant. *Schechter*, followed to its logical, inevitable end, required America to "go back to a government of forty-eight states and see what happens"—a country of "forty-eight nations," each utterly incapable of addressing national needs. It was "a perfectly ridiculous and impossible situation."

Would Americans stand for that? Or would they give their federal government—like that of "every other nation in the world"—the power to apply national solutions to national problems? "That actually is the biggest question that has come before this country outside of time of war," Roosevelt said calmly, "and it has got to be decided. And, as I say, it may take five years or ten years. . . . In some ways," he mused, *Schechter* was "probably the best thing that has happened to this country for a long time . . . because it clarifies the issue." And then, in the final moments of this impressively disciplined, almost perfectly calibrated performance, Roosevelt let the mask slip. "We are the only nation in the world that has not solved that problem," he snapped. "We thought we were solving it, and now it has been thrown right straight in our faces. We have been relegated to the horse-and-buggy definition of interstate commerce."

For nearly ninety minutes, the correspondents had scribbled in silence. "We have been talking an awful lot," Roosevelt said. Noting the time, he took two questions. "Can we use the direct quotation on that 'horse-and-buggy stage'?" asked a reporter. "I think so," replied Roosevelt. "Just the phrase," Early interjected. The unwritten rule of these press conferences was that reporters could characterize what Roosevelt had said, but could not quote him directly without permission.

"You made a reference to the necessity of the people deciding within the next five or ten years," said another reporter. "Is there any way of deciding that question without voting on a constitutional amendment or the passing of one?"

"Oh, yes; I think so," Roosevelt responded.

"Any suggestion as to how it might be made, except by a constitutional amendment?"

"No," he said, "we haven't got to that yet."

"Or a war?" someone asked. And for the first time that morning, everyone laughed.

"Horse-and-buggy" touched off a firestorm in the press. Out of context—which is how the comment was almost invariably presented—it sounded like a slur against the Nine Old Men of the Supreme Court. It gave the impression, strenuously promoted by conservative editors, that FDR's even-tempered monologue had been a harangue, a "jeremiad." A *New York Times* editorial called it a "cry of despair."

Roosevelt's apparent pessimism was the focus of much clucking and chortling in the conservative press. "New Deal Dead—F.D.," read one headline. This was a recurrent theme: that the New Deal, as the *Wall Street Journal* argued, "cannot be encompassed within the limits of the American Constitution." Papers like the *Journal* and other right-wing critics had been making this claim for nearly two years, but now Roosevelt himself seemed to have conceded the point. Indeed, he had gone to some lengths in his press conference to suggest that the once irresistible force of the New Deal had met, and been halted by, the immovable object of the Supreme Court.

There was, however, a distinction between what Roosevelt was saying and what the press was contending. Roosevelt's complaint in 1935—as it had been on the campaign trail in 1932—was not with the Constitution, but with a Court that read the Constitution as a set of limitations. He did not see any inherent, unavoidable conflict between the New Deal and the Constitution; he never had, and *Schechter* did not change his views. Even so, his evident frustration with the system of checks and balances made it easy for his opponents to claim that he was seeking a radical restructuring of the government. *Time* asserted that FDR was "obviously" launching "a trial balloon to see whether the U.S. would rally to a constitutional amendment giving the federal government centralized powers which it has never had."

Roosevelt, declared Jouett Shouse of the Liberty League, "has renounced entirely the theory of states' rights." *The Washington Post* took the same line, arguing that the real significance of the press conference was that FDR had "definitely turned his back on the traditions and principles of his party." It was left to Ellison ("Cotton Ed") Smith, the hulking, ill-tempered senator from South Carolina, to spell out which traditions, exactly, were at risk: amending the Constitution, shouted Smith, pounding his desk in the Senate chamber, "would involve more than destroying our form of government. . . . It would involve the race question. . . . I cannot conceive of the southern people making such a disgraceful surrender of their rights."

Roosevelt's "horse-and-buggy" remark aroused such violent condemnation that it might have been expected to put an end to any serious talk of amending the Constitution. This was not, in fact, the case. In a remarkable reversal, some of the senators who attacked the idea in the hours after the press conference then declared themselves, a day later, willing to consider an amendment of some kind.

What had happened overnight? Senators had heard "from home." A torrent of telegrams—praising FDR and supporting the idea of rewriting the commerce clause—flooded Senate offices. Roosevelt had once again demonstrated his ability to clarify an issue and to shape, in an instant, public opinion. For all the fulmination in the press, Arthur Krock believed that FDR's press conference had changed the situation to his advantage. Small businessmen, leading industrialists, farmers, consumers, and other groups might not have liked the NRA, but they shuddered at Roosevelt's picture of forty-eight disputatious states trying to tackle the problem, each in its own, inept way.

Democratic leaders who had firmly closed the door to the prospect of amending the Constitution now opened it back up. Even Charles McNary, the Senate Republican leader, declared himself interested in the idea. The *New York Times* observed "a marked change of front" among members of both parties; suddenly, "a constitutional amendment was not such a bad idea." Two successive headlines in the *Times* told the story: "Many in Congress Oppose Roosevelt," the paper declared the morning after the press conference. Then, the next day: "Senators Veering to Roosevelt View."

But what was Roosevelt's view?

On June 10, FDR—now at home in Hyde Park—wrote a Harvard classmate that "you . . . have got the wrong idea if you think I am trying to appeal to the people over the decision of the Supreme Court. I am, on the contrary, most loyally carrying out the ruling of the Supreme Court." Beyond this, he was noncommittal. "Time alone," he wrote, "can tell what constitutional procedure can accomplish the results or whether constitutional amendment is advisable, as it has been in a number of cases in the past." That same day, he answered a letter in which Henry L. Stimson, who had served as Hoover's Secretary of State, implored him to "stop, look and listen. I certainly do not know any mind in this country omniscient enough and farsighted enough to draft in a constitutional amendment the necessary provisions for the delicate readjustment of state and national powers required." Roosevelt replied, cryptically, that "somewhere between your thought and my Friday [press conference] statement the truth lies! I can assure you," he added, "that I am trying to look at several angles and that I hope something practical can be worked out."

The need was pressing. On June 20, Homer Cummings informed Roosevelt that in the fall, "we would have our hands full" with "quite a number of laws that would have to run the gantlet of the Supreme Court." The vulnerable legislation, which Cummings itemized in his diary, began with "the Wagner [Labor] Bill, which I regarded as of rather doubtful constitutionality. The Guffey Coal Bill, which I thought was clearly unconstitutional. The A.A.A. Amendments, which were not in good condition to meet the constitutional test, and which would have to be strengthened to give them any chance at all. In addition . . . there was the Social Security Act, the T.V.A., and quite a number of other measures of high importance." In the near term, Cummings saw two alternatives: either to stand aside and let the trains wreck; or, more responsibly, to correct the flaws in these bills, defend the legislation vigorously when it reached the courts, and expect that the Supreme Court would strike down most, if not all, of it.

In the long term, something drastic would have to be done. Court-packing, however, appeared to be out of the question. "If it [the Court] had split 5–4 again, we should have had by now a bill to increase the membership," a friend of Van Devanter's wrote to him after *Schechter*. "About that I think there can be no doubt." Indeed, the 9–0 decisions of Black Monday—and, not long before it, the 8–1 hot oil decision—made the idea seem absurd. The columnist Raymond Clapper wrote that "talk of blackjacking the court by enlarging its membership collapsed when all nine justices joined in the decision. That subterfuge of packing the court, a weak and uncertain one at best, becomes ridiculous to think of now."

This made a constitutional amendment more likely. Over the decades, Roosevelt—like most politicians with progressive roots—had backed amendments providing for a federal income tax, the direct election of U.S. senators (both in 1913), and women's suffrage (1920). In each case, liberals and progressives had come to see an amendment as their only recourse since the Court had cut off other avenues to reform. Indeed, the income tax amendment was a direct (if long-delayed) response to

Pollock v. Farmers' Loan and Trust Co. (1895), a controversial decision that effectively prevented the government from imposing an income tax. Similarly, in 1924, Congress proposed a child labor amendment in an attempt to undo the notorious *Hammer v. Dagenhart* (1918), in which the Court ruled that a federal child labor ban was "repugnant to the Constitution" on the grounds that the act exceeded the authority of Congress to regulate commerce. (By 1935, half the states had ratified the amendment, but the effort had stalled.)

But in 1935 Roosevelt was not sold on the approach. To begin with, reformers were far from agreeing on what sort of amendment was required. Then there was the difficulty of enactment. Article V of the Constitution requires that an amendment, once proposed, be ratified by three fourths of the states. As FDR frequently reminded his advisers, this meant that the legislatures of the thirteen smallest states could block an amendment favored by the other thirty-five. Even if this hurdle were cleared, enactment was no guarantee of effectiveness. Unlike, say, Prohibition or repeal, most of the amendments under consideration in 1935 were highly complex, involving the recalibration of federal and state power and the meaning of ambiguous terms like "due process" and "general welfare." For this reason, as Louis B. Boudin, a leading left-wing critic of the Court, warned in *The Nation*, it was "very dangerous" to trust in amendments. "Not only can amendments be interpreted away; they can also be made, by interpretation, a source of new and undreamed-of ills."

Moreover, Roosevelt still believed what he had declared on Inauguration Day: that the Constitution was "simple and practical" enough to permit the nation to meet any new challenge. He took issue with reformers who claimed that the Constitution had grown "obsolete." Indeed, his entire presidency can be seen as an attempt to disprove this. In his inaugural address he also said that if "the normal balance of Executive and legislative authority" proved inadequate, he would ask Congress for broad new powers. During his first two years as president, that had not proven necessary; he had shown just how much authority was inherent in the office, should one choose to exercise it. But now he found those powers curtailed by a Supreme Court with every intention, it appeared, of disassembling the New Deal act by act, piece by piece, and denying the government any means to replace it. The White House, Court, and Congress had reached an impasse. Stalemate, Roosevelt believed, could only result in more suffering, violent unrest, and, in the end, collapse. "If the Court does send the AAA flying like the NRA," Roosevelt told a Justice Department official, "there might even be a revolution."

"It is common sense," he once said about public policy, "to take a method and try it: If it fails, admit it frankly and try another. But above all, try something. The millions who are in want will not stand by silently forever while the things to satisfy their needs are within easy reach." Now, in that same spirit, he began to forward "extremely interesting articles" and "various suggestions" for amendments to Cummings, Reed, and Frankfurter, seeking comment; he also sought meetings with senators and labor lawyers to trade ideas. The attorney general, meanwhile, instructed his aides to explore these and other options. Through the summer of 1935, as the crisis atmosphere of Black Monday receded, FDR seemed satisfied with the direction of the Court project and confident in its outcome. He felt certain that whenever he finally confronted the Court, the American people would stand behind him. "There is no question," he wrote to a senator in June, "that we are on the right track, not only logically but popularly as well."

Yet Roosevelt recognized that he had work to do. Though the public seemed open to his arguments, he knew this did not equal a movement for constitutional change—let alone for any specific amendment. And so, as the summer drew to a close, he decided to send up a trial balloon. It appeared in *Collier's*, the weekly magazine he had often used for such purposes. Roosevelt had been friendly with its Washington correspondent, George Creel, since both men served in the Wilson administration. When *Collier's* claimed that "few men are able to write more authoritatively of the President's purposes" than Creel, it was not an idle boast. "Time after time," Creel recalled, "he used my articles . . . to test public opinion." Not only that: Roosevelt dictated entire paragraphs, even noting which words, exactly, should appear in italics.

Creel and Roosevelt's latest collaboration appeared in the September 7 issue of *Collier's*, beneath a charcoal illustration of workers cringing at the base of an insurmountable wall labeled: "Constitution of the United States"; vultures circled overhead. The article was equally unsubtle. "It is the deep conviction of Franklin D. Roosevelt," the piece began,

> that the Constitution was never meant to be a "dead hand," chilling human aspiration and blocking humanity's advance, but that the founding fathers conceived it as a living force for the expression of the national will with respect to national needs. . . . He knows, as few seem to remember, that the founding fathers were not doddering octogenarians, fearful of change, but young and ardent men who had just thrown off the shackles of Old-World despotism.

All this had come from Roosevelt. As did the following:

> In the next few months, the Supreme Court will hand down fresh pronouncements with respect to New Deal laws, and it is possible the President will get another "licking." If so . . . if it is held that one hundred and fifty years of change have no bearing on the case, and that the present generation is powerless to meet social and economic problems that were not within the knowledge of the founding fathers . . . then the President will have no other alternative than to go to the country with a Constitutional amendment that will lift the Dead Hand, giving the people of today the right to deal with today's vital issues.

"Fire that," Roosevelt had said to Creel, his expression grim, "as an opening gun."

The piece was a bust. It roused no one to action. "Nothing," recalled Creel, "was more plain than the lack of public interest." Clearly, absent any immediate grievance provided by the Court, it was going to be harder to enlist the public than FDR had expected. A Gallup poll, conducted just after the issue of *Collier's* hit the newsstands, showed little support for curtailing the Court's power to overturn acts of Congress: while 31 percent favored the measure, 53 percent opposed it, and the rest had no opinion. The public's concerns about the Court's obstructionism, having been stirred by Black Monday, had not yet translated into a desire to do something about it.

Privately, some administration officials began to express impatience.

They wished that FDR would make use of the bully pulpit. A government lawyer wrote to Tom Corcoran that no amendment would have "a fighting chance" until the president was willing to "throw his powerful personality into the struggle, with every instrument at his command, not forgetting radio 'fireside talks.'" Still, Roosevelt was not yet ready to act. While he continued to search for a solution, he would wait for the Court, which reconvened in the fall, to make the next move.

Chapter Ten

VIGILANTES

"THE ROOSEVELT TIDAL wave has receded," *Time* observed. "How far no man knows. One extreme view: the wave is going out as rapidly in 1935 as it came in in 1933." Though "the great bulk of plain people," as *Time* called them, were still solidly behind him, there was no doubt that Roosevelt's popularity was steadily declining. Since February 1934, FDR's approval rating had been dropping at a rate of about 1 percent a month, reaching a low, in September 1935, of 50 percent. Roosevelt himself remained more popular than the New Deal. As George Gallup explained in a radio interview, "people say that they think the President is trying to do the right thing but is being misled by the Brain Trust." This was hardly a vote of confidence in Roosevelt's leadership.

His growing vulnerability emboldened his critics on Capitol Hill. The Seventy-fourth Congress, recalled Ray Moley, a member of the Brain Trust, was "a good deal talkier and balkier than its predecessor." Despite predictions by the Liberty League that members of Congress, in the wake of the 1934 election, would "crawl like spaniels to the heel of the Executive," the legislative branch asserted its independence over issues as varied as U.S. participation in the World Court, which was rejected by the Senate; a work relief bill that angered labor by setting wages too low; the fate of the NRA, before the Court dispensed with that; a shortfall in patronage (most of the jobs, Moley said, had already been handed out); and, not least, Roosevelt's inaccessibility and "childish peevishness," in the view of the Senate Republican leader, Charles McNary, and quite a few others.

Every step now seemed a stumble. In the winter, when Roosevelt appeared indifferent to events on the Hill, Democratic leaders complained about a lack of presidential leadership. In the late spring and summer, when he reengaged, they carped about being browbeaten to back priorities that they did not share. One summer night at the White House, after dinner on the south porch, FDR told Felix Frankfurter that southern senators "like Joe Robinson, though he has been loyal, and Pat Harrison, are troubled about the whole New Deal. . . . They just wonder where that fellow in the White House is taking the good old Democratic Party. They are afraid there is going to be a new Democratic party which they will not like. That's the basic fact in all these controversies and that explains why I will have trouble with my own Democratic party from this time on." If they stood in the way of reform, Roosevelt said, he would appeal over their heads to the American people.

In the "jungle heat" of the Washington summer of 1935, as the session stretched on, Arthur Krock reported that the situation was growing combustible. Congress was "exhausted, irritable, nervous and uncertain. . . . Tempers explode on slight provocations." Roosevelt made matters far worse by sending up tax legislation after promising he would do no such thing—and shoehorning it into an already overcrowded list of bills that he said "must" be passed before adjournment. The tax bill—largely an attempt, as he conceded to Moley, to "steal [Huey] Long's thunder"—proposed to raise taxes on the highest incomes and to create an inheritance tax, a gift tax, and a graduated corporate income tax. "Pat Harrison's going to be so surprised he'll have kittens on the spot," Roosevelt told a horrified Moley on the eve of introducing the bill. The Senate, roiling with resentment, pared the bill down dramatically before passing it. The president claimed victory for principle. Yet even this partial success had been "dearly bought," as Moley later wrote. "It had inflicted wounds on the party that would fester and corrupt. It had thrown the business community into paroxysms of fright. It had alienated thousands of Roosevelt sympathizers."

Despite these difficulties, the congressional session that ended on August 27, 1935, had been a remarkable one; indeed, one of the most productive in history. Social Security; the National Labor Relations Act (or Wagner Act), which guaranteed, after decades of struggle, labor's right of collective bargaining; reform of public utility holding companies and the banking system; relief; public works; stabilization of the coal industry; an important shift in the tax structure; a new railway pension system and farm mortgage law to replace what the Supreme Court had thrown out in May—all this and more had been accomplished, but at a cost to Roosevelt's standing on Capitol Hill and, it was clear, to his state of mind.

Summer's end found the president grim-faced, irritable, and exhausted. He confessed to Henry Morgenthau that he was "so tired that I would have enjoyed seeing you cry, or would have gotten pleasure out of sticking pins into people and hurting them." Most of those people, presumably, were members of Congress, for whom the feeling was mutual. Democrats left Washington embittered and exhausted. Republicans, by contrast, felt a renewed sense of purpose. For the first time, as Krock pointed out, they were "facing 1936 with their chins and hopes . . . high."

"Can Roosevelt be beaten?" The mere fact that anyone was asking the question—and many were, in the summer and fall of 1935—roused Republicans out of their long spell of grief, self-doubt, and complacency. They could hope again; and perhaps, soon, they could win again.

For the GOP, Roosevelt's troubles, not least his conflict with the Court, were "manna from heaven on a silver plate," as the columnist Ray Clapper put it. The party had spent more than a year positioning itself as protector of the Constitution and had been greeted in 1934 by a collective national yawn. Now the strategy seemed filled with promise. At a conference in New York, hundreds of Republican women cheered strenuously as Edith Roosevelt, Theodore's widow, implored them to defend the Constitution, protector of "the liberty that we stand in terror of losing." An old Hoover hand on the Republican National Committee sent a letter to thousands of county chairmen, city officials, and young Republicans, dismissing the "scared-rabbit talk" of recent years as "a lot of hooey!" The party, he said, could take back the White House with "the battle cry 'Save the Constitution' " and "a leader with some guts for the fight." Hoover himself, still his party's leading man, began a determined effort to show that he was the one with the guts, the vision, and the popular support to lead Republicans out of the wilderness. He toured the country, slashing, at every stop, at the New Deal, and defending the property rights he said were in "deadly peril."

These were signs of life for a party that, the previous November, had been delivered last rites by the American electorate. Still, the party's ranks had thinned considerably. Also, it had nothing to offer by way of an alternative to the New Deal, and its conservatives and progressives remained locked in a decades-long battle for control. On the right, the real vitality belonged to the American Liberty League, which was looking more and more like a third party than a "non-partisan" pressure group. In 1935, the League raised more and spent twice as much money as the GOP, much of it, apparently, on distributing crisp, white anti–New Deal pamphlets and on establishing its presence in every congressional district in America. "When next I go to the polls," declared the League's secretary, Captain William H. Stayton, in a nationwide radio broadcast, "I must ask myself whether my party candidate has helped to pass a law violating the Constitution he swore to preserve."

The League also showed a new breadth of vision. Its basic mission remained the same: the administration, said Jouett Shouse, "must be stopped" from "perverting the form of the American government." But as the League's ambitions grew, so did its interest in the world beyond the Constitution. That summer, at the University of Virginia, the organization played host to an extraordinary five-day conference that attracted members of Congress, union leaders, and other major figures. The speeches and panel discussions, broadcast over NBC as a series called *You and Your Government*, were surprisingly wide-ranging: John L. Lewis of the United Mine Workers spoke of "revolution"; black educators and reverends addressed "the church in a changing world"; and a round table of scholars considered U.S.-German relations, calling for greater "understanding" of the "New Germany." There were also, of course, heated exchanges over the fate of the Supreme Court; but this was a new, broad-minded Liberty League, offering opinions on most anything.

The press lavished attention on the League. Every pamphlet—whether another denunication of the New Deal or a comparison of FDR to Hitler, Mussolini, Stalin, and George III (all in a single pamphlet)—was news. When the League published its twelve-point plan to deconstruct the New Deal, the *New York Times* printed the plan in full, word for word, starting on the front page, as if it were a party platform. In a sense it was: if the League had its way, the plan would be the basis for the 1936 GOP platform. "As the campaign warms up," noted the *Times*, "the league sheds one by one its false whiskers and appears as a guerilla ally of the Republicans."

An ally—not an alternative. For all the League's ambitions, its leaders did not aim to replace the GOP; rather, they sought to co-opt it. In the summer of 1935, James M. Beck—who had resigned his House seat rather than continue as "one four-hundredth part of a rubber stamp"—convened a series of feverish meetings to develop a plan. He and his allies—Theodore Roosevelt, Jr.; David Reed; Colonel Robert McCormick, publisher of the *Chicago Daily Tribune*; John W. Davis; and others—hoped to draw Jeffersonian, states' rights Democrats into an alliance with Republicans, thereby splitting the Democratic Party, putting conservatives in control of the GOP, and defeating FDR. "The coalition idea is in the air," announced Beck, calling for cross-party cooperation on "the broadest grounds of patriotism."

The publishing tycoon William Randolph Hearst smiled on these efforts. Hearst—who, after backing Roosevelt in 1932, had turned violently against him—liked Beck's idea of running an "independent" Democrat against FDR. Bainbridge Colby, Secretary of State under Wilson, announced his intention to hold a separate, anti–New Deal convention after the two political parties had staged their own. At the encouragement of Hearst and Beck, Colby and others set about building a nationwide conservative coalition. Similar efforts were underway in the South under the leadership of Eugene Talmadge, the brutal and autocratic governor of Georgia. By the fall of 1935, Talmadge's Southern Committee to Uphold the Constitution claimed a membership of 50,000 anti-Roosevelt Democrats.

The Constitution had no shortage of protectors. Other groups, loosely modeled on the Liberty League, began to proliferate; some, by their vehemence, made the League look weak-kneed. America First! Inc., a fairly typical example, promised to deploy "a field force of vigilantes" to track politicians' commitment to the Constitution, and pledged "to give the New Deal an X-ray exposure." Also joining the fray was Rear Admiral Richmond P. Hobson, a well-known hero of the Spanish-American War who had served briefly in the House. In the decades since, Hobson had been waging wars against various vices: alcohol, narcotics, and, more recently, "bad" motion pictures. *Time* called him a "professional zealot." By 1935, his chief concern was the Constitution. From his vantage point on the Liberty League's advisory council, Hobson saw "certain weaknesses" in the organization. In August of that year he and other retired military officers launched the Constitutional Democracy Association in an attempt to "apply scientific warfare" (whatever that meant) "against the enemies of the Constitution."

One of Hobson's ideas was to recruit the 10 million Americans (Hobson's estimate), mostly war veterans, who at some point in their lives had taken a pledge to defend the Constitution. These "Oath of Office Men," as Hobson called them, would start "Defend the Constitution" clubs across the country and "entrench constitutional democracy in the conscious affections" of the public. Through 1935 the admiral tried with little success to enlist the likes of Hearst, the du Ponts, Henry and Edsel Ford, Andrew Mellon, and John D. Rockefeller, Jr., in his cause. Still, he kept at it. "Radical amendments" were coming, said Hobson, who vowed not to rest until he had built a thirteen-state barrier against ratification.

In June 1935, the Liberty League, flush with money and purpose, launched a new effort: the Lawyers' Vigilance Committee. Its roots, like those of the League itself, lay in the repeal movement. In 1927, leaders of the New York bar had come together to undo the Eighteenth Amendment, arguing that Prohibition invested too much power in the federal government. Working with Jouett Shouse and the Association Against the Prohibition Amendment, these lawyers helped speed repeal by developing plans for each state to hold its own ratification convention, rather than wait for instructions from Congress.

Now, under the auspices of the Liberty League, many of the same attorneys—fifty-eight of the most respected corporate lawyers in the nation—volunteered to scrutinize New Deal legislation with an eye to its constitutionality. The lawyers solemnly pledged not to concern themselves with the merits of a given law, only whether it passed constitutional muster. The Vigilance Committee also planned to find and argue test cases and build a nationwide network of like-minded lawyers. Recruitment was easy. Thousands offered their services for free, seeing this as a good way of representing existing, paying clients like Consolidated Gas and Bethlehem Steel.

Indeed, it was no coincidence that the subcommittee charged with reviewing the Wagner Labor Act was chaired by the chief counsel for Weirton Steel, Earl F. Reed, who had led that company's fight against the NRA Labor Board. In September 1935, the committee issued its first verdict: that the Wagner Act constituted "a complete departure from our constitutional and traditional theories of government." Labor relations, the lawyers said, had no bearing on interstate commerce; and the act's wage agreements infringed workers' freedom of contract. The "ruling" was unanimous: "58 Lawyers Hold Labor Act Invalid," announced the front page of the *New York Times*, which failed to ask whether a self-appointed panel of lawyers had the power to hold laws valid or invalid. Earl Reed certainly believed that it did—and that its word, moreover, was binding. "When a lawyer tells a client that a law is unconstitutional," he said, "it is then a nullity and he need no longer obey that law."

This sparked a cry of protest that resounded for months in liberal and legal publications. The *United States Law Review* observed that the report could have only two purposes: to put pressure on the courts to reject the legislation or to erode public confidence in courts that did not. The administration's only official comment came from the irascible Harold Ickes, who mocked "Chief Justice Shouse and his fifty-seven varieties of associate justices." (Shouse, in response, denounced Ickes as a "persistent denouncer," not entirely unfairly.) At Roosevelt's prompting, Felix Frankfurter derided the League's "super-supreme court" in an unsigned editorial for *Today*. Frankfurter marveled at the idea that "while on Monday, Wednesday and Friday, they are paid handsomely [by their clients] to prove that a law is unconstitutional, on Tuesday, Thursday and Saturday, they can sit in impartial judgment upon the same law."

In the fall, the American Bar Association (ABA) weighed a formal complaint against the group: that it was encouraging litigation by offering free legal assistance. Indeed, both Shouse and Beck had offered to represent any American whose constitutional rights were in jeopardy. Calling their bluff, the American Civil Liberties Union asked for help in defending leftist radicals. Shouse referred the matter to his executive committee, where it disappeared without a trace. Calls for disciplinary action grew louder. In October, Democratic Party officials made public a letter in which Raoul Desvernine, chairman of the Lawyers' Vigilance Committee, urged Justice John F. Carew of the New York Supreme Court to sign the group's labor ruling. "I regard this as impudence," the judge scrawled across the invitation before returning it and, apparently, handing a copy to the Democrats. Regardless, the ABA not only cleared the great fifty-eight of any wrongdoing but publicly praised their selfless patriotism.

None of the committee's subsequent reports generated quite the same level of interest. Still they kept coming: a succession of subcommittees reviewed (and found wanting) the AAA, TVA, Social Security, and the Potato Control Act ("flagrantly unconstitutional"). Even the conservative press began to ignore their activities—a sign the attorneys might be overplaying their hand. "The legal profession certainly seems bent on making an exhibition of itself these days," sighed Justice Stone in a letter to Frankfurter. "The performances of the American Bar Association and the recent Lawyers Committee makes one despair of ever attaining better things."

And yet: as Sam Rosenman recalled, "Roosevelt's friends took the American Liberty League seriously. So did he." Though the League at times approached self-parody, it was well funded, increasingly well organized, and spoke for a conservatism that clearly had some life left in it. And if the League's lawyer-vigilantes were unpracticed at press relations, they were devastatingly effective in the nation's courtrooms, where they led the continuing legal assault against the New Deal.

Roosevelt knew he was vulnerable to their persistent charge. When the Vigilance Committee declared the Guffey Coal Act unconstitutional, it was only stating what most of Washington believed and what the president himself, in a moment of candor, conceded as Congress debated the bill. "A great many people think that it is constitutional," he said at a press conference—hardly a ringing endorsement. The attorney general, too, was equivocal. Cummings dodged congressional hearings for days because "I could not give them much comfort on the constitutional features of the act." When he finally appeared, he refused to express an opinion, arguing only that the need for action was so great, the legislation should be allowed to "take its chances with the courts."

Indeed, conditions in the coal industry could hardly have been more dire. What progress had been made since 1933 was quickly being lost. Even before the Court had overturned the NRA—taking the coal codes down with it—operators had begun slashing prices and overproducing. For months the threat of a debilitating strike hung in the air, averted only by the prospect of the Guffey bill, which aimed to stabilize prices, wages, trade practices, and production levels. Hoping to placate the Court, Congress declared the coal industry to be affected with a public interest and rested the authority of the new, National Bituminous Coal Commission on the taxing power—seemingly more secure grounds than the commerce power, which, along with unlawful delegation, had proved the undoing of the NRA. Under the Guffey bill, all coal companies were to pay a 15 percent excise tax; mine operators who obeyed the new codes were then to receive a 90 percent rebate.

This was not enough to quiet concerns about the bill's constitutionality. Opponents of the New Deal bottled up the legislation in a subcommittee chaired by Representative Samuel B. Hill. On July 5, looking to break the logjam, Roosevelt sent Hill a letter urging action. "I understand that questions of the constitutionality of some of its provisions have arisen . . . ," Roosevelt began. Then, after making the case that the bill was constitutional—stressing the national character of the coal industry and the impact of industrial strife on interstate commerce—the president admitted that

> no one is in a position to give assurance that the proposed act will withstand constitutional tests, for the simple fact that you can get not ten but a thousand differing legal opinions on the subject. But the situation is so urgent and the benefits of the legislation so evident that all doubts should be resolved in favor of the bill, leaving to the courts, in an orderly fashion, the ultimate question. . . . I hope your committee will not permit doubts as to constitutionality, however reasonable, to block the suggested legislation.

Conservatives seized on Roosevelt's letter as further evidence—if any were needed—of his casual contempt for the Constitution. "President Roosevelt has come perilously close to what some people call impeachable grounds," declared Bertrand Snell, the House Republican leader. The coal bill spent another five weeks in purgatory before passing by a narrow margin. Roosevelt got his victory, but Republicans got another "good talking point" for 1936.

Appearances aside, lawmakers were taking increasing care in the drafting of legislation. Justice Stone, after *Schechter*, had privately scorned "the general sloppiness of everything" associated with the Recovery Act and hoped that "Congress will now undertake to do its job." Indeed, both Congress and the White House, mindful of the Court, were proceeding with greater caution. Legislation was no longer the slapdash affair of the Hundred Days. None of this, of course, was acknowledged by New Deal critics, who had long ago made up their minds that Roosevelt cared little for the Constitution. His detractors, including those in the mainstream press, took an increasingly conspiratorial view. "Washington," declared *Time*, saw "a deliberate policy by the President to overwhelm the Supreme Court with a mass of New Deal legislation of doubtful constitutionality" and dare the justices to throw it all out in an election year. And if they did so, "Washington" believed, Roosevelt would go to the country and seek a mandate to strike back at the Court. Such was the established wisdom.

September 17, 1935, was Constitution Day. The holiday, which had lost something of its spark during the first years of the Depression, was enjoying a renaissance as Roosevelt revived right-wing fears of socialist rule. Accordingly, the celebrations in 1935 were more elaborate than in recent years: at City Hall in New York, foreign nationals, dressed in their native costumes, took the oath of allegiance, after which members of six veterans' organizations, rechristened "Minute Men of 1935," pledged to defend the Constitution. At Faneuil Hall in Boston, the national observance looked like a meeting of the Liberty League's advisory council: Beck, McCormick, Talmadge.

"A great holiday, hitherto little noticed but now suddenly press-agented into prominence, is being used for political purposes," complained an editorial in the *New York Post*. "The ideals of Madison, the Father of the Constitution, had little in common with those of the great corporation lawyers, the semi-Fascist 'patriotic' groups and the Hearsts who are using today's celebration to grind their own axes." Their Constitution, charged the *Post*'s editors, was "synonymous with privilege, poverty and insecurity, gag laws, concentration camps for strikers, and foreclosure."

President Roosevelt paid this no mind (though someone on his staff clipped the editorial and placed it in a file marked "Speech Materials"). As the autumn began, he was "more tranquil, generous, indulgent" than he had been all year, according to Ray Moley, who visited him in Hyde Park in September. That fall his mood, like his popularity, began to recover. His promise of a "breathing spell" for business—essentially a freeze on further regulations—had been well received by the public and had quieted, for the moment, many of his critics on the right; the *sturm und drang* over the NRA was past; the economy continued its slow march out of the depths; and even stocks were on the rise, toward their highest mark since Roosevelt took office. In addition, the greatest political threat to FDR's reelection, Huey Long, was gone. On September 8, Long had been shot as he strode through the Louisiana Capitol. He died two days later. For Roosevelt this news, horrific though it was, could not have been entirely unwelcome.

Of course, as *Time* pointed out, "disturbances loomed": a battle over federal spending; the possibility that the Supreme Court would strike down the AAA; and trouble overseas. Italy's invasion of Ethiopia was stoking fears of a wider conflict. Caught between the League of Nations, which favored economic sanctions, and the American public, which opposed them, Roosevelt felt powerless to intervene. "I'm walking a tight rope," he told an aide in November. Meanwhile, the presidential election was only a year away, and despite the slight boost to his approval ratings, discontent with Roosevelt remained strong on both ends of the political spectrum. Could he win back disaffected liberals without driving away his conservative supporters, or further inflaming his opponents? It did not seem likely. While the left grumbled that FDR was abandoning the New Deal, business, fearing the opposite, resumed its offensive.

In 1935, Robert Jackson recalled, "'hell broke loose' in the lower courts." That summer, about five new lawsuits were filed each day against the Agricultural Adjustment Act alone. During this period, more than 100 district court judges held acts of Congress unconstitutional; federal courts issued more than 1,600 injunctions blocking the enforcement of New Deal laws. "At no time in the country's history," Felix Frankfurter later argued, "was there a more voluminous outpouring of judicial rulings in restraint of acts of Congress." If this were not enough to inflame tensions among the branches of government, judges were also increasingly in the habit of making stump speeches from the bench—"reminiscent," wrote Frankfurter, "of political harangues by early Federalist judges which involved the federal judiciary for the first time in the conflict of politics."

Ominously, the Supreme Court's thick, gray, clothbound docket was heavy with what Cardozo called the "alphabetical combinations"—not just the AAA, but the TVA, SEC, and other New Deal creations. In mid-November, barely a month into the new term, an obscure case emphasized anew the sharp split in the Court. The case concerned a 1916 law, the Federal Warehouse Act, which provided for the storage and marketing of farm products, especially cotton. During the argument, the conservative justices assailed the assistant attorney general, who defended the law, while the liberals directed their fire at the Liberty League's James M. Beck, who denounced it (along with the AAA, the Potato Control Act, and, for good measure, the defunct NRA) as unconstitutional.

That afternoon, the president had a long lunch with Harold Ickes. The two men discussed the coming campaign. Roosevelt expressed hope that the Republicans would nominate Hoover, which Ickes found unlikely. The conversation turned to the Supreme Court. Ickes asked whether Roosevelt thought any justice would retire and give him the chance to appoint a liberal. Roosevelt did not think so. "Then," Ickes wrote in his diary, FDR "said that while the matter could not be talked about now, he believed that the way to mend the situation was to adopt a constitutional amendment" that would require the Court to offer an advisory ruling on any bill, at the administration's request. If the justices considered an act unconstitutional, the last word would belong to the American people: the following election, Roosevelt said, would serve as a de facto referendum on the Court's finding. If the majority party prevailed at the polls, Congress could pass the legislation a second time. The act, thereby "purged of its unconstitutionality," in Ickes's words, would now lie beyond the reach of the Supreme Court.

Such an amendment would do one other thing, Roosevelt said: it would acknowledge the Court's veto power over acts of Congress—authority that, he insisted, was not provided by the Constitution and that had been rejected "on three or four occasions" by delegates to the Constitutional Convention. In effect, Roosevelt was saying that the Court had been operating outside the bounds of the Constitution since at least 1803, when Chief Justice John Marshall asserted the right of judicial review in *Marbury v. Madison*. Not only Roosevelt but many of his advisers, members of Congress, and reformers agreed with Ray Clapper, who wrote that the justices "get away with" striking down legislation only "because John Marshall . . . did. Nothing in the Constitution says they can."

The charge, in fact, was nearly as old as the nation. It was technically accurate in that the Constitution did not *expressly* vest the power of judicial review in the Court; but then, the power was generally understood by the framers to exist, implicitly, in Article III, which established the judiciary. (Contrary to Roosevelt's claim, the framers never rejected judicial review. They did reject Madison's notion of an executive-judiciary "revisionary council" possessing veto power, and Roosevelt may have been confusing the two.) Still, there was enough ambiguity about their exact intentions—and enough continuing anxiety about the role of judges—that judicial review was periodically and at times aggressively challenged throughout the nineteenth century and into the twentieth. Virtually every time a group of legislators, federal or state, felt aggrieved by the Court, the cry of "usurpation" was raised.

It was, however, more an expression of resentment than radicalism. Few of the Court's critics actually saw its exercise of power as illegitimate, and even fewer were prepared to do violence to the system of checks and balances in the manner of Robert "Fighting Bob" La Follette, the Wisconsin senator who said in the early 1920s that he wished to "put the ax to the root" and destroy "at one stroke" the "usurped power of the Federal courts." As Charles Warren, the renowned historian of the Court, observed, most of the opposition to judicial review "was directed not so much at the *possession of the power* of the Court to pass upon the validity of Acts of Congress, as at the *effect of its exercise* in supporting or invalidating some particular measure."

This was likely true of Roosevelt. It is possible that by the fall of 1935, his conflict with the Court so clouded his perspective that he had come to see the justices' exercise of power as illegitimate; more likely, though, his argument against judicial review was little more than an argument in favor of judicial self-restraint. "What is wanted," Robert Jackson reflected, speaking for himself and FDR, "is . . . a return to the spirit with which our early judges viewed the function of judicial review of legislation—the conviction that it is an awesome thing to strike down an act of the legislature approved by the Chief Executive, and that power . . . is not to be used save where the occasion is clear beyond fair debate." One of those early judges, Bushrod Washington—the nephew of George Washington and a justice of the Supreme Court—said in 1827: "It is but a decent respect due to the wisdom, the integrity, and the patriotism of the legislative body, by which any law is passed, to presume in favor of its validity, until its violation of the Constitution is proved beyond all reasonable doubt."

This is what Roosevelt sought: judicial restraint and humility, judicial deference to the other branches of government. "This presumption of constitutionality . . . ," he wrote a few years later, "is not a technical lawyer's rule. It is part of the very fabric of our scheme of government, obedience to which is indispensable." And if the judges would not exercise self-restraint, then the president would impose restraint by other means. In the guise of a concession to the Court, the amendment Roosevelt described would sanction—but at the same time weaken—judicial review. He would leave the justices with a say in matters of national importance; a say, but no longer the last word.

Apparently, though, this was not the only approach he was considering. "The President's mind," Ickes recalled, "went back to the difficulty in England, where the House of Lords repeatedly refused to adopt legislation sent up from the House of Commons." Roosevelt said that when the Lords refused to approve an Irish Home Rule bill, Prime

Minister David Lloyd George asked the king to create several hundred new peers, enough to outvote the Lords. This threat alone, Roosevelt said, had been enough; the Lords let the bill go through.

Roosevelt's analogy was off—but significant. He was somewhat misremembering a constitutional crisis in which the Lords had stood in the way of reform and, as a result, lost much of their power. Between 1909 and 1911, the Liberal government of Herbert Henry Asquith hit an impasse with the conservative Lords; the peers' resistance to the "People's Budget"—its taxes on property, its redistribution of wealth—led to a showdown. When Asquith convinced George V to create, if necessary, hundreds of Liberal peers, the Lords yielded, and, in an unprecedented act of self-emasculation, gave up their power to veto certain types of legislation. The Commons also gained the ability to override the Lords by reenacting, in three successive sessions of Parliament, any bill the Lords had rejected.

In retelling the story, Roosevelt did not even mention this outcome. Rather, what he emphasized to Ickes—and repeated, soon after, to the entire cabinet—was the fact that the British government had threatened to pack the House of Lords with Liberals, and the conservatives had backed down. Was FDR mulling the same idea? Did he think that the mere threat of packing the Court might cow the justices into upholding the New Deal? If so, he did not say. But his interest in the analogy spoke for itself.

It said much, in fact, about Roosevelt's view of the problem. Even now—despite all the talk about amendments to the Constitution and about adjustments to the system of checks and balances—Roosevelt was consistent in his belief that the real problem was not one of law per se, but of law being twisted by ideologically driven, outcome-oriented judges. At a meeting on November 15, Roosevelt informed the cabinet that a district court had just upheld the Coal Act—which other courts had tried to shut down. "Apparently," he said, "it made a great deal of difference what judge decided the question."

Cummings agreed. As he told his colleagues, he was reminded of something Charles Evans Hughes had said when governor of New York: "We are under a Constitution, but the Constitution is what the judges say it is."

Chapter Eleven

SLOW POISON

ON THE AFTERNOON of November 20, 1935, Attorney General Cummings put on his cutaway coat and top hat and took his official sedan up Pennsylvania Avenue to the new Supreme Court Building. He was there to escort the justices to the White House for their annual, formal call on the president.

The visit was meant to have taken place more than a month earlier, when the Court's October term began. But President Roosevelt, at that time, was busy catching sailfish near Cocos Island, southwest of Costa Rica, and had been so busy since his return that the reception was put off indefinitely. In November, as another presidential vacation approached—this one to Warm Springs—an invitation was hastily sent.

Seven justices—all but Brandeis (who generally did not bother with social engagements outside his apartment) and Van Devanter (who was out of town)—greeted Cummings and then joined him in the small procession of black limousines. Cummings rode with Chief Justice Hughes. The two made pleasant conversation on the brief ride to the White House, where, a few minutes later, the president and Mrs. Roosevelt welcomed the justices to tea in the Blue Room. The meeting was cordial. After an hour or so, the president excused himself to make a southbound train to Georgia.

Roosevelt "seemed strong and happy," Cardozo wrote to Felix Frankfurter the next day. "To have a picture of him talking with McReynolds would be precious." The professor passed Cardozo's comment along to Roosevelt, adding, "Can we not have such a photograph!? It would be a superb campaign poster—or might McReynolds enjoin you from exhibiting it!"

"I think the Chief Justice pulled a fast one on me," Roosevelt replied from Warm Springs. "After he had been talking with me himself for ten minutes he got up, said he thought some other members of the Court should have a talk with me, and went across the room and brought McReynolds and plumped him down. The Chief Justice," he added, "has a sense of humor though few people realize it. Thank God no photographers were present."

Almost three weeks later, on December 9, Cummings put his coat back on and returned to the Court—this time for oral arguments in the AAA case, *United States v. Butler*.

The administration, still shaken by *Schechter*, approached the test with trepidation. The AAA—like that other pillar of the recovery program, the NRA—was a complex, innovative, and ambitious arrangement, patched together at a time of desperate urgency. Like the NRA, it stood on shaky constitutional ground; aroused an intense, emotional sort of opposition; and by 1935 had come to be seen as a cumbersome relic. And now, the AAA seemed to be headed for the same fate, by the same hands.

The Agricultural Adjustment Act had been one of the proudest achievements of the Hundred Days. It was Roosevelt's answer to a tangle of problems afflicting farmers: production was too high, prices were too low, and previous administrations had done little to stop the vicious cycle. Under the AAA, farmers were paid to plant fewer acres, produce less corn or cotton, raise fewer cows or chickens or hogs. The payments came from a new tax on the processing of farm goods: canning, milling, meatpacking, textile manufacturing. The U.S. Treasury operated as something of a conduit, collecting the revenues and passing them through to farmers. "I tell you frankly," Roosevelt cautioned Congress in 1933, "that it is a new and untrod path, but I tell you with equal frankness that an unprecedented condition calls for the trial of new means."

Conditions began to improve. In the short span of two years, farm incomes more than doubled; food prices rebounded nearly as much; and the wave of rural violence that crested in 1933 finally receded. It was never clear how much of this improvement was due to the AAA, or to the growing national economy, which buoyed demand for farm goods, or to the dust storms that spread their thick, suffocating clouds across the heartland and stifled production. What was clear was that the improvement, while real, was not enough. Farmers were still suffering. And by 1935, the AAA seemed to be running out of remedies. Its "best work," judged the *New York Times*, "lies behind it." Too little, for example, was being done about soil erosion, and too many farmers were opting out of the benefit scheme.

The public's view remained something of a mystery. On the one hand, the *Times* called the AAA "the most popular measure of the New Deal," while, on the other, Gallup showed that nearly 60 percent of the public opposed the AAA (though it was possible that these two results did not contradict). Some Americans, clearly, had never come around to the notion of paying farmers *not* to produce—even to plow under crops and slaughter and burn livestock—at a time when many of their fellow citizens were starving. Business groups, eager to exploit this discontent, had waged a massive public relations offensive in the spring and summer of 1935, hoping to head off congressional improvements to the AAA. Leaping to the aid of the processing industries, the Liberty League unleashed a new flurry of pamphlets and press releases that showed a newfound solidarity with sharecroppers, farm laborers, and other helpless victims of the AAA's "fascist control."

Meanwhile, the AAA was under assault in the courts. By the end of the year, more than 1,700 suits were pending. Grain millers, meatpackers, and clothing manufacturers sued to recover taxes paid—despite the fact that they had passed those taxes along to consumers in the form of higher prices—and to enjoin the government against collecting taxes due. Judges granted injunctions in 90 percent of all cases. The processing tax was not, in truth, the companies' primary complaint with New Deal agricultural policy, which they loathed for an abundance of reasons; the tax was a target because the tax, as they could see, was the AAA's Achilles' heel. The administration recognized this as well. Henry Wallace, the Secretary of Agriculture, told a fellow cabinet member that he wished the Court would go ahead and overturn the processing tax so that Congress would be forced to place the AAA on more secure footing—perhaps by drawing its funding from general tax revenues.

But of course, Achilles' vulnerability had been fatal. The AAA's looked to be, too. In the *Butler* case, lawyers for the Hoosac Cotton Mills, a Massachusetts firm, claimed that the processing tax was not, in fact, a tax at all. They saw it as a back door scheme to "control and regulate" agriculture—a local matter that, they said, lay outside the reach of Congress. In June 1935, an appeals court in Boston agreed, sustaining Hoosac Mills right down the line.

A long dormant debate was thus resumed. Article I, Section 8, of the Constitution gives Congress the "power to lay and collect taxes" for the "general welfare of the United States." That power, James Madison had argued, was limited to congressional functions specifically enumerated by the Constitution: raising armies, for example, or maintaining post offices. Regulating agriculture was not among them. This, the Madisonian position, was the one taken by Hoosac Mills and endorsed by the Court of Appeals in *Butler*. Alexander Hamilton, by contrast, had seen the general welfare clause as a broad and undefined grant of power, permitting Congress to tax and spend essentially as it saw fit. This was the position taken by the administration—that the clause, as the government's Supreme Court brief contended, "should be construed in the Hamiltonian sense to include anything conducive to the national welfare," and that the definition of "general welfare" belonged "primarily to the judgment of Congress," not the courts. On that basis, the administration appealed to the Supreme Court.

It was to be the first argument of consequence in the new Supreme Court Building. The walls and floor of the great hall were made of Alabama marble, said to be the whitest in the world; the friezes of the courtroom were Spanish marble; the Ionic columns, Italian (Mussolini himself had helped in the selection)—"marble, marble, more marble than in any other building in the world," noted Drew Pearson and Robert Allen. It was all too tempting to view the building as metaphor. "It is a dead white," they wrote, "colorless, relentless—an atmosphere of austere, Olympian dignity, that yields to no one, that has no soul. . . . The corridor inside is like the entrance to a tomb. . . . At the far end is the court chamber itself, again in icy marble, like the ordeal room of the grand inquisitor."

After seventy-five years as a "temporary" resident in the Capitol Building, the Court had traded the intimacy of the Old Senate Chamber—its muted gray-green columns, its deep mahogany, its wrought-iron balcony—for this stark, imposing, impersonal space, and most of the justices instantly regretted it. "I fear I shall never be reconciled to surroundings so pompous and pretentious," groused Stone. He said that whenever he looked at the building, he felt he and his brethren should ride to work on elephants. McReynolds did not mind the building from "an artistic standpoint," he told his brother, but "from a practical standpoint, it is a mess." The gilded ceiling was so dark that it required repainting, at great expense. The acoustics in the courtroom were so poor that the justices had to lean forward to hear oral arguments or one another. The lighting was so bad and unalleviated by natural light that they were unable to see clearly—though some New Dealers said old age was the reason.

As arguments in the AAA case approached, Roosevelt traveled to Fremont, Nebraska, to make the case for the program—not just its success, but its consistency with American ideals. "I like to think that agricultural adjustment is an expression, in concrete form, of the human rights those farmer patriots sought to win when they stood at the bridge at Concord, when they proclaimed the Declaration of Independence, and when they perpetuated these ideals by the adoption of the Constitution of the United States. Methods and machinery may change," Roosevelt declared, "but principles go on, and I have faith that, no matter what attempts may be made to tear it down, the principle of farm equality expressed by agricultural adjustment will not die." Statements like "the true function of government under our Constitution [is] to promote the general welfare" were not mere banalities. Roosevelt was offering a preview of the *Butler* brief, then being drafted in long, late night sessions at the Justice Department. Cummings thought the brief "masterly."

The oral argument, however, was another matter. On December 9, 1935, the new courtroom—though it held more than three times as many spectators as the Old Senate Chamber—was filled well beyond capacity. At the stroke of twelve on the great gold clock above the dais, the justices stepped through the red velvet curtain and slipped into their seats. The session began badly for the government—with an argument, of sorts, among the justices. Before hearing from the two sides in the AAA case, the Court delivered decisions in a pair of earlier cases—each one a blow against the federal government and a victory for states' rights.

The first opinion held that the Home Owners' Loan Act, a product of the Hundred Days, had intruded upon powers reserved to the states. This was unanimous. The second ruling was not: a familiar six-man majority, led by Justice Roberts, overturned a federal tax on liquor dealers. Roberts's stridency here—his angry insistence that Congress should not be taken at its word, that its professed intentions disguised a darker motive—was no greater than in the railroad pensions case, earlier in the year, but it was startling nonetheless. He held that the liquor tax, if upheld, would "obliterate the distinction" between national and state power and "would open the door to unlimited regulation" of state activity. Cardozo and the other two dissenters, Stone and Brandeis, issued a warning that obviously applied to the case they were about to hear: "One branch of the government," Cardozo said, "cannot encroach on the domain of another without danger."

Thus the oral defense of the AAA, which immediately followed, began on a note of futility. Stanley Reed's presentation did not help. Under fire from the conservative justices, the solicitor general hedged, contradicted, and ultimately disowned the grander claims the government's written brief had made about the delegation of power and the general welfare clause. Reed was no match for opposing counsel. Hoosac Mills—or, rather, its receivers, for the mill had gone bankrupt and was now controlled by the chairman of Armour & Company, the meatpacking giant—was represented by George Wharton Pepper, the former Republican senator from Pennsylvania. Tall, imposing, and famously theatrical, Pepper was a performer—"a carnival pitchman," wrote Pearson and Allen. He was also a mentor to Justice Roberts. Pepper had taught law to Roberts at the University of Pennsylvania; had urged Coolidge to appoint Roberts to the Teapot Dome investigation in which he made his name; and, it was said, had lobbied Hoover to appoint Roberts to the Court on which he now sat, arms folded across his black robe, listening to the oratory of his friend and patron.

Pepper argued that the government's brief went well beyond Hamilton; it was, Pepper charged, "the general welfare clause gone mad." If the AAA were allowed to continue, he said, echoing the opinion Roberts had just delivered on the liquor tax, Congress would be "subject to no restraint except self-restraint." He painted the AAA's benefit scheme as inherently coercive—not acknowledging that the owners of one quarter of all the cotton acreage in America had opted out of the program, as they were permitted to do. (Pepper's "solicitude for the independence of the farmers was truly touching," observed Robert Jackson archly.)

Pepper built toward a crescendo, the sort of performance for which he was known. "May it please your Honors," he declared, his volume rising, his voice swelling with emotion, "I believe I am standing here today to plead the case of the America I have loved; and I pray Almighty God that not in my time may 'the land of the regimented' be accepted as a worthy substitute for 'the land of the free.' " With this, Pepper concluded his peroration, returned to his seat, and broke down in quiet, if not inconspicuous, sobs.

The "twilight war" between the branches, as Tugwell called it, was escalating. Washington was riveted. At the Gridiron Dinner on December 14, the press corps made malicious fun of the conflict. Following a skit about the Schechters (which, bizarrely, portrayed the Jewish Schechter brothers bringing their chickens to race at the Olympic Games in Berlin. "Heil Hitler!" the brothers shouted. "Heil Roosevelt! . . . Heil with 'em all!"), the six justices in attendance were asked to rise from their seats at the high table to be applauded by the other dinner guests, including the president.

Then began the final skit of the evening: nine journalists, dressed as ancient Athenian soldiers, marched onto the set of a grand marble temple and were introduced as "the nine wisest men in the entire world." After a song about Supreme Court "revelations" ("you'll hear what folks were thinking in eighteen hundred ten . . ."), the identities of the wise men were revealed: Shouse, Beck, and other leaders of the Liberty League. "Gentlemen," said one, "permit me now to exhibit the historic charter upon which our freedom rests." From a gold chest, he extracted a list of the League's contributors.

The real justices, according to Pearson and Allen, "looked on with fixed smiles. Those of Hughes and Stone were genuine. They even contributed several deep belly laughs. But the smiles of Van Devanter, McReynolds, and Butler were of that glassy variety developed to perfection by chorus girls." Ickes, who was in the audience, hoped that the justices were sufficiently humbled.

As tradition dictated, the president drew the evening to a close. After enduring another round of "semi-annual flagellation," Roosevelt said, "I suppose I should be in a mood of appropriate humility and contrition for all the sins I have committed and all the wisecrack statesmanship which I have failed to display. I do not feel depressed, however, because, sitting here in 'buggy-drivers' row,' it is obvious to me that as long as the Gridiron Club is in general supervision of our government, there is a final appeal to that Gridiron Court of sublime judgment, to which all of us can appeal." This last line he added, in pencil, to his reading copy of the speech.

Most of what followed was lightly sardonic. He closed, however, on a serious note, as in years past. "I am not one of those who fears for the survival of our political institutions," he said, "or of the broad structure of our national economic life. I believe that part of the genius of our form of government is its adaptiveness to the needs of changing times. The wise and sound general principles upon which our government rests, and from which our peace and happiness are derived, were not intended to become rigid formulae, inflexible, resistant to the stresses and strains . . . out of which true progress arises."

It was, in a sense, his closing argument in the AAA case. When the president returned to his place at the center of the dais, Hughes, who sat one chair away, leaned in and warmly congratulated him. To Pearson and Allen, watching from one of the long banquet tables below, it appeared that "Mr. Roosevelt had made at least one convert." McReynolds, however, was unmoved. Writing to his brother the next day, he pronounced Roosevelt's speech "a failure—bad taste and very flat."

• • •

There had been no conversion. On December 16, just two days after the dinner, Hughes joined the five conservatives in an unprecedented ruling. In *Colgate v. Harvey*, the Court set aside a Vermont law that taxed income from out-of-state loans at a higher rate than from loans originating within the state. They did so by holding that the tax violated the "privileges and immunities" clause of the Fourteenth Amendment, which forbade certain kinds of state discrimination against out-of-state citizens. Never before—not once in its history—had the Court struck down a state law on this basis. Forty-four times it had considered the possibility; forty-four times it had declined. When the justices discussed the Vermont case in conference, Hughes had dismissed the idea of invoking the clause. He argued, instead, that the tax was a denial of equal protection under the same amendment; and Sutherland soon circulated an opinion to that effect.

Then Stone fired back with a draft dissent so blistering that Sutherland shifted ground. With Hughes's blessing, he disinterred the privileges and immunities clause and put it to use. "As citizens of the United States," Sutherland now wrote, "we are members of a single great community consisting of all the states united, and not of distinct communities consisting of the states severally." The irony, indeed the perversity, of that statement—coming as it did from a justice who had stood, so consistently and stridently, for the rights of those distinct communities above those of the nation—proved too much for Stone. "Feeble indeed," he snapped in his dissent. The Court, he said, had turned itself into a "superlegislature," dictating "what shall and what shall not be taxed" by the states. "To me," he wrote to his sons a few days later, "this was a rather shocking extension of judicial power, with little to warrant it."

The *Colgate* decision drew little comment in the press. In the law schools, however, the news was explosive. "We are intellectually outraged here," said Thomas Reed Powell of Harvard. He decried the Court's tendency to "pick new, strange clubs out of the air to swat anything that it doesn't like. . . . The Supreme Court is riding high, wide and handsome," he added, "and I see no likelihood of any serious movement to curb its power." His colleague Felix Frankfurter was apoplectic. "Gosh it is unbelievable," he wired Stone. "Apparently history and precedents mean nothing. I don't think I have ever been more shocked." Twice that night Frankfurter awoke, searching his mind for a Supreme Court decision that was more indefensible than *Colgate*. He could not think of one. *Colgate*, he wrote to Stone the next day, was "the end of the limit. After that, anything may be expected."

Stone agreed. "The tendency to press constitutional restrictions to their limit and beyond," he wrote to Frankfurter, "gives me serious apprehension for the future capacity of the Court to render useful service." He found the whole experience "rather shocking." In Stone's view, the majority's "overstimulated inventive genius," its resort to a long forgotten clause as "a happy afterthought," made the process "even more alarming than the results." His disdain for Hughes reached new depths. He had long disliked what he saw as Hughes's arrogance and mania for order. He also (still) resented being passed over for Chief Justice and then being relegated to "unimportant, junky cases," as one of Stone's clerks put it. Now he faulted Hughes for lacking courage. "If the inventor would only sponsor his invention in public," Stone wrote to Frankfurter, "I think I could write a really effective dissent." For now, however, "I am only a voice crying out in the wilderness."

But not a lone voice. The bloc of three dissenters was secure. It was also, of course, badly outnumbered. First they had lost their occasional ally, Roberts, and now Hughes seemed to have abandoned them as well. The rift within the Court was widening. During the 1920s, under Chief Justice Taft, the conservatives had begun meeting on Sunday afternoons to talk strategy, and later rode to and from the Court together. Now Stone and Cardozo gathered at Brandeis's stuffy, overheated apartment on Friday afternoons to agree on their approach in advance of the weekly Saturday conference.

Beyond this, the justices had little to do with one another. Apart from arguments and conferences, nearly all nine continued to work at home—by choice and habit rather than necessity, now that the new building was open and each justice, for the first time, had his own chambers. They communicated mainly by messenger. On occasion, justices might see one another socially; some affection existed, even across ideological lines. Cardozo felt fondly toward Sutherland, Van Devanter, and especially Roberts, in spite of their views; and Brandeis tried not to let personalities interfere with working relationships.

This was not always possible. The hostility that Butler and McReynolds directed toward Brandeis, for example, was so pronounced that the Chief Justice, as the host of two annual Court dinners, made sure to seat other guests between them to prevent an embarrassing incident. "The mastiffs have been inconsiderate," Brandeis told Frankfurter, noting that Benjamin Cardozo, the gentlest justice, showed "shocks at the treatment received" by the conservatives. Brandeis advised Cardozo to "ignore it, brush it aside," which Cardozo was never able to do; the Court, he told friends, was a "prison house"—impersonal, severe, and frequently cruel.

In mid-December, the Court announced that it would return from its holiday recess on January 6, 1936, a week earlier than originally planned. This made the front pages. It heightened the sense of tension, of looming crisis, in Washington. Clearly a decision in the AAA case was coming.

The cabinet met on the afternoon of December 27. Roosevelt had a bad cold. To avoid being wheeled to the West Wing, he held the meeting in the White House residence. His private study, the Oval Room (not the similarly shaped Oval Office), had the appearance of a nautical museum: oil paintings of old sailing vessels lined the walls, frame above frame, nearly to the ceiling; elaborate model ships rested on tables, on the mantel, and in glass cases. The setting gave the meeting an intimate, informal feeling; to Cummings, it felt like a family gathering.

FDR, despite his health, was in an expansive mood. He talked at length about many things—among them the certainty, as he saw it, that the Supreme Court would nullify virtually everything of significance that the administration had done. It would not be long, he said, before the nation's streets were filled with marching farmers, marching miners, and marching factory workers. He saw three possible ways to prevent this: first, by packing the Court—"a distasteful idea"; second, through a series of constitutional amendments specifically addressing the Court's objections; and third, by amending the Constitution to give Congress the power to override decisions. Roosevelt asked the cabinet to consider this last method carefully, then moved on without requesting anyone's views.

• • •

On January 6, 1936, Justice Owen Roberts fixed his glasses, looked out at the courtroom, and began to read his opinion in *United States v. Butler*. For the next thirty minutes, as he spoke, he scarcely lowered his gaze. He glanced left, then right, as if delivering a lecture. Though the pages of the opinion lay before him, Roberts had committed them almost entirely to memory. Later that day, reporters who scoured the published opinion were hard-pressed to find discrepancies between the text and Roberts's oral presentation. His voice carried well, despite the room's terrible acoustics, and he spoke firmly but dispassionately. "Never did a judge kill a legislative creature with more elegance and soft grace," recalled one observer.

Roberts began by affirming the appeals court ruling: the AAA's processing tax, the six-judge majority agreed, was not a tax at all. In three recent opinions, including the one concerning the liquor tax, Roberts had frowned upon any use of the taxing power other than to raise revenue; here, in *Butler*, he expanded the doctrine. The word "tax," he said, "has never been thought to connote the expropriation of money from one group for the benefit of another." The AAA, he continued, did exactly that—taking from processors and giving to farmers in a scheme to control agricultural production.

Roberts paused. A muted *thump*, *thump* was heard from the press benches as pneumatic tubes carried the news from the courtroom to the press office in the basement. Within minutes, the verdict would be on the wires, even before Roberts had finished reading his opinion. Now he resumed—reflecting, for a moment, on the role of the judiciary. "It is sometimes said that the court assumes a power to overrule or control the action of the people's representatives. This," Roberts insisted, "is a misconception. . . . When an act of Congress is appropriately challenged in the courts . . . the judicial branch of the government has only one duty; to lay the article of the Constitution which is invoked beside the statute which is challenged and to decide whether the latter squares with the former. All the court does, or can do, is to announce its considered judgment upon the question. The only power it has, if such it may be called, is the power of judgment. This court neither approves nor condemns any legislative policy." It was as pure a statement of "automatism"—judicial decision making as a precise, impersonal, mechanical act—as any justice had made in recent memory.

Then—in what was for many the greatest surprise of the day—the Court endorsed, for the first time in history, Hamilton's sweeping view of the general welfare clause and rejected Madison's more circumscribed notion. The "broader construction," Roberts announced, was "the correct one." This seemed to contradict what he had said only moments before. If Congress was indeed free to tax and spend as it saw fit for the general welfare, was it not then free to tax for the sake of curtailing agricultural production?

It was not, Roberts said, for two reasons: because the processing tax was not really a tax, and agriculture was "a purely local activity," reserved under the Tenth Amendment to the states. Dust, drought, rotting surpluses—these were not, by the logic of the majority, national problems; they reflected, instead, "a widespread similarity of local conditions." By "no reasonable possibility" did they fall within the powers of the federal government. Hamilton, said Roberts, in a final, cruel thrust, had never intended that "the general welfare of the United States . . . might be served by obliterating the constituent members of the Union."

Stone answered sharply. One of his main concerns, as he sat down to draft an opinion, was to avoid writing anything that he might, down the line, feel the need to take back. A wry and temperate Yankee, he was hardly given to bursts of pique. But by 1936, Stone had grown deeply troubled by the majority's tendency to "slop over" the boundaries of a given case and to overrule, in unrestrained fashion, the will of the people as expressed by their elected representatives. On New Year's Day, 1936, as he drafted his *Butler* dissent in his wood-paneled study, Stone gave full vent to his outrage. The resulting draft was a cri de coeur. When Stone circulated it among the justices, Roberts was so taken aback that he appealed to Hughes to intervene. Hughes suggested that Roberts take it up with Brandeis instead. Stone, possibly at Brandeis's urging, softened his language—but only a bit.

On decision day, Stone was harder to hear than Roberts; the chamber seemed to swallow his words. Still, as he barked out one phrase after another, there could be no mistaking that his was, as the *New York*

Times observed, a "hot dissent." Robert Jackson thought it "hardly paralleled in the century and a half of the Court's existence for its scathing rebuke to the majority." The dissent, joined by Brandeis and Cardozo, attacked not only the majority's decision but the philosophy behind it. Stone rejected out of hand Roberts's notion that the payments to farmers were coercive—a "groundless" suggestion contradicted by the facts. He also took aim at Roberts's contention that the taxing power, while legitimate, had been applied toward illegitimate ends. The power of Congress to promote the general welfare, Stone replied, necessarily entailed—indeed, required—the ability to make conditional grants of money. Otherwise the power was meaningless. "It is a contradiction in terms," Stone declared, "to say that there is power to spend for the national welfare, while rejecting any power to impose conditions reasonably adapted to the attainment of the end which alone would justify the expenditure. The limitation now sanctioned must lead to absurd consequences. The government may give seeds to farmers, but may not condition the gift upon their being planted in places where they are most needed or even planted at all. The government may give money to the unemployed, but may not ask that those who get it shall give labor in return, or even use it to support their families."

Stone had even less patience for Roberts's blithe claim that judges, as a general matter, did nothing more than lay a statute beside the relevant article of the Constitution, see if they squared, and announce the results—what Roscoe Pound, dean of Harvard Law School, called the "slot machine" theory of judicial review. This affectation of powerlessness infuriated Stone, given the majority's willingness, even its eagerness, to impose its own judgment over that of the Congress. Where Roberts had raised the specter of an out-of-control Congress, unchecked by the courts, Stone answered that judicial power could be even more easily abused—because "the only check upon our own exercise of power is our own sense of self-restraint."

In the end, what offended the dissenters most was the arrogance of presuming "it is the business of courts to sit in judgment on the wisdom of legislative action." In closing, Stone issued a stinging indictment of judicial supremacy: "Courts," he said, "are not the only agency of government that must be assumed to have capacity to govern."

• • •

"Well, I guess we've been 'Schechtered,' too."

This was heard at the Department of Agriculture, in the outer office of Secretary Wallace, as the ticker rattled off the news of the decision. Henry Wallace himself was already in the Oval Office, where he and other officials were wrapping up a meeting with Roosevelt about new farm relief legislation. An assistant entered the room and laid a news bulletin on the president's desk. Roosevelt held the sheet in front of him and smiled. He seemed wholly unsurprised, undisturbed, and even, in a strange sense, pleased.

"Please resist all—say nothing," his press secretary, Steve Early, advised him. Word filtered quickly through the administration that none were to comment until the president had chosen a course of action. At 2:30 p.m., Roosevelt summoned the attorney general and a handful of others to the White House to review the opinions. They began with the dissent. Cummings read it aloud, stopping frequently for discussion; Roosevelt followed suit with Roberts's opinion, pausing to comment.

"Never before," Robert Jackson recalled, "had a blow of such force been struck" at the finances of the federal government. The sums involved were staggering—nearly a billion dollars collected from processors now entered a kind of legal purgatory: were processors entitled to refunds, even though they had, in most cases, already passed the tax burden on to consumers? And what of national agricultural policy—could such a thing exist anymore? Was the American Liberty League right in charging that the Department of Agriculture itself was now unconstitutional? The *Butler* decision was "so sweeping," according to the *New York Times*, that replacing the AAA would be "desperately difficult."

Conservatives were overjoyed. "The lawyers and business men and really good citizens in general thank God we still have a Supreme Court," a friend cabled Van Devanter. "Constitutional government still lives," declared Henry P. Fletcher, chairman of the Republican National Committee, at a Union League luncheon. The crowd cheered for several minutes. The conservative press believed the end of the New Deal was in sight: constitutionalism, said the *Chicago Daily Tribune*, had triumphed over "Hitlerism"; and the *Philadelphia Inquirer*, hometown paper of both Owen Roberts and George Wharton Pepper, saw in the rubble of "regimented monstrosities" like AAA the rebirth of "plain, old-fashioned Americanism." Not all were ready to declare victory: in a letter to his brother, Justice McReynolds warned that the nation was not yet free from danger. "The forces who control R[oosevelt]," he wrote, "are really seeking confusion & wide discontent in order to bring about the most radical changes. . . . He probably lacks brains to understand what he is doing." Still, McReynolds took comfort in the notion that thanks to the Court, "the New Deal is on the rocks."

After a day's reflection, many Republicans grew more restrained. "There was peace along the Potomac," observed *Time*, "the peace that arises on those infrequent occasions when politicians admit that something surpasses their understanding." It was difficult for either party, especially the GOP, to orient itself in a landscape now devoid of both the NRA and the AAA. The Guffey Act, the Wagner Act, Social Security—each presented a new potential target but none, as yet, brought conservatives' blood to a boil as readily as the two defunct programs once had. Stone, who was still socially and temperamentally aligned with the GOP, wrote a party member that "the Supreme Court has robbed your Republican friends of a good campaign issue."

The virtual silence lasted for days. "The tongues of politicians were frozen stiff with fright," *Time* reported, "fright of what farmers might be saying by their kitchen stoves." What they—or other Americans—were saying, no one really knew. At a movie theater in Manhattan, a few days after the decision, the audience hissed a newsreel image of the Supreme Court. But this was New York. In rural America, initial reactions showed a deep split. While the Farm Independence Council (its name something of a giveaway) hailed the Court's blow against "bureaucrats masquerading as benefactors," the leader of the American Farm Bureau Federation declared that "the fight is on. And this time," he promised, "all gloves are off." On January 7, in Ames, Iowa, the justices who had struck down the AAA were hanged in effigy: six life-sized, cardboard figures, identified by name and draped in black, ersatz robes. Police came to cut them down.

Among liberals, a consensus quickly took hold that however one might have felt about the AAA, the majority opinion was political, unreasonable, logically incoherent, and possibly dangerous. *Butler* angered them far more than *Schechter* had. Partly they had been stirred by the moral force of Stone's dissent. Also, increasingly, they were just fed up. "The Constitution is the Lord," sneered *The New Republic*, "and the Supreme Court is its prophet!" Ray Clapper, rarely one to get carried away, could not contain his disgust. The day after the decision, he wrote that the rest of the New Deal was to be "mowed down" just as soon as the Court

> can find the technical legal pretexts to support its political opinions. . . . [Roosevelt] can yield to its political philosophy which would confine the Federal Government largely to running the Army, the Navy and municipal affairs in the District of Columbia. Or he can accept the challenge as a political one, which it is, and go to the country to determine whether the people want to be governed by their elected President and their elected Congress or by a lame-duck judicial dictatorship. There is no use being dainty any longer in discussing the court. It is in politics up to its neck. . . . Roosevelt has his issue now, if he wishes to accept it.

He did not. So, at least, it appeared on January 7, the day after the decision, when he held a press conference in the Oval Office. By one account it drew the biggest attendance on record; reporters, it appeared, were hoping for a reprise of "horse-and-buggy." If so, they were disappointed. Roosevelt opened, as usual, with a broad grin and a benign joke, stating that there was no news except that the DNC's Charles Michelson, who sat nearby, needed a haircut. Roosevelt rocked back in his chair and deflected the first question, which concerned the future of agricultural policy. Again and again, reporters rephrased the question, trying different angles of approach, hoping to bait him into responding. After a while Roosevelt grew visibly annoyed. Finally, someone blurted, "What do you think of the Supreme Court decision?" The correspondents laughed, but not Roosevelt; instead, he smiled slowly and repeated that he had no news. He said he was still studying "both opinions" in *Butler*—Roberts's and Stone's—implying that he gave equal weight to the two.

The next night, he said the same thing to a cheering crowd at the Mayflower Hotel. At the annual Jackson Day Dinner, Democratic partisans happily accepted the incongruity of putting on formal attire and paying fifty dollars a plate (five for dinner, forty-five for the party's coffers) to hear tributes to Andrew Jackson, the smasher of special privilege. The president's speech was broadcast by special radio hookup to two thousand similar dinners across the country. FDR was in terrific form, using every oratorical tool in his arsenal—gestures, laughter, carefully deployed derision—and the audience of 2,100 delighted in it all. The more he talked about Andrew Jackson, the clearer it became that he was talking about himself. The people loved Jackson, he said, "for the enemies he had made. . . . An overwhelming proportion of the material power of the nation was arrayed against him. The great media for the dissemination of information and the molding of public opinion fought him. Haughty and sterile intellectualism opposed him. Musty reaction disapproved him. Hollow and outworn traditionalism shook a trembling finger at him. It seemed sometimes that all were against him—all but the people of the United States."

Then, lest the parallel escape anyone: "History repeats." Roosevelt noted that 1936 was an election year, and that "the basic issue," as it had been under Jackson, "will be . . . the retention of popular government." He turned briefly to *Butler*. "I know you will not be surprised by lack of comment on my part tonight on the recent decision," he said, adding that he needed time to study carefully "two of the most momentous opinions" in history. "The ultimate results of the language of these opinions," he concluded, "will profoundly affect the lives of Americans for many years to come."

Several blocks away, at the Willard Hotel, Eleanor Roosevelt was the guest of honor at a dinner of Young Democrats. There she heard Florence Jackson Stoddard, a descendant of Old Hickory, read a composition of her own: "Ballad of the Nine Old Men." It told of "nine old men who sat on a bench" and "read the law as they wanted it read." Its closing stanza: "Shall we let them lead till we all are dead?" The first lady, observed the *New York Times*, "joined heartily in the applause." This did not escape notice, at least on the right. *King's Business*, a journal published by Protestant fundamentalists, said the incident showed how little separated Eleanor Roosevelt from the "Bolshevistic hoodlums" who had hung the six justices in effigy.

• • •

The following night, the justices attended the annual judicial reception at the White House. One by one they entered the receiving line in the Red Room, where the president and Mrs. Roosevelt stood before a row of potted palms. The Secret Service, as a rule, forbade guests from approaching the president with their hands concealed, though for high officials this was often waived. Tonight, however, a pair of overzealous agents leapt forward and yanked the hands of two justices—conservatives, no less—from their pockets. Indignant, the justices briskly shook the hand of the president and moved to the State Dining Room for a requisite sip of lemonade; but before long, they retrieved their hats and went home. Making matters worse, the president turned to Stone, who had been dean of the Columbia Law School back when FDR had been a student, and said, "I am glad that *you* taught me law"—loud enough for Roberts, who stood nearby, to hear.

Stone accepted the compliment; but by this point, he had received about as much praise from New Dealers as he could bear. From the start, despite his association with Hoover, Stone had been a favorite of New Deal liberals; now he had become a hero, lionized in the press and lauded by the president's circle. "Your dissenting opinion is on a high plane—sound, constructive & human," Cummings had written him on January 8. "It may not be the law *now*, but it will be the law later, unless governmental functions are to be permanently frozen in an unescapable mold. You spoke at a great moment & in a great way. Congratulations!" Stone replied: "When one finds himself outvoted two to one he should be humble and perhaps skeptical of his own judgment. But I have a sincere faith that history and long-time perspective will see the function of our court in a different light from that in which it is viewed at the moment."

"The joke of it," Stone confided to his sons, "is that I haven't very much confidence in the A.A.A." In fact he deplored it. He thought the program economically unsound and administratively a mess. "But the Constitution," he observed later, "does not command wisdom on the part of Congressmen." If the role of judges was to get rid of laws they disliked, "I should have been on the other side" in *Butler*. Two weeks after the decision, Stone wrote a letter to his old friend, Hoover, praising a speech in which the ex-president attacked the

AAA. Stone grew increasingly uneasy with the plaudits of liberals, many of whom misread his dissent as a wholesale endorsement of the New Deal; some even floated his name as a new running mate for Roosevelt. At a dinner party, Stone sat in uncomfortable silence as Henry Wallace and James Roosevelt talked as if Stone were a New Dealer, a liberal, one of the team. Finally Stone reached his limit. "My duty as a judge," he snapped at the men, "is simple and explicit. It is to see that the Constitution functions. It is not for the judge to approve or disapprove social policy." As for the surviving New Deal programs, Stone added ominously: "it is only a question of time before many of these things will have to be scrapped."

Stone's concern, in the end, was not what the Court was doing to the New Deal, but what the Court was doing to the Constitution, and to itself as an institution. "I do not question the motives of my brethren," he insisted to a former colleague on the Columbia faculty, Howard Lee McBain, but "I do question a method of thinking" that presumes that a "bad or unwise" law is necessarily unconstitutional. "The judgment of what is good or bad, which is essentially a legislative function, is likely to be affected by the passions and prejudices of the moment. Such an approach to constitutional construction tends to increase the dead areas in the Constitution, the lacunae in which no power exists, either state or national, to deal with the problems of government."

"Frankly," McBain replied, "I do question the motives of your colleagues." Frankly, Stone did, too—particularly the motives of Roberts and Hughes, the "two variables," as *Time* had christened them. Stone had once held out high hopes for Roberts. No longer. But what of Hughes, who, in the past, had shown such awareness of economic imperatives, and such appreciation of the responsibilities only government could fulfill? "What bothers me most," Frankfurter wrote to Stone, "is the Chief Justice's role in all this business. I understand those whom Learned Hand calls the 'mastiffs' or 'the Battalion of death.' Nor is Roberts unintelligible. . . . But . . . something deep in me just balks at that assumption of obtuseness in Hughes."

"I don't know that I shall ever reach a satisfactory answer," Stone answered, "but perhaps it can be summed up in two phrases which you have doubtless heard me repeat before: 'lack of vision' and the unwillingness of certain gentlemen to trust their own intellectual processes. . . . I think there has never been a time in the history of the Court when there has been so little intelligible, recognizable pattern in its judicial performance as in the last few years." Stone cited a series of recent decisions. "It just seems as though, in some of these cases, the writer and those who united with him didn't care what was said, as long as the opinion seemed plausible on its face, if not compared with any other. The worst of it," he concluded, "is that the one that you find it most difficult to understand is the one chiefly responsible."

Some believed that Hughes had thrown his lot in with the conservatives to avoid the embarrassment of another 5–4 split. Others said he was finally revealing his true colors—which, it turned out, were no different than those of McReynolds. All this was surmise; as Stone made clear, even Hughes's colleagues had little sense of what compelled him. In conference, the chief tended to align himself with the conservatives, trying first to narrow the grounds of decision, and then, having invariably failed, lending his name and credibility to a broad, antigovernment opinion. *Colgate* was one example, *Butler* another.

In the latter case, Hughes had recommended that the act be struck down as an excessive delegation of power to the Secretary of Agriculture, but found no takers. Then he argued that the act invaded the reserved powers of the states. With this, the conservatives agreed. Curiously, there was no mention in conference of what Hughes would later identify as the most important aspect of the opinion: the Hamiltonian view of general welfare. Hughes may, in fact, have approached Roberts separately and urged him to take this position. Years later, Roberts implied as much in a note to Frankfurter: "I . . . often wonder why the hell I did it just to please the Chief!" If this, indeed, is why Roberts did it, Hughes's motives were again inscrutable: was he directing (a possibly unwitting) Roberts to open the door to upholding New Deal statutes in the future? Whatever the truth, whatever his endgame, Hughes appeared increasingly to Stone and the dissenters as a man without bearings—still the chief, but no longer the leader.

"My how they do push the Supreme Court these days," Stone's sister Helen wrote in mid-January. "Why don't you retire and have some fun before you die?" But Stone was not ready for retirement. In a very real sense, after a decade on the Court, Stone was just getting started—and relishing his role. He may not have been having fun, exactly, but his playful letters to family, friends, and his growing number of admirers showed that he had lost neither his sense of humor nor his faith that the Court would, in time, correct its own errors. "Keep up the good work," a former clerk urged him. "Roberts cannot hold out forever."

The *Butler* decision had not settled the matter. There was still the question of what to do with more than a billion dollars in processing taxes that the Treasury had collected and distributed, as well as the millions more that courts had impounded. In 1935, Congress had passed an amendment to the Agricultural Adjustment Act forbidding processors from suing to recover taxes that had, in fact, been paid by consumers in the form of higher prices. That provision, of course, was promptly challenged by processors—which meant that the Supreme Court was not yet done with the AAA. On January 13, only a week after striking the program down, the Court dealt the government a second blow, holding unanimously that $200 million in impounded tax payments had to be refunded to processors. Henry Wallace called the decision "probably the greatest legalized steal in American history"—drawing calls for his impeachment from House Republicans.

That same day, the Court also dismissed, on technical grounds, a constitutional test of the Bankhead Act, a law establishing government control of the marketing of cotton. This was, at best, a stay of execution. Another test of the statute was already on the Supreme Court's docket, and Roberts—in a strange breach of judicial practice—had already, in his *Butler* opinion, condemned the Bankhead Act as even more damaging to farmers than the AAA tax.

Cummings, "puzzled . . . and disturbed," went that afternoon to the White House, where he and the president spent two hours reviewing opinions, trading gossip about the justices, and asking themselves where this was all leading. Using a phrase of Frankfurter's, FDR said that the Court was taking "slow poison." He believed, as Cummings noted in his diary, that the majority was "moving in two parallel lines, one to restrict the States within such narrow margins that the States cannot deal effectively with economic conditions"—Roosevelt mentioned *Colgate*, the Vermont tax case—"and, at the same time, limiting the power of the Congress." Neither man put much stock in the

Court's acceptance of the Hamiltonian view—"lip service," Cummings scoffed. Clearly the majority intended for the Court, not the Congress, to determine what policies advanced the general welfare of the American people.

In the press, the conflict was usually portrayed as a battle between the president and the Court. But there was, of course, another branch involved—and Congress, no less than FDR, had come to resent that the conservative justices were overturning its actions, overriding its prerogatives, and questioning, often with brusque condescension, its stated intentions. In a sign of the times, the national college debate proposition that year was "Congress or the Supreme Court: Which Shall Rule America?" The very premise was an affront to congressional leaders. At the same time, they recognized the grim reality of the situation: that no degree of care or cleverness in drafting legislation seemed likely to satisfy the Court's conservatives, and that much of what was happening on Capitol Hill, therefore, had an air of futility.

Congress was not without tools to subdue the Court: the Constitution gave legislators the power to impeach judges, withhold funding, pack the Court, or restrict its jurisdiction. These were blunt instruments—too blunt, really, to be applied without creating collateral political damage. Partly for that reason, Congress had rejected them all at various points over the past century and a half. But in early 1936, angered by the Court, frustrated by Roosevelt's reluctance to act against it, and genuinely concerned about the nation's ability to endure, without violent discontent, another year or two of this standoff, members of Congress revived old methods to curb the Supreme Court, and came up with new ones as well.

The proposals came in a cascade: "Enlarge Supreme Court to fifteen members. Have bill introduced in House immediately," a newspaper publisher wired the Postmaster General, James Farley (who passed the telegram on to FDR). In the days after the *Butler* decision, at least two such bills were introduced in the House: one for a Court of fifteen, another for eleven. The latter was proposed by Congressman Ernest Lundeen, a Farmer-Laborite from Minnesota: "New blood," he said, "will mean a more liberal outlook on constitutional questions." In the Senate, Lynn Frazier, Republican of North Dakota, called for a law abolishing judicial review, adding that any judge who voted to invalidate an act of Congress should be automatically impeached. (Remarkably, this was not a new idea: in 1917, an Oklahoma senator proposed that any judge who tried to void a federal law was guilty of violating the constitutional standard of "good behavior" and should be removed.) Peter Norbeck, a South Dakota Republican, introduced a bill to prevent the Court from overturning an act of Congress unless seven or more justices voted to do so. Joseph O'Mahoney of Wyoming thought the vote should be nothing less than unanimous. On January 10, he reported to FDR that he had been floating the proposal among their fellow Democrats, who were embracing it "with enthusiasm. . . . It avoids the delay and difficulty involved in a long campaign for a constitutional amendment."

All three Senate proposals, in fact, marked a shift away from amendments and toward curbing the Court by statute. Yet Frazier was the only one to acknowledge that the Court would probably strike down any law limiting its powers. (Itching to impeach the entire tribunal, Frazier dared the justices to go ahead and try.) For this and other reasons, some continued to urge amendment. "There has been a great deal of talk about the sanctity of the Constitution," said Senator Burt Wheeler. "But I suggest that constitutions are made for men, not men for constitutions." Wheeler added that he had never favored the AAA's crop production controls, "but now I feel that if we are going to help the farmers we may have to amend the Constitution to do it." *The New Republic* bitterly suggested that any law on any serious matter should take the form of a constitutional amendment, unless Congress preferred to abdicate and let the Court run the nation.

Uncertainty reigned on Capitol Hill. There was growing agreement that the Court must be curbed—but a searching and fumbling over the means. "Knowing some of the members of the Court, a couple of them fairly well now," Hiram Johnson, the progressive warhorse, wrote to his son, "the system . . . ought, in some fashion, to be altered, and [judicial] power should have upon it some other restraint than self-restraint of just common, ordinary individuals, for they are that, after all." The constitutional system of checks and balances, the careful weighing of state and federal responsibilities—these, many now believed, were indulgences, to be bought at the expense of economic recovery and social stability. As Lloyd K. Garrison, dean of the Wisconsin Law School, observed: "What we face now . . . is the question, not how governmental functions shall be shared, but whether in substance we shall govern at all . . . our national problems appear to have outrun our constitutional capacity to deal with them." Action or disintegration, that was the choice, Garrison said. "We have got to take some chances."

Roosevelt did not disagree. All the same, he moved cautiously and, as yet, without clear direction. For all his cheerful self-confidence, genuine courage, and sense of himself as a "snap-judgment man," as he once put it, Roosevelt was not by nature impulsive. When he gambled—and he frequently did—it was rarely for grand stakes. Though he tended to act quickly and decisively, he nearly always waited for just the right moment. He did not yet believe this was one of them.

Still, the pressure to act, to do *something*, was weighing heavily on him. It came from friendly columnists like Ray Clapper, who urged him to present the constitutional issue to the people, and from unfriendly papers like the *Wall Street Journal*, which goaded him to do the same, for "it might, in fact, be the deciding factor whether Franklin D. Roosevelt is a great president or an ex-president." Similar sentiment was building within the administration. Assistant Attorney General John Dickinson sent Cummings a memo urging that FDR adopt "the position taken by Lincoln in regard to the Dred Scott decision, namely, an appeal to the people based on an express purpose of trying to get the Court to reverse its position." At a cabinet meeting on January 17, Roosevelt looked drawn and tired, even nervous, as Cummings railed about "judicial autocracy" and Wallace and Ickes declared themselves ready for a fight.

A week later, Roosevelt told the cabinet that word was coming to him from across the country that people were starting to show interest in constitutional issues, but the key word here was "starting." Polls taken in the two weeks after the AAA decision showed a significant majority—66 percent—in support of requiring justices to advise lawmakers about the constitutionality of legislation before it took effect. Yet a much smaller majority, 53 percent, favored requiring a "supermajority" or unanimous vote by the Court in order to overturn an act of Congress; and only 43 percent backed an amendment giving the federal government power to regulate agriculture and industry. Clearly, there was work to be done in what Frankfurter had called the "quiet" education of the people.

"It is plain to see from what the President said today and has said on other occasions," Ickes wrote in his diary on January 24, "that he is not at all averse to the Supreme Court declaring one New Deal statute after another unconstitutional. I think he believes that the Court will find itself pretty far out on a limb . . . and that a real issue will be joined on which we can go to the country."

Chapter Twelve

A PROJECT OF GREAT IMPORTANCE

EVEN AFTER ALL the seats had been assigned, requests for tickets continued to come in at the rate of 700 a day. By January 25, 1936, the night of the banquet, the Liberty League had turned away 4,000 hopefuls. The Mayflower Ballroom—where the president, barely two weeks earlier, had spoken on Jackson Day—was packed so tightly with guests it was difficult for anyone to move: the women in black velvet dresses, the men in white ties and tails, the ushers in Confederate gray mess coats and black pants. James M. Beck was there, of course, and Raoul Desvernine, of the Lawyers' Vigilance Committee. Dissident Democrats, veterans of the "Stop Roosevelt" movement as well as apostates of more recent vintage, were seated prominently; but Republicans, including the party's astringent grande dame, Alice Roosevelt Longworth, were more plentiful. Along with bankers, lawyers, and assorted socialites, they had come to hear and applaud a keynote speaker that many of them had worked assiduously to defeat in 1928: Al Smith. Now they embraced him—both for his bitterness toward Roosevelt, which they shared, and for the gloss of bipartisanship he lent to the League.

The event was the kickoff of the group's campaign against Roosevelt. Like the rest of the opposition, the League had begun the election year in high spirits. One trouble after another beset the president: the AAA decision, the fiscal crisis, the threat of Democratic defections. On the eve of the banquet, Arthur Krock portrayed FDR at low ebb, "more on the defensive than in any period since he took office." His path to reelection, Krock concluded, was steep. A new Gallup poll appeared to confirm this: Roosevelt clung to a slender majority in the electoral college. The New Deal itself, if put up for a vote, would either eke out a victory or lose in a landslide—poll results differed.

The League had been girding itself for this fight. Over the past year, it had built an organization that rivaled the national committees of both political parties. The League's offices in the National Press Building in Washington contained publicists, economists, researchers, messengers, field organizers. A membership of 100,000—missionaries, all, for constitutional government—was deployed across the country, and increasingly eager to do more than distribute pamphlets (3.5 million so far). In January, a member of the League's executive committee announced that the group was prepared to throw its weight, financial and organizational, behind the GOP—"if," he said, "the Republicans behave well."

For all its swagger, the League had something to prove. After more than a year on the offensive, it had yet to show that voters would rally in meaningful numbers to "preserve the Constitution." Toward the end of 1935, national polls showed that the issue ranked well below reducing unemployment, staying out of war, balancing the budget, and cutting taxes. Among Democrats, it failed to make the list at all—casting doubt on the League's claim that the Constitution was the wedge that would split open the party.

The banquet, then, was an important test. If Al Smith, the "Happy Warrior," could not drive other Democrats to ditch FDR, it was unlikely that anyone could. Smith, to be sure, would give it his all. Huddling with Robert Moses, New York's parks commissioner, and other advisers, Smith had spent more time preparing this speech than any he had given in years. And now, as the audience roared in anticipation, he stepped to the podium, gestured broadly like a winning candidate, and gave a performance to remember. He began on a sorrowful note, noting the pain of breaking with a Democratic administration. "It is not easy," he insisted. "It hurts me." Then, with biting wit, sarcasm, and sheer delight, came the assault: the New Deal, he charged, was pitting the workingman against the businessman, bankrupting the nation, and strangling liberty. Smith leaned into the microphone, twisted his mouth into a familiar sneer, and barked that he and like-minded Democrats "can either take on the mantle of hypocrisy or we can take a walk, and we will probably do the latter."

The crowd cheered wildly. The applause went on so long it consumed much of the airtime allotted by the networks; Jouett Shouse, calling for quiet, smashed his gavel so hard that it splintered in his hand. Finally, Smith built toward his climax: "This country," he said, "was organized on the principles of a representative democracy, and you can't mix socialism and communism with that. . . . That is the reason why the United States Supreme Court is working overtime throwing the alphabet out of the window, three letters at a time." Then, his voice rasping, his fist upstretched,

> There can be only one capital, Washington or Moscow. There can be only . . . the clear, pure, fresh air of free America, or the foul breath of communistic Russia. There can be only one flag, the Stars and Stripes, or the flag of the godless Union of the Soviets. . . . There can be only one victor. If the Constitution wins, we win. But if the Constitution—stop! Stop there. The Constitution can't lose. The fact is, it has already won, but the news has not reached certain ears.

"It was perfect," gushed Pierre S. du Pont, one of a dozen du Ponts in the room that night. Smith, said a lawyer for the coal industry, "is the greatest apostle of the common people in America." The next day, more than 1,000 telegrams of support flooded into the League's headquarters; over the following week it received more than 9,000 requests for copies of the speech. "The people," proclaimed Shouse, "have awakened." Justice McReynolds, who had listened to the speech at home on his radio, felt the stirrings of new hope. Smith "would have pleased me better by saying that he would take off his coat & fight the gang in power with all his strength," McReynolds wrote his brother, "but he made a helpful talk. There is only one way of escape—put Roosevelt & all his gang on the outside. To do this will require a real fight, but 'tis a fight for existence."

Democrats expressed bitterness at Smith's betrayal and disgust at his embrace of, and by, the business community. Some fretted that Smith would make good on his threat to "take a walk," but others doubted that many delegates would follow if he did. The speech might even be a stroke of luck for the party: Senator Elmer Thomas of Oklahoma, who attended the event, said afterward that the Democrats should "hire Smith to make that speech everywhere"; Smith's serenade to the greatest gathering of concentrated wealth in recent memory was enough, in Thomas's view, to ensure Roosevelt's reelection.

Still, Democrats did not intend to leave Smith's charges unanswered. Three days later, Joseph Robinson, the Senate majority leader and Smith's running mate in 1928, delivered a rebuttal. Earlier that evening, Roosevelt hosted Chief Justice Hughes, five associate justices, and about ninety other guests at the annual judiciary dinner. After the meal, the president asked Hughes and Sutherland to come sit beside him. "Don't let them corrupt you," Stone joked to Roosevelt. Though only three weeks had passed since the AAA decision, the bitterness seemed well behind (or beneath) them. The president, Hughes observed to Pierce Butler, looked exceedingly well—as if he had not a care in the world. (No doubt it helped that McReynolds stayed home.) This was quite remarkable, Hughes said admiringly, given the pressure FDR was facing.

Shortly after 10 p.m., the attorney general and his wife, Cecilia, slipped into a White House office to hear the radio broadcast of Robinson's rebuttal. The majority leader spoke with barely contained rage. "It was strange to see you in such company, Governor Smith," he said. "The brown derby"—Smith's humble trademark—"has been discarded for the high hat."

The tit-for-tat continued, at increasing volume. Robinson was followed the next night by Eugene Talmadge, the Georgia governor and leader of the Southern Committee to Uphold the Constitution, who addressed a convention of 3,500 Democrats in Macon. "Pour it on!" a supporter shouted from the balcony; and that was exactly what Talmadge did, standing in a green suit beneath a Confederate flag, railing against Negroes, the New Deal, and Karl Marx, and brandishing a photograph of Eleanor Roosevelt being escorted to her car by a black man (as it happened, a member of the Howard University faculty). The Roosevelts, Talmadge charged, had handed the reins of government to Socialists, Communists, and Negroes. Give FDR four more years, and he would get the chance to appoint successors to "such stalwart men" as Hughes and McReynolds.

Two days later, the president publicly blessed a proposal by Senator Robinson: to set up a special committee to investigate campaign expenditures and possible violations of the Corrupt Practices Act. "Among such organizations that might come under the purview of the proposed committee," reported the *New York Times*, were the "Liberty League [and] the Constitutional Democrats organized by Governor Eugene Talmadge."

Washington, in the first months of 1936, was a massive, rolling constitutional convention. Debates took place not in grand halls but at supper clubs and dinner parties, in newspaper columns and Capitol Hill cloakrooms. "Nooks and crannies about Congress . . . ," noted *Time*, "concealed embryonic constitutional amendments" of countless kinds. Lawmakers issued a great wave of proposals—more than a hundred altogether—aiming to enhance the powers of Congress, limit those of the Court, or both. Homer Cummings, pressed by reporters for his reaction, said he was considering such proposals "as a mere matter of routine."

In truth he was doing far more than this. For the past year, Cummings, Stanley Reed, and a few sharp young assistants had been reviewing amendments and statutes, remedies and reprisals. After the AAA decision, these efforts intensified. The junior lawyers worked not as a unit but as individuals, isolated from one another and unaware of any larger design. The attorney general told them only that they were contributing to a "project of great importance." They understood, of course, that it had something to do with curbing the Court. But as Cummings later recalled, he "parceled out work so that no one person knew what the whole thing was about."

At this stage, the attorney general himself did not know what the whole thing was about. It was only beginning to take shape in his mind—his and Roosevelt's. After three years of talking, on and off, about taking action against the Court, the pair was now in fairly constant conversation about different approaches. "What was the McArdle [*sic*] case . . . ?" Roosevelt asked on January 14. "I am told that the Congress withdrew some act from the jurisdiction of the Supreme Court." Within forty-eight hours, Cummings responded with a three-page analysis on *Ex parte McCardle* (1868), a Reconstruction-era case dismissed by the Court after Congress removed the Court's jurisdiction over certain *habeas corpus* appeals. *McCardle*, Cummings reported, "is one of the classic cases to which we refer when considering the possibility of limiting the jurisdiction of Federal Courts." He promised to study the idea further. That same week, Reed asked two Justice Department lawyers whether Congress had the power to "excise" constitutional questions from the lower courts. Both rated the prospect poorly.

The "project" was still in its infancy. FDR and his advisers had yet to answer some basic questions—including whether they should address the issue by statute, by constitutional amendment, or simply by waiting for the Court to reverse itself or for justices to retire. Within Roosevelt's circle there was an astonishing lack of agreement on any of these points. Each adviser seemed to have his own, idiosyncratic ideas about the source of the problem, the shape of the solution, and the right moment to strike. While Rex Tugwell and others urged immediate action, Felix Frankfurter—virtually alone—counseled patience. "Go slowly," he said, "and you will carry the Court with you."

Roosevelt doubted that. He saw no indication that this Court could be "carried" by anything but its own presuppositions. Roosevelt's instincts were also leading him away from the idea of amending the Constitution. After a year of considering amendments, he still had not found one he liked. A few had excited him for a moment and then struck him, on reflection, as impractical, ineffective, or unwise. The justices seemed to hold all the trump cards. If an amendment gave Congress broad new powers, the Court could narrow them to nothing. "It would be difficult to frame an amendment broader than the general-welfare clause," the historian Charles Beard observed. "But see how that clause has been neglected, mauled, manhandled, and whittled away!" If an amendment granted authority in a more limited realm, such as agriculture, the Court could restrict this power, too. And what about mining, manufacturing, or other areas of economic activity? Would each require its own amendment—and, if so, would this not turn the Constitution, as one writer charged, "into a book of permissive statutes"?

The experience of Prohibition had tempered many Americans' enthusiasm for embedding in the Constitution what properly belonged, if anywhere, in the statute books. Even some progressives saw it this way. In 1922, Robert La Follette complained that "we cannot live under a system of government where we are forced to amend the Constitution every time we want to pass a progressive law." Roosevelt, more than a decade later, took a similar view. But where La Follette had favored amending the Constitution regardless, FDR had soured on the prospect. This reflected the pragmatic bent of the New Deal. Indeed, it would have been surprising if Roosevelt had concluded that the problem of an excessively formalist reading of the Constitution could be solved by adding a new formula to that document. The issue, as Roosevelt saw it, was the foolishness of men, not the fallibility of the Constitution.

On the afternoon of January 29, he told Ickes that he had come to the conclusion he could accomplish his goals by congressional statute rather than by amendment. The pronouncement had a note of finality. Roosevelt still liked the idea of requiring the Supreme Court to issue advisory opinions, and giving Congress the right either to rework the legislation or to simply pass it again, over the Court's now impotent objections. But now he thought an act of Congress would suffice. For good measure he also hoped to withdraw the right of lower federal courts to rule on questions of constitutionality.

Ickes replied that the Court would surely overturn an act like this. Of course it would, Roosevelt responded. "To meet that situation," Ickes wrote in his diary, "his plan would be somewhat as follows: Congress would pass a law, the Supreme Court would declare it unconstitutional, the President would then go to Congress and ask it to instruct him whether he was to follow the mandate of Congress or the mandate of the Court. If the Congress should declare that its own mandate was to be followed, the President would carry out the will of Congress through the offices of the United States Marshals and ignore the Court."

Almost a year earlier, when he had feared an adverse decision in the gold clause cases, Roosevelt was prepared to defy the Court. Here again he raised that prospect—no less staggering in its implications, no less an affront to American constitutional traditions. As Roosevelt had made clear in his recent speech, he fancied himself a present-day Andrew Jackson; and part of the mythology of Jackson was that he had once declared, following a Supreme Court decision he did not like, "John Marshall has made his decision—*now let him enforce it!*" This was probably not what Jackson said and almost certainly not what he intended; but Ickes, believing it so, leapt to praise Roosevelt for "taking a leaf out of the book" of Jackson.

Ickes hoped that FDR would make this the defining issue of his campaign for reelection. "It will have to be fought out sooner or later," Ickes believed, and told Roosevelt that "the President who faced this issue and drastically curbed the usurped power of the Supreme Court would go down through all the ages of history as one of the great Presidents."

The following day, January 30, Roosevelt received a ruminative—and, it turned out, pivotal—letter from his attorney general. "The real difficulty," Cummings stated up front, "is not with the Constitution but with the Judges who interpret it." Amending the Constitution, he wrote, presented "enormous difficulties. . . . No one has yet suggested an amendment that does not do either too much or too little, or which does not raise practical and political questions which it would be better to avoid. If we had liberal Judges, with a lively sense of the importance of the social problems *which have now spilled over State lines*, there would be no serious difficulty."

This much was obvious. Liberal judges were the answer; liberal judges would end the impasse. The question was how to create room for them on a court where every justice seemed a permanent fixture. Around this time, Henry Ashurst, chairman of the Senate Judiciary Committee, delivered a prophecy to FDR: "It will fall to your lot to nominate more justices . . . than any other president since General Washington. . . . Father Time, with his scythe, is on your side." Roosevelt was not so sure. Neither was the Metropolitan Life Insurance Company, whose actuaries predicted that all the justices would survive not only the remainder of Roosevelt's first term but the entirety of his second, should he win in November.

With that in mind, Cummings urged Roosevelt to give "some serious thought" to a constitutional amendment mandating the retirement of all federal judges, or at least all Supreme Court justices, at the age of seventy. "It may very well be that life tenure lies at the heart of our difficulty." His qualms about amendments notwithstanding, Cummings believed that "such an amendment would probably encounter less opposition than almost any other I can think of. It would have the advantage of not changing in the least degree the structure of our Government, nor would it impair the power of the Court. It would merely insure the exercise of the powers of [the] Court by Judges less likely to be horrified by new ideas."

It had been three years almost to the day since William McAdoo, then a senator-elect, had lobbied Cummings to draft a bill edging the "old fossils" off the Court. Roosevelt had liked the idea, then let it drop. Now McAdoo's proposal reemerged, announcing itself as the best of all possible amendments. From this point forward, it would shape Cummings's search for a solution—a search that, in another year's time, would resolve itself in a plan to pack the Court with young, liberal justices.

"Nine Old Men." No one could be sure when the phrase had entered the popular lexicon, but it was well before these particular nine old men put on their robes. As far back as 1867, the *New York Herald* denounced the Supreme Court as "a relic of the past, nine old superior pettifoggrts [*sic*], old marplots, a formidable barrier to the consummation of the great revolution." At the turn of the century, the *New York Times*'s fictional fount of small-town wisdom, "Silas Larrabee," cast a jaundiced eye on the justices of his time and declared them "long past their wood-choppin', elbow-wrastlin', leap-froggin' days. . . . This," Larrabee concluded, "is an old man's gover'ment, and . . . it's always goin' to be an old man's gover'ment."

It had always been so. There had never been a time when the Court was not composed mostly or entirely of venerable men. Their age was a tempting target—particularly for critics on the left, who, like a Socialist Party leader in 1932, saw the Court as a brake on progress and the justices as "nine old men consecrated to the mistakes of their forbears."

The complaint became commonplace during the New Deal era. Pearson and Allen, the political columnists, made a sport of savaging the nine old men (not all nine, actually, but the five or six conservatives). Shortly after the AAA decision, the columnists announced they would publish a book by that name: *The Nine Old Men*. "Most of us are coming to fit the part," Justice Stone joked to a friend.

Age defined outlook. So, at least, contended Cummings and others—notwithstanding the examples of Holmes, who had only recently retired at ninety, or Brandeis, seventy-nine in 1936. Roosevelt himself tended toward this view: as early as 1926, in his speech at Milton Academy, he had mocked modern-day "Rip Van Winkles" who "have not been physically asleep, but . . . have come to view the world with eyes of the past." Even Brandeis, he complained to Ickes in late 1935, was losing sight of the fundamentals as he grew older. "That they are behind the times is very plain," a Los Angeles man wrote to Roosevelt after the AAA decision. "All you have to do is look at Charles Hughes' whiskers."

Others, such as Robert Jackson, felt the problem was not age, but longevity. There was a difference. Owen Roberts, for example, was not an old man—in early 1936 he was only sixty—but he had been appointed before the New Deal era, by a president, Hoover, whose system of beliefs had since been repudiated. "The judiciary," Jackson later wrote, "is thus the check of a preceding generation on the present one . . . and nearly always the check of a rejected regime on the one in being." Of course, the longevity of Cardozo and Stone did not trouble New Dealers; and Roosevelt, like all presidents, intended for his appointees to remain on the bench long after he himself had left office. This was one reason why, as a rule, he appointed only men under sixty as federal judges. In general, though, holdovers from past regimes were seen to cause trouble. They served to prevent sharp turns in national direction, even when events, and the people, demanded it.

Life tenure had long been a focus for reformers. In 1894, the House Judiciary Committee favorably reported a bill to limit the terms of all federal judges to ten years. Dozens of similar proposals were made over the following decades. Many states, moreover, set compulsory retirement ages for judges; New Hampshire had done so as early as 1792, and Alexander Hamilton, in *The Federalist No. 79* (1788), condemned such laws as a foolish response to "the imaginary danger of a superannuated bench." So the idea of term limits or age limits was hardly new; and while McAdoo may have been the first to urge it on FDR, he and, later, Cummings were not the only ones to do so.

After *Butler*, the idea gained currency. In March, Arthur Krock—whose column was one of the best places to learn what "that man" in the White House was thinking—published an article on the political biases of Supreme Court justices, and concluded: "Probably the faults of the system could be reduced if there were an age limit for justices who have served more than a certain number of years. Aged men often grow remote from the world, unsympathetic to change, shackled to their prejudices." Krock cited an "eminent" author who had once considered an age limit of seventy-five to rid the bench of judges who have "stayed too long." The author, Krock revealed, was Charles Evans Hughes.

"I am glad that you found my 'favorite author' a useful source," Hughes wrote to Krock. The chief hastened to add that the oldest justices, Brandeis and Van Devanter, "are still going strong." Hughes was too gentle with Krock, who had taken the line entirely out of context from a 1928 collection of lectures. "The community has no more valuable asset than an experienced judge . . . ," the passage began. "Contrary to general opinion," Hughes had written, "the work of the court tends to keep a man keen-witted and earnest." He never argued, as Krock had implied, that old age colored a judge's views. Rather, his concern was "decrepitude": judges whose tenure had outlasted their physical and mental health. This was quite a different matter.

In February 1936, the Justice Department began an exhaustive investigation of the issue. They considered the example of Britain, and pulled together a thick file of research on the findings of a recent Royal Commission on aged judges. "One's receptive faculties," the commission had concluded, "begin to diminish after a man gets to a certain age." Still, it exempted Britain's highest courts from its proposed age limit of seventy-two because it saw the role of an appellate judge as "rather more of a contemplative one . . . knowledge, experience and ripe judgment are more valuable in judicial work than energy or power of initiative."

A contrasting view—also noted by Cummings—had been expressed by William Howard Taft in his *Popular Government* (1913). Some judges, Taft acknowledged, were still up to the task after reaching the age of seventy. But in most cases,

> they have lost vigor, their minds are not as active, their senses not as acute, and their willingness to undertake great labor is not so great as in younger men, and as we ought to have in judges who are to perform the enormous task which falls to the lot of Supreme Court justices. In the public interest, therefore, it is better that we lose the services of the exceptions who are good judges after they are seventy and avoid the presence on the Bench of men who are not able to keep up with the work.

Taft urged an amendment mandating retirement at seventy. Cummings, delighted by this discovery, sent the text to Roosevelt, who forwarded it to the chairmen of the House and Senate Judiciary Committees. Henry Ashurst appeared unmoved. The idea of an age limit, he replied, was worth careful study, adding a bit curtly that this session was not the time to raise the issue. "Will you speak to me about this?" Roosevelt asked Cummings in late February. Despite the cool reaction on Capitol Hill, neither was prepared to let the matter drop.

The old men were still capable of surprises. On February 17, by a margin of 8–1—McReynolds alone dissented—the Court backed the government in its first test of the Tennessee Valley Authority (TVA), a massive program to distribute electrical power and create economic opportunity across the South. In Knoxville, factories and mills sounded whistles in a joyous shriek at news of the decision; a high school band marched the streets. Throughout the winding valley, people planned dances and celebrations. New Dealers, hailing the victory, touted plans for new "little TVAs" across the nation. "It was naturally a day of considerable rejoicing in administration circles," noted Cummings. He talked at length with Roosevelt—who, despite his stated wish to have the Court knock down the entirety of the New Deal, shared in the satisfaction and took a little credit. "It did those babies good to criticize them a bit," Roosevelt said. Stone, who saw no sign that his conservative colleagues had yielded to external pressure, fretted, privately, that this was "the popular impression."

The administration's joy, in any event, was overblown. Hughes had confined his opinion to the question of whether the TVA could sell power generated by the Wilson Dam in Alabama—a single function of a single dam in a single state. The opinion made no promises about the constitutionality of TVA writ large, a program with far grander ambitions than building dams or supplying electricity; it made no broad pronouncements about governmental power. "The Court," observed Ray Clapper, "narrowed the opinion to the smallest possible territory while in AAA and NRA it took in all the territory in sight." A friend of Van Devanter wrote to express his relief that the decision was "most carefully and definitely limited."

Narrow though it was, the ruling did relieve some of the heat on the Court. Some critics had been quieted. "Not the least of [the] excellences" of the decision, judged the *New York Times*, "is that it may help to dispel the foolish notion that the court is composed of nine old men bent on imposing their will on Congress and writing their private prejudices into the Constitution." *The Nation*, which did not consider this idea foolish at all, warned its readers: "We have all burned our fingers so many times with wishful zeal over what seemed to be a new turn in the court's attitude. . . . We must not dance too joyfully around the TVA decision."

This was prescient. April brought a new, if familiar, assault on the New Deal. The case, *Jones v. Securities and Exchange Commission*, concerned J. Edward Jones, a dealer in oil royalties who had filed a registration statement with the SEC, declaring his intention to issue securities. The commission, finding reason to doubt Jones's facts and figures, issued a subpoena—at which point Jones withdrew his statement. That, he said, should end the matter. The government disagreed—as did a federal district court, which ordered Jones to appear before the commission and to bring his private papers with him. The Court of Appeals affirmed that order. And now, six justices of the Supreme Court reversed it. "An abandonment of the application," George Sutherland wrote for the majority, "was of no concern to anyone" but Jones himself. "The possibility of any other interest in the matter"—meaning a public interest—"is so shadowy, indefinite, and equivocal that it must be put out of consideration as altogether unreal." Sutherland compared the SEC's investigatory power to the "intolerable abuses of the Star Chamber" of England under the Stuarts, a body famously ruthless in its suppression of dissent. Though the majority stopped short of ruling the SEC unconstitutional, "it might just as well have," observed *The Nation*.

"Sutherland writes as though he were still a United States Senator, making a partisan speech," Frankfurter complained in a letter to Stone. The professor again found it "saddening and incomprehensible" that Hughes should sanction such a ludicrous opinion by joining it. "It was written for morons," Stone replied, "and such will no doubt take comfort from it. But I can hardly believe that intelligent people, trained in the law, will swallow such buncombe." It was, he said, "the Supreme Court at its worst. . . . When our Court sets at naught a plain command of Congress, without the invocation of any identifiable prohibition of the Constitution, and supports it only by platitudinous irrelevancies, it is a matter of transcendent importance."

"I am happy to report," said Chief Justice Hughes, "that the Supreme Court is still functioning." He made that pronouncement with a smile to a meeting of the American Law Institute in May, and paused for two minutes as his audience laughed and applauded. ("*Hubris*," carped Frankfurter.) He shrugged off complaints that his Court was divided. "How amazing it is," said Hughes, that in a time of great controversy, one would expect unanimity. "In the highest ranges of thought—in theology, philosophy and science—we find differences of view." On the most difficult questions of legal principle, he said, "we do not suddenly rise to a stratosphere of icy certainty."

Unanimity, to be sure, was elusive. Icy certainty, however, was in no short supply in the opinions of the Supreme Court majority. On May 18, in *Carter v. Carter Coal Co.*, the Court—as predicted—overturned the Guffey Act. Frederick H. Wood, the Wall Street lawyer who had successfully represented the Schechter brothers, now prevailed on behalf of James W. Carter, whose company shipped 97 percent of its coal outside its home state of West Virginia but contended in court, without fear of contradiction, that mining was a local activity. Seven coal-producing states, however, filed *amicus curiae* briefs insisting that the act did not infringe their rights, and that without federal regulation of prices and of labor conditions in the mines, the industry would collapse. Carter, for his part, asked that the entire act be thrown out—an audacious move in at least two respects. First, it was unclear what harm Carter could possibly claim from the act's provisions on wages, hours, and labor rights, which had not yet been put into effect. Second, Congress had declared the price-fixing provisions "separable" from the labor provisions, which meant that even if Carter prevailed against the former, the latter—and therefore the rest of the act—would still stand.

Sutherland, writing again for the majority—this time absent Hughes—rejected out of hand the claim of separability. The two parts of the act, he said, went down together. He thereby freed himself from addressing the only part of the act that had actually affected the Carter Coal Company: the price-fixing provisions. This nimble act of avoidance kept Roberts on board—for it was Roberts who, in *Nebbia*, had upheld the power of Congress to do exactly what it had done in the Guffey Act, that is, to regulate prices. Sutherland trained his sights instead on the act's labor provisions, which he considered an excessive and "obnoxious" delegation of power, a violation of due process and an infringement on state sovereignty. Coal production, Sutherland said, was a "local activity"; the evils that attended it were "local evils." Labor conditions, moreover, had no "direct" effect on interstate commerce because there was an intermediate step: by the majority's logic, if a strike was followed by a halt in coal production, it was not the strike itself, but the halt in production, that impeded interstate commerce. The strike's effect was indirect. And the magnitude of that effect—say, the potential of a single strike precipitated by conditions at a single mine to paralyze the nation's railroads (which ran on coal) and devastate the national economy—mattered not a bit.

Cardozo thought this absurd. He wrote another impassioned dissent for himself, Brandeis, and Stone. Hughes, meanwhile, stood alone. Like the liberals, he believed that the labor and price provisions were separable, and that the latter were valid, and therefore should stand. But like the conservatives, he viewed the labor provisions as unconstitutional, and so he voted with the majority. Whether he agreed that mining was a purely local activity, whether he, like Sutherland, saw the magnitude of the effect on interstate commerce as an irrelevance, Hughes's concurring opinion did not say. "Perhaps when you have read it all," Stone wrote to Frankfurter, "you will tell me what it was the Chief thought should be decided and why." Brandeis offered Frankfurter a different perspective on Hughes. "He is deeply unhappy," Brandeis said two days after the decision. "He has no control over the Court."

Stanley High had never seen his boss so dejected.

Recently recruited to write campaign speeches, High had not worked for Roosevelt very long. This made it especially unnerving for him to see the president, for the first time, as anything less than the most carefree man in the room (or indeed in the nation). High had arrived at the White House on the afternoon of May 18, only a few hours after the *Carter* decision came down, and found FDR looking tired and discouraged. Marvin McIntyre, the president's appointments secretary, tried a few wisecracks to no avail. After a few minutes, though, Roosevelt's mood brightened. He ridiculed the Court for a bit, blew off some steam, and appeared to cheer up considerably. The following afternoon, Cummings found him "in fine humor," taking perverse delight in the majority opinion. The attorney general, too, was feeling fine, for he perceived a "small crack in the door": Sutherland's avoidance of the price-fixing issue. To Cummings this suggested that not only Hughes but also Roberts might join the liberals in sustaining price controls in the future, should Congress revive that half of the Guffey Act.

As Roosevelt and Cummings ate lunch, an aide handed them a memo that Stanley High had just written. The men paused to read it. High, dispirited by the Court's decisions, argued that the New Deal had been so badly damaged by the Court that in the course of the campaign, FDR would have to say what he planned to do about it. Homer, Roosevelt asked, what do you think? Cummings took issue with High's basic premise. In January, after the AAA decision, Cummings had stalked the Cabinet Room in anger, but now he took a more sanguine view. The only real casualty, he said calmly, was the NRA. The AAA was being reenacted by other means; Guffey could be, too; the TVA and SEC had, at least for now, survived; the administration had prevailed in the gold clause cases; and the government's spending power, Cummings added, had gone essentially unchallenged.

Even if High were right about the state of the New Deal, Cummings continued, there was "no political justification" to open the Pandora's box of judicial reform in an election year. The economy was improving, the opposition was weak, and the chance of losing in November was "exceedingly remote"—unless the president made careless mistakes. "I want to hear very potent reasons," Cummings said sternly, "before shifting tactics in the face of the enemy."

"President Will Dodge Issue of Supreme Court. Too Dangerous for Campaign," asserted the *Chicago Daily Tribune*. On this, the president and the paper found rare agreement. It seemed wise, as one citizen wrote Roosevelt, to avoid the subject "till after the campaign, so as not to supply ammunition to the 'constitution cryers.'" Even Ickes—who more than any other member of Roosevelt's circle had been bruising for an election-year battle over the Court—had cooled on the idea. By late May he had come to believe that it might take years to lay the groundwork for such an assault. He shared none of the attorney general's confidence about the election—after a meeting with Emil Hurja, who conducted polls for the Democratic Party, Ickes felt more alarmed than ever—but he did agree, as did Frankfurter, that "the Constitution should not be brought into this campaign as an issue."

There was another good reason to avoid the issue: Roosevelt was doing just fine without it. The spring had marked a revival of his political fortunes. His popularity had begun to climb in January—precisely when the Supreme Court killed the AAA. As Hurja told a reporter, Roosevelt's recovery came only after the Court had eliminated the NRA and AAA; what FDR once thought "his greatest achievements" were, Hurja said, the "very things that were sinking him in 1935." Arthur Krock found it significant that in 1936—unlike the year before—Roosevelt was seen to be accepting the Court's verdicts, working within them, and making progress despite them. His refusal to be provoked—to make another "horse-and-buggy" slip—revealed, in Krock's view, a newly "chastened obedience to the organic law." This had improved Roosevelt's approval ratings—and his prospects for the fall. So had his promise of a balanced budget. "This," declared Krock, "is the Spring of his content."

It helped, too, that as the summer approached, the "constitution cryers" were using their remaining ammunition to shoot themselves in the foot. Republicans were squandering the euphoria of the winter months on old, internecine battles, now played out among candidates for the party's nomination. And where was the Liberty League? The Al Smith banquet—the League's exuberant kickoff to the election year—now appeared, with hindsight, to have been its swan song. Many commentators traced Roosevelt's revival to that January night when the Happy Warrior and the captains of industry swooned, for all to see, in a suffocating, mutual embrace.

The League, by the late spring, was dying of a thousand cuts—many inflicted by Hugo Black of Alabama, the relentless chairman of the Senate Lobby Investigating Committee. With a ferocity that unsettled the press, champions of civil liberties, and, not least, the executive council of the American Liberty League, Black launched an exhaustive investigation into groups that he said were concealing "sinister activities behind lofty names . . . sonorous phrases" and pledges of "non-partisanship." In March, Jouett Shouse boasted carelessly that Black was welcome to any information he wanted, for the League had "no skeletons in its closet." Black made him regret this. The committee subpoenaed the League's leaders, its telegrams, checkbooks, balance sheets, everything. This enabled Black to reveal, among other things, that the Farmers' Independence Council—which was trying to turn farmers against the New Deal—was a front group that operated out of the League's headquarters, bankrolled by the League's benefactors. "Do you know whether Mr. Jouett Shouse devotes much of his time to farming?" Black demanded at a public hearing. "About as much time as I do," admitted the witness, a publicist on the League's payroll.

The more that the committee exposed the League and its affiliates to the light, the more ridiculous—or outrageous—they appeared. Made public by Black, the correspondence of one patriotic society, the Sentinels of the Republic, revealed its concern with the "Jewish threat" to the United States and its leaders' desire for "a Hitler." The Sentinels' financial supporters were shown to include Alfred P. Sloan of General Motors; J. Howard Pew of Sun Oil; George Wharton Pepper, the lawyer who had argued the AAA case; and Irénée du Pont—the same list of contributors as the Liberty League, the Southern Committee to Uphold the Constitution, and even a small Texas group that had applied the donations toward distributing copies of the photo that Eugene Talmadge had waved to great effect at a rally, the photo of Eleanor Roosevelt "going to a Negro meeting with a Negro escort on either side of her." (This was the caption in the *New York Times*; the Texans used less genteel terms.)

Shouse, increasingly a subject of public scorn, cried "subterfuge" and "terrorism." In a year when he had hoped to apply the League's money and momentum toward defeating Franklin Roosevelt, he was instead defending his own organization against legal sanction for violating its "non-partisan" tax status. In April, in another blow to the League, James M. Beck, its leading authority on the Constitution, died suddenly of coronary thrombosis, less than a week after prevailing in *Jones v. SEC.* The self-proclaimed defenders of the Constitution, despite all the help they were getting from the Supreme Court, were having a surprisingly bad year; and the president's men watched with rising satisfaction. Told by a reporter about the League's latest activities, James Farley grinned. "The more they work," Farley said, "the happier we are."

Chapter Thirteen

NO-MAN'S-LAND

RARELY IN ITS history had the Supreme Court aroused so much sustained controversy, scrutiny, and scorn—or played for such grand stakes—as it did during the term that began in fall 1935 and ended, in a last spasm of contention, on the cusp of summer, 1936.

On May 25, almost as a prelude to the final act, a 5–4 majority struck down the Municipal Bankruptcy Act as an invasion of state sovereignty. The act had given cities, counties, and other local units the same relief that Congress granted to private corporations—the ability to scale down their debts in federal courts, so long as that state and a substantial majority of creditors allowed it. Writing for the majority, McReynolds cried "interference" with states' rights, even though the plaintiff in the case was not a state but a "water improvement district." He argued, in effect, that states' rights implied cities' rights, and counties' rights, and water districts' rights, and so on—each subdivision sovereign, no matter how small. The decision, Stone scoffed in a letter to Frankfurter, was "a form of indecent exposure. Thank heaven the term is approaching its end."

On the last day of the term, June 1, the Court again considered how far a state could go in protecting workers from exploitation. In 1934, the Court was thought to have settled the question: in the Minnesota mortgage and New York milk cases, it gave states more room to regulate economic activity in the public interest. But much had happened since, and that pair of decisions, however emphatic, offered no indication of the Court's next move. In the two years since, the majority's solicitude for states' rights had seemed to depend less on precedent than on which rights, in particular, a state tried to exercise.

In the case now before the Court, *Morehead v. Tipaldo*, the state was New York; the right it asserted was to set a minimum wage for women. This it did for good reason: in 1933, a third of the working women in New York City made less, often much less, than what city officials estimated it took to stay alive. Forced to choose (if there really was a choice) between food and rent, many women were sleeping in the subways. "Laundry girls" had it especially rough. The work itself was brutal, the conditions were wretched, and the pay, even after the minimum-wage order came down, was slight. Joseph Tipaldo, manager of the Spotlight Laundry in Brooklyn, was one of many operators who ignored the mandate and falsified payrolls to suggest otherwise. For this he was locked up in the city jail. Yet the stakes in his case were greater than one man's freedom. When Tipaldo made bail, his lawyers ushered him back behind bars so they could sue for his release on the grounds that the minimum-wage law was unconstitutional.

New York was prepared for this fight. Its minimum-wage statute, crafted with great care by Felix Frankfurter and Ben Cohen, was designed to overcome a noxious 1923 Supreme Court precedent, *Adkins v. Children's Hospital*, in which a 5–4 majority struck down a Washington, D.C., minimum wage as a violation of the liberty of contract—in this case, the liberty of a twenty-one-year-old elevator operator and her boss to sit across the table from one another and, in the words of Sutherland's opinion, exercise their "equal right to obtain . . . the best terms they can." Sutherland's position was so extreme that even Chief Justice Taft had been moved to dissent, and strongly. Yet between the lines of the majority opinion, Frankfurter and Cohen had found a little room for maneuver. They did their best to meet Sutherland's objections. To some minimum-wage advocates, the new approach smacked of appeasement. "I know this sounds awfully meagre for you," Frankfurter pleaded with Molly Dewson, a leading reformer, adding that "as a practical woman, I am sure you will want to meet the prejudices, let's call them such . . . of the Supreme Court."

The *Tipaldo* case was the test. New York argued that its minimum-wage law could be distinguished from D.C.'s, and was therefore not controlled by *Adkins*. The state also called for "a reconsideration" of *Adkins*—a polite way of asking the justices to overrule it. Brandeis, Cardozo, and Stone were ready to do that. The chief was not. He was prepared to dissent, but only on narrow grounds. More practiced than the others in the art of fine shadings, more inclined to inch away—by often imperceptible degrees—from a troublesome precedent than to overrule it, Hughes was prepared to differentiate and uphold New York's statute, assail the absolutist doctrine of liberty of contract, and leave *Adkins* standing—irrelevant, apparently unloved, but still standing. The remaining five justices took the less complicated position that two laws resting on essentially the same premise should meet the same fate. Showing uncommon restraint, Justice Pierce Butler limited the initial draft of his opinion to this point and circulated it for comment by the brethren.

Stone, frustrated by what he saw as Hughes's timidity—by the "sad business," as Stone saw it, of standing on "trifling differences between the two statutes"—wrote his own dissent, attacking *Adkins*. This provoked the majority to respond in kind: angrily, and in sweeping terms. Butler's next draft not only reaffirmed *Adkins* but also, with brusque efficiency, dismissed any attempt by any state to set a minimum wage as "repugnant" to due process. This was *obiter dicta*, incidental to the issue at hand; it was not, strictly speaking, legally binding. But it certainly appeared to be. It was impossible to imagine any minimum-wage law passing muster with these five men.

The gloves were off, as they had been all term. The passions of the past several months could not be contained in the measured, narrowly construed opinions that Hughes and Butler had drafted at first; the rage sought release. And while Hughes still clung to the center, it was an illusion, a vacuum, a vanishing point. On either side of him the combatants swung wildly, and connected. Stone now openly questioned the motives of his colleagues: "It is difficult to imagine any grounds," he thundered, "other than our own personal economic predilections, for saying that the contract of employment is any the less an appropriate subject of legislation than are scores of others, in dealing with which this Court has held that legislatures may curtail individual freedom in the public interest." The due process clause of the Fourteenth Amendment, he said, "has no more embedded in the Constitution our preference for some particular set of economic beliefs than it has adopted, in the name of liberty, the system of theology which we may happen to approve."

At long last, the Supreme Court term was over. For Ray Clapper, it brought to mind the final act of a Shakespearean tragedy, the stage strewn with dead bodies. Stone thought the term "in many ways one of the most disastrous in its history. The Court," he wrote to his sister, "has been needlessly narrow and obscurantic in its outlook. I suppose no intelligent person likes very well the way the New Deal does things, but that ought not to make us forget that ours is a nation which should have the powers ordinarily possessed by governments, and that the framers of the Constitution intended that it should have." Having forbidden government at any level from protecting exploited workers, the Court, he said, had "tied Uncle Sam up in a hard knot."

Over the seventeen months between the hot oil ruling and *Tipaldo*—"the climax to this course of destruction," as Roosevelt called the latter decision—the majority not only had knocked out the central pillars of the New Deal but had also constricted the powers of the president, Congress, and, to a lesser degree, the states in decisions that covered the constitutional landscape. While some were rooted in the usual grounds of substantive due process and the commerce clause, others drew upon the doctrines of delegation of power, the privileges and immunities clause, the taxing and spending power, and the president's power of removal. The New Deal's only notable victories during this period were the Court's grudging approval of the gold clause policy and the TVA.

A little more than a year later, Roosevelt wrote in the introduction to his *Public Papers* that "history . . . may well refer to those [seventeen] months of 1935 and 1936 as the time of the 'Nullification Decrees' promulgated by the Supreme Court. . . . It was a complete breakdown of the system of government by three independent but theoretically cooperating branches." While this overstated the case, there could be little doubt that Roosevelt saw it this way, and many others did as well.

"Positively medieval," snarled Harold Ickes in his diary. "The sacred right of liberty of contract again—the right of an immature child or a helpless woman to drive a bargain with a great corporation. If this decision does not outrage the moral sense of the country, then nothing will."

The condemnation, this time, was well near universal. Even the Court's most consistent defenders felt compelled to denounce the decision. The (Albany) *Knickerbocker Press* snapped that "the law that would jail any laundry-man for having an underfed horse should jail him for having an underfed girl employee." *The Washington Post* found it "difficult to escape the conclusion that the Court has gone out of its way" to rein in the states. Regret, bafflement, even indignation rippled through the press: out of 344 editorials on the *Tipaldo* ruling, only 10 supported it. Not only that: dozens of the most conservative papers went a step (perhaps several steps) further and said that if the states lacked any power to fight sweatshop conditions, then the Constitution might have to be amended after all.

Here, at last, was the wave of national revulsion that had been expected for years and had failed, until now, to materialize. When the Court had overturned the NRA, the AAA, and the Guffey Coal Act, when it chiseled away at states' rights in other decisions, there had been protests, clamor, but nothing like this. The difference, in part, was that the minimum wage, focus of fierce battles in past decades, had, by 1936, quietly accomplished something that the New Deal, for all its fanfare and manifest success, had not: overwhelming popularity. More than a third of the states had such laws on the books, in some cases for decades. The minimum wage served an obvious and desperate human need. And though the policy did reflect a certain paternalism, it was no weird concoction of the Brain Trust, it had put down deep roots, and even the Liberty League could hardly be roused to condemn it.

With *Tipaldo*, the issue had finally transcended the New Deal. The question confronting the nation—whether government at any level had any power to address the most vicious inequities of modern life—could no longer be clouded by nonsense about sick chickens, "Russianization," or a *Führer* in the White House; it could no longer be tangled up in the labyrinthine twists of the "stream" of commerce or obscured by legal language. For most Americans, "the liberty of contract" was an abstraction; "the liberty to starve," as *The New Republic* put it, was, for many, reality.

"Increase number of jurists in Supreme Court with men in their fifties," a Brooklyn man wired Roosevelt. The public's interest in curtailing, punishing, or otherwise remaking the Court reached new levels. Stanley High advised FDR on June 2 that *Tipaldo*—"more than any previous decision—may solidify opinion in favor of an amendment." High attached that morning's *Washington Post* column by Franklyn Waltman, Jr., a prominent conservative writer, calling the decision "one of the best political breaks" Roosevelt had received in months and noting that the Court had created a void in which no government, state or federal, could govern. High marked that passage for Roosevelt and wrote in the margin: "The Twilight Zone."

At 4:10 that afternoon, in the three hundredth press conference of his presidency, FDR seemed far less troubled than Waltman (or anyone else, for that matter). When a reporter once again asked how the New Deal could possibly be squared with recent Supreme Court decisions, Roosevelt smiled and offered to rephrase the question: "Have you any comment on the Supreme Court decision?" At which point he paused, puffed his cigarette, and answered his own question in the negative; no, he had no comment. He did, however, urge Americans to read "all three" opinions in the case—Butler's, Hughes's, and Stone's—because together they defined the boundaries of a "'no-man's-land' where no government can function."

"How can you meet that situation?" asked a correspondent.

"I think that is about all there is to say on it," Roosevelt replied. The reporters laughed, knowing that there was plenty to say, but that none of it was going to be said—not today, not any time before November, most likely—by FDR.

"The issue," observed *The Nation*, "is packed with the most deadly dynamite." Historically, election-year attacks on the Court were a losing proposition. In 1896, the Democratic candidate, William Jennings Bryan, suffered at the polls for having criticized the Supreme Court. In 1912, former president Theodore Roosevelt—leading an insurgent, third-party campaign to reclaim the White House—paid dearly for his very vocal support of the popular recall of decisions and judges. More recently, Robert La Follette, the Progressive candidate for president in 1924, drew fire from both mainstream parties over his proposal to allow Congress to override Supreme Court decisions. Republicans, in particular, used the issue to discredit the entire Progressive program. The GOP deployed two leading authorities on the Constitution—Charles Evans Hughes, then the Secretary of State, and Harlan Fiske Stone, then the attorney general—to paint La Follette's proposal as the end of liberty. "If the proposal of the Third Party were adopted," Hughes boomed at a rally, "everything you have, the security of your person and life, would be held at the mercy of Congress. And they call that progress!"

In 1936, Senator Burt Wheeler, the Montana Democrat who had been La Follette's running mate, sent word to FDR to avoid the Court issue at all costs, lest history repeat itself. Roosevelt needed no convincing. He had made his decision. *Tipaldo*, however, made it much harder for Roosevelt to avoid what commentators like Ray Clapper called the "No. 1 political issue." Labor leaders, Democratic politicians, and ordinary citizens urged the president to present a plan. For if he did not, his opponents just might come up with one of their own.

The previous week, that idea would have been laughable. But now, on June 2, Hamilton Fish, a New York Republican, stood on the floor of the House of Representatives and urged his party to support an amendment to the Constitution. Failure to take the lead, he said, would cost the GOP a million votes in November. Republicans, said Fish, had freed 3 million slaves during the Civil War; now it must "emancipate three million women and children workers." To the applause of his fellow Republicans, Fish pledged to carry the issue to the party's national convention in Cleveland a week hence. Others had the same idea. On his way to the convention, Herbert Hoover voiced support for an amendment. "Something," he said, "should be done to give back to the states the power they thought they already had," adding that minimum-wage laws in his home state of California had "done a great deal of good."

"Don't let the Republicans get ahead of you," a supporter wired FDR. For the moment, though, he seemed content to do just that.

Republicans were in a panic. The Court's majority, Arthur Krock observed, had "landed on the front steps of the Cleveland convention as a problem child." *Tipaldo* had put two planks of the party's platform at odds: its cheerleading for the Supreme Court and its increasingly ardent support for states' rights. Of late, the party of Lincoln and Theodore Roosevelt, the party inclined toward strong assertions of federal power, had been waving the banner of states' rights just as vigorously as any Southern Democrat might. "What brought about this remarkable change of clothing?" asked the journalist George Soule in *Harper's Magazine*. "Why are Republicans now acting like Democrats?" It was certainly not due to any newfound solicitude for the right of states like New York to conduct experiments in social policy. Rather, it flowed from the Republicans' identification with the captains of industry and finance, who had come to see the doctrine of states' rights very much as Southern Democracy did in the era of human bondage, and as the enforcers of Jim Crow still did: as a means to prevent the federal government from placing constraints on their power. "The doctrine of State Rights . . . ," observed Irving Brant, a leading commentator on constitutional issues, in 1936, "is a defense mechanism of great corporations and industrial fortunes against governmental control. The forty-eight states, acting separately, are powerless to cope with these huge aggregations of wealth. If [corporations] escape federal control, they escape altogether."

But *Tipaldo* exposed the limits of the GOP's commitment to state sovereignty. The party's conservatives were less aggrieved by the Court's abridgment of New York's freedom to govern than by the efforts of Republican moderates and progressives to go on record against the decision. "The Republican Party must not let the Democrats fire the first shot in the new battle for human freedom," urged William Allen White, the influential editor of the *Emporia Gazette* and an intimate of Alfred M. Landon, the Kansas governor who had emerged as the near-certain nominee. Landon headquarters in Topeka issued a swift denial that White was speaking for the governor—then promptly installed White on the resolutions committee, charged with drafting the party platform. This was no small matter. With the presidential nomination essentially sewn up, the platform became "the chief issue at Cleveland," as one reporter observed.

In the convention hall, to the tune of "Oh! Susanna," a trio sang without fear of contradiction: "Landon, Oh! Landon / Will lead to victory / With the dear old Constitution / And it's good enough for me." But was it good enough for Landon? He had recently declared himself a "constitutional liberal." By this he meant not to align himself with Brandeis, Cardozo, and Stone, but to contrast himself with the unconstitutional liberal in the Oval Office. Still, Landon's comment hardly endeared him to conservatives, who already saw him as insufficiently intent on rolling back the Roosevelt revolution. Indeed, Landon's appeal was that he stood squarely in the middle of the road—as a sensible alternative, or corrective, to the excesses of the New Deal and the orthodoxies of the old guard. He endorsed the aims of the New Deal while leaving, as much as possible, the responsibility for achieving them to the states.

Tipaldo had made this position untenable—constitutionally and politically. Stuck in "no-man's-land," Landon searched for a way out. Through an emissary, Harlan Fiske Stone counseled Landon to be patient: members of the Court, Stone said, were only human, and some had taken great offense at Roosevelt's conduct as president. But that anger, Stone believed, would spend itself eventually. Wait, and the Court would correct its own errant course. Landon, however, was unwilling to wait. The forecast of Hamilton Fish hung like a pall over the convention: if Fish were right, the price of patience might be 1 million votes and four more years in the wilderness. So Landon resolved, as his friend White had urged, to "fire the first shot."

As the delegates gathered, right-leaning newspapers implored them to think twice. "Slow on Amendments, Please!" shouted the *Boston Herald*, admonishing Republicans not to abandon their "rightful possession [of] a strong and appealing slogan—the preservation of the Constitution." The *New York Times*, too, cautioned against "a hasty surrender to impetuous innovators." And as the resolutions committee began work on the platform, the conservative "bitter-enders," as Landon once called them, forced concessions on plank after plank. Over Landon's protest, the plank committing the party to a minimum-wage amendment was thrown out. On the eve of his anointment, as Landon sat restlessly in his office in Topeka, the old guard appeared to be taking back control by degrees; Landon weighed the idea of filing a minority report and staging a floor fight.

Into this contentious mix strode Roosevelt, cheerfully. While the Republicans churned in Cleveland, FDR embarked a few minutes after midnight on a 4,000-mile loop through the Southwest. Arriving in Hot Springs, Arkansas, on the morning of June 10, Roosevelt was wheeled from the train platform to a police "riot car" painted apple blossom pink in honor of the state's centennial, which he was there to celebrate. Under a steady rain and stifling heat, Roosevelt was taken to the bathhouses of Hot Springs, then to an old-fashioned camp meeting, featuring churchgoers dressed as pioneers, soldiers, and Native Americans, and finally, by train, to Little Rock, where, that evening, an estimated 50,000 to 60,000 people sat in temporary stands in a half-completed stadium to hear him give a speech his aides had billed as "historical"—not at all political.

Standing against a 35-foot-high backdrop painted with portraits of heroic Arkansans, Roosevelt began by talking about the Louisiana Purchase, which had brought Arkansas and other states into the union. He said that Jefferson, in making the deal with France, showed "the courage, the backbone, to act for the benefit of the United States without the full and unanimous approval of every member of the legal profession." To those who warned that the Constitution did not expressly authorize him to acquire new territory, "Jefferson replied that there were certain inherent qualities of sovereignty which could not be separated from the Federal Government, if such a Federal Government was permanently to endure." So he went ahead—and "nobody," Roosevelt added, "carried the case to the Supreme Court." The crowd, silent to that point with rapt attention, now erupted with laughter and applause.

Why, he then asked, had a state government been set up in Arkansas? Because, he answered, certain problems exceeded the capacities of town or county governments. For similar reasons, a strong national government was needed to address twentieth-century concerns like low wages and long hours that, "with growing intensity, now flow past all sectional limitations." The Constitution, Roosevelt continued, was "the best instrument ever devised" to strengthen self-government at all levels. "Under its broad purposes," he declared, "we intend to and we can march forward, believing, as the overwhelming majority of Americans believe, that the Constitution is intended to meet and to fit the amazing physical, economic and social requirements that confront us in this modern generation."

At that very moment, Republican delegates were voting on a platform that asserted wages could be raised and hours limited "within the Constitution as it now stands." The old guard, having won its very public argument with the Landon forces, had hoped in this way to provide a stark contrast with Roosevelt. Instead, in one deft move, Roosevelt had neutralized the issue, positioned himself as a true believer in the wisdom of the founders, and left Landon as the only candidate in the race who thought that the U.S. Constitution might need adjustment. All was commotion on the convention floor. "Totally unexpected," sputtered the *New York Times*. "Platform Carpentry Hit," read the next morning's headline, as conservative Republicans carped that FDR had stolen—and used—their best ammunition.

That night, Herbert Hoover, stepping to the podium to rapturous, frenzied applause, set the record straight for anyone who indulged, even briefly, the notion that the two parties had anything in common. "The American people," Hoover said, hands twitching, knees trembling, "should thank Almighty God for the Constitution and the Supreme Court," for these were all that stood between FDR and fascism. Had Roosevelt been able to appoint his own justices, Hoover charged, America would have slid into violence, repression, the obliteration of freedom. "Have you determined to enter in a holy crusade for liberty . . . ?" asked the ex-president. The delegates roared an unrestrained "Yes." "Here in America," shouted Hoover, his words underscored by claps of thunder outside, "where the tablets of human freedom were first handed down, their sacred word has been flouted. Today the stern task is before the Republican Party to restore the Ark of that Covenant to the temple in Washington. Does this issue not transcend all other issues?"

At this, the delegates stood on their seats, screamed, cheered, chanted, wept. The same spirit animated the platform—which, thanks to the exertions of conservative members of the resolutions committee, read like a summons to revolution. The document had the feel of an underground circular, written by members of the resistance at a time of martial law and then posted, under cover of darkness, on signposts, walls, and fences. "America," it began, "is in peril." It went on to paint a dystopic picture of a "tyrannical" regime that had usurped all power, centralized all authority, flouted the Constitution, launched a class war, suffocated free enterprise, and harassed and intimidated citizens with "swarms of inspectors." The platform owed much, in form and content, to a recent pamphlet by the Liberty League.

At the same time, Landon's men had managed to hold their ground on a number of key questions. Beneath the platform's layers of invective and its apocalyptic call to arms was a tacit acceptance of unemployment relief, labor rights, federal regulation of securities and public utilities, and other elements of the New Deal which, it appeared, were here to stay. Lest there be any doubt, Landon, on June 11, sent a telegram to the convention "interpreting" certain planks of the platform to mean precisely what he wished them to mean. And though the platform said nothing of the sort, he pledged his party to seek a constitutional amendment if other state minimum-wage laws met the same fate as New York's. When Landon's chief of staff stood before a microphone and read the telegram aloud, the delegates listened in disconsolate silence. The platform, in the words of one newspaper, had been "Landonized"; but it appeared unlikely that the party had, too.

"I think we should be more than human," Benjamin Cardozo wrote to Stone during the convention, "if we failed to sit back in our chairs with a broad grin upon our faces as we watch the response to the minimum-wage decision. Is it possible that both political parties hold the view that legislation condemned by the majority of our brethren as an arbitrary and capricious assault upon liberty is so necessary and beneficent that we cannot get along without it? Perish the thought!"

Cardozo was not the only one who found in the furor some measure of vindication. The three dissenters, bound even more tightly together by the term that had just ended, traded letters of support through the summer. "The reception given your minimum wage [dissent] must please you," Brandeis wrote Stone from his summer home in Chatham, on Cape Cod. "The consternation of the enemy is encouraging." Stone, too, considered the whole business "amusing"—and somewhat encouraging. "It seems to be dawning on a good many minds that after all there may be something in the protest of the so-called liberal minority," he replied to Brandeis.

The conservatives, too, tracked the public discussion. "My dear Pierce," Van Devanter wrote to Butler, "herewith is a clipping from the *New York Sun* relating to the minimum wage decision. George [Sutherland] sent it to me. . . . You will notice his pencil notation at the top of the article. I do not know the author, but it is evident that he has a better understanding of the situation than many who have written or talked about the decision." Rarely had judges in the majority felt so embattled and misunderstood. Stone's dissent in *Tipaldo* had cast a harsh light on their "predilections," and now, to an unsettling degree, it was these men as individuals, not just their decisions, that drew fire in the press, the law schools, and the political arena.

After *Tipaldo*, many of the Court's keenest observers came to believe—and to assert with new intensity—that the problem was five or six men, not the Constitution. That summer saw publication of *Storm Over the Constitution* by Irving Brant, a leading liberal writer and friend of Stone. "The Brant thesis," as Henry Wallace wrote in the Introduction, was that "adequate powers are in the Constitution, provided adequate men are named to the Court." Brant therefore opposed amending the Constitution; but this was far from his greatest concern. He believed that a more radical, even violent response was likely if the conservative justices continued to stand athwart history. "A judiciary out of sympathy with the striving of the people for well-being," Brant argued, "does not constitute a restraint upon the turbulence and follies of democracy. It is a frustration of government; the negation of democracy; a stimulus to fascist or communist revolt."

From Isle-au-Haut, his wooded retreat off the coast of Maine, Stone offered Brant an enthusiastic review. "I am delighted with [your book] . . . ," he wrote. "You are quite right in saying that there is no satisfactory solution for our problem except in the character of the judges appointed to our Court." Brandeis, another fan, wrote Stone with a "wish [that] the fairies would make our Junior from Pennsylvania read it."

That was Owen Roberts. The youngest justice was spending the summer on his sprawling farm and was, without doubt, following events as closely as his brethren. Even more intensely, perhaps: shortly before the Republican Convention, the *New York Times* had reported the likelihood of a "substantial 'native son' vote" for Roberts by the Pennsylvania delegation. The state had the second largest bloc of electoral votes in the nation; party officials said a third of its votes might go to Roberts. Several days later a friend informed Stone that "some of the bankers . . . are confidentially reporting that the dark horse to be nominated is Justice Roberts. Whether they speak with any authority, or whether the wish is father to the thought, will soon be told."

The Roberts boomlet had begun a year earlier. Republican strategists, frustrated by their lack of appealing candidates, had thought of Roberts: he had been baptized politically by Coolidge and Hoover, had won acclaim during Teapot Dome, and was young, attractive, and good with the press. Even his ambidexterity on the Court made him seem an ideal "liberal conservative" to put up against Roosevelt. Other Republicans eyed Stone. But Stone, unlike Roberts, "put his foot down," as *Time* reported. (That was before Stone's dissents in *Butler* and *Tipaldo* put an emphatic end to Republican interest.) At that time, Senator William Borah—who coveted the Republican nomination himself—charged that the justices-for-president talk had another, more sinister motivation. The rumors, he said, were a "subtle" inducement for justices to toe the line—to render the sort of decisions that pleased party leaders.

"I never had the notion" of running for president, Roberts insisted years later, and issued a stern warning to his successors on the Court: "However strong a man's mentality and character, if he has this ambition in his mind it may tinge or color what he does." None could say with authority whether Roberts himself ever had it in mind. What does seem clear, however, is that he said nothing—nothing publicly, at least—to squelch the reports of his interest. What put an end to those rumors, finally, was not a disavowal by Roberts. It was *Tipaldo*. On the eve of the Republican Convention in 1936, Arthur Krock noted that, thanks to the minimum-wage decision, "the fine idea" of a Roberts nomination was "gone utterly."

Whether he received this news with disappointment, relief, or indifference, Roberts, it can safely be said, was having a difficult summer. Owen Roberts was a man who cared greatly, perhaps too greatly, about his public reputation; in the view of a reporter who knew him socially, Roberts was "too anxious for worldly approval." And when, in 1936, he and the rest of the conservative majority became objects of widespread scorn and ridicule—when even Republicans began to hold them at arm's length—the public lashing may have hurt Roberts more deeply than the others. More than any of his brethren, Roberts remained a presence in Washington, a "man about town," it was said, seen at dinner parties and other events. He refused to recede behind the velvet curtain or retreat to Olympian heights. He was open; he was exposed; and now he was a target.

This was also true within the confines of the Court. In the AAA case, where Roberts had written the majority opinion, Stone had taken him on directly in a dissent that dripped with derision. In the press, Roberts suffered by comparison to Stone. The consensus was that the dissent, as *Fortune* put it, was "better law and better logic" than the majority opinion. *The New Republic* imagined how a debate between the two justices might go. Unsurprisingly, Stone won hands down. Even in cases where Roberts had not written the opinion, he was not safe from Stone's wrath. In *Tipaldo*, for example, Stone's dissent implied that Roberts had strayed from his celebrated opinion in *Nebbia*, which, if applied in the minimum-wage case, would have dictated a different result. "You hit him hard," the renowned New York lawyer Charles C. Burlingham wrote Stone, "and perhaps, despite his robust health, he may wake o' nights with a start and see the word NEBBIA in fiery letters on his bedroom wall."

That summer, the Chief Justice and Mrs. Hughes paid a visit to Roberts's estate. They spent about twenty-four hours at Bryncoed, during which the two men (and, separately, the two women) were in near-constant conversation. The first day, Hughes and Roberts went for a walk and never got farther than the terrace. "They walked up and down that terrace for hours," Elizabeth Roberts recalled. "I said to myself, 'Owen is no walker. His feet will drop off. What in the world is the Chief Justice talking to him about so much? Why don't they stop this?' " Twice she called them in for tea. Twice they replied, "Just a minute," and kept right on talking.

That evening, after dinner with their wives, Roberts turned to Hughes and said, "I want to show you some old Pennsylvania court records that I've got . . ." and led him across the house to the library, where they spent the rest of the evening. "Much use we had of them. Much conversation we had out of those men," Elizabeth said later. "Mrs. Hughes and I talked to each other about the children, the servants, gardens, the weather, Washington gossip. We got to the end of our rope, but those two men still stayed in there." The next morning, the justices went back to the library and talked some more. About what, none but the two would ever know.

Now it was the Democrats' turn. Roosevelt's speech at Little Rock, though it succeeded in roiling the Republicans, had failed to quiet liberals who wanted an amendment plank in the Democratic platform. In mid-June, as the convention approached, letters flooded the White House urging planks on everything from devaluing the dollar to ending tuberculosis to a "pledge to the sportsmen." Many suggestions concerned the Constitution—planks to praise it, fix it, rewrite it. An Illinois congressman proposed a plank to create a commission of "impartial experts" that would recommend changes to the Constitution. Another correspondent, a lawyer, warned FDR against an amendment plank as "it would be poor strategy."

It was getting harder to hold the line. Landon's promise to seek an amendment (if necessary) heightened tensions within the Democratic Party, just as it had for the GOP. On June 20, three days before the delegates convened in Philadelphia, Cummings warned FDR of a "growing conviction amongst our friends" that the platform "should contain some affirmative statement dealing with a Constitutional Amendment. . . . The primary difficulty, however, seems to be that if we attempt to deal specifically with this problem we must go so much further than the Republican Platform, or its candidate, that an entirely new situation is apt to be created which may shift the emphasis of the campaign." Cummings seconded what Roosevelt had been saying recently—that the platform should be framed in terms of general principles, not specific prescriptions.

Around the same time, Roosevelt summoned Sam Rosenman, his longtime adviser and speechwriter, to the White House, and set him up to stay, as usual, in one of the guest rooms across from the study. Rosenman was there to work with Stanley High in drafting the acceptance speech. But that night, the president asked them both to work on the platform as well. Keep it short, Roosevelt said; base it on that line in the Declaration of Independence: "We hold these truths to be self-evident." With that, he was wheeled out of the room and to bed.

High manned the typewriter. Forsaking food and coffee, he and Rosenman wrote nearly all night. They believed their draft was faithful to Roosevelt's brief instructions but was missing important pieces. "Most pressing," Rosenman said later, "was what to suggest about the recent Supreme Court decisions." In the morning, Roosevelt received the draft in bed along with his breakfast. When the writers reached the bedroom, Donald Richberg was already there. A few days earlier he had taken a shot at drafting an amendment plank; this morning he had a carbon in his pocket and handed it to Roosevelt to read. After a moment, FDR whistled softly. "I think this is it," he said. He read it to the others, who agreed.

Richberg's language was intentionally vague. It signaled the Democrats' intention to act without specifying what, exactly, the action would be. It pledged, in the likely event that the Court kept up its blockade, to seek some kind of "clarifying" amendment—not creating new powers, but instead clarifying or restoring powers that Congress and the states had traditionally possessed and, in this fashion, forcing the Court to acknowledge the fact. Even this, though, was too much for some of Roosevelt's advisers. A few days after Richberg handed his draft to the president, Tom Corcoran and Ben Cohen read it over dinner with Ray Moley and panicked (at least by Moley's account). It was suicidal, they insisted, to go ahead—just as Republicans had hoped they would—and suggest that there might, after all, be something wrong with the Constitution. Frantically, Corcoran and Cohen tried to alter the draft, but it was too late. FDR was already making his final changes to Richberg's version, which had survived almost perfectly intact.

In Philadelphia, the delegates adopted the platform without incident. Despite the worries of Corcoran and Cohen, the plank had its intended effect. "The Democratic party," judged the *New York Times* approvingly, "recognizes the authority and respect which the Supreme Court enjoys. It does not regard the court as beyond criticism . . . but it proposes no limitation on the present powers of the court; it will abide by its decisions and seek to shape its program in accordance with them. . . . It is possible that further amendment of the Constitution may be necessary . . . but the Democratic party covets no power that would deprive the States of the right to deal locally with local responsibilities."

Convention speakers reinforced this message, albeit at higher decibel levels. Alben Barkley of Kentucky, one of the greatest orators in a Senate overpopulated by them, delivered an impassioned address that praised the New Deal while taking potshots at the Court. "Over the hosannas of Hoover for the tortured construction of the Constitution," Barkley said, to roars of approval, "I place the tortured souls and bodies" of working men, women, and children. "Is the Supreme Court beyond criticism?" Barkley demanded. "No!" the delegates shouted. "May it be regarded as too sacred to be disagreed with?" "No!" they repeated. "Thomas Jefferson didn't think so," Barkley declared. "Andrew Jackson did not think so. Abraham Lincoln did not think so. Theodore Roosevelt did not think so."

It was abundantly clear that Franklin Roosevelt did not, either. But Barkley's bare-fisted address, having made the point plain, freed FDR from having to say so himself. On June 27, under a cloud-filtered moon at Franklin Field, the president delivered his acceptance speech, a stirring summons to a "rendezvous with destiny." His only reference to the Court that night was an oblique one: "Economic royalists complain that we seek to overthrow the institutions of America," Roosevelt said. "What they really complain of is that we seek to take away their power. In vain they seek to hide behind the Flag and the Constitution. In their blindness they forget what the Flag and the Constitution stand for. Now, as always, they stand for democracy, not tyranny; for freedom, not subjection; and against a dictatorship by mob rule and the overprivileged alike."

The "new despotism," the president said, had been "wrapped . . . in robes of legal sanction." But the "fight," he promised, "will go on." He, and America, would win the "war for the survival of democracy."

"We had everything set in pretty nice shape," Alf Landon said later, "then the Old Guard moved in and took control." A large part of the problem, from Landon's perspective, was his own running mate. The delegates at Cleveland had chosen Colonel Frank Knox to join Landon on the ticket. Knox was a vigorous veteran of the Spanish-American War, the First World War, and Bull Moose insurgency, who fashioned himself, as a public persona, in the mold of Theodore Roosevelt. Knox was also the publisher of the *Chicago Daily News*—conservative, like its hometown rival, Colonel McCormick's *Daily Tribune*, but showing, like Knox himself, a greater suppleness of mind. Early in the campaign he had made clear that he favored a "slashing, frontal attack" on Roosevelt and the New Deal, and soon he chafed at Landon's patient insistence that the Constitution was a losing issue for the GOP. In late June, when Landon took an extended vacation, Knox—joined by the like-minded party chairman, John Hamilton—stepped into the void, which they filled with warnings, harangues, and maledictions.

They ran the campaign that Landon had resisted. Knox charged FDR with "leading us toward Moscow." Hamilton alleged that New Dealers were scheming to replace the Constitution with "some other mechanism." The head of the ticket, meanwhile, was silent for weeks, turning his campaign into an exercise in self-contradiction. It was no coincidence that the Liberty League—battered by Hugo Black, disowned by Republicans, and denounced by Barkley as the "illegitimate brother" of the GOP—chose this moment to reemerge, opening a "nonpartisan" drive to defeat Roosevelt. This was unwelcome news for the increasingly troubled Republicans. "The political liability of the League was so great," Arthur Krock observed in August, that even Hamilton "would have walked a mile out of his way rather than be seen in the company of a leaguer."

When Landon finally emerged, he veered uncertainly between right and left—pleasing no one, confusing everyone. In a single speech he might appear to refute his running mate and then, in the next breath, to echo him. "The governor's campaign seems to me to have disintegrated into a rather sad affair," Ray Clapper, a friend of Landon, wrote to William Allen White in October. "The constant harping on Roosevelt undermining the American system of government adds a grotesque capstone to an unworkable and contradictory group of specific policies. . . . I have gone overboard completely for Roosevelt."

On the eve of the election, conservatives charged Roosevelt with a secret plan to pack the Court. Landon—perhaps against his better judgment—picked up the allegation. At a thunderous rally in Madison Square Garden, he blasted the president for having "publicly belittled the Supreme Court . . . [and] publicly suggested that the Constitution is an outworn document." That was an applause line. This one, however, was not: "If changes in our civilization make amendment to the Constitution desirable, it should be amended. It has been amended in the past. It can be in the future." At risk of losing his audience, Landon tried the politics of insinuation: "What," he wanted to know, "are the intentions of the President with respect to the Constitution? . . . Will an amendment be submitted to the people, or will he attempt to get around the Constitution by tampering with the Supreme Court?

"The answer," said Landon, "is no one can be sure."

Roosevelt himself was unsure. The problem remained on his mind, despite his steadfast refusal to break what *The Nation* called his "conspiracy of silence." Stanley High noted in his diary in late October that Roosevelt "frequently returns to a discussion of the Supreme Court—wonders how long some of its ancient judges will hold out."

Roosevelt's self-discipline was strong. Among intimates, he talked frequently about the Court, wondering how long some of the older justices would hold out before retiring. ("I just saw Van Devanter. He looks very bad," Tom Corcoran told Roosevelt and a group of advisers, prompting laughter all around.) Publicly, though, no degree of Republican goading could get him to drop his pose of sublime indifference to the issue. The strategy, even this late in the game, had its holdouts: "It was a pretty good speech," Eleanor Roosevelt said with a shrug after her husband delivered a major end-of-the-campaign address at Madison Square Garden. "But," she added, turning to his top campaign hands, "I think he should have said something about the Constitution." ("She has a genius," High observed, "for saying the wrong things.")

"There's one issue in this campaign," Roosevelt told Moley. "It's myself." He went forward in confidence that the people, as always, were with him. The polls were less certain. The Republican ticket, despite its disarray, made a strong showing right down to the end: in the last days of the campaign, while Gallup showed a growing lead for FDR, the *Literary Digest* poll, well praised for past accuracy, predicted a substantial victory for Landon. After the fact, winning presidential campaigns achieve an aura of inevitability, Roosevelt's more than most;

but in the final stretch of the 1936 race it was still possible to believe—or at least to hope—that the electorate was about to send FDR the way of the NRA and the AAA.

"There seems a growing feeling that Roosevelt may be defeated—but I've not been about enough to have [a] definite view," McReynolds wrote his brother in July. Van Devanter did not get out much, either, but had friends who did, and in October they assured him "that Landon has a very real chance." Van Devanter himself made no predictions, as he told his sister on November 2, the day before the election. Still, citing "the consensus of newspaper opinion," he was willing to venture "that the election will be close, save for unforeseen undercurrents."

It was anything but close. At his family's home in Hyde Park, as the sound of Tom Corcoran's accordion competed with teletypes in the smoking room, Roosevelt was handed an early bulletin from New Haven. He was winning so big he refused to believe it. He asked that the figures be double-checked. Ensured they were correct, Roosevelt leaned back in his seat and blew a smoke ring at the ceiling. "Jesus," he said. It was over already. He had not even eaten dinner yet.

Chapter Fourteen

PLANS AND PURPOSES

THE SCALE OF it defied description. "It is very difficult to analyze a tornado," remarked the *Albany Times-Union.* Of the forty-eight states, only two—Maine and Vermont—resisted the Roosevelt sweep. In neighboring New Hampshire, after the election, someone hung a sign on the bridge to Maine: YOU ARE NOW LEAVING THE UNITED STATES.

"I am at [an] absolute loss for words," Speaker William Bankhead wrote to Jim Farley. "Nothing of this sort has ever happened before." It was only a slight overstatement. Roosevelt had won the widest margin of victory in the electoral college since 1820—523 votes to Landon's 8—and a staggering 61 percent of the popular vote. A woman wrote Landon a condolence letter: "The Republican Party chose you for fulfilling a mission impossible to man or God." Indeed, even the Schechter brothers, whose lawsuit had brought down the NRA, had voted for Roosevelt.

The landslide brought the nation closer to one-party rule than at any point since Reconstruction. During his first term, Roosevelt had enjoyed a comfortable majority on Capitol Hill. During his second, the imbalance of power would be even greater. The new Senate, in January 1937, would contain seventy-six Democrats—so many that a dozen would have to cross the aisle and sit in the traditionally Republican section. The Senate opposition, such as it was, totaled twenty, most but not all of them Republicans. The *New York Times* found it necessary to report that the GOP "is not dead," that Landon, after all, had won nearly 40 percent of the popular vote. Yet there was no denying the totality of Roosevelt's triumph—or of the repudiation of the Republican Party. "I agree with you that the mess is pretty complete," Ogden Mills, a close associate of Herbert Hoover, wrote to the former president. "How to revitalize the Republican party under such conditions looks almost impossible. So far as I can see, then, the only thing for us to do is to wait and see and to be guided in the immediate future by the course which events may take."

To win, Roosevelt had lifted, forcibly, his flagging popularity. He energized supporters who had grown complacent and humbled enemies who had grown emboldened. He brought record numbers of immigrants, union members, Catholics, women, and African-Americans into the Democratic Party, creating a massive new coalition and obliterating the third-party threat, only recently seen as potent. By the power of his words and the force of his personality, he conveyed a sense of steady purpose and a message of mutual obligation that was heard above the din raised by his critics and the conservative press—"a crescendo of hate such as had never before been heard in our time," according to the *New York World-Telegram*. He had weathered attacks on his patriotism, a whispering campaign about his health and his sanity, ongoing controversy about the New Deal, and setbacks by the Supreme Court. He had survived all this and emerged, in many respects, stronger than ever.

"And now will come the test of the President," wrote Hiram Johnson, the old California Republican, in a letter to his son. The test, in Johnson's view, was whether FDR could resist hubris. Johnson was not the only one with this concern. The day after the election, the nation's editorial pages were filled with calls—not calls, really, but pleas—for Roosevelt to "act with restraint," as the *Cincinnati Enquirer* urged. The *Times-Union* hoped Roosevelt would be "far more careful" than in his first term. The *Baltimore Sun* wished for a "sense of humility." Hugh Johnson, for one, was not optimistic. Roosevelt "loves the dramatic," he complained. "His mentality is so restless it has to have something new daily." General Johnson was sure that "Roosevelt during this next session will give free rein to his imagination. There will be nobody to stop him, and but a few to protest. . . . He will really feel that he has been given a mandate by the people to do as he pleases."

Indeed, he did. The rest of Johnson's critique was open to question, but on this last point, he was more correct than he could have known. On November 6, at the first post-election meeting of his cabinet, Roosevelt declared that he now had a free hand. "I owe nothing" to anyone, he told Missy LeHand a week later. "I promised nothing." He had run on a set of principles, not a set of policies; and the overriding issue in the campaign, as he had intended, was Roosevelt himself. It was the man—not his program, not his party, but the man—that had received the ringing endorsement of the people. It followed that the man could act essentially as he saw fit. "The President's check in 1936 was even blanker than it was in 1932," said one observer. Going one considerable step further, Steve Early told Ray Clapper: "Roosevelt elected himself."

Yet this did not mean that Roosevelt was going to break loose from his moorings and act rashly, despotically, or punitively. Visitors to the White House were struck by his sober, realistic view of the challenges ahead. They saw no signs of smugness or megalomania. This should not have been surprising: if Roosevelt tended, as his critics charged, toward "absolutism," then surely he would have assumed dictatorial powers in 1933 as so many had urged; or nationalized the banking system as some had wanted; or "wrapped . . . up" the Constitution "and laid it on the shelf" as Al Smith had advised. Roosevelt had done none of these things. This made it unlikely that he would do so now, despite the scale of his triumph.

"Now he stands as victor, with whip in hand if he wants to use it," observed the *World-Telegram*. "Will he?" To compel Congress to pass his programs, quite possibly. To flay his enemies, not likely. As angry as Roosevelt certainly was at the press and, as he put it, "the reactionary element," he assured his old friend Josephus Daniels on November 9 that "we have—all of us—been leaning over backward in taking the general victory calmly and in asserting that there will be no reprisals." (Some had other ideas: on election night, a crowd of Roosevelt supporters surrounded Tribune Tower in Chicago, headquarters of the city's right-wing newspaper, and heaved bricks through a window.)

Looking ahead, Roosevelt saw an opportunity to add expansively to the achievements of his first term. Yet he knew the opportunity would be fleeting. The economic recovery that was now, at long last, gaining momentum—lifting incomes, production, and prices—threatened to erode the public's appetite for further reform. On the eve of the election Roosevelt had insisted that "we have only just begun to fight"—to fight for the millions of Americans, more than 15 percent of the workforce, who remained unemployed; for the men, women, and children who still toiled in sweatshops for starvation wages; for fairness and dignity and security. But he knew that if these battles were not engaged quickly and decisively, they might well be lost, with dire consequences for democracy in the United States and around the world.

Other obstacles loomed. "Today there is war and rumor of war," Roosevelt had said during the campaign. "We want none of it." He spoke not only for himself but for the vast majority of the American people. As a bloody civil war consumed Spain, as Hitler and Mussolini intervened to aid the Fascists, the official U.S. posture continued to be one of neutrality. The national attitude was one of indifference. But Roosevelt knew that the policy of non-intervention could not be maintained for long, and that both alternatives—action and inaction—put America at great risk. Also, FDR had watched as the First World War made a casualty of Wilson's New Freedom, and he knew the same might befall the New Deal.

It might also run aground on Capitol Hill. Few second-term presidents had fared well with Congress. "Mr. Roosevelt is likely to break this precedent as he has broken all others," predicted a writer for the *New York Times*. But the discontent of progressives and of conservative Democrats was like a slow-burning fuse. Even the size of his new majority presented problems. Roosevelt told LeHand that he had not wanted such a large majority; left-wing Democrats who rode in on his coattails were likely to get out of hand and send him bad bills he would have to veto—and, he said, they might have the votes to override him. He knew that Congress was almost certain to balk. The question was when, and at what provocation.

There was a more immediate threat to Roosevelt's plans: the Supreme Court. At that first cabinet meeting, FDR talked at length about the Court. The attorney general was away, playing golf in North Carolina. Stanley Reed, attending in his place, told the president that Justice Stone was seriously ill. (In fact, Stone was near death. Hit by dysentery, he spent six weeks fighting to stay alive; not until late December did he have the strength to travel to Sea Island, Georgia, to recover in the sun. He would return to Washington in late January 1937.) FDR replied that he expected McReynolds still to be on the bench at the age of one hundred and five.

Roosevelt instructed Reed to press rapidly ahead with the New Deal cases—concerning Social Security, the National Labor Relations Act, and other major reforms—pending in the courts, adding that he expected to lose the whole lot of them. Harold Ickes got the sense that when that happened, Roosevelt—finally—would take the issue to the people. "The President," Ickes believed, "is getting ready to move."

But would the Court move first—out of Roosevelt's way? Many people thought it might. The solicitor general was one. On November 5, Reed urged Roosevelt to expedite the Court test of the Social Security Act on the notion that "there may be growing changes in the attitude of the Supreme Court following the election." FDR rejected the suggestion—and its premise. But others saw the tantalizing possibility that the swing men on the Court might decide to end the crisis. Ray Clapper pointed to conciliatory signs that were coming from some of Roosevelt's bitterest critics. "Now that we see that anything can happen . . . ," Clapper mused, might "some members of the Supreme Court . . . lend a hand, with similar good-will, toward helping the Government cope with the problems on its doorstep? . . . All of this talk about packing the Court, stripping it of its powers of review, tinkering with the Constitution, would disappear if men like Hughes and Roberts would relent." Some saw it as an obligation. "Either the election was only a mirage . . . ," Robert Jackson argued, "or the Court must yield."

The Court was watched for signs of amenability. Observers said the atmosphere in the courtroom had changed dramatically since the election: the conservative justices treated government attorneys with greater respect—or at least with less overt hostility. Soon came an indication that Hughes and Roberts may have at least "squinted sideways" at the election returns, as one law school dean put it. On November

23, the Court upheld a New York unemployment insurance plan that was similar to the Railroad Retirement Act overturned in 1935. With Stone still recuperating, the vote was 4–4. In the Supreme Court, a tie automatically affirms the decision of the court below, and the Court of Appeals in New York had held the law to be constitutional. A tie also means that no decision is written and no announcement is made of which justice voted which way. But in this case it seemed clear that Hughes and Roberts had joined with Brandeis and Cardozo in validating the law. Frederick Wood, the lawyer who had won the *Schechter* case, had tried to tie the unemployment law to the railway pensions plan, claiming that the New York payroll tax took employers' property without due process of law; but Wood failed, it appeared, to persuade Roberts, the author of that earlier decision. Though the November ruling concerned state, not federal, power, some predicted that the Court was now certain to uphold the Social Security Act. Cummings was more cautious. "The result is encouraging," he wired Roosevelt, "since it indicates increasing liberalism" on the part of Roberts; but Cummings thought it "throws little light on the constitutionality of the federal social security statute."

Two weeks later came other "halting steps," as Jackson called them. On December 7, the Court unanimously upheld the "fair trade" acts of two states. Fourteen other states had similar laws, which fixed retail prices in a way that, in effect, replicated parts of the National Recovery Act through state action. That same day, in another unanimous decision, the Court gave the government protection from an onslaught of injunction suits against the Public Utility Holding Company Act, a major achievement of Roosevelt's first term. Administration lawyers were jubilant, telling the *New York Times* that "the decision would go far toward preventing what some . . . call 'the gang-up' method of attacking" New Deal measures. Though the Court essentially annulled the decision on a technicality a week later, few noticed; the impression was setting in that the justices had heard—and were heeding—the people's verdict.

Despite the prevailing mood, lawyers at the Department of Justice steeled themselves for the task ahead. Though the Social Security tax had not yet taken effect, the legal battle had already begun; administration officials expected a flood of lawsuits when taxes came due in

January 1937. On top of this, five cases concerning the National Labor Relations Act were pending in the Supreme Court. Until these were resolved, enforcement would be badly compromised. The TVA, meanwhile, was under attack by the power companies; a mid-December, lower court injunction brought the program to a virtual standstill. The Public Works Administration faced a similar barrage: several dozen local utility projects, involving half the states in the union, remained in legal limbo.

The problem transcended the cases at hand. A confidential Justice Department memo expressed concern about the "general attitude of law defiance" encouraged by the Court's rulings. "So far as the business population is concerned it is like the old prohibition enforcement situation over the whole wide field of [the] New Deal. . . . A law is now *the* law only after every last detail has been fought through every last court. Agencies that ought to be smoothly functioning administrative institutions are completely dominated—as the price of survival—by their legal fighting machines. . . . It makes for strain all around."

While some continued to hope that one or more of the justices had seen the error of their ways, or would give in to popular pressure or retire, there was a growing sense that the crisis had entered a new, perhaps final phase, and that due to the election, the Court, as a *Washington Daily News* headline put it, was "No Longer 'Untouchable.'" Ray Clapper, who was talking frequently with White House insiders, wrote that it was now "certain that President Roosevelt will not be thwarted throughout his second four years by five or six members of the court who happen to hold a political philosophy contrary to that which dominates the federal administration, most of the state governments, and more than 60 percent of the voters." Even foreign observers saw action against the Supreme Court as inevitable. "If the first American president with the overwhelming support both of the people and of Congress behind him does not tackle this problem, who will?" asked the *Manchester Guardian*.

Yet it was far from clear that Congress and the American people supported Roosevelt on the issue of the Supreme Court. Congress, reported Turner Catledge of the *Times*, was still in something of "a stupor" because of the election, and FDR had made no attempt to assess congressional attitudes toward any specific approach, or even toward court reform generally. As for the public, Gallup polls presented a mixed picture. Though nearly 60 percent of the public wanted the Court to take a "more liberal" view of the New Deal, this did not equal a desire to curb the Court: only 41 percent favored limits on judicial review. Support for that approach had risen over the past year—but so had opposition to it. And when Americans were asked to name the nation's most pressing issue, neither the Court nor the Constitution even made the list.

This, for Roosevelt, was the cost of avoiding the issue in 1936. In denying ammunition to his opponents, he had also denied himself a valuable chance to educate the public—to prepare it for what he might do and enlist it in what many believed would be a difficult fight. Robert Jackson later wrote that the Court was an "issue on which the President had no need to speak"—because his position was resoundingly clear. Others, though, saw a missed opportunity. Roosevelt's silence, argued Oswald Garrison Villard of *The Nation*, ensured that any move against the Court would touch off a "tremendous debate in and out of Congress, perhaps the most vital constitutional debate in our history."

"Now that the election is over," a reporter asked the president on November 6, "will you discuss your attitude toward amending the Constitution?" To which Roosevelt replied: "Why spoil another happy day?"

Indeed, these were happy, even euphoric days. For all his awareness of the challenges ahead, FDR was still taking great delight in discussing the campaign—recalling every moment when he had outguessed and outmaneuvered the Republicans. When Homer Cummings returned from his golf vacation in mid-November, Roosevelt greeted him at the White House with a roar of self-induced laughter, saying he had heard rumors that when he had won the attorney general's reliably Republican hometown of Stamford, Cummings had "gone off on a protracted bender" and was not heard from for weeks. That was "more than half true," Cummings replied. The two men sat for a while and made merciless fun of their opponents' mistakes, including the failure to interest anyone in the constitutional issue.

Cummings brought up a topic that had, increasingly, been on both men's minds: the need for more judges. For more than a year, he and Roosevelt had been assaulted with letters, telegrams, charts, lists, and assorted appeals from a tireless judge on the Ninth Circuit Court of Appeals in San Francisco: William Denman, whose consuming cause, beyond his own advancement, was the expansion and reorganization of the judiciary. Silver-haired and tall, with hardened, Roman features, Denman, in C. C. Burlingham's view, was a man of "colossal self-love and ambition." For decades he had been known in California as an energetic reformer. In 1934, Roosevelt yielded to Denman's relentless campaign for a judgeship—even his wife wrote a letter urging his appointment—and named him to the federal bench.

Three days after taking his seat, Denman began lobbying FDR and Cummings to increase the number of federal judges. "Emergency!" he wrote to Cummings. The Ninth Circuit, Denman argued, was typical of a judicial system that was overburdened, "sluggish," and filled with men of "fading memory, declining mental power, or . . . indolence and similar impairments." The result was a loss of public confidence in the court system and the "social and economic evil [of] delayed justice." The judiciary, Denman told FDR, was incapable of reforming itself—in part because the Judicial Conference, a body of circuit judges created by Congress to help govern the system, was dominated by Republicans who had no desire to expand the bench to make room for Roosevelt appointees. To prove his point, Denman supplied an eight-page document (then making the rounds among liberal judges) listing political affiliations, judge by judge.

After the election, Denman stepped up his campaign. ("If he would stay home and do the same amount of work that the other judges are doing," a California lawyer later wrote to Justice Stone, "there would be no need of increasing the court.") On November 7, he sent FDR a letter that began not with congratulations but this familiar plea: "The New Deal needs more federal judges."

Roosevelt was increasingly drawn to the idea. As governor, he had streamlined New York's slow, overcrowded, and unaccountable court system; and Ray Moley, who helped lead that effort, had drawn the same connection that Denman later did between a judge's age and efficiency. Roosevelt went one step further, connecting age and outlook: he saw the courts as a haven for purblind Republican partisans, reflexively hostile to new ideas. But he was not then convinced that the answer to either the congestion or conservatism of the courts was more judges: "There are, of course, legitimate demands for additional judicial manpower in sections where the population has grown rapidly," he said at the time. "But . . . to apply this remedy in all cases is to add to the ravages of the disease, to contribute to the confusion, and . . . to burden still further an already seriously embarrassed taxpayer."

As late as 1934, Roosevelt felt the same way. "Do you think that many additional judges are absolutely essential?" he wrote Cummings that year. "I have my doubts." But by the fall of 1936, Denman had exerted an influence on both men's thinking. What Denman did was to fuse, into a unified line of argument, three elements of the problem—age, inefficiency, ideology—and provide a neat answer: "More judges." If one could not rid the courts of old, Republican judges, one could try to outnumber them with young Democrats. Denman's concern did not extend as far as the Supreme Court—he had never once mentioned it—but this would be a short, easy leap.

On November 18, Roosevelt embarked on the USS *Indianapolis* for a month-long tour of South America. His purpose was to attend a peace conference of Latin American nations in Buenos Aires, but the trip was also a much needed vacation: 12,000 miles of deep-sea fishing, poker, and "sleep and sunlight," as he wrote to his mother. Cummings sent him off with two massive binders: one containing all the constitutional amendments they were still considering; the other, all the court-curbing bills pending in Congress. At every port Roosevelt received more material from Cummings: memos, clippings, expert opinions. It was unlikely that Roosevelt made his way through much if any of this. He rarely read any memorandum that was longer than ten pages; he preferred to be briefed in person by the author. Either way, en route to his first appearance, in Rio de Janeiro, the president was enjoying the longest stretch of idle time he could remember having. The Court could wait.

When the ship docked in Rio, FDR was greeted by wildly cheering Brazilians and by the country's repressive president, Getúlio Vargas. "*Viva la democracia! Viva Roosevelt!*" screamed the crowds, as the men made their way through the city in an open car. Vargas, hearing in this a personal rebuke, turned to FDR and said: "Perhaps you've heard that I am a dictator?" Roosevelt, grinning and waving his hand as the car drove on, replied: "Perhaps you've heard that I am one, too."

On December 1, after opening the conference in Buenos Aires, Roosevelt returned to the *Indianapolis*. The sidewalks along the way were again lined with crowds of thousands, their cheers undiminished by the heavy rain that fell. FDR, though, felt the gloom. That morning, as he rose, he had been told that Gus Gennerich, his bodyguard and dear friend for nearly a decade, had died suddenly of what appeared to be a heart attack. The loss was a heavy one for Roosevelt, who had relied on Gennerich not just for protection or companionship but for the perspective he provided: Gus, he had told friends, was "my humanizer," his "ambassador to the man on the street." He had run ideas by Gennerich, read speech drafts to him to test the language. "The tragedy of poor Gus," FDR wrote to Eleanor, hung over them all on their long voyage home.

The death of Gus Gennerich compounded another, even more devastating loss. In April 1936, after a long period of wretched physical decline, Louis Howe had died in his sleep. For a quarter century, ever since Roosevelt was a state senator in Albany, Howe had been his indispensable man. Howe had a room of his own in FDR's house in Manhattan, and at Hyde Park, and then the executive mansion in Albany, and then, in time, the White House. He was a small, shriveled figure, with a face like a bulldog's and a personality no less persistent. It was Howe who, almost single-handedly—and certainly single-mindedly—had salvaged Roosevelt's political career after FDR contracted polio in 1921. To Howe, recalled Sam Rosenman, Roosevelt was "a kind of religion." If so, it was free of worship; Howe did not regard Roosevelt with blind idolatry. Howe could be counted on to say no more often and more emphatically than anyone else—not only no, in fact, but "You damned fool!" and "Goddammit, Franklin, you can't do that!" and, when sufficiently provoked, "*Mein Gott!* That's the stupidest idea I ever heard of!"

Roosevelt had relied on this. He deeply trusted Howe's political judgment and, even more important, his understanding of Roosevelt's own psychology—knowledge that Howe applied, with ruthless and often tactless determination, to prevent FDR from indulging his worst instincts. On more occasions than either man could remember, Howe stopped Roosevelt from accommodating his enemies too fully—or lashing back at them vindictively. Howe functioned as a substitute, in essential respects, for Roosevelt's own capacity for self-examination or self-control. He was Roosevelt's balance wheel. Or, as Howe himself put it, "My job is to supply the toe-holds."

And now, as Roosevelt began his second term as president—with a sweeping if undefined mandate and challenges on many fronts—that anchor was badly needed. FDR would not lack for either companionship or counsel. He would surround himself, as ever, with a frequently shifting cast of brilliant, lively characters—people he trusted, whose company he enjoyed, whose advice he often heeded, and who even, from time to time, were heard to tell him no. But as Eleanor Roosevelt later reflected, "no one quite filled the void." This was true to the end of FDR's life. It was especially true now.

As Roosevelt sailed home, Homer Cummings, whose instinct—and most valued ability—was to find some way to tell the president yes, was at work on a solution to the problem that had vexed them since their first days in office: what was to be done about the Supreme Court?

The answer, always elusive, now appeared within reach. After nearly four years of false starts, dead ends, and half-baked ideas, the pieces of a plan clicked rapidly into place in the weeks between Thanksgiving and Christmas 1936. This suddenness was partly due to the election results—to the sense of confidence and opportunity they engendered in the president and his advisers. But it was also a product of circumstance, of ideas that flowed in from many sources but appeared to fit neatly together, reinforcing one another and suggesting, in Cummings's mind, a pattern, a natural coherence, a kind of inevitability.

But first the path had to be cleared of the detritus of old ideas. Momentum was building for some kind of amendment to the Constitution. Since the election, many New Dealers had come to view this as a foregone conclusion. "Personally," declared Molly Dewson, leader of the Women's Division of the DNC, "I don't see any substitute." Cummings grew concerned that Congress, early in the coming session, would yield to the pressure and unite behind an ill-conceived amendment of one kind or another, leaving Roosevelt to react rather than lead. Mainly for this reason, Stanley Reed approached Ben Cohen in late November and asked him to investigate "some of the problems" afflicting various amendments—as well as statutes—aimed at curbing the Court.

Cohen immediately dashed off a series of letters to Frankfurter and other law professors. "Can you lend me a helping hand?" he asked. Cohen "start[ed] with the proposition that there is probably nothing in the Constitution itself properly interpreted which stands in the way of legislative progress, federal or state," as he wrote to Charles E. Clark, the dean of Yale Law School. Yet Cohen recognized that Congress or even Roosevelt (if pushed) might propose an amendment regardless; so, as he worked to weed out the bad ideas, he made one last attempt to see whether any good ideas existed. Cohen quickly dismissed the notion that either the commerce clause should be expanded or the due process clause contracted. "I am pretty much of a pragmatist," Cohen observed; he doubted that any redefinition of those concepts could stand the test of time. Instead, he inclined toward an amendment that would allow Congress to override the Court—just as the president, with his veto, could override Congress. That, said Cohen, was the only amendment consistent with his belief that "highly questionable decisions of the Court," not the provisions of the Constitution itself, were at the heart of the trouble.

To the extent that Cohen had any interest in an amendment, it may have been as a means of turning up the heat on the justices. "The important thing at this time," he wrote Dean Clark, "is to bring to the foreground the need for action," not to settle on an approach. After a public discussion of all the possibilities, "we shall be in a better position to make up our minds." Clark agreed that pressure on the justices might result in better decisions. "It is merely wishful thinking," Clark replied, "to expect the Court to retrace its steps merely of its own accord. At least agitation for an amendment is necessary, if not actual amendment itself."

Meanwhile, in the Justice Department, a young lawyer was conducting an intensive, one-man research project of enormous importance. The lawyer was Warner W. Gardner, a Frankfurter protégé who had clerked for Justice Stone and then became a star within the greatest constellation of legal talent in the government: the Solicitor General's office. In October 1936, Gardner, hardly a week past his twenty-seventh birthday, was summoned to the attorney general's wood-paneled office, where Cummings let him in on a startling fact: that the president intended to move swiftly against the Supreme Court after winning reelection. Cummings asked Gardner to consider every sensible alternative to amending the Constitution, and to report back after the election.

Gardner had contributed to the "project" before: in the summer of 1935, Reed had asked him to determine whether Congress had the power to limit judicial review. In response, Gardner had raised a long list of objections. He brought a similar skepticism to his new—and more urgent—assignment. On December 10, 1936, after two months' effort, Gardner handed in a remarkable 65-page memorandum, rich with historical detail and legal precedent, measured in tone, and unmistakably dubious of every possible course of action. Among other things, Gardner argued that the power of judicial review had deep historical roots and should not be impaired; that Congress had no power to require a "super-majority" vote by the Court; and that "little can be hoped for" in terms of limiting the jurisdiction of the courts, not least because of "the judicial distaste at relinquishing . . . power." Gardner showed even less patience for what he called "the most cynical of the proposals": the suggestion some had made to place judicial pensions on a sliding scale—so that the longer a judge stayed on the bench after reaching the age of seventy, the lower his pension would go. "Congress would not only be seeking to curtail their power, but would be insulting them in the bargain," Gardner wrote. He added that "age is not even a tolerably accurate gauge of constitutional backwardness."

He also briefly considered the idea of packing the Court. "This proposal," he wrote, "is the only one which is certainly constitutional and . . . may be done quickly and with a fair assurance of success." Still, it raised serious concerns. Among them was "the superficial character of the remedy—the problem would recur, probably, every decade" because a number of justices, once appointed, could be expected to lose their liberalism over time. Also, perhaps with Stone in mind, Gardner warned that Congress might need to add "as many as nine or ten new justices" to compensate for "antagonizing the present liberal justices to a point where they would retaliate by voting against the constitutionality of legislation." Swelled by these additions to grotesque proportions, the Court, Gardner said, would become a behemoth—"cumbersome and unwieldy" and virtually impossible to manage.

Yet Gardner did not dismiss the idea entirely. The "administrative difficulties" of a larger Court were not, in his view, "insuperable," and might be mitigated by making the expansion temporary. As for the "political disadvantages," he said, they "might possibly be offset by an 'educational campaign' " stressing the need for a modern interpretation of the Constitution. As Gardner saw it, this left FDR with two options: "The choice must be made between a constitutional amendment and increasing the size of the court. . . . Only the former of these alternatives," Gardner judged, "would seem to offer a lasting solution to the problem."

Cummings saw in Gardner's memo that which he wished to see—that which confirmed the trend of his own thinking. While the memo did not make the case for Court-packing with any particular conviction, it did argue convincingly against every other approach. If the choice really was between packing the Court and amending the Constitution, then the decision, for Cummings, was clear. On December 11 or 12, a day or two after receiving the memo, he called the young lawyer back to his office for a follow-up assignment. He directed Gardner to draft a bill enlarging the Supreme Court.

The bill's "central provision," Gardner later recalled, came from Cummings himself and had "a perverse charm." For months, this particular idea had been hiding in plain sight—in Cummings's files, on his desk, always within arm's reach, never noticed until recently. It appeared within the pages of a book Cummings had just written with an assistant, Carl McFarland: a thick history of the department, *Federal Justice*, due to be published in the next several weeks. In the closing pages, Cummings and McFarland had mentioned—almost in passing—"the problem of age." The book explained that in 1913, during the Wilson administration, one of Cummings's predecessors as attorney general complained of judges "who have remained on the bench long beyond the time that they are able to adequately discharge their duties, and in consequence the administration of justice has suffered." Wilson's attorney general had a novel solution: an act providing that any time a federal judge, other than a Supreme Court justice, refused to retire at the age of seventy, the president would have the power to appoint a younger judge to sit beside the older one. "This," the attorney general advised Congress, "will insure at all times the presence of a judge sufficiently active to discharge promptly and adequately the duties of the court."

The suggestion had gone nowhere; Wilson's attorney general, a year after proposing it, had moved on—to the Supreme Court, in fact. He was still there in 1936, the year he turned seventy-four. He was James C. McReynolds.

In December 1936, Roosevelt sent up another trial balloon. He brought his collaborator, George Creel of *Collier's*, back to the White House, where they spent an entire afternoon and evening at work on the piece. FDR talked for a while about his achievements, his goals, and the obstacles ahead, especially the Court. "I've thought of a better way than a constitutional amendment . . . ," he told Creel, with apparent satisfaction. "What do you think of this?" From a desk drawer, Roosevelt produced a well-thumbed copy of the Constitution. He turned to Article III, which established the judiciary. "Where is there anything in that," he challenged Creel, "which gives the Supreme Court the right to override the legislative branch?" Then, answering his own question, Roosevelt quoted at length from Madison's journal of the Constitutional Convention and Jonathan Elliot's *Debates* to support his long-held belief that the framers had rejected the notion of judicial review; John Marshall, Roosevelt said, had asserted the power in *Marbury v. Madison* "to block the progress of a new order that he resented and distrusted." (Gardner's scholarly memo, which devoted twelve dense pages to debunking these claims, appears to have had no effect on FDR.)

The solution, Roosevelt insisted, was simple. The next time Congress passed legislation regulating wages and hours, or child labor, or housing, for example, it could attach a rider to the bill instructing the Court to recognize that Congress was acting within its power to "provide for the general welfare." But what, Creel asked, if the Court ignored the rider? He later recalled Roosevelt's response: "'Then,' said the President, his face like a fist, 'Congress can enlarge the Supreme Court . . . to permit the appointment of men in tune with the spirit of the age. And what is there radical about it? The country started out with six justices and has had as many as ten.'" Creel was struck by FDR's evident "belief in himself . . . not shaken by a single doubt." When Creel asked him whether he intended to consult congressional leaders about the matter, Roosevelt "shrugged off the question." To Creel, it seemed powerfully clear that Roosevelt "regarded the election as a purely *personal* victory."

The piece, titled (by Roosevelt) "Roosevelt's Plans and Purposes," hit newsstands in mid-December. "Looking back on November 3d," it began, "in no sense does he regard it as a personal victory." (Creel, it appears, was writing fiction.) Roosevelt lacked even "a single bitterness." To make that plain, Creel went to some lengths to establish that the real controversy was between the Court and Congress, not the Court and FDR. The piece then tracked what Roosevelt had dictated about the general welfare and judicial review, and ended with a threat that if other approaches proved "ineffective, Congress *can enlarge the Supreme Court*, increasing the number of justices from nine to twelve or fifteen." The emphasis was Roosevelt's own.

Again—as they had in August 1935, the last time they had collaborated—Roosevelt and Creel awaited an explosion. Again, none came. Perhaps the approach of the holidays led Congress, the press, and others to overlook the article; or it may just have been that after years of Court-packing rumors attributed to FDR and his circle, none of this seemed out of the ordinary. There was another possible interpretation: that as the election results indicated, the American people stood behind Roosevelt to such an extent that he could attack the Court, even threaten to pack it, with impunity.

The *Collier's* article was out of date the moment it reached the stands. Only two or three men, though, were aware of this, and Roosevelt was not one of them. Through the month of December, the "working party" of Cummings and Gardner made great strides toward completing what the latter called their "joint product," but were not yet ready to spring it on Roosevelt. Stanley Reed, meanwhile, knew about the project but, as Gardner recalled, "distanced himself as far [from it] as was feasible," either out of a "natural conservatism" or simple discomfort at the idea of conspiring against the Court, when it was Reed's job, as solicitor general, to represent the government before those same justices.

The bill took shape quickly. Early in the drafting process, Cummings asked that Gardner broaden the legislation to include all federal courts—not just to add judges, but to reform the way the courts were administered. Here was the influence of William Denman—and again of McReynolds, whose proposed reforms of judicial administration had applied to the lower courts. Gardner incorporated these changes, handing Cummings a new draft every few days, at which point the two men would sit down for an hour or two and go through the bill, word by word. The McReynolds provision—tying expansion to the refusal of judges to retire at seventy—struck Gardner, on repeated inspection, as "ingenious and entirely sound." He added what he considered "a most important corollary, that no successor be appointed when the old codger who held on past seventy finally retired." This idea, first raised in his December memo, avoided the permanent expansion of the Court. Within a week or two, Gardner recalled, "we had . . . a bill which I found entirely satisfactory."

And then a letter arrived. In Cummings's frame of mind it must have appeared a meaningful sign. The letter came from Edward Corwin, the Princeton professor of jurisprudence who, as Cummings informed the president in early 1936, had been "giving us aid, comfort and assistance" on constitutional questions for some time. The attorney general regarded Corwin with a special reverence—an article of Corwin's on the *Schechter* case, Cummings once wrote him, was "quite beyond praise"—that few would have seen as misplaced. Hired and anointed by that great Princetonian, Woodrow Wilson, Corwin was well admired for his scholarship. In 1936, on the occasion of its three hundredth anniversary, Harvard honored Corwin alongside Albert Einstein, Niels Bohr, and others as one of the world's greatest thinkers. A leading exponent of a "living Constitution," Corwin shared Roosevelt and Cummings's reservations about what he called "the gross, fumbling hand of amendment."

Corwin was on record as an opponent of Court-packing. In early December, he argued in a newspaper article that Court-packing, while constitutional, had the "obvious" flaw that it would need to be "repeated indefinitely until the Court, loaded with superfluous members and [having] become the football of politics, would have lost all semblance to a judicial tribunal and all claim upon popular regard." Corwin preferred an act of Congress or—if absolutely necessary—an amendment setting an age limit of seventy for federal judges.

Corwin's article sparked something in Arthur Holcombe, a professor of government at Harvard. On December 7, he wrote Corwin with a suggestion: "What would you say to an act of Congress providing that judges under the age of 70 should always comprise a majority of the Court . . . ?" Holcombe proposed that the president should have the power to name as many additional justices as it took to restore a majority of younger men. At present, this would give Roosevelt four appointments, assuming none of the older justices retired. "My feeling," he added, "is that the threat of such an act . . . might persuade some of the older justices to resign . . . , but if not, I believe the public would support the general proposition" that the Court should be dominated by young men. Corwin replied that the scheme was "*most* ingenious, devilishly so. . . . I'm going to pass the idea along, and we'll see what comes of it." On December 16, he wrote Cummings: "it is probably Utopian to hope that the Court will supply the needed remedy for a situation which it has itself created." Action, he said, must be taken. To that end, he offered Holcombe's "ingenious suggestion."

It was not a new idea, but a variation on an increasingly familiar theme. The common element linking Holcombe's proposal to the "roughly similar" formulation that Gardner had already put in his draft bill was the idea of outnumbering older judges, of essentially crowding them off the bench. The important thing about the Corwin letter was its timing. Arriving when it did, the letter provided confirmation—even better, independent and unsolicited confirmation—that Cummings was on the right course. If the great Corwin had arrived, of his own accord, at the same place as Cummings at the same time, then it had to be said that the stars were aligning. That is, if one wished them to align, and was prepared to ignore any sign to the contrary.

Cummings wrote Corwin back right away, expressing enthusiasm. "Of course," the attorney general acknowledged, "I realize that there is a good deal of prejudice against 'packing the Court.' I have been wondering to what extent we have been frightened by a phrase."

Cummings, for one, was frightened no more. The past few weeks—full of hard but exhilarating intellectual labor, of sudden insights and happy coincidences—had changed everything. On December 22, he scribbled a note to President Roosevelt, asking to meet. "I am 'bursting' with ideas [about] our constitutional problems," he explained, "and have a plan."

Chapter Fifteen

WARNING BELL

On Saturday, December 26, 1936, Cummings went to his office at the Justice Department to review, one last time, a thick stack of documents on the Court situation. At 5 p.m. he drove the short distance to the White House, arriving at the gate with his arms full of briefing books and memoranda. For the next two hours, Cummings and FDR talked in the Oval Room—interrupted only by the president's son, James, who appeared with tea and toast, and then quickly excused himself.

The president, still tan from his month overseas, spoke expansively and unhurriedly about his recent trip, as if nothing in the world interested him more than the question of which of the gifts given to him by South American officials should be kept and which donated to the Smithsonian Institution. Gesturing to a large leather box on the floor nearby, he prompted Cummings to open the case and admire the silver teaset inside. Finally, after exhausting the subject, Roosevelt declared himself ready to discuss the constitutional issue—and then launched into another digression, this one concerning his upcoming annual message to Congress, the budget, and his inaugural address.

By this meandering route he found his way, at long last, to the matter at hand. Go ahead, he told Cummings. Tell me what you have in mind. Cummings began with a request: do not laugh at me when I say I have the solution. At this they both broke out laughing.

The attorney general grew serious. He told Roosevelt that he had surveyed the subject prayerfully for a long period of time and found "serious objections" to every conceivable option. "So it seemed to me," he continued, "that we had to go back to fundamentals and diagnose our trouble before seeking to apply a remedy." He described the trend of recent Court decisions, calling particular attention to the liberals' dissents. These, he said, made plain "that the real difficulty," as he wrote in his diary, "was not with the Constitution but with the manner in which it had been interpreted and, as we believed, misinterpreted."

"Go on," Roosevelt said, "you are going good. I wish I had a stenographer present."

Cummings had concluded that his instincts were right all along—that it made no sense to amend the Constitution, to invite delays and to risk damaging the system of checks and balances when there was, in fact, "nothing the matter with it." Look closely, he said, at the crowd now rallying—or, rather, hiding—behind various amendments. Conservatives, in growing numbers, backed the idea only because it had no chance of succeeding and had, at the same time, a high likelihood of entangling the administration in a distracting, losing battle. It was time, Cummings urged, to dismiss any last thoughts of an amendment from their minds, and focus on the real problem: the men on the bench who were dangerously, perhaps willfully, "out of tune" with modern life.

Roosevelt interrupted to pass along a rumor. He said that a source close to McReynolds had told him that this present term might be the last for McReynolds, Sutherland, and Van Devanter—that all three might retire. But Roosevelt did not think he could afford to wait and see whether this came true. Neither did Cummings. Time, he said, was their enemy; something had to be done before the end of the Court's current term, lest the matter drift into the next session of Congress, the mid-term elections, the end of Roosevelt's second term. "The thing chiefly required," Cummings argued, "was speed." Not just speed, but "speedy justice." Judge Denman had been right all along, Cummings said: the federal courts were a travesty, a mess; they were understaffed and unable to keep pace with the flow of litigation. Many citizens had decided against filing a perfectly legitimate lawsuit because they feared they would go broke or die of old age before their case was decided. "Speedy justice," the attorney general said, "was the crying need of the day, and the present situation was a reproach to our standards of civilization." More judges were needed.

Cummings had not made clear what, if anything, this had to do with the Supreme Court. As Roosevelt knew, Denman's concern about overloaded dockets had been limited to the lower courts. Then Cummings shifted direction again, taking another "by-path," he said, toward his destination. He mentioned something that Taft had once said: that the failure to require judges to retire at seventy amounted to a "defect" in the Constitution. And here, finally—having proceeded by careful, logical, half-steps; by large, inductive leaps in reasoning; and by strange, seemingly disconnected digressions—the attorney general reached his conclusion. "If the Federal Judiciary as a whole should grow in numbers," he said, "there was no particular reason why the Supreme Court should not grow in numbers as well." In fact, he saw a good reason why it should: the Court too often refused to hear important cases. Clearly, it needed more judges. If this was packing the Court, well, Cummings said, "we were probably unduly terrified by a phrase."

The solution, he told Roosevelt, was simple: a law providing that when any federal judge refused to retire at seventy, the president would have the power to appoint an additional judge. Roosevelt got the point immediately. If no one retired, this would give him six appointments overnight—one for each of the current justices older than seventy. A three-man liberal minority would become, virtually overnight, a nine-man majority. Of course, Congress would first have to pass the plan, but Cummings predicted that a bill expanding the courts "could be put through quickly. . . . The whole thing could be over with in sixty days, and the excitement would subside and the job would be done." He acknowledged that "there might be some mistakes made, and the plan might miscarry at some point, but generally speaking it seem[s] to me pretty sound."

Roosevelt thought so, too. He did not even pause to approve the plan; rather, he began talking about strategies to pass the bill. Yet he did ask about a contradiction he saw at the heart of the plan. If a seventy-year-old judge stayed on, he would be "supplemented" by another judge. But if the old judge retired, he would be replaced in the ordinary manner, resulting in no net gain of a seat. How, in that event, would this relieve congestion in the courts? Were younger judges so much more efficient than older ones that no additional seats would be required? Cummings had no good answer for this. He saw nothing to do but "try it and see how it worked out," and if a large number of judges resigned, Congress might have to expand the bench in a more direct fashion.

The two men had been talking for well over an hour now and were starting to lose focus. Cummings—having said what he had come to say and having heard, apparently, what he needed to hear—delighted FDR by quoting a series of "salty observations" that Theodore Roosevelt had made decades ago about aged justices. The president grew quiet. "Shall I go ahead," Cummings asked him, "or are you thinking?"

"I am thinking," Roosevelt replied. He was silent for some time.

Then, abruptly, he changed the subject. He said he had heard a rumor that Cummings and his wife, Cecilia, were hoping that someday they would get to the Philippines—to take up the post of Governor-General that FDR had offered him in 1933. Cummings told him, no, there was nothing to the rumor. (Indeed, there was nothing to the suggestion that Cummings had ever wanted to go to the Philippines in the first place, though he was too politic to say so.) That was good, Roosevelt said, because he strongly preferred that Cummings continue as attorney general. "Do you really want me to stay, Mr. President?" Cummings asked, promising that he would remain loyal either way. "No, I mean it," the president replied, "and I would like to have you stay with me." Cummings responded in a rush of grateful, unembarrassed tributes to FDR's "unfailing kindness."

The purpose of all this was unclear. It was highly unlikely that FDR, if he had heard such rumors, put any stock in them at all; he knew how eagerly, even desperately, Cummings had sought his present post, and how loath he must be to leave it. Neither did he need a pledge of loyalty from Cummings, whom he trusted implicitly. Whatever the reason, as the two men paused at the start of an uncertain path, they took the opportunity to reaffirm the ties that bound them together. The clock now approached 7 p.m., and Cummings gathered his papers to go. Before he left, he and FDR reminisced a bit about the first days of the Roosevelt administration. Back then, Cummings recalled, "I had to depend pretty largely on hunches."

"Your hunches," said Roosevelt, "have been generally right."

• • •

Over the holidays "our circle of court-packers," as Warner Gardner later called it, widened a bit. The group now included Carl McFarland, the young assistant attorney general who had co-written *Federal Justice* and whom Gardner considered "an able but not thoughtful administrator." Gardner thought even less of Alexander Holtzoff ("neither thoughtful nor able"), an assistant without portfolio and a favorite of Cummings. Holtzoff had already been active at the margins of the "project," and now he was brought into the center of things. More significantly, a few of Roosevelt's closest advisers were briefed on the bill. One morning toward the end of December, Sam Rosenman greeted Gardner on the ground floor of the White House and escorted him up to the president's small, surprisingly austere bedroom, where Gardner spent a thrilling hour answering Roosevelt's questions about the provisions of the Court-packing bill. A day or two later, he was asked to repeat this performance over lunch with James Roosevelt, who had just joined the staff as his father's chief assistant, and a small group of aides.

If objections were raised, none were recorded. On the contrary, the bill received a warm reception. Around this time, Cummings invited Ben Cohen and Tom Corcoran to his office for a long discussion; Gardner, who walked them through the workings of the bill, recalled that Cohen and Corcoran "were in strong support and without suggestions for change." Cohen, with Corcoran's help, was still at work on an analysis of constitutional amendments, and an early draft of that memo reveals their enthusiasm. Reflecting what they had just learned from the attorney general and Gardner, they made an impassioned argument for "the new mechanism proposed by the President." Court-packing, wrote Cohen and Corcoran, was "long overdue."

"Not a single appointment has been made to the Court since the depression," they insisted (inaccurately, for Hughes and Roberts had been appointed in 1930, and Cardozo in 1932). "Not one of the Justices has had to struggle with the problems of a depression more serious than war." This was an echo of a Brandeis dissent—and not the only sign in this memo that "Old Isaiah" was on the minds of Cohen and Corcoran, who had so often sought his advice and done his bidding. They knew that any attack on aged justices—no matter how well couched or hedged—was sure to be seen, by Brandeis and others, as a slur against a perfectly able and thoroughly progressive old judge. Thus they took pains to stress that the plan "does not require Justices over 70 to retire. Any Justice over 70 who feels that his voice and his judgment will carry weight with new and younger Justices as equally devoted to the Constitution as he is, may have good reason to remain upon the Court. The President's proposal merely provides that a passing generation of Justices shall not be the exclusive guardians of a Constitution which belongs not to any one generation but to successive generations."

As a sales pitch, this needed work. Was age an inherent problem or was it not? Cohen and Corcoran seemed unsure. On the one hand, their memo acknowledged that wise old justices might have "good reason" to remain on the Court. On the other, they cited the fact that two of the three justices younger than seventy had voted to uphold New York's minimum-wage law in *Tipaldo*, while only two of the six justices over seventy had voted that way. In other words, younger justices were twice as likely as older ones to view key economic reforms as constitutional. "The conclusion is inescapable," the memo argued, that "it is difficult for the average jurist . . . after he has passed three score and ten to understand . . . changed social and economic conditions." This ambivalence about age was a weakness not only of the memo but of the plan itself; and though Cohen and Corcoran, two of the brightest minds in the administration, had made a reasonable first attempt at sketching lines of argument, the case they made was, as yet, less than persuasive.

And perhaps it was already moot. Starting in November, the Court had issued a series of opinions that indicated it might be yielding to the popular will. That trend continued into the new year. On December 21, a 7–1 Court (Stone was still absent; McReynolds alone dissented) gave the president virtually unlimited authority over the "vast external realm" of foreign affairs. Though it said nothing about the domestic powers of the office, the decision was still more sweeping than anyone had expected; in his majority opinion, Sutherland was like "a Psalmist lauding the Almighty," according to *Time*. Two weeks later, an 8–0

Court rejected the arguments of a Liberty League lawyer and maintained a ban on the shipment of prison-made goods into states that forbade their sale. Liberals cheered the decision—along with the prospect that the justices no longer saw the commerce clause as an insurmountable obstacle to banning child labor or regulating wages and hours. And on January 11, 1937, in yet another unanimous opinion, the Court sustained a federal tax on speculation in silver. Only a year after the AAA case, in which a six-man majority held that the processing tax was not really a tax at all, not a single justice appeared troubled by what Robert Jackson called "a frank use of the taxing power for non-revenue purposes."

"Is the Court Shifting?" asked the *Washington Daily News*. The Court, said the editors, had so far avoided the kind of "destructive decisions" that characterized the last term, and the justices were avoiding constitutional questions when other, narrower points could decide a case. While the real tests lay ahead, the editors saw reason to believe that the Court would continue to "mend its opinions" and thus spare the nation a wrenching conflict among the branches of government.

At the moment, it was not unthinkable. Everywhere one looked, the New Deal's worst critics appeared to have been cowed (if not quite converted) by the election results. The newspapers, after running—not just reporting on—a fierce campaign against FDR, had grown quiescent. Wall Street, gratified by Roosevelt's pledge to balance the budget, spoke of "encouraging trends" in fiscal policy. Commentators began to write of a new "era of good feeling." Some remained skeptical. Felix Frankfurter wrote to FDR about a recent conversation with a prominent corporate lawyer. "I asked him if there was really to be another 'era of good feeling,'" Frankfurter wrote. "He replied, 'Yes—provided that man in the White House becomes sensible.' Aren't they amusing?" But for the moment, the political waters, so recently roiling, had been stilled. After a brutal campaign, Arthur Krock observed in the *Times*, "the country can use the rest, even if it be proved that it was dwelling briefly in a fool's paradise."

Of course, the peace that prevailed in the winter of 1936–37 was not a permanent one; it was more of a cease-fire, born of exhaustion and a certain confusion. The election results, so resounding that they had seemed to answer every question, now appeared, on reflection, to have settled very little. At the most basic level, it was unclear whether voters wanted to press ahead with further reforms, or simply improve existing New Deal programs. Nor was it apparent what Roosevelt wanted to accomplish. He had let it be known that when Congress convened on January 5, 1937, its first order of business should be to strengthen the Neutrality Act in order to keep the United States out of the Spanish Civil War. He had also begun to describe his ambitious plans to restructure the executive branch—to streamline the sprawling system of independent and quasi-independent agencies, commissions, and boards, and to bring them under greater presidential control. Beyond this, however, little could safely be assumed about Roosevelt's second-term agenda.

Even less was known about the disposition of the new Democrats in Congress. Few of them had any real idea whether they owed their election chiefly to FDR's popularity or their own, or the flow of New Deal benefits to their states and districts or the general rise in prosperity. While the public assumed that the new members would "goose-step along to the directions of the White House," as Turner Catledge put it in the *New York Times*, many in the capital felt that "the Seventy-Fifth Congress cannot be counted upon for any such performance. . . . Surprises may be in store." For all of Roosevelt's enhanced power after his reelection, members faced powerful countervailing pressures from constituents and lobbyists. At the same time, the ability of FDR and congressional leaders to compel good behavior was waning: the reservoirs of patronage and public largess had, by 1937, largely been tapped. Also, the expectation of Roosevelt's retirement in 1940 brought the revival of personal ambition. Senior Democrats, for all these reasons, looked ahead with foreboding. They paid no mind to the few remaining Republicans; "their main concern," Catledge concluded, "is their own crowd."

Congressional leaders, too, were concerned about the Supreme Court, despite its recent decisions. When Joe Robinson, the majority leader, returned to the Senate on January 2, he declared that the Court still stood in the way of reform and that something would have to be done about it. He saw no alternative to amending the Constitution, even though it "would provoke much debate and require time." Speaker

William Bankhead agreed on both counts: amendment, he said, was "a long, torturous process, but if we are to meet the issue, and we must meet it, then it should be done head-on."

The conservative *New York Herald Tribune*, in its pre-session survey, painted a slightly different picture, citing southern conservative leaders who were cautious about the Court, indifferent to constitutional issues, and "obviously not eager to become embroiled in such problems." Though most said they would support any reasonable reform put forth by the president, they saw the economic recovery as proof that the government could get along perfectly well without changing the Constitution. People back home, these congressmen said, were "tired of controversy" and wanted nothing more than "results with a minimum of annoyance." This portrait was not entirely at odds with the one in the *New York Times*; Robinson and Bankhead, southern conservatives both, showed no enthusiasm for amendment, just a recognition that Congress had to assert itself somehow against the Court—rhetorically, at the very least. It is also possible that, like other conservatives, they had gotten behind the amendment drive as a means to forestall other options: such as packing the Court.

Most observers expected that Roosevelt would have something to say about the Supreme Court on January 6, in his annual message on the state of the union. Initial drafts of the speech had a confrontational tone, quite out of keeping with the "era of good feeling." For example, the first version conceded that the NRA had been poorly administered, but argued that it had been fully capable of reforming its methods and meeting its goals—"if the Supreme Court, by its decision, had not outlawed the whole" of it. The line survived two rounds of editing, but Roosevelt struck it from the third draft, along with a reference to "powers recognized by a minority of the Court." He further rejected a suggestion that he quote Hughes to the effect that the Constitution was an adaptable instrument. Through successive sessions, FDR and his speechwriters rounded off these sharp edges, rejecting provocation in favor of conciliation and appealing to the Court to join the other branches in strengthening the "essential powers of free government."

And if the Court refused? A late draft of the speech stated flatly that "these powers must be implemented—without constitutional amendment if possible—with amendment if necessary." Roosevelt tinkered with the sentence a bit, then crossed it out. It was not his style to issue ultimatums. And while he was eager to discuss the problem of the Court, he was not inclined to tip his hand about a solution.

On the afternoon of January 5, the day before the speech, Roosevelt read the final version to his cabinet. Ickes thought it a "subtle speech. It raised the Supreme Court issue very clearly and very cleverly but very inoffensively." He did, however, have one concern, which was quickly echoed in the meeting by Henry Wallace: the speech seemed to rule out an amendment. "The President insisted that his message didn't close the door on any method that . . . might be necessary . . . to put the Supreme Court in its place. It seemed to me that it did," Ickes recalled, "but I could do no more than raise the point."

At 2 p.m. the next day, Roosevelt entered the House chamber on James's arm and was hailed as a conquering hero. As he gripped the sides of the lectern, the cheers came over him in waves, and finally gave way to an expectant silence. The speech was brief and delivered with vigor. Roosevelt drew frequent applause, but generated little excitement—until, about halfway through, he reached this passage:

> During the past year, there has been a growing belief that there is little fault to be found with the Constitution of the United States as it stands today. The vital need is not an alteration of our fundamental law, but an increasingly enlightened view with reference to it. Difficulties have grown out of its interpretation; but rightly considered, it can be used as an instrument of progress, and not as a device for prevention of action.

Democrats leapt to their feet, cheering madly in the sort of demonstration one might see at a campaign rally. Republicans, so few in number they could hardly be found, sat tight-lipped and seething. In the galleries above, spectators applauded mildly, more out of respect, it seemed, than agreement.

Roosevelt continued, citing the debates of the Constitutional Convention 150 years before. The framers, he argued,

> were fully aware that civilization would raise problems for the proposed new Federal Government, which they themselves could not even surmise; and that it was their definite intent and expectation that a liberal interpretation in the years to come would give to the Congress the same relative powers over new national problems as they themselves gave to the Congress over the national problems of their day. . . .

Then, what Rosenman called the "warning bell":

> It is not to be assumed that there will be prolonged failure to bring legislative and judicial action into closer harmony. Means must be found to adapt our legal forms and our judicial interpretation to the actual present national needs of the largest progressive democracy in the modern world.

At a time when freedom was under siege around the world, America, said the president, "must continue the task of making democracy succeed." All three branches had to do their part. He explained what that meant for each, concluding with the judiciary. "We do not ask the Courts to call non-existent powers into being," he insisted, "but we have a right to expect that conceded powers or those legitimately implied shall be made effective instruments for the common good."

This brought another roar from the Democrats. "Roosevelt," the *New York Times* noted, "appeared in complete control of the new Congress." Still, as he surveyed his audience, he felt a touch of disappointment. Tradition dictated that at least a few members of the Supreme Court would be in attendance. Yet he could see that not a single one had come. Roosevelt suspected that someone had shown the justices an advance copy of the speech and that they had stayed home out of spite (rather than, say, a desire to avoid having to sit impassively through a presidential sermon directed at them, outlining their obligations to the nation). More than a week later, the apparent slight was still on his mind—though, as he wrote a friend, he took some satisfaction in hearing that the justices had "at least read the remarks which pertained to them. I hope so!"

If they had, indeed, read Roosevelt's remarks about the Court—and it is hard to imagine that any of them had not—their response cannot be known. Roosevelt's words were ambiguous enough to inspire highly divergent reactions. To Rosenman, who helped draft the words, they constituted a veiled threat. To some commentators, like Arthur Krock, they represented a "conservative approach," for Roosevelt had not proposed any kind of radical solution but had, instead, implied that the Court should correct its own course. Agreeing with Krock, the editors of the *New York Times* wrote that Roosevelt did "not speak like a man thinking of new experiments and new crusades." His message was "not a summons to battle. It is, rather, a note appealing for peaceful cooperation" and was, therefore, "an augury and guarantee of many good things to follow."

On Capitol Hill, however, many assumed that Roosevelt was just playing for time, and that when the Court again showed its true colors, he would move quickly to limit its powers—if members of Congress did not beat him to it, as many now seemed inclined. Only hours after applauding FDR's comment that the Constitution needed no changes, the leaders of both houses of Congress went before the press to contradict him directly. Joseph Robinson went on the air that night to repeat his insistence that "the most practical way to deal with the subject, and the safest way, is through an amendment." Speaker Bankhead seconded the thought: "I still do not see how we can escape a constitutional amendment," he said the next day.

In just the first ten days of the session, members proposed nearly fifty amendments to the Constitution: amendments allowing Congress to override a Court decision; empowering Congress to legislate for the general welfare; requiring "super-majority" decisions to overturn acts of Congress; limiting the Court to an advisory role; and ending judicial review altogether. A handful concerned other matters, including equal rights for women; another would ban "war for any purpose." But most aimed to impair the Court. A few members had other methods in mind. On January 10, Congressman Emanuel Celler of New York, a member of the Judiciary Committee, announced in a radio address that "if the Court again sends back our measures there will be but one course to follow—and Congress will follow it—pack the Court." He called for an immediate increase to eleven justices.

Constitutional reform groups—scores of them—began to proliferate. If anything was to come of all this, someone would have to bring order out of chaos. In January, a delegation of lawyers, economists, and labor groups approached Nebraska senator George W. Norris to see whether he might be willing to play that role. Bow-tied and boyish at seventy-five, Norris was a progressive Republican—so progressive, in fact, that the *Chicago Daily Tribune* refused to acknowledge that he was actually a Republican; it referred to him as "George W. Norris (Radical, Neb.)." Norris was known as the "father of the TVA." As such, his chief complaint with the judiciary was that injunctions had "virtually paralyzed" his program. So the delegation found a willing sponsor. (Burt Wheeler was another.) Norris agreed to chair a March conference with the goal of finding common ground. "Those who would deal with the situation," he declared, "first must compromise among themselves." Morris Ernst, a prominent civil liberties lawyer, wrote to inform Roosevelt about the gathering. "We hope to have a fair sprinkling of congressmen, governors and judges," Ernst told the president. "The implications of the conference," he added, "may be more than subtle."

Roosevelt could not have been pleased by all this activity. It complicated things, muddied the waters. But then, he should not have expected any different. In his annual message, he had refrained from announcing a plan, hinting that one was forthcoming, or ruling out any course of action. Thus there was no reason for members of Congress—or anyone else, for that matter—to hold back and wait for the president to act. Not a single congressional leader had been brought into the president's confidence on the Court issue. Each, therefore, felt entirely free to pursue his own ends, on his own timetable, in his own manner.

Roosevelt's lieutenants on the Hill had every reason to expect that if the president had a plan, he would not only tell them about it but ask for their input, or even get behind their collective recommendation (assuming they had one). This, after all, was the approach he was taking on the executive reorganization bill. In early January, he brought Democratic leaders to the White House, gestured to a large humidor of Cuban cigars on the table, and as the room filled with smoke, he leaned forward, made eye contact, listened intently, and freely took their tough questions—the very picture of openness and accommodation. The bill was a tough sell; in its pursuit of effective government, it would strip the Congress of many cherished prerogatives. Understanding this, Roosevelt "jumped around like a cat, three steps ahead of everyone," as a staff member recalled.

Though FDR did not acknowledge (or explicitly deny) it, his message to Congress on executive reorganization had already been written before that meeting. But openness—or the appearance thereof—had an obvious and essential function: it helped keep Congress in line. The popular notion of a "rubber-stamp" Congress had always been, as Roosevelt well knew, largely a fiction. The extent to which Congress went along with the White House depended directly on the hours (by FDR's own reckoning, three or four a day while Congress was in session) that Roosevelt spent listening, flattering, humoring, persuading, and pressing party leaders to fulfill his wishes—and leading them to believe, in many cases, that his initiatives had been their idea. He strove to avoid the impression that he was, as he put it, "cracking the whip of a dictator." This was also a matter of self-protection. By encouraging Hill leaders to take the initiative on controversial matters like banking reform or Social Security, "he let his shock troops bear the brunt of the fighting while he stayed safely behind the lines," as Pearson and Allen observed.

Roosevelt loved discussion. He loved to talk (and liked to listen). "Well, Cordell," he would say, reaching his Secretary of State by telephone, "what's on your mind?" This was what he did all day. It was his sport and his sustenance. "Huddles and 'bull sessions,'" observed George Creel, "were the delight of his soul." They were also, in large part, how he made decisions. Roosevelt knew that a small circle—particularly a small circle around a president—tended to become an echo chamber, a chorus of yes-men. His process, by contrast, was pluralistic. He welcomed opposing views, invited dissent, brought outsiders into the mix. The result, quite often, was administratively a mess—a jumble of conflicting and overlapping directives. But by these means, gaps in his thinking were usually filled, and flaws in his reasoning exposed and corrected.

On occasion, however, he worked in secret, hiding his plans from close allies and aides. The most egregious example had been his "wealth tax" message of 1935—his response to Huey Long's "Share

Our Wealth" plan—which Roosevelt had drafted without talking to congressional leaders and then demanded action on precisely the terms he had dictated. "This precipitate action," judged Pearson and Allen (and nearly every other observer), "caused more bickering among Congressional Committees and more resentment against the President than any other act of his administration."

What explained the shift from solicitude to high-handedness? The answer, in part, was that Roosevelt had expected conservative Democrats to resist his plan; and so, instead of running it by them, he sought to impose it upon them. This was a mistake—one that he appeared, in short order, to recognize. His old attentiveness was soon in evidence. But the problem—and, as the tax furor demonstrated, it was indeed a problem—ran deeper than any particular case. It went to the core of Roosevelt's personality: his love, in Rosenman's words, "of the dramatic and climactic."

"I'm going to spring a bombshell," Roosevelt often told advisers, prompting, more often than not, alarm. He delighted in surprises: political and personal, large-scale and small, "clever, cunning and quick," as Hugh Johnson recalled. "He likes to shock friends as well as enemies." "Can you keep a secret?" FDR asked Missy LeHand one day in 1936. He told her he planned to adjourn that afternoon's cabinet meeting a bit early and lead everyone outside for a "big surprise": Claude Swanson, Secretary of the Navy, who had been ill for some time, would be waiting in a car. "We'll have a reunion," the president said, his eyes sparkling. (LeHand did not have the heart to tell him that the cabinet was unlikely to share his excitement about Swanson, an able public servant but something less than a luminary.) In the political realm, this manifested itself, from time to time, in a desire to startle not just enemies but supporters—to confound expectations. When he did so, it was because he had calculated that the public would back him. He was often right about this—often, but not always, as the tax fight showed. Accordingly, Roosevelt tended not to take big, bold steps in this fashion. Instead, he made small steps look bigger and bolder by announcing them with a bang.

Secrecy, at times, became an end in itself. "He loved mystery," remembered Rosenman; too often, this meant that in dealings with congressional leaders or even his own advisers, FDR took pleasure in hiding crucial pieces of information. "Not that Roosevelt sought to deceive; he just did not let them in on the whole tale," his speechwriter said. "He seemed not to want any one person to know the whole story."

Roosevelt could talk all day, but conversation did not equal candor. "Never let your left hand know what your right hand is doing," he once advised Henry Morgenthau. "Which hand am I, Mr. President?" asked Morgenthau. "My right hand," Roosevelt replied, "but I keep my left under the table." This bred resentment and internecine conflict when staff members discovered, usually by accident, that the president had asked more than one of them to complete a related request. "Sometimes," Rosenman reflected, "I thought it was because it gave [FDR] a sense of power—which he loved—to be the only person who knew everything about a project. After a while you accepted this failing of his even though it was an inefficient way of doing things."

It could be worse than inefficient. It could be reckless. Such was the case with the Court-packing proposal. "How is your plan coming along, Homer?" the president teased at a cabinet meeting toward the end of 1936. It was a private joke. Except for Cummings, the cabinet was completely in the dark about the "project." Ickes and Wallace, who for years had pressed for aggressive action against the Court, knew nothing about the plans. Neither did Frances Perkins, the Secretary of Labor—who, from a jurisdictional perspective, had the most at stake in the pending Court tests of Social Security and the National Labor Relations Act. Neither did Vice President John Nance Garner, FDR's chief liaison with Capitol Hill. At Friday afternoon meetings, as cabinet officials engaged in weekly complaints about the Court, Roosevelt smiled inscrutably to himself or conspiratorially at Cummings. Sometimes he even participated in the conversation—saying something but revealing nothing, and giving every appearance of open-mindedness, even after he had settled on a solution.

Beyond his love of mystery, Roosevelt may have seen no need for further discussion. He already knew what Ickes, Wallace, and Perkins thought he should do about the Court. He had been consulting widely on the matter for years—seeking a range of informed views, exploring every possibility in depth, and weighing the constitutional and political repercussions of each. He and Cummings had steeped themselves in these questions so long that, by 1937, it was hard to imagine an angle they had failed to consider. And so, at the critical moment, the decision point, Roosevelt closed the door to additional debate. None of the men who knew about the plan—Gardner and the other assistants—were in a position (or of an inclination) to challenge it openly. Any who might have done so were shut out systematically. Cummings had long despised the loose clique of intellectuals around FDR, men like Frankfurter, who considered the attorney general a hack. Cummings took no small pleasure in disregarding them now.

All this secrecy, Roosevelt said later, had a single purpose: to protect the Court plan from being leaked to the press. But to accept this explanation is to believe that the element of surprise was somehow more critical to the plan's success than to the passage of the NRA, or Social Security, or any other reform that he had discussed in advance, even in public, with congressional leaders and White House correspondents. Roosevelt never said why he believed more could be gained by surprising—and, almost inevitably, humiliating and infuriating—congressional leaders than by working with them toward a solution. These were the tough questions FDR might have faced had anyone around him—anyone but Cummings—known enough to ask.

Roosevelt's conflict with the Court, it appears, had clouded his judgment, had brought out some of his most self-destructive tendencies. His love of the covert; his preference for the sly over the straightforward; his occasional vindictiveness; his eagerness to astonish—all these came together in the Court-packing plan. The man who delighted in surprises now had one of the biggest that any president had ever sprung on the nation. He would not share it before he was ready, and, before then, would not expose it to any who might question it. He and Cummings had their solution—the very shrewdness of which seemed, to its authors, proof of its perfection. In the bubble they had built around themselves, these two—this constitutional convention *à deux*—fell victim to their own cleverness. Locked in an embrace of mutual reinforcement, these smart and seasoned politicians came to see a radical solution as precisely what they wished it to be: practical, moderate, reasoned, and wise.

Chapter Sixteen

PRESERVE, PROTECT, DEFEND

WARNER GARDNER WAS appalled. For the better part of the past month he had been busily drafting and redrafting the bill to pack the Court. He had been given the privilege, at the age of twenty-seven, of briefing the president of the United States about the plan. He had begun to feel, as one might, a certain pride of authorship. And then, in the first weeks of January 1937, he learned that the bill would not, as he had expected, be presented as an answer to the Court's obstructionism, but as a means to lighten the load on overworked judges.

Gardner had clerked at the Supreme Court. He knew that whatever the situation might be in the lower federal courts, the highest court was in no way overwhelmed by its caseload. And so "a constitutional confrontation that men could fight for," Gardner said later, had become a "trick," an "effort to market deceit," an "exercise in Madison Avenue sleaze." Gardner wondered whom to blame for the change in approach; his best guess was Carl McFarland, "who was very close to Cummings and of a notably practical cast of mind." This was not a compliment.

Gardner may have been wrong in assuming that a shift had taken place. It is unclear that Cummings had ever considered making a direct attack on or even a direct reference to the Court majority's conservatism. In December, when he presented his plan to Roosevelt, Cummings was already tying the need for more judges to congestion in the courts. There had been no reason for him to tell Gardner about this. Cummings tended to parcel out information on a need-to-know basis, and Gardner, who was drafting the bill, did not need to know how the plan was to be packaged.

Regardless, when Gardner made that discovery, he dropped out of the project. In early January, he handed Cummings another draft of the legislation, made a last-ditch argument (which he won) for a ceiling of fifteen justices, and that was that. Years later, he could not quite remember whether he had dodged additional work on the bill, or simply emitted such strong disapproval for it that Cummings went elsewhere for help. Either way, Gardner was out, and deeply dismayed by the turn things had taken.

So were Ben Cohen and Tom Corcoran. In December, they had cheered the plan (or what they knew of it); their draft memo on Court proposals included a rousing call to get the old, out-of-touch conservatives off the bench. But when the two men learned, in early January, that the case would be made on grounds of efficiency rather than ideology, they recoiled. They had no problem with Court-packing per se; what they could not abide was Court-packing on false premises. Aghast at the bill's new rationale, Corcoran and Cohen promptly turned their memo into a brief for the opposing side, making an impassioned, if ultimately pointless, attempt to change Roosevelt's mind.

Old age, they now wrote, did not always make justices more "arbitrary in their judgments or . . . unsympathetic with the needs of the present." In fact, "some men acquire serenity" with age, growing "more tolerant of experiments." Moreover, adding seats to the Court would cause justices to behave like legislators—riven by factionalism, prone to "speech-making," occupied with "crude bargaining for . . . votes." Cohen and Corcoran expressed doubt that such a proposal could possibly receive a fair hearing in Congress or the nation. It would look, to all, like an assault on the independence of the judiciary. "At best," they concluded, "enlarging the Court is a temporary expedient which may fail [to fulfill] its purpose." As an alternative, they halfheartedly proposed amending the Constitution to give Congress veto power over the Court's decisions. On January 7, they handed in the memo and promptly disowned it. That afternoon, Corcoran turned up in Ickes's office and said it would be impossible to ratify an amendment and foolish to try. "It may be that the only course left to us is to enlarge the membership of the Court," Ickes wrote in his diary, glumly conceding Corcoran's point. Ickes wanted real reform—a permanent crippling of the Court. That, he believed, would have to happen eventually.

In mid-January, on the eve of his second inauguration, FDR sat down for an extended interview with Anne O'Hare McCormick of the *New York Times*. She found him looking hale, full of energy and optimism, as if the burdens of the presidency were, in her words, "a stimulant to buoy him up." She was struck by the sense that "he is always the same Roosevelt; it would be difficult to find a man who changes less, in manner or substance. But the accent has definitely shifted. There is a difference in the interpretation he puts on his policies." Four years earlier, facing an economic crisis, he had spoken of reform and recovery. Today, his goals were more fundamental: "the vindication and strengthening of democratic government."

To that end, as he had made clear in his annual message on January 6, Roosevelt sought change in the Court—but not, he assured McCormick, by constitutional amendment. The president, she reported, was "so little desirous of raising that issue" that he was willing to adjust his own methods in the interest of avoiding confrontation. She "doubted whether he would abridge, if he could, the powers of the Supreme Court. All he asks of that body, he says, is that it should be reasonably contemporary. He holds that the court should live and think in the same decade as the other branches of government—and that is a condition any president can help realize by the exercise of his appointive power."

This was a dangerous game. In the span of a few weeks, Roosevelt had gone from threatening in *Collier's* that action was imminent, to implying in his annual message that it was not, to telling McCormick explicitly that he was content to wait for justices to die or resign. Roosevelt was doing more than playing coy about his plans: he was going to greater and greater lengths to deny even the possibility of doing what he had already, in fact, resolved to do. All these comments were made on the record—rendering it almost certain that sometime soon, critics would confront him with his inconsistent, misleading, even outright dishonest statements, and hold him to account. It is hard to see in this any kind of deliberate strategy, beyond a desire to throw people off the trail—to maximize the surprise they would feel when he finally revealed his proposal. Clearly, Roosevelt was anticipating a big reaction. "Very confidentially," he wrote to Frankfurter on January 15, "I may give you an awful shock in about two weeks. Even if you do not agree, suspend final judgment and I will tell you the story."

In 1937, for the first time in history, the presidential inauguration would take place on January 20 rather than March 4. The Twentieth Amendment, ratified in 1933, had closed the gap between election day and the swearing-in ceremony—a gap that, in the winter of 1932–33, had been so fraught with uncertainty. Now, four years later, the festive spirit of the holiday season extended all the way to mid-January. As Roosevelt prepared to take the oath of office a second time, Christmas trees and lights were replaced by banners and bunting across Washington. In the red-carpeted corridors of the White House, the poinsettias remained in place.

Yet worries about the weather had hung over the event since the amendment was first proposed. These concerns, it turned out, had been only slightly misplaced. Snow did not fall on January 20, 1937, as had been predicted, and temperatures did not plunge; what came down in torrents was rain and sleet, whipped by the wind at great velocity. Just before noon, as Harold Ickes and Henry Morgenthau—fortifying themselves from a flask of scotch—stepped out of the Capitol Building onto the reviewing stand, the rain hit them full force, like spray from a firehose. On the grounds below, thousands of spectators, ankle-deep in mud, huddled for hours under useless umbrellas. Several thousand more had arrived at Union Station and, seeing what they were up against, went no farther, content to read Roosevelt's address in the evening papers.

Across the street, in the Supreme Court Building, seven justices were steeling themselves. Stone was still recuperating, and Brandeis, as a rule, never attended public functions. But the rest of the "Nine Old Men," fearful, as old men might be, of the bad weather, prepared themselves to go out in it. At 11 a.m., following tradition, they met in the courtroom, wearing their robes. The Chief Justice made a formal announcement that the justices would attend the inauguration. At this they rose, removed their robes—which were then neatly folded and given to messengers—and took elevators to the basement, where cars were waiting to ferry them, for the first time in more than a year, to their old chamber on the Senate side of the Capitol. There, after a short delay—the messengers, lacking the proper passes to enter the building, argued with the guards before being admitted—they put their gowns back on and stepped outside.

The robes offered scant protection from the slashing rain. Most of the justices pulled heavy overcoats over their shoulders and covered their heads with little black skullcaps. As the seven men entered the inaugural pavilion, making their way along a runner of red carpet that was as saturated as a sponge, attendants tipped their chairs forward to pour off the puddles. George Sutherland sat down and shivered. Nonetheless, when James McReynolds, his senior on the Court, was escorted onto the platform, Sutherland stood up and offered his seat. He had it back about five minutes later. Afraid of catching pneumonia—and not the least bit interested in hearing the inaugural address—McReynolds left the reviewing stands and went straight home. ("He didn't have what it took," sneered Ickes, who watched from nearby.)

"If they can take it," Roosevelt said of the crowds, "I can take it." He left the windows of his limousine open as he drove up Pennsylvania Avenue to the Capitol. He cast aside his silk hat and left his coat open at the neck. He did, however, agree to wait for half an hour inside the building in the hope that the rain would eventually let up. When it did not, he proceeded, on the arm of his son James, up the long ramp to the platform where Chief Justice Hughes, removing his skullcap, stood to greet the president and to issue the oath of office.

The oath, even more than the speech that would follow, was what thousands had endured the weather to witness. Roosevelt and Hughes—antagonists in the greatest constitutional crisis since the Civil War—stood barely a yard apart. As the Chief Justice spoke the words of the oath, a sodden presidential flag, bearing four stars and an eagle, was raised. Between and slightly behind the two men stood the Clerk of the Supreme Court, who held FDR's twenty-pound, two-hundred-year-old family Bible, now covered with a sheet of cellophane to protect it from the rain. Roosevelt placed his left hand on the Bible and raised his right hand. He listened intently to Hughes, then repeated the oath in full. Roosevelt did not smile, but jutted his jaw as he spoke, giving certain words special emphasis:

> I do solemnly swear that I will faithfully execute the office of President of the United States, and will, to the best of my ability, *preserve . . . protect . . . and defend* the *Constitution* of the United States. *So help me God!*

"It was not what was said but the way in which it was said," observed the *New York Times*. "The emphasis was not lost on the crowd. Under the umbrellas men and women turned to one another. They understood."

And then they turned to go, many of them. Roosevelt's address could be heard on one of the many radios set up in hotel lobbies and restaurants—though the weather made even this difficult. The steady rain on the canopy of the inaugural stand made a sound that radio engineers at first thought was static; when blasts of sleet hit the podium, it sounded more like a drum roll. People with seats near the president fared little better: a clerk to Justice McReynolds found he "couldn't hear a word Roosevelt said."

Still, those who remained, including the six justices, leaned forward and listened. It had been rumored that Roosevelt would allude, in his speech, to the Court. Tom Corcoran had pressed him to attack not only the Court but the Liberty League lawyers who advised their clients to ignore New Deal laws until the Court had ruled on them. "Never again," read the first draft of the speech, "will patriotism be a cloak for reaction. Never again will the names of the founding fathers be invoked against a modern application of the founding fathers' faith." But the president had taken this out. There would be plenty of tough language in the speech, plenty of scorn for "heedless self-interest" and "hard-heartedness," but FDR wanted to leave the League out of it.

As for the Court itself, he settled for an oblique but pointed reference. Echoing his first inaugural, he expressed his faith in the Constitution as the founders had conceived of it—namely, its creation of "a strong government with powers of united action sufficient then and now to solve problems utterly beyond individual or local solution." He paused to brush water from his face. "Today," he continued, "we invoke those same powers of government to achieve the same objectives. . . . The Constitution of 1787 did not make our democracy impotent." As he had in his annual message, he called on all three branches to do their part. The American people, he said, "will insist that *every* agency of popular government use effective instruments to carry out their will." Sam Rosenman watched Hughes's face as Roosevelt spoke this sentence. "There was no doubt," Rosenman said later, "that the Chief Justice understood what the President meant."

Talking later with Rosenman, Roosevelt said that when reciting the oath, he had felt like saying to Hughes, "Yes, but it's the Constitution as *I* understand it, flexible enough to meet any new problem of democracy—not the kind of Constitution your Court has raised up as a barrier to progress and democracy." Roosevelt's critics, of course, saw the irony differently. A lawyer on Park Row in New York wrote to Hughes the day after the ceremony: "It has been a long time since I have had anything which has given me more pleasure and satisfaction than listening yesterday to your administering the oath of office to the President and requiring him to swear, right before your face, to 'support the Constitution of the United States.' This must have been a bitter pill to him, after the sarcasm and contempt which he has seen fit to try to bestow upon the Constitution and the Supreme Court." Hughes, ever proper, wrote a curt reply: "I have no comment to make on the matter you mention."

Word of the plan was getting out. Roosevelt's advisers, and possibly even Roosevelt himself, were growing careless in the hints they dropped, and to whom. Just before the inauguration, the president had met briefly with Senator Sherman Minton of Indiana, a faithful supporter. Incredibly, as Minton strolled out of the White House, he told a group of waiting reporters that FDR was planning a big meeting with congressional leaders to develop a plan to curb the Court. Minton cautioned that he was speaking for himself, not the president. A White House aide affirmed this. Still, the story made the front pages. Speculation was increasing that Roosevelt's "attitude . . . of watchful waiting," as the *New York Times* called it, was a pose.

Donald Richberg was similarly—shockingly—indiscreet. In early

January, Richberg, the former head of the National Recovery Administration, had presented Roosevelt with a draft bill to mandate retirement from the Court at age seventy. FDR and Cummings had told him it was unconstitutional. Apparently they, or someone else, had told Richberg more than that. On the evening of January 20, he held a post-inauguration cocktail party, which he used as an opportunity to take credit for Roosevelt's inaugural address and to share confidences with the columnist Ray Clapper. At some point that night, presumably after a highball or two, Richberg took him aside and confided, as Clapper recorded in his diary, that

> Rvt has a number of bombshells ready to shoot which will astound country—says Rvt is in audacious mood and is even thinking of proposing to pack Supreme Court by enlarging it. . . . He says Rvt is determined to curb the court and put it in its place, and will go ahead even if many people think it unwise.

Clapper kept this scoop to himself. He was, by his own account, a "75 percent New Dealer," and sympathized with the White House in its struggle with the Court. Others, feeling less beholden, went to press with whatever they had heard. In some cases, this was impressively close to the mark. The Washington bureau of Scripps Howard notified its entire chain of papers that the president was considering an increase in the Court's membership. Pearson and Allen, in a column filed just after the inauguration, even had the number right: six justices. The move, they said, was imminent.

The number of potential sources for the leak was increasing. In January, Cummings for some reason revealed the plan to Breckenridge Long, until recently the ambassador to Italy. Roosevelt himself ran the proposal by Charlton Ogburn, counsel of the AF of L, and John L. Lewis of the Congress of Industrial Organizations (CIO), who was at that time trying to negotiate an end to the sit-down strike at the GM plant in Flint, Michigan. Roosevelt's courting of these union leaders may have reflected, more than anything, his eagerness to convince them that he had a long-term solution to rising labor unrest—a reconstituted Supreme Court that would, before long, affirm workers' rights.

For these reasons it could not have surprised Roosevelt when the journalist Irving Brant wrote him on January 24 that "several senators have told me that you expect to make a statement about the Supreme Court within a few days. If it is a statement critical of the court, or intended to put heat on it, I would urge you not to do so," Brant implored him.

> What you have already said has opened the way to criticism by others and it will keep coming. . . . Anything said by you now would start a backlash. . . . I think that the strongest pressure you can exert is that which now prevails—the pressure of uncertainty, and I hope you'll keep the reactionaries in suspense. From talks with liberal justices I am sure there will be a fundamental shift in constitutional interpretation.

Brandeis, Cardozo, and Stone heard the rumors from Brant. McReynolds, too, picked them up somewhere. "The Justice has been tipped off to something," noted John Knox, McReynolds's perceptive law clerk, in a letter to his parents, "but I don't know yet what it is. He is either fearing inflation or being forced to resign. He has had me go through his records back to 1903"—when McReynolds had first taken a job in Washington—"and he has been calling up his stock brokers, etc. A millionaire from Wall Street came down to advise him to ship part of his money to Canada and England. Beyond that I don't know what happened but will find out in due time, I suppose."

It was now a matter of weeks. The speculation in the press, along with the determination of many inside and outside Congress to take immediate action, led Roosevelt to step up his timetable. He believed the Court bill might take a bit of time to pass. After that, the new, liberal justices would have to be selected and confirmed. It was important, therefore, to launch the plan early in the session—both to get it out of the way and to let it take effect as soon as possible. Only then could the administration and Congress pursue meaningful reforms with confidence that the Court, newly constituted, would no longer stand in their way.

Inspecting the calendar, Roosevelt saw a very small window of opportunity. The annual Judiciary Dinner at the White House was scheduled for February 2. It would be embarrassing (whether to himself, the justices, or everyone present, he did not say) to launch the plan before then. Six days later, on February 8, Solicitor General Stanley Reed would appear before the Court to argue the labor act cases. Presenting the plan after that, while the justices deliberated, would, Roosevelt feared, look a lot like a threat. (For some reason, he did not worry that unveiling the plan on the eve of the argument would be seen the same way.) That left three possible weekdays. Of these, Roosevelt chose the third: Friday, February 5, barely two weeks after Inauguration Day.

On Saturday, January 30, Sam Rosenman traveled from New York to Washington for the President's Birthday Ball, an annual benefit for the fight against polio. Missy LeHand had urged Rosenman to arrive early enough to attend a very important lunch meeting that day. About what, she did not say, and Rosenman did not ask. He reached the White House at the same time as a contingent of movie stars, in town for the ball. Initially, Roosevelt had been scheduled to eat lunch with the group, but declined in favor of meeting with his aides. As Rosenman rode the elevator to the second floor, he felt an acute discomfort. He knew that something serious was on the agenda; it was not for nothing that FDR would skip lunch with the likes of Jean Harlow.

The table in the Oval Room was set for five: the president, Rosenman, Cummings, Reed, and Richberg. As the meal proceeded, Rosenman's confusion grew, for the conversation lacked focus; the men chatted about nothing in particular. FDR cracked that the peaceful luncheon reminded him of a British "Q-boat" from the First World War. When a German submarine would surface, the Q-boat, disguised as an ordinary merchant vessel, would appear to surrender—then drop its false hull sidings and open fire. All the guests laughed except Rosenman. At this point he realized he was "the only one of the five still in the dark."

The table was cleared and the doors were closed. Roosevelt moved to sit behind his desk. He glanced sideways at Cummings and told the group he wished to read aloud two documents: a draft message to Congress, and a letter by the attorney general that would be attached. FDR read each in turn, slowly and gravely. "Delay in the administration of justice is the outstanding defect of our federal judicial system," began Cummings's letter. "It has been a cause of concern to practically every one of my predecessors in office. It has exasperated the bench, the bar, the business community and the public. . . . The evil," it continued, "is a growing one." The letter made the case for adding "a sufficient number of judges" to the courts—judges "of a type and age which would warrant us in believing they would vigorously attack their dockets, rather than permit their dockets to overwhelm them." It concluded with statistics establishing that district courts were indeed overburdened.

The draft message to Congress picked up where Cummings's letter left off. It grounded the case for more judges in experience, present need, and the obligation of Congress to maintain "the useful and up-to-date functioning of the federal judiciary." The message and the attached bill—the one on which Gardner had labored—aimed to "invigorate all the courts by the persistent infusion of new blood" and other means, among them the creation of a "proctor" to expedite cases in the lower courts; temporary transfers of judges to the most congested courts; and, for cases involving constitutional questions, direct and immediate appeals to the Supreme Court. As Roosevelt read on, rambling across the landscape of judicial administration, not once did he acknowledge the real issue: the conservative bias of the Supreme Court majority.

Rosenman's initial unease was now a deeper sort of dread. His unhappy task, it became clear, was to polish these documents for public consumption—even though he found it "hard to understand how [FDR] expected to make people believe that he was suddenly interested primarily in delayed justice rather than in ending a tortured interpretation of the Constitution." Rosenman was utterly unconvinced by what he had heard. But he knew the president well enough to understand why it had appealed to him: "the cleverness, the too much cleverness."

Richberg and Reed had the same, sinking feeling. The plan, Richberg warned Roosevelt, had the "appearance of deceptiveness"; he argued for a frank, direct attack on the Court's reactionaries. Reed, meanwhile, warned that it would be difficult to make the case that the justices were behind in their work. As solicitor general, it was his responsibility to track the movement of cases on and off the Supreme Court docket. Only one year earlier, he had given a speech to the New York State Bar

Association—a speech reviewed and approved by the White House—in which he had praised the Court's dramatic "progress towards prompter decision" over the decades. "While the Legal Tender Act was not finally upheld until six years after its passage" in the 1860s, he said, "the Gold Clause Resolution was sustained in less than two years." Income taxes had been in effect for thirty-four years before the Court, in 1895, had struck them down; by contrast, the AAA was overturned after less than three years. An unfortunate decision, perhaps, but at least it had come swiftly. On top of this, Reed and Cummings had just submitted reports to Congress stating that the federal courts, all the way up to the Supreme Court, were free of congestion. The reports praised the Court for refusing to hear many cases. Reed had even argued that the Court should exercise stricter discretion, because, he had written, "a very large majority of the cases . . . do not . . . warrant consideration on the merits"—a point of rare agreement, in recent decades, between liberals like Frankfurter and conservatives like Van Devanter.

The president listened to his advisers' concerns and dismissed them summarily. He had made up his mind. He often took a long time—in this case, years—to reach a decision. But once he had done so, he quickly moved on. FDR's manner now made clear that he had invited these men to the White House to improve his message, not to question it. At 4 p.m., the lunch meeting ended. As the men filed out, FDR told Rosenman that "the message in its present form leaves me cold" and it needed to be "pepped up." And so the draftsman went straight to the Cabinet Room, where he spread the papers across the long table and worked on the message until evening, when it was time to put on his black tie and gold FDR-SIR (Samuel I. Rosenman) cuff links, a gift from the president, and go downstairs for the birthday dinner and ball.

Rosenman went back to work on the message the next morning, a Sunday, and had a new draft in the president's hands by lunchtime. This one went as far as Rosenman felt he could go toward addressing the real issue: the Court's conservatism. He hoped that by inching closer to the truth of the situation, even if FDR would not address it directly, the message might appear more credible. Rosenman's draft, while maintaining the "crowded dockets" argument, emphasized the infirmities of age and the "natural conservatism" of old men. But this approach had problems of its own. Rosenman's discussion of "mental or physical decrepitude" ran a real risk of insulting not only the old men of the Court but, more dangerously, the old men of the Congress—who would control the fate of the bill.

While Rosenman worked at the White House, Reed and Richberg spent Sunday afternoon at Cummings's house making other changes to the papers. By Tuesday, February 2—the day of the Judiciary Dinner—most of the pieces had settled into place. That afternoon, Roosevelt spent the better part of three hours considering whether the increase in the number of justices should be temporary, as Richberg argued, or permanent, as Cummings insisted. FDR sided with his attorney general. Soon, as the clock approached 7 p.m., the men left to dress hurriedly in white tie and tails for dinner with the justices.

Don Richberg rushed home to change clothes, then rushed back to the White House, arriving late to the reception—a serious breach of protocol. Then, as he whipped off his overcoat in the cloakroom, three studs popped off his shirt. An attendant inserted them with such force that he left big thumbprints on the shirt, before hurrying Richberg and his wife into the East Room, where the Roosevelts and seven Supreme Court justices were already making pleasant conversation.

The work was nearly complete. By the evening of February 3, after almost five hours in conference with the president, all that remained were the finishing touches—statistics and such. When the others had left the room, Roosevelt asked Cummings whether it might be time to let the cabinet and key congressional leaders into the fold. Cummings agreed. He considered it "very important" that the leaders be notified, "so that they would not be caught by surprise and that the whole affair might move off more smoothly." Since FDR intended to launch the Court plan at an 11 a.m. press conference on Friday, Cummings suggested that the leaders be called to a 10 a.m. meeting. This would be their advance notice: one hour. "The President thought this was a good idea," Cummings wrote in his diary.

Meanwhile, Rosenman prepared to take the train back home to New York. Missy LeHand pulled him aside. "The President," she said, "is terribly nervous about this message. I think it would be helpful and comforting to him if you stayed over until the thing is finally . . . put to bed." In almost a decade of working with Roosevelt, Rosenman could not recall a single time when Roosevelt had seemed nervous after making a decision. So Rosenman stayed. It was just as well that he did: at 8:30 p.m., the others returned to the White House and worked on the papers for a few more hours.

On the afternoon of February 4, as the group—minus Reed, who had business to conduct at the Court—went over the final draft. By now, Roosevelt appeared quite confident. He called his press secretary Steve Early into the study, handed him the message, and enjoyed his startled expression. Early had to be told because he needed time to prepare for the inevitable flood of press inquiries. But even at this late hour, Roosevelt could still keep a secret from a senior aide. When he asked Marvin McIntyre, his appointments secretary, to summon cabinet members and congressional leaders to a meeting the next morning on a "confidential matter," he did not tell Mac the reason for the meeting. Neither would he permit the message, letter, and bill to be mimeographed that night, lest a copy somehow find its way into the hands of a White House correspondent. FDR instructed that his staff start the machines at six thirty in the morning. "Unprecedented precautions," Rosenman recalled.

It was the end of the social season at the White House, and on the evening of February 4, FDR was scheduled to attend another East Room reception—this one of 1,200 military leaders, cabinet and departmental officials, labor leaders, reporters, and others. Many of those whom he would see in the morning were gathering downstairs as he read the final draft of his message aloud, one last time, to the circle of confidants that now included James Roosevelt and Steve Early. "All of us," recalled James, "emitted war whoops."

Some of these, though, may have rung hollow. While FDR attended the reception, Betsey Roosevelt, James's wife, held a small dinner for Rosenman, Tom Corcoran and his girlfriend Peggy, Missy LeHand, and another assistant, Grace Tully. They talked about nothing but the Court-packing plan. Corcoran, uncharacteristically grim, kept imagining the reaction of "Old Isaiah," the eighty-year-old Justice Brandeis. "I've got the Boss' O.K.," Corcoran said, "to go down [to the Court] and tell him what's coming. He sure won't like it."

If Franklin Roosevelt shared this worry, not a soul in the East Room could detect it. He was, that night, at his best: kinetic, expansive, evidently unburdened by a care or concern. To a group of several guests, including a reporter or two, he said with delight that "there will be big news tomorrow." When they pleaded to know what the news would be, the president only laughed.

Chapter Seventeen

THE BEGINNING OF THE END OF EVERYTHING

"WHY ARE YOU here?"

Henry Ashurst, chairman of the Senate Judiciary Committee, and Hatton Sumners, his sour-faced, tart-tongued counterpart in the House, had been the first to arrive in the Cabinet Room on the morning of February 5, just before 10 a.m. Each had the same question for the other, and neither had an answer. They stood together on the periphery of the room, waiting for someone to come and tell them what they were there to discuss.

Before long the others filed in: Vice President Garner; Senator Robinson; Speaker Bankhead; Sam Rayburn, the House majority leader; and nearly all the members of the cabinet. At the entrance stood Ross McIntire, the White House physician, stationed like a sentry. James Roosevelt had placed him there as a private joke—on the notion that the news that the president was about to reveal might cause someone to faint, or perhaps have a heart attack.

President Roosevelt wheeled himself into the room in a hurry. He was trailed by a secretary, her arms full of papers—freshly mimeographed—which she distributed up and down the long table. Sitting down, the group glanced at the document, but its cover page revealed nothing of its purpose. Roosevelt greeted them amiably, using first names, and apologized for his haste; in less than half an hour, he told them, the White House press corps would be steps away in the Oval Office, awaiting the same news.

He then revealed the contents of the papers: a plan to reorganize the federal judiciary—a companion, he said, to his proposal to reorganize the executive branch. He explained that he had rejected the idea of a constitutional amendment. In New York, he said, Liberty League types were earnestly insisting that the only way to proceed was the "time-honored American" method of amending the Constitution—even as they collected a large sum of money to block any attempt. Roosevelt said that he had also decided against legislation preventing acts of Congress from being overturned by anything short of a two-thirds or three-quarters majority of the Supreme Court; that approach, he said, was almost surely unconstitutional, and would leave him right where he started.

And so Roosevelt presented his alternative. He spent the better part of an hour reading the documents aloud, interrupting himself here and there to elaborate. He paused at one point to say that he had attached a draft bill—"something into which Henry and Hatton can sink their teeth." Cummings eagerly scanned the group for its reactions. John Nance Garner, he thought, looked troubled: "his face was all screwed up." Ickes, who was also keeping an eye on Garner, believed this was the only time the vice president had ever remained silent at a meeting—which did not bode well. But as Roosevelt continued reading, Garner appeared to relax. At one point he even winked at Cummings—who concluded, with relief, that there was "no doubt about [Garner's] wholehearted support." Joe Robinson was harder to read. As Senate majority leader, he would bear primary responsibility for passing this bill; and as a man whose greatest aspiration was a seat on the Supreme Court, his fate was wrapped up in the success or failure of FDR's plan. Staring at the table, Robinson murmured assent, but his face turned a deep purple.

Speaker William Bankhead maintained a poker face, solemn and inscrutable. Sumners did, too, though he showed some satisfaction when FDR said that the legislation provided full pay for retiring justices; this had long been a goal of Sumners's. Henry Ashurst, meanwhile, appeared to listen intently, sitting straight up in his seat, his head tilted back, his eyes fixed at a point on the ceiling. When FDR finally finished speaking, Ashurst was the only one to utter a word; he said that until now, he had sought an amendment, but that Roosevelt had swayed him and could count on his support.

That was the extent of the discussion. Roosevelt promptly excused himself for the press conference as Joe Robinson, dutifully, rose and followed him into the Oval Office. The other congressional leaders, creasing the documents and slipping them into suit pockets, pushed their way through the crowd of reporters in the hallway and filed wordlessly out of the White House. The attorney general lingered a few moments in the room to savor the congratulations of his cabinet colleagues. All, in his view, were "greatly pleased"—none more than Henry Wallace, who had been "wreathed in smiles" throughout the presentation. "You and the president make a great pair," Wallace said. Frances Perkins told Cummings she had watched him during the meeting, and that he had worn the self-satisfied grin of the cat that had swallowed the canary.

The chieftains of the congressional majority, accompanied by Garner—himself a great force on the Hill—made their way back to the Capitol in a pair of sedans. These men had not been warned, they had not been consulted, and now, it appeared, they were not even being courted; the president expected them to fall right in line. But as the cars pulled out of the White House gates and rounded the Treasury, there were already rumblings of rebellion. "Boys," announced Hatton Sumners, "here's where I cash in my chips."

In the Oval Office, the correspondents were waiting. Nearly two hundred stood in a semicircle around the president's desk. Windows revealed the South Lawn, newly blanketed by snow. FDR entered a few minutes before eleven. He appeared relaxed, even euphoric—a bright and buoyant counterpoint to Joe Robinson, who proceeded glumly to his seat on the edge of the room. Robinson spotted Charley Michelson, a like-minded publicity man from the DNC, and shook his head mournfully.

Roosevelt took his place behind the desk and leaned back in his chair, grinning broadly. He announced that he had a "somewhat important matter" to address—the subject of the text that he held in his hand.

"Copies will be given to you as you go out," the president said. "Don't anybody go out until that time," he added, following the instructions of his press secretary, who feared that reporters might leave early, go to Capitol Hill, and solicit comments from congressmen before anyone had actually seen the presidential message. "We brought our lunches," a newsman said, and the others laughed. "I am glad you did," Roosevelt replied.

He paused, shot expectant glances around the room. Then he laughed. "As you know," he said, "for a long time the constitutionality of laws has been discussed." The reporters broke out in a round of "ah"s and the president grinned. "We have," he said, "come to the very definite conclusion that there is required the same *reorganization*"—he leaned on the word—"of the judiciary as has been recommended to this Congress in the case of the executive branch." He began reading the letter from Cummings. His pace was brisk, his voice tense, even breathless with obvious excitement. He moved quickly through the letter and onward to his message to Congress.

In one deft sentence, Roosevelt identified the need and the precedent for action: "Since the earliest days of the republic," he declared, "the problem of the personnel of the courts has needed the attention of Congress." The legislature, he said, had been adjusting the number and the responsibilities of judges since George Washington's time, when justices were required to "ride circuit"—travel across the country and help lower federal courts dispose of cases. "I might add," Roosevelt said, "that 'riding circuit' in those days meant riding on horseback. It might be called a pre-horse-and-buggy era." This broke up the room. "That," he said with delight, "is not in the message." More laughter.

He then, in some detail, described "overcrowded federal dockets," interminable delays in court trials, and the Supreme Court's "heavy burden." Unable to keep up with its work, the Court, he said, had refused—"without even an explanation"—to hear 85 percent of the cases presented to it by private litigants. "That," he said, "is an amazing statement," one that "brings forward the question of aged or infirm judges—a subject of delicacy and yet one which requires frank discussion." He paused, looked up, and again, to his evident satisfaction, the correspondents broke up in laughter.

Sam Rosenman had carefully crafted that sentence, and now the president played it like a punch line. Roosevelt's presentation—his mock earnestness and ironic asides—made it hard for reporters to take the text of the message, or even the substance of the proposal, at face value. FDR seemed to be letting them in on a grand joke: asking them "to applaud the perfections of his scheme, to note its nicely calculated indirections," recalled Joseph Alsop and Turner Catledge, a pair of political reporters who shared a byline in the *Saturday Evening Post*. "While [it] was obvious he realized historic importance of occasion," Ray Clapper typed in his journal that day, there "was nothing solemn about his handling of it"; Roosevelt, he observed, was eager to "wring . . . laughs out of sideswipes at court, particularly in passages regarding retirement or age." Referring to an 1869 act providing pensions for judges, Roosevelt said it was intended to stop judges from staying in office "to the very edge of the grave." More cackling. "I am talking about 1869," he protested—meaning, not 1937—and this time the laughter was explosive.

Generous pensions, he continued, were at best a "partial solution," for aged judges were sometimes "unable to perceive their own infirmities. 'They seem to be tenacious of the appearance of adequacy,' " he added, quoting "a very important judge . . . you will have to find out who said it. I am not going to tell you." That judge, many reporters knew, was Charles Evans Hughes.

Roosevelt's refusal to name Hughes was, of course, part of the fun; it was also to tweak Cummings, who, while the message was being drafted, had argued strongly against bringing Hughes into it. In a similar vein, Roosevelt had been eager to attribute the core idea of the Court-packing plan to James McReynolds—to the reforms he had proposed as attorney general—but Cummings had talked him out of that, too. What remained in the text was a reference to past "attorneys general." But here, once again, Roosevelt could not contain himself. "I will end the suspense. . . . That was McReynolds," he told the press, prompting the biggest laughs of his entire performance.

Finally, the president turned a shade more serious and made his case for expanding the judiciary.

> Modern complexities call . . . for a constant infusion of new blood in the courts. . . . A lowered mental or physical vigor leads men to avoid

an examination of complicated and changed conditions. Little by little, new facts become blurred through old glasses fitted, as it were, for the needs of another generation; older men, assuming that the scene is the same as it was in the past, cease to explore or inquire into the present or the future. . . .

Life tenure of judges, assured by the Constitution, was designed to place the courts beyond temptations or influences which might impair their judgments: it was not intended to create a static judiciary. A constant and systematic addition of younger blood will vitalize the courts and better equip them to recognize and apply the essential concepts of justice in the light of the needs and facts of an ever-changing world.

Then Roosevelt ran through the highlights of the draft bill—even as he dismissed it, less than credibly, as "simply something for [Sumners and Ashurst] to work on to save them the trouble of trying to put the language together." After a while, when the language became more technical, he grew tired of reading it and quickly wrapped up. He looked out at the correspondents and smiled. "And that," he declared, "is all the news."

"Thank you, Mr. President," said someone in the front row. "For background," a reporter jumped in, "is this intended to take care of cases where the appointee has lost mental capacity to resign?"

This, like so much that had preceded it, was intended—and received—as a joke. But the president had had his fill. "That is all," he said curtly; he would take no questions. He told the correspondents they had enough material for one day—and if they stuck around much longer, they were sure to get scooped. The men rushed to the doorways of the Oval Office, shoving each other in a scramble for copies of the letter, message, and bill, while Franklin Roosevelt sat in his wheelchair, coolly observing the chaos he had created.

The last time Tom Corcoran had, in his words, "crashed the sacred robing room" of the Supreme Court, it was on Black Monday, at the invitation of Justice Brandeis, who had a message to deliver to the president: he had been "living in a fool's paradise." This time, on the morning of

February 5, Corcoran visited the Court at his own initiative—and with FDR's approval—to give Brandeis a bit of advance warning about the Court-packing bill. Corcoran hoped this small kindness would "soften the blow." Roosevelt had considered calling Brandeis himself, but did not want to "get into an argument."

Corcoran caught a cab outside the Treasury Building. This was a minor subterfuge: FDR had rejected Corcoran's idea of taking an official White House car, lest it attract attention before the bill had been delivered to Congress. Arriving at the Court, Corcoran entered the robing room to scowls of disapproval from Hughes and McReynolds; oral arguments were only five minutes away, and the justices did not welcome the intrusion. Brandeis appeared startled. While the others headed to the courtroom, Brandeis stayed behind for a moment, gesturing for Corcoran to join him down the hall.

The president has sent me, Corcoran said. He handed Brandeis a press release. If there had been any way to exclude you from the plan, Corcoran continued, the president would have done so; no offense was intended. Brandeis scrutinized the release, was silent for a moment, then looked up. He asked Corcoran to thank the president for the courtesy. But "tell your president," Brandeis said gravely, "he has made a great mistake. All he had to do was wait a little while. I'm sorry for him." Corcoran wondered what Brandeis meant by "wait," but lacked the nerve to ask. With that, Brandeis shook the young man's hand and passed through the red velvet curtain.

In the courtroom, a crowd had gathered. The usual contingent of lawyers was augmented by gawkers and gate-crashers, "thronging to the building in large numbers," as a Supreme Court clerk recalled. The news was out, despite Roosevelt's careful stage-managing of the press corps. Much of the public now knew what the justices (Brandeis excepted) did not. So many people wanted a firsthand look at the Nine Old Men—to see whether they would show any strain—that the courtroom had filled quickly, and hundreds more people spilled onto the steps outside.

The justices' reaction, when it came, was muted. Just after noon, a White House messenger delivered a sheaf of mimeographed papers to the Clerk of the Court. As the justices sat on the bench, listening to oral argument, the clerk emerged from behind the curtain and handed the papers to Chief Justice Hughes; then a pageboy distributed copies to the others, all along the length of the bench.

The spectators stirred. The lawyer in the case at hand froze at the rostrum, for it was suddenly clear that not a single justice was listening to a word he was saying. Reporters strained to see whether the justices were reading the message or some other document; it was impossible to tell from their seats in the press section. Brandeis switched on his desk lamp and appeared to read carefully, wearing a faint smile and occasionally scratching his ear. Cardozo scanned the document, then put it down. Sutherland and Stone appeared to read the whole thing. Hughes, looking up, asked the poor lawyer a question, then went back to reading. He whispered something to Van Devanter, who gave a grim smile. Roberts stroked his chin, flipping pages quickly and pausing, at one point, to scrutinize a passage. He exchanged looks with Butler, and the two men chuckled.

After the oral argument, McReynolds returned to his apartment, which also served as his chambers. His clerk, John Knox, had been there all day. McReynolds made no mention of the Court-packing plan as they worked, mostly in silence, through the afternoon; Knox did not learn of the proposal until he saw the evening newspapers. The papers carried no comment from the justices, of course, but did quote unnamed Supreme Court "attachés," who said, brusquely, that the Court was up to date with its work.

Across the street from the Court, in the Capitol Building, members of Congress filtered onto the House floor and saw that microphones were hastily being set up: the networks were about to broadcast something from the floor to the nation. But what? The chamber filled quickly.

A few minutes after noon, the Clerk of the House read aloud the president's message on the judiciary. Only one month earlier, in his annual message, Roosevelt had stood in this same chamber and vowed to find "means . . . to adapt our legal forms and our judicial interpretation" to modern realities. It was the biggest line of the speech. But now, as the means of reform were revealed, no cheering was heard. News of the plan, observed *The Washington Post*, "burst like a bombshell" in a Congress already shell-shocked by FDR's proposal to reorganize the executive branch. The Court plan was met with "anguish and acclamation . . . , dividing unprepared members into cliques of the faithful, the doubtful and the outspokenly opposed." In the cloakrooms of both houses, they clustered in small groups, anxiously debating what to think, say, and do. For all their prior discussion of the Court issue, for all their efforts to devise a solution, no one—not even the most ardent supporters of Court reform—had been prepared for this. As he intended, Roosevelt had thrown them all off balance.

Discontent spread instantly. House Republicans, snapping out of their post-election sulk, settled right into talk of "fascist and communist dictatorship," like a needle finding a well-worn groove. Bertrand Snell, the minority leader, saw in the plan "the beginning of the end of everything. . . . The President has Congress groveling at his feet now and he will have complete power when this bill is passed." This was to be expected—as were the objections of conservative Democrats, who, according to the *New York Times*, "gagged" upon hearing the president's message. More surprising, though—and more portentous—was the performance of Vice President Garner, who, as the message was read, stood in the doorway of the cloakroom, holding his nose and making, for all to see, a thumbs down gesture.

Few, however, were incited to open rebellion. Loyalty to FDR was strong, resentment of the Court was running high, and political timidity, never in short supply on Capitol Hill, was seen in abundance. Not many Democrats were prepared to defy a popular president absent a clear command from their constituents—and it was simply too early to tell what the American people thought. In the House, only a single Democrat said a word against the bill. In the Senate, most Democrats, whatever their actual beliefs, shuffled into line behind Joe Robinson, who offered a tepid endorsement. "The program . . . ," he said, "is in no sense a violent innovation." Senators gamely—in a few cases enthusiastically—voiced their support. "A splendid solution," chirped Joseph Guffey. Hugo Black cited its "unanswerable . . . logic." South Carolina's James Byrnes went so far as to call the proposal "conservative. I do not know that it goes far enough, but I am in favor of it." Even Garner, after indicating his true feelings in the cloakroom, allowed himself to be photographed smiling, literally, upon the message as he flipped through it with Ashurst and another senator, both smiling as well.

The most curious response came from Senate Republicans. Most refused to react at all. Only a few days before, in a nationwide radio address, William Borah had denounced the idea of interfering with the Court. But now that Roosevelt had revealed his plan, Borah struck an almost comically neutral pose. “This,” he said, “is a very important message. There are some things in it which seem to be all right. There are some that I do not see my way clearly to support.” Refusing to clarify or to comment further, Borah would only state the obvious: “this matter,” he said, “will be thoroughly discussed.”

The bill would be discussed, assuredly at high volume. It might even instigate, as the *Chicago Daily Tribune* predicted (and hoped), “the greatest legislative battle since the League of Nations covenant went down to defeat two decades ago.” But no one was betting against FDR. “There will be real opposition on the Democratic side,” the *New York Times* forecast the next morning, but thought it beyond doubt that the bill “will be moved steadily to passage.” The *Baltimore Sun* agreed: “The President happens to have too much power for the opposition to overcome. . . . Power in terms of patronage, of prestige, and of vast sums of money.”

Initial reports appeared to confirm this. A “tentative survey” that day by the *Wall Street Journal* indicated little opposition in the House and a favorable split in the Senate of 53–43. “The situation looks promising,” agreed Homer Cummings, who spent the afternoon in his office, dodging press calls. He foresaw “some opposition,” as he wrote in his diary, “but not as much as probably might have been expected.” His assistant Joseph Keenan, having spent the day canvassing opinions, “told me that the Senators with whom he talked agreed that it was a remarkable piece of work and they were disposed,” Cummings wrote, “to give me credit for it.”

At the White House, where the president and a few aides crowded into Missy LeHand’s office to hear reactions over the radio, the mood was similarly upbeat. Charles West, FDR’s congressional liaison, returned from the Hill that afternoon with a bullish report. “The high spots,” James Roosevelt recorded in his diary, “seem to be that the conservatives are red in the face and furious. Most of the others think this is a grand method to make constitutional changes when necessary." That night, FDR had dinner in the Oval Room with James, his wife Betsey, and Missy LeHand. They listened for a while to radio commentary on the Court proposal. "Some good—some bad," noted James. After dinner they played a couple of sets of bridge "midst great hilarity. Father certainly can't bid," James observed, "but he can play pretty well."

However futile the fight appeared, the nation's newspapers were not inclined to concede it. The press, by Roosevelt's estimate, had been 85 percent against him in 1936. (The DNC put it closer to 60 percent.) Now the conservative papers charged back into battle—"banners flying and trumpets blowing, hell-bent for salvation," as *The New Yorker* put it a few weeks later. One right-leaning New York newspaper dedicated as many front-page columns to FDR's announcement as it had to the sinking of the *Lusitania* in 1915, while another, according to *The New Yorker*, "just took off all its clothes and stood screaming in the middle of the market place."

But it was not only conservative papers that lined up against the plan. A survey taken at the time showed that more than two thirds of the newspapers that had backed Roosevelt's re election in 1936 now opposed him on the Court bill, and more than half of these did so "vigorously." More ominously, while pro-administration papers supporting the plan had a combined circulation of 3.1 million, pro-administration papers opposing it reached an audience that was four times larger. "I do not recall any single issue affecting the Government that has caused the spilling of so much printer's ink . . . ," Harold Ickes observed. "The President has a first-class fight on his hands."

In the first few days after the launch of the plan—while most members of Congress, waiting for public opinion to declare itself, kept silent—the press took the offensive against the plan on several fronts. Nearly every argument that would ever be made against the plan during the coming months appeared on editorial pages in early February. Attacks came in such a rush that it was hard, at first, to keep up; the White House began tracking press arguments in a series of internal memos. One of the most widespread accusations was that FDR, as the first White House memo put it, had "double-crossed the country" by refusing to discuss his plans during the campaign. "Breach of faith" was the charge. "Mr. Roosevelt never once asked and certainly never received a popular mandate for the course he now proposes," complained *The Washington Post*. "On the contrary, he effectively lulled to sleep" any discussion of Court-packing. A few commentators thought this naive: Arthur Krock of the *New York Times* wrote that voters had certainly understood that Roosevelt planned to—indeed had to—do something about the Court. Hugh Johnson, the former NRA chief and now a columnist, declared, "what we have here is a man doing what he was elected to do": making democracy work. But the prevailing opinion was that Roosevelt had hidden his plans—that he had, as the *Baltimore Sun* alleged, "been disingenuous with the people."

This might not have mattered had Roosevelt, on February 5, gone before the nation, described, in plain language, the dangers of a conservative Court, and presented his plan as the best and most moderate means of reform. Instead, he wrapped his concerns and his goals in a cloak of "sweet reasonableness," as *Time* observed. "Seldom has there been a state paper in this country as ingenious, seemingly plausible and convincing" as the Court message, wrote Franklyn Waltman, Jr., in *The Washington Post*. "Yet for all its suavity and argumentative skill, the message does not conceal that Mr. Roosevelt's real objective is to make the Supreme Court amenable to his will."

Indeed, for all the talk in the papers about the plan's great "cleverness," its rationale had fooled no one. Worse, the whiff of "political trickery," as an internal White House memo called it, persuaded many that Roosevelt was hiding deeper, darker aims. Form followed function: the shape of the scheme, its deceptive design, seemed proof of its evil intent. "It is a hard thing to say of the President of the United States," wrote the *Los Angeles Times*, but "this program cannot be offered in good faith." *The Washington Post*, disputing the claim that court dockets were overcrowded, found it "impossible . . . to escape the conclusion that the President is wittingly or unwittingly distorting facts in an effort to foist this revolutionary change upon Congress." To others, like the *Emporia Gazette*'s William Allen White, Roosevelt's "elaborate stage play" was worse than dishonest; it was precisely the sort of "trick" being played in Moscow, in Rome, in Berlin. The plan, by this rendering, was not simply a con; it was a putsch.

"This is a bloodless coup d'état," cried Walter Lippmann in a column titled "The Seizure of the Court." "No issue so great or so deep has been raised in America since secession." At issue, according to Lippmann, was whether one man "shall by indirection become the master of all three branches of the government and of the fundamental law as well." This—dictatorship—was the most common charge. Editors and columnists likened FDR to the unholy trinity of Hitler, Mussolini, and Stalin. With tyranny on the rise in Europe, warned William Allen White, "this court message . . . seems strangely like the first looming American symptom of danger. Surely Mr. Roosevelt's mandate was to function as the President, not as *Der Fuehrer*." (Adding force to the argument, the Nazi press hailed the Court-packing plan, portraying Roosevelt, the Associated Press reported, "as a champion of vigorous leadership against 'outworn' methods of government." According to an Italian official, *Il Duce*, too, cheered America's "trend toward Fascism's idea of strong, central authority.")

The plan, if enacted, "would end the American state," pronounced the *New York Herald-Tribune*. The paper provided, for reference, what the White House privately conceded was a "very clever diagrammatic table" drawing parallels among the Mussolini, Hitler, and Roosevelt regimes. Each of the three, explained the *Herald-Tribune*, had taken power during times of distress; each had used social unrest as a pretext to turn the legislature into a rubber stamp. The final item on the Fascist checklist—"courts abolished"—was all that remained to make the analogy complete. Of course, the same apocalyptic charge had been hurled at Roosevelt since the start of his presidency, but now it seemed, at least to some, credible. Not just right-wing papers but also "respectable" ones were filled with premonitions of "one-man rule." Four years into the Roosevelt presidency, it was hard for editors to maintain that FDR wanted supreme power. But it was easy to believe that one of his successors might; and Roosevelt, it was said, had opened the door. The next president might even be "the creature of a Ku Klux Klan party," observed the *Chicago Daily Tribune*, "with all the fanatical belief in racial and religious intolerance which goes with it."

But how was this supreme power to be exercised? How was the Court to be controlled, its decisions predetermined? Cartoonists portrayed the Court as "another rubber stamp" within Roosevelt's reach, right next to one labeled "Congress." H. L. Mencken wrote that if the plan passed, "the court will become as ductile as a gob of chewing gum, changing shape from day to day and even from hour to hour as this or that wizard edges his way to the President's ear." William Mitchell, attorney general under Hoover, charged that anyone willing to accept a Supreme Court seat under these circumstances would "know they must listen to their master's voice." And if, in the end, Roosevelt's justices failed to obey him, he would simply pack the Court again—and again, and again—until, "in time," as the White House memo put it, mocking the notion, "all our children will be drafted to serve as justices."

This criticism assumed that Roosevelt had some means of influencing "his" justices after appointing them—or that even without White House pressure, they would remain reflexively loyal. Of course, after going to the trouble of passing a Court-packing bill, FDR was not going to be cavalier about selecting new justices. He would nominate reliable liberals. At the same time, what he expected in a justice was not fealty, but a basic sympathy with his belief in a living Constitution. This, in Roosevelt's view, was the most he could do to ensure the right kind of decisions. He knew there were no guarantees. Many, perhaps most, of FDR's predecessors had complained—bitterly and with cause—of "betrayal" at the hands of their own appointees. Theodore Roosevelt later regretted selecting Holmes, and Wilson never forgave the advisers who had urged him to name McReynolds. FDR knew that once a man had put on the judicial robes, he could not be constrained or controlled. Moreover, as Irving Brant wrote, it was unlikely that men of the caliber of Holmes, Brandeis, Cardozo, and Stone—Roosevelt's archetypes of great liberal jurists—would, once appointed, sheepishly follow the president's dictates.

Still, most commentators accepted the idea uncritically. One had to search far and wide during those first days of February 1937 to find an editorial page willing to give Roosevelt the benefit of the doubt in this or any respect. There were, of course, a few supporters of the Court-packing plan: the *Philadelphia Record*, for example, exulted that it "lays siege to the citadel of special privilege. . . . The stock market broke on receipt of the President's message yesterday, but the worker in the sweatshop, the farmer on his wasted lands, will not share the ticker's grief. . . . How much longer must an entire Nation be held in legalistic chains welded by five elderly, conservative men for the benefit of vested rights and special interests?" Among the columnists, Ray Clapper did his best—sometimes using arguments supplied by Cummings—to knock down criticisms of the Court bill, a proposal that, Clapper insisted, was "the mildest" of all possibilities. But voices like these were hard to hear amid the shrieking. Whether newspapers had really been 60 or 85 percent (or some other proportion) against Roosevelt in 1936, they were now nearly unanimous in condemning his Court plan. The White House, in its ongoing survey of press reactions, did not even bother to track arguments in favor of the plan, because they were so few in number.

The question of who spoke for the American people, the press or the president, seemingly resolved in November, was now wrenched back open. The public's reaction to the Court-packing plan could not be assessed overnight. Still, in 1937 there was one instant, if incomplete, measure of popular opinion: the telegram. And by that benchmark, Roosevelt's plan was, from the start, in very serious trouble.

Congressional offices quickly found themselves overwhelmed, not only by the volume of correspondence (Henry Ashurst received a thousand telegrams in a single day) but by the intensity of public opposition to the plan. Only the merest handful of telegrams urged Congress to pass the bill. Meanwhile, at the White House, the wires were distressingly quiet. For the past four years, nearly every important action and major announcement had prompted a flood of positive telegrams to the president. The response to the Court-packing message, however, was unusually light. Of the "night letters" the president did receive, some were enthusiastic: a Chicago woman wrote that his "splendid message" showed that "the government is really moving . . . back to the people. If we needed proof, the evening papers have published it in the anguished cries of the lawyers—hirelings of our invisible government—who rend their garments and shout 'dictatorship.' We pray for your success." But to the chagrin of White House aides, the telegrams consisted, by and large, of requests that FDR deliver a fireside chat to better explain the change he was seeking.

When the newspapers hit the stands on the morning of February 6, forecasting the bill's fast track to passage, the prediction already felt out of date. Clearly, now, there was going to be a fight. Not a feeble, pro forma protest as the bill became law—as had often been the case since 1933—but a genuine fight, fueled by ideology and anger, and by fear, on both sides, for the survival of the American system of government.

Chapter Eighteen

THE FIRST WEDGE

"WHAT A GRAND fight it is going to be!" Roosevelt wrote George Creel. But from its very first days, the Court fight, as it quickly became known, did not unfold as Roosevelt had expected. The actors in this national drama stubbornly refused to get on script.

On February 8, three days after FDR's announcement, Steve Early invited Ray Clapper to the White House to talk on background about Roosevelt's strategy. Early confided that for the time being, the president would "[hold] his fire . . . , let opposition blow itself out and then move in." According to Clapper's notes, Early said that Roosevelt "was holding back the whole Cabinet," including Attorney General Cummings, who would "make his blast" whenever the judiciary committee held hearings. Early "said Rvt would not go to country . . . said was bad stuff to go over head of Congress and never saw it win—said it was something to be used only in desperate situation." Clapper typed a note to himself on Scripps-Howard letterhead: "If Rvt does go to country on this, will know he really worried."

At the moment, Roosevelt gave no sign of concern. Still, he was a bit startled by the reaction of Democratic leaders. Speaker Bankhead told a colleague that FDR had kept Congress in the dark "because he knew that hell would break loose." He should have known, at any rate. But it was clear right away that he had failed to anticipate the rage, hurt, humiliation, and betrayal that his Court-packing plan would unleash among his faithful—if often resentful—lieutenants.

They were aggrieved for multiple reasons. First, there was the fact that for months Roosevelt had sat, Sphinxlike, in silence as members of Congress prattled on publicly about their own pet solutions to the Court problem—giving nationwide radio speeches, musing on the record with reporters, lending their names and prestige to groups advocating one approach or another, usually amendment. With a quiet word behind the scenes, a slight hint that his own answer was forthcoming, Roosevelt could have quieted this talk and spared congressional leaders the inevitable embarrassment. Instead, he let them get farther and farther out on a limb. Now any leader whose leverage depended, at least in part, on the perception that he had the ear of the president had been proven a fool. This was especially true of Robinson and Bankhead—"shown up as clear out of step," as Clapper noted in his diary. And as Alsop and Catledge observed, Roosevelt's decision to draft the bill without congressional input made it seem "as though . . . erasure of the merest comma would not be allowed." Finally, to make the indignity complete, Roosevelt clearly expected Democratic leaders to defend Court-packing on the dubious grounds he had provided.

It was no wonder that on February 6, only one day after FDR's press conference, Henry Ashurst saw Congress as "an angry ocean of adverse opinion." That morning, Roosevelt gathered Garner, Robinson, Bankhead, and others to talk strategy and spent much of the meeting explaining why he had hidden his plans from them. "Their feelings," James Roosevelt noted in his diary, "were somewhat hurt at being left out"—an understatement that, coupled with his father's continuing air of unconcern, suggested the White House had a ways to go toward correcting its original offense, and might, in fact, still be compounding it.

Roosevelt's high-handed treatment of congressional leaders showed how fully he had come to take them for granted. He was not unaware of this and neither were they. In a sense he relished it. He took a certain malign pleasure in pushing these workhorses farther and faster than they wanted to go, no matter how they bridled and brayed. "One of the things that I am proud of," the president told an adviser in 1936, "is that I made men like Joe Robinson . . . swallow me hook, line, and sinker."

Franklin Roosevelt on the eve of his second term, January 1937, showing no sign of the urgency he felt. (Courtesy of the D.C. Public Library, *Star* Collection, © *Washington Post*)

Columbia University
in the City of New York

SCHOOL OF LAW

RESULT OF EXAMINATION OF
F. D. Roosevelt

First Year Class	Second Year Class		Third Year Class
Contracts	Admiralty		Corporations
Criminal Law and Procedure	Agency ✓	C	Equity Jurisprudence
Elements of Law	Bailments ✓	B	Evidence
Equity	Bankruptcy		Mortgages
Pleading and Practice	Damages		Partnership
Real Estate and Personal Property	Equity Jurisprudence ✓	B	Pleading and Practice
Torts	Negotiable Paper ✓	D	Real and Personal Property
	Pleading and Practice ✓	C	Suretyship
	Quasi-Contracts ✓	B	New York Trusts
	Real and Personal Property ✓	C+	Wills and Administration
	Sales of Personal Property		American Constitutional Law
	Administrative Law		Conflict of Laws
	Law of Officers		International Law
	Comparative Constitutional Law ✓	P	Municipal Corporations
	Institutes of Roman Law		Modern Civil Law
			Law of Taxation

Note.—A=Excellent; B=Good; C=Fair; D=Poor; F=Failed

Registrar

Portrait of an indifferent law student, 1907. Roosevelt never got his degree, but he did pass the bar. (Franklin D. Roosevelt Library)

The "Nine Old Men" of the Supreme Court, 1932. Standing, left to right: Owen Roberts, Pierce Butler, Harlan Fiske Stone, Benjamin Cardozo. Seated, left to right: Louis Brandeis, Willis Van Devanter, Charles Evans Hughes, James McReynolds, George Sutherland. (Harris & Ewing, Collection of the Supreme Court of the United States)

Chief Justice Charles Evans Hughes. To many observers, no man had ever looked, sounded, or acted more like God Almighty. (Library of Congress)

Justice James McReynolds, the most strident of the "Four Horsemen," so despised Roosevelt that he vowed "never [to] resign as long as that crippled son-of-a-bitch is in the White House." (Library of Congress)

Owen Roberts, the swing justice, at his 700-acre Pennsylvania farm. His deciding vote made him a rival to Roosevelt as the most powerful man in America. (AP Images)

Harlan Fiske Stone, whose ferocious dissents turned this Republican into a hero of New Dealers. (Harris & Ewing, Collection of the Supreme Court of the United States)

Attorney General Homer Cummings, mastermind of the Court-packing plan. To Cummings, the cleverness of his approach was proof of its perfection. (AP Images)

Felix Frankfurter, the renowned Harvard law professor, warned Roosevelt in May 1935 that "a general attack on the Court," while justified, would play into his opponents' hands. (Library of Congress)

Jouett Shouse: defender of the Constitution, scourge of Franklin Roosevelt, president of the Liberty League. The League's "vigilante" lawyers waged war on the New Deal in the courtrooms. (AP Images)

Harold Ickes, the Secretary of the Interior, told FDR in January 1936 that if he curtailed the Court's power, he "would go down [in] history as one of the great Presidents." (Library of Congress)

A crowd gathers in the Supreme Court building, 1937. On decision days, spectators arrived at dawn, forming long, snaking lines. (Library of Congress)

Roosevelt and Hughes, at center, face off beneath the driving rain at FDR's second inaugural ceremony, January 20, 1937. (Library of Congress)

Hatton Sumners and Henry Ashurst, chairmen of the House and Senate Judiciary Committees, respectively, leave the White House after meeting with FDR about the Court plan, February 8, 1937. Neither man had been consulted in advance by Roosevelt; neither man would help him now. (Library of Congress)

Senator Burton Wheeler, Democrat of Montana, believed that FDR had "betrayed" liberals in a quest for "one-man power." Wheeler pledged to beat the Court bill and destroy the president. (Library of Congress)

"NEW BLOOD."

A common view of the kind of men whom Roosevelt would appoint as justices. (*St. Louis Post-Dispatch* Collection, Courtesy of the State Historical Society of Missouri, Columbia)

MASS MEETING

THE PRESIDENT'S COURT PLAN

CHICAGO STADIUM

1800 West Madison Street

SATURDAY, APRIL 10TH - 8 P. M.

Speakers { SECRETARY OF THE INTERIOR HAROLD ICKES
U. S. SENATOR ALBEN W. BARKLEY

Admission Free

637

Countless rallies, for and against, took place across the nation. (Library of Congress)

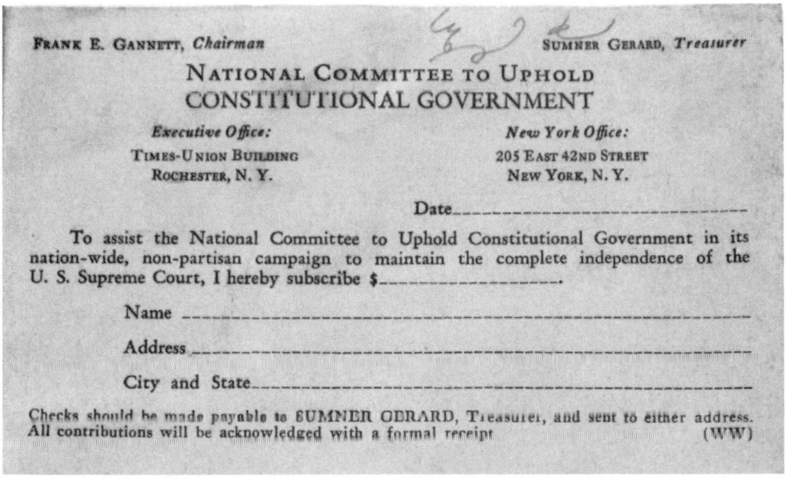

FRANK E. GANNETT, *Chairman* SUMNER GERARD, *Treasurer*

NATIONAL COMMITTEE TO UPHOLD
CONSTITUTIONAL GOVERNMENT

Executive Office:
TIMES-UNION BUILDING
ROCHESTER, N. Y.

New York Office:
205 EAST 42ND STREET
NEW YORK, N. Y.

Date____________________

To assist the National Committee to Uphold Constitutional Government in its nation-wide, non-partisan campaign to maintain the complete independence of the U. S. Supreme Court, I hereby subscribe $______________.

Name ____________________

Address ____________________

City and State ____________________

Checks should be made payable to SUMNER GERARD, Treasurer, and sent to either address. All contributions will be acknowledged with a formal receipt (WW)

Hundreds of groups sprang up overnight to fight the Court plan. Publisher Frank Gannett's National Committee to Uphold Constitutional Government was the biggest. (Library of Congress)

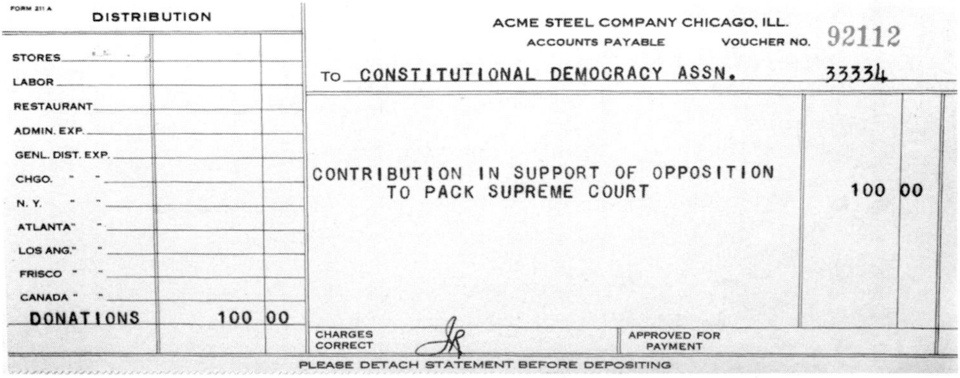

FORM 211 A

DISTRIBUTION

STORES
LABOR
RESTAURANT
ADMIN. EXP.
GENL. DIST. EXP.
CHGO. " "
N. Y. " "
ATLANTA " "
LOS ANG. " "
FRISCO " "
CANADA " "
DONATIONS 100 00

ACME STEEL COMPANY CHICAGO, ILL.
ACCOUNTS PAYABLE VOUCHER NO. 92112

TO CONSTITUTIONAL DEMOCRACY ASSN. 33334

CONTRIBUTION IN SUPPORT OF OPPOSITION
TO PACK SUPREME COURT 100 00

CHARGES CORRECT APPROVED FOR PAYMENT

PLEASE DETACH STATEMENT BEFORE DEPOSITING

Checks like this, large and small, filled the coffers of opposition groups. (Library of Congress)

When the Court bill was introduced, Vice President John Nance Garner stood in the Senate, held his nose, and gestured thumbs down. When the fight got close, he went fishing. (Library of Congress)

In a fireside chat on March 9, 1937, FDR denied that he would appoint "spineless puppets" to the Court—but refused to "yield our constitutional destiny" to the Court's conservatives. (Courtesy of the D.C. Public Library, *Star* Collection, © *Washington Post*)

Joseph Robinson, the Senate majority leader, at the Democratic National Convention, June 24, 1936. Promised a Supreme Court seat by FDR, he threw himself in the fight for a Court-packing bill in which he did not believe. (AP Images)

Roosevelt was elated by the victory of a "remarkable young man"—Lyndon Baines Johnson—who had run for Congress as a champion of Court-packing. Here they shake hands in Galveston, May 11, 1937. Between them is Texas governor James Allred. (Lyndon B. Johnson Library / Photo by Jack Miller)

Senators Burt Wheeler and Edward Burke shake their fists in defiance of FDR, May 21, 1937. (Library of Congress)

Willis Van Devanter on June 1, 1937, his last day on the Supreme Court. His carefully timed retirement dealt a blow to the Court-packing bill. At right is Chief Justice Hughes. (Library of Congress)

In June 1937, his back to the wall, FDR invited all 407 Democrats in Congress to a Chesapeake Bay resort for what one reporter called "mass wooing." Seated at far left is party chairman James Farley; second from right, in the bowtie, is Senator Tom Connally of Texas. (AP Images)

The last word? On September 17, 1937—Constitution Day—FDR told a crowd of 65,000 on the grounds of the Washington Monument that his judiciary bill had caused the Court to overrule itself. (Library of Congress)

"O, Death! O, Change! O, Time!" The caption came from a nineteenth-century poem that continued, "Without you, O the insufferable eyes / Of these poor Might-Have-Beens / These fatuous, ineffectual yesterdays." (Herblock cartoon, 1937, © The Herb Block Foundation)

Robinson, though, was a special case. During the Hundred Days, as Robinson labored to pass programs in which he did not believe, FDR had offered him a quid pro quo—asking Robinson, in effect, to name his price. This, for Robinson, had been easy to do. There was one job he wanted more than anything else. He wanted to become a Supreme Court justice.

He had never been shy about admitting it, this preacher's son who, despite his lack of formal education, had served at age twenty as a judge's apprentice, reading Blackstone's *Commentaries* in the back of a law office in Lonoke, Arkansas, before rushing home to manage the family farm. Ever since, for all his volubility, for all his coarseness and his skill at the tactile arts of horse-trading and browbeating, Robinson had yearned for the quiet dignity of the black robe. Thus Roosevelt's promise had sustained him through the difficult and, at times, humiliating work of carrying—on his "stableboy shoulders," in *Time*'s phrase—the New Deal to passage. "Roosevelt," observed Alsop and Catledge in their *Saturday Evening Post* column, "uses him to push and pull, butt and bludgeon his ideas into legal existence." FDR did not always show Robinson the gratitude he was due. Also, members of the president's inner circle—the intellectuals, at least—looked down their noses at this unrefined example of rural Arkansas, excluding him from policy discussions, disdainful of his ideas though reliant on those sturdy shoulders.

More than once, their condescension had nearly provoked him to rebel. But Robinson prized nothing more than loyalty, and this is what he gave his president. There was also, in the distance—maybe nearer—Roosevelt's pledge, which loomed larger in Robinson's mind as the years passed, as his acts of courage and miracle work multiplied, and as his patience with the role of good soldier was tested, again and again, never more so than by the Court plan that ran counter to his every last political instinct. Even so, bound to FDR by honor, duty, and self-interest, Joe Robinson would lead the charge for the president's goals—one more time, perhaps the last.

Yet he could make no promises that his colleagues would follow. By 1937, FDR and the Democratic leadership were like an old, unhappily married couple, nursing innumerable grievances but unwilling, or unable, to separate. They needed one another—and resented it fiercely. Both sides recognized that Roosevelt had the upper hand in the relationship. Their indignation did not change that fact; and in this instance, as in most others, he did not expect it would change the result.

For Roosevelt, the petulance of the Democrats was far less troubling than the silence of the conservatives. "Liberty League folded up too soon," Clapper noted on February 5. "Shouse will have to revive it." This was Roosevelt's fervent hope. As *Time* observed, "a good resounding denunciation from the Liberty League" would be "a great help to him" in the fight for the Court bill. "The Liberty League and the Du Ponts and that whole crowd" remained, in William Allen White's words, "black beasts in the popular imagination," and he hoped they could be persuaded to keep a low profile. So did Admiral Sumner Kittelle, a leader of the Constitutional Democracy Association. He wrote the group's founder, Admiral Richmond P. Hobson, that wealthy constitutional crusaders should "work quietly by opening their purses and then [go] sail-fishing off Miami" for the duration. The "Save the Constitution" crowd had never shown much capacity for self-control. But their silence in February 1937 suggested they had learned something over the past year: they could be more effective if they remained in the background.

Senate Republicans quickly came to the same conclusion. The day after FDR's message, Oregon's Charles McNary, the shrewd Senate minority leader, met with William Borah, the Idaho progressive, and Arthur Vandenberg of Michigan, a leading conservative, and the three men decided to "let the boys across the aisle do the talking," as McNary put it. After years of issuing shrill attacks on the New Deal, restraint did not come naturally to most Republicans. Through 1936, their strategy had been almost to berate the public, in the manner of the stereotypical American abroad who, discovering that no one around him comprehends English, speaks it loudly and slowly in a belief that this will allow him to be understood. But Republican leaders, too, had learned something in 1936. "If this is beaten," Borah explained to a friend, "it must be beaten by Democratic votes." So Senate Republicans resolved to hang back for a week or more and see how things developed. Vandenberg, who was better suited for a brawl, privately called this "the hardest job of self-control I ever undertook." Still, he held his tongue: "the main thing," he reminded himself, "is to *win*."

Meanwhile John Hamilton, the GOP chairman, pledged to do whatever he could to stifle the party's other putative spokesmen. When members of Alf Landon's staff notified the press that the governor planned to attack the Court-packing plan in an address in New York on February 9, party representatives mobilized. As Landon changed trains in Chicago, he—with his rough draft—was intercepted by Robert McCormick, publisher of the *Daily Tribune*, who convinced him to rewrite his speech. The mission had been arranged by none other than Jouett Shouse. Later, Landon expressed relief that Shouse had stopped him from "sticking my foot in my mouth." As Landon explained to Stanley High, "we want to make it as easy as possible for the Democrats who want to oppose the President."

Not everyone was so easily persuaded. On February 6, Herbert Hoover issued an acerbic statement from his suite at the Waldorf-Astoria, charging FDR with subordinating the Court to his "personal power." That same day, the former president phoned Vandenberg and expressed his eagerness to join the fight. The senator, uncomfortably, implored him to stay out. "Who's trying to muzzle me?" Hoover exploded. "Here," Vandenberg wrote in his diary, "is one of the tragedies of life. Hoover is still 'poison'—(the right or the wrong of it does not matter). . . . What a bitterly unfair contemplation! That an ex-President must efface himself! Yet the need is . . . true." It took a round of calls and other intercessions before Hoover acquiesced—temporarily. He maintained a grudging silence for two weeks. Then, in a speech to the Union League of Chicago, he erupted, decrying the Roosevelt plan as the end of liberty, a fateful step down the path of dictatorship. "As we watch the parade of nations down that suicide road," Hoover said, "every American has cause to be anxious for our republic. . . . Ladies and gentlemen, I offer you a watchword—'Hands off the Supreme Court.'"

Hoover notwithstanding, nearly all senior Republicans maintained what *The Washington Post* called a "strategic silence." The party's self-discipline was unsettling to supporters of the bill. Senator Robert La Follette, Jr., who had left the GOP in 1934 to become a Progressive, sounded the alarm. "Do not be misled," he warned in a radio address. "The same forces which opposed the President in November are opposing him now. For strategic reasons other leaders will doubtless be chosen. . . . Democratic reactionaries will be relied upon to lead the fight."

In the vacuum left by the GOP, dissident Democrats, as if on cue, began to announce themselves against the Court plan. The old Confederacy rumbled with concern. Josiah Bailey of North Carolina was among the first to take the offensive. In 1935, the senator had denounced any attempt to amend or interfere with the Constitution as a "violation of our American holy of holies, the laying of profane hands upon the Ark of the Covenant." Now, to no one's great surprise, he promised to fight the president's plan. "My regret is inexpressible," Bailey intoned. "I have no doubt of my duty in the matter." Neither did Carter Glass, the diminutive, combative, seventy-nine-year-old Virginia senator whom Roosevelt called "the unreconstructed rebel"—not a term of endearment. "Of course I shall oppose it," said Glass, who had opposed most of the New Deal. "I shall oppose it with all the strength that remains to me. But I don't imagine for a moment that it will do any good. Why, if the President asked Congress to commit suicide tomorrow, they'd do it."

They were joined in insurgency by Thomas Connally, a valuable addition. The Texan, who sat on the Judiciary Committee, was a grand orator of the southern school. When he strode onto the Senate floor in a black suit and string tie, silver hair curling over the back of his standup collar, it appeared to Joe Alsop that the chamber had just "gained a visitor from the nineteenth century." Connally was tireless and, in debate, relentless. He was also a fairly faithful New Dealer. Roosevelt had rewarded him for services rendered—directing patronage and federal largess to Texas, and backing him in a tough fight for reelection. (Connally "came crying to the White House and Roosevelt saved him," a White House aide said sourly.) But to Connally, the Court plan was a worrying sign that Roosevelt, in his second term, was forsaking reform for radicalism.

"The issue of packing the Supreme Court . . . ," observed *The Wash-*

ington Post, "may be the first wedge to widen the breach between the old line Democrats of the South and the New Dealers." Southern politicians and FDR had a deeply, mutually ambivalent relationship. Ironically, Roosevelt had run for the party's nomination in 1932 as the candidate of the South and West, against the urban bosses of the northeast, who favored Al Smith. For Roosevelt, this was not merely a marriage of convenience. He had great affection for the South. He had adored Georgia, in particular, since arriving in Warm Springs (then Bullochville) in 1924 to spend hours a day in the pool, working to regain the use of his legs. He loved the countryside and the food—barbecue, turnip greens, even on occasion possum. He liked the politicians, too: their earthiness and vitality, the languid pace of their conversation—all pleasant contrasts to the stiff and aloof northern elites whose company he typically kept.

And the feeling, to a surprising degree, was mutual. During the early days of the Roosevelt administration, southern "common folk"—tenant farmers, millworkers—found that this Hudson Valley patrician shared many of their economic concerns. Through programs like the TVA and AAA, the New Deal had begun a slow-rolling modernization of the region's economy, and inspired intense loyalty across the South. With it came political obeisance. Southern congressmen, wrote a contemptuous northern colleague, "have been trained by subsidies for education and highways, for the boll weevil and fruit fly, and for rural electrification"—all of which had turned them from "strict constructionists," alert to any reform that infringed on states' rights, into "broad constructionists, with a patriotic flair for large expenditures."

But this was too cynical. States' rights remained the central article of the southern political faith, just as it had been in the decades before the Civil War, when the doctrine was invoked by plantation owners and their political guardians as a bulwark against abolition. The New Deal's emphasis on national concerns above state sovereignty and its energetic exercise of federal power clashed with traditional southern sensibilities. So did its evident disdain for old, established social hierarchies. For all their discontentment with the economic order and their public support for the New Deal, most southern politicians viewed Roosevelt's experiments with unease. The rise in federal spending and indebtedness, and, not least, the empowerment of labor, filled them with dread. Businessmen in the South felt singled out by new regulations, particularly by

NRA code agreements. Many of the NRA's fiercest critics were big men in small towns who resented their apparent loss of autonomy and of cheap labor. Furthermore, they detested the fact that the codes' guarantees of wages and hours applied equally to blacks and whites.

The New Deal, and its apparent indifference to race, had earned Roosevelt the gratitude of a growing number of black Americans. "You have fed the poor, clothed the naked . . . ," one man wrote the president. "You have healed broken hearts. . . . We Negroes see things in the Democrat[ic] party that we had never seen before. . . . You are the next 'Moses' that God has sent to lead the country to the promise[d] land."

This aside, to placate his southern base of support, Roosevelt moved only imperceptibly—if at all—on matters of race. Though he favored anti-lynching legislation, he refused to back a federal ban; he feared it would inflame racial tensions and undermine his efforts to seek economic justice for all Americans. When it came to Jim Crow, Roosevelt's policy, simply put, was to look the other way. Even so, senators like Bailey, Connally, and Glass saw the New Deal—and its popularity back home—as a mortal threat to their primacy and the "Southern way of life." What these men perceived, correctly, was that FDR was trying to shake up southern political alignments, so long defined by race, and to bring blacks and whites together in shared support for his programs, his principles, and himself.

Fears of eclipse were not without reason. Southerners still, for the most part, ran Congress. But they had been losing their hold on the Democratic Party since the 1920s. The nomination of Smith in 1928, a major blow, had effectively ended their control of the national ticket; eight years later, at the 1936 convention, the party made it official. Under pressure from the White House, southern Democrats yielded their century-old veto power over the party's presidential nomination, agreeing to repeal a controversial rule that had required candidates to collect two thirds of all delegates rather than a simple majority. Then, that November, Roosevelt's margin of victory was so wide that he would have been re-elected even if the whole of the South had abandoned him. (It did not. He swept the region.)

The Court-packing proposal, following so closely on the heels of these humiliations, inflamed southern concerns. Bailey wrote a friend after the launch of the plan that the president "is determined to get the Negro vote, and I do not have to tell you what *this* means." It meant, in the view of Bailey and others, that the Court, after being packed with Roosevelt appointees, would end segregation. The resulting rush of black voters into the Democratic Party would consign white southerners like themselves to political (and economic and cultural) oblivion and give FDR control, for the first time, of a truly liberal party. All this by the addition of seats to the Supreme Court.

For the old-school Democrats of the deep South, then, the Court fight was a struggle for survival. As the Democratic Party became larger and more diverse, they saw themselves becoming a smaller minority within it—a constituency not only outnumbered by but also at odds with the union members, urban dwellers, immigrants, and, indeed, the blacks who had finally begun to abandon the party of Lincoln and to vote (to the extent that they had access to the ballot) Democratic. Following the landslide of 1936, Roosevelt's dream of a party no longer divided between reform and reaction seemed closer to reality. His talk of realignment sent a very clear message to southern Democrats: change or get out. None of this was lost on the southern leadership of Congress, which chafed increasingly at its ties to Roosevelt, or on the trio of Democratic rebels that now saw the Court fight as the old Confederacy's final stand.

In the days after Roosevelt's launch of the Court plan, another disaffected group asserted its independence: Senate progressives. Roosevelt had expected these men, regardless of party affiliation, to fall in line behind the bill. This was not unreasonable. Progressive senators had been expressing concerns about the judiciary—its power, its membership, its decisions—far longer, in some cases, than Roosevelt had. For decades, Republicans like Hiram Johnson and George Norris and Democrats like Burt Wheeler had been sounding the alarm about judicial supremacy and pressing for curbs on the courts. Johnson, as Theodore Roosevelt's running mate in 1912, had backed his proposal to recall judges and decisions; Wheeler, in 1924, had sought a congressional veto over Court decisions; and Norris had long been a voice for curtailing judicial review. These were radical reforms—considerably more so than expanding the Court. Each would have drastically altered the balance of power among the branches of government. If any senators were especially likely to see Court-packing as moderate, prudent, and justified, it was, therefore, this group of senators.

Yet their suspicion of judicial power had been tempered, in recent years, by an appreciation of the Court's role as a defender of civil liberties. In the 1920s, the Court had begun to incorporate key parts of the Bill of Rights into state law, and a substantial majority of the justices, liberals and conservatives alike, had joined in decisions supporting the freedoms of speech, press, assembly, and religion, and backing the rights of the accused, irrespective of race or ideology. These rulings won praise from progressives, among others. By the mid-1930s, as Robert Jackson recalled, many minority groups had come to believe "that the Court was the only protection they had against arbitrary majorities. . . . Negroes felt that it was their only real protection against the white tyranny. Catholics felt that the Court had protected the parochial schools. Minorities felt a certain security . . . that they didn't think would exist if the Court were too much under the control of the executive or legislative branches." Many progressives, like many minorities, felt that the "political" branches were a greater threat to liberty than an independent judiciary could be.

Progressives' wariness toward executive power per se was reinforced by their distrust of FDR personally. These were, of course, intertwined. The idea of giving any president, particularly Roosevelt, the authority to remake the Supreme Court virtually overnight was abhorrent to Senate progressives. Hiram Johnson was, in this way, typical of the group. His reasons for opposing the plan were at once personal, political, and ideological. A fixture in the Senate, Johnson was a perpetual insurgent, a menace to presidents of both parties. Few, if any, politicians could match the ferocity of Johnson once provoked. His bellicosity increased with age: by 1937, at the age of seventy, he had given up his dreams of either the White House or a Supreme Court seat and had grown ever more embittered toward Franklin Roosevelt.

"We're on the road to Fascism," Johnson wrote his son the day after Roosevelt launched the Court plan. "He will make himself an absolute dictator. . . . I am under no illusions about the puny power one man in opposition wields, but it is better to die fighting a fight like this." This was not mere melodrama; Johnson was sick and weak and truly believed that the exertion might kill him. Still, he seemed prepared to risk it all, for he knew that his power was not puny at all. By his obstinacy, his sheer contentiousness, he exerted a kind of influence over the other progressives—even though, as Alsop observed, Johnson "looked as though he might bite one of his colleagues at any time." Johnson "undoubtedly is in a position to do considerable damage to the president's cause," wrote Harold Ickes, a few days after the senator returned from a long period of recuperation in Florida and condemned the Court-packing plan.

Johnson's defection was followed, in short succession, by that of other Senate progressives—one or two a day during the first week—each damaging in itself and worse in the aggregate. Though they gave the opposition little in terms of sheer numbers, they endowed it with experience, credibility, and diversity—creating the appearance, if not yet the reality, of a broad, bipartisan movement against Court-packing. The alliance between western progressives and southern conservatives (even if it was, like most political unions, a marriage of convenience) had great symbolic power. When George Norris once praised by FDR as "the very perfect gentle knight of American progressive ideals"—declared himself "not in sympathy with the plan," Roosevelt, for all his confidence, was shaken.

A heavier blow fell on February 13. The *New York Times* had seen it coming: "Wheeler Plans Revolt." Not a "break," like the others, but a full-scale "revolt." Indeed, only Wheeler, among the bill's initial opponents, had the skills and stature to instigate a large-scale rebellion. He was, for one thing, comfortable in the company of others, while men like Johnson seemed happiest alone. Wheeler, George Creel observed, "is essentially cooperative. . . . He loves to feel other elbows touching his own." He was "a senator's senator," *Time* magazine judged. Broad-shouldered and lanky, piercing blue eyes behind octagonal spectacles, Wheeler shambled through the Capitol, cigar between his teeth and well-worn Stetson in his hand, eager for conversation and open for business. His geniality masked, just barely, a ruthlessness. Wheeler's smile was boyish but also, *The Nation* noted in 1924, "cool and deadly"—a paradox that captured his appeal.

> He is exigent; but he is attractive. He is attractive perhaps precisely because he is exigent and uncompromising and—it might be said—politically bloodthirsty. There is something soft in many reformers. There is nothing soft in Wheeler. . . . He is humane in his policies. Personally he is hard-boiled, hard-bitten, hard-fisted.

He had to be. Wheeler was a product of the political crucible of Montana. He was not a native: he retained the accent, the broad "a," of Massachusetts, where he was raised, the tenth son of a small-town shoemaker. Wheeler made his way westward in stages, first to law school in Michigan and later to Butte, where, according to legend (his own) he landed after being cleaned out by card sharks on a train bound for the coast. In 1910, he won a seat in the Montana House of Representatives, from which he crusaded against the copper mining companies that dominated the state. During the First World War, as the youngest federal district attorney in America, he was fearless in defending civil liberties. His refusal to prosecute alleged "pro-Germans" for sedition got him run out of Dillon by a mob and made him a liability for Thomas J. Walsh, the U.S. senator who had arranged his appointment. Wheeler resigned to protect Walsh—then joined him in the Senate, where together they led investigations into the Harding administration scandals. This, too, made Wheeler a target. The Justice Department sent agents into Montana to follow him, ransack his office, tap his telephone line, and find some dirt; failing in this, it tried to frame him on corruption charges. When the case went to trial in 1925, the jury acquitted Wheeler after thirteen minutes' deliberation. He was a fighter—and a survivor.

If Wheeler saw enemies all around him, in the shadows, he was right as often as not. But suspicion had a corrosive effect on his character: it curdled him. He was forever in feuds, forever acquiring, nursing, and relishing grudges. And there was no one he resented more than Franklin Roosevelt.

The relationship had gone sour almost from the start. In April 1930, both men addressed a Jefferson Day Dinner in New York. Roosevelt spoke strongly against the concentration of wealth in the United States. Wheeler rose to praise him. "As I look over the field for a general to lead the people to victory under the banner of a reunited, militant progressive party, I cannot help but fasten my attention upon your Governor. The West is looking to Roosevelt to lead the fight and with him I feel sure we can win." Wheeler did it, he said later, "to head off another race by Al Smith." Regardless, Wheeler had now become the first major Democrat to back FDR publicly for president and thus, as the *New York Times* reported, "launched a boom for the governor." Roosevelt, of course, was delighted. But in an ill-considered effort to distance himself from efforts being made on his behalf, he waited more than a month to contact Wheeler—leaving him, all the while, to wonder if he had somehow offended Roosevelt. "I was made very happy by your reference to me," he finally wrote Wheeler in June. By this point, however, seeds of suspicion had been sown.

While distrustful of FDR, Wheeler was nonetheless instrumental in lining up support—most important, that of Huey Long—for his nomination at the Chicago convention in 1932. This was partly a ploy to join the ticket. Wheeler "wanted the vice-presidential nomination desperately," recalled a fund-raiser for Roosevelt. Wheeler would have been a risky choice—many Democrats were still angry that he had left the party, if only briefly, to run as the Progressive nominee for vice president in 1924. Still, Wheeler wanted the job and was angered by Roosevelt's selection of John Nance Garner. "Being passed over in 1932 was what originally soured Wheeler on Roosevelt," the fund-raiser said. "He never was wholeheartedly for him after that."

The indignities mounted. After the election, Wheeler traveled to Warm Springs to meet with the president-elect. "I was not invited . . . I invited myself," Wheeler said later. FDR asked whether Wheeler's political patron, Thomas J. Walsh, might be persuaded to leave the Senate and become attorney general. Both senators had some hesitation about this, fearing that if Walsh resigned, Montana's governor would fill the seat with a nemesis of theirs—a Democratic Party official and mining company lobbyist, J. Bruce Kremer. Still, Wheeler promised to raise the matter with Walsh (who, in the end, accepted the post that he would not live to fill). That day in Warm Springs, Wheeler also voiced some concerns about Roosevelt's legislative agenda. "I told the Governor," Wheeler soon recounted to Cummings, "that when he got through his goddamned palliatives, he would find that they wouldn't work and that unless something was done to check the fall of prices, that the slaughter of our party two years hence would be something terrible. The Governor," Wheeler added cheerfully, "seemed shocked." Wheeler's answer—and obsession—was bimetallism, the coinage of silver. As Cummings recalled, Wheeler boasted that "he was beginning to think well of himself as a prophet"—but also, clearly, as a scourge.

Walsh's death en route to the inauguration in March 1933 was a terrible blow to Wheeler, who for a quarter century had seen him almost as a father. "I am grieved beyond words," Wheeler said, though that grief turned to rage when Homer Cummings took Walsh's place as attorney general. Wheeler later denied that he wanted the job for himself; either way, he deplored Cummings, who was in his view unworthy of the job. Even worse, Cummings was a friend of Bruce Kremer. Though the governor of Montana, John Edward Erickson, appointed himself, not Kremer, to fill the empty Senate seat, Kremer seemed certain to reap undue rewards in terms of patronage and influence—making him a power in both Washington and Helena. It was almost more than Wheeler could bear.

All this before Inauguration Day.

Over the next four years, Wheeler's list of grievances grew long and varied. As early as 1935, he sat in his Senate office and railed to reporters, off the record, about Roosevelt's misdeeds. Behind every reform, every advance—most of which Wheeler supported—he saw corrupt bargaining and creeping conservatism. Wheeler "has lost all faith in FDR," Rex Tugwell observed in 1935. "He complains of wobbling, of his catering to business, of unfriendly acts toward his logical supporters . . . and of general administration failure to strike out boldly for economic reforms." Wheeler charged that Roosevelt had sold out to big business and its champions in Congress—senators like Joe Robinson and Pat Harrison of Mississippi, who, Wheeler warned, "will never be for him and will sooner or later cut his heart out."

What Wheeler resented most of all was that fate had fulfilled his own prediction of 1930: Roosevelt had become the "general" of the progressive forces—balky though they might be. Though senators like Wheeler loathed FDR for, they believed, betraying progressive ideals, they had to be aware that outside the Congress, reform-minded leaders and voters felt quite differently. Even those who saw the New Deal as imperfect—and many did—saw Roosevelt as the vehicle for realizing all the deferred hopes and unfulfilled dreams of the past twenty or thirty years. To Senate progressives, it was galling and exasperating, this hold that the president had on their issues and their followers. "Who does Roosevelt think he is?" Wheeler barked at a White House aide. "He used to be just one of the barons"—like Wheeler himself, or Huey Long. Now, Wheeler said, Roosevelt was "like a king trying to reduce the barons."

Indeed, Roosevelt was cutting Wheeler out of the picture. From time to time the White House relied on Wheeler's parliamentary skill. But mostly Roosevelt refused to consult Wheeler—even on issues that the senator felt passionately about, such as silver. In 1934, when Wheeler was up for reelection, FDR crossed Montana without once mentioning his name—an almost unthinkable affront. These slights were hard for a proud man to take, but for a time Wheeler swallowed them. Having contracted "the presidential virus," as a reporter put it, Wheeler could not risk a break with a popular president of his own party. In 1936—with his eye on 1940—Wheeler hit the trail for FDR, grousing all the way about being underutilized. Though Roosevelt urged his campaign managers to use Wheeler to the full, the complaints kept coming. In August, Wheeler wrote Corcoran that Minnesota would be lost if Roosevelt's lieutenants continued to "throw over their friends. . . . One thing people do not like is ingratitude and that is surely what is being shown those people who went out and fought for them four years ago."

By 1937, Wheeler's sense of duty had been discharged and his patience exhausted. "He was determined to pull Roosevelt down, with a very great feeling," judged a reporter who knew him well. On February 5, Wheeler, on a trip to New York, picked up a newspaper. "FDR," he could see, "had dropped a political bombshell." He withheld comment at first. But he saw his course with perfect clarity. Burton Wheeler was no friend of the Court; packing it, however, he would not abide. It struck him as a sham, another power grab in the guise of reform. "I discovered," Wheeler said later, "that the only way to deal with Roosevelt was to stand up to him." And so he would fight the Court-packing plan. Not only that—he would lead the fight, and make it his own.

Before Wheeler had publicly declared his intentions, Thomas Corcoran asked him to lunch at the Grace Dodge Hotel on Capitol Hill. The two men had worked together closely and had, until recently, been fond of one another. But for some reason—most likely Corcoran's growing closeness to Roosevelt—Corcoran found himself on the long list of those who had "betrayed" Wheeler. The senator made no secret of his contempt for the young man. Now, as they sat together in the Dodge's dimly lit dining room, they bickered, sotto voce, about the Court bill.

Later, each gave a different account of the lunch. Corcoran said that he had begun, "in all friendliness . . . , with a pitch that if the Court plan should go through as proposed I should hope Roosevelt would appoint [Wheeler] one of the liberal new justices and make up for not appointing him attorney general." Wheeler recalled no such offer, only an invitation to "sit in on the naming" of new justices. Either way, he was not buying. After several minutes, according to Corcoran, the senator had worked himself into a rage.

"Do you remember Huey Long?" Wheeler snapped. Yes, Corcoran said, of course I do. Well, Wheeler replied, if it hadn't been for me, Huey wouldn't have backed Roosevelt in 1932; and if it hadn't been for Huey, Roosevelt wouldn't be president. Then, shaking his finger, Wheeler reached his crescendo. "Did you see what Roosevelt did to Huey?"

Corcoran paused. "You don't think Roosevelt had him killed?"

Wheeler did not answer directly. "I've been watching Roosevelt for a long time," he said instead. "We picked him as one of us to be our president. Now after what he did to Huey he is on the way to destroy the rest of us." Then, ominously: "He's made the mistake we've been waiting for for a long time—and this is our chance to cut him down to size."

Corcoran sputtered about the Court, about the evils of "what McReynolds is doing to us all," and implored the senator to "think it over"—before warning that whether Wheeler liked it or not, "something's going to pass." Wheeler—by both accounts—smashed his fist on the table. "No it's not . . . It's not going to pass. And what's more," he shouted, "I'm going to fight it with everything I've got."

Shaken, Corcoran returned to the White House to relay the news. Roosevelt listened and was silent for some time. "Huey," he said finally. "My God—they don't believe—"

"I don't know," said Corcoran. "Burt is a terribly passionate man—that's his strength. . . . But clearly from now on this isn't a legislative fight about the Court; this is a baron's revolt against you and I'm afraid you'll have to fight it that way." He urged the president to "send for Burt right now" and set things right.

The next day, February 13, Charles Michelson, publicity director of the DNC, phoned his old friend Wheeler and asked to see him. Michelson did this on his own initiative, not Roosevelt's. Wheeler stalled a bit. Only after releasing a statement opposing the Court bill did he invite Michelson into his office. Michelson said he had come in search of a way to "avert further hostilities"; he was sure that Wheeler and FDR wanted, in the end, the same thing. He urged Wheeler to "thrash the matter out" over dinner with Roosevelt.

"Charley," Wheeler replied (by his own recollection), "the President ought to save the plate for someone who persuades more easily. He should get some of those weak-kneed boys and go after them because he can't do anything with me." He handed Michelson a copy of the statement. "At best," it read in part, "the president's proposal is a mere stopgap which establishes a dangerous precedent. . . . There is nothing democratic, progressive, or fundamentally sound in the proposal."

No White House meeting followed, no rapprochement. Instead, Wheeler dined with other dissidents at the home of Senator Millard Tydings of Maryland. It was not a dinner so much as a coronation. The long table was lined by about a dozen opponents of the Court bill. Though this was the first time Wheeler had joined the group, it had been meeting regularly since Roosevelt's announcement. It included conservatives from both parties, along with a few moderate Democrats and progressive Republicans. Tom Connally was there, and Josiah Bailey, and Carter Glass, as well as Vandenberg and Borah. They were not natural allies. Yet they had joined together in a spirit of common purpose, and tonight they anointed Burt Wheeler as their leader.

Wheeler stood and gave a short speech. It struck some of the others as a lecture. Still, they were willing to bear it—and, more important, to subject themselves, as Wheeler now insisted they do, to his leadership. "Wheeler is absolutely *essential* to us in this fight," Arthur Vandenberg noted in his diary. "He has taken a courageous stand against the President and is entitled to any co-operation we can give him."

"Burt, we can't lick it, but we'll fight it," said Harry Byrd, a Virginia Democrat, at dinner that night. The sense of noble futility was real—and profound. Given the strength of the president and the size of the Democratic majority, a split, a fissure, in its ranks was not going to stop the bill. It was going to take a schism.

"I would judge that the battle lines were forming and that we would have to hold the hands of a few wavering souls," James Roosevelt noted calmly in his diary on February 8. Hand-holding was the first order of business for the "White House strategy board," of which James was nominal leader. Not yet thirty, James had just been named an assistant to his father over the objections of his mother, who had questioned whether their firstborn son was ready to withstand the pressures of the job.

In certain respects, he was well groomed for it. James had grown up in politics. In 1928, as a junior at Harvard, he had hit the hustings in the evenings, after football practice. The night his father was nominated for governor, James spoke for the Democrats in a radio debate. (Speaking for the GOP: Elizabeth Hughes, daughter of Charles Evans Hughes.) After graduating, James stayed in Cambridge, got married, went into the insurance business, and, while still in his mid-twenties, entertained thoughts of running for governor of Massachusetts. He was a strapping figure, amiable and attractive, and close to his father—none of which endeared the "crown prince," as he was known, to FDR's aides. In January 1937, FDR announced that his son would be joining Steve Early and Marvin McIntyre as a presidential secretary—a position last held by the late Louis Howe.

James filled the vacancy, but not the void. Though FDR intended his son to serve as a substitute for Howe, this was an order that no one could (or would ever) fulfill; certainly not James. He had none of

Howe's shrewdness or stubbornness. Neither was he likely to be heard reprimanding FDR as a "damned fool," as Howe had. James's diaries, littered with pairs of exclamation marks ("!!") and banal observations about men ("I like his attitude") and events (the Court plan, he had predicted, would "cause considerable comment"), betrayed a lack of political sophistication. Yet here he was, expected to "work out strategy for Father" in what was proving, already, to be one of the most ferocious, unpredictable, and consequential fights of the Roosevelt presidency.

The board he now led was an ad hoc creation. It was a small, informal collection of men who, for the most part, had never worked together as a team or hoped for the opportunity. Mutual suspicions ran high. Now, however, they shared two main responsibilities. First was managing "the list": the daily head count of congressional supporters, detractors, and fence-sitters (these, for now, the majority). Board members operated as FDR's agents on the Hill, showing up in the Capitol to issue promises, IOU's, and threats—typically the province of House and Senate leaders, but in this case the president did not think he could count on Robinson and the rest. Instead, he relied on James, Corcoran, Charles West, and Joseph Keenan, the compact, round, red-faced investigator who handled judicial patronage for Cummings. Keenan had an insinuating manner and a frankness that politicians thought reassuring—almost as much as they found Corcoran's exuberance and showy brilliance irritating.

Corcoran, though, was well suited to the board's second task: making the case for the Court plan. This meant supplying the best arguments to the bill's proponents inside and outside Congress, conducting research, drafting speeches, and dispatching speakers to conferences, radio programs, town hall meetings, and the House or Senate floor. Because the bill had caught everyone by surprise, supporters were literally at a loss for words. They spent an anxious week waiting for the White House to send talking points, data, relevant bits of judicial and legislative history. The president himself had a hand in this. He sent a sheaf of papers to Cummings with a note attached: "Don't you think that most of this material, which is excellent, should be put into the hands of the appropriate Senators and Congressmen for use in the coming debate, together with all the other things we suggested for their use? F.D.R." He passed along other fragments for Corcoran to use. Nothing—not even the suggestions of a Maricopa County, Arizona, superior court judge, whose letter made it to the president's desk—was to be overlooked in the search for strong arguments.

Corcoran worked in tandem, as usual, with Ben Cohen. Neither had any real enthusiasm for packing the Court, but Corcoran loved a fight, and Cohen, driven more by a sense of duty, threw himself into the effort. They recruited their friend Milton Katz, formerly a lawyer at the NRA, to help with speeches—even though Katz saw Court-packing as "lunacy" and refused to write a word of praise for the plan. (Instead, he wrote attacks on the Court; this he could stomach.) Joining them was Charley Michelson—"the ghost," he called himself, alluding to his role as the party's ghostwriter. Michelson, in Corcoran's view, was "stiletto-minded," a gimlet-eyed man with "a brilliant pen." A cartoonist portrayed him as a ventriloquist, a yapping "senator" dummy on one knee, a "Cabinet member" on the other, and a bunch of others at his feet. Michelson was not a young man; his long face had a tired look, and some believed his best days were behind him. James Roosevelt had always considered him "quite an aged and incompetent person," but quickly discovered that he was "very active and canny."

Michelson's ability was never really in question. His loyalty was. This was due in part to the company he kept: it was Jouett Shouse, future founder of the Liberty League, who plucked Michelson from the Washington bureau of the *New York World* in 1929 and installed him at party headquarters, where Shouse was director. Their bond, forged in battles against Hoover, remained strong. Even after Shouse's apostasy and Michelson's public ridiculing of the League's lawyer-vigilantes, the two friends were spotted, on occasion, eating lunch in a corner of the Mayflower dining room, leaning forward in quiet conversation, their heads almost touching over the small table.

"As to the New Deal," Michelson later remarked, "somebody has to give me a clearer definition of that term before I know whether or not I am a New Dealer." This was in 1944, more than a decade after Roosevelt took office. Michelson's cool, agnostic outlook almost certainly extended to the Court plan—an impression he did not seem at pains to dispel. Later he denied that his personal views mattered either way. "I was merely a propagandist," he shrugged. This he was, and a good one, which helped explain why he was given a role in the fight rather than be left to his own devices. Steve Early believed Michelson would be dangerous (never more so than now) if he were to fall back into the embrace of Shouse, Al Smith, the du Ponts, and other old compatriots.

The strategy board met in groups of three or four over breakfast or lunch, or huddled in the narrow hallways of the West Wing, reviewing the latest reports from Capitol Hill. Their first recommendation to FDR was that he call members of Congress—waverers and supporters both—to the White House to talk about the plan. Roosevelt liked the idea, and invitations were extended immediately. For all the tension in the air, the sessions were civil. "A very interesting and pleasant talk, open, frank," declared Nevada senator Pat McCarran, a skeptic, after seeing Roosevelt on February 10. Some senators, though, could not contain their anger: at a meeting on February 13, William H. King of Utah spoke so harshly to the president that the others, appalled by this breach of protocol, felt a rush of reflexive loyalty to FDR. Affable as ever, Roosevelt was so conciliatory, so alert to the senators' concerns, that some got the feeling he was open to a compromise. Yet most could see that he was resolute—absolutely determined to pass his bill.

Through most of February, he held one or two of these meetings a day. To *Time*, "it looked almost as if the President meant to conduct a seat-by-seat canvass of the Senate." Soon he began to wonder whether it was worth the effort. While he did not ask his guests to commit themselves to vote for the bill, he expected at least some of them to volunteer. None did. And after dozens of senators and congressmen had come to hear his pitch, not a single opponent switched positions.

Indeed, some sharpened their critiques. These included George Norris, the Nebraska progressive. Though his initial pronouncement on the plan—"I am not in sympathy"—was hardly an endorsement, it did not seem to place his support entirely beyond reach. Norris, after all, was a leading advocate of amending the Constitution; perhaps he might be persuaded to pack the Court instead. Roosevelt called him to the White House—then kept him waiting for an hour. This did much to erase whatever remained of his goodwill. Progressives like Norris had often complained of contemptuous treatment by Marvin McIntyre, FDR's fairly conservative appointments secretary, who tended either to ignore their requests for a meeting with Roosevelt or to make them wait interminably. By 1937, their belief, as Pearson and Allen observed, was that "a camel could get through the eye of a needle more easily than one of them could get past McIntyre." This was a problem, as James Roosevelt could see. "It is things like that which may seem unimportant," he noted in his diary, the day of the Norris meeting, "but often make the difference between the warm-hearted and luke-warm supporter."

Or an ice-cold opponent. Emerging from his meeting with FDR, Norris showed no signs of softening. Quite the opposite, in fact. "I think the President's plan is bad and I won't make any bones about it," he announced that day, vowing to continue his pursuit of fundamental reform by constitutional amendment. If the Court were packed now, Norris added, it would end up being packed again and again "until it's as big as the House of Representatives. Then we'd have to build another marble palace."

The conferences continued—with a shift in tone. "Father outlined new plan of strategy," James recorded on February 14: the president would now see senators "one by one and take down what they suggest as alternate proposals and then show the hopelessness of such proposals." He began each meeting by referring to a well-known British cartoon from the First World War: "Well," says one soldier to another, as shells explode above their foxhole, "if you knows of a better 'ole, go to it." He pressed members of Congress to say whether they really believed that a constitutional amendment—of any kind—could be ratified in anything less than a few years, or even at all. Most of the time, this met with silence. No better 'ole, Roosevelt said.

"Can you tell us what the senators have been telling you about your judiciary reform bill?" Roosevelt was asked at a press conference. "You don't want to be here all day, do you?" he replied with a grin. But there was a steeliness to his manner. *Time* noted that while he had coasted to many big victories in the past, he was clearly now "rolling up his sleeves. . . . Never before had observers seen Franklin Roosevelt go so earnestly to bat for anything. It was an omen that the beginnings of the Supreme Court battle were but a mild foretaste of what is yet to come. . . . It meant also that the outcome of the battle is more uncertain than that of any which the New Deal has yet fought."

• • •

Still, he was confident—and not without cause. "All odds [are] that the President [will] get what he wanted," *Time* predicted in mid-February, and it was hard to find anyone in Washington who disagreed. White House advisers, cabinet members, House and Senate leaders and backbenchers, Capitol Hill reporters—all took it for granted that Roosevelt would prevail. It might take longer than initially expected, he might have to work harder than planned, but the outcome seemed assured. "The President has, of course, the better of the situation," grumbled Hiram Johnson, who wrote his son that "the chances are ten to one" in FDR's favor.

Liberal support appeared to coalesce. "It is becoming clearer," *The Nation* reported, "that the labor, farmer, and progressive sentiment of the country is supporting the proposal." It seemed to be the one thing that various labor factions could agree on. The leadership of the AF of L (after considerable argument) formally endorsed the Court bill on February 17, while the Labor Non-Partisan League, created in 1936 to campaign for FDR, sent letters to every member of Congress expressing the group's expectation that every friend of labor would get behind the plan. ("I am sure we will be asked for the quid pro quo for this support," wrote James Roosevelt in his diary.) And farm groups, with the notable exception of the National Grange, began to line up behind the bill—partly at the incitement of Henry Wallace, who told a conference of farm leaders that if the Court plan passed, the administration would be able to revive the AAA in a slightly modified form. Indeed, the White House took this opportunity to suggest that it might reconstitute much of the original New Deal, including parts of the NRA—the parts that labor unions liked.

"Roosevelt Will Win," declared *The Nation*, adding that soon, the shouting would die down, the bill would pass, and "there will be nothing left to do but see which of the justices decides to be lead-off man on the retirement list." The press was already speculating about the identity of Roosevelt's eventual appointees. Robinson, Ashurst, Sumners, Richberg, and Frankfurter led most lists; also mentioned were Corcoran, Cohen, Rosenman, and Robert Jackson, as well as Senators Black, Byrnes, Harrison, Minton, and Wagner. Friends of Roosevelt began lobbying him on behalf of their own preferred picks. "I respectfully recommend to you Mr. Owen D. Young," wrote Thomas Watson of IBM. Young, he noted, was chairman of the board at General Electric and possessed "a very deep appreciation of the changing conditions in our country."

This was all a bit premature. A Gallup poll taken during the week of February 15 showed an even split in public opinion: 45 percent in favor, 45 percent against, with 10 percent undecided. A week later, opponents had gained a slight advantage. Roosevelt had work to do in building public support. Still, these mixed results could be seen as good news. Even though he had not yet begun to fight—he had not uttered a word publicly in defense of his plan since the day of its unveiling—roughly half the nation was behind him. Also, even among opponents, polls showed overwhelming support for the premise of the Court plan: that something must be done to liberalize the Court. Roosevelt told associates that as people came to understand the Court-packing plan, more and more would back it.

Reports from across America reinforced the president's optimism. Irving Brant wrote Corcoran in mid-February that a *St. Louis Star-Times* poll showed three-to-one support for the plan in that city—far greater than Gallup's numbers for the nation. Why? "I believe it is due to long preparation" of public opinion through the newspaper's editorials critical of the Court, Brant wrote. In other parts of the country, where that preparation had not occurred, it did not seem too late to make a difference. On February 11, the editor of the *Athens Banner-Herald* wrote to Harllee Branch, one of James Farley's chief assistants at the DNC: "I fear that some of our representatives have the feeling that Georgia is so conservative that any change in the court . . . will not meet the approval of their constituents. As things now stand, that may be the true situation, but I am confident that if an educational campaign were conducted in Georgia . . . , public opinion in this state would crystallize in favor of the plan of Mr. Roosevelt." Branch passed the note along to the president.

Moreover, after the first week or two, the tide of angry telegrams appeared to recede. In mid-February, Maury Maverick, a congressman and fervent New Dealer, told FDR that mail from his Texas constituents had at first run two-to-one against the bill, but now that they were learning more about the issue, his mail was running three-to-one in favor. This might have been in response to Maverick's public enthusiasm for the Court bill; but members of Congress who did not support the plan reported a similar shift. Also, a good many of the angriest letters, subjected to scrutiny, were seen to be written on embossed stationery by precisely the sort of people—members of the outraged upper class—that had voted against Roosevelt the previous fall. This did not a movement make. "It may be possible that these letters have their influence," Senator Royal Copeland of New York wrote a member of the DNC, "but I doubt it."

As the *New York Times* observed, many in Congress were maintaining a "prudent silence, waiting to see how the cat of public opinion will jump." They were confused by the polls and the mail and the contradictions between them. For all the fury being expressed on Capitol Hill, publicly and privately, members of the new Congress did not appear ready for rebellion in sufficient numbers. The House majority whip, based on an internal poll, was still forecasting victory by a margin of 100, while in the Senate, men like Black and Minton—"New Deal bitter-enders," as Alsop and Catledge called them—stood by the president. Though Joe Keenan returned from his daily surveys of the Senate a bit battered, he did not signal defeat, only difficulty. In mid-February, his tally showed a third of senators in support of the plan, a third opposed to it, and a third uncommitted. Nearly all of the last group were Democrats—thus likely, in the end, to back FDR. Little wonder, then, that when congressional leaders approached the president about seeking a compromise, they found him unyielding.

Homer Cummings was enjoying himself. "What do you think of recent developments? Some of the dry bones are rattling like cast[a]nets just now," he joked in a letter to Edward Corwin. The attorney general was untroubled that the Court plan had been roundly condemned as "ingenious," in the worst sense of the word. The plan's basic premise was sound, he told Ray Clapper, so what difference did it make if its presentation was a bit too clever? At a press conference on February 10, Cummings shrugged off another of the most distasteful aspects of the plan—its unsubtle suggestion that judges older than seventy-five, including the beloved Brandeis, should retire. "We lose some good judges and some we will hate to see go," Cummings said, "but generally the farewell is not a source of deep regret."

The attorney general felt so assured of the plan's success that he began a not so quiet campaign to take credit for the idea. "I have been very much amused by the gropings of newspaper correspondents to find out how the bill originated. They have now resorted to reckless guessing," he noted in his diary. Cummings was in fact less than amused: in a meeting with James Roosevelt, he "talked at length of the historic value of this proposal and of his satisfaction at his part in its authorship. Made it quite plain that he resented the newspaper stories that Ben Cohen and Tommy Corcoran had anything to do with it!!" Cummings sat down with Ray Clapper to set the record straight, describing in great (if not entirely accurate) detail how he had put the plan together. "Said neither Corcoran nor Cohen in on it at all," Clapper recorded. "Robt Jackson not in on it."

Neither was Felix Frankfurter, though most observers believed that he was. Given his relationship with FDR—his role, in effect, as the president's chief outside counsel—it was almost impossible to believe that he had not been in on it. On February 8, the newspaper columnist Frank R. Kent cited the "general feeling" that Frankfurter was the mastermind of the Court plan.

This presumption filled the professor with dread. For a host of reasons, he wanted nothing to do with the plan, beginning with the fact that he did not believe in it. "There is no magic in the number nine," he had written in a 1934 entry in *The Encyclopedia of the Social Sciences*, "but there are limitations to effective judicial action. . . . Experience is conclusive that to enlarge the size of the Court would be self-defeating," for an increase would make it harder for justices to confer and deliberate effectively. But Frankfurter was not merely a pragmatist. He was also something of a romantic. His righteous anger at many recent decisions reflected his reverence—"love" was not too strong a word—for the Supreme Court as an institution. He retained a certain faith that the Court would, in time, overrule itself, and was dead-set against changes to its structure or function.

But Frankfurter's vehemence had another source: ambition. Of all possible responses to the constitutional crisis, Court-packing was among the most provocative. Clearly it would not behoove Frankfurter, who dreamed of serving on the Court, to associate himself with such an idea. As early as 1935, when the whispering began that the professor was urging FDR to pack the Court, Frankfurter acted quickly to correct the impression. In a sharply worded letter, he rebuked a Philadelphia attorney who had written him asking for comment on the rumors. "Lawyers at least ought to have a sense of responsibility," Frankfurter snapped, "and not indulge in . . . tittle-tattle."

Frankfurter's fears were, it turned out, well grounded. Within two days of the launch of the Court plan, his detractors were using his presumed involvement as a brush with which to tar his reputation and ruin his chances of a Court appointment. On February 7, in a letter to Harold Laski, the prominent British political scientist and a friend of Frankfurter's, Ben Cohen described "a subtly instigated movement over here to create the impression that Felix is too radical to win confirmation and that the President would defeat his own purposes by taking on the fight."

Roosevelt, too, had anticipated this and tried to forestall it. After unveiling the plan, he called Frankfurter in Cambridge and asked for help in passing it—but by this he meant covert assistance, not public support. The president told Frankfurter, in effect, to keep his head down for the duration so that FDR could appoint him to the Court someday without incident. But even this special dispensation left Frankfurter in a state of distress, feeling torn between his loyalty to FDR and his devotion to Brandeis, who was the oldest of the nine old men and therefore, by the cruel and sweeping logic of the president's February 5 message, yet another judge who viewed the world through "blurred glasses."

Still, Frankfurter had no doubt of his duty. His true feelings aside, he left Roosevelt with the impression that he not only approved of the plan but admired its manner of presentation. "You 'shocked' me by the deftness of the general scheme . . . ," he wrote the president on February 7.

> You "shocked" me no less by the dramatic, untarnished secrecy with which you kept [it]. . . . Dramatically and artistically you did "shock" me. But beyond that—well, the momentum of a long series of decisions not defensible in the realm of reason nor justified by settled principles of Constitutional interpretation had convinced me, as they had con-

> vinced you, that means had to be found to save the Constitution from the Court, and the Court from itself. . . . And so it was clear that some major operation was necessary. Any major action to the body politic, no less than to the body physical, involves some shock. But I have, as you know, deep faith in your instinct to make the wise choice.

Later, Frankfurter recalled that he had sat at his desk for an hour before composing those lines—a measure of his psychic torment. Through the spring of 1937, however actively he offered advice, encouragement, language for speeches, and other support to FDR, the Court fight was hard on Frankfurter. His periodic neuritis flared up again; the pain was so acute that he had trouble sleeping or even sitting up. Among his intimates—Ben Cohen, Tom Corcoran, and other "Frankfurterians," as the press called them—he gave vent to his true feelings. David Ginsburg, another protégé and young New Deal official, recalled that "Frankfurter was vociferous on the point that [the Court plan] was very bad and dangerous and . . . that it could not serve Roosevelt's purpose."

But outside this small, protective circle, Frankfurter was tight-lipped—even among friends. Grenville Clark, a prominent lawyer and critic of the Court plan, wrote him demanding to know "why, at a time like this when everyone is seeking light, you of all others should remain silent." Frankfurter replied cryptically that if he were to speak out, he would be seen not as a constitutional scholar but as "the symbol of the Jew, the 'red,' the 'alien.'" To others, he offered varying but always unsatisfying explanations. "I know almost too much about the Supreme Court and its doings . . . to be as free to talk as some people," Frankfurter insisted to a leading New York attorney, with some basis in fact—though he had never been shy about discussing the Court in the past.

For now, he appeared content to let others lead the national conversation. "My formula . . . ," he wrote to the renowned Judge Learned Hand of the U.S. Court of Appeals for the Second Circuit, "is, 'tell the truth about the Court for a good stretch of time and then I don't care what remedy you propose or oppose.'" Frankfurter had, in fact, privately urged FDR to "take the country to school," to educate the American people about the Court's proper role and how conservative justices had overstepped it. But Frankfurter's affectations of disinterest only encouraged more "tittle-tattle." That spring, when he addressed a small gathering of the Harvard Club in New York, he said virtually nothing about the Court fight, baffling his audience. Some left muttering that the professor must be opposed to the plan, and that Roosevelt had bought his silence with the promise of a Supreme Court seat.

Frankfurter was not the only presidential adviser to swallow his doubts. One by one, even those who had voiced doubts in January now fell in line: Tom Corcoran, Donald Richberg, Sam Rosenman. The onset of battle, a rush of loyalty to Roosevelt, and the sight of familiar enemies filled them all with a determination to win. "The court debate now raging in the press is very reminiscent of June and July in the last campaign," Rosenman wrote FDR in mid-February.

> It is the grand opportunity of third and fourth raters to make the first page by yelling at the President. The louder they yell, the bigger the space in the newspaper. . . . I do not know what sentiment you are getting from the millions who are inarticulate so far as newspaper media are concerned. I have a feeling that there is an overwhelming sentiment that this is the only way to break through the wall and get a really working democracy. It was a thrill almost equal to the campaign to have been permitted to watch this thing be born. . . . I know how determined you are in this fight—and how right! Compared to other fights you have won, this is not half so hard as it looks. Cheerio!

The line between determination and self-delusion was hard to tread. As the clash moved from the cloakrooms to the House and Senate floor and to the broader battleground of the nation, there were signs that the White House, or at least some within it, teetered toward a dangerous overconfidence. A diary entry of James Roosevelt's captured this perfectly: "We are . . . going to do some heavy work on Senator Wheeler," he wrote on February 15, "in the hope that we can swing him back in line."

Chapter Nineteen

PUNCH DRUNK

THE CLAMOR WAS unrelenting. From the morning of February 5, a great roar of opinion—for and against—issued forth from the radio, editorial pages, newspaper columns, town halls, church pulpits. Switchboard operators argued between calls. Waitresses passed petitions. In state capitals and in Washington, the mailbags were full and the wires alive with implorings of one kind or another, sent to anyone with a potential say in the matter. A din like this had not been heard since the League of Nations fight of the early 1920s, or perhaps since Reconstruction—commentators were unclear when, if ever, Americans had made this much noise.

In February 1937, it seemed that the only place one could go and not get an earful about the fate of the Supreme Court was the Supreme Court. The Court was, in fact, quieter than ever, and had been since February 5, when a group of reporters strolled into George Sutherland's chambers, found him in conversation with Owen Roberts, and asked the two justices for comment on the Court plan. Affably, they declined. After that, newsmen had been barred from that part of the building, and all one could hear, in its long corridors, was the muted tapping of typewriters and the click and the squeak of shoe heels on marble. The justices, reported the press, had gone into "deeper seclusion than ever."

But not entirely. On the evening of February 6, Henry Wallace held a small dinner party in honor of Chief Justice Hughes and Justice Butler. Daisy Harriman, the socialite, social reformer, and Democratic Party leader, was surprised at how smoothly it went—how buoyant everyone appeared. Still, she thought that Hughes, at times, had a worried look; she wondered if the merriment was perhaps a bit forced. Butler, though, seemed wholly at ease. He talked with Harriman at length, drifting, after a while, onto the subject of age. He said he used to think seventy was old—but not any more. Then he grinned.

The public face of the Court remained inscrutable. On Monday, February 8, the justices heard their first oral argument since the launch of the plan. On the ride to the building that day, McReynolds's clerk, John Knox, made the mistake of mentioning the president's plan to McReynolds, who made clear he did not want to discuss it. He stared out the window in silence, his eyes fixed on the traffic. Knox, pretending to notice a passing car, glanced nervously at the justice. "His facial expression was grim," Knox later wrote, "and he reminded me of a general in the midst of a decisive battle who is sorely puzzled as to just what move to make next."

Outside the courtroom, in a long, snaking line, two hundred spectators stood hoping to catch a glimpse of the justices or perhaps to hear arguments in a pair of major cases—one concerning labor rights, the other free speech. Also, it had been rumored that the justices were ready to announce their decision in a Washington State minimum-wage case, so the room was tense with excitement. The crowd in the chamber stared at the clock above the bench. Then, precisely at the stroke of twelve—nothing happened. A minute passed—an eternity in the Hughes courtroom. The chief was well known for his punctuality, so the audience, conditioned to expect his appearance at noon, took note of the delay. Finally it was not Hughes but Brandeis who appeared. He looked around, and, obviously confused and embarrassed, began to slip back behind the curtain when, suddenly, the gavel cracked and Chief Justice Hughes emerged. Later, correspondents joked that Brandeis was the only justice not afraid to face the public.

Other lapses in protocol followed. Hughes leaned forward in his seat, cleared his throat, and invited applicants to the bar to come forward—something he had never done as the first item on the agenda. On Mondays, the Chief Justice invariably handed down opinions and issued Court orders. Today, he did neither. Ray Clapper, in the press seats, felt like he was watching a sit-down strike; aside from admitting attorneys to the bar, no business was being transacted. "My God," said the press room clerk, "the Court is punch drunk."

To varying degrees, the justices were reeling from the news of Roosevelt's proposal. "'Off the record,' and not for transmission," Cardozo wrote to his cousin, "I am with you altogether in opposition and amazement." To his clerk, Joseph Rauh, he stressed that he opposed the plan—"no judge could do otherwise"—but Cardozo said this plaintively. Even now, he remained devoted to FDR. Brandeis, too, privately expressed dismay. He had long objected to what he called the *Kunststücke*—"clever tricks"—of the New Deal. The plan, again, showed Roosevelt's tendency to be "smart." Also, as Tom Corcoran had anticipated, Brandeis was angered by the impugning of old men. Brandeis told Arthur M. Schlesinger, Sr., the Harvard historian, that conservatism was a product of genes, not years; in fact, he said, as men aged, they tended to become more financially secure, and—freed from the pressures of making a living—more liberal in outlook. On that score, *The New Yorker* agreed:

> The men of eighty whom we know are on the whole a more radical, ripsnorting lot than the men of seventy. They hold life cheaply, and hence are able to entertain generous thoughts about the state. It is in his fifty-to-seventy phase that a man pulls in his ears, lashes down his principles, and gets ready for dirty weather.

Harlan Fiske Stone—the Court's fiercest internal critic—was quick to concede that "the Court has brought it all upon itself," as he wrote his sister. He had long seen this coming. "I know," Felix Frankfurter wrote him, "that the present posture of things cannot give you any satisfaction—any more than Cassandra could have been happy when she was finally vindicated. But there may be inner harmony without elation—the sense of having done one's job fully and having given ample warning of the dangerous consequences of pursuing wrong directions. That feeling of tranquility surely must be yours." Frankfurter guessed wrong. "To see [the Court] become the football of politics fills me with apprehension," Stone confided to a friend. To another, he wrote: "Granting all the faults that are attributed to the Court, it still embodies in its traditions and habits of work, and in the performance of its functions essential to our form of government, values which are inestimable. I fear that in the emotional stress of the moment these may be sacrificed."

Though Stone was still weak from his illness of the previous fall, and taking most of his meals through a straw, he resented the Court plan's picture of enfeebled old men. "While it is couched in terms of speeding up the court and enabling the 'Nine old men' to do their work, no one accepts it at face value," he wrote his son. "The truth is that the Court doesn't need any speeding up and the members of it, young and old, are as able to do their work as any group of judges in the world." Stone predicted a long fight and a close vote. His friends on Capitol Hill told him that if the bill's fate could be decided by a secret ballot, it would be rejected out of hand, but Stone knew that fear of reprisals—and hunger for patronage—might dictate a different result.

In the end, whatever Stone felt about the Court's missteps, he could not agree either with this plan or its fundamental premise—that something had to be done right away about the Court, lest the New Deal collapse and, with it, the entire social and political order. "I do not think the country is likely to go to pot in the next two years whether any of the desired legislation is passed," he wrote his son. Besides, he added, "the attitude of courts change and I think that the country will probably see a change within a reasonable time . . . through the normal change of personnel and the softening of the rigid views which have prevailed, and this long before the country will go to smash through the inability of Mr. Roosevelt to carry out all his pet projects."

And these were the liberals. Warner Gardner, Stone's former clerk and a key contributor to the proposal, had been right to worry about antagonizing Roosevelt's few allies on the Court—though it was unclear whether they would go so far as to retaliate by overturning New Deal programs, as Gardner had feared. Either way, the disaffection of the liberal justices was a kind of collateral damage, an unintended (if not unforeseen) consequence of Roosevelt's battle with the Four Horsemen.

The conservatives reacted in characteristic ways. James McReynolds simply withdrew from the world—from all but his official duties and closest friends. "All of a sudden and without warning," John Knox recalled, "the gates began to close." This had something to do with the mail McReynolds was receiving—hate-filled, threatening mail. "Some people never learn anything—*human* or *real*," read one such postcard, from Chicago. "You old Crab are one of them. If you'd had some heart, some sense, some regard for the rights of the poor the Lord would not now have left you . . . to a well deserved fall. May you *land hard*." Another card, from Denver, had a newspaper photo of McReynolds pasted on the back, with a bandit's mask drawn across his eyes and the word "R E S I G N" printed carefully on his forehead. The caption read "Enemy 'No. One.'"

After the first week or two, Knox stopped giving McReynolds postcards like these. But Knox could do nothing about the letters, whose contents he could not see; McReynolds had denied him permission to open sealed envelopes. This McReynolds did on his own, behind the closed door of his study. Then, every morning, after McReynolds had read the letters, Knox smelled smoke. The justice was burning his mail. This was something he did from time to time, burning personal letters one at a time on a metal tray. If this gave him release, he showed no sign of it now. Some days, after putting the fire out, he grew restless and gathered his things to go for a walk. "Better let me go with you," said his long-serving (and long-suffering) messenger, Harry Parker, on more than one occasion. "Somebody might hit you over the head if you go walking alone!" McReynolds would glower. "I'll go alone—like I always have!" he would say. "If anybody dares hit me, why, why, I'll strike him with this walking stick! I can put up a good fight yet!" Then he would jerk the door open and, for a moment, look back at his messenger and clerk with disdain. "To think," McReynolds once said, before walking out, "that the president would bring us to this!"

McReynolds was agitated—but defiant. "It is definite that McR. is not going to resign voluntarily," Knox wrote his parents on February 21. "This is the inside dope, but don't tell anybody!! He said so himself. However, he seems to think the bill may go through." So did Knox, and it filled him with dread; he feared losing his job. Clerks "are out the moment a Justice is out," Knox informed his parents, and while this was true, he did not seem aware that the bill would not compel any justice to retire. Some, however, might resign in protest—though McReynolds had ruled this out, Roberts told intimates that if the bill passed, he would quit the Court. So clerks followed the debate in Congress with anxiety. "Van Devanter's secretary [clerk] has four children to support," Knox wrote. "I pity him if he loses his job. I am not as bad off as I might be." Still, as an insurance policy, Knox began applying for other jobs. One partner at a Chicago law firm, replying that he had no openings, blamed FDR: "I am very sorry . . . ," he wrote Knox. "The New Deal is not increasing the volume of real work for a lawyer, but it is increasing a lot of the clerical work which must be handled before the various bureaus to the sacrifice of what used to be and what ought to be much more important." One more reason to resent Franklin Roosevelt.

The only other justice to record his initial reaction to the plan was Willis Van Devanter. He greeted the news fatalistically, almost as if he had seen it coming. In December, he had warned an old friend to steel himself against impending "troubles which we cannot prevent," advice that Van Devanter himself appeared to have taken. "When it is not one thing it is another," he shrugged. "The outcome cannot yet be foretold with any certainty. I naturally refrain from discussing the subject." Instead, Van Devanter immersed himself in his consuming passion—the work of his farm in Howard County, Maryland. As the storm raged around him, he wrote long, precise letters on Supreme Court stationery to his son, Isaac, who managed the family property. He instructed Isaac exactly where to install electric fencing and a pair of small troughs ("one for slop and one for water"), specified the proportion of salt water to be mixed with corn fodder (too much salt water, the justice cautioned, would upset the digestive system of most livestock), and solicited advice from fellow farmers ("Is there a swine breeders journal or magazine which you have found helpful?").

None of the justices made any public comment on Roosevelt's plan. This was to be expected, though NBC Radio, ever hopeful, telegraphed Hughes on February 5 with an offer to make its broadcast facilities "available for any member of the Supreme Court to discuss the proposal." A secretary replied that the chief "thanks you but he does not care to take advantage of it." CBS tried as well: Edward R. Murrow, the network's director of talks and education, sought a meeting with Hughes to discuss the possibility of a radio address. Murrow, too, was refused. Then, on February 13, Pathé News distributed its weekly reel to movie theaters around the nation. "Roosevelt's plan to change the Supreme Court has become the greatest public issue since slavery," the narrator began, and then introduced an "exclusive statement on the Supreme Court itself by Chief Justice Hughes." Though the narrator made no mention of the fact, the footage in question was six years old. Hughes, deeply concerned by this misappropriation, called J. Edgar Hoover, head of the Federal Bureau of Investigation. Hoover, applying the powers of persuasion for which he was rapidly becoming known, convinced Pathé to pull the film clip.

The justices' silence continued. "[A]fter Roosevelt launched his amazing attack . . . ," John Knox recalled, "much of the enjoyment of being with the Court vanished. The [justices] went into a chilling retirement from then on." Yet it was an open question whether they could remain mute for long. One senator on the Judiciary Committee declared that when hearings began on the bill, he would call all nine men to testify.

Roosevelt's opponents were, for the most part, realists. They did not expect to defeat the Court bill. They sought instead to weaken, modify, or possibly supplant it—to force the president to accept a compromise. Their first attempt concerned judicial pensions, which, for the justices, had been a source of anxiety ever since 1932, when Congress, in a trivial gesture of fiscal prudence, had slashed the pension of the newly retired Justice Holmes in half. Though it was later restored, the remaining justices never shook the fear that their own pensions "might at any time be cut off," as Stone wrote to Irving Brant on February 6. "The disposition of Congress to tinker with the Judges' retirement allowance," Stone added, had become a "serious drawback to retirements from our Court." Indeed, had it not been for this concern, both Van Devanter and Sutherland would almost certainly have retired at the start of FDR's presidency—and spared the nation the struggle that followed between its branches of government.

Roosevelt later tried to remedy the situation—to put Supreme Court justices on an equal footing with lower court judges, who were permitted by Congress to "retire" rather than "resign" and thus to remain (if only technically) on duty, drawing full paychecks for the rest of their lives. In early 1935, at the administration's prompting, Hatton Sumners of the House Judiciary Committee had introduced a bill guaranteeing a lifetime salary to any justice older than seventy who had served at least ten years on the bench. In a macabre irony, the House rejected the measure on March 6, 1935—a day when the Capitol was filled with florid tributes to Holmes, who had died that morning at the age of ninety-three. Sumners reintroduced the pensions bill in January 1937, seeing it as an incentive for justices to retire and thereby end the crisis. Again, "I expressly approved of the idea," Roosevelt wrote a friend a few weeks later, yet he does not appear to have taken much interest in it. Neither he nor Cummings seem to have considered the effect the retirement bill might have on their own. Neither anticipated that, within days of the Court message, members of Congress would seize on the bill as an alternative to Court-packing and a way out of the whole mess.

On February 9, the *New York Times* described a serious effort underway in the House to "shove through" the Sumners bill "in the somewhat desperate hope" that justices might be persuaded to retire. The next day, a member of the Judiciary Committee went on the radio and helpfully identified McReynolds and Van Devanter as likely candidates. "Of course," the congressman conceded, "their dignity may be deemed considerably ruffled" by the idea of retiring under such circumstances. "Self-respect may also prompt them to refuse." Still, he urged them to do it. If they were willing to step aside, then Congress could either abandon the Roosevelt plan, or, as some suggested, modify it by adding two (rather than six) seats to the bench—giving Roosevelt, all told, four or five appointees.

Having blessed the pensions bill, Roosevelt now eyed it warily. This rush of solicitousness for the financial security of Supreme Court justices was proving a distraction. He resented the pressure "to put his strength behind the [Sumners] bill," as Ashurst urged him. Bankhead, too, pressed Roosevelt to see Sumners "*alone* at as early a moment as possible" to work out a deal. The president chafed at the suggestion. "I do not like to have anybody hold a pistol to my head and demand that I do something," he once said—a general rule that surely held here. Roosevelt was also highly irritated with Sumners, who had just called a press conference and denounced the Court-packing plan as "infamous." Steve Early reported to Roosevelt that Sumners had been "savage in attack" and gave the proposal "hell, specifically and generally." Neither did it help that Sumners, asked by reporters when he intended to introduce the Court-packing bill in his committee, shrugged and said, "We'll let nature take its course."

Sumners "needs to be straightened out," James Roosevelt snapped. On the morning of February 10, FDR met with Sumners in an attempt to do just that. "Didn't make an awful lot of headway," James observed afterward. Regardless, the pensions bill passed the House that day by a vote of 315–75, a margin that failed to obscure the deep divisions among members. The floor debate, in fact, had grown so heated that Speaker Bankhead gaveled it to an abrupt close and changed the subject, ordering a clerk to read aloud a presidential message on the less contentious question of drought relief.

Moments after the passage of the pensions bill, word was carried across First Street to the Supreme Court, where the justices were hearing arguments on the Wagner Act—the most pressing New Deal case on its docket this term. A brief typewritten note was handed from left to right along the bench. Each justice, in turn, put on his glasses, read the note, smiled, and passed it on, until the last of them had seen it. They whispered briefly to one another, then returned to the matter at hand.

To Hiram Johnson, the retirement bill was "a bait and a lure." He wrote his son that "the damned scrubs who were presenting this thing in the hope it would save timid, shrinking souls from having to take a stand, were playing a contemptible game." If it was, indeed, a game of sorts, then it was being played for very high stakes, and Sumners appeared to be winning. Flush with the success of his bill, Sumners paid a visit to James Roosevelt and tried to cut a deal. Radiating a sly self-confidence, he suggested that the bill that had just passed the House now be rushed through the Senate, and that the president then give him six weeks to convince at least two justices to retire. In return, he asked that FDR settle for fewer judges.

Sumners's leverage in this discussion had less to do with the pensions bill than with the fact that he had persuaded a majority of the Judiciary Committee to join him in opposing the Court bill. Forecasts of a wide margin of support in the House would mean nothing if Sumners were able to block the bill in committee. The White House, in that event, would have two alternatives: abandon the bill or dislodge it by force, suspending the rules and forcing its way to the floor. Speaker Bankhead and Sam Rayburn, the majority leader, pleaded with the president not to divide the House in this way; the acrimony, they said, would be so extreme that it would doom Court reform and a whole lot else.

At the time of James Roosevelt's meeting with Sumners, the strategy board was divided over the question of whether the White House should steamroll Sumners—as Corcoran and Keenan believed—or forgo standard procedure and introduce the bill in the Senate rather than the House, as Charlie West and the House leaders wished. The Roosevelts, father and son, were uncertain. But James emerged from his meeting more inclined to avoid Sumners altogether: no deals, no compromises, but no needless provocation. "Two things seem obvious," he wrote in his diary. "(1) I doubt if [Sumners] can deliver" any retirements; and "(2) It wouldn't really cure the situation even if he succeeds, and from a political point of view, it is bad strategy not to have the President put through his own plan. Talked with Steve [Early] who agrees." James added that he was "taking it up with father"—who, as James predicted, permitted the retirement bill to be put through the Senate, but showed no interest in making concessions to Sumners, or anyone else, for that matter. The president decided to bypass the House for now, and come back to it after the Senate had passed the Court bill.

In Congress, the frantic search for a compromise continued. Nearly every faction—the bill's reluctant supporters, its nervous opponents, and those too afraid to take a stand either way—was eager to avert an all-out fight. If the Sumners bill would not accomplish that, then perhaps a constitutional amendment might. All the familiar variations on this theme were revived, whether in earnest or out of cynicism or sheer desperation. Not one of them stood "more than the slightest chance of adoption," in the view of the *New York Times*. Still, "proponents hope that Congress might turn to them if the close division over the President's proposals continues."

"Nothing new," scoffed White House aides. They described the president as equally unimpressed by any of the alternatives being discussed in Congress. Roosevelt, they said, had already considered—and rejected—

all these possibilities. This was true. Having spent two years examining almost every conceivable amendment to the Constitution, Roosevelt was well armed (and inclined) to shoot down each proposal.

And now it seemed he might have to. When Roosevelt launched his Court plan, he had expected liberals to see it as moderate, practical, achievable—and preferable, therefore, to amending the Constitution. Many did view it that way. But two weeks into the fight, the president could see that the plan left some liberals cold, whether because they were concerned about the possible threat it posed to the system of checks and balances, or because they believed that the real problem was not this particular group of justices but judicial power per se. Hence the continuing appeal, on the left, of a constitutional amendment. Some advocates of amendment were willing to pack the Court now and curtail its powers later. Harold Ickes was one of them. He saw Court-packing as "fully justified. . . . But in my opinion, it won't do as a final solution since . . . the disposition of the Court always will be to whittle down all powers except its own." Ickes believed that "in the end, we must have an amendment."

But some on the left—inclined, as a general matter, toward moral or political absolutes—insisted on "an amendment or nothing." In their view the time had come, after decades of judicial arrogance, for a storming of the citadel. To "the more ardent New Dealers," as *The New Republic* explained, Roosevelt's plan was "deeply disappointing." They "had dug in their heels for a great constitutional tug-of-war"—a "glorious" struggle to subdue the Court permanently by limiting or perhaps eliminating judicial review. They had no patience for an approach that they saw as a mere expedient and, worse, as a substitute for real reform. "They are opposing the President's plan," complained Robert H. Jackson, "because they want to get an amendment that will end judicial power." Though they constituted no more than a small minority, even among liberals, their numbers were great enough—and their volume high enough—to provide cover for conservatives whose real agenda was to defeat any kind of judicial reform.

"To hell with their sincerity," snapped the left-leaning columnist Heywood Broun about this group of liberals. "Damn their stupidity." A dismayed Donald Richberg noted the "great glee" with which conservatives greeted the most radical proposals. *The Nation* warned its readers against "playing into the hands of the reactionaries. They will inveigh against 'packing' the court, grow hysterical about the supposed blow to the independence of the judiciary, and insist that the only method of change is through an amendment. Do not be trapped by them. The only thing they value in an amendment is the delay it would involve and their hope finally of being able to beat it."

Roosevelt could not have put it better himself. He came close, however, in an exchange of letters with his friend Charles C. Burlingham, the reform-minded grand old man of the New York bar. Burlingham had been outspoken in favor of an amendment. On February 19, dismayed by the Court plan, Burlingham wrote and urged the president to change course.

Dear Franklin,
I haven't bothered you for quite a spell.

You can't feel more strongly than I about the majority opinions, especially AAA, Minimum Wage and Roberts J.'s silly talk about railroad pensions. *BUT* I don't like your method. I suppose you are in a hurry and this is *your* Congress. It's all very well to refer to previous changes in the size of the Court. Only one involved a desire to affect decisions of the Court—the appointment of Bradley and Strong by President Grant . . . [but] that episode . . . has always been regarded as more or less scandalous and discreditable to Grant.

Let me give you a plan that would work:

1. Pass the retirement bill so that no justice can be treated as scurvily as Holmes was.

2. Pass a joint resolution . . . for an Amendment making retirement at 75 compulsory. This, however, should not apply to the present sitting justices. I am confident that if such a joint resolution is passed, all the justices over 75—Brandeis, Hughes, Van Devanter and McReynolds—would retire without waiting for the adoption of the Amendment itself. . . . It would not be decent for them to hang on after Congress had adopted such a resolution. I told this to Molly Dewson [of the DNC] this morning, and she said "Produce their signatures and I will believe it!"

A few days later, Roosevelt replied:

> I agree with Molly Dewson! Strictly between ourselves there are two difficulties with any amendment method. . . . The first is that no two people agree both on the general method of amendment or on the language of an amendment.

Second, Roosevelt deemed it "next to impossible" to get a two-thirds vote in Congress for any amendment within the next two years.

> Those people in the Nation who are opposed to the modern trend of social and economic legislation realize this and are, therefore, howling their heads off in favor of the amendment process. They are joined by many others who do not know the practical difficulties.

Finally, FDR cautioned that if, somehow, Congress were to pass an amendment,

> You and I know perfectly well that the same forces which are now calling for the amendment process would turn around and fight ratification on the simple ground that they do not like the particular amendment adopted by the Congress. If you were not as scrupulous and ethical as you happen to be, you could make five million dollars as easy as rolling off a log by undertaking a campaign to prevent ratification. . . . Easy money.
>
> Therefore, my good old friend, by the process of reductio ad absurdum, or any other better-sounding name, you must join me in confining ourselves to the legislative method of saving the United States from what promises to be a situation of instability and serious unrest if we do not handle our social and economic problems by constructive action during the next four years. I am not willing to take the gamble and I do not think the Nation is either.

Roosevelt made the same point emphatically in his closed-door sessions with senators. Still, the futility of answering critics one by one—whether by mail or in person—was becoming clearer. It was getting to the point that he could not hold a press conference without someone asking whether he had plans to "go on the air" to defend his proposal. "No," he replied, invariably. Yet he was no longer willing to cede the airwaves to his adversaries. If the opposition would not, as he had hoped, blow itself out, then perhaps, he thought, it could be drowned out.

Chapter Twenty

THE REAL MISCHIEF

THE COUNTEROFFENSIVE BEGAN on February 13, 1937. Roosevelt, the *New York Times* reported, had decided to use his "heaviest artillery"—starting with Senator La Follette—to answer the rising chorus of critics.

The choice of La Follette was intended to show that progressives were sticking with the president. In an NBC radio address drafted by Tom Corcoran, La Follette pointed out that most of those now urging amendment were the same people "who before last November were talking about the sacredness of the Constitution and the sinfulness of amending it." Reviewing, one after another, the main arguments against the Court plan, La Follette sought to turn each on its head. The president, he said, was no dictator; "but when the Court substitutes for the will of the people of this country its own will; when it supplants the prevailing economic theory with its own smug theory of days gone by . . . then it has become a dictator and we have succumbed to a Fascist system of control." As for the charge of "packing" the Court, La Follette retorted that "the Court has been 'packed' for years—'packed' in the interests of Economic Royalists, 'packed' for the benefit of the Liberty Leaguers, 'packed' in the cause of Reaction and Laissez-faire."

Next in line, on February 14, was Homer Cummings—a Sunday night broadcast over all the major networks. Privately, Cummings remained tranquil as ever, confident about the outcome of the fight; yet he had, by this time, become aware that "we are in for quite a job," as he wrote Stanley Reed. He aimed in his speech to stiffen the spines of wavering senators. "Only nine short days," he began, had passed since the launch of the plan; "yet in that brief time, unfriendly voices have filled the air with lamentations and have vexed our ears with insensate clamor." Cummings, by contrast, was the sweet voice of reason, gliding, in his silky way, through the case for packing the Court. But the congestion argument, by now, was badly discredited, and Cummings did little to bolster it with new facts or insights. Not until the end of his speech did he stray more than slightly from what he or Roosevelt had said previously, and this was only to denounce the "virulent attack" on FDR as a revival of the 1936 campaign. The Court bill, Cummings concluded, "meets legitimate need. It is reasonable, it is moderate, it is direct, it is constitutional." Then, having said his piece to his own satisfaction, the author of the plan packed his bags and left for a few weeks' vacation on the golf courses and beaches of Florida.

The barrage continued. Senator Sherman Minton went on the air on February 16, and then, a few days later, Ickes traveled to Austin to address a joint session of the Texas legislature. This was hostile territory. A week earlier, the Texas State Senate had fired one of the first shots in a rebellion that spread from one state capital to the next. When legislators in Austin introduced a resolution attacking the president's proposal, the White House responded with alarm, calling on Governor James Allred and Vice President Garner, a Texan, to shut down the revolt. The resolution, however, passed almost unanimously. Within days, the Maine legislature denounced Court-packing as a "covert attack" on the Constitution, the Minnesota House debated whether it would lead "toward fascism and dictatorship," and critics in Albany declared "war" on the plan. Some states backed FDR; but most defied him—largely out of fear that the New Deal, unchecked by a liberal Court, would spell the end of states' rights.

Enter Ickes, who relished a fight. Escorted by Allred, he strode into the Texas State Capitol with a set of notes in his hand—some of them dictated by Roosevelt himself. Ickes had not advertised the topic of his speech, so legislators did not know what to expect. He began by talking about public works and the oil industry—all in his domain as Interior Secretary. Then, abruptly, he shifted gears, announcing his intention to discuss the Court. Gasps were heard. "I waded right into the constitutional issue with both feet," Ickes later recalled—and, he should have added, with both fists. He insisted Roosevelt had a mandate to do whatever it took to defend the New Deal, charged that the Court had usurped its authority, and called it a shame that "one could not be impeached for being too old." It was a bare-knuckled speech.

That same day, Democratic leaders carried the fight to the floor of the U.S. Senate, where Robinson and Ashurst gave speeches—dreary, perfunctory speeches—in support of the plan. The contrast with Burt Wheeler, who spoke that evening on NBC, could not have been greater. Opening with a cheery "Hello, folks," the leader of the opposition was by turns slashing, scathing, and mocking. From his place in the pulpit, clearly savoring his role as the high priest of "true liberalism," Wheeler dripped condescension and hurled invective. The president, he said, wanted "one-man power"—wanted "to make each and every one of the branches of the government subservient to him." True liberals, Wheeler said, could not abide this. "A liberal cause," he intoned, "was never won by stacking a deck of cards, nor by stuffing a ballot box, nor by packing a court."

Having thus claimed the high ground, Wheeler could not resist making a bitter, personal thrust at the attorney general. He ridiculed Cummings's speech—especially its lament that "unfriendly voices . . . have vexed our ears." "So they vexed the Attorney General," Wheeler scoffed. "What a pity . . . ! What unrealized arrogance this reveals! 'On what hath this, our Caesar, fed, that he hath grown so great!' " Revealing more, perhaps, about his motivation than he might have intended, Wheeler invoked the memory of his beloved Tom Walsh: "If he had been attorney general, the present deplorable controversy would never have occurred. He would never have advised his president to pack the Supreme Court. And . . . ," Wheeler added, if Roosevelt had gone ahead regardless, "he would have had to look for a new attorney general."

The columnists Pearson and Allen, with Wheeler very much in mind, wrote that "behind the opposition of almost every liberal or Democratic Senator fighting Roosevelt on the Supreme Court issue is some hidden factor other than conviction. Conviction, principle, and saving the country are what he [the liberal] talks about. But these high-sounding phrases are camouflage. There is always something underneath." Of course, to be fair, some Democratic senators opposed the Court bill out of conviction. But in Wheeler's case, there was plenty underneath—and his camouflage, clearly, did little to disguise it.

The air war continued without relent—nightly sorties, bombardments of oratory. But this was not, primarily, a war of words. There were other, more direct forms of pressure, and Roosevelt applied them all. Public works, public money, public appointments—this was the currency of doing business on Capitol Hill. It could be offered—or withheld. Either way, it was a powerful inducement, for without federal jobs and dollars to dispense, a senator had little leverage back home. It was therefore entirely possible that the fate of the Supreme Court, the New Deal, and, indeed, the nation would hang, in the end, on the allocation of dams, bridges, post offices, and appointments to the Bureau of Customs. As Postmaster General, James Farley managed the flow of federal patronage. Roosevelt instructed him to hold up judicial and other appointments in states where both senators opposed the plan. In states where the two senators were split on the plan, all patronage would flow to the one who stayed loyal. Arkansas's Joe Robinson demanded patronage as the price of his support for the Court bill, and there seemed little doubt that he would receive it. By contrast, Utah's William H. King, who not only opposed the bill but had lectured Roosevelt about it, was cut off completely. "In view of his attitude on the Court program . . . ," Farley wrote in his diary, "no consideration would be given Senator King's recommendation of anything."

Undecided senators weighed, anxiously, the cost of defiance. Charles O. Andrews, a first-term Democrat from Florida, was chastised by his son for taking a "straddling attitude" on the Court plan. "I do not see," his son wrote, "how you can stand to go against the President. . . . Your being in Washington you cannot realize the absolute necessity of patronage and you have not gotten one little bit and you have got to have it." Prodded by Joe Keenan of the White House strategy board, the state's governor, Fred P. Cone, wired Senator Andrews that 90 percent of Floridians favored the plan and that if Andrews failed to toe the line, "your . . . usefulness to [the] state will be effected [*sic*]."

Pressure could be exerted from various angles. A member of the

Judiciary Committee, William Dieterich of Illinois, was known to be wavering, so Tom Corcoran placed a call to Chicago's powerful Kelly-Nash machine, which turned the necessary screws. Similar requests were made of the Pendergast machine in Kansas City and other Democratic organizations, with similar results. State officials were also enlisted. When Marvel M. Logan, a Democratic senator from Kentucky, refused to back the bill, the state's governor paid a suspiciously well-timed visit to the White House to request flood control money. Logan got the message—and got in line. Roosevelt was even less subtle in dealing with Gerald Nye, a Republican from North Dakota. After newspapers reported that Nye was preparing to speak against the bill, the president summoned him to the White House and talked at length about the federal projects being undertaken in North Dakota. Roosevelt never mentioned the Court plan, but his meaning was clear. "We were one hundred and ten percent dependent on the federal government out there," Nye recalled. He went ahead with his speech regardless—even after a North Dakota farm leader, dispatched by the White House, turned up at his home on a Sunday morning to warn him against it.

In a sense, the Court bill itself—namely, the scores of new judgeships it would create—was "a mass patronage scheme," as one former judge put it. This, some said, was part of its genius. "With from thirty to fifty such jobs to hand out," wrote Frank Kent, a conservative columnist, "cynical Senate observers are convinced the President could put through a bill to make members of that body black their faces every Friday afternoon and wear lilies in their hair or do any other fool thing desired." Senators themselves may have yearned for the jobs. Many looked to the federal bench—the power and quiet majesty conferred by the robe, the seat above the fray and beyond the reach of voters, lobbyists, and other special pleaders—as the natural terminus of a career in public life.

Yet this also made senators protective of the judiciary, its powers and prerogatives. "An attack on the Supreme Court," Rex Tugwell observed, "was felt vicariously by every prospective member of the judiciary," a group that included most members of the Senate. Few wished to serve on a neutered court; and few doubted that this would be the effect of the Court bill. For this and other reasons—among them, Roosevelt's wish for a balanced budget, which would necessarily curtail the number of government projects—the lure of patronage and federal largess was neither as strong nor as enticing as it once had been. "The [Supreme Court] issue was too big," noted Alsop and Catledge; "the senators were too much excited by it to be affected by the petty political bullying and legal bribery which are ordinarily so useful to all administrations."

And Roosevelt was not an especially good bully. Though willing to play the patronage game, there were limits to how far he would go. Veiled threats were one thing; following through another. When Tom Corcoran urged him to "play rough" with Henry Ashurst—the Judiciary Committee chairman whose support for the bill, despite his public statements, was in doubt—Roosevelt refused. Like Nye's North Dakota, Ashurst's home state of Arizona was at that time essentially a piece of federal property; its economy was highly dependent on government subsidies. Tom Corcoran advised Roosevelt to shut off the spigots. "I never quite understood how the President failed . . . to use his power in this instance," Corcoran said later. But Roosevelt had little taste for this brand of politics. He knew that when the Court fight was over, he would need to rely on Ashurst again. "I don't devour them in the end," Roosevelt told a close Senate ally.

Every day, in a hidden corner of the Capitol, the opposition forces met to compare notes, make adjustments in strategy, and get their latest orders from Wheeler. Roosevelt might have the powers of the presidency, but Wheeler and his men had experience, ability, and the significant advantage of fighting a battle on their own terrain. With ruthless, remorseless efficiency, they waged a campaign of what Wheeler called "intensive lobbying." What this meant was that each member of the "steering committee" was assigned to the uncommitted senators he knew best and then stalked them like quarry—in the Capitol, the cloakroom, the Senate Office Building, at cocktail parties, at stag dinners. Committee members made the usual arguments about the Court and Constitution but also—perhaps with greater force—stoked their colleagues' fears of dominance by an all-powerful president and of the next wave of New Deal legislation, more radical than the last, and unchecked by the Court.

At their daily meetings, committee members gave status reports. But the best intelligence came from the other side. Leslie Biffle, an assistant to Joe Robinson, called Wheeler every night to share his knowledge of which senator was leaning which way. Why would Biffle do this? "I never knew for certain," Wheeler later reflected. He wondered whether the majority leader himself had been behind it—perhaps in an attempt to strengthen the opposition and force Roosevelt to compromise. "Robinson," said Wheeler, "had no more stomach for the Court-packing fight than we did." (Wheeler, of course, had plenty of stomach for the fight.)

For Wheeler especially, this was strange, uncharted territory. The old alignments were breaking down and new ones—born of ideology, expediency, ambition, and spite—were taking shape. The emerging picture was a jumble; it did not yet cohere. Very little about it made sense. What to make of a world in which Burt Wheeler's bitterest enemies—Old Guard Republicans, Liberty Leaguers, bankers, corporation lawyers, captains of industry, even Montana copper moguls—were now his greatest enthusiasts? Politics, went the cliché, made strange bedfellows, and rarely stranger than these. But it was the press barons, the great newspaper magnates, whose embrace must truly have made Wheeler squirm. The "lords of the press" stood adamantly, often hysterically opposed to all that Wheeler believed, which had long made him a target of theirs. In the pre–New Deal years, their dailies had denounced him as a "wealth distributor." During Roosevelt's first term, they had derided Wheeler for cowering, along with the rest of the Congress, "in the shadow of the rubber stamp." Now, in the clarifying light of the Court battle, they took a different view. They saw a man of integrity, of independence, of deep commitment to democratic rule. Wheeler, they cheered, was "sav[ing] the country." He might still be an "extremist," as McCormick's *Tribune* warned; but he was, for the moment, their extremist.

For one of these publishers, he was also a partner. This was Frank E. Gannett, one of the lesser lords. While other press barons, most conspicuously William Randolph Hearst, lived an outsized existence, Gannett—despite his taste for flashy suits and shiny shoes—could walk without recognition through the modestly sized cities and small towns his papers served and celebrated. His chain of "clean, wholesome, educational and entertaining newspapers" (so described in their mission statement) was concentrated in New York State, where he owned, among others, the *Knickerbocker Press* in Albany; his flagship, the *Rochester Times-Union*; and what had once been its chief rival, the *Democrat & Chronicle*, a paper that Gannett, in 1886, had tossed onto doorsteps as a ten-year-old newsboy. From his earliest days, the press had been his passion—not merely as a vocation or a business but as an instrument of mass persuasion. At his high school commencement in rural Bolivar, New York, Frank Gannett, Class of '93, stood before his eight classmates and their families and delivered an oration on "The Press and Public Opinion." The text was later lost; but the speech had served notice that Gannett, even at the age of seventeen, saw the power of print to shape, arouse, inflame, and direct public sentiment.

He was an armchair evangelist. He loved a crusade. Prohibition was one. Even after repeal, Gannett, a teetotaler, maintained the ban on liquor advertisements in all his newspapers. Another enduring concern, as his official biographer explained, was the question of "how one may better his lot." Gannett was a particular sort of self-made man—the kind that made it his business to inspire thrift, industry, and enterprise in others. He was, to that end, a purveyor of platitudes, a fount of homilies and maxims ("little strokes fell big oaks"), each uttered with meaning and not a trace of self-consciousness. "Gannett is sincere, humanitarian, a man of good intentions, and one of the most confused persons in public life," observed George Seldes, a progressive journalist.

That jab referred to Gannett's social, economic, and political views, which, in fairness to Gannett, were no more confused than those of any other member of the chamber of commerce. Gannett was hardly the only businessman who started off supporting the New Deal, only to change his mind when the federal government began to regulate his industry. Like most publishers, Gannett bitterly resented the provisions of the NRA's Newspaper Code (loophole-ridden though it was) as well as Roosevelt's belief that the industry's battalions of newsboys constituted child labor. Gannett later cited FDR's "horse-and-buggy" press conference as the event that, as his biographer put it, "severed [his] last frayed strand of hope" in Roosevelt's leadership, but surely the strand had already been broken. By 1936, Gannett's chauffeur described him as "violent against Mr. Roosevelt."

Early that year, Gannett found a new crusade: the nomination of the seventy-year-old Senator William Borah to lead the Republican ticket. "I am very busy . . . promoting your cause," Gannett reported to Borah, in one of a steady stream of letters describing his efforts and offering advice. "Unless you are nominated," Gannett wrote him in the spring of 1936, "Roosevelt will be re-elected, the Supreme Court will be remade and the Constitution will be thrown into the discard." The Constitution was not, however, Gannett's chief concern. In another letter to Borah, Gannett placed the Constitution fifth on his list of priorities—below unemployment, agriculture, free enterprise, and business expansion. "The great mass of people . . . ," the publisher advised, "are not so much concerned about the Constitution and Supreme Court as they are about having jobs and opportunity."

For his efforts, Gannett won a seat on the Borah ticket—for the Ohio primary, in which presidential candidates were required to select a non-binding running mate. In May 1936, Borah lost badly to Robert Taft, eldest son of the former president and Chief Justice and a "favorite son" of Ohio. In a telegram to Borah, Gannett attributed Taft's victory to "powerful organization, plenty of money, and vicious misrepresentation." In June—without success—Borah tried to install Gannett on the Landon ticket, but the nod went to Frank Knox, a rival publisher. "We fought a good fight, did the best we could, and have little reason for remorse . . . ," Gannett wrote Borah after the convention. "I want you to keep up the fight for the principles in which we believe. I want to co-operate with you at all times."

The chance came sooner than either man could have expected. Nine months after the Ohio primary, Roosevelt launched his Court plan. Gannett promptly flew to Washington to consult with Borah. As Gannett remembered (or refashioned) it, the senator pointed his finger at the publisher and said, "With . . . your background, you can inform the people back home of the dangers of this bill. You are especially fitted for this task. . . . Get busy; and get busy fast, or it's all over." Gannett needed no such encouragement. He had already gotten busy. Within a day of Roosevelt's bombshell, Gannett had wired a statement from his winter home in Miami Beach to every newspaper in the United States: the president, he wrote, had "cleverly camouflaged a most amazing and startling proposal for packing the Supreme Court. Do we want to give to this man, or any one man, complete control of these three departments of government . . . ? This proposal . . . ," Gannett concluded gravely, "is a step toward absolutism and complete dictatorial power."

The coming days brought fevered discussions by telephone with New York Republicans, followed by a decision to send, at his own expense, a "test mailing" to 10,000 prominent Americans calling for "immediate, aggressive action—and enough money to carry the cost of awakening public opinion." Checks came in, yielding more than $1,000 a day. Returning to New York, Gannett mailed another 49,000 letters and then, on February 14, announced the formation of the National Committee to Uphold Constitutional Government. Its goal, he said, was to "mobilize and coordinate individual and mass protest against the proposed undermining of an independent judiciary." Gannett spent the next day on Capitol Hill, formalizing what would soon become a productive partnership with Wheeler and the rest of the Senate opposition. Borah aside, Gannett steered clear of Republicans. "We preferred to have the Committee made up of liberals and Democrats," Gannett said later, "so that we would not be charged with having partisan motives." The committee's roster included historians, journalists, clergymen, farm leaders, businessmen, veterans—a fair sampling of "nonpartisan" elites. This, however, was largely for show. Most members, even the Democrats, were fierce critics of the New Deal. And when there was real work to be done, Gannett turned covertly to the Republican National Committee, whose publicity man, William Hard, served as a liaison between Gannett and Wheeler.

Gannett's group settled into a large factory loft on East 42nd Street in Manhattan. Fifteen young women sat at typewriters in the vast, open room, broken up by makeshift cubicles and long pine tables, each of which was stacked with multigraph and photo-offset direct-mail material. This seventh-floor office, such as it was, belonged to another group with a grandiose name: the Committee for the Nation to Rebuild Prices and Purchasing Power, founded by businessmen in 1933 to fight deflation. The two organizations shared more than office space. They had a common lineage and worldview. Gannett was a leading member of the monetary group, as was the strange, furtive figure who occupied a littered desk in the corner of the loft: Edward A. Rumely, a master of mass mail campaigns who now ran the daily operations of Gannett's National Committee.

Dr. Rumely (*Doktor der Medizin*, University of Freiburg, 1906) was ruddy-faced and stocky, outwardly genial, but brooding and domineering. "Emphatic and oily," judged one longtime acquaintance. Rumely was something of a polymath (he had also studied at Oxford and Notre Dame) and, politically, a lapsed Progressive who had drifted rightward. He was also a traitor. In 1920, Rumely had been found guilty of serving as a German agent during the war: using $1.4 million provided secretly by the Kaiser's government, Rumely had purchased the *New York Evening Mail*, turned it into an outlet for pro-German, anti-British propaganda, and covered his tracks in an elaborate, if ultimately unsuccessful fashion. Coolidge later pardoned him. Rumely retreated for a time to his hometown, La Porte, Indiana, where he became a pioneer in the sale of vitamin-enriched foods. During Roosevelt's first term, Rumely reemerged, applying his considerable energies toward pressuring Congress through direct-mail campaigns. He had in mind to inflame the masses. "There is a psychology in cheers and enthusiasm," Rumely once wrote, "which catches up in the maelstrom millions of men who are not sufficiently intelligent to analyze their emotions."

Gannett's triumvirate was completed by Amos Pinchot, a leading New York lawyer who, along with his brother, Gifford, had helped found the Bull Moose Party in 1912. (Gifford later served as governor of Pennsylvania.) Amos Pinchot remained, for the most part, a progressive; what united him with Gannett and Rumely was his contempt for FDR; a deep, mortal fear of the New Deal; and his practice in the art of political pamphleteering. Pinchot and Rumely were unlikely but enthusiastic partners. A man who dined at Pinchot's Park Avenue apartment one evening described the atmosphere as "a three-ring circus, with messengers dashing in to hand notes to Rumely, Rumely dashing off to make mysterious long-distance phone calls, and the general attitude of Hitler's headquarters the night before a purge."

Gannett disliked the term "propaganda" (though with something short of actual loathing). "'Propaganda,'" he once mused, "cannot manufacture sentiment. It can only reveal and release it." This, he said later, was the goal of his committee: "to arouse that already existing sentiment and fear" and "direct" it "upon Washington." This it did, by the ton. During the first month of the Court fight, the Gannett group dropped a half million pieces of printed matter into the U.S. mail—not dropped so much as aimed, for every piece was targeted to the great and the good, the prominent and persuasive, the politically active and financially secure. At its headquarters, the National Committee maintained massive lists and card files bearing the names and addresses of 161,000 lawyers, 121,000 doctors and dentists, 68,000 businessmen, 100,000 Protestant clergymen, 35,000 priests, 3,100 rabbis, many thousands of city and state officeholders, "school men," and others, each categorized and cross-tabulated. Rumely had no interest in expanding these lists because, in his view, they "covered completely the 700,000 individuals who comprise this country's leadership" and shaped the views of the "unthinking" masses. Robert Jackson received a letter. So did Tom Corcoran. "My dear Mr. Corcoran," it read, "we write to you as one who, in 1936, showed concern over the problems of government by making a substantial contribution to either the Democratic or the Republican Party, and who therefore now is keenly interested in the Supreme Court issue."

What these "leadership individuals" received, courtesy of the committee, was essentially a subscription to the most current—and most vicious—polemic produced anywhere in the nation against the Court plan. Gannett's research staff sorted through every available public statement, distilled the strongest stuff, and reprinted, by the hundreds of thousands, newspaper columns; transcripts of speeches by opposition senators; pamphlets, booklets and tracts; "open letters" to Congress by National Committee members; and, not least, articles by the man on the masthead, Gannett himself, for the benefit of those who had not already read them in one of his papers. Gannett reprinted his editorials poster-size—for display, he suggested, "on bulletin boards in factories, schools, Y.M.C.A.'s, etc." A typical commentary began:

> President Roosevelt stands charged with helping to break down respect for our courts and respect for law. His attacks on the Supreme Court

> because all the justices do not agree with him [have] . . . fostered the idea everywhere that our courts were something to be laughed at, overridden and disregarded.
>
> It is no wonder that those who understand the situation are panic-stricken . . . every minority group is becoming anxious. . . . Jews, Catholics, various Protestant sects and Negroes who in turn have been persecuted and prosecuted are beginning to realize what all this may mean to them.
>
> What can you do about it? Bestir yourself. . . . Awake America before it is too late! Awake or government of the people, by the people and for the people will perish in America.

These packets of material were followed, in due course, by further fund-raising appeals—arriving in crisp white envelopes that bore one-and-a-half-cent commemorative stamps of Warren G. Harding and were emblazoned, in vivid red, "IMMEDIATE Action Required."

Gannett looked to amplify his message. He paid for hundreds of thousands of reprints of speeches against the Court proposal, which were then sent out under senators' "frank"—their right to mail letters without paying postage. In other words, Gannett provided the copies and the mailing list, and taxpayers paid the remainder of the tab. Gannett also acquired recordings of such speeches and mailed the vinyl discs to three hundred broadcasters across the nation. An accompanying note asserted darkly that Court-packers had been dominating the airwaves; your listeners, it said, deserve to hear the other side of the argument. Similar letters went to small-town newspapers like *The Post*, in Worcester, Massachusetts: "You can serve your readers . . . ," Gannett advised the editor, "if you will call attention to these programs that are to be put on the air by your local radio station."

These small-town papers were an important outlet. Gannett, better than most, understood their hunger for copy; and this he supplied them, column inch by column inch. But he wanted more than outlets. He wanted allies. He wrote every newspaper editor in America, asking them to enlist in his campaign. The response was favorable; most editors, of course, were already crusading against the Court plan. At least one, however, took strong exception. William T. Evjue, editor of the *Madison Capital Times*, fired back in an open letter that Gannett's appeals were "becoming more and more nauseating. You big moguls in the American publishers' association are hypocritically using the freedom of the press to promote your own selfish special interests. . . . I am not going to help you play the game of the selfish big newspaper publishers who hate the Roosevelt administration."

But then, the *Capital Times* was not a Gannett paper. Gannett claimed with pride that he had never once dictated the editorial position taken by any of his papers. His editors, it was true, were used to a wide degree of discretion; in 1936, a few had even dared endorse FDR. But as the Court fight intensified, and Gannett's public role in it increased, it was hard for these editors to view an urgent appeal written on the boss's personal letterhead as anything other than a direct order. It was no surprise, then, that news coverage—no less than editorials—toed the company line on Court-packing. In mid-February, furious reporters at the *Knickerbocker Press* charged their editors with burying stories showing public support for the Court plan. Writers demanded that their new contract affirm the importance of "a full, accurate, truthful and fair presentation of the facts." Management rejected the clause on the grounds that it impugned the integrity of Frank Gannett.

In 1933, commentators from Walter Lippmann to Al Smith had suggested that Roosevelt might have to suspend the Constitution in order to save it. Now, four years later, Gannett seemed to take the same view of freedom of the press. The line between his newspapers and his packets of propaganda grew increasingly blurry. The Gannett chain grew chilly toward competing views. In February, the business manager of United Feature Syndicate warned Ray Clapper that his support for Court-packing was hurting sales of his column: "too many publishers," he explained, "are violently opposed," and none more so than Gannett. "I am taking the only attitude that I could logically take," Clapper replied, "and will just have to take my chances." A few weeks later, the business manager was ready to make another sales pitch to the Gannett papers. "Things look bright," he told Clapper, "unless you get going on the Supreme Court again."

Gannett measured his impact as a publisher might: by circulation. He kept careful count of letters sent, reprints ordered and distributed, and contributions received. Beyond this, however, the effect of his efforts was impossible to gauge. *The New Republic*, while identifying the National Committee as "the chief organized group so far," hastened to add that few in Washington took Frank Gannett seriously: the magazine reported that "he is not considered to be much beyond the pre-kindergarten stage of politics." Critics pointed out that Gannett was preaching mostly to the converted. Yet there can be little doubt that Gannett helped fuel the panic of those inclined toward panic, and helped arm opponents with arguments against the plan. He turned up the volume and the heat. If his goal, as he proclaimed, was "to arouse . . . existing sentiment and fear," then surely he succeeded.

The American Liberty League was essentially defunct by 1937. But its politics and methods were very much alive. So was the alliance it helped to forge between strait-laced, leading citizens like Pinchot and unsavory characters like Dr. Rumely. The National Committee to Uphold Constitutional Government revealed anew the extent to which the captains of industry and high finance had not merely co-opted the cranks but had themselves become cranks—unhinged by the New Deal and muttering, as Pinchot did, about an "international conspiracy," with Franklin Roosevelt at its helm, "to destroy private enterprise." For men like these, the Court fight was largely, as Pinchot confided to Gannett, a "fight against managed economy. That is the major consideration."

Frank Gannett was a man of principle. He cared deeply for the fate of free institutions and free markets. But like the du Ponts, who had bankrolled the Liberty League, or like Henry Ford, who had intervened (with no success) on Rumely's behalf at the time of his indictment as a German agent, Gannett had aligned himself with a cast of characters who could be reasonably described, as Rumely's acquaintance put it, as "100% racketeers and opportunists who . . . have nothing but self-interest at stake, are entirely mercenary soldiers of fortune attempting to wreck in order that they may loot."

Gannett had no monopoly on patriotic zeal. Admiral Richmond P. Hobson, the longtime crusader for various causes, had been preparing for an assault on the American system of self-government since 1935, when he established the Constitutional Democracy Association. The CDA had done little of note in the two years since, but now, its sense of purpose renewed, it looked to create a nationwide movement against the Court plan.

"The fight will be won or lost 'back home,'" Hobson's lieutenants believed, and they launched a massive campaign to mobilize opposition in small cities and rural areas. They reached out to luncheon clubs and a menagerie of fraternal associations (Elks, Eagles, Lions, and more), and blanketed the country with letters to newspaper editors in towns like Oroville, California, and Xenia, Ohio. "We are anxious," Hobson wrote them, "to learn the names of organizations in your State, county and community which have recorded their objections to the President's proposal . . . and of citizens who have formed committees adopting resolutions to oppose this measure. Would it be possible for you to supply us with this information?" Most editors happily did.

Within a few weeks, Hobson's group had built a network of more than five hundred such committees. "Many of these . . . were formed at our suggestion," one CDA leader boasted to another. Indeed, they had followed a CDA template for the recruitment "of influential people who would form a temporary group such as 'Smithville Committee to Uphold the Supreme Court.'" The committees also received mimeographed instructions on how to craft press releases, conduct letter-writing campaigns, train "a corps of speakers" for the radio and town halls, and assemble petitioners to stand at the factory gates at closing time. The CDA even scripted—down to the last detail—the sequence of a typical town hall meeting. "THIS IS HOW TO DO IT," a memo declared: the singing of "America," an invocation by a local minister, speeches by upstanding citizens, and then "a musical selection would be in order" while ushers passed out pencils to tally votes on resolutions against the Court plan. Finally, it said, meetings should close with "The Star Spangled Banner."

Not all these groups, though, were CDA creations, and not all shared its singular focus on the Constitution. For years, Hobson had been cultivating relationships with a wide range of patriotic and religious organizations, from the mainstream of respectable society to its outer margins. He had forged a partnership with the American Coalition, a vast umbrella group dedicated "to keep[ing] America American." The coalition included everyone from the Paul Reveres to the

Sons and Daughters of the Pilgrims, the Dames of the Loyal Legion of the United States, the Old Glory Club of Flatbush, Inc., and, not incidentally, the Immigration Restriction Association. Together they saw a "movement afoot to condemn, weaken and destroy the American Constitution and to slur and repudiate the American Flag, and to extol many alien theories, and to inject them into our political and family life." The Court bill, they said, was "oriental despotism"—though among their eight goals, preserving the Constitution ranked seventh, below "deport[ing] undesirables" and "resist[ing the] efforts of unassimilated or hyphenated groups" to hand control of the United States to "foreign governments."

Farther toward the fringes, Hobson found an ally in the America for God Crusade, which sounded the alarm against "militant godlessness and all faith-destroying and subversive activities." (These included packing the Court.) Countless fundamentalists answered the call. Among them was Gerald B. Winrod, an increasingly notorious Kansas preacher and author of *The Jewish Assault on Christianity* (1935). Winrod, whose movement of tens of thousands came to be known as the Jayhawk Nazis, threw himself into the campaign against the Court plan, sending his followers a fiery letter under the banner "The Crisis Hour Is Here." Roosevelt, he charged, "WANTS to be an absolute DICTATOR . . . THE END OF CHRISTIAN AMERICANISM IS TODAY IN SIGHT!"

Pro-packing groups were weak-kneed by comparison. Groups like the National Popular Government League sent out mailings and made fundraising appeals, but with something less than religious fervor. At the grass roots, most of the intensity belonged to the other side. Leaders of the opposition in the Senate, keenly aware of these efforts, kept in close contact with agitators back home, offering encouragement and coordinating strategy.

The "wizard of public relations" was out of spells. Or so it appeared, for the first time anyone could remember. Charley Michelson's Democratic publicity operation clattered and sputtered, looking not at all like the well-oiled machine of the previous fall. "Weak, fumbling, almost, it seemed, halfhearted," judged Alsop and Catledge, who had the feeling that Michelson was going through the motions. Talk of establishing a citizen's committee to promote the bill under the leadership of Joseph P. Kennedy, the former head of the SEC, came to nothing. True, Michelson did set up an "independent" Committee for Public Information to counter Gannett's group, news bulletin by news bulletin, pamphlet by pamphlet; and Corcoran and the others continued to draft speeches and arrange radio appearances for pro-administration senators. *The New Republic* called these efforts "technically flawless." But this was a minority view. In the face of the Gannett onslaught, Michelson's propaganda looked paltry, and among Roosevelt's allies there was muttering about the quality of materials; one senator cast a narrowed eye on a speech draft he had been given, then refused to deliver a word of it.

The real problem, though, was not any lack of commitment or ability by the president's propagandists, but rather the hand that Roosevelt had dealt them. In his message of February 5, FDR had laid out his case for packing the Court—a case that was, as widely noted, incomplete, misleading, and unconvincing. Still, it remained his case, for his bill, and from his supporters he expected some degree of fidelity to the picture he had painted of congested court dockets and aged justices refusing to hear important cases ("denying writs of certiorari," in the dry language of the law) out of sheer exhaustion. With few exceptions—such as Ickes, who said whatever he pleased—speakers in support of the plan felt compelled to march through these arguments before saying something in which they actually believed. No wonder that many speakers sounded tentative—or confused. The February 5 message was thus the original sin. It was visited upon every successive messenger.

In late February, Robert Jackson traveled to upstate New York, his home as well as the president's. "In Jamestown," Jackson recalled, "the people that I would have expected to support nearly anything that the President proposed were baffled by the Court plan. They hadn't sensed the necessity for it." Roosevelt had not done enough to prepare them—and now, it appeared, was doing little to persuade them. When Jackson returned to Washington, he delivered the sort of blunt, even harsh assessment that Roosevelt had not received elsewhere. "I have returned from some time among the plain people," Jackson wrote him on February 22,

> and regret to report to you that, in my opinion, support is not increasing for your court reform but rather decreasing. This, I think, is distinctly due to the terms in which the problem is approached. We can not expect the general public to understand the significance of "certiorari denied." To begin with, they do not know what certiorari is. . . . They do not understand calendar congestion and nobody ever yet went into a fight over a set of statistics. . . . Instead of talking about cases the court would not take, let us talk about the cases they did take.

Jackson urged Roosevelt to make the case more simply and clearly and to seize "the fighting issues": how the Court had made itself a superlegislature, how the conservative justices had "gone out of their way" to cut off every avenue for economic reform, how they were twisting the meaning of the Constitution. "The people," wrote Jackson, "are unquestionably ready to support you to the finish if they understand that this is a fight to make the court a contemporary and nonpartisan institution. I am utterly unable to get any response to the statistical approach and I do not see that anyone else has."

Sam Rosenman, Stanley Reed, and others had made the same argument three weeks earlier, on the eve of Roosevelt's launch of the plan, to no avail. But much had changed since then—including, apparently, Roosevelt's mind. On February 25, in a White House meeting with Jackson and Reed, he was surprisingly quick to yield. "It is a pretty terrible platform to stand on, isn't it?" Roosevelt acknowledged. Years later, he reflected that "I made one major mistake when I first presented the plan. I did not place enough emphasis upon the real mischief—the kind of decisions which, as a studied and continued policy, had been coming down from the Supreme Court." It had taken him three weeks to admit this mistake—three crucial, costly weeks—ample time for his credibility to be battered, enemies emboldened, and goals put at risk. And so, in the final days of February, he resolved to do what he should have done from the start: to take the fight directly to the Court and put the real issue before the American people.

He had always intended to deliver a fireside chat around this time—"to dwell," as he wrote Frankfurter on February 9, "on the reorganization of the judiciary, at the same time that I speak of the reorganization of the executive and of flood relief, etc." Clearly, such a speech was needed now. Roosevelt acknowledged this. Still, he did not seem in any particular hurry to actually deliver the address. He was happy to table the matter until he had taken a long postponed two-week vacation in Warm Springs. This, recalled Jackson (with some understatement), "greatly troubled" Roosevelt's advisers; the president "had overruled [them] all." At his White House meeting, Jackson "waded into it," strongly urging FDR to speak to the country before heading south. "I told him I was afraid public sentiment would form against him in his absence," Jackson recalled. Roosevelt took the matter under advisement.

Around this time, the White House reacted angrily to press reports that Roosevelt was planning to stump the country in support of his plan. "False," barked Steve Early, who blamed the rumors on "hostile forces." He might have been right. Speaking to the country was one thing; "going to the country," in the terminology of the time, was quite another, and Roosevelt was dead-set against it. The last president to travel the nation on behalf of a controversial proposal was Woodrow Wilson, in 1919; famously, he had embarked on an exhausting—and in the end debilitating—tour to rally support for ratification of the League of Nations. "Dare we reject it," Wilson had asked, "and break the heart of the world?" The nation answered: "Yes." Ever since, *Time* observed, "the stigma of failure" had clung to the idea of a tour. If Roosevelt so much as stepped on a train to give a speech outside Washington, he might just as well have waved a white flag.

But Roosevelt, as *Time* pointed out, "had something that Woodrow Wilson did not have: the all-pervasive radio." On February 26, a day after his meeting with Jackson, FDR held his Friday press conference and announced that in two weeks' time he would deliver the first fireside chat of his second term. Perhaps "announced" was not the word: Roosevelt delivered the news offhandedly, in response to the same question he had received week after week from White House reporters: "Are you considering making a radio speech on your court program?"

"I think I will," he said this time. "I was talking to Steve [Early] about it last night. The usual fireside talk on the general state of the nation."

"Including the Court?" someone asked.

"Usual broadcast on the state of the nation," Roosevelt repeated.

This was a strange bit of indirection. Every reporter in the room knew there was nothing "usual" about a fireside chat; since taking office, FDR had delivered only eight, nearly all of which had concerned matters of high importance. "It will include a great many things, as usual," he said breezily. "Don't get yourselves out on limbs. I think Steve got the ninth of March for it, at 10:30 P.M. Columbia, National, Mutual—I don't know what else. Usual thing."

Though Roosevelt did not inform the press, he had decided to deliver not one but two speeches about the Court. The first would come several days before the radio chat, at a big gathering of Democrats at the Mayflower Hotel on March 4. That event—and more than a thousand like it from coast to coast—was being billed as a "Victory Dinner," a chance to celebrate the party's triumph in 1936 and, perhaps more important, to help retire its campaign debt. FDR's speech would be broadcast to every one of these dinners across the nation. It was a terrific opportunity to rally Democrats behind the plan. At the same time, it risked giving a partisan coloring to a matter that should have transcended party politics. There was, as James Roosevelt recorded, "considerable debate" among the president's advisers "as to whether the $100 [a plate] Victory Dinner was a good place" to make a speech about the Court. But FDR, in the end, concluded that it was.

"Looks like a working weekend," James wrote in his diary on Friday, February 26. Sam Rosenman was summoned, as usual, from New York. Tom Corcoran was told to come to the White House the next morning. So were Donald Richberg and Harry Hopkins. After weeks of letting countless others, on both sides of the fight, do the talking, FDR now had two opportunities to speak for himself—two speeches, James noted, "upon which much of our hopes are based."

Chapter Twenty-one

THIS NEW ROAR

"PA IS BOTH nervous and tired," Eleanor Roosevelt wrote their daughter, Anna, on March 3. "The court hue and cry has got under his skin." He was "edgy," she observed, as he and his speechwriters worked on the Victory Dinner draft. It came together quickly—an impressive feat, since initial drafts had not dealt even remotely with the Supreme Court. Tom Corcoran's original notes had envisioned an aggressive call to action: "Progress," he had written, "will have to be forced over a strong opposition." The line stayed ("That is grand," FDR commented in the margin); but as the speech evolved, "strong opposition" came to refer not only to that familiar bête noire, "economic royalists," but to their allies on the Court. By March 4—the day of the speech and the fourth anniversary of his first inaugural—Roosevelt had in hand "a fighting speech," as Homer Cummings noted in his diary, adding that it "will stir up a good many dry bones."

That evening, in forty-three states (and a few territories and possessions), more than half a million Democrats put on formal wear and attended one of 1,263 Victory Dinners. For many attendees, particularly those at the Mayflower in Washington, the mood was less than celebratory. The glow of the November triumph had dissipated; the Court fight had rendered the very idea of an "era of good feeling" a bitter joke. While most Republicans remained happily mute—"as meek as skimmed milk," sneered Harold Ickes—Democrats slashed at Democrats. The Court fight was a family quarrel. In the Senate, Democratic tempers were rising, and the rhetoric—overheated from the beginning—continued to escalate, becoming, in pitch and in tone, like a stuck whistle.

Just a few days earlier, Joe Robinson had given a speech on the Senate floor denouncing the opposition's "unfair" propaganda, drawing a stinging retort from Edward Burke of Nebraska, who, as a junior Democrat, might have been expected to treat the majority leader with deference. The next day, in an address at the state house in Austin, Senator Thomas Connally drew an analogy between the present crisis and the "dark and dismal period" of Reconstruction—a time, he said, when "a rabid majority in the United States Congress . . . enacted the most oppressive and the most rigorous laws which all the deviltries of passion and prejudice could devise." The Civil Rights Act of 1875, he said, had made it a felony to refuse "to place yourself upon social equality with the colored people. . . . Thank God," he exclaimed, that the Supreme Court had overturned the law and said, in Connally's words, "Mr. Government, Mr. Congress, and Mr. President, you cannot invade the rights of the southern people . . . thus far can you go, and no farther."

These were the sounds of stalemate, reflecting the frustration and futility of "trench warfare," as Alsop and Catledge put it, in the most apt of the martial metaphors being applied to the conflict. Ground was gained, ground was lost, nobody moved. Gallup, on March 1, reported that public support for the plan had dropped 4 points, to 41 percent, while 48 percent disapproved. A groundswell for the opposition? Perhaps. But mail to members of Congress seemed to point in the other direction. Neither side, in short, had much to show for a month's worth of making speeches. And so, without a sense of what else to do, the combatants made more speeches—and attacked one another with growing abandon. By March, broadcasters had reached their limit. Like his counterparts at NBC and Mutual, Edward R. Murrow of CBS refused to air even one more speech on the Court plan until the president had delivered his own.

At the Mayflower, cabinet members, senators, lobbyists, and assorted hangers-on and job-seekers assembled in the ballroom, taking their places at immaculate white tables. It was a largely male crowd, *Time* noted dryly, "for most Democrats did not put up an extra $100 to feed their wives." The crowd rose and cheered as Sidney's Mayflower Orchestra struck up "Hail to the Chief," signaling the arrival of the president and first lady, and cheered even louder when the band shifted to "Happy Days Are Here Again." Southerners made rebel yells. Perhaps there was some good feeling left.

Roosevelt and the 1,300 Democrats dined on Diamondback Terrapin Soup, Breast of Capon on Smithfield Ham, and, pointedly, Salade Victoire. At 10:30 p.m., Roosevelt was helped from his armchair to the podium and began to speak. His manner was solemn, even stern; his audience ceased its whistles and war whoops. He recalled their attention to that day, exactly four years ago, when "we faced and met a grave national crisis. Now," he declared, "we face another crisis—of a different kind but fundamentally even more grave." This, he said, would be his subject tonight—and five nights hence, in his fireside chat.

"We are celebrating the 1936 victory," he said, though his tone belied it. "That was not a final victory." He noted that "the tumult and the shouting have broken forth anew—and from substantially the same elements of opposition. This new roar," he argued, "is the best evidence in the world that we have begun to keep our promises, that we have begun to move against conditions under which one-third of this nation is still ill-nourished, ill-clad, ill-housed." His voice grew hard. "We gave warning last November that we had only just begun to fight. Did some people really believe we did not mean it? Well—I meant it, and you meant it." This line, like so many others, was Roosevelt's own, a last-minute addition in his slanted handwriting.

He paused to tell a story—sidling up to the issue at hand. A few days ago, Roosevelt said, a member of Congress had come to see him

> to talk about national problems in general and about the problem of the judiciary in particular. I said to him: "John, I want to tell you something that is very personal to me—something that you have a right to hear from my own lips. I have a great ambition in life."
>
> My friend pricked up his ears.

> I went on: "I am by no means satisfied with having twice been elected President of the United States by very large majorities. I have an even greater ambition."
>
> By this time, my friend was sitting on the edge of his chair.

So were his friends in the Mayflower ballroom. Everyone had heard the rumors that FDR planned to run for an unprecedented third term.

> I continued: "John, my ambition relates to January 20, 1941."
>
> I could feel just what horrid thoughts my friend was thinking. So in order to relieve his anxiety, I went on to say: "My great ambition on January 20, 1941, is to turn over this desk and chair in the White House to my successor, whoever he may be, with the assurance that I am at the same time turning over to him as president, a nation intact, a nation at peace, a nation prosperous, a nation clear in its knowledge of what powers it has to serve its own citizens, a nation that is in a position to use those powers to the full in order to move forward steadily to meet the modern needs of humanity—a nation which has thus proved that the democratic form and methods of national government can and will succeed. . . .
>
> "I do not want to leave it to my successor in the condition in which Buchanan left it to Lincoln."

Roosevelt had delighted in dictating this passage to his writers, and delighted even more in delivering it to a rapt audience at the Mayflower. But here again he grew severe, confessing his "anxiety" that democracy in America might not survive. "As yet," he warned, "there is no definite assurance that the three horse team of the American system of government will pull together. If three well-matched horses are put to the task of plowing up a field where the going is heavy, and the team of three pull as one, the *field . . . will . . . be . . . plowed.*" The rhythmic movement of his head—up, down, up, down—punctuated his words. "If one horse lies down in the traces or plunges off in another direction, the *field . . . will . . . not . . . be . . . plowed.*

The Democrats whistled and cheered—here and around the country, where they listened by live radio hookup. Now, at last, the president had engaged the issue—and though he did not once, in this speech, refer to the Court by name, he laid the threats to democracy, unmistakably, at its feet. When he chided "the unthinking, those who dwell in the past," there was no doubt whom he meant. He reminded his audience about the AAA and the premise on which it rested: that Congress had "full constitutional authority" to address national problems. "You know who assumed the power to veto, and did veto that program," Roosevelt said darkly. He mentioned the NRA next: "We tried," he said, "to establish machinery to adjust the relations between the employer and employee. And what happened? You know who assumed the power to veto, and did veto that program." He continued listing the names of the fallen: the Railroad Retirement Act, the Guffey Coal Act, and the New York minimum wage—the demise of which established, beyond any doubt, that

> it pleased the "personal economic predilections" of a majority of the Court that we live in a nation where there is no legal power anywhere to deal with its most difficult practical problems—a No Man's Land of final futility.

Roosevelt had, to this point, been addressing the nation, but he directed his final appeal to the Democratic Party. "Let our minds be bold," he urged. The nation, he said, expected its ruling majority to find solutions "free from legal doubt." But the people's patience was not without limit. "If we do not have the courage to lead the American people where they want to go, someone else will." His implication was clear: pack the Court, or forfeit the right to rule.

Finally, voice rising, arm thrusting outward, he launched into his peroration:

> Here is one-third of a nation ill-nourished, ill-clad, ill-housed—*now!*

He spoke this last word softly, emphatically.

> Here are thousands upon thousands of farmers wondering whether next year's prices will meet their mortgage interest—*now!*
>
> Here are thousands upon thousands of men and women laboring for long hours in factories for inadequate pay—*now!*

Here are thousands upon thousands of children who should be at school, working in mines and mills—*now!*

Here are strikes more far-reaching than we have ever known, costing millions of dollars—*now!*

Here are Spring floods threatening to roll again down our river valleys—*now!*

Here is the Dust Bowl beginning to blow again—*now!*

If we would keep faith with those who had faith in us, if we would make democracy succeed, I say we must act—*now!*

A "fighting speech" indeed. It was a tremendous performance—by many accounts, one of his greatest. Roosevelt's supporters were overjoyed. For a very long month they had waited for this. "The speech was a crackerjack," said Speaker Bankhead. "They will eat it up where I come from," exclaimed Clyde Herring, a Democratic senator from Iowa. Telegrams, full of praise, flowed into the White House. One said simply: "Now." The liberal press hailed FDR's new directness and forcefulness. The *Philadelphia Record* echoed Roosevelt's sense of urgency: "The ill-nourished, the ill-clad, the ill-housed," wrote the editors, "may not wait until Sutherland, McReynolds, Van Devanter, Butler, Roberts and Hughes are gathered to their fathers. They may not be content to underfeed their children for another decade, waiting for the slow process of amendment to work itself out. . . . We dare not stand still."

"If the country now faces a crisis," countered the *New York Times*, "it is a constitutional crisis, and it is of the President's own making." Most editorial comment, as usual, was negative, and harshly so. Even E. B. White of *The New Yorker*, who generally did not deign to comment on politics, was roused to denounce Roosevelt as "an Eagle Scout whose passion for doing the country a good turn every day has at last got out of hand. His 'Now' remarks were a giveaway—the utterances of a petulant saviour. America doesn't need to be saved today; it can wait till tomorrow. Meanwhile, Mister, we'll sleep on it."

For Democrats opposing the Court plan, the most objectionable part of the speech was its appeal to party loyalty. It was one thing for Roosevelt to argue that Court-packing was consistent with Democratic ideals; it was quite another to say, as he had, that the price of disloyalty was defeat. Worse, he had implied that his Democratic opponents were essentially one and the same with the Republicans, Liberty Leaguers, economic royalists, and "defeatist lawyers" who had aligned against him in 1936. Outraged, these Democrats resolved to work even harder to expose the "innate wickedness" of packing the Court. If the president kept fighting for his plan, they said, they might well bolt the party. "Had Mr. Roosevelt deliberately sought an issue to drive a wedge through the center of the Democratic Party," *The Washington Post* observed, "he could have found nothing more effective than his [Court] proposal."

But had the speech made a difference? It was hard for anyone to imagine that it had not. Roosevelt's persuasive power was so legendary that some Americans, according to *The Nation*, had actually "refused to listen to [the speech] on the radio, lest . . . they be seduced into agreement with it." Many newspapers, on the basis of abundant anecdotal evidence, declared that the president had won himself many converts. Roosevelt himself, eager to cement this impression, placed piles of telegrams on his desk before that morning's press conference. "Mr. President," asked a correspondent, taking the bait, "is that your fan mail?"

"That is part of it," Roosevelt replied, adding that seven out of eight telegrams supported his plan.

Opposition senators refused to believe that the Victory Dinner address, "despite its power and deadly earnestness," would change minds in Congress. But privately they conceded that they were worried about its effect on public opinion. Senate sources told a leader of the Constitutional Democracy Association that "in the final analysis they would have to follow the opinions of the majority of their home state voters," whose verdict had not yet been clearly rendered. The opposition, then, saw no alternative but to keep up the fight, a bit more gloomily than before, while "hoping that some of the justices will take the hint and resign as a way out of the dilemma."

The Victory Dinner speech was the first of two acts—the second being the fireside chat—and Roosevelt appeared satisfied with the reviews. On March 7, James Farley wrote in his diary that he had "never seen the President in a better frame of mind. . . . He said he was a bit tired, but all right" and "looking forward to getting a rest in Warm Springs."

Farley believed that Roosevelt was happiest when he was in the middle of a fight—this one especially. The Court proposal, it was clear, "is close[r] to his heart than almost anything else."

The boost to his spirits was short-lived, however. Visiting the White House on March 9, Ickes found the president "in a bad way," complaining about the draft of the fireside chat he was scheduled to deliver that evening. Corcoran, Rosenman, and Richberg had given it their best; Frankfurter, from Cambridge, had contributed language and ideas; but "the speech simply would not go," Ickes noted. Roosevelt thought he might have to start from scratch. Ickes replied—reasonably if a bit unhelpfully—that it was probably too much for Roosevelt to expect that he could give two great speeches on the same subject in the span of five days.

It was true that the president, his speechwriters, and his secretaries were spent. An early draft of the fireside chat stretched to fifty double-spaced pages—evidence of lack of focus. Missy LeHand, retyping Draft #4 late one night, got giddy with exhaustion (Grace Tully, another secretary, called this "the silly stage") and started inserting parenthetical comments to the speechwriters: "The appointment of new judges calls for the selection of honorable and able candidates (That leaves about three available). . . . President Harding appointed four judges in less than two years (Look at him now). . . . And so today I am seeking the legislative means within the Constitution in the hope that the difficult process of constitutional amendment may be averted (My back is breaking at this moment) (I also want a soda, and I bet you bozoes [*sic*] are having one—Curses)."

By nightfall on March 9, Roosevelt had made his peace with the draft. He underlined key words for emphasis in his reading copy, triple-spaced and typed with blue ribbon. The White House had no broadcasting studio; instead, Roosevelt gave his fireside chats from the Diplomatic Reception Room—an oval-shaped space on the ground floor, which did in fact happen to have a fireplace. Ushers brought in a desk and furnished it with a reading light, a pitcher of water and a drinking glass, a watch, and three heavy microphones—one for each of the national broadcasting networks. The rest of the room was cluttered with radio equipment, lights for the newsreel cameras, and uncomfortable folding chairs, about thirty in number, to seat friends, family members, house guests, and public officials.

Roosevelt entered about 10:20 p.m., ten minutes before airtime. Taking his seat at the desk, he smoked a cigarette and nervously considered the pages of his speech—collected, as usual, in a black leather looseleaf notebook. From a small, heart-shaped silver box, he removed a single-tooth bridge; he disliked wearing it, but knew that without it, he slightly whistled certain words. He took tremendous care with his voice when preparing to speak over the radio—even, at times, bringing in the White House physician to cleanse his sinus passages two or three hours before the speech. "He was perfectly aware," Tom Corcoran recalled, "that everything depended on the tone of voice. . . . He thought of his voice . . . as an opera singer thinks of it."

He was the master of his medium. This had been clear as early as 1924, when a writer for the *New York Times* identified Roosevelt as one of the few politicians in America who passed the "radio test": while most orators shouted at the microphone, as if their words were meant to reach someone in the back of a noisy convention hall, Roosevelt had a "knack at making things sound personal and informal." He made listeners feel that he had dropped by the parlor for relaxed conversation. "People felt this," Frances Perkins said later, "and it bound them to him in affection." Roosevelt had begun giving radio speeches as governor and had used them to great advantage ever since. His language was deliberately plain: his use of "I" and "you" and homespun metaphors gave these chats their intimate feel, even as he delivered them in an ornate room, floodlit by press photographers, to 60 or 70 million "friends."

This Thursday night, Roosevelt was preceded on the NBC Red network by Fred Astaire, who introduced a few songs from the Gershwin musical *Shall We Dance?*; on Mutual by a mystery sketch; and on CBS by a fourteen-year-old Judy Garland. Roosevelt looked at his watch, put out his cigarette, took a drink of water. The chief radio engineer nodded, and the president began speaking.

This, too, was a fighting speech. Like the Victory Dinner address, it began somberly and marched briskly toward its purpose. Again, Roosevelt harked back to the banking crisis, this time to remind listeners of his actions to rein in the supply of gold. When that policy came before thc Supreme Court, he said, "its constitutionality was upheld only by a *five-to-four* vote." He leaned so hard on these words, "five-to-four," that it seemed as if that fact alone—the fact of a divided decision—was itself an affront to democratic rule. "The change of one vote," he continued, "would have thrown all the affairs of this great nation back into hopeless chaos. In effect, four justices ruled that the right under a private contract to exact a pound of flesh was more sacred than the main objectives of the Constitution to establish an enduring nation."

There was nothing coy here—none of the arched eyebrows and "you-know-who"s of five days before. This speech, in contrast to the last, not only mentioned the Supreme Court but also, for more than half an hour, subjected it to the most unsparing series of attacks any president had ever made—publicly, at least—against the judiciary. "The Court," Roosevelt charged, "has been acting not as a judicial body, but as a policy-making body," setting itself up as "a third House of the Congress—a super-legislature, as one of the justices has called it—reading into the Constitution words and implications which are not there, and which were never intended to be there. We have, therefore, reached the point as a nation where we must take action to save the Constitution from the Court and the Court from itself."

Defending his proposal, Roosevelt barely acknowledged a word of what he had said in his February 5 message to Congress; instead, he now declared that his "plan will save our national Constitution from hardening of the judicial arteries." He insisted that there was "nothing novel or radical" about changing the number of justices; Congress had done it several times. Neither was there anything exceptionable about encouraging the oldest judges to retire; forty-three states had such a requirement, and the Army, Navy, civil service, and countless large companies and universities mandated retirement at seventy. Here was Roosevelt in a familiar and effective role: the nation's schoolmaster, informing and instructing, never talking down, patient, benevolent, wise.

But this time he was angry. He had spent a month listening to the worst sort of invective about his motives, much of it from "friends" invoking the very Constitution he was trying to save. "The President," recalled Rosenman, "was extremely sensitive about the charge of 'packing' " and had dictated a pointed rebuttal:

> Those opposing this plan have sought to arouse prejudice and fear by crying that I am seeking to "pack" the Supreme Court and that a baneful precedent will be established.
>
> What do they mean by the words "packing the Court"? Let me answer this question with a bluntness that will end all *honest* misunderstanding of my purposes.
>
> If by that phrase "packing the Court" it is charged that I wish to place on the bench spineless puppets who would disregard the law and would decide specific cases as I wished them to be decided, I make this answer: that no president fit for his office would appoint, and no Senate of honorable men fit for their office would confirm, that kind of appointees to the Supreme Court.
>
> But if by that phrase the charge is made that I would appoint and the Senate would confirm justices worthy to sit beside present members of the Court who understand modern conditions, that I will appoint justices who will not undertake to override the judgment of the Congress on *legislative* policy, that I will appoint Justices who will act as *justices* and not as *legislators*—if the appointment of such Justices can be called "packing the Court," then I say that I, and with me the vast majority of the American people, *favor doing just that thing—now.*

To critics who shouted, "hands off the Supreme Court," Roosevelt made clear that

> Our difficulty with the Court today rises not from the Court as an institution but from human beings within it. But we cannot yield our constitutional destiny to the personal judgment of a few men who, being fearful of the future, would deny us the necessary means of dealing with the present.

Having justified his plan, Roosevelt turned to the question of a constitutional amendment. He was aware that the idea continued to gain momentum. According to Gallup, popular support for an amendment giving Congress more power over industry and agriculture had jumped 13 points since December, to 58 percent. When drafting the speech, some members of the White House strategy board had pressed Roosevelt to say that he would drop the Court-packing plan if the opposition could agree on an amendment that met his goals and could guarantee its ratification—both impossible conditions. He rejected the obviously cynical suggestion. Still, he had to say something to stem the tide. He decided to stress the difficulties of drafting an amendment, building consensus for it, ratifying it, and getting it to survive the justices' scrutiny. Slyly paraphrasing Hughes, he cautioned that "an amendment, like the rest of the Constitution, is what the justices say it is rather than what its framers or you might hope it is."

His voice heavy with sarcasm, Roosevelt spoke directly to the "newspaper publishers, and Chambers of Commerce, and bar associations, and manufacturers' associations who are trying to give the impression today that they really do want a constitutional amendment. . . . I do not think you will be able long to fool the American people as to your purposes." To liberals "who honestly believe" in amending the Constitution, he said that the process was too slow to answer present difficulties and warned that their newfound conservative allies would, in the end, "sabotage" any worthwhile amendment. "Look," he said sourly, "at these strange bedfellows of yours. When before have you found them *really* at your side in your fights for progress?"

Finally, Roosevelt returned to a theme of his first inaugural address: keeping faith with the founders. In the closing lines of this fireside chat, Roosevelt said that the Court had "tipped out of balance" the powers of the branches of government "in direct contradiction of the high purposes of the framers of the Constitution. It is my purpose," he insisted, "to restore that balance. You who know me will accept my solemn assurance that in a world in which democracy is under attack, I seek to make American democracy succeed. You and I will do our part."

The radio engineer signaled that the president was off the air. As the networks played "The Star-Spangled Banner," the small audience in the Diplomatic Reception Room rose, paused in deference to the song, then offered thanks and congratulations to FDR, who remained at his desk for a few minutes to allow photographers to take pictures of him rereading passages of the speech. Then he and his aides went upstairs to the Oval Room for cocktails and sandwiches and a brief sampling of the first batch of telegrams. One was from Eleanor, who was traveling through the South on a lecture tour. "GRAND TALK," it said.

Most of his supporters agreed, while detractors like Wheeler found his arguments "very clever . . . but wholly unsound." Comments ran, in both directions, along preestablished lines. The next day, Gallup went into the field to determine what the people thought; but until the results were in, the only evidence was anecdotal. Senators' mail showed a spike in sentiment for the plan—a good sign for Roosevelt. But hostility to the plan appeared undiminished. On March 11, Justice Stone and his wife went to see a movie in a Washington theater. He wrote his sons the next day: "The news reel displayed a picture of President Roosevelt making his assault on the Court at the Victory Dinner and repeated some of his most telling passages. There was practically no applause. But when it was followed by Senator Burke's speech assailing the President's proposal the applause was general and loud."

Stone, presumably, was too discreet to participate. To friends, however, he expressed irritation that the "best ammunition" in Roosevelt's two speeches—phrases like "a super-legislature" and "personal economic predilections"—had come from Stone's own dissents.

On the morning of March 10, Henry Ashurst of Arizona, chairman of the Senate Judiciary Committee, woke up early and went to a Turkish bath. By this means he prepared himself to open the hearings on the Court bill. For weeks the White House had been pressing him to "get going," as James Roosevelt put it. "No haste, no heat; no hurry, no worry," was Ashurst's reply, a lack of urgency that greatly annoyed the president. But after years of observing Ashurst, he could not have expected otherwise. For a quarter century Henry Fountain Ashurst had meandered through the Senate, gliding through hearing rooms and across the floor like a Shakespearean actor bemused that, somehow, he had found himself in summer stock. He wore a wing collar, a spade-tailed coat, and a pince-nez tethered by a flowing black ribbon. His speeches flowed, too; he had, by his own admission, "a mania . . . for talking," something that he did, at length, in polysyllables. Henry Ashurst was never in a hurry.

This applied to the issue at hand. In January 1936, after the Court overturned the AAA, Ashurst had counseled FDR to wait for "Father Time" to change the Supreme Court. On constitutional and economic questions, Ashurst's views were more in line with Herbert Hoover's than with Franklin Roosevelt's. Though he had gone along with most of the New Deal, Ashurst had recently called Court-packing "the prelude to tyranny." At the same time, Ashurst had a somewhat remote relationship with his principles, and despite his earlier statement showed no discomfort, on February 6, in describing the Court plan as "the best thing" the Judiciary Committee would ever accomplish. "I am," he said on one occasion, "the Dean Emeritus of Inconsistency." And, on another: "In the Senate you are on roller skates. You go partly where you like to go and partly where the skates take you."

On March 10, with Chairman Ashurst in the lead, the eighteen members of the Judiciary Committee marched in solemn procession into the ornate, marble-tiered Senate Caucus Room. First Ashurst took a seat, followed by the rest. The chairman banged his gavel. "The committee," he said, his voice crackling through loudspeakers, "is here to consider S. 1392, a bill to reorganize the judicial branch of the government. The committee observes the presence here of the attorney general of the United States."

Homer Cummings was the first witness. For all the nervous energy in the room, most of the committee seemed to regard him with indifference, as if they wished him to finish his statement as quickly as possible and clear the way for someone more interesting. Indeed, Cummings had little to add to his previous statements on the subject. His only new line of argument was to turn the "dictator" charge on its head. It was "preposterous," he said, to call the Court plan a power grab, since no president could fill the Court with loyal stooges without the assent of the Senate and the appointees themselves. "Dictatorships," Cummings argued, "grow from ill-adjusted economic conditions, out of distress, out of fear, out of injustices"—the very things that the Court's defenders would, by their intransigence, perpetuate.

Having finished his statement, Cummings paused, smiled, and half-raised his hands. "If there are any questions, gentlemen, I shall try to answer them." This was what spectators had come to see. For days, the Court plan's opponents had been promising a fierce cross-examination of the attorney general. They did not deliver. There were a few testy, rapid-fire exchanges, a bit of give-and-take, but at no point did the hearing become truly contentious, and, as Turner Catledge reported in the *Times*, not once did Cummings lose his "appearance of suavity, complete self-containment and amusement." When a senator complained that Court-packing was not a "permanent remedy," Cummings again smiled. "Oh, senator," he said, "there is no such thing as permanence in life. Those who dream of permanence are dreaming an idle dream." Senator Norris, lost in a reverie of his own, idly snapped a rubber band against a pad of paper. The crowd, too, was growing restless, prompting Ashurst to leap to his feet and shout: "Will senators and spectators kindly stop moving about the hall, shifting, ruffling papers—and snapping rubber bands!"

Robert Jackson, the next witness, made a very different impression. Two weeks earlier, Assistant Attorney General Jackson had alerted Roosevelt to the fact that "there might be some difference" between Cummings's testimony and his own. Roosevelt was untroubled by this. And so, on the morning of March 11, Jackson went before the committee and completely disregarded what his boss had said the day before. Jackson spoke calmly, clearly, dispassionately, sounding more like a potential justice (as he was rumored to be) than a politician (as Cummings had seemed). The New Deal, Jackson argued, was "in peril," at risk of "being lost in a maze of constitutional metaphors." The system of checks and balances, the tradition of judicial deference to the legislature and the popular will—nothing had succeeded in containing the Court. "Self-restraints," he said, "are proving no restraints." And amendments would not correct the balance. "Judges who resort to a tortured construction of the Constitution may torture an amendment," Jackson warned. "You cannot amend a state of mind."

"Hearty congratulations upon your superb argument today," Ashurst scribbled on a sheet of Senate notepaper. Praise came from many directions. "Nothing abler and clearer . . . has emerged from the entire debate," enthused *The Nation*. Stone, in a letter to his sons, wrote that Jackson had given "a powerful exposition" of the view that "the Court has misused its powers. . . . There is too much truth in it for the comfort of those who have been responsible for the Court's action in recent years."

• • •

At 3 p.m., two hours after Jackson's testimony, Roosevelt boarded a special train for Warm Springs. William C. Bullitt, the U.S. ambassador to France, came along to brief the president on the situation in Europe. (A few weeks earlier, Bullitt had told him that a full-scale European war would not be long in coming; but now, despite Italy's ongoing provocations, especially its intervention in Spain, Bullitt brightened his prognosis a bit.) Leisure, though, was the main item on the agenda for Roosevelt's long-delayed vacation. Though he promised to track events via the direct telephone and telegraph lines he had installed in his cottage on Pine Mountain, he planned to spend most of his time at rest or at play—swimming in the famous pool, tossing rubber balls with the children who, like Roosevelt himself, had been stricken with polio and moved more freely in the water than they ever would on land; driving the rutted red clay roads of the Georgia hills in his little, brown, hand-controlled Ford Phaeton convertible; reading; sitting in the sun; and tending to his stamp collection in front of a pine fire.

For the first time since he had proposed to pack the Court, he could afford to relax. After his two speeches, support for the plan had begun to climb—only marginally, but for the White House, the trend was encouraging. Senators' mail, too, showed the shift. Perhaps more important, patronage had begun to exert its unsubtle influence. Senator Rush Holt of West Virginia, a Democrat who had criticized the Court bill, said that before the controversy, "I was consulted about even a janitor in the government service," but that since then, his views had been ignored. An opposition group observed that "many who spoke against strongly first now sorry they are out 'on limb' but trying desperately to find compromise to back off on."

The Senate opposition was getting nervous—and a bit smaller. Hiram Johnson wrote his son that "they are picking off occasional men from the opposition," enough, he believed, to pass the bill by a comfortable margin. George Norris, who had been outspoken against the bill, now made conciliatory noises, perhaps because the pro-amendment group whose conference he was supposed to chair in late March had unanimously endorsed FDR's plan and then, not long after, called off its meeting.

While the president rested, members of his administration launched a drive to press their advantage. Some went south, where popular support for the Court plan was strong (two-to-one in some states, three-to-one in South Carolina), putting voters sharply at odds with certain of their senators. This was one of the paradoxes of the Court fight. The enthusiasm of southern citizens for Court-packing may, in part, have reflected the relative poverty of the region: in general, the least affluent Americans were the most likely to back the plan, whether out of loyalty to FDR and the New Deal or hostility toward a Court that had seemed, so often, to tilt against their interests. Either way, southern senators, ostentatiously concerned with abstractions like state sovereignty and judicial independence (not to mention concrete realities like the loss of southern control of the Democratic party), had fallen badly out of step with many of their constituents and left themselves vulnerable to charges of betrayal. Thus did Jim Farley, on a visit to Tom Connally's Texas, warn that Democratic defectors lent "aid and comfort to the enemy," while Ickes, in Josiah Bailey's North Carolina, won enthusiastic applause from a crowd of 2,000 Democrats by charging that many opponents of the Court plan did not even deserve "credit for sincerity." Arthur Krock, reviewing these performances, expected them to make "a tremendous impression on members of Congress."

Momentum was building; events were conspiring to help pass the bill. Even a growing domestic crisis—the gathering storm of labor unrest—appeared to strengthen the case for Court-packing. As recently as January, there had been 25 such strikes, in which workers seized and shut down factories; in March, there were 170, involving 160,000 workers, and carrying the threat of wholesale economic disruption. Across the nation, increasingly militant unions and bitterly obstinate companies engaged in lengthy, costly, and sometimes bloody standoffs over labor conditions and the right of unions to negotiate on behalf of an exhausted and desperate workforce. In February, an ongoing United Auto Workers (UAW) strike at a GM facility in Flint, Michigan, had turned violent, and not for the first time. Company police, supplemented by hired thugs and armed with pistols, tear gas bombs, blackjacks, and clubs they had made in the Chevrolet woodshop, clashed with union workers until 1,200 National Guard troops imposed order by bayonet. "Something is seething in America today . . . ," said Morris Ernst, a founder of the American Civil Liberties Union, at a town hall meeting. "We are either going to get out of this mess by a change in the Court or with machine guns on street corners."

By the time of Roosevelt's trip to Georgia, the Senate was at full boil over the strikes. "A crisis is approaching," Joe Robinson declared. He extracted a private pledge from FDR to meet with congressional leaders immediately upon his return to Washington. (Within hours, Roosevelt's pledge was front-page news. "That," he groused to reporters, "shows why it was impossible to talk to them before I announced the Supreme Court thing." Members of Congress could not keep a secret.)

Supporters of the Court plan, such as Hugo Black of Alabama, laid the blame for the strikes on the steps of the Supreme Court, which he called "an insuperable, impossible obstacle" to addressing the root causes. Robinson announced that the Senate would take no action of any kind until the Wagner ruling came down—for if the Court, as expected, held manufacturing to be a local concern, as it had mining in the *Carter* coal case, then the federal government would be rendered powerless to stop the strikes. Thus did all the hopes of "labor and the middle class," according to *The Nation*, appear to rest on the outcome of the Court fight. And thus did FDR, in a telephone conversation with Ickes one night from Warm Springs, sound cheerful. "It seems to me," Ickes noted afterward, "that with a Court dillydallying on this decision, there is something to be said for the proposition that the Court is more responsible than the president for the present industrial unrest."

Roosevelt's opponents, despite steadily lengthening odds, kept fighting. The night after FDR's fireside chat, Wheeler went on the radio himself to accuse the president of "haste and hate." Two nights later, a fervent crowd of 4,000 gathered at Carnegie Hall in Manhattan to sing patriotic songs and cheer a lineup of senators who strove to outdo one another in strident condemnation of the Court plan. The winner was Senator Edward Burke, who appropriated the signature line of FDR's 1936 acceptance speech: "At this very moment," Burke declared, "we do have our 'rendezvous with destiny.' It is no exaggeration to say that constitutional democracy in America has a rendezvous with death. Democracy is face to face with death, death to all semblance of sovereignty in the states, death to the separation of governmental power into three departments . . . death to an independent judiciary."

If so, the judiciary did not intend to go quietly. On March 16, James

McReynolds broke the justices' silence on the Court-packing bill. He became the first to comment publicly on the controversy that he, as much as any man, had helped to create. That evening, he addressed an annual dinner of his college fraternity, Phi Delta Theta, at the Carlton Hotel in Washington. McReynolds had spoken at the banquet in past years, but these tended to be nostalgic affairs, full of manly remembrances and tributes to brotherhood. Tonight, though, he stepped to the lectern and said tentatively that he might speak about current events; the crowd of 125 urged him on. He began by saying that the framers intended for local entities to solve local problems, while leaving "only certain large things" to the federal government. These things did not, apparently, include the Depression, which McReynolds described as a "temporary inconvenience"—one that the American people could overcome without government intervention. "We must," he said, "awaken the citizens to their obligations, rather than their so-called rights."

In a high-pitched voice he spoke steadily, making no gestures. The audience broke in frequently with applause, not least at McReynolds's personal creed: "I have," he said, "taken an oath to do justice to the best of my ability, to do justice to rich and poor alike. That obligation I try not to forget. I try to protect the darky in the hills of Georgia as well as the man of wealth in a mansion on Fifth Avenue. . . . Without that spirit of justice, and without having an arbiter to settle your disputes, this government cannot function." (In its report the next day, the genteel *New York Times* replaced McReynolds's racial epithet with the less objectionable but hardly analogous "backwoodsman.")

His tone ranged from defiant ("put yourself in the place of the court and see if you could have done better") to fatalistic. "I should like to be optimistic," he said. "I should like to tell you that the situation is rosy. I can't. But I like to believe in the courage of the American people, and I hope they may make a solution of which they may be proud." McReynolds made no reference to FDR or the Court plan, but his allusions were clear enough. "The evidence of good sportsmanship," he declared, "is that a man who has had a chance to present a fair case to a fair tribunal must be a good sport and accept the outcome."

McReynolds had believed his comments were off the record, but perhaps he should have known that one of his fraternity brothers was, in fact, an Associated Press reporter, who had a sense of professional obligation that superseded the ties of Phi Delta Theta. In the morning, McReynolds's comments shouted from the nation's front pages. Congressional opponents of Court-packing, who had been waiting eagerly for the justices to weigh in, felt a bit disappointed; McReynolds was hardly the spokesman they would have chosen. Indeed, his speech drew angry rebukes from many quarters, including the NAACP. A newspaper editor wrote Cummings that "McReynolds has done you a great service. . . . Of course the whole issue is that the present Supreme Court is *not* a 'fair tribunal.' " In a radio rebuttal, Joe Robinson called attention to a related irony: "Nowhere in legal literature does a judge stand more emphatically condemned by his own testimony as a poor sportsman." He might have added that the Chevy Chase Country Club had stopped just short of expelling McReynolds for persistent unsportsmanlike behavior, but Robinson thought better of it (perhaps because he himself had been "permanently suspended" by the club for punching a fellow golfer in the face near the eleventh hole).

In the view of many observers, outbursts like McReynolds's were a sign of weakness—the cries of a failing campaign, raging against the dying of the light. "There seems to be a breakdown of the intellectual side of the opposition," Robert Jackson wrote a friend, "leaving them nothing but an emotional persistence." The tide had turned; "the psychology has changed," as Cummings reported to FDR in Warm Springs. "Of course you are going to win," Molly Dewson wrote him that same week, and promptly renewed her lobbying for potential Court appointees. When Farley talked to Roosevelt on March 21, the two agreed that the opposition, in Farley's words, was rapidly "cracking up . . . losing ground . . . and breaking down." Field reports, sent to Warm Springs, described "especially fine progress in our Supreme Court campaign" in western states, where a margin of "at least two and one-half to one" of the public was believed to support the president's plan. In Washington, meanwhile, the Senate hearings went on—to the detriment of the plan's opponents, who appeared, as Roosevelt himself put it, "somewhat confused among themselves" in their questioning of administration witnesses.

Brimming with confidence, the White House decided to rest its case before the Judiciary Committee earlier than planned. The strategy board, under the guidance of Corcoran and Keenan, had selected and coached an impressive series of witnesses—from labor leaders to law school deans, federal judges, and leading commentators like Edward Corwin and Irving Brant (who observed that "the conservative justices . . . are honest and sincere. So was Marie Antoinette when she said . . . 'Let them eat cake' "). It was all going fairly well, from FDR's point of view. But two weeks into the hearings and about halfway through their witness list, Corcoran and Keenan had come to a strongly held view that opposition senators were, in effect, filibustering—asking long-winded, elliptical questions, repeating themselves and one another (even more than usual), on and on, day after day.

To the strategy board, these stalling tactics suggested that leaders of the opposition were not ready to present their own witnesses. So Roosevelt forced their hand. On Saturday morning, March 20, the White House called its last witness—giving Burt Wheeler, first to speak for the opposition, only forty-eight more hours to prepare his testimony. Critics of the Court plan placed their remaining hopes in his hands. In an internal memo, one opposition group reported that Wheeler, "according to well informed sources," was "expected to 'shoot the works.' "

Chapter Twenty-two

THE YIELDING

On Monday, March 22, several hundred spectators filled the Senate Caucus Room to hear Burt Wheeler launch the opposition's case against the Court bill. The crowd's excitement was palpable. *The Washington Post*, however, could not help wishing that the opening argument was being made by one or more of the Nine Old Men. The *Post*'s editorial read like a lament. "There will be widespread regret," it observed, "that Congress must decide the most vital issue in American history concerning the Supreme Court with no word of advice from members of that tribunal." But this, the paper insisted, was to the justices' credit. Their silence revealed them as "more interested in preserving the independence of the judiciary, with all that implies, than in defending their own reputations against heedless attack."

At 10:30 a.m., Henry Ashurst called the committee to order. "Senators," he said, with even more pomp than usual, "we are signally honored this morning. We have before us one of the most, if not the most distinguished member of the United States Senate, Senator Burton K. Wheeler of Montana." Wheeler sat at the table and faced his colleagues. "It is with some reluctance that I appear here this morning," he began, striking the first of several false notes. He wanted it known that he meant no disrespect toward President Roosevelt, with whom he was "exceedingly friendly. . . . There has never at any time been anything but the most cordial relations between us." Wheeler blamed the idea of Court-packing not on FDR but on "young men"—clearly, Tom Corcoran and Ben Cohen—who, he said, had offered the same proposal to him a year earlier, "probably without [FDR's] knowledge or consent." Wheeler recalled telling "these young men at that time that I was opposed to it; that I thought it was wrong in principle, and that the American public would never stand for it." (According to Corcoran and Cohen, it was a speech draft, not a bill, and they had written it at Wheeler's request.)

"Shocked and surprised" by the president's proposal, Wheeler described his efforts to get to the bottom of its assertion that the Court, made up of old men, had fallen behind in its work. In his search for the truth, Wheeler said, he had consulted books, law journals, and Justice Department reports. Then "I went to the only source in this country that could know exactly what the facts were . . . better than anyone else." He reached into his suit pocket and pulled out a document. "I have here now," he said with relish, "a letter by the Chief Justice of the Supreme Court, Mr. Charles Evans Hughes, dated March 21, 1937, written by him and approved by Mr. Justice Brandeis and Mr. Justice Van Devanter. Let us see what these gentlemen say about it."

The letter began on a coolly defiant note: "The Supreme Court is fully abreast of its work." It proceeded, point by point, to destroy the myth of the Court's incapacity. Senators were incredulous. Spectators leaned forward, making sure to catch every word. The knitting ladies of Washington (as they were known), long a fixture in this hearing room, dropped stitches and let their needles fall into their laps. A man was so transfixed he forgot he was holding a cigarette—until his fingers had been burned. Wheeler, unable to contain his delight, could not resist adding comments of his own, prompting senators to ask whether these were Hughes's words or Wheeler's own "personal observations."

Hughes turned the tables on Roosevelt, arguing that an increase in the number of justices would make the Court less efficient. "There would be more judges to hear, more judges to confer, more judges to discuss, more judges to convince and to decide." As for the idea—suggested by some proponents—that a new, larger Supreme Court should split into "divisions" to hear cases, Hughes was dismissive. "The Constitution," he wrote, "does not appear to authorize two or more Supreme Courts," or any practice that approximated two Supreme

Courts. On this and all questions addressed in the letter, the chief made clear that he spoke for a unanimous Court. "On account of the shortness of time," he acknowledged, he had not been able to consult with every member of the supreme bench, but was "confident" that his statement was "in accord with the views of the justices," not only Brandeis and Van Devanter.

The letter was explosive, and Wheeler had played it for full effect. Though his testimony continued for some time thereafter, salted with attacks on Roosevelt and Cummings, and infused with Wheeler's chronic sense of martyrdom ("I have suffered for my liberalism as perhaps few of you have suffered"), he had accomplished his purpose in the first few minutes, and the rest was epilogue. When Wheeler finally rose from the witness chair, committee members who supported the Court plan furiously scribbled rebuttals, while opponents, for the first time in two weeks of hearings, smiled beatifically. The plum red carpet beneath Wheeler's feet was littered with the detritus of his performance: notes, wads of scratch paper, and cellophane wrappers and ashes from the cigars he had wielded throughout. The afternoon session, featuring the president of the Farmers' Union, was, after Wheeler's bombshell, a bore; reporters noticed senators glancing distractedly away from the witness to a blond secretary in the front row.

Wheeler had succeeded where many had failed. Over the preceding six weeks, numerous parties had tried to draw the Chief Justice into the Court fight—to give a speech, grant an interview, go on the radio, say something, anything, on the record. "Please be assured," read a typical telegram, "that The New York Times will esteem it a privilege to publish anything you may choose to send us." Hughes demurred. He declined, politely, every invitation. He remained, until the Senate hearings, "the central, if silent, figure of the Court debate," as *Time* put it (forlornly).

Or so he intended it to appear. For all his pious refusals to comment, Hughes was, all the while, working intently behind the scenes to undermine the Court bill and safeguard his own reputation. That work had begun within days—hours, even—of the launch of the Court plan on February 5. Franklyn Waltman, the *Washington Post* reporter and columnist, called on Hughes at that time and found him surprisingly willing to talk, off the record. Hughes told Waltman there was no link between the age of judges and congestion in court dockets. Besides, he added, the Supreme Court was not behind in its work. He pointed Waltman to sources that proved it—studies by the Judicial Conference, which the Chief Justice headed; reports that the Justice Department had made to Congress; detailed surveys of Supreme Court dockets over the past decade; and so forth. Keeping his source confidential, Waltman turned this research into a devastating series of front-page articles debunking the central claim of FDR's message.

This was not all. Hughes had long been irritated—never more so than now—by liberals' use of a comment he had made thirty years earlier when governor of New York. "We are under a Constitution," Hughes had said then, "but the Constitution is what the judges say it is." By 1937, that quote had, for liberals, come to embody their critique of the courts. They flung it back at Hughes like a self-incriminating slip—an accidental admission that judges (as Brandeis, Cardozo, and Stone freely, unashamedly acknowledged) were indeed in the business of judging, of interpreting the Constitution as they saw fit, not merely of transmitting the document's original, inviolable, unmistakable meaning (as conservatives insisted). Liberals had no problem with the sentiment Hughes expressed; it reflected their view of the judge's role. What they deplored was the unwillingness of the conservative majority (which sometimes included Hughes) to concede the truth of his statement. In the *Butler* case, for example, Roberts had destroyed the AAA while denying that he was exercising any personal judgment whatsoever.

The Hughes quotation appeared in news stories and columns, labor union circulars, books, speeches—always as an indictment of the Court majority. The original context of the comment had largely been forgotten—but not, of course, by Hughes himself, who knew exactly what he had meant so long ago, and was now determined to set the record straight. In March, he sought help from Ogden Reid, publisher of the right-leaning *New York Herald Tribune*. Hughes lent Reid an old volume of his speeches, which indeed proved that in 1907, Hughes had been making a very different point, namely, that courts should be left to address constitutional questions and not be burdened by complex regulatory issues that were better left to administrative agencies.

Obligingly, Reid published an editorial on the quote's real meaning. "I am very grateful to you and to your editorial staff," Hughes wrote him afterward, "for giving adequate publicity to the text of my statement, which has been so grossly misused."

It is unlikely that Wheeler knew about any of Hughes's backchannel efforts; and in mid-March, as the opposition began to line up witnesses for the Senate hearings, he could not have dreamed that Hughes would be interested in making the list. But he was—as Wheeler learned by accident. Around this time, Wheeler's daughter, Elizabeth Colman, had given birth to a son, and one day Alice Brandeis, the justice's wife, stopped by to see the baby. The Wheeler and Brandeis families had been friendly for more than a decade. In the mid-1920s, when Wheeler was indicted on phony corruption charges, the justice had invited the Wheelers to his apartment for dinner and "cheering up." Now, as Alice was about to leave the Colmans' house, she turned to Elizabeth and said, "Tell your father the justice is in favor of his fight against the Court bill." Elizabeth called her father before the car had left the driveway.

Thus emboldened, Wheeler went to see Brandeis. Hoping not to offend the justice's sense of propriety, Wheeler ventured only a factual question about the docket. Brandeis replied that Wheeler should ask the Chief Justice. "Yes," Wheeler agreed, "but I don't know the chief justice."

"The chief justice knows you, and what you're doing," Brandeis said, and led Wheeler to the telephone to call Hughes then and there.

On Thursday, March 18, Wheeler, William King of Utah, and Warren Austin, a Vermont Republican, visited Hughes at his home at 2223 R Street. In his plainly furnished chambers, the chief justice sat in a high-backed chair he had used as governor and listened as the senators formally invited him to testify against the Court plan. They found him, in his own words, "entirely willing." Still, "I thought it inadvisable," Hughes later recalled, "in view of the delicacy of the situation, that I should appear alone." He wanted another justice to join him, "preferably Justice Brandeis—because of his standing as a Democrat and his reputation as a liberal judge." But later that day, when Hughes reached Brandeis, the latter strongly opposed the idea that any justice should appear before the committee. Hughes had another idea. He asked Brandeis, what if Senator Wheeler were to ask me, in writing, for my views on certain questions? And what if I were to answer in writing? Brandeis considered this perfectly appropriate. So did Van Devanter, the only other justice whom Hughes consulted.

In the morning Hughes placed calls to King and Wheeler (and took the unusual step of transcribing the conversations). "I find that there is a strong feeling that the Court should not come into this controversy in any direct or even indirect way," Hughes told King, not mentioning Brandeis. "I feel that it would be better in these circumstances that I should not appear. That is a deliberate conclusion after my consultations—for your own ear. I think you will appreciate the reasons. Now," he added, "if the committee should desire information as to the work of the Court. . . ." Hughes made his pitch to King, then did the same to Wheeler. "If they will address a communication to us in writing, we will answer it in the same way and give whatever facts are necessary."

The next day—Saturday—Wheeler agreed to the proposal. He told Hughes that he hoped to have the letter in hand Monday morning so he could use it to launch the opposition's case. "This gave me very limited time," Hughes said later, but went immediately to work and, by Sunday morning, had a draft to show to Brandeis and Van Devanter. "Each went over it carefully and approved it." Hughes later insisted that he "had no time to consult the other Justices," even though Cardozo lived in the same building as Van Devanter, Stone lived only two blocks away, and—this being a Sunday morning—both men could presumably be found at home. In the afternoon, Hughes summoned Wheeler to his house. As Wheeler walked in, Hughes handed him the letter. The Chief Justice said solemnly: "The baby is born."

"Bull's Eye!" cheered an editorial cartoon the morning after Wheeler's testimony, picturing the Hughes letter as a cannonball that had blown a massive hole in Roosevelt's arguments. The *New York Times* wrote that the "authority and suddenness" of Hughes's "objection" had stunned the administration, sending supporters "scurrying to strengthen their defenses."

Stunned, certainly; but "scurrying" overstated the case, at least as far as the central players were concerned. Roosevelt spent the morning of Wheeler's testimony in the swimming pool at Warm Springs, then rested in his cottage until the University of Georgia literary society visited in the late afternoon to present him with an honorary membership. Talking with Ickes two days later, Roosevelt sounded untroubled by the Hughes letter. Ickes, while calling the letter "good tactics," noted that "we abandoned this ground"—congested court dockets—"some time ago." Cummings showed a similar lack of concern. Several hours after Wheeler's presentation, Cummings recounted the day's events in his diary and failed even to mention the letter, though he did see fit to review a play he had just seen at the National Theatre—Katharine Hepburn in *Jane Eyre* ("on the whole a remarkably fine performance"). The next day he conceded that Hughes's statement had "created quite a sensation," but added that "it is easily answered."

In the press, much attention was paid to Hughes's statement that "the Constitution does not appear to authorize" the Supreme Court to split into separate divisions. This had the ring of a judicial opinion—which, in light of Hughes's known objections to expressing judgment on anything but an actual case, was surprising, even shocking. "An advisory opinion run riot," charged *The New Republic*, in an editorial ghost-written by Thurman Arnold, an administration official. The Hughes letter, it continued, "throws all judicial discretion to the wind. . . . It violates every tradition of our judicial process. . . . Here we have the final step in the usurpation of judicial power—a statement in advance to Congress of the kind of laws which the Court intends to condemn." Not everyone deemed this a terrible thing. Arthur Krock described a "widespread and hopeful" feeling in the capital that the Hughes letter signaled a new era in which the Court would join the White House and Congress in a "cooperative 'look-before-you-leap' arrangement among the three branches"—just what Roosevelt had long desired.

This was unlikely. Hughes had given himself license to bend (or break) long-established practice, not to overturn it. Also, Cardozo, Stone, and possibly other justices strongly objected to what Hughes had done in the name of the Court as a unit. It had taken some nimbleness for Hughes to convey the impression that all of his brethren endorsed his letter in its entirety—an impression that most of the press accepted uncritically. The *New York Times*, for example, inferred that the Chief Justice spoke for "a united Court." This made Cardozo—

the gentlest, most forgiving justice—angrier than the Court-packing plan had.

Stone, too, was furious. "I simply cannot believe that you . . . would have concurred in giving the advisory opinion," Frankfurter wrote him. Stone replied: "You are right! I did not see the C.J.'s letter, or know of it until I read about it in the papers. I certainly would not have joined in that part of it which undertakes to suggest what is and what is not constitutional." But Stone's reaction to the episode was more complex than he let on. He actually agreed with much of what Hughes had written, including his contention that a larger Court would be less efficient. "The intimate conference . . . ," Stone wrote to Irving Brant around this time, "would be increasingly difficult with increasing size." And Stone did not object to Hughes's tactics. He had employed some of them himself. Like Hughes, Stone had sent factual material to journalists to help them puncture the notion that the justices were overburdened. (Using Brant as a conduit, Stone even encouraged FDR to propose a constitutional amendment requiring judges to retire at seventy-five.) He also flirted with appearing before the Judiciary Committee. In the end, though, he pulled back from making a public statement on the Court plan—concluding, a bit sadly, that one of the burdens of being a justice was that "one must remain silent under unfair and unjust criticism and various types and degrees of misrepresentation, relying only on his published opinions" to speak for his "intelligence and character."

Louis Brandeis, by contrast, had let Hughes speak for his. This lent the letter most of its power. It also broke the hearts of Brandeis's acolytes—in one case irrevocably. "Brandeis had up to that time been one of the lodestones of my life," Tom Corcoran said later. "After the conversation with him [on Black Monday] . . . I still felt the same. But when he joined with Hughes and Wheeler in what I knew would be the knife in the back . . . , I never called on Brandeis again." Frankfurter, too, felt betrayed. He drafted a sharply worded note to Brandeis—"I resent the C.J.'s putting you in the front line even with your approval"—but thought better of mailing it. (Instead he sent a version without the sting.) Frankfurter did, however, unburden himself to FDR:

> *That* was a characteristic Hughes performance—part and parcel of that pretended withdrawal from considerations of policy, while trying to

> shape them, which is the core of the mischief of which the majority have so long been guilty. That Brandeis should have been persuaded to allow the Chief to use his name is a source of sadness to me that I need hardly dwell on to you.

Roosevelt, no doubt, took a similar view but kept his feelings about both justices to himself. Despite the strains on his relationship with Brandeis, he regarded "Old Isaiah" with deep respect and affection. For Hughes, in many ways his most powerful rival, FDR maintained a kind of grudging admiration. It may have been mutual. At their occasional meetings, they called each other "governor." It was a meaningful bond. Roosevelt chafed anytime his advisers spoke harshly about Hughes. And though he did not relish being outmaneuvered, he had to acknowledge, as he said years later, that Hughes was "the best politician in the country."

In later years, Hughes professed to be unrepentant. But his recollections showed at least a touch of defensiveness. In his autobiographical notes, he insisted that "at the very first opportunity, when the justices were all together," he had explained why he had only been able to consult two of them, and said he hoped that they all approved of what he had done. "Several justices at once spoke up, saying that they did," Hughes recalled, "and the others seemed to me to acquiesce." Presumably he knew better. If Stone and Cardozo were, indeed, acquiescing, it was only because the letter had already been released. "No objection to letter voiced," Hughes later wrote in a note to himself—or, really, to history, for Hughes knew that he had forsaken actual unanimity for the appearance thereof. To avoid weakening his letter with compromises of the sort that often diluted Supreme Court opinions, he had consulted just enough justices—one liberal, one conservative—to imply that, together, they spoke for the rest.

That aside, Hughes was proud of what he had wrought. "This letter," he wrote later, with evident satisfaction, "appears to have had a devastating effect." Others thought so, too. Rex Tugwell believed that the letter "so conclusively refuted the arguments Franklin had made in his message . . . that it ended any chance for passage the bill might have had." Robert Jackson judged that the letter "pretty much turned the tide." But those assessments came long after the fact. In March 1937,

Jackson still thought "there is no question that the President's plan will go through"—as well he might. As Ickes had seen, the Hughes letter had laid waste to an abandoned fortress. It left untouched and perhaps even reinforced the argument Roosevelt was now making with increasing force: that the Supreme Court was a political body, and willing to cross the bounds of precedent and propriety to oppose him at any cost. That point, Hughes had made persuasively.

While the Hughes letter was being hatched, FDR was working on a surprise of his own. It, too, involved a Supreme Court justice—but in this case, a retired one. John H. Clarke, eighty years old and full of vigor, was the only living ex-justice. Appointed by President Wilson in 1916, Clarke had aligned himself with Holmes and Brandeis and developed a reputation for speaking his mind from the bench. But after only six years on the Court, he resigned in order to campaign for the League of Nations and "the outlawry of war." President Harding filled the seat with the staunchly conservative George Sutherland, and liberals—Wilson among them—were dismayed. "I have been counting on the influence of you and Justice Brandeis to restrain the Court in some measure from the extreme reactionary course which it seems inclined to follow . . . ," the former president wrote Clarke. "The most obvious and immediate danger to which we are exposed is that the courts will more and more outrage the common people's sense of justice and cause a revulsion against judicial authority which may seriously disturb the equilibrium of our institutions."

Over the next decade, in which the United States steadfastly refused to join the League of Nations, Clarke retreated so fully from the national stage (*Time* called him the "forgotten justice") that his occasional public statements had the ring and the power of a voice from beyond the grave. In March 1937, the White House began pressing him to speak on behalf of the Court bill. He quickly agreed. And then, just as quickly, he began placing conditions on his statement: he would not criticize the Court as an institution, or its members, or its decisions; he would not issue a ringing defense of the bill. Roosevelt began to grow concerned that Clarke's speech, if tepid, could do the cause more harm than good.

Urgent interventions followed—letters, telegrams, and phone calls from James Roosevelt and others. On FDR's behalf, George Creel warned a close associate of Clarke that the justice's speech, as it then stood, would be an "anti-climax." Creel urged, "I do wish you would try to rid his mind of this obsession about proprieties. I cannot imagine why he has them, for God knows he had experience enough with McReynolds, Sutherland and Van Devanter to make him understand that these people themselves have no sense of propriety or even of common decency. . . . This is no longer an argument. It is a struggle to the death."

Clarke was unyielding. Finally, bowing to his "sense of delicacy," FDR suggested that the ex-justice make one, simple point: that Court-packing was "entirely constitutional." This would give the speech the feel of an argument—when it was really only stating the obvious. Critics had called the Court plan ruinous, pointless, fascistic, rash, and worse, but few had questioned its constitutionality. Regardless, on the night of March 22—only hours, it turned out, after the Hughes letter was made public—Clarke went on the radio and talked for fifteen minutes. He said virtually nothing of interest. He did, however, make the argument Roosevelt had asked him to make: "It has become so widely asserted" that the plan was unconstitutional, Clarke said, that he felt it his "duty as a citizen" to say otherwise.

"Apparently," chided *The Washington Post*, "he was under the misapprehension" that this was "an important part of the controversy." As Roosevelt had feared, Clarke's speech was portrayed not as backing the plan but "damning it with faint praise." Another paper called "the much-heralded speech" a "pronounced 'dud.'" Clarke made no apologies. "Had I interpreted the proprieties as liberally as the Chief Justice did," he wrote FDR a few days later, "I could have gone much further than I did in support of your program and in criticism of the Court." Surely Roosevelt wished that Clarke had done exactly that.

On Monday, March 29, a record crowd of 53,000 spread across the South Lawn of the White House in what *Time* called the "biggest non-industrial . . . mob scene" that month in a nation plagued by strikes: the annual Easter Egg Roll. Boys and girls, trailed by their mothers, hunted for eggs, put them in baskets, pushed them up the slope with spoons, and hurled them at one another. In a holding pen outlined with rope, children who had eluded their guardians played tag. It was a sunny spring afternoon—Roosevelt's first day at work since returning, over the weekend, from Warm Springs. Wearing an old gray felt hat, he stood on the south portico, gripping the railing for support; beside him, in a green crepe dress, was Eleanor. FDR told the children he would have loved to be down in the grass with them, but "I had my eggs for breakfast." The crowd cheered, and the president went back inside to work.

Roosevelt was well rested. He had largely succeeded at keeping events—the Court fight, the sit-down strikes, the churning in Congress over next year's budget—at arm's length while he played cards and swam. Now that he had returned, many in Washington expected that he would press these rolling crises toward resolution. Yet it was clear that the next move belonged to the Supreme Court. Two important decisions were pending, each with massive implications for the Court bill—and much else. The first was not, in fact, a single case, but a cluster of them concerning the landmark Wagner Labor Act and workers' right to organize—a matter very much on the public mind as sit-down strikes spread like a prairie fire. The Court had heard arguments in early February; in the weeks since, government at all levels, from the White House to local police precincts, had been steeling itself for the explosion that all believed would follow a decision against labor.

The second, somewhat incredibly, was a minimum-wage case. Not even a year had passed since the 5–4 *Tipaldo* decision overturned New York's expertly drafted law. Now the Court was taking up the question again—even though the statute at issue, a quarter-century-old Washington State minimum-wage law, was almost identical to New York's and, for that matter, to the Washington, D.C., law struck down in the *Adkins* decision of 1923. The new case, *West Coast Hotel Co. v. Parrish*, concerned a chambermaid, Elsie Parrish. She had sued her employer, the Cascadian Hotel in Wenatchee, Washington, for $216.19: the difference between what she had been paid and what the state's minimum-wage law for women required. The Cascadian offered to settle the case for $17. Parrish took the case to the state Supreme Court, where she prevailed. The hotel, citing *Adkins*—specifically, its holding that minimum-wage laws deprived not only employers but also workers of their "freedom of contract"—appealed to the U.S. Supreme Court.

Given the recentness of *Tipaldo* and the vehemence of its reaffirmation of *Adkins*, it was wholly predictable that when the *Parrish* case came before the justices in October 1936, the four conservatives would vote in conference against hearing the case. And they did. The surprise was that Owen Roberts, who had joined the majority in *Tipaldo*, voted the other way. "What is the matter with Roberts?" one conservative justice muttered to another.

On December 16 and 17, 1936, the Court heard oral arguments in *Parrish*. Months then passed without a decision. The eagerness of certain justices to revisit the issue was not matched by any apparent haste in resolving it. "Why the delay?" taunted the White House strategy board, in a set of talking points for use by supporters of the Court bill. "The questions involved are not new. . . . Can it be that the Court has special reasons for withholding its decision? . . . Can it be that the Court is affected by the President's proposal . . . ? Can it be that the Court fears the justified public resentment that would be aroused by a reaffirmation of the *Adkins* case . . . ? Can it be that the Court which ought to be above politics is playing politics?"

On March 29, thousands of tourists thronged the Court, eager for answers and untempted by the Easter Egg Roll, fifteen blocks away. Their hopes for a decision on the Wagner Act brought them here in such numbers that John Knox, McReynolds's clerk, could hardly push his way through the main hall to the courtroom. At noon, the justices came through the curtain and eased into their leather chairs. There followed a flurry of decisions—nearly twenty overall—the Wagner cases not among them. Cardozo, McReynolds, Stone, and Sutherland each delivered three majority opinions; Roberts one; and so on, all along the mahogany table, until all but Hughes had spoken. Only a few of these excited much interest in the room. One that did was a 9–0 decision validating the 1934 Railway Labor Act, which required railroad companies to negotiate with repair workers—an extension of the commerce power into the back shop. Also unanimously, the justices sustained a non-revenue use of the taxing power to curb trafficking in firearms. Another newsworthy decision upheld the revised Frazier-Lemke Act, a relief measure for indebted farmers. On Black Monday in 1935, it had been Brandeis who, on behalf of a unanimous Court, pronounced last rites on the original act; now, speaking again for all nine, he declared that Congress, on its second attempt, had corrected its constitutional errors.

The spectators were beginning to flag. The Chief Justice was not. Hughes, throughout, had been scanning the room intently for people's reactions, and even on occasion allowing a hint of his own. As Stone read the railway decision, for example, Hughes leaned back in his chair, the slight suggestion of a smile on his face. Now, finally, the moment was his. Hughes leaned forward and lifted some papers. Suddenly, McReynolds stood, collected his things, turned around, and walked out of the room. He knew the result in the case. He could not bear to hear it presented.

"This case," Hughes began, "presents the question of the constitutional validity of the minimum wage law of the State of Washington." The room snapped to life. The Chief Justice raised his head, paused, then continued.

As most of his audience was aware, Hughes had been in the minority in *Tipaldo*. It had been, in effect, a minority of one. Rather than joining Brandeis, Cardozo, and Stone in calling for *Adkins* to be overruled, Hughes had dissented separately on narrower grounds. He alone believed that New York's minimum wage law could be distinguished from the D.C. law struck down in *Adkins*. That precedent, in his view, was not at issue in *Tipaldo*, had not been challenged by New York's lawyers, and should therefore remain standing. Stone had called this "an interesting bit of technique"—and by "interesting" he meant cynical and contemptible. In liberal legal circles, Hughes's unwillingness to address what most considered the central issue—*Adkins*—had earned him a fair bit of abuse.

But now, in *Parrish*, Hughes saw many reasons why "fresh consideration" of the *Adkins* decision was "not only appropriate, but we think imperative." The Supreme Court of Washington's refusal to adhere to *Adkins*; the number of states having minimum-wage laws similar to Washington's; the narrow division in the *Adkins* decision; and, not least, "the economic conditions which have supervened" in the ten months since the New York minimum-wage decision—all this, Hughes declared, "necessarily presented" the question of *Adkins*'s status. He did not acknowledge that most of these conditions had existed in June 1936, at the time of the *Tipaldo* ruling.

At the heart of both previous minimum-wage cases was the freedom of contract—long held to reside in the due process clause of the Fourteenth Amendment. In his tentative *Tipaldo* dissent, Hughes had called this "a qualified and not an absolute right." Now he made the same point, with far greater feeling. "What is this freedom?" he asked, his voice booming. "The Constitution does not speak of freedom of contract. It speaks of liberty and prohibits the deprivation of liberty without due process of law." Liberty, he continued, was not "uncontrollable. . . . The liberty safeguarded is liberty in a social organization which requires the protection of law against the evils which menace the health, safety, morals, and welfare of the people. Liberty under the Constitution is thus necessarily subject to the restraints of due process, and regulation which is reasonable in relation to its subject and is adopted in the interests of the community is due process."

Was a minimum wage for women reasonable? Did it serve the community's interests? Hughes and four other justices—the three liberals and, remarkably, Roberts—answered yes on both counts. "What can be closer to the public interest," Hughes asked, "than the health of women and their protection from unscrupulous and overreaching employers?" Women received less pay than men for similar work, had weaker bargaining power, and were "ready victims" of exploitation. It was, he continued, entirely reasonable for state legislators to address these inequities—not on behalf of a special interest, as minimum-wage recipients were often regarded, but instead, on behalf of the broader community, which, in the form of relief payments and the taxes that sustained them, bore the cost for employers' "selfish disregard of the public interest." As he had three years earlier, in *Blaisdell*, Hughes took "judicial notice" of reality—here, the "alarming" demand for relief—though he did not dwell on it. "It is unnecessary," Hughes said sharply, in a clear rebuke to the four dissenters, "to cite official statistics to establish what is of common knowledge through the length and breadth of the land."

Hughes was now ready not only to uphold the minimum-wage statute but to declare the *Adkins* decision "a departure from the true application of the principles governing the regulation by the state of the relation of employer and employed." To that end, he cited a series of precedents, including—pointedly—*Nebbia*, the 1934 case in which Roberts, writing for the majority, had established "reasonableness" as the test for state economic regulations and had broadened substantially the concept of "public interest." Following Roberts's own reasoning, Hughes marched to the finish. *Nebbia* had crippled the doctrine of substantive due process, and now *Parrish* finished it off. "Our conclusion," the chief said triumphantly, "is that the case of *Adkins v. Children's Hospital, supra,* should be, and it is, overruled."

Roberts, whose switch had made this possible, seemed to take no pleasure in it at all. He appeared instead to wish he could retreat from the room. Eyes closed, he leaned back in his chair. The question that one conservative had asked another in conference—"What is the matter with Roberts?"—had never really been answered, and the outcome of *Parrish* only heightened the sense of mystery about his motives. The next day's headlines would say that the Court had reversed itself on the minimum wage, but it was really Roberts, and Roberts alone, who had switched positions from the previous summer. Hughes took a different position regarding *Adkins* than he had before, but he—like every other justice but Roberts—voted for the same result as he had in *Tipaldo*. Had Hughes's affirmation of *Nebbia* brought Roberts on board? Perhaps, but Hughes had cited *Nebbia* in his *Tipaldo* dissent as well—to no discernible effect. Did Roberts agree with any of the reasons that Hughes said required "fresh consideration" of *Adkins*? Perhaps—but again, one could only speculate. Roberts, on this day, was maddeningly mute.

George Sutherland now leaned forward, eyes on the spectators, alert to their smiles, their obvious enjoyment at the sight of a court overruling itself. Many then began to leave. Calmly, almost indifferently, Sutherland picked up the pages of his dissent and began to read it aloud. His voice, at first, was so soft it could hardly be heard. Then he paused, sipped a glass of water, and seemed to find his strength, reading with rising passion and rapping his knuckles on the table to emphasize key points. The remaining crowd stayed put in the courtroom.

The dissent itself was a serial scolding. First, of Roberts, for bowing to public opinion or the pressure of his peers:

> Undoubtedly it is the duty of a member of the Court, in the process of reaching a right conclusion, to give due weight to the opposing views of his associates; but in the end . . . the oath which he takes as a judge is not a composite oath, but an individual one. And in passing upon the validity of a statute he discharges a duty imposed upon him, which cannot be consummated justly by an automatic acceptance of the views of others. . . . If upon a question so important he thus surrenders his deliberate judgment he stands forsworn. He cannot subordinate his convictions to that extent and keep faith with his oath or retain his judicial and moral independence.

Roberts, with reason, looked annoyed. He touched a handkerchief to his lips and glanced coldly at his accuser. Then Sutherland moved on to Stone, who, in his celebrated dissent in the AAA case, had accused the conservatives of lacking self-restraint and acting on their "predilections":

> The suggestion that the only check upon the exercise of the judicial power . . . is the judge's own faculty of self-restraint, is both ill considered and mischievous. Self-restraint belongs in the domain of will and not of judgment. The check upon on the judge is that imposed by his oath of office, by the Constitution, and by his own conscientious and informed convictions. . . . It is the right of those in the minority to disagree . . . in terms which, however forceful, do not offend the proprieties or impugn the good faith of those who think otherwise.

Next came Hughes, who had suggested that events required reconsideration of *Adkins*. "The meaning of the Constitution," Sutherland lectured, "does not change with the ebb and flow of economic events."

Finally, he seemed to address Franklin Roosevelt and acknowledge the Court bill:

> If the Constitution, intelligently and reasonably construed in the light of these principles, stands in the way of desirable legislation, the blame must rest upon that instrument and not upon the Court for enforcing it

according to its terms. The remedy in that situation—and the only true remedy—is to amend the Constitution.

For "a more complete discussion" of the dangers of annihilating the liberty of contract, Sutherland, in a final, defiant note, pointed to *Adkins*, now overruled, and *Tipaldo*, almost universally deplored. He was taking nothing back. With a grim expression, he laid his dissent on the dais and rocked back in his chair.

"What a day!" rejoiced Robert Jackson, who had sat at the government counsel table. "The Court was on the march!"

Joe Robinson, handed the news by messenger, roared his approval on the Senate floor, interrupting Wheeler midway through another attack on the Court bill. Robinson's face was flushed; his fists, clenched in victory, shot into the air above his head and stayed there as he spoke. "Today," he proclaimed, "the Supreme Court has completely reversed itself!"

"I am sure the Senator from Arkansas is delighted," Wheeler snapped.

"Certainly I am delighted," Robinson said, and began reading from the majority opinion, smashing his heavy hands down on the mahogany desk to make a point, wagging his finger at opponents of the Court plan, and generally relishing his own performance.

"Fine," Wheeler interjected.

"Yes, fine," Robinson shouted. "Talk about accepting in all cases Supreme Court decisions as binding and above question! Here is a case where the minority opinion at last after many years becomes the majority opinion!" One person in the gallery began to clap—until attendants gave him a stony glare. As the argument went on, both sides claimed vindication: to Robinson, the *Parrish* decision showed the importance of having the right men—and more of them—on the bench; to Wheeler, it revealed the Court's capacity to correct itself.

Or so they now said. Previously, Wheeler had never put much faith in the idea that the Court, of its own accord, would remedy its own worst errors—so little faith, in fact, that he had been pushing a constitutional amendment to give Congress the power to override decisions.

Robinson, in continuing to press for packing the Court, also found himself at odds with his earlier position, as Franklyn Waltman, with glee, pointed out in his column: "He thinks the Supreme Court should be packed when it invalidates New Deal legislation and he thinks it should be packed when it upholds New Deal legislation. You just cannot satisfy some people."

Parrish had scrambled the pieces. In the days after the Court's reversal, no one could tell which side stood to gain politically. The decision's impact on the Court bill—and vice versa—was a matter of intense debate. "Economic predilections do not yield to skilled draftsmanship," Homer Cummings said in an official statement, referring to the expertly crafted minimum-wage law the Court had struck down in *Tipaldo*, "although sometimes they yield to the pressure of events. The whole episode indicates in vivid fashion the soundness of the President's proposal." Taking, as ever, the opposite view, the *Chicago Daily Tribune* proclaimed that the *Parrish* ruling "Wrecks Argument for Packing Supreme Court." Both contentions were plausible. It was certainly possible, as some claimed, that in the span of a single week, the Hughes letter and the Hughes opinion had blunted FDR's momentum. Unless they fueled it by reinforcing the argument that the Court was a political body. As William Borah wrote to an associate on March 30, "the situation here is difficult to diagnose. . . . We do not know 'where we are at.' "

The administration moved quickly to seize the advantage. This required a shift in the public rationale for the plan. In February, Roosevelt had said that the Court was behind in its work. When that claim collapsed, he began to make the case that the justices were behind the times—a barrier to social progress. Now that the Court, in *Parrish*, had given liberals a long sought victory, the grounds for Court-packing had to change again. Senior officials picked up a line of argument that Robert Jackson had provided during his Senate testimony: "Even government victories by 5-to-4 decisions are unsatisfactory," Jackson had said in early March, foreseeing the possibility that the administration might, sometime soon, win a case. "A state of the law which depends upon the continuance of a single life or upon the assumption that no justice will change his mind is not a satisfactory basis on which the government may enter into new fields for the exercise of its power."

Cummings, in an official statement, hit the same refrain. "Only by the shift of the vote of a single justice were the constitutional rights of the state legislatures reinstated. So it happened," he said with disdain, "that the Constitution on Monday, March 29, 1937, does not mean the same thing that it meant on Monday, June 1, 1936"—the date that the Court had struck down New York's minimum-wage statute. The problem, in the view of the administration and its supporters, was not simply that the liberal justices had only a one-vote majority; it was that the one vote belonged to Owen Roberts. More than once in recent years, Roberts had swung from side to side, carrying liberals from joy (*Nebbia*) to despair (the railway pensions and AAA decisions; *Tipaldo*). When—and where—did a pendulum come to rest? "We do not want to be ungracious and eternally dissatisfied . . . ," wrote the editors of *The Nation*. "Nevertheless, no clear mind today will be lulled into optimism because some needed legislation has finally been validated, or because a 'bad' judge seems to have become a 'good' judge. . . . Roberts' very changeable mind . . . is not a sturdy enough peg on which to hang the garment of one's hopes."

By contrast, "the hard-boiled four," as Harold Ickes called them, stood fast. Sutherland's opinion had made that very clear. In a letter to his sons, Stone expressed "fear . . . that the dissent of the four so-called conservatives, expounding their views of a rigid and changeless Constitution, apparently to be applied always in the same way, no matter how much the subject matter to which it is applied may change, will stimulate the criticism of the Court and give emphasis to the demand that it be reformed." Not even the unanimous decisions on "White Monday" (as March 29 became known to New Dealers, in contrast to that Black Monday of two years before) suggested that the four had actually tempered their views; their willingness to abide these limited constitutional advances showed how limited they really were. "Shotgun liberalism," *The Nation* scoffed. A sudden change of direction did not necessarily indicate a change of heart.

"Mr. President," a reporter asked at a press conference on March 30, "do you think the Supreme Court is curing itself?" Roosevelt shrugged. "I don't think there is any news in it. To tell you the honest truth, I haven't even had time to read the opinions." He said only that he planned to talk to the attorney general about whether the D.C. minimum wage, struck down fourteen years earlier in *Adkins*, had been revived by *Parrish*. If so, asked another correspondent, "would you explore the possibility of having other laws, such as NRA and AAA—" Roosevelt cut him off. "You are getting too 'iffy,' " the president said.

"Isn't everything today exciting?"

Molly Dewson, a leader of the long fight for the minimum wage, wrote a colleague that the struggle of the past few decades was finally on the verge of being won. Two days after the *Parrish* decision, representatives of eight states with minimum-wage laws based on New York's (the one the Court had overturned in *Tipaldo*) were meeting in Washington to discuss reenactment. Some legislators even talked about expanding the scope of such laws to protect men as well as women. "Just to think that silly Roberts should have the power to play politics and decide the fate of minimum-wage legislation," Dewson wrote. "But, thank God he thought it was politically expedient to be with us!"

Felix Frankfurter, who had fought those same battles, shared Dewson's enthusiasm about the outcome of the case, but could not cheer as heartily as she did. To Frankfurter, who was deeply devoted to the Court as an institution, the decision was "one of life's bitter-sweets," for he could only see Roberts's "somersault" as "a shameless, political response to the present row." Frankfurter wrote FDR on March 30 that "with the shift by Roberts, even a blind man ought to see that the Court is in politics."

This was a common view on the left. The fact (as opposed to the result) of Roberts's reversal was not to be celebrated; it was, rather, to be scorned, ridiculed, and feared. A *Philadelphia Record* editorial titled "Owen J. Roberts, Rex," asked whether the justice, "an ex-corporation lawyer, [is] a king that . . . can safely govern our destinies." One Democratic senator drew a more ominous analogy: "There has been much talk about the danger of a dictatorship in this country," said Lewis Schwellenbach of Washington, "but . . . Roberts has more power than Mussolini, Stalin, Hitler, or anybody else."

For Roberts, this must have been a painful period—not unlike the summer of *Tipaldo*, when he had taken the brunt of the abuse directed at the Court even though Pierce Butler had written the offending opinion. All Roberts had done then was sign his name. But that had been enough to place him, in many people's estimation, to the right of Herbert Hoover. It also ended any lingering notion of Roberts as a "liberal-conservative" and a possible candidate for president. If any justice could have shrugged off the criticism, that justice was not Owen Roberts. He cared greatly—too greatly, some of his friends believed—about his reputation. Now, not long after that wretched summer, he was again being singled out, mocked, attacked. He saw no choice but to suffer in silence. Like Stone, he believed that a justice's only real line of defense was his published opinions. This may have been cold comfort: in *Parrish*, as in *Tipaldo*, Roberts had allowed another justice to speak for him.

Years later, after retiring from the Court, Roberts did try to explain his actions. In a three-page memorandum published posthumously in 1955, Roberts revealed the truth, as he saw it, behind the so-called switch. The memo was no mea culpa. Writing in flat, impenitent prose, Roberts sought not to justify the switch but to deny it, contending that his position had remained perfectly consistent all along. In making this claim, he laid the blame for the whole upheaval—the wave of national revulsion against the Court after *Tipaldo*; the almost universal assumption that he had switched sides in *Parrish* for political reasons—on a technicality.

In its *Tipaldo* petition, New York contended that *Adkins* did not apply because the state's minimum-wage law was sufficiently different from D.C.'s. "The argument seemed to me to be disingenuous and born of timidity," Roberts recalled. New York, he said, had been too meek to ask the Court to overrule *Adkins*. In the Washington State case, by contrast, "the authority of *Adkins* was definitely assailed and the Court was asked to reconsider and overrule it." And therefore he could.

Here was the crux of Roberts's contention. He had not changed his mind; he had merely changed sides, for the simple reason that Washington had given him an opportunity to do so. Some accepted this rationale. "If counsel for the parties [in *Tipaldo*] did not want the *Adkins* case overruled, it was none of his business as a judge to go ahead and do it," said Erwin Griswold, dean of Harvard Law School, at the time of Roberts's death. Roberts had taken "a good lawyer's approach."

Yet other good lawyers had seen it differently—Brandeis, Cardozo, and Stone among them. In *Tipaldo*, all three had been prepared to overrule *Adkins* irrespective of what New York's petition did, or did not, contain. "I know of no rule or practice," Stone wrote in dissent, "by which the arguments advanced in support of an application for *certiorari* restrict our choice between conflicting precedents in deciding a question of constitutional law which the petition, if granted, requires us to answer." No legal principle, including *stare decisis*, requires the Court to apply bad precedent.

Moreover, Roberts's recollections were wrong. It was New York State in *Tipaldo*—not Washington State in *Parrish*—that expressly challenged *Adkins*. While New York had undeniably staked its case primarily on the grounds of distinguishing the statutes, it also hedged its bets. The state's petition called for "reconsideration of the *Adkins* case in the light of the New York act and conditions aimed to be remedied thereby." New York, it seems clear, was suggesting that *Adkins* be cast aside. The state's attorneys had marked out dual paths to the same result. Hughes had taken one; Stone, Brandeis, and Cardozo the other. Roberts took neither. Instead, he stood pat with the "hard-boiled four."

"My proper course," Roberts conceded in his memo, "would have been to concur specially on the narrow ground I had taken. I did not do so." He never explained why. Roberts had to have known in 1936 that by signing the *Tipaldo* opinion, he was endorsing it in full: its forceful, ringing reaffirmation of *Adkins* and of the discredited doctrines of liberty of contract and substantive due process. Whatever his true feelings at the time of the decision, Roberts gave not only the appearance, but the fact and full effect, of a wholehearted embrace.

The timing of the Court's reversal did not strike many as coincidental. The belief that Roosevelt's proposal had cowed Roberts into changing sides—that the justice had wilted in the heat of the Court fight—was well near universal, and eagerly promoted by the president's allies. The truth was that Roberts, Hughes, Brandeis, and Cardozo voted to affirm the minimum-wage law on December 19, nearly two months before the launch of the Court plan. Harlan Stone, at that time, was still dangerously ill. His vote was not needed—a 4–4 split would automatically sustain the statute—but as Roberts recalled, "it was thought that this would be an unfortunate outcome" and that Stone, as soon as he was able, should be given the chance to make it a majority decision rather than one by default. Hughes therefore held the case until Stone was healthy enough to attend conference, which he did on February 6, 1937—the day after Roosevelt had announced his Court plan and turned, in that single instant, the liberal justices' triumph in *Parrish* into what they knew would now look to all the world like a capitulation.

Hughes withheld his announcement of the decision a bit longer, hoping to undercut that likely impression; yet as the Court fight approached its third month, the delay itself was becoming a liability. Hughes bowed to the inevitable. Proprieties prevented the justices from revealing the true sequence of events; what happened in conference was supposed to be kept in the strictest confidence. But the facts, as Roberts later insisted, would seem to establish "that no action taken by the President . . . had any causal relation to my action in the *Parrish* case."

Perhaps not. But even though the *Parrish* decision preceded the launch of the Court plan, a credible case can be made that Roberts and Hughes were influenced by the criticism of *Tipaldo*; or by rising popular exasperation with the Court; or the indignation of the legal journals; or the scale of Roosevelt's reelection, which surprised the justices; or, through 1936, the mounting threat—or certainty—that either FDR or Congress was about to take serious action to curb the Court. If any of this had an effect on the decision, it can never be measured; nor would it suggest that either justice changed his basic beliefs in the face of events. It may, however, have made each more likely to examine his beliefs and then act on them—to take a bold step, to confront a tough choice and no longer avoid it.

"Few speculations," Felix Frankfurter observed, "are more treacherous than diagnosis of motives . . . in Supreme Court decisions." Yet one need not speculate wildly to posit that some of these events, to some degree, weighed on the minds of Roberts and Hughes and placed a finger on their internal scales. This would explain their relief when the minimum-wage issue came back before the Court so soon after *Tipaldo*. Indeed, when Roberts told Hughes that he would vote to uphold the Washington minimum-wage law, the chief nearly hugged him. Their later protestations aside, it is hard to escape the conclusion that they shed their self-imposed restraints and faced the fundamental issue because events had led them to see *Parrish* as precisely what they wished it to be: a second chance, a shot at redemption.

Chapter Twenty-three

BLOOD OR INK

NO ONE WAS conceding a thing. The Court's dramatic reversal on the minimum wage produced no defections, no weakening of resolve on either side. On the night of March 29, 1937, several hours after the Court handed down its decision, Carter Glass was helped from his sickbed, where he had been recovering from a long illness, and was taken to a studio by his physician to deliver an hour-long broadside against the Court plan. "I am speaking tonight from the depths of a soul filled with bitterness," the senator said, his voice cracking over the air. He called the president's proposal "utterly destitute of moral sensibility. . . . There has been no such mandate from the people to rape the Supreme Court."

Coughing frequently, the frail Virginian spoke with obvious emotion, making the sort of sectional appeal that one sometimes heard from southern senators—if rarely, as in this case, before a nationwide audience. He denounced "visionary incendiaries" like Harold Ickes, who, according to Glass, "recently reproached the South for providing separate public schools for the races [and] urged repeal of every statute and ordinance of segregation. . . . This infuriated propagandist for degrading the Supreme Court practically proposes another tragic era of reconstruction for the South." *The Washington Post* cheered the attack: "The moment had come to call a spade a spade. . . . In many parts of the South the response to his plea is likely to be . . . definite and electric."

FDR was not retreating, either. On April 1, at lunch with James Farley and Senator Hugo Black, the president was buoyant, insisting that all he needed to do in order to win was to give another good speech. Farley, second only to FDR in his overconfidence, agreed, though he added that it might take longer than Roosevelt expected. Black warned that the bill's opponents were planning to use parliamentary tricks to delay a vote as long as possible. "We'll smoke 'em out," Roosevelt replied, and "press for an early vote."

That same day, FDR sent a message to be read at a celebration of the fiftieth anniversary of the Interstate Commerce Commission, which regulated (with only partial success) the railroads and served, in this instance, as a useful metaphor. Roosevelt noted that private interests had opposed the creation of the ICC and had predicted it would bring economic ruin. "Those," Roosevelt wrote, "were the opinions of holdovers from the old 'public-be-damned' days—economic fossils which, like the poor, are always with us." But the ICC had proven that "an obviously national need can be met only through obviously national action" and a liberal reading of the Constitution. The *New York Times* had little trouble in decoding his meaning. "President Renews Battle Over Court," read the next day's headline.

Meanwhile, in the Senate Caucus Room, the hearings of the Judiciary Committee played every morning to a packed house. "The opposition is putting on a great show," Farley admitted to an associate; indeed, it would have been hard to deny. Ashurst, the chairman, presided with relish over a variety performance of labor leaders and farm union officials, law school deans, columnists, historians, stockbrokers, presidents of patriotic societies, theologians, bishops, and rabbis—united only by their abhorrence of the Court-packing plan. Roosevelt's decision to cede the stage to this motley collection of antagonists had proven a mistake. Opposition senators turned out to be shrewd in their selection and skillful in their coaching of witnesses—who provided, week after week, an earnest, instructive, and often entertaining filibuster against the president's plan. Ashurst, despite his pledge to support the bill, showed no inclination to hurry things along. "It is splendid mental stimulation," he said cheerily. "Besides, if we weren't doing this we might be doing something a damned sight worse."

Typical testimony—if there was such a thing—began with an avowal of admiration for FDR. "I am a lifelong Democrat and a Roosevelt man by conviction," declared one witness. Most insisted that the problem was not the president but his proposal—and what a future president, less scrupulous than Roosevelt, might do once Court-packing had been established as precedent. C. C. Burlingham, who described himself, fairly, as "an admirer and a friend" of FDR, reminded the committee that "all the Huey Longs are not dead, and as the political pendulum swings we may have reactionary presidents and reactionary senators, who . . . may make a new Court responsive to their will."

Others were unwilling to take Roosevelt's good intentions on faith. The influential foreign correspondent Dorothy Thompson, who had recently been expelled from Nazi Germany, suggested darkly that "this is the way" that despots take power. "The modern coup d'état . . . ," she said, "does not destroy the legal apparatus of the state." Thompson pointed out that Hitler had left the Weimar constitution in place—had even sworn his loyalty to it—then simply ignored it. Harold W. Dodds, the president of Princeton University, made a similar analogy. Calmly puffing on his pipe, Dodds likened the Court controversy to the rise of Nazism. "Shrewd and forceful political leaders . . . ," he explained, "know how to take advantage" of "emergency psychology." They manufacture a crisis, then use it as a pretext to justify exceptional new powers.

Across the country, despite the economic recovery, the feeling of emergency was as acute as at any point since 1933. The hearings played out against a backdrop of strikes and civil disorder. "Sit-down fever," *Time* observed, "flashed like heat lightning over the land." During a single week, workers shut down nine GM plants in Flint and Pontiac. In Wilmington, Delaware, striking truck drivers roamed the streets, heaving bricks through the windows of trolleys, buses, storefronts, anything. In Albert Lea, Minnesota, when police hit a union building with tear gas, employees of a gas machine plant overturned automobiles, burned one police car, and dumped another into the river. Union leaders seemed to be losing control of their members. Public opinion—and certainly congressional opinion—started to run against the strikers. A sense of siege hung over the Caucus Room. "This nation is on fire!" shouted William Lemke, a North Dakota congressman who had run for president the year before on the populist, anti-Roosevelt "Union Party" ticket that Huey Long and Father Charles Coughlin had forged.

This was no Reichstag fire—no conjured crisis—though there were those who suggested otherwise. William McDowell, a Michigan attorney, provided senators with a terrifying account of a rally in Detroit's Cadillac Square, in which 40,000 to 60,000 striking auto workers cheered the leader of the UAW, Homer Martin, as he stood on the back of a small truck and denounced the Supreme Court justices. "We know that nine old men have been on a sit-down . . . ," Martin had proclaimed on March 23. "The Supreme Court of the United States is the greatest threat to democracy in America outside of police fascism. We as workers are going to get everything that is ours, even if we have to move every public official out of office to get it." McDowell, in the Caucus Room, let this sink in. "If 40,000 peaceable citizens will boo the Supreme Court of the United States," he said, "you have got a dangerous situation." He accused Roosevelt of encouraging the sit-downs to intimidate the Court.

In this climate, it was no surprise that the hearings were heavy with portents of violence—of the "bloodless assassination of the justices," as one witness put it, or, in the words of Harvard Law School's Erwin Griswold, Court-packing as a "genteel" equivalent of "tak[ing the justices] out and shoot[ing] them." Senator Connally used the appearance of John P. Davis, secretary of the National Negro Congress, as an opportunity to stoke southern fears of desegregation. Connally subjected Davis to lengthy cross-examination about the ultimate goal of packing the Court with liberals.

Connally: You complain about Jim Crow schools. . . . You . . . expect the new Court to hold unconstitutional any state statutes in the South providing for segregation in the schools of white and colored, do you not?

Davis: Yes, I believe they are inconsistent with the—

Connally: You favor . . . the admixture in the schools of the white and the colored on the same terms and on the same social plane, and all that?

Davis: Yes, for the reason that experience—
Connally: I do not care for an argument. I just want to know if you do. You do?
Davis: Yes.
Connally: So . . . the purpose of some of the proponents of this bill is to do away with either state or federal laws that interfere with complete social equality of the races. Is that right?
Davis: That is right, Mr. Senator.

Still, there were lighter moments, many of them unintentional: the head of the Supreme Court Defense Association of Texas introducing the senators to a member of his group, a "Mr. Jones, from Russ County, a dirt farmer"; Burlingham's literate assault on Roosevelt's haste ("Emerson said, 'Why so hot, my little sir?' "); and, not least, senators' fulsome tributes to the "prophetic gifts" and "intuitive faculty" of the few women called as witnesses. Fears of the death of democracy aside, the hearings veered frequently into farce, and hundreds of spectators roared with appreciative laughter.

On the whole, the hearings were perhaps surprisingly substantive, drawing deeply on the debates of the Constitutional Convention, landmark cases, legal doctrines, British common law, even the practice of judicial review in France and Argentina. Though rarely matching the expertise of their witnesses, senators were well prepared and made, in general, a respectable show of themselves. Of course, being senators, they talked and preened and talked some more, issuing, in Alsop and Catledge's words, "steady barrages of oratory, long gas attacks." After a while, senators began to bore even themselves. But all that talk made a difference. "It is easy to make fun of such public speaking . . . ," reflected the two reporters, who sat through six weeks of hearings.

> Turgid, repetitious, crammed with non-sequiturs, richly ornamented with appeals to prejudice and self-interest, couched in an English which would have made Edmund Burke weep for very horror at the fate of the language—most of it was all these things. But it gave the country a chance to think the issue over. By sheer force of its repetitions it dinned the arguments for and against into the ears of the electorate.

But mostly against. Corcoran—who more than anyone had pressed for an early end to the administration's testimony—still talked big about "breaking" the opposition, but as the weeks passed, the hearings, along with his other responsibilities, took a toll on his confidence and his health. His weight shot up twenty-five pounds. He grew exasperated with Ashurst. The chairman, in his view, "was deliberately extending the hearings until such time as the public could be whipped up to think of Roosevelt as dictator." Or, more likely, until an event of some kind—a Court decision, a retirement—tipped the balance in favor of the opposition. Three times, Roosevelt's supporters on the committee tried—and failed—to shut down the hearings. After the first attempt, at the end of March, opponents responded by scheduling fifty more witnesses.

The president appeared untroubled. He wrote Frankfurter on April 5 that "we are carrying out the dignified process of keeping still and watching each new witness damn the proposal and offer a new remedy. My last count runs to over two hundred amendment proposals and over one hundred legislative proposals. It is quite clear that the utter confusion of our opponents among themselves means success for us even though it may be deferred until June or July. The opposition has daily epilepsy because we are 'keeping our shirts on.' "

"Nine men will decide whether we have peace or violence," wrote Morris Ernst, the civil liberties lawyer, in 1937. "What type of men will write this chapter of the United States? And will they write it in blood or in ink?"

All this and more seemed to rest on the fate of the National Labor Relations Act, better known as the Wagner Act. By either name, it was a thin reed on which to rest the survival of democracy. The act guaranteed workers' right to organize and to bargain with employers through union representatives; it also banned unfair labor practices and gave the National Labor Relations Board new power to resolve disputes. These were perfectly worthy goals, in most people's view. The trouble was that almost no one believed the act was constitutional—not the legal community; not the many members of Congress who voted for the bill solely out of a fear of provoking unions, while hoping and expecting that the Court would eventually strike it down; not Homer Cummings, who "regarded [it] as of rather doubtful constitutionality" and had urged Roosevelt to veto it; and, lastly, not Roosevelt himself, who had resisted signing the bill until the Court, by voiding the NRA in the *Schechter* decision of May 1935, left him no viable political alternative. Though Senator Wagner and the bill's drafters had made, as one of them noted, "a number of obvious specific changes" to the legislation in response to *Schechter*, the act took what one government lawyer considered "a rather extreme position" on the matter of federal power under the commerce clause. It was sure to be challenged, and vigorously.

With this in mind, the drafters wrote a preamble to the act that read like a legal brief. It took pains to establish that labor issues were not—as many, perhaps most, of the justices believed—a local concern, but instead a part of a current of commerce that stretched, unbroken, across the nation. The act's sponsors argued that strikes and other standoffs over wages, hours, pensions, and working conditions had a direct effect on interstate commerce. When workers walked out or sat down, plants were shuttered; when plants were shuttered, goods could not flow. The first step led inevitably to the last.

To liberals, this seemed obvious. To the Court's conservatives, it seemed specious in the extreme. In the *Carter Coal* decision of May 1936, the four conservative justices, joined by Roberts, had ruled that labor disruptions had at most an indirect effect on interstate commerce. And that was not, in their view, enough to sustain the Coal Act. According to commerce clause doctrine—inexact and inconsistent though it was—some activities had an immediate, direct, or proximate effect on interstate commerce; others, arguably, did not. Some industries were "affected with a public interest," others were not. Some companies were located amid the "current" of commerce, others at its beginning or end. All these considerations would have some bearing on the Supreme Court's verdict on the Wagner Act.

The NLRB's lawyers knew that the Wagner Act would be impossible to enforce until the Court had given it a clean bill of health. Indeed, with its constitutionality in question, the act was brought to a standstill by lower court injunctions and corporate defiance, stoked by lawyers who invoked the "higher law" of property rights. (The act was the subject of the first "ruling" by the lawyers' committee of the Liberty League, which unanimously held that it marked a "complete departure" from constitutional principle.) So rather than sit, wait, and settle for whatever cases came their way—the approach that helped doom the NRA—the lawyers of the Labor Board developed a master plan for testing the Wagner Act's constitutionality. They scoured the dockets of appellate courts across the country for labor cases that combined the most abusive practices, the most sympathetic victims, and the most auspicious set of legal issues. The government's lawyers carefully selected cases concerning large companies and smaller ones, major industries and lesser ones, businesses that manufactured goods, businesses that provided services—all with direct bearing (the board's lawyers believed) on interstate commerce.

By petitioning the Supreme Court to hear these particular cases—five, in the end—the goal was not simply to win each one and sustain the Wagner Act, but to break new constitutional ground and pave the way for future extensions of federal power. Together, these cases constituted a broad, coordinated assault on the conservative majority's notion of the commerce clause. The government was, in effect, ganging up on the doctrine, coming at it from several angles at once.

In February 1937, only days after the launch of the Court-packing plan, the justices heard arguments in the five Wagner Act cases. Attorney General Cummings, satisfied by the government's presentation, reported to FDR that "the matter now rests in the bosom of the Court." This was on February 11. Two months later, it rested there still. No decision had been issued; and with each passing week, more and more critics of the Court argued that its delay was creating a vacuum in which lawlessness and violence would breed.

"The sit-down," observed *The Nation*, "has reached the point where people no longer reason about it: they can only give spluttering expression to their hopes and terrors." Abbott Lawrence Lowell, the former president of Harvard, called the strikes a form of "armed insurrection . . . anarchy, mob rule, and ruthless dictatorship." For once, middle-class Americans found themselves in agreement with the *Wall Street Journal*: the strikes, it seemed, would lead to revolution. By the end of March, the Senate was so agitated about the strikes that members—for a week, anyway—actually stopped fighting about the Court plan and began arguing, with just as much vehemence, about the sit-downs. The loudest opposition came from representatives of the South, where John L. Lewis and his CIO were beginning a big push to organize workers in the textile mills; Lewis's stated aim was a union of 1.25 million members (many of them, not incidentally, black) and an end to cheap labor. On April 7, the Senate overwhelmingly condemned the sit-downs as "illegal and contrary to sound public policy." This resolution was no more than a formal, collective complaint; it lacked the force of law. Hiram Johnson, among other senators, sought to shift responsibility to the White House. "This is a case," he insisted, "where the president may act and it is his duty to act."

These were assertions, and open to question. The White House took the position that sit-downs were a local law enforcement issue, and that the president lacked authority to intervene except where local officials had asked the federal government to do so. None had. Either way, it was reasonable to expect, as many did, that Roosevelt would step up to the bully pulpit and exercise the authority he had in abundance. He did not. He kept silent. Not only did he fail to indicate disapproval of the strikes, but he did nothing to distance himself from the strike leaders who erroneously claimed his support. A rising chorus of incredulous critics in Congress and the press charged that Roosevelt's silence had been bought in 1936, when Lewis had thrown the considerable weight of his union behind the reelection effort. This Faustian bargain also, presumably, included labor's support for the Court-packing bill.

If so, Roosevelt got the worst of the deal. His acquiescence earned him little tangible support for his plan. Unions generally—not just the CIO—were making all the right noises and endorsing the bill, but their actions, to date, had been paltry. The whole effort lacked urgency. One labor leader wrote James Roosevelt in praise of Minnesota unions, which had sent "a personal letter to every Democratic precinct worker" urging support of the bill, while in Nebraska, "telephone contacts have been made with various outstanding liberal leaders." This was a far cry from 1936, when labor had put itself to work for the president with something approaching religious zeal. That campaign was a crusade, its aim nothing short of deliverance—deliverance from starvation wages, endless workdays, inhuman conditions on the shop floor. These were still labor's goals, of course, and Roosevelt was still their greatest hope. So where had all the passion gone?

In part, it was sapped by infighting among the factions of the labor movement. Having joined together to fight the GOP, they then returned to the familiar business of battling one another: the established craft unions of the AF of L versus the militant, ascendant CIO. This crippled their joint creation, the Labor Non-Partisan League, rendering it unable to fulfill its promises "to rise and support this great undertaking" of passing the Court bill. Labor, simply put, was distracted and divided—not least by the strikes.

Ironically, leaders of the warring factions did agree on one thing: that Roosevelt was not to be trusted. The AF of L's Bill Hutcheson and William Green complained that the president was aiding the rival CIO, while Lewis complained no less bitterly that the president was not doing enough to help his group. Roosevelt could do little to mollify them. Hutcheson, who had served on the Republican Campaign Committee, was implacable, while Lewis, a sometime ally of FDR, was shrewd enough to see that by withholding labor's active support for the Court plan, he increased his leverage over the president. Neither side, therefore, was especially eager to help Roosevelt augment his power through the appointment of six sympathetic justices; and both were content to wait and see what the Supreme Court had to say about the Wagner Act.

For now, they steadfastly resisted provocation. Administration spokesmen, to little avail, tried to draw labor into the fight. On March 24, in a debate with Senator Edward Burke at the Economic Club of New York, Robert Jackson laid the blame for labor unrest at the courthouse steps: "Our judges sowed repression and we reap violence." Later that night, at a rally of the American Labor Party, Jackson told an audience of 2,000 at Carnegie Hall that the Supreme Court had substituted the "law of the jungle" for the law of reason. In "the whole war between capital and labor," he said, the justices' message was to forget about peaceful deliberation and, instead, "fight it out with such weapons as you have." Over the coming weeks, as the Court maintained its silence on the Wagner Act, the administration and its allies continued to ratchet up the rhetoric. On April 10 at Chicago Stadium, Harold Ickes and Senator Alben Barkley addressed a mass meeting of labor and progressive groups ("PACK THE STADIUM," urged the planning committee) and issued a slashing attack against "sit-down judges" who, Ickes said, were preventing Americans from getting back to work. The crowd of 12,000 roared its approval.

The implicit invitation to turn up the heat on the justices (by whatever means) was not taken up. Attacks on the Court might well draw cheers, but the animus of rank-and-file union members flowed more freely in the direction of scabs, strikebreakers, senior management, phony "company unions," hired thugs, and "fascist" police than it did toward the Nine Old Men. Union leaders, for the most part, paid only lip service to Roosevelt's notion that the Court—more than these other, obvious, proximate causes—was responsible for the plight of workingmen and women.

"How is your Court fight coming along?" Homer Cummings asked Roosevelt on April 8. The president laughed. "What do you mean, 'How is *your* Court fight coming along?' " he said. Cummings replied that he thought the president had "considerable responsibility in the matter."

If there was an edge in either man's voice, Cummings's diary does not record it. But they both knew, of course, that they had conceived this plan together, to what had been their mutual satisfaction. In February, the attorney general had let it be known (to colleagues, reporters, dinner party guests) that he—not Corcoran or Cohen or Frankfurter or anyone else—was the mastermind behind the plan. He had run around town like a proud new father, handing out cigars, seeking congratulations. But the next two months had been hard on Cummings. While still proud of his handiwork, he had become a scapegoat for its failings. C. C. Burlingham, in his Senate testimony, wondered aloud why Cummings "would not have resigned his office rather than condone or have any part in such a shabby enterprise." Others put it more bluntly. Frank Kent, the conservative columnist, charged that Cummings had knowingly given the president false information about the Court's workload and ought to resign. Cummings passed along the column to FDR with a note attached: "No doubt," he wrote, "you have seen this grossly libelous article. Much the same tactics are being employed [elsewhere]. Perhaps we should take account of it before long."

There was really nothing to do but endure it. Cummings made a good show of this at the Gridiron Dinner on April 10, when he sat at the high table and laughed good-naturedly at a skit portraying him as "a rather incompetent chancellor" who shouts: "I've won a case in the Supreme Court at last!" A Gridiron member introduced the skit as a glimpse "a few years into the future . . . of what the Supreme Court will be, maybe—and maybe not!" At this, fifteen reporters marched onto the stage, each dressed as a cross between a Supreme Court justice and Caspar Milquetoast, the droopy, submissive character from a comic strip of the period. "Oyez, oyez," called a clerk, "this more or less honorable, and more or less Supreme Court is now in session." To the tune of Cole Porter's recent hit, "It's De-Lovely," a character identified as "Associate Justice No. 13" delivered the Court's verdict on Roosevelt's plan:

The Court is young, its docket clear,
But if you want our opinion here,
It's delib'rate, it's deceptive, it's de-lousy!

"Come on, get a move on," snapped a White House messenger, "and hold these new laws constitutional. The President wants them. It took him almost two hours this morning to get them through Congress. There's a crisis. . . . You don't have to know what's in 'em. Even Congress doesn't know that."

"Gentlemen of the Court," said Chief Justice Milquetoast, "let us go to work. Get out your rubber stamps!"

Roosevelt, from his vantage point at the center of the dais, joined in the laughter. A few seats away sat Cummings, and next to him, Justice Stone. Between skits, Cummings and Stone had "a long and very intimate conversation," as the attorney general recorded in his diary. "I observed that the President's Court bill was a natural development from the long suffering we had endured at the hands of reactionary judges, and that I thought the Court had it coming to them. He said they certainly have." Stone had "told his associates it was due to come sooner or later." Cummings asked how Roberts had come to reverse himself in the minimum-wage case. "Stone said he had not the remotest idea. He said he could not understand it." Cummings ventured that "the chief, in his [*Parrish*] opinion, built a bridge for Roberts and that the latter walked over it. [Stone] said, 'Yes, of course, that is what happened, but he ought not to have come over on that bridge. He might better have written [a] four- or five-line concurring opinion, simply stating he had been wrong before. . . .' [Stone] thought that would have been a franker approach and the better in the long run."

Turning to the Court bill, Stone expressed hope that the number of justices would not be increased by too many. The attorney general, a bit stiffly, replied that this was up to the oldest justices; if they did the right thing and resigned, the overall number would remain unchanged. Finally, Stone cautioned that whatever the size of the Court in the end, the president should take great care in selecting nominees; it was, he said, a very hard job. Cummings agreed. He asked Stone for the name of any Republicans who, if placed on the bench, would join the liberals. The justice was stumped. "He said the Republican Party had gone into such a condition of dry rot," Cummings wrote, "that they had no available live timber."

Late in the evening, just before the salad course, a chorus of journalists assembled on stage. They pointed in unison to Chief Justice Hughes, who sat, smiling broadly, at the high table. Then, in unison, they sang "Happy Birthday to You." The next day, Hughes would turn seventy-five. When the song was through, the Gridiron Dinner guests—among them Wheeler, Connally, Ashurst, and Sumners—rose in a standing ovation that lasted a very long time. Long enough to make its point clear.

"My dearest and my gallant 'old soldier,'" Hughes's wife, Antoinette, wrote him on his birthday, "how can I be grateful enough . . . that we are together, that we are well and sound of mind and, above all, that our love has grown deeper and truer with the years? With these blessings," she added, "we can bear anything, even 'the slings and arrows' of an outrageous Court plan."

Indeed, Hughes seemed to be bearing them quite well. To a friend, who had also offered birthday wishes, the Chief Justice replied that "the only calendar which engrosses me is the calendar of the Supreme Court and that I am glad to say is in good shape."

Chapter Twenty-four

THE SWITCH IN TIME

THE SUPREME COURT building, on Monday, April 12, was choked with the sort of crowds seen week after week since the Court fight started; indeed, since the whole trouble with the New Deal had begun more than two years before. Tourists, many of them in town to see the city's famous cherry trees in full bloom, waited in line from the early dawn hours in the hopes of getting a seat. One who succeeded was "Woody" Van Dyke, director of the "Thin Man" pictures; he said the scene reminded him of a major motion picture premiere.

Certainly the Chief Justice could not have been better cast. He strode into the courtroom at noon, barely glanced at those seated, and nodded to Owen Roberts at the right end of the bench. "I am directed," Roberts began, "to announce the opinion of the Court in No. 365, *Associated Press v. National Labor Relations Board*." The fate of the Wagner Act had finally been decided.

Roberts read opinions in this case and one other, concerning a bus company. Both were victories for the government but could not, in themselves, be considered a breakthrough. In the AP case, for example, the four dissenters—Butler, McReynolds, Sutherland, and Van Devanter—did not contest that the AP was engaged in interstate commerce; rather, their objection was that the Wagner Act interfered with freedom of the press. And since interstate bus companies were clearly in the business of carrying people across state lines, the second opinion was unanimous in upholding the authority of the NLRB.

Only when Hughes began reading the opinion in a steel company case, *N.L.R.B. v. Jones & Laughlin Steel Corp.*, did the courtroom come alive. Speaking for a five-man majority, the Chief Justice not only upheld the Wagner Act but seemed to consecrate it; he read his opinion, as Alsop and Catledge observed, with "an overtone of infallibility which made the whole business sound like a rehearsal for the last judgment." His voice boomed and his white beard bobbed up and down with his words. He acknowledged no difficulty, no particular complexity, in deciding the matter; he sounded, to one of the Labor Board's astonished lawyers, as if "the law had always been this way, that there had never really been any dispute about it."

Of course there had, a serious dispute; and much of the difficulty had concerned *Carter Coal*, the 1936 ruling in which a 5–4 Court held that coal production was a local activity with no direct bearing on interstate commerce. In preparing for conference on the NLRB cases, Cardozo had tried to draft a memo arguing that the Court could uphold the Wagner Act without overruling *Carter Coal*—then quit because he could not find a way around it. So he was shocked when two justices said in conference that they could: Roberts, who had joined the majority opinion in *Carter*, and Hughes, who had written a concurrence in that case, establishing a bit of distance from the conservatives but siding with them in the end. Cardozo was even more shocked—and delighted—when Hughes's opinion in the steel case curtly dismissed not only *Carter* but *Schechter* as "not controlling here." Hughes simply brushed those cases aside, giving them the constitutional equivalent of the back of his hand. "Yes, sir, a magnificent opinion!" Cardozo wrote to Hughes.

This it was, and a combative one, as well. Hughes declared that the ability of employees to organize and to select representatives to bargain on their behalf was "a fundamental right" and, he added pointedly, "often an essential condition of industrial peace." To the conservatives, who had long maintained that labor unrest exerted—at most—an indirect effect on interstate commerce, Hughes answered not with competing doctrine but "actual experience." What did experience teach here? That "stoppage of [the steel company's] operations by industrial strife would have a most serious effect upon interstate commerce. In view of [the] respondent's far-flung activities, it is idle to say that the effect would be indirect or remote. It is obvious that it would be immediate and might be catastrophic."

Here the Chief Justice delivered his sharpest rebuke yet to a conservative bloc that had, for decades, applied the "direct-indirect" test in a narrow, mechanical fashion:

> We are asked to shut our eyes to the plainest facts of our national life and to deal with the question of direct and indirect effects in an intellectual vacuum. . . . When industries organize themselves on a national scale, making their relation to interstate commerce the dominant factor in their activities, how can it be maintained that their industrial labor relations constitute a forbidden field into which Congress may not enter when it is necessary to protect interstate commerce from the paralyzing consequences of industrial war?

Though Hughes emphasized that the steel company was a massive, national enterprise, the magnitude of the operation was not the deciding issue. This became clear in the two opinions that followed *Jones & Laughlin* that day. These, too, were decided by the same 5–4 split, but they concerned smaller businesses (one a trailer company and the other a manufacturer of men's clothing). The government's victory was now complete.

As Chief Justice Hughes triumphantly read the opinions, one member of his majority, as Ray Clapper observed, looked "as if [he] had been through hell." This was Owen Roberts, and he had looked that way for months. During the Wagner arguments in February, and again during argument of the Social Security cases in April, Roberts was "quiet and sulky," Cummings told the cabinet. Roberts, he said, "has not looked at a government attorney." Neither had the justice asked counsel a single question. Charles Wyzanski, who argued some of the Wagner cases for the government, had found Roberts "rather ominously silent." And now, although Roberts had voted for the government in all five labor cases, it was clear from his countenance that he shared none of Hughes's self-satisfaction.

Perhaps that was because, to reach this point, the two men had traveled different roads, and Roberts had the more difficult passage. Hughes had taken an expansive view of the commerce power for many years: as long ago as 1916, Hughes, then an associate justice, had argued that interstate commerce was "a department of practical affairs" and that no abstract doctrine could dictate where to draw the line between state and federal authority or between activities that had "economic unity." His concurrence in *Carter* twenty years later was an aberration, born less of conviction than a desire to avoid the embarrassment of another 5–4 split. Hughes's failure to stand up to the conservatives in *Carter* may well account for his born-again fervor in *Jones & Laughlin*, a decision that marked a return to form.

Roberts, by contrast, had tended to take an orthodox view of the commerce power. He had signed the majority opinion in *Carter*. Moreover, his own opinion in *Alton*, the 1935 railroad pensions case, had not only questioned but ridiculed the idea that labor relations had anything to do with interstate commerce. But much had changed since then. The same pressures—doctrinal, political, personal—that had nudged Roberts into the liberal camp on the minimum wage had also, it now appeared, changed his mind about the commerce clause. "Actual experience"—in the form of the sit-down strikes—may too have had an effect. While Roberts may have been "naturally conservative," as Erwin Griswold recalled, he was not, like Sutherland and the rest, doctrinaire; he retained, in Griswold's view, "an open and alert and receptive mind. . . . His judgment was not static. It moved, but slowly." Slowly—and significantly.

Roberts had joined the liberals before, only to return to the right. But to the Four Horsemen, this shift had the feel of permanence. They considered Roberts gone for good—and with him the fight for all they believed in. As decision day approached and they worked together on their dissents in the Wagner cases, the loss registered on their faces. When McReynolds's clerk, John Knox, entered the living room during one of these conferences, he felt he was "witnessing the end of an era in the law and the death of an entire way of thinking."

Indeed, Sutherland's dissent in the AP case had an elegiac quality: it seemed to suggest that the Court had bowed out of the battle to save the Constitution, and it was left to the "people of this land" to wage a last stand for liberty. "Let them withstand all beginnings of encroachment," the justice declared. "For the saddest epitaph which can be carved in memory of a vanished liberty is that it was lost because its possessors failed to stretch forth a saving hand while yet there was time." Sutherland's "homily," Homer Cummings wrote in his diary, "was almost tearful in effect."

McReynolds's dissent, which covered all three manufacturing cases, had a very different tone. As Hughes delivered the opinion in *Jones & Laughlin*, McReynolds's face, as John Knox observed, "was set in granite, and he was staring straight ahead—seeing nothing." Yet when McReynolds started speaking—extemporaneously, as usual—a sardonic smile crept across his face. He spoke calmly, conversationally, but with bitterness, jabbing his pencil at the crowd to underscore a point, and sounding, at least to Cummings's ear, as if he was delivering a lecture to Roberts and Hughes.

If one followed the majority's reasoning, McReynolds said, "almost anything—marriage, birth, death—may in some fashion affect commerce." He joked that more marriages meant more babies, and more babies would mean, in time, more employees. Then he grew serious. A few moments before, Sutherland had closed with a lament; McReynolds, in keeping with his character, ended with an eruption. "Are our states obliterated?" he snapped. "This decision is wider than the people of this country can dream. The cause is so momentous and the possibilities for harm so great that we felt it our duty to expose the situation as we saw it."

When the justices had finished their business and retreated, once more, behind the scarlet curtain, a prominent lawyer rose from his seat, turned to a colleague, and said, "Chief Justice Hughes has saved the Supreme Court."

"I think," his colleague replied, "he has saved the United States as well."

On the afternoon of April 12, as news of the decisions made its way around Washington, some imagined that FDR was in a cold rage, cursing the Chief Justice for outmaneuvering him again and denying him the last good reason to pack the Court. In fact he was elated. When Cummings arrived at the White House to discuss the decisions, he found FDR "in fine humor." Farley phoned the president and heard the exultation in his voice. Not just Roosevelt but his entire circle was overjoyed.

The government's victory was monumental. "Nothing short of a miracle," *The Nation* cheered. Millions of workers were now free to organize without fear of repression, free to negotiate with their employers from a position of strength—for these liberties, so long in doubt, had finally been sanctioned by the Court. Labor regulations now had teeth. Moreover, "these decisions," as Robert Jackson told Ray Clapper in the Court's cafeteria, "go back to John Marshall's conception of nationalism"—of a federal government with all the authority it needed, unencumbered by the doctrine of state sovereignty. More than any ruling in a hundred years, *Jones & Laughlin* opened the door to a dramatic expansion of federal power. "What a change in the center of gravity," Cardozo wrote to Frankfurter the day after the decision.

In a quip that made the rounds in Washington, *Jones & Laughlin* was the "switch in time [that] saved nine." It was never clear who thought to adapt the eighteenth-century maxim ("A stitch in time saves nine") in this way, but many later claimed credit. The line caught on because it captured what virtually everyone on both sides of the fight believed: that the Supreme Court, seeking to save itself from being packed, had simply surrendered. The Court had bent so as not to break. "R[oosevelt] proposal forced this change," Clapper wrote in his diary. "Congratulations on the Wagner Act decisions," Morris Ernst wrote FDR, "the first real effect of your Supreme Court message."

While a few attributed the decisions to the sit-down strikes, even FDR's most implacable opponents credited him with (or blamed him for) forcing the retreat. "This would not have happened three months ago before the agitation about the Supreme Court . . . ," Hiram Johnson wrote to his son. "I think they [Hughes and Roberts] voted right this time, but I have damn little respect for them. In my opinion, they permitted themselves to be bludgeoned into voting to sustain the Act. I don't think the Court, from the standpoint of its personnel, at least a portion of it, is worth fighting for, and if it were not for the immensely bigger thing at stake, I would not be engaged in this contest."

The Chief Justice's "rather adroit piece of work," as Cummings put it, left even some liberals feeling as Johnson did: pleased by the outcome, appalled by what they saw as the cravenness behind it. "After today," Frankfurter wired FDR, "I feel like finding some honest profession to enter."

"The Court bill is dead," Senator Burt Wheeler declared; and for once, he had given voice to the hopes of most of his colleagues. The president, he said, now had no "excuse for wanting fifteen members on the Court." Even Harry Truman of Missouri, a backer of the bill, had to admit that "it looks like the Supreme Court has reformed." Opponents of the plan were harsher, of course, in their assessment: Tom Connally called the bill "a car with two flat tires"—punctured by *Parrish* and *Jones & Laughlin*. "If the president were smart," said another opposition leader, "he'd jerk his bill today. The whole country would honor that attitude." Only Senate leaders like Robinson and Ashurst—bound, against their better instincts, to support the bill—were prepared to say otherwise; but "such remarks," as *The Washington Post* observed, "were accompanied by twinkles of the eye and tongue-in-cheek gestures that belied the words."

The moment was ripe for a compromise on the Court plan. Supporters did not know if they had the votes to pass the bill, opponents were unsure whether they had the numbers to kill it, and both sides were exhausted by their two month-long siege. Both were also anxious about the political consequences (of either crossing the president or standing by him) and eager to move on to other, pressing business, of which there was no shortage. The Court fight had created a terrible bottleneck of urgently needed legislation. "The session is making a record for aimlessness and inertia . . . ," Frank Kent complained in his column. "For three months [Congress] has done nothing." Conceding the point, Joe Robinson told reporters that he could not remember a session that, at this stage, had so few bills of importance on its calendar. The 75th Congress was farther behind in the appropriations process than any Congress in a generation: only one of eleven spending bills had been passed.

The day after the Wagner decisions came down, Robinson summoned Joseph Keenan, FDR's Senate liaison, to his office deep within the Capitol and proceeded to walk him, step by step, through the opinions. Right down the line, Robinson said, the president has gotten exactly what he wanted—not a bigger Court, but a liberal one. "Settle this thing right now . . . ," he told Keenan. "If the president wants to compromise I can get him a couple of extra justices tomorrow. What he ought to do is say he's won, which he has, agree to compromise to make the thing sure, and wind the whole business up."

Keenan carried this message to Roosevelt, who was hearing similar advice from others. Ernest Lindley, a journalist who had covered Roosevelt since Albany, sent word that he should "ease up and get things calmed down again"—not by abandoning the bill, but by refusing to press it, and instead leaving it to hang like a sword of Damocles as the Court weighed the fate of Social Security. Around this time, Irving Brant wrote Roosevelt that "the number 15 has become a symbol of terror" in the country and that he should instead seek an amendment mandating the retirement of justices at age seventy-five. Though Brant refused to disclose his source (Stone), he warned Roosevelt that "the chief fear of the [Court's] liberals is that the prestige of the Court will be damaged if the transition to liberal control is forcible."

But those who counseled compromise misjudged both FDR and his antagonists. While most opposition senators would have settled for modifying the bill, the leaders of the revolt—Wheeler, Burke, and others—fiercely regarded adding even "two [justices] as bad in principle as six," as William Borah wrote an associate. The president, too, was full of fight. This was entirely in character. In 1933, even before Roosevelt had taken the oath of office, Drew Pearson discerned that "under that disarming amiability . . . runs a vein of steel—steel hardened by years of suffering and years of victory over an almost incurable disease. The steel is inflexible. Sometimes Roosevelt is slow to make up his mind. . . . But once he makes a decision, it stands." Thus on April 12, 1937, FDR told Farley that he was still convinced his proposal was necessary. "He is as firm as ever for the plan," noted Cummings. There was another reason: FDR was not used to losing. In fact, as a general matter, he had a hard time believing he could lose; and in this case, though it was not the sort of thing he acknowledged out loud, the cost of losing or giving in seemed too heavy to bear.

At a press conference the next day, Roosevelt professed that he had "not had a chance to read [the opinions] with any care" and so could not comment—before spending the rest of the session doing exactly that. "Off the record," he said with a grin, "and really off the record and just in the family, I have been chortling all morning ever since I picked up the papers. I have been having a perfectly grand time." In the "dear old *Herald-Tribune*," he said, there was an editorial that morning entitled "A Great Decision." This, he went on, had brought his mind back to September 1935, when a group of "very, very distinguished lawyers . . . operating under an organization known as the American Liberty League—" He paused, still smiling. "This is all off the record. What are you taking this stuff down for?"

The correspondents laughed. "You may change your mind," one of them said.

Roosevelt explained that on a hunch, he had asked his press secretary Steve Early "to do a little digging for me, and he found just what I thought he would find, and it is a joy": "a beautiful editorial" from the *Herald-Tribune* dated September 21, 1935, praising the Liberty League lawyers' "ruling" against the Wagner Act. That editorial, Roosevelt said, was titled "Thumbs Down on the Wagner Act."

"Well, I have been having more fun," Roosevelt grinned, and the reporters laughed again. "And I haven't even read the *Washington Post* and . . . the *Chicago Tribune* yet." He was indeed having fun, and so were the newsmen. "Today," he said, "is a very, very happy day." He added, to the further appreciation of his audience, a comment he attributed to one of his aides: "In the last two days the 'No Man's Land' has been eliminated, but see what we have in place of it—we are now in 'Roberts' Land.' "

Only when a reporter raised "the central question"—the effect of the Wagner opinions on the Court bill—did Roosevelt stop cracking wise. The decisions, he replied, were limited to collective bargaining. He said he had asked his advisers whether the decisions applied to child labor, or minimum wages, or maximum hours; their reply, he said, was, "the Lord only knows!" As for "the average man and woman on the street," he imagined their views would be this: " 'So far, so good, but—' and then, perhaps, the old phrase, 'So what?' "

This was implausible. With the papers full of grand pronouncements—talk of "a new era in labor relations" and "a turning point in American economic and political life"—it was going to be hard to convince anyone that what the Court had just done was insignificant, that the decisions, as Roosevelt insisted at another press conference, had merely restored "a very small, infinitesimal part of the N.R.A." But Roosevelt's skepticism was not just for show. It reflected a consensus among his advisers that while the administration had reclaimed a bit of lost ground, two thirds of all workers—those in service jobs and in industries that were clearly intrastate in character—had nothing to gain from the decisions. Also, as Robert Jackson recalled, Roosevelt and his aides felt that as great as the victory appeared, the justices were "now going to whittle it down by decision of individual cases until it won't mean anything."

Analyses by Justice Department lawyers concluded that "the new definition of interstate commerce rests on a precarious foundation" and that the Court still "may not sustain any of" the wages and hours bill that Cohen and Corcoran were drafting. Federal regulation of that nature might still be out of constitutional bounds. The *Jones & Laughlin* decision, as some (including Hughes) pointed out, was not wholly out of keeping with existing doctrine; it modified existing paradigms (the "direct-indirect" test; "stream of commerce" theory) rather than upending them. And because the opinion had not overruled *Carter* or *Schechter* but merely dismissed them as "not controlling here," they could still be cited as precedent. Though Hughes spoke with clarity, he had sown confusion.

Also, as with *Parrish*, there was the matter of the 5–4 margin. "Our national destiny," *The Nation* worried, "hangs on the slender thread of a single justice's vote." Roosevelt, too, was concerned. With so much at stake—legislation to raise wages and limit hours, to ban child labor and unfair trade practices, to protect investors and farmers and the aged, to build housing and prevent floods, erosion, and drought—it seemed reckless to go forward when the president could only count on the votes of three or, at most, four justices. He told aides that even if he could depend on Hughes, Roberts was unreliable. Virtually all the men around Roosevelt felt that the switch was born of fear rather than conviction, that it was tactical, temporary. This was not, in their view, a liberal Court—as Cummings put it in a radio address, it was "a reactionary court . . . in a liberal mood."

So Roosevelt saw no choice but to keep on fighting, firm in his conviction that he had been right all along, and still confident, if a little less so, that he was winning. At a press conference on April 16, he laughed at a recent compromise proposal: "There is a new one every ten or fifteen minutes," he said. He laughed, too, on opening day at Washington's Griffith Stadium, when he and the rest of the crowd looked up from the field (where the Washington Senators were trailing the Philadelphia Athletics) to see a small plane pulling a massive red sign: PLAY THE GAME—DON'T PACK THE COURT.

Some of this was false bravado. Roosevelt could see that in the Senate, the margin for the plan was narrow. He had begun to worry that Robinson would agree to a compromise without consulting him. Yet on balance, the president was upbeat enough to raise others' spirits—to put "wind into [the] sails, air into [the] flat tires" of a previously deflated Felix Frankfurter, who visited the White House in late April to help plot the next moves in the battle. After a few hours in Roosevelt's company, "I flew out . . . on wings," Frankfurter wrote him. By the end of April, FDR was feeling optimistic enough to take a fishing trip in the Gulf of Mexico—leaving the battle, for two full weeks, to his lieutenants.

On April 28, Roosevelt sped southward on a special presidential train. From the windows he could see the textile mills of the Carolinas and Georgia, where the CIO, in the wake of the Wagner decisions, was stepping up its drive to unionize the workers. He passed through Gastonia, North Carolina, site of one of the most storied, and violent, strikes in U.S. history, in 1929. In New Orleans, he visited the Bonnet Carré Floodway, credited with saving the city from the past winter's floods, and then, his thoughts on the massive schools of tarpon seen running at Aransas Pass, Texas, he put to sea on the presidential yacht *Potomac*, escorted by a flotilla of Navy destroyers.

His yield was poor. By May 9, he had only two catches; at port on the Texas coast, when cameramen asked him the size of the fish, he smiled, extending his forefinger and thumb about two inches apart. On May 11, the *Potomac* docked at Galveston so that Roosevelt could disembark, make the rounds of a few nearby cities, and greet the governor, James Allred, and a few local pols.

One of them was the congressman-elect from the Hill Country—a rangy twenty-eight-year-old named Lyndon Baines Johnson. On

April 10, two days before the Court ruled on the Wagner Act, Johnson, the former state director of the National Youth Administration, had defeated a crowded field of candidates in a special election to fill the seat of a congressman who had died in February. Johnson was an unknown; his strategy, as he and his advisers agreed at the start of the campaign, was to distinguish himself as "Roosevelt's man." This meant full support for Roosevelt right down the line, including his Court plan—which the Texas legislature had roundly condemned. "Now, Lyndon," said his closest counselor, "of course it's a bunch of bullshit, this plan, but if you'll flow with it, Roosevelt's friends will support you." Privately, Johnson expressed no opinion on the plan one way or the other. "It didn't make a rat's ass [of difference] to him," recalled a member of his circle. What mattered was winning.

Johnson came out swinging for the Court proposal. "I am willing to stand or fall on that issue," he said in his maiden speech. Only two of the eight candidates openly opposed the plan, but Johnson faulted the others for "hanging back like a steer on the way to the dipping vat." Standing on the back of a flatbed truck, his big hands gesturing broadly, Johnson told Texans that "this is the first and only test at the polls in all of the United States of the president's program. . . . A vote for me will show the president's enemies that the people are behind him. This is the test. Mr. Roosevelt is in trouble now. When we needed help, he helped us. Now *he* needs help. Are we going to give it to him?"

This they did, with roars of approval and a solid plurality for Johnson on April 10, though it was less than clear whether the people agreed with Johnson's position on the Court. Either way, his energy and intensity were greater assets than his identification with the Court bill. Still, he shrewdly sought to cement the impression. Minutes after his victory, Johnson telegraphed his friends at the Associated Press and other wire services that he had won a vote of confidence for the president's plan; he also prodded supporters to send the message to FDR himself. In a typical telegram, Thomas B. Love, former Speaker of the Texas House, wired Roosevelt that the judiciary bill had just "won a big victory in Texas. . . . Lindon [*sic*] Johnson, champion of the president's proposal, [was] elected by a wide [margin]."

Roosevelt got the message, and was gratified by it. He had quietly aided Johnson's campaign and was "elated by this victory," as Tom

Corcoran recalled. Here in Texas, seemingly, was evidence that the people were still with him—never mind that a Gallup poll showed declining support for the plan. In a meeting with Governor Allred, during a brief stop at Port Aransas in the middle of his fishing trip, Roosevelt had shown intense interest in the details of Johnson's campaign, and raised the question of what committee assignment the new congressman might prefer.

Johnson's first reward was a photograph, greatly coveted and carefully arranged. On May 11, Johnson stood grinning on the pier at Galveston Bay and wearing, on the lapel of his double-breasted pinstriped suit, one of the white oleanders for which the city was known. Roosevelt, also grinning, shifted his weight down the gangplank with a hand on each rail. Finally he reached the dock, where Allred introduced him to the champion of his Court plan. FDR shook Johnson's hand. (Later, Johnson would have Allred's image airbrushed out of the photo.) Roosevelt was so delighted by Johnson's presence that he invited the young man to join him on the presidential train for the three-hour trip to College Station. "That was all it took, one train ride," Corcoran recalled—though in fact, Roosevelt and Johnson ended up spending the entire day together, traveling another 200 miles to Fort Worth before parting. The president scribbled a phone number and the name "Tommy" on a scrap of paper and told the congressman-elect that if he needed anything, he should call Corcoran.

In Roosevelt's retelling, Johnson's election was soon transformed into an epic triumph in which a "remarkable young man"—a man who, Roosevelt added, might someday become president—had defied the party establishment to run as "Roosevelt's man," and then stood alone in support of the Court plan. Meanwhile, Johnson, who had pledged to go to Washington "for one reason"—to join the Court fight—never said another word about it. Not publicly, at any rate. He did, however, turn up at Corcoran's office, bearing maps that showed exactly where along the Pedernales River he wanted the federal government to build dams and rural electrification projects.

While the president chased tarpon in the Gulf, Corcoran was back in Washington, having a case of nerves. Since February, he had been swaggering around town, boasting that "the thing is in the bag." In reality, the steady drone of the hearings and the drumbeat of gloom from Senate leaders had sapped his confidence. He huddled with Ben Cohen and Robert Jackson to devise a new strategy. The three men agreed that Roosevelt should drop the bill for now and take it up next session, by which time he could line up sufficient support. To save face, the White House could say that the Court's switch had deferred—but not eliminated—the need for "new blood." Joseph Keenan and Charlie West, the two members of the strategy board in closest contact with congressional leaders, both agreed that this was best.

As for their putative leader, James Roosevelt found himself cornered by Joe Robinson, Alben Barkley, and Pat Harrison in a Capitol hideaway office. The senators told him in no uncertain terms that the president had lost the fight for six additional justices, and that, by refusing to face the truth, he was tearing apart the Democratic Party. "Mr. Roosevelt," said Robinson, "you tell your poppa that he'd better leave this whole thing to us to get what we can out of it. We'll do our best for him."

The next day, May 4, James convened the strategy board over lunch at the White House. Cummings, too, joined the group. "There is a good deal of defeatist talk going on around on the Hill amongst some of our friends," Cummings wrote in his diary that day. James repeated what the senators had told him, and the consensus at the table was that the president needed to hear the message in full and without delay. Eager aides tried to reach FDR right away by telephone, but found that he was on the water. Thus it was resolved that the following week, James should intercept his father's train along the journey home and see if he was willing to modify his plan, or at least to postpone it.

If James conveyed this advice, the president did not take it. On May 13, moments after James boarded the special train in St. Louis, FDR called reporters into his dining car and reminded them of the pledge he had made during last year's campaign: "I have just begun to fight." His trip to Texas, he said, had given him a "view of the people," and he could see that they were just as committed to his goals as they had been last November. He did not cite the Court plan specifically, but reporters got the message.

Later that afternoon, during a stop in Indianapolis, Jim Farley joined the traveling party and holed himself up in a private car with the president. He gave FDR the names of a dozen or more wavering senators who might be won over if proper pressure were applied. Farley urged him to call each of these men to the White House for a one-on-one meeting in the evening, usher everyone else out of the room, close the door, and put the screws to the senator. Farley told Roosevelt he could not afford to be beaten.

Returning to the White House on May 14, the president promptly summoned Robinson, Bankhead, and Rayburn to his office, where he presented them with a new "must list" of legislation for the current session: $1.5 billion for work relief; an act banning child labor and regulating hours and wages; a farm tenancy program; an excise tax bill; a balanced budget for fiscal year 1938; legislation for flood control, soil conservation, and hydroelectric power; and, not least, reorganization of the judiciary. On the last of these, Robinson pressed for compromise and, again, got nowhere. Instead, he and his colleagues got a lecture that they were out of touch.

"Washington," the president told them, "is a vacuum." If they would only "go out into the country" as he had (never mind that he had spent far more time on the water than on land the past two weeks), then they would see, as FDR later wrote to a friend, that "there is no question about the temper of the country . . . we have the overwhelming majority of Democratic voters with us and a substantial majority of all the voters." The people are with me, FDR insisted, and would make their views known "eventually"; to that end, he said, he might have to take the issue to the country in 1938—or 1940.

These men had seen Roosevelt bluff before; but he did not seem to be bluffing now. In fact, he had rarely seemed more sure of himself. His veiled threat to campaign against opposition Democrats during the 1938 congressional primaries—or, more incredibly, to seek a third term on the basis of the Court issue—sent Robinson and the others into a cold rage. Emerging from the meeting, Bankhead and Rayburn muttered to reporters that Roosevelt "has on his fighting clothes." Robinson added brusquely, and a bit wearily, that he saw "no prospect" of modifying the bill. The next day's *New York Times* left no doubt of FDR's intentions: "Court Battle Set to Go to a Finish."

Chapter Twenty-five

CONSENT

At 8 a.m. on May 18, the telephone rang at John Suter's house. "Mr. Suter," said a voice, "Justice Van Devanter wants to know if you can drop by his apartment on the way to the office."

The call itself was unremarkable. Suter, who covered the Supreme Court for the Associated Press, had been dropping by the homes of justices for years now; many members of the Court, Willis Van Devanter especially, regarded Suter as a confidant and friend. At seventy-one, he was also their peer. The justices never spoke to him about pending cases, only past decisions and general questions of law, but they did sometimes share secrets, and never once had the reporter broken a confidence. Now, on this bright Tuesday morning, Suter hailed a taxi, and on the ride to the majestic building at 2101 Connecticut Avenue, he wondered what Van Devanter wished to discuss. "There was only one story I could think of . . . ," the reporter recalled, "the justice's retirement."

The story, indeed, was in the air. Three days earlier, Suter's colleagues at the AP had filed a report under the banner: WATCH FOR COURT RETIREMENTS. The piece cited "hints in some high quarters" that Van Devanter was about to quit, a development that "might suddenly change the entire course of the battle." Rumors like this, complained *The New Republic*, constituted "the deadliest attack yet" on the Court proposal, because they encouraged undecided senators to wait for the crisis to resolve itself. Thus the talk rattled the White House. At various points, four or more justices were said to be on the verge of retirement—possibly in protest. In April, a former senator told Joe Keenan that he had learned from sources on Capitol Hill that "Brandeis is going to resign and give the President hell for his bill and then, if that [does] not defeat the bill, and Congress goes ahead with it, the whole crowd is going to resign—the whole darn crowd." There was, the source said, "no doubt."

Many conservatives, too, were alarmed by the prospect. While a well-timed departure might indeed kill the Court plan, it would also, of course, give Roosevelt the chance to appoint a liberal—or worse, a "Red." "For the sake of our country and friends *STICK*," a woman wrote Van Devanter in April 1936, on his seventy-seventh birthday. Every year around that time, Van Devanter's advancing age led to a new wave of letters—anxious entreaties from family members, from former fraternity brothers, from businessmen, from a New York lawyer claiming to speak for "thousands of America-loving Americans"—urging him to stay put. "Save us from having a communist . . . filling that vacancy," a friend beseeched him. Every justice received letters like these—more and more as the Court fight continued. To one such appeal, James McReynolds replied reassuringly that he was following the admonition of a preacher who had told him to stay put. "We will save the Court and the Constitution," the preacher had said, "if it takes a revolution to do it!" And "think," McReynolds added, "what my successor would be!"

As Suter settled into a chair in Van Devanter's spacious study, its walls lined with books and signed portraits of colleagues, past and present, retirement seemed the furthest thing from the justice's mind. For fifteen minutes Van Devanter puffed his pipe, talking in an animated way about Suter's health, dispensing advice. He appeared every bit as vigorous as he had at Court the day before, when he delivered, in a strong, clear voice, an oral opinion for more than half an hour. Though frail-looking, Van Devanter led a more energetic life than most of the justices: his greatest pleasure was his Maryland farm, where he tramped around purposefully in knee-high boots. He also remained an avid duck-hunter, and spent part of every summer at a sportsmen's club in Canada, where he hunted, fished, and played golf. As Van Devanter talked, Suter thought to himself that his reporter's instinct had been wrong, that retirement was out of the question.

Then the justice said abruptly: "What I really wanted to see you about is that I'm going to notify the president of my retirement." He handed Suter a copy of a short letter to FDR declaring, "I desire to avail myself of the rights" specified in the recent judicial pensions act, and to retire from the bench on June 2, the final day of the term. Having given his old friend this scoop, Van Devanter asked Suter not to publish the letter until a copy had reached the White House. "Be sure and visit me on my farm," he added, as Suter left the apartment, prize in hand.

The letter reached the president on a tray, brought to his bedside along with his breakfast. Roosevelt read what Van Devanter had written; then he asked his valet for some paper on which to draft a reply. "My dear Mr. Justice Van Devanter," Roosevelt began, forgoing the usual warmth ("Dear Willis") of such letters. He offered the justice "every good wish. Before you leave Washington for the summer," he concluded, "it would give me great personal pleasure if you would come in to see me." That was all. The letter, soon to be typed onto the heavy, faintly green-tinted stationery reserved exclusively for the president's use, failed either to thank Van Devanter for his twenty-six years of service on the Court or to praise his contributions to the law and the life of the nation, though it was customary to have done so.

The members of the Judiciary Committee were handed the news just as they entered the hearing room. They had not come to debate; rather, they were here to vote on whether to recommend Roosevelt's plan to the full Senate. Their verdict, a foregone conclusion, took no time to render: 10 to 8 against the bill. The Democrats split evenly, denying Roosevelt even a slight majority of members of his own party. The committee then delivered a second blow to the proposal and Roosevelt's prestige. Despite Roosevelt's hard line against compromise, all but one of the bill's supporters voted for a substitute measure, put forth by Marvel Logan and backed by Joe Robinson, to allow a temporary increase in the number of justices at the rate of no more than one a year; this, too, was defeated, 10–8.

The timing of these two developments—the committee's vote and

Van Devanter's announcement—may have been coincidental, but seasoned observers doubted it. "Justice Van Devanter was long in politics," noted Arthur Krock. Others pointed out that William Borah and Van Devanter were friends who lived in the same apartment building; not only William Borah but also Burt Wheeler, according to *Time*, were "credited . . . with an assist." This was not just surmise. Wheeler had recently received a tip from the writer Marquis Childs, who frequently served as a conduit between the senator and Brandeis. During a recent conversation, Brandeis had told Childs that one of the justices might retire if encouraged by the right parties. Omitting the name of his source, Childs passed the message along to Wheeler. "Your friend is right, whoever he is," Wheeler replied. "Tell him it's going to be done." It was then Borah who did it—despite his later denials. ("I think I have a fair amount of nerve, but I would not undertake such a job as that," he insisted.)

Among the Court plan's opponents, the news met with mixed reactions. Some believed that Van Devanter had yielded under duress; others thought he had outfoxed Roosevelt. "You have done a most courageous thing under the circumstances, a patriotic thing," Hatton Sumners, the man behind the pensions bill, wrote the justice. To Hiram Johnson, the old irreconcilable, the retirement was "perhaps fortunate" and "most unfortunate" at the same time. "I ought not to quarrel with Van Devanter because he is seventy-eight years old, and has been sick," he wrote his son, "but . . . I would have died on the bench before I would retire at this time." Van Devanter himself confessed to "mingled feelings of regret and relief" about leaving the Court at that point, but mostly, as he wrote his cousin, he felt eager "to be free from the work and turmoil." He was, as Louis Brandeis had sensed, ready to go. For all his remaining vigor, Van Devanter wrote a friend that he was "conscious that time has been running with me and has been registering as it passed along. . . . Perhaps also there is an increasing tendency to discouragement, but this last may be an incident of the times rather than of increasing age."

Either way, the announcement had its intended effect. A cartoon in *The Washington Post* pictured a grim-faced Van Devanter, pistol in hand, shooting an anthropomorphized Court bill in the head—to thumbs-up approval from the Senate opposition. In Congress and the press (if not, it appeared, in the country), the calls for FDR either to make major concessions on the bill or give it up altogether reached a high and steady pitch. "Mr. Roosevelt is 'on the spot,'" observed the *Boston Transcript*. Still, he gave no sign of it. On the afternoon of May 18, when Farley called the president "to kid him about" the cool tone of his "amusing" letter to Van Devanter and its suggestion that the justice pay him a visit, Roosevelt laughingly replied that if McReynolds ever resigned, no such invitation would be extended. FDR, Farley wrote in his diary, "appeared to be in very good humor and not at all disturbed by the agitation." At a press conference that afternoon, Roosevelt refused to speculate on the effect the retirement might have on the Court plan. "I don't think there is any news in that," he said. Asked about his long-sought opportunity to appoint a justice, the president simply shrugged. "I haven't thought about it at all," he said. "Absolutely no consideration."

Roosevelt wasn't fooling anyone. On the Senate floor that afternoon, Democrats and Republicans alike were gathered around Joe Robinson, pounding him on his broad back, hugging him, grabbing his arm, shaking his hand, calling him "Mr. Justice." It had been widely known for years that during the Hundred Days, FDR had promised Robinson the next open seat on the Court—a supreme reward for services rendered.

Within hours of Van Devanter's announcement, Senators James Byrnes and Pat Harrison moved quickly to claim, for Robinson, this IOU (This was hardly an act of altruism: both men wanted the majority leader's job.) They called the White House and asked to see Roosevelt the next day. The meeting went badly. FDR had said many times that he did not like to have a pistol held to his head, and that was distinctly the feeling he got from these two senators—that, in an inversion of the rightful, constitutional order of things, the Senate presumed to pick the next Supreme Court justice and asked the president to advise and consent (but mostly the latter). More irritating still, two leading Republicans, Borah and Charles McNary, wrote Roosevelt expressing their party's approval of the imminent selection of Robinson. They promised to confirm him without delay. In baseball, this is known as the "suicide squeeze," in which the runner at third dashes for home before the pitcher has even released the ball.

A promise, of course, had been made—and made public—which

made it unthinkable that Roosevelt could go back on his word. Yet "the Robinson suggestion," as Harold Ickes noted in his diary, "distinctly puts the President in a hole." The majority leader, observed Ickes, "isn't anything but a conservative at heart. And now it is proposed that he go on the Supreme Court as 'new blood' and as exemplifying a 'more liberal mind' than the irreconcilables on that Court. It really is an occasion for sardonic laughter." Robinson's age—sixty-five in August—was the least of his liabilities. The real problem with Robinson, as Ickes pointed out, was that he was widely regarded as a closet reactionary. He had, of course, backed the New Deal right down the line, but few believed that his heart had been in it. His pre–New Deal record on reform was more progressive than most liberals were prepared to acknowledge; he had, in fact, fought for social insurance and against child labor before FDR came along, and had a strong identification with the common man. Yet he also had an allegiance to the utility company magnates who dominated his region; and, while hardly a race-baiter, he had no apparent objection to Jim Crow, and turned a blind eye to the desperate plight of black sharecroppers in the cotton fields of eastern Arkansas. If Republicans and southern Democrats were excited about a Robinson nomination—and they manifestly were—it was largely because he was, as *Time* put it, "not at all the kind of dyed-in-the-fleece New Dealer that the Administration would feel sure of on the bench."

"Robinson Will Not Do!" cried *The Nation* in protest. Liberal groups and publications, which had looked forward to a Supreme Court vacancy in the way that the faithful await the Rapture, now erupted in righteous fury. The certainty of Robinson's nomination had been reported in the press for years; but now that liberals had come face to face with the fact, it was too much to bear—especially if the Court bill was rejected and this ended up being Roosevelt's only appointment for some time. Walter White of the NAACP wrote Eleanor Roosevelt that black Americans were deeply upset by the possibility; she passed the message along to the president. Around the same time, a group of sixty well-known labor, civil rights, and other progressive figures—including A. Philip Randolph of the Brotherhood of Sleeping Car Porters; Reverend Adam Clayton Powell, Jr., of Harlem; and the Socialist leader Norman Thomas—drafted a petition to FDR declaring that "we would regard the appointment of Senator Robinson as a blow to every movement for social justice in America." Robinson had other detractors in high places. "For the last two years," Irving Brant informed Tom Corcoran, "Stone has been dreading the appointment of Robinson more than anything else that could happen."

Anticipating this, perhaps, Roosevelt had begun looking for a way out of his pledge as early as March. He asked a leading attorney whether Robinson might be disqualified on the basis of the Ineligibility (or Emoluments) Clause of the Constitution, which provides that members of Congress cannot be appointed to an office that they helped create (in this case, by voting to increase the number of justices), or for which they had increased the pay (as Robinson had done in supporting the pensions bill). Roosevelt did not pursue the point, probably because Robinson's allies made clear that they were unimpressed by the argument.

Roosevelt was in a terrible bind. The liberals were right: to appoint Robinson after months of insisting that the Court needed young, modern, progressive men would smack of betrayal. At the same time, Roosevelt understood that a refusal to fulfill his promise to Robinson could, as *Time* observed, "stir up a bigger nest of hornets" than the Court bill had. Already, senators were muttering openly about mutiny. For Roosevelt, it seemed that the only way out of his predicament was to persist in packing the Court. "If I had three vacancies I might be able to sandwich in Joe Robinson," he told Henry Morgenthau. But he did not—not yet, anyway—have three (or six) vacancies to fill. He had only one; and despite his continuing optimism, he knew he could no longer take for granted that he would get any more than that.

The situation was replete with ironies: for Robinson, the sad spectacle of fighting to pack the Court with, among others, himself; for Roosevelt, the fact that the retirement of a conservative justice, so long and eagerly awaited, brought him not elation but frustration. Though he once called himself "a snap-judgment man," this was never really true. He did often decide quickly—few presidents in the course of American history could match Roosevelt's ability to consider an issue in its entirety, strip it of needless complexities, weigh its implications, make the call, and move on. But when faced with alternatives that he could not reconcile, he tended to freeze, stall, play for time that he did not always have to spare. This was one of those cases. He neither nominated Robinson nor declined to nominate him. He decided nothing—except to delay. He refused even to talk with Robinson, lest the majority leader force his hand.

"Do you intend to confirm the Senate nomination of Senator Robinson to the Supreme Court?" a reporter asked FDR, to the approving laughter of the White House press corps, in an Oval Office session on May 21. "Get out your rubber stamp!" joked another.

"I'm afraid I will have to tell you the truth," the president replied, with an air of benign indifference. "I have not considered the Supreme Court vacancy at all. Really, not at all. And I don't expect to for some time and, when I do, I am not going to tell you. Anything you write should be headed, 'Surmise Number 23.' There isn't any news on it and, by gosh, there won't be any news on it."

Robinson made no secret of what he thought of this. "Everybody's told me they're for me except that fellow in the White House," he snapped to Senator Harry Byrd, vowing, "I won't say a word to him until he says it first to me." And so the lines of communication between the president and the majority leader went dead for days. Only when Roosevelt had resolved that his instinct was right—that he could not afford a Robinson appointment until it could be counterbalanced by more than one liberal—did he send an emissary, Jim Farley, to convey the news. While feelings were raw, Roosevelt thought it best to keep a safe distance. He also wanted to be able to say, if asked, that he had not discussed the appointment with Robinson, so no bargain had been made for Robinson's support.

"Mr. Justice," Farley began warmly. He reassured Robinson that his nomination was not in jeopardy. "Sit steady in the boat, and [don't] rock it," Farley advised. Once the Court bill had passed, the seat would be his. Robinson expressed relief. He did not, however, give up his grudge. He waited, again in vain, for an invitation to the Oval Office and a presidential apology—even an acknowledgment might have sufficed. The estrangement continued. It was hardly the first time FDR had treated Robinson shabbily, but it may have been the first time Robinson responded in kind, denying the White House the daily head-count he had been providing on the Court bill.

Presidential aides scrambled to determine where exactly things stood—and, increasingly, voiced their discontent with the whole damned business. And with one another. "As our campaign's failure became manifest," Charles Michelson recalled, "tempers became strained, misunderstandings multiplied, and the disposition of everybody to blame somebody else increased." Party operatives like Michelson and Farley charged Keenan and Corcoran with arrogance and naïveté, blaming them for antagonizing senators. White House advisers like Corcoran, for their part, charged the Democratic National Committee with passivity, and mocked Farley for traveling around the country and giving what one Brain Truster called "weak and even silly" speeches on the Court for the purpose of building interest in his quest for the presidency in 1940. James Roosevelt, charged with the miserable and probably impossible task of holding this fractious group together, was manifestly not up to it.

Some blamed the president himself. FDR "never actually took charge of the Court fight," Corcoran said later. Robert Jackson complained to Ray Clapper that "the whole thing had been badly handled" from the beginning, that Roosevelt should have acted before the election or waited for an egregious decision—because nothing the Court had done this term justified packing it. The Court, Jackson said, had cut the ground out from under the president, and if it upheld Social Security, as it might do any day, it would be unclear what else FDR could want from the Court. Clapper said the same thing in a column: that Roosevelt, having forced the Court to reform itself, ought to declare victory and end the fight. At the White House the next morning, Clapper ran into Charlie West. "That was a fine piece you had yesterday," West told him, "but don't quote me." Steve Early, too, agreed that withdrawing the bill "would be a sporting thing to do," Clapper noted in his diary.

Even Farley—who, just a few days before, had swaggered out of a cabinet meeting and, in response to a reporter's question, laughed and said, "Why compromise?"—now privately conceded that a two-judge bill would "save everybody's face." In a memo for his files, Farley wrote that a compromise would also clear away the logjam of other legislation. Also, by giving opposition senators something to support, it would "relieve a lot of fellows from embarrassing situations" and allow them "back on the bandwagon as quickly as possible." But that opportunity might be fleeting. Farley thought it essential that FDR act now to strike a deal—for "the Supreme Court bill has engendered almost as much bitterness, if not more, than did the campaign."

Farley felt the brunt of this. He was not just an enforcer; he had long been a skillful broker and peacemaker among competing factions of the party. His easy geniality, his frankness and openness, well suited him to this role, which had made him indispensable to the president. But now, Farley—like Roosevelt himself—found that his charm was getting him nowhere.

On May 24, in a trio of decisions that, by now, could not have been entirely unexpected, a divided Court upheld the Social Security Act. Ironically, Cardozo, who wrote the two key opinions—one sustaining the unemployment insurance provisions of the act, and the other, the old age pension—had voted with Stone, Brandeis, and Roberts in conference to dismiss the challenge to the pensions provision on the grounds that the plaintiff lacked standing to sue. Hughes, however, had insisted on hearing the case, possibly with an eye to ending the term emphatically with another landmark liberal decision. In conference, he joined the four conservatives (whose motives, surely, were different than his) in voting to consider the act on the merits.

Oral arguments, presented in April and May, were notable mostly for their target: Owen Roberts. "I was arguing to a one-man court," Robert Jackson confided to Clapper. "I stressed the arguments that would appeal to conservatives," Jackson said. For example, he emphasized that Social Security promoted thrift and benefited "the man who works." Jackson was not the only one "working upon . . . Roberts" that day, according to Irving Brant; other justices, liberal and conservative, asked questions of counsel that appeared "aimed at holding Roberts in line." The effect of all this had been impossible to gauge. Roberts, observed Jackson, "has the best poker face on the Court. The Chief Justice, when you score a point, you can see his eyes twinkle. . . . But Roberts gives you no clue at all."

Apparently, the strategy worked brilliantly. Roberts joined both of Cardozo's opinions, which together took an even more expansive view of the federal taxing and spending power and the general welfare clause than the most optimistic government attorneys had thought possible. The decisions not only upheld the Social Security program but also gave Congress far greater authority to induce states, through conditional grants of federal funds, to take actions prescribed by Washington. Out of the ashes of the AAA case of 1936—in which Roberts had broadened the interpretation of the general welfare clause, only to conclude that agriculture was a local issue—the new Court majority, which included Roberts, was building a new constitutional order.

In Clapper's view, Cardozo "went out of [his] way to salve Roberts and Hughes by saying that this opinion was consistent with AAA decision. . . . That apparently was [a] sop or payoff to Roberts for coming over in this case." This was only partly true: Cardozo did affirm the portion of the AAA ruling that concerned the general welfare clause, but effectively reversed the part that constrained the taxing and spending power. Roberts joined him anyway. In fact, Cardozo rooted his pensions decision so deeply in the reasoning of the AAA decision that even Sutherland and Van Devanter felt compelled to come aboard. This left McReynolds, on behalf of himself and Pierce Butler, to deliver another of his harangues from the bench—wearing, throughout, a vicious smile as he denounced both Social Security and the majority opinions as intellectually soft. "No citation of irrelevant statistics and no appeal to feelings of humanity can expand the powers granted to Congress," McReynolds snapped. Watching from the courtroom, Clapper found the performance "despicable. . . . No imagination or sympathy. Just meanness."

It was a fitting end to a term in which McReynolds and the conservatives had suffered a rout. The Court had not struck down a single New Deal measure since it had convened in October. By June 1, 1937, when the Court adjourned for the summer and Van Devanter, looking cheerful and chewing gum contentedly, made his final appearance in the courtroom, "the New Deal's victory was complete," declared *The Washington Post*. The papers scored the session 12–0 for Roosevelt. "No such rapid advance . . . in constitutional interpretation has been made in this country before," let alone in a single term, wrote Arthur Krock in the *New York Times*.

Harlan Fiske Stone rated the term "one of the most exciting ones in the entire history of the Court." Still, as he wrote his sons, "it has not been a very happy one for me." During the first half of the term he had been gravely ill, and "the last half we have all been working under the strain of constant assaults upon the Court and misrepresentation of it and its work." Stone was, at least, "enjoying the dismal comfort" of knowing that he had been warning the conservatives against overreaching since Taft had been Chief Justice, "and now that some of the Brethren are seeing the error of their ways, I am not obliged to take back anything I have said." Looking ahead, though, Stone was "fearful." First, because he doubted "the permanence of sudden conversions"; and second, because he worried about the kind of man that Roosevelt would install in Van Devanter's seat. "I have not much faith in appointing men because it is thought they will vote in a particular way," Stone wrote Frankfurter, adding, "How I wish it would be you!"

Frankfurter (who wished that, too) felt "pretty low" about the Court's reversal—not because of the results, which he praised, but "because of the political somersaults (for such they are) of the Chief and Roberts." The swell of praise for Hughes—for his liberal vision, for his deftness in bringing Roberts to heel and his strength in asserting control of the Court—was too much for Frankfurter to bear. "When I see how a synthetic halo is being fitted upon the head of one of the most politically calculating of men," he wrote Stone on June 2, "it makes me, in the sanctified language of the old gentleman [Holmes], 'puke.' "

Frankfurter overstated the case. Hughes had certainly won some praise, and his manner in the courtroom made clear that he regarded every constitutional advance as a personal triumph. But he was also taking some tough criticism, especially from liberals. "Mr. Hughes has played high politics these last three months," wrote the columnist Robert S. Allen, "and played it with boldness and agility"—a compliment, perhaps, but a backhanded one. Early in June, Irving Brant wrote Roosevelt about a case-by-case study he had been conducting of Hughes's record. Brant published the findings in *The New Republic* under the heading: "How Liberal Is Justice Hughes?" His answer: Not very. On key questions, Brant argued, Hughes was "more reactionary than Justice Roberts." This he deduced from Hughes's votes during "quiet" periods when the public was not paying particular attention to the Court. But when popular opinion demanded it, Hughes, he said, became a crusading liberal. "When Charles Evans Hughes is a liberal, he proclaims it to the world. When he is reactionary, he votes silently and allows somebody else to be torn to pieces by the liberal dissenters."

In his letter to Roosevelt, Brant added a postscript: "I think more than ever that the court program should be shaped toward [Hughes's] retirement." White House aides agreed. Corcoran complained to Ickes that "Hughes has played a bad hand perfectly while we have played a good hand badly." Outmaneuvered—"checkmated," as Robert Allen put it—the president's men surveyed the Constitution to see whether they might, by some means, forcibly replace Hughes as Chief Justice. They came up with nothing.

"That is just what I expected," Roosevelt said to Steve Early, who had just brought him the news about Social Security. At a press conference the following afternoon, Roosevelt declared himself "very, very happy over the decisions of yesterday," but again, just as he had after the Wagner rulings, he tried to minimize the significance of what the Court had done. "We are all hopeful," he said, "that in the days to come the same human point of view will prevail; but of course there are a great many things that have not been passed on yet—an enormous number of things." He recited the now familiar list: a ban on child labor, wage and hour regulations, flood control measures, "and so it goes. . . . There are half a dozen other things that have not been ruled upon as yet by the Supreme Court and they are all very, very vital propositions."

That week, in fact—and the timing was not a coincidence—Roosevelt introduced one of the most wide-ranging pieces of legislation of his entire presidency, a bill that, among other things, would prohibit factory work by children and create a Labor Standards Board to regulate wages and hours in businesses engaged in interstate commerce. In a sharply worded message to Congress, FDR implied that the legislation was on its way toward what Cummings privately called "a head-on collision with *Hammer v. Dagenhart*"—the much maligned decision of 1918, in which a bitterly divided Court had ruled that a child labor ban exceeded the congressional power to regulate commerce.

In drafting the bill, some Roosevelt aides had thought it better to avoid, if possible, confronting *Hammer*, but the president chose the riskier path of forcing the Court either to sustain the precedent or overrule it. "If *Hammer v. Dagenhart* could be gotten out of the way once and for all," Cummings noted, "the fetters on Congressional action would be largely stricken off. . . . It would be a great advance." Holmes, in that case, had written one of the most important dissents in the Court's history, one that became, over the following two decades, a liberal lodestar; and it was this dissent that FDR quoted at length in his wages and hours message. "Although Mr. Justice Holmes spoke for a *minority* of the Supreme Court," he added pointedly, "he spoke for a *majority* of the American people."

The labor standards bill was not just an attempt to remedy social ills or knock down a long-standing barrier to reform. It was also aimed at changing the subject. Roosevelt, complained Hiram Johnson, "is filling the Congress so full of work now that he hopes to distract their attention from his Court scheme, and suddenly, he will pull a fast one." While FDR did, without doubt, hope to give Congress something other than the Court bill to talk about, he was less intent on pulling a fast one than on giving his Democratic critics a reason to get "back on the bandwagon" before the 1938 elections, as Farley had written. Roosevelt took care to consult Congress this time around; unlike his message on the judiciary, the labor message supplied only the outlines of the legislation, not every last detail.

Yet here again, he miscalculated. For some opponents of the Court plan, the labor bill provided a way to appear loyal to Roosevelt while in the act of undercutting him. Others, though, quickly rejected the labor bill as an unconstitutional political trick—or, in the case of southern senators, as an attack on low-wage manufacturing industries in their home states. "To ask them simultaneously to support a national wages-and-hours law" and the Court bill, *The New Republic* observed, "is probably to ask more than human flesh is capable of."

It had become, in Krock's phrase, an "era of ill-feeling." Roosevelt's relationship with Congress was worse than it had ever been; his standing on Capitol Hill was at its lowest ebb. The Court bill was both cause and symptom: it reflected what congressional leaders saw as Roosevelt's imperious manner. "He freezes up" at bad news and refuses to listen, one Democratic senator complained to Krock. He "laughingly" dismisses our advice, said another. And "he won't let us do anything ourselves." There was a restiveness in Congress, and in the party generally, that predated the Court fight—but the Court fight had given it focus, expression, and a noble purpose. What had begun as a struggle between the president and the Court was now a struggle between the president and Congress. Senators, in significant numbers, were finally prepared to make a stand. "We have retreated from one battle to the other during the last four years," one told a reporter. "But this is Gettysburg."

This sort of talk made it harder, surely, for Roosevelt to contemplate retreat. Publicly and privately, through the end of May, he gave every indication of keeping up the battle. "Apparently," Clapper believed, "he would rather meet defeat than . . . weaken." That, however, put it too strongly. Roosevelt had never considered defeat as an option—because he had never believed defeat was possible. Until now.

It had been an astonishing, often bewildering period. Less than three months had passed since Roosevelt gave his pair of speeches on the Court and seemed, virtually overnight, to seize the advantage in the fight. Then, just as quickly, his position began to erode. The Hughes letter; weeks of public abuse of the Court plan by opposition witnesses; Roberts's stunning switch on the minimum wage; sweeping government victories in the Wagner Act and Social Security cases; Van Devanter's retirement—these took a collective toll. None of these developments had, in itself, killed the Court plan. After each, it was still possible—and in important respects perfectly reasonable—for Roosevelt to believe that victory was within reach. Some of the events—especially the Court's reversal—that opponents portrayed as setbacks for the plan could also be (and were) interpreted by supporters as arguments in its favor. But by June 1937, the collapse of the effort could not be denied. Opinion polls showed a marked decline in support for the Court plan since Van Devanter announced his departure; and despite Roosevelt's faith that the people were with him, the overall trend of public sentiment was worrying. His own popularity had slid substantially since the election: in June, a *Fortune* poll marked the most precipitous decline of his presidency.

For the first time during the four-month-long fight, Roosevelt could see that defeat of the bill was not only possible but likely. None of his advisers was willing to suggest otherwise. Corcoran, Cohen, and

Jackson pressed him to suffer the slings of appointing Robinson to Van Devanter's seat; declare a provisional victory for the idea of a living Constitution; and withdraw the plan until the next session of Congress. "I pointed out to him," Jackson recalled, "that he was in a position to claim . . . victory in the Court if not to claim one over the Court." Aides had already drafted a presidential statement claiming credit for the switch: "Recommendations that I have made have already done much to clarify the constitutional situation and to improve the judicial process," it read.

Roosevelt leaned against shelving the plan. Anything could happen between now and the next session. He seemed inclined to accept as many additional justices as Congress was willing to give him—now. Seeing this, his advisers argued against accepting the two-judge compromise that many senators favored. "If you're going to pack a Court, you've got to really pack it," said Corcoran and the others. As Corcoran wrote to his colleagues on the White House strategy board, "if we get over the emotional hump of packing the Court"—pausing, he crossed out "if" and replaced it with "after"—"the common-sense thing to do is to finish off the job—not to swallow the two or three judges who won't be enough to do the job but to take the whole six in stride to neutralize the four reactionary votes and the two cagey ones of Hughes and Roberts."

But there was another powerful incentive for Roosevelt to take whatever he could get, and to take it now: such was the cost of his pledge to Joe Robinson. The only way he could justify the Robinson appointment to New Dealers was to pair it with the appointment of at least one liberal. Since the majority leader would be occupying an existing seat on the Court, a two-judge compromise had the virtue of allowing FDR to name two liberals at the same time as he appointed the (reputedly) conservative Robinson—yielding a net gain of one liberal vote. This offered no guarantees in terms of future decisions. Hughes and Roberts might well switch back to the conservative camp, as Roosevelt expected, and if Robinson joined them there, the Court of eleven would feature a six-to-five bloc against the New Deal. But that might, under the circumstances, be the best Roosevelt could do.

On June 3, the president sent James to the majority leader's office on the pretext of some matter of patronage. During the meeting, James, as planned, remarked casually that it had been too long since Robinson had visited the White House. "Father's been wishing you would come to see him, senator. In fact," James added, "he's rather hurt that you've stayed away so long." Robinson grumbled that he had not wanted to be seen as seeking the Supreme Court seat. Shrugging this off, James reached for the telephone and got his father on the line. This, too, had been arranged beforehand. FDR was blithe as ever—as if he had not left Robinson dangling abjectly on a limb for two weeks, as if he himself were not backed into a desperate corner. He invited the majority leader to dinner that night.

A few hours later at the White House residence, neither regrets nor recriminations were heard; only a frank, businesslike assessment of where things now stood, and what might possibly be salvaged from the original proposal. They talked for two hours. Roosevelt said that if there was to be a bride, there would also have to be bridesmaids. Four, ideally. Robinson, no doubt, got his drift.

On his way out, the senator encountered a group of newspapermen waiting on the White House steps. He flatly rejected reports that the Court bill was being abandoned. Then he added cryptically: "It is felt that during the last months some changes have occurred which have modified the situation, but there still exists the necessity for the injecting of new blood into the Court." Robinson allowed that he might offer amendments to the bill. None of this confirmed a change in strategy. It was, at most, "A Hint," as the front page of the *New York Times* proclaimed the next morning. But Robinson's grin—"ear to ear," wrote one observer—suggested that there was more to this story.

Chapter Twenty-six

STRIKING A BLOW FOR LIBERTY

"TELL US ABOUT your conversation with Senator Robinson last night," a correspondent asked Roosevelt on June 4, at his weekly press conference.

"He told you about that?" Roosevelt answered, implying that he had not seen the morning papers—before revealing that he had. "All you people down here were all right," he said, "but on the Hill they wrote the story yesterday afternoon that the court reform had been abandoned. Of course, that is just plain silly."

Immediately, though, he signaled a shift in approach, or at least in emphasis. For the first time since his fireside chat of March 1937, Roosevelt spoke in broad terms about judicial reform—"all the way up or down, from the district court to the Supreme Court." Now that the Court seemed to have conceded the argument about ideology, Roosevelt revived the question of the efficiency of the judiciary. In some districts, he told reporters, people waited years for their cases to be heard. As for the Supreme Court, Roosevelt derided the justices for going on summer recess when so many important cases—concerning, for example, the Public Works Administration, regulation of power companies, and other vital programs—remained undecided.

"They have a perfect right to take a holiday," Roosevelt said. "Nothing in the statutes to prevent it." Yet he added, pointedly, that he had "checked up" and found that while the Court was required to begin its term on the first Monday in October, "nothing . . . except the Court's volition" determined when it should adjourn, or for how long. His unsubtle implication was that old and presumably tired justices had been worn out by their work. True, they may have cleared their docket before leaving town, but that docket was short, and their vacation was long—four months long.

"The country," said the president, "sees the forest and a lot of people in Washington are all busy seeing the trees." Asked repeatedly what number of additional judges he would be willing to accept, Roosevelt lost his patience. "Again . . . ," he said, "I am talking about court reform and you are talking about trees."

"How many trees make a forest?" a reporter asked. On this note, the discussion ended.

Joe Robinson, having emerged from purgatory, now enjoyed a somewhat exalted status in the Senate. His authority finally acknowledged by FDR, his Court appointment no longer in doubt, Robinson was at the peak of his celebrity—"just as an expectant mother," quipped *Time*, "commands a certain ethereal prestige above other women." Never once in four years had Roosevelt handed him the reins. Robinson now relished the chance to resolve the Court controversy on his own terms—and then, having rendered his final act of service to the president, ascend to a position, unlike any other he had ever held, where he would be utterly unbeholden to any person, party, or interest.

Two compromise measures drew his attention. The first, proposed by Senator Charles O. Andrews of Florida, would create a Court of eleven: ten associate justices, each representing one of the ten federal judicial circuits, and a Chief Justice, appointed at large. This would give the Court the feel of a federal commission, with seats awarded in the manner of lower court appointments—that is, on the basis of strenuous lobbying by state politicians and senators. For patronage-minded politicians, this was precisely its appeal. Unfortunately, the map revealed that Joe Robinson's circuit, which stretched from Arkansas all the way up to the Canadian border, was already represented on the Court by Pierce Butler, a Minnesotan. This pretty well doomed the idea.

Roosevelt was inclined toward a second alternative—perhaps

because it looked so much like his original plan. Senator Carl Hatch of New Mexico proposed that the president be authorized to add a new seat to the Court for every justice who refused to retire at the age of seventy-five. Aside from this increase in the age threshold—FDR's bill had set it at seventy—the Hatch plan contained another change. New seats could not be added at a rate of more than one a year. Senator Marvel Logan suggested a slight modification: that any additions be temporary. When a justice inhabiting one of the newly created seats retired, that seat would cease to exist. The Court would expand and contract. Cummings called this the "accordion plan."

Robinson asked Logan—a heavyset Kentuckian who had served as chief justice of his state's court—to work with Hatch in drafting the substitute bill. Under ordinary circumstances, its terms would have been dictated by the White House. The strategy board, however, had become a casualty of Roosevelt's ceding of control. The president's "young men," so irritating to the Senate leadership for so long, were finally relieved of duty. Of the board members, only Joe Keenan, a favorite of Robinson, was included in the discussions about a substitute. Cummings, the old party man, had a role as well. He met almost daily with the majority leader in long sessions at the Capitol and the Justice Department. Canvassing, too, had become an internal Senate matter. From here forward the business of browbeating recalcitrant senators and coaxing others off the fence became the responsibility of men like Alben Barkley, Hugo Black, Sherman Minton, and Robert La Follette.

It was an onerous task. Had Roosevelt declared himself willing to compromise right after the Van Devanter announcement, the Senate, grateful for the president's good sense, might well have granted him a face-saving solution. But the two-week period in which he had let Robinson dangle had cost FDR dearly. It confirmed everything being muttered (or shouted) in the cloakroom about his imperiousness; it provided an outlet for senators' discontent not just about Court-packing but about the sit-down strikes, the budget, and, more generally, Roosevelt's insistence on further reforms at a time when the economic emergency finally seemed to be passing. The president was demanding completion of the rest of his agenda—seven key measures in all—before the summer heat stifled the capital and congressmen fled for cooler climes.

Compromise in whatever form had appealed to both sides when it seemed to offer the only way out—that is, the only way short of giving the president exactly what he wanted. But now that the original plan was dead, and goodwill toward Roosevelt was on the wane, the battle for half-measures was distinctly uphill. While public support for FDR's six-judge plan now stood at 40 percent—the lowest level yet—only 42 percent favored a two-judge substitute. This did not compel combatants to abandon entrenched positions. Among Roosevelt's allies, the Labor Non-Partisan League, roused to a previously unseen level of militancy, urged its friends in Congress to reject any substitute; seeing an opportunity to reassert its relevance, the League preferred to bring the issue before the voters in 1938 or 1940. FDR's opponents, too, maintained their firm stand. "We'd be the laughing stock of the country," said Senator Edward Burke, "if we should . . . consent to adding two justices . . . after we've licked the six-judge increase."

There was, however, a nervousness in their ranks. They knew that Robinson had now invested his whole self in the fight—that he was no longer restrained by the White House or his own ambivalence. And Robinson unbound was something to behold. In June, he began his campaign quietly, patiently, meeting one-on-one with colleagues in his Senate Office Building suite, two or three every morning, listening to their complaints, echoing their concerns. "Well," he would say, "how are you going to stand?" Sometimes he got the answer he sought, sometimes not; but as the days passed, he seemed to be gaining ground. Soon, pressing his advantage, he summoned, in groups of fifteen, senators who had made a commitment—however vague—to back a substitute. Here he ratcheted up the pressure. He made a short, emphatic speech about the bill being drafted and about his most cherished virtue: loyalty. At the end of each rally Robinson declared that every man in the room was now firmly committed—unless someone wanted to step forward and say otherwise. Only one senator did, and he asked merely for more time to think.

On June 11, after a cabinet meeting, Vice President John Nance Garner told "the boss" he was going fishing.

In a sense, the trip was unnoteworthy. There was little that Garner enjoyed more than fishing with his old friends back home in Uvalde, Texas, eighty miles west of San Antonio. Not the deep-sea, sport fishing that Franklin Roosevelt preferred—big boats, big fish—but the kind that involved sitting on a quiet lake, drifting, and waiting. This suited Garner. Despite his wealth, a fortune built of small-town banks, shops, cattle, mohair goats, and pecan orchards, he remained, fundamentally, a man of modest tastes. He and his wife, Ettie, who had also been his secretary since their arrival in Washington in 1903, had lived in boardinghouses for most of his long climb toward becoming Speaker of the House in 1931 and then, a year later, vice president. His only known indulgences were poker, which he played for fun and occasionally for money, and bourbon, a fine bottle of which he kept in the medicine cabinet above the washstand of his office. As early as ten in the morning, he made a ritual of pouring three fingers' worth into tumblers for himself and his guests, and proposing, as he raised his glass, to "strike a blow for liberty."

The interesting thing about Garner's fishing trip was its timing. Not once in thirty-five years in Washington had he gone on vacation before the end of a congressional session. And this, Garner knew, was no ordinary session. If ever his influence was needed, it was now. Garner once said, famously, that the vice presidency was not worth "a bucket of warm piss," and he made no great claims of usefulness in that office; in January 1937, taking the oath for a second term, he promised four more years of silence. But this understated his power and regard on Capitol Hill. He was more popular in Congress than any of its members. His blue eyes alight beneath a thatch of white hair and bristly white eyebrows, "Cactus Jack" held court in the rear of the Senate chamber, dispensing advice. *Time* called Garner "one of the President's chief behind-the-scenes wirepullers, arranger of neat political compromises, legislative uncle of the New Deal." Garner and Robinson were an effective tandem: the majority leader imposing order by the measured application of force, the vice president winning votes with homespun wit, charm, and shrewdness. All in service of an agenda in which neither man fully believed.

"The dates for this trip were set weeks ago," Garner protested when news of his vacation made the papers. "I told the boss that I would . . . return immediately if he needed me." This assuaged no one in the White House, least of all Roosevelt. The sunfish and bass of the Nueces River would be jumping in July and August no less than in June, and Garner had no good reason for deserting—indefinitely—not just at the climax of the Court fight but as Roosevelt was trying to push the rest of a contentious agenda through Congress. "Unfortunate conclusions," as Cummings put it, were drawn immediately by the press, which surmised that Garner was leaving "in a 'huff' " over the Court plan—an impression that senior Democrats were happy to confirm.

The huff, if that was what it was, had only partly to do with the Court plan. Garner's true feelings about the proposal were hard to determine. Estimates ranged from "strongly in favor" (Farley) to "lukewarm" (Ickes) to violently opposed (all who had seen Garner, the day the plan was announced, stand in the Senate lobby, hold his nose, and gesture thumbs-down). But Garner's chief complaints with Roosevelt were that his hands-off approach to the sit-downs was emboldening the strikers, and that federal spending, especially on relief, was out of control. Garner was an old school, agrarian, Jeffersonian Democrat—more New Freedom than New Deal—and while he made certain allowances for changing times, FDR's labor and budget policies were an affront to his reverence for property rights. He made no secret of that belief. The president, he wrote Jim Farley that summer, had "overreached in some things [and] . . . arrived at conclusions which to my mind can't be sustained from a standpoint of statesmanship or patriotism."

By the spring of 1937, Garner's irritation had trumped the public "pledge of fealty" he had sworn to his "commander." Thus he went "off the reservation," as Tom Corcoran complained. "He is almost in open revolt," agreed Ickes. When Garner's congressional allies stepped up their attacks on the relief program, White House aides saw the not so hidden hand of the vice president. The conflict reached a breaking point on May 14. While the cabinet waited outside to begin its weekly meeting, Roosevelt dressed Garner down in the Oval Office, lecturing him about the strikes, the budget, and the Court plan's popularity in Texas. Twenty minutes later, the two men entered the Cabinet Room. "The vice president," Ickes observed, "looked as if he had had a thoroughly sound spanking." During the meeting, FDR made obvious attempts to placate Garner, to bring him into the discussion, but this met with stony, disapproving silence.

And so, on June 11, Garner announced his trip to Texas. "He selected the right psychological moment," noted *The Nation*, and that was hard to deny. White House aides muttered (off the record) that the real reason Garner was leaving town was that he was "cracking up"; but Jack Garner, despite his sixty-nine years, had never been taken for a doddering old man. He knew precisely what he was doing, and to what effect. During his three decades on Capitol Hill, Garner, when inserting the knife, had done so in some hidden corner of the cloakroom; now, however, he was sending "the boss" a very public message that in this time of testing, no Democrat, not even his vice president, could be taken for granted.

On June 13, Garner got in his chauffer-driven car and left Washington. The next day, the members of the Judiciary Committee stepped without fanfare onto the Senate floor. One of them, Pat McCarran, carried a 48-page document, which he handed to a Senate page. ADVERSE REPORT, it read at the top. Weeks earlier, the committee had rendered its verdict on the Court bill: 10 to 8 against. Here now was the written opinion of the ten-man majority, seven of them Democrats. Henry Ashurst, the committee chairman, affected indifference, writing busily at his desk. Abruptly he rose to denounce the report as a "monstrosity." No one in the galleries paid him much mind, for none of them yet had seen the document in question.

The report was no dry-as-dust legal analysis. It was as caustic, contemptuous, and apocalyptic as anything that Justice McReynolds had ever uttered in the courtroom. It laid waste to every premise, provision, and stated purpose of the bill, granting nothing to Roosevelt, not even the good faith of his intentions.

McCarran and Joseph O'Mahoney of Wyoming, a Roosevelt-before-Chicago man, were the principal authors, though some of the more forceful phrases came from Wheeler, who was not a member of the committee, and from Borah, who was. (Borah later resented that O'Mahoney had received more than his share of the credit.) The Court bill, they declared, "applies force to the judiciary. It is an attempt to impose upon the courts a course of action. . . . Can there be any doubt that this is the purpose of the bill? . . . No amount of sophistry can cover up this fact."

Citing "the futility and absurdity of the devious . . . method," the report struck repeatedly at the artifice of Roosevelt's presentation of the plan. It also addressed the mostly forgotten aspects of the bill—those concerning the lower federal courts. In a recent column, Frank Kent had sounded the alarm, reminding readers that FDR was just as eager to pack the district and circuit courts. With this concern in mind, the senators argued that adding judges based on age, not on need, would fail to relieve congestion anywhere it did exist.

For all their attention to the particulars of the bill, the senators returned, again and again, to the basic principles they saw at risk. The Constitution, they wrote, "is in our hands now to preserve or to destroy." They implored their colleagues:

> Let us, of the Seventy-fifth Congress, in words that will never be disregarded by any succeeding Congress, declare that we would rather have an independent Court, a fearless Court, a Court that will dare to announce its honest opinions in what it believes to be the defense of the liberties of the people, than a Court that, out of fear or sense of obligation to the appointing power, or factional passion, approves any measure we may enact. We are not the judges of the judges. We are not above the Constitution.

In their closing passage, the authors summoned the nation's founders—a fitting point of reference, since the report ended with a litany of attacks that resembled, both in form and obvious intent, the charges against George III in the Declaration of Independence.

> We recommend the rejection of this bill as a needless, futile, and utterly dangerous abandonment of constitutional principle.
>
> It was presented to the Congress in a most intricate form and for reasons that obscured its real purpose.
>
> It would not banish age from the bench nor abolish divided decisions. . . .
>
> It would not reduce the expense of litigation nor speed the decision of cases.
>
> It is a proposal without precedent and without justification.
>
> It would subjugate the courts to the will of Congress and the Presi-

> dent and thereby destroy the independence of the judiciary, the only certain shield of individual rights. . . .
>
> Its ultimate operation would be to make this Government one of men rather than one of law, and its practical operation would be to make the Constitution what the executive or legislative branches of the Government choose to say it is. . . .
>
> It is a measure which should be so emphatically rejected that its parallel will never again be presented to the free representatives of the free people of America.

Every one of these arguments had been made before, but never with such collective force. "Bitter document, extremely rough," Ray Clapper wrote in his diary. "It reads almost like a bill of impeachment." To reject the plan was one thing, he added, "but to brand it as a violation of every sacred principle of Americanism, etc., is to practically brand Roosevelt as an enemy of his country." Harold Ickes agreed: "If the President is guilty of what this report says, then he should be impeached." Ickes took equal offense at the report's implication that the Court was, in his words, "like the Pope—infallible."

Liberal journals—suspending, for the moment, their disaffection with FDR's failing strategy—launched a counterattack on the adverse report. *The New Republic* took aim at its Court-worship and "hysterical intensity," while *The Nation* derided it as "a political broadside, studded with vague stereotypes and filled with often nonsensical fears about the future of our government. The only group that has reason to be happy over the report," the editors concluded, "is the Republican National Committee."

The GOP, of course, was beside itself with joy—not least at the fact that seven of the ten signatures on the report belonged to Democrats, making this the clearest evidence yet of a party at war, increasingly, with itself. Indeed, from the political sidelines to which they had been relegated, the Jeffersonian Democrats of the Liberty League rejoiced. "Complete vindication," Raoul Desvernine boasted to Jouett Shouse. Publicly, their ally Frank Gannett praised the Judiciary Committee for a "masterful presentation"; privately, he thanked certain members for leaking him a copy of the report, which, days before its official release, he had reproduced and airmailed to every daily newspaper in America.

The conservative press, too, exulted. "Prepare Burial Rites for Court Packing Fiasco," declared the *Chicago Daily Tribune*. This was not so much reporting as wishful thinking, but it did reflect a widespread and rational assumption that the president had been defeated.

At the very least, he had been dealt "the worst public humiliation he had ever had," as Rex Tugwell recalled. Adding to the affront, the Court bill's supporters on the committee failed to mount any kind of defense of the president, refusing even to file a minority report. (Corcoran, showing a typical disregard for Senate proprieties, had drafted one and tried to impose it on Ashurst, who turned him down flat.) Publicly, Roosevelt appeared unbowed. At his press conference on June 15, he claimed not to have read the report, though he promised to do so over the weekend, along with "ten or twelve other reports" on different subjects. He was clearly eager to move beyond it. What he wanted, he said, was "a vote; the sooner the better. The country wants it, too." A vote on the original bill, or a substitute? "A vote in the Senate," he said, not really answering. "In other words, not a filibuster. I don't think the country wants a filibuster. I think they want a vote."

Privately, of course, he was enraged. During the Senate hearings, opposition witnesses had gone to some lengths to avoid attacking Roosevelt personally. The adverse report, by contrast, painted him (without mentioning his name) as a liar, as power-mad, as hell-bent on crushing the Court and wrecking the Constitution. As Arthur Krock argued, this could only be intentional—an act of cold, premeditated, political patricide that, in the end, had less to do with beating the Court bill than with seizing control of the party. Only five months into Roosevelt's second term, the race to succeed him had already begun. That is, if he did not succeed himself—a widespread rumor he refused to squelch.

It was not just a matter of who would become president in 1941, but what kind of party he would lead: one with a split personality, as it presently existed; a solidly conservative party, largely southern and rural, incorporating right-leaning elements of the Democratic Party and the GOP; or a truly liberal party, with labor at its core, uniting progressives of both parties. (The Republican Party, at this point, was less focused on reclaiming the White House than surviving to see another election.) The realignment was coming, Marvin McIntyre told Ray Clapper; but the outcome, he said, was wholly unclear.

"Will the Democrats Divide?" wondered *The Nation*. Vice President Garner's departure and the release of the adverse report brought "the under-surface struggle," as Cummings called it, into plain sight. In Krock's view, the Democrats who signed the report had fired the "first gun" in the battle for 1940 and aimed, with this single shot, to take Roosevelt out of the picture. It was a risky strategy. The rebels might, instead, be handing FDR the issue on which to run for a third term. Also, as Krock pointed out, the president had "an impressive record of retaining and executing grudges." Should the authors of the report ever wish, for any reason, to eat their words, it was "unlikely that a man of the President's temperament would forgive them."

On June 16, only two days after the Judiciary Committee issued its report, President Roosevelt, the very picture of magnanimity, threw open his arms and invited every Democrat in Congress—all 407—to a "harmony meeting" at the Jefferson Island Club, a party retreat in the Chesapeake Bay. This had been Robinson's idea. "Mass wooing," Turner Catledge called it. The majority leader believed that the Roosevelt charm, turned up to full wattage in the summer sun, might solidify support for the substitute bill. Republicans gleefully mocked the picnic, comparing Democrats to "school boys" about to get "a lecture from their teacher." Ickes considered the meeting a fine idea indeed, and wrote FDR a note urging him to "let the people at Jefferson Island know where [to get] off." Roosevelt replied that he would enjoy "cracking the whip." The White House, however, made clear that the weekend's agenda was purely social and that the president would not even think of scolding insurgents. That is, those who showed up. More than a dozen opponents of the Court plan, including Carter Glass and Edward Burke, hastily declined the invitation. So did Rush Holt of West Virginia. "You know, there's an old Roman custom," Holt said, laughing; "first feast them and then acquire them. And I don't want to be acquired."

If nothing else, the retreat would give Roosevelt a chance to dispel, for a moment, the pall that hung over his presidency. "Everything very depressing," Ray Clapper wrote in his diary, describing the mood in Washington and the country. "Everything seems [to] be going sour. People have jitters and seem [to] have lost senses." Roosevelt was "being denounced daily in Congress, public sentiment seems [to] be turning on him for letting labor get wild. . . . Most serious ebb of Rvt sentiment since he took office." In the Senate, James Byrnes, Garner's proxy, launched a campaign to strip the federal government of much of its responsibility for the relief program and to vest control in local communities. The press called this the "Garner revolt"—until Robinson, surprisingly, stepped forward to lead it. Piling on, General Hugh Johnson, the former NRA director, denounced Roosevelt's second-term agenda as the prelude to revolution. The *Macon Telegraph*—in the state, Georgia, that FDR considered his second home—even called for his impeachment.

Meanwhile, Chief Justice Hughes, before leaving on a motoring trip to Alberta, Canada, delivered a pair of commencement addresses that, to Roosevelt, must have felt like a slap in the face. At Amherst College, where a grandson was graduating, Hughes went after "crusaders"—a term that, decades ago, had been applied to him. Where, Hughes asked, "shall we look for the balanced judgment, the sane appraisements and the reasonable methods?" Two days later at Brown University, his alma mater (where another grandson was receiving a degree), Hughes again avoided mention of the Court fight, but seemed to paraphrase the adverse report: "The arch enemies of society," he declared, "are those who know better but by indirection, misstatement, understatement and slander, seek to accomplish their concealed purposes."

All this weighed heavily on Roosevelt. With his confidant Louis Howe and his friend and bodyguard Gus Gennerich both gone, with Eleanor out of town much of the time, the president was a lonely figure. He spent night after night working alone in the White House residence. His aides worried about his growing isolation.

The Jefferson Island retreat would provide relief—at least for a weekend. On the morning of Friday, June 25, about 130 members of Congress and other officials arrived on a contingent of Navy patrol boats. This was the first wave. Two others would follow, one each on Saturday and Sunday. The long, white, colonial clubhouse had too few beds for a crowd this big, so only the president and some members of his cabinet would stay overnight. Francis Perkins was not among them. The Jefferson Island Club, founded in 1931 by a group of Democratic senators, was off-limits to women, so neither the Labor Secretary nor the six female members of Congress were welcome at what the invitation called "'stag' parties." "The men," said one congresswoman, "might feel hesitancy about letting down their hair, taking off their coats and perhaps their shirts—I don't know—with us along."

Arriving on the island, a number of the men shed not only coats and shirts but the rest of their clothes, then stepped over stones into the clear, green waters of Jefferson Narrows. Some of their colleagues, meanwhile, sat sweltering in flannel suits or, more wisely, summer whites, drinking mint juleps and cold beer, eating blue crabs, and playing cards on the wide veranda of the clubhouse. Others, scattering like children across the club grounds, shot skeet, sang songs ("The old G.O.P., she ain't what she used to be," went one), cast a line for bluefish or croakers, challenged each other to hog-calling contests, and played sloppy baseball games. One ended in a 6-to-6 tie. "We put the decision up to the Supreme Court," a congressman laughed.

And there, near the water's edge, was their host. In white linen trousers and a white, short-sleeved shirt open at the neck, Roosevelt sat in the shade of an old tree and warmly greeted his guests, many of whom had never met him in person. Six hours a day he sat, shaking hands, making jokes and posing for photographs with clusters of sweaty men who refused to remove their neckties. A group of congressmen inducted him into the Demagogues Club—a not so secret and not so serious society—during a ceremony in which he repeated their pledge never again to be consistent in his views. Correspondents, confined to the wharf, claimed to hear FDR's familiar laugh ringing out across the water.

He was having a terrific time. He resisted attempts to talk shop. The few congressmen who arrived with briefcases and arms full of documents went away disappointed. Most guests, however, were thrilled to be freed from workaday concerns; there was not even a telephone on the island (though the *Potomac*, anchored offshore, maintained contact with Washington). Only at night, after the last boatload of revelers had left, did Roosevelt and a handful of remaining guests settle into serious discussions. The attorney general huddled with Robinson and Roosevelt about the shape of the substitute Court bill; but in keeping with the spirit of the weekend, these conversations gave way to what Cummings called "very merry" poker games.

The Jefferson Island outing was a success. It was not just a picnic, it was a "love feast," as the press mockingly but accurately referred to it. The mood was nothing short of giddy, unspoiled by the few passing showers or by the presence of malcontents like Burt Wheeler. Not only that: as Sir Ronald Lindsay, the British ambassador to the United States, reported to London, Democrats "returned to the capital in a far more malleable spirit." Many congressmen agreed. "I think he won some who might have been slipping," said one. It seemed likely that Roosevelt had clinched a few votes—just enough, perhaps, to make the difference. If so, he had done it not by persuading Democrats, pressing them, or making them promises, but rather, as Arthur Krock argued, by "his geniality, apparent forbearance and high charity," all shown in abundance. "The dramatization was perfect," Krock added; "the hero played his role flawlessly; and the audience began to forget his faults and indignantly to recall his aspersed virtues." The seven senators who wrote the adverse report were said to have been shunned on the island; they were reported to worry they had gone too far.

"Nobody got religion," scoffed Senator Josiah Bailey, but this was a hope, not a fact. A few days after the Democrats' return, *The Washington Post* decided that opponents like Bailey had been "entirely too optimistic in their assumption that the court-packing plan is dead." Newspapers reported that fifty-four senators had lined up behind the compromise bill—a number that, give or take two or three, matched the confidential tallies produced by each side. Robinson had done it—he had built a majority. There was no guarantee that he could hold it; but for now, at least, he had the votes to win. Wheeler, accordingly, stopped boasting or bluffing that he could beat any compromise. "You know what that means," Hiram Johnson wrote his son. It meant a filibuster.

This now seemed inevitable. Even before the island retreat, opposition leaders had begun drafting the interminable speeches with which senators held the floor during a filibuster. (Of course, in the practiced art of talking a bill to death, speeches per se were not required. Anything would do: the works of Shakespeare, the most recent *Congressional*

Record, year-old election returns, biographies of Abraham Lincoln or Jefferson Davis.) The opposition had also split its forces into "quints," teams of five senators that were charged with talking for twenty-four hours—to be relieved, if necessary, by a "reserve squad" of experienced filibusterers. "I will stand in the Senate until I drop," announced Pat McCarran. Opposition senators also prepared a poison pill amendment aimed at inducing southerners to join the filibuster: they planned to attach an anti-lynching bill to the substitute Court bill. This, they said, would have the salutary effect of reminding the Old Confederacy that a Court packed by Roosevelt would be a Court that would uphold a federal law against lynching—should one someday confound the odds and pass.

There were other time-worn tactics to blockade a bill. One Senate rule forbade members from speaking more than twice per day on a given piece of legislation; but a senator was free to offer as many amendments to the bill as he wished, and could then speak twice on each new amendment. This created a nearly infinite range of possibilities for mischief. In early July, Senator Burke procured a stack of official amendment blanks and charged a group of young American Bar Association lawyers with the task of filling them in. After a day and a half, the lawyers had drafted no more than fifteen amendments, each of which substantially altered the Court bill. Exasperated, the men paid a visit to Senator Bailey, who laughed out loud at their paltry output. Reaching for a copy of the bill, he told one of the lawyers to take dictation. Bailey pointed to the provision that set a limit of fifteen justices, and instructed the lawyers to replace "fifteen" with "fourteen." Then "thirteen." Then "twelve." And so on through the various sections of the bill. Having received this lesson in legislative hair-splitting, the lawyers produced 125 neatly typed amendments by the next morning—enough to permit 250 speeches.

Before the Jefferson Island picnic, most of Roosevelt's Senate supporters had lacked the will to ride out a filibuster. But after their return, infused with new resolve, they readied parliamentary maneuvers to break the rebellion. Robinson and his deputies were confident that as the weeks dragged on and the heat of the Washington summer grew more and more oppressive, the opposition would suffer defections. Hiram Johnson, a veteran of many filibusters during his twenty years in the Senate, feared that Robinson was right. "I know how men tire," Johnson wrote his son, "and though these men,—The Democrats, I mean—have . . . a pertinacity that is admirable . . . , I imagine that one by one they will be broken down."

In the event of a filibuster, Arthur Krock wrote, "public opinion will select the victor." At the moment, according to Gallup, the American people were just about evenly divided on the question. But most observers expected that once the blathering began, the balance would shift decisively against a filibuster. Burt Wheeler and Tom Connally were already feeling heat back home for their apparent obsession with the Court issue, and before long, most opposition senators were sure to face popular pressure to attend to other, urgent business. Farmers, for example, were loudly demanding some form of a new AAA, and workers wanted passage of the wages and hours bill. Their patience was not unlimited.

Neither, one imagined, was their tolerance for a spectacle of the sort that would be seen on the Senate floor, hour after hour, week after week. After a while, even Americans who opposed the Court plan might well recoil from tactics that, as *Time* described a 1927 filibuster, "turned Senators into a pack of snarling, sleepless animals." *Time* later noted that Senator Huey Long's "orations of obstruction," his frequent filibusters against, among other things, the National Recovery Administration—however unpopular that program might be—had "stirred revulsion in and out of the Capitol."

By July 3, union members in New York had collected 2,000 signatures on a petition warning Senator Robert Wagner against joining a filibuster. Efforts like this, presumably, were just the beginning. With that in mind, Democratic moderates on both sides of the contest began to cast about for another solution—some way to settle the matter short of an ugly, intraparty brawl on the nation's center stage. The odds seemed increasingly in their favor.

Their success would depend on Robinson's ability to craft a compromise that would satisfy both the White House and a majority of the Senate. By the start of July, Robinson had won commitments from fifty-four colleagues—but this was before the substitute bill had been drafted. Once senators saw it, would they stick? Here, too, the fates seemed to smile on Robinson's labors. After returning from Jefferson

Island, he quickly worked out the language of a new bill in meetings with Cummings, Stanley Reed, and Senators Marvel Logan and Carl Hatch. "We . . . had very little difficulty in coming to an understanding," the attorney general wrote in his diary. On July 2, "the die was cast," Cummings declared, adding proudly that "the bill as now drafted is substantially as it was originally proposed, except in the matter of the Supreme Court." This was a rather large exception. Still, it mattered greatly to Cummings (if few others) that the lower court reforms in the original bill had survived intact. When the substitute passed, he could claim vindication for "our entire theory of speeding Justice, clearing clogged dockets, [and] infusing new blood into the judiciary."

When it came to the Supreme Court, the substitute bill was different than Roosevelt's; but was it different enough to satisfy the Senate? For all the hard work of Robinson and the rest, the latest version of the bill retained much of what critics found so objectionable about the first: it expanded the Court; it allowed the number of justices to reach fifteen; and it rested on the rationale of the original. Yes, the age threshold, at which a justice's refusal to retire would prompt a new appointment, was now set at seventy-five rather than seventy—a minor concession. And yes, the creation of additional seats was now limited to one per calendar year, as Logan had suggested. But under this arrangement, taking the current justices at their word that none planned to retire during the next term, FDR would be able to appoint three justices almost immediately: one to replace Van Devanter; one for the year of 1937; and, a mere six months later, one for 1938; creating, all told, a Court of eleven. This was still packing the Court—packing in slow motion.

Yet, for Roosevelt, it constituted a retreat. Not a surrender, but certainly a retreat from what he had proposed in February and had then demanded, without modification, for the next four months. Not once in his presidency had he lobbied this hard for something this significant and then backed down, even a half-step. So the substitute Court bill—galling as it would no doubt be to the intransigents—might be enough to end the long impasse. Not all of FDR's opponents, after all, wanted him humiliated and permanently weakened; many senators were looking for a way to remain in his good graces.

In the shade of that tree on Jefferson Island, Roosevelt may not have won the undying affection of his party, but he did seem to have earned back the benefit of the doubt. Animus no longer flowed so freely in his direction. This was not merely a measure of his charm; it reflected the degree to which he had been chastened. For while he had not sacrificed much in terms of the Court bill's provisions, he had given up something significant: control, which now rested firmly in Joe Robinson's hands.

The headlines confirmed it: "Court Bill Shelved by Senate Chiefs; Substitute Ready," the *New York Times* announced on July 2. That day, Robinson introduced the legislation that he would take to the Senate floor. The fight was his now—and it was a fight that most expected him to win.

Chapter Twenty-seven

TO FIGHT AGAINST GOD

THE HEAT BUILT up over the Great Plains, searing the fields. Then the winds carried it slowly eastward. By the second week of July 1937, two thirds of the nation was sweltering. Shops, offices, and factories shut down. City and state governments sent workers home, where they found little if any relief. In Atlantic, Iowa, temperatures reached 102°F. In Boston, the streets were deserted as residents fled for the beaches. In Manhattan, the heat loosened cornices on buildings; stones fell from facades, prompting police to rope off sidewalks in the financial district. On a single Friday night in the Bronx, seven fires were started when the summer heat melted Sabbath candles near their bases, causing them to topple out of candlesticks onto tablecloths and drapes.

Newspapers kept daily tallies of "heat deaths and prostrations"—grim, matter-of-fact accountings of heart attacks suffered on the job by butchers, gardeners, and waiters; of people collapsing and dying as they stepped out of automobiles to fill up the gas tank or walked down the street; of children drowning in overcrowded swimming pools and waterways. Across the nation, more than a hundred deaths were registered.

The residents of Washington, D.C., were more familiar than most Americans with appalling, ceaseless, tropical heat, but this was unlike anything in recent memory. The banks of the Potomac were lined with people seeking even the slightest hint of a cool breeze; parks were filled all night with families who had fled stifling apartments and rowhouses, carrying pillows and blankets, and parcels of food for the next morning's breakfast. In the haze of this heat spell, the U.S. Senate began its great debate. Though the Senate chamber was one of the relatively few air-conditioned rooms in Washington, senators regarded this as something of a mixed blessing. Their jobs required movement in and out of the Capitol, and senators—one third of whom were over sixty years old—complained of the brutal transition between unnaturally chilled offices and the ungodly heat outdoors. They did not want to go home because their houses had no air conditioning; what they wanted was to leave town; and tempers rose like mercury at the recognition that, for the foreseeable future, the Court fight would keep them here.

Debate on the substitute bill was scheduled to begin on the afternoon of Tuesday, July 6. By mid-morning the Senate galleries, which wrapped round the room, were packed well beyond capacity. Diplomats and senators' wives sat in the gallery reserved for notables. Hundreds of neatly dressed Boy Scouts, in town for their annual jamboree, were scattered throughout the rest. When the seats were filled, spectators lined the back walls, standing pressed between white marble busts of the early vice presidents. Outside the maple doors to the galleries, others waited four abreast in long lines, hoping for a chance to see the debate. Meanwhile, on the floor below, senators filtered slowly to their desks, which faced the dais in semicircular rows.

For the moment, the leader of the opposition to the Court bill was not among them. Senator Burt Wheeler was in a cab on his way to the White House. At eleven o'clock, about an hour before the debate was to begin, he had received a call from a colleague, Homer T. Bone of Washington, a loyal New Dealer who was already in the Oval Office with Roosevelt. Inviting Wheeler was Bone's idea; he had just told the president that Wheeler might be open to finding a way out of a bruising public battle. Whether Bone had good reason for his hunch was unclear, but Roosevelt quickly acceded. The Montanan arrived several minutes later.

"Burt," the president began, as Wheeler was brought in, "I just want to give you a little background on the Court matter." He talked about the English judicial system—its crisp efficiency, its flexibility. That, he said, was all he wanted. This did nothing but provoke Wheeler, who was, as ever, in a fighting mood. Changing tack, Roosevelt appealed to the senator's sense of loyalty to the Democratic Party. Hang back, the president urged him; let the Republicans lead the fight. This, too, got him nowhere. Wheeler replied coldly that he planned to continue to lead the opposition. "Well, let's keep the bitterness out," Roosevelt said.

Wheeler would not agree even to this. "The Supreme Court and the Constitution are a religion with a great many people in this country," Wheeler remembered replying, "and you can't keep bitterness out of a religious fight." He did promise, though, that if FDR were willing to drop the bill, two justices would resign and make room for Roosevelt's appointees. "How can I be sure?" Roosevelt asked. Wheeler gave his word. Of course, it had been years since Wheeler's word counted for anything with Roosevelt. Their hour-long meeting ended without resolution.

Emerging from the White House, the senator declared himself unshaken in his opposition. "I am your friend," he claimed to have told Roosevelt, "and this will kill your popularity. It is the difference between you coming out as a great president or as a bad one. I don't want to see that happen to you."

Joe Robinson entered the green-carpeted Senate "pit," as it was known, like a bull charging into the ring. Such was his force—and in his opening speech he applied it in full. Within minutes he was pounding his desk with his fist, slashing the air with his arm, and bellowing at his opponents, who jumped up frequently to interrupt and heckle. All at once, several senators stood and asked him to yield for a question. "I'll yield to everybody," Robinson shouted, narrowing his eyes. He was taking all comers.

His speech was long, and not without its rhythms. He slowed down, sped up, roared, ruminated, and quipped. He delivered a thoughtful review of the bill's provisions and then a blistering attack on the Court, its decisions, and its defenders. The presentation was far from eloquent, but none could deny that it was effective. Robinson seemed, as one reporter wrote, "rejuvenated"—in command of the chamber, more so than in years. Often he played to the audience above: "Men are not always conscious of the time when they have passed the climax of their usefulness," he said, eliciting a laugh from the crowd, and leading some to wonder whether he was referring to himself. "I have often thought that politics is not an occupation," he continued, "it is a disease; and, by the eternal, when it gets in the blood and brain, there is no cure for it." Another appreciative roar from the galleries.

Robinson dared his opponents to try to outlast him. Surrender, he taunted them; avoid "putting the Senate to the embarrassment and inconvenience of staying here long days and long nights in a test of physical endurance. Much as it might surprise the Members of the Senate, I would probably come out of that kind of a test better than those who are in the opposition. . . . I think I could endure it longer than could the Senator from Montana," he added, to more laughter above.

Wheeler jumped up. "Will the senator yield?"

"Yes; with pleasure," Robinson said.

"I am in very good physical condition. I have been training for it."

"Very well," Robinson said, shrugging. "Before he gets through, he will not feel so confident as he feels today."

"I do not feel cocky about it," Wheeler snapped, "I never have felt cocky about it, and I am not threatening the senator with a filibuster." He said he merely thought it would take "considerable time to discuss" the bill.

"Oh, yes," Robinson answered, his voice heavy with sarcasm. "Do not imagine, my dear friend, that I am going to interfere with that freedom . . . but I think I will know when you turn from a debater into a filibusterer, and then, as the old saying goes, it will be 'dog eat dog.' "

The spectators liked that one, too, but Robinson, by now, had grown weary of the exchange. "All right," he said wearily. "These things have to come to an end." Forgetting the rule against smoking in the chamber, he fumbled to find a cigar in his pocket, struck a match on the Senate floor—then, realizing what he was doing, threw the match down abruptly. Edward Burke stood and asked him to yield. "No, I am through," Robinson said. "No more questions today. . . . Reserve them until next week." He waved his arm. "Goodbye!" he shouted, to uneasy laughter in the galleries, and stalked toward the cloakroom looking pale.

. . .

The next two days unfolded in the same manner: a clamor of charges, countercharges, and personal attacks, and the useless banging of the chairman's gavel, as Key Pittman of Nevada—presiding over the debate in the place of Vice President Garner—shouted, "Let there be order" in the galleries and on the floor. The only respite came on the afternoon of July 7, when the Senate adjourned early so members could attend the all-star game at Griffith Stadium, where, in the stifling heat, they watched FDR throw out the first pitch and saw the American League, led by a pair of Yankees, Lou Gehrig and Joe DiMaggio, crush the National League, 8 to 3.

Then the hostilities resumed. A good deal of the bitterness concerned Robinson's decision to invoke a long-ignored rule preventing senators from yielding the floor to one another for statements (as opposed to questions) and limiting each senator to two speeches a day on a given subject. The catch here was that Robinson, in an effort to forestall a filibuster, defined "day" to mean not a calendar day—which of course lasted twenty-four hours—but a "legislative" day, which could go on indefinitely. During a tariff debate in 1922, one legislative day lasted 105 calendar days. But that was the last time anyone could remember the rules being applied so strictly. Robinson, noted *Time*, was breaking "the great unwritten rule of the Senate: that its written rules are not rigidly enforced. . . . This was far closer to steamroller tactics than the U.S. Senate usually sees. Many of the elder members . . . fumed with anger at the breach." Discussion of the bill nearly came to a stop as senators bickered about the rules. Order collapsed; confusion reigned; the line between a question and a statement was inherently blurry, and over those two days, Pittman had to rebuke his colleagues dozens of times for breaking the rules.

Shedding their self-restraint, supporters of the bill went after the Court with a vicious kind of glee. Not just the Court's decisions, but its swing justices, Roberts and Hughes. Senator Joseph Guffey, who had sponsored the Coal Act that the Court had struck down in 1936, attacked the Chief Justice for "campaigning" against the Court bill. He launched into a scathing review of Hughes's long career as a "supremely clever politician," a "real master of tactics." The chief was "a high-grade" politician, Sherman Minton agreed, "a high-paid one, and a very good one." Roberts, he charged, had switched for one reason: "he was listening to the siren voice of the political chief justice . . . the wee small voice of the chief justice that was talking politics to him. There is no other explanation." Court-packing, Minton argued, was therefore essential, for without it, "when [Roberts] has accomplished his political purposes he will turn back. . . . He will backslide."

Mostly, however, the senators attacked one another—Democrat against Democrat. Republicans, meanwhile, maintained a "silence as deep as the grave," as Joseph Guffey complained. The most frequent target was Burt Wheeler. Addressing him at times directly, Wheeler's fellow Democrats shook their heads in exaggerated sorrow at the company he had been keeping: Frank Gannett, the Liberty League, the ABA. "He has turned his back," said a mournful Marvel Logan, "on everything he has ever stood for since he has been in the Senate, and is lending aid and comfort to those who, he knows, would destroy the government if they were not restrained."

The bill's supporters also laid into the seven apostates—the Democrats who had signed the adverse report of the Judiciary Committee. This was not simply score-settling; it was central to the administration's strategy. After the Jefferson Island trip, Roosevelt's allies had come to see the report as a great asset—an opportunity, as Arthur Krock described it, "to pin the badge of presidential persecutor" on the rebels and prompt other Democrats to rush to FDR's defense. The strategy was working well enough that some of the senators in question were privately insisting that they had not really read the report, but had signed it after being misled about its contents. And now, as Logan now stood in the well of the Senate and waved a copy of the report in the air, threatening to read it aloud, its authors did their best to interrupt him. Logan denounced them as naïfs who must not have known the impact of their words. There was, he said, "a movement" in progress to create a new, conservative party. "The worshipers of the golden calf are really behind it all. They do not like Mr. Roosevelt; they have never liked him. They are starting out now to destroy him." And these dissident Democrats, Logan charged, were aiding the reactionaries.

Still, amid this kind of talk, a serious debate was taking place. Senators addressed some of the fundamental questions that, a century and a half before, had concerned the framers: the balance of power among the branches; the ability of judges to overrule the will of the people; and others. "What is liberty," asked Sherman Minton, if liberty depended on the shifting views of a single man on the Supreme Court? And could there be any check on a Court gone wrong? "It may go wrong willfully," Logan warned. "It may be an absolute monarch." Yet "senators tell me that no one has the power to do anything about it, that the Court may destroy our government, and no one has the power to do anything about it." Logan disagreed. The Constitution, he insisted, gave Congress "control" over the Supreme Court.

During the first few days of the debate, the opposition did not send its own speakers to the floor. Preserving their strength for the long siege, they contented themselves at first with mocking, harassing, and relentlessly interrupting supporters of the bill. Then, on Friday, July 9, Burt Wheeler rose—and spoke without cease for the next three hours. The only sign that he might be flagging came at the two-hour mark, when he signaled for a Senate page to bring him some milk, which arrived periodically in small paper cups.

It was a characteristic Wheeler performance: self-righteous, belligerent, defensive, defiant. He answered, one after another, the charges that had been made against him, sometimes striding up to an accusing senator's desk and wagging his finger in the man's face. He derided the idea that any senator—even those who had been swept into office as part of the Roosevelt landslide in 1936—should back the bill out of a feeling of loyalty. "Those of you who rode in on the coattails of the President of the United States will ride out on the coattails of the President of the United States if that is the only reason you are here," Wheeler warned. Also, once again, he played the victim, claiming that men "on the government payroll" had been sent into Montana to stir up union members against him.

And finally, leaving nothing out, he put Roosevelt's words in the mouths of tyrants. "Mr. Hitler," Wheeler said, "acted 'to meet the needs of the times.' Mussolini . . . set up his own court, in order that he might 'meet the needs of the times.' . . . There are courts in Germany," Wheeler concluded, "there are courts in Italy, there are courts in Russia, and men are placed on them to meet the needs of the times as the dictators see the needs."

On Friday, Saturday, and again on Monday, members of the opposition held the floor, pushing themselves to ever greater heights of hyperbole. "Toilers of America, awaken! . . . Come to our aid!" rasped Pat McCarran, who was seriously ill. He declared the cause "worthy of any man's life." Josiah Bailey drew the now-familiar analogy to Reconstruction, when "the bayoneted soldiers of the federal government" marched south "to put the Negroes in power, and give them their so-called rights"—until "an independent Court" put an end to the reign of terror. And so they continued, speaker after speaker invoking apocalypse.

They were gaining ground. Robinson walked off the floor during Bailey's speech and placed a phone call to Joseph Keenan of the White House strategy board: "I tell you I'm worried," Robinson said. A headcount on July 10 showed some attrition: Roosevelt's 54-vote majority was now down to 51 or, at best, 52; two days later, it fell to 50. Supporters began scrambling for a new compromise—a substitute to replace Robinson's substitute. But no one really knew what was happening. Tom Corcoran argued that the opposition was claiming votes it had not locked down, but both sides were probably inflating their own numbers. Only one thing was clear, as Arthur Krock pointed out: that "all the morale seems to be on one side."

Before the noon session on Monday, July 12, Robinson had an early lunch with Joseph Keenan. Keenan thought the majority leader looked awful—energetic, somehow, but awful. For days, Robinson's stomach had been troubling him; he was living on a diet of little more than buttermilk. Keenan pleaded with him to stop working so hard, to let his deputies manage the debate, but Robinson waved him away with a joke.

The toll the debate was taking on him was even more apparent that afternoon. On the edge of the pit, Robinson sat in his red leather swivel chair as Joseph O'Mahoney stood above him, jabbing his finger. Robinson's face turned crimson. He started to his feet several times, looking like he might take a swing at O'Mahoney. Finally, Robinson exploded with rage. He felt a stabbing pain in his chest. All his breath left him. Looking drawn, he made his way out of the chamber and onto the north portico—where the hot air hit him like a blow to the head. Gasping, he sat down in an old wicker rocking chair. Two attendants brought him hot water mixed with common soda, which seemed to revive him. He sent for Alben Barkley and other lieutenants, issued instructions for the afternoon, and excused himself to rest at home.

He crossed the street to the Methodist Building, which occupied a triangle of land along Maryland Avenue between the Capitol and the Supreme Court Building. There, in his narrow, overheated apartment, he sat by himself for the remainder of the day. His wife was in Little Rock, caring for her sick brother. That night Robinson went out to the movies with an old friend from Arkansas, but still felt weak enough that his friend spent the night in the apartment, in case Robinson needed help.

The rest seemed to do him some good. In the morning, he arrived at his office at 9:30 a.m. for an interview and a charcoal sketch by the journalist and portraitist S. J. Woolf. Robinson, in a white suit, smoking a black cigar, complained that he was not feeling well, but Woolf doubted this. "He seemed strong, vibrant and vital," Woolf recalled. "His mind worked with startling keenness and his body seemed physically fit." As the artist drew, Robinson talked. Chewing his cigar until the end of it frayed, sitting beneath framed WPA posters and an oil painting of his wife, Robinson spoke at length about the fight he was waging.

"I'd hate to think that when the founders of this country got together to give us a Constitution they were so blind to the future that they . . . felt the 'horse and buggy' age would never pass away. . . . I am sure that when the Supreme Court was created by the framers of the Constitution they intended that it should in no way attempt to thwart the will of the people." It was Congress, he said, that gave the Court its power, and Congress that must curb the abuse of that power. "What we want to do is to see to it that the Court will stick to the job cut out for it. We want men on the bench who will interpret laws and not pass on the wisdom" of legislation.

Robinson mused about the likelihood—the inevitability, as he saw it—of a major shift in the political landscape. "I haven't any doubt," he confided to Woolf, "that the time is not very far distant when this country will see an entirely new political alignment, when men with forward-looking ideas will be members of one great party—let's hope it's the Democratic—and the men who are content to live in the past will band together in the other." Aware that most observers would place him in the latter group, Robinson called himself a "radical," a man at ease with new ideas. "I don't know why they call me conservative," he protested, before showing exactly why they did: he made the case for restricting the activities of the federal government. "We cannot go along indefinitely borrowing money," he said.

Finally, Woolf had finished his sketch. It was a handsome, robust rendering—Robinson's head in two-thirds profile, his eyes narrow, his expression pensive. The majority leader signed the portrait at the bottom and Woolf collected his things to go. "Well, Senator," he said as they parted, "I hope that you will let me draw your picture again and give me another interview when you assume the next office which I am sure you will hold." A smile crossed Robinson's face. "I don't believe in counting my chickens before they are hatched," he replied.

Moments later, Robinson ushered about thirty senators into his office. The opposition, he complained, was "cutting to pieces the president's bill." The majority leader addressed each senator in turn and demanded to know when he would speak on behalf of the bill. He reached Ashurst. "Henry, when will you speak?" Ashurst replied: "My physician will tell you when I may speak, and you, Joe, should not speak unless your physician permits."

Robinson, in fact, had no intention of rejoining the debate—that day, at least. After the meeting, he went back to his apartment to spend the rest of the day there. Thus he was at home, in bed, as Congressman Hatton Sumners stood in the House chamber, denounced the Court bill as "a meat ax" that would wreck "Anglo-Saxon institutions," and—to the wild applause of his colleagues—pledged that, as chairman of the Judiciary Committee, he would never let it pass the House. Robinson was in bed as Key Pittman defied his direct orders and decreed, from the chair, that every new amendment constituted a new subject, allowing each senator to speak twice on it—thus permitting opposition senators to speak without cease. Robinson was in bed as his lieutenants wrung their hands and worried that if they failed to stop the debate, the party would be torn asunder, irreparably so. He was in bed as four senators—three of whom Robinson had counted as likely supporters of the bill—let it be known they would not only vote against it but would go to the White House and urge FDR to abandon the fight.

Meanwhile at the Methodist Building, an elevator boy, knowing that Robinson was all alone, knocked on his door and asked if he needed some company. "Quite all right," the senator said. His answer was the same when his chauffeur stopped by later.

It rained that night—a brief thunderstorm that interrupted the heat wave. The morning of Wednesday, July 14, was not cool exactly, but it was pleasant—more so than any day in weeks. At the usual time, eight o'clock, Robinson's maid let herself into the apartment. She made his coffee; and when it was done, she waited. Robinson did not appear. This was unusual. The senator was always punctual.

She made her way to the bedroom, glanced through the crack of the door, and could see that the light was on and the bed was empty. Where had Joe Robinson gone? Unsettled, she went into the hallway and found the elevator boy. Together, they eased open the door to the bedroom. And there they found Robinson: on the floor beside his bed, wearing his pajamas. He was dead. His reading glasses and a volume of the *Congressional Record* lay just beyond his outstretched hand.

Half an hour later, Roosevelt was still in bed. Steve Early called with the news. Corcoran telephoned as well, reaching Missy LeHand. He warned her to prepare the president for a battery of calls telling him to drop the Court bill. Indeed, within fifteen minutes, Bernard Baruch, the well-known financier and friend of Robinson, was on the line, urging Roosevelt to quit the fight and avoid killing any more senators. Roosevelt replied sharply that if anything put senators' lives at risk, it was the threat of a filibuster, which was preventing the Court bill from passing quickly.

Before leaving bed, the president dictated a short statement for the press: "A pillar of strength is gone. A soldier has fallen with face to the battle." He spoke of Robinson as a "greatly beloved friend" and a progressive: "Those who knew Joseph Taylor Robinson best," Roosevelt said, "recognized in him the qualities of true liberal thought."

At noon, Senator Hattie Caraway of Arkansas, wearing a black dress, rose in the Senate chamber to make the official announcement of the majority leader's passing. Expansive tributes followed. "With a grim gameness he traversed the long, hard path of duty," said Henry

Ashurst, "bearing aloft a flambeau of idealism. . . ." There was much more in this vein. But many eulogies had an edge of bitterness—not toward Robinson, certainly, but toward Roosevelt, for driving the man, it was said, to his death. "Some of us felt he was carrying a greater load than he should have been given," said one senator. Picking up the president's metaphor, William Borah wanted it known that the fallen soldier was "faithful to his general, though not always agreeing with the line of battle." Robinson's reluctance was widely noted, not only by partisans. Ray Clapper considered the death "a pretty high price to pay" for what the columnist deemed "very much a matter of personal pride on the part of Roosevelt." Even the *New York Times*, an ostensibly neutral party, cited the Court fight—rather than, say, a lifetime of overexertion—as the cause of death.

A few blamed his opponents. "You are a murderer of Joe Robinson," a Salt Lake City woman wrote Borah, "for there was no need for debate. . . . Shame!" But inevitably, most observers saw Robinson's death as a final, fitting, damning verdict on Roosevelt's plan. "Had it not been for the Court bill," Burt Wheeler charged, Robinson "would be alive today. I beseech the President to drop the fight lest he appear to fight against God."

"Finish trip," an assistant wired an outspoken opponent of the bill who had gone on a family vacation. "Court-packing killed for this session." This seemed a safe assumption. Newspapers predicted that Roosevelt would abandon the fight and use this moment of shared grief as an opportunity to heal the breach in his party. FDR's instinct was exactly the opposite. He resolved to press ahead, harder than before. "Happy news," said Harold Ickes. But Roosevelt himself was not so much happy as grimly determined. His entire presidency seemed to hang in the balance. "If he stands pat and refuses to be bluffed or stampeded," wrote the columnist Robert S. Allen, "there is every likelihood he will have his way on . . . other measures. If he weakens and runs he is all washed up, not only for this session but for the rest of his term."

For many of Roosevelt's Democratic opponents, the battle had always been bigger than this particular bill—or even this issue. To some, the Court fight represented a chance to halt the drive for reform. To others, it was an opportunity to remove the "rubber stamp" label from Congress and assert their independence from the White House.

And to those with presidential ambitions, it was a means to wrest control of the party from Roosevelt and dictate (or become) the party's nominee in 1940.

For all these overlapping reasons, the cease-fire that followed the news of Robinson's death gave way, a mere twenty-four hours later, to renewed and bitter sniping. On July 15, opposition leaders announced that they had the votes to send back (or, in Senate parlance, "recommit") the bill to the Judiciary Committee, a move that was the legislative equivalent of euthanasia; White House spokesmen, meanwhile, insisted that the president was not backing down. That morning, when four freshman senators pleaded with him to stop tearing the party apart, FDR gave them a lecture about the preexisting divide in the Democratic Party—the split, as he put it, between the Al Smiths and the Joe Robinsons, the Tories and the true liberals.

"Mr. President," one of them mustered the courage to say, "it's the hardest thing in the world to tell you something you don't want to hear." With that, the senators reiterated their intention to go against him on the bill, and returned to the Capitol.

There, another fight was brewing: the battle for Robinson's job.

The contest had been underway before Robinson's death. The moment it became clear that he was bound for the Supreme Court, senators began jockeying to take his place as majority leader. One contender was Alben Barkley. As Robinson's chief deputy, he had become acting leader on the news of Robinson's death. He had been close to Robinson but was even closer to the White House. Full of fire, a violent New Dealer, Barkley was popular among senators who had come in on Roosevelt's coattails, but not much liked by the others.

James Byrnes, a second possibility, was adept enough to have maintained the trust of both Roosevelt and Garner; but Barkley's real competition for the post was Pat Harrison of Mississippi, a tall, portly, shambling figure who was probably the Senate's favorite senator. Harrison had backed the New Deal down the line and without complaint. But in his heart, it was clear, he was no New Dealer. Harrison was cozy with the bankers and the big manufacturers and the power companies. A Harrison victory, wrote the liberal columnist Heywood Broun, would mean "a 99.78 percent sabotaging" of FDR's second-term agenda. Still, Harrison had the edge in the contest. This was due, in part, to his role in the Court fight—or, rather, his refusal to play a role. Dutifully, he had backed the bill, but never exerted himself on its behalf. When Robinson asked him to make a speech for the bill, Harrison declined. He had not been a partisan. Senators thought he might, therefore, be a healer.

The choice, of course, was the Senate's to make. But Roosevelt's preference was not hard to discern. It was Barkley, not Harrison, whom he called to the White House on the evening of July 15 for an emergency meeting, along with three other ardent New Dealers. This alone tipped his hand. Then, after the ninety-minute meeting, the president dropped even the pretext of neutrality. Before heading to bed, he dictated an open letter to Barkley and released it to the press.

"My dear Alben," it began warmly, "I am glad you called my attention to certain events of yesterday and today"—a reference to the opposition's boasts that it now constituted a majority, and to rumors that Roosevelt planned to withdraw the bill. "Lest there be any misunderstanding in regard to judicial reform," Roosevelt continued,

> please let me clarify the situation. Since the untimely death of our Majority Leader, I had hoped with you that at least until his funeral services had been held a decent respect for his memory would have deferred discussion of political and legislative matters. It is, therefore, with regret that I find that advantage is being taken of what, in all decency, should be a period of mourning. Because of this situation, however, I am compelled in the public interest, though against every inclination, to write to you. I do this because you are the Acting Majority Leader in the Senate. . . .
>
> The situation of the civilized world has been, for several years, at a point of extreme danger. This has been caused by three factors—aggression and armament, economic crisis and major social needs. The United States is happily free from any thought of aggression or armament for aggression, but the people of the United States have called for economic security and for major social improvements. National safety demands them. . . .
>
> An abandonment of judicial reform . . . places the responsibility squarely on the Congress of the United States. May I, therefore, tell

> you very simply once more that the objectives of the President, and, I believe, of the great majority of our citizens, remain the same, and that I believe that it is the duty of the Congress, and especially of the members of the majority party . . . , to pass legislation at this session to carry out the objectives.

"I have no doubt," Homer Cummings wrote that night, "the letter will create something of a sensation." This it did. Krock called it "militant." "Sheer buncombe," scoffed the *Portland Oregonian*. "Almost pitiable," said the *New York Sun*. The *Los Angeles Times* wondered why Roosevelt "has stirred up a new hornet's nest. . . . All Washington seems to be affected by the heat, including the President." Senators stormed around the chamber, saying things like, "Whose Senate is this?"

Wheeler, again seizing the moral high ground, expressed disbelief that the president "would make political capital out of a tragedy of this sort, but if it is so, he must have accepted poor counsel in an hour when men who have lost a friend are particularly susceptible." But not Wheeler. "When Joe Robinson passed away," Wheeler told reporters, "I canceled all engagements and forgot the Court bill completely."

"What the president is trying to do . . . ," William Borah wrote a friend, "is to stop what was thought to be a stampede." Borah thought that Roosevelt's nerves had been rattled by the four senators who had visited that morning and urged him to drop the bill. Indeed, Roosevelt told Jim Farley that when those senators went back to Capitol Hill, they spread the word that he was about to give up; the purpose of the "Dear Alben" letter was to counter that impression. Steve Early confirmed this in a conversation with Ray Clapper. "Steve said [the] lines were crumbling," Clapper wrote in his diary; "morale [was] shot to hell and they had to act at once or have [the] whole thing collapse."

On the morning of July 16, as the Senate seethed, Roosevelt put on his morning coat and made his way to the chamber for the state funeral of Joe Robinson. The casket, covered with flowers, rested in the "pit" where Robinson had uttered his last recorded word as leader: "goodbye."

Hattie Caraway sat next to his empty, red leather chair. Wheeler and

Barkley, the two chief combatants in the Court fight, sat next to each other, a gesture of unity. Roosevelt, hands clasped in his lap, sat with his cabinet in front of the coffin. Across the aisle from the president was Justice Pierce Butler—the lone representative of the Supreme Court, for he had been its only member within traveling distance of the capital.

The service was short and somewhat rote. There was no eulogy, no funeral oration, only the doleful incantations of the House and Senate chaplains and the singing of hymns. At the end, Roosevelt was helped to his feet, cast a sympathetic glance at Ewilda Robinson, and was escorted to the lobby. A contingent of senators trailed him there—Pat Harrison among them. Greeting him coolly, Roosevelt asked him to meet at the White House later that day, just a few hours before Harrison and dozens of colleagues were to board a train to Little Rock for Robinson's burial. The president would not be attending. Overruling his advisers and offering a series of disconnected, unconvincing excuses, Roosevelt refused to travel to Arkansas—yet another cause for resentment in the Senate.

Despite his increasingly dire predicament, Roosevelt remained—at least by appearances—the least agitated man in Washington. For senior members of the White House staff, it was a day of some desperation; but if Roosevelt shared it, he did not show it. Visiting the White House that afternoon, Farley found him "in a fine frame of mind." The day before, Roosevelt had remarked that Robinson's inability to relax, or to take bad news dispassionately, had been his undoing. Clearly, it would not be Roosevelt's. He could be bitter, or hold grudges, or act cruelly or vindictively, but rarely did he lose his cool. And he seemed in no danger of doing so now. Without any apparent sense of alarm, he dispatched Keenan to accompany the senators to Arkansas in the hopes of securing a last-ditch compromise. That afternoon he also told Harrison that under no circumstances would he intervene in the leadership fight—a statement that Roosevelt did not mean and Harrison did not believe.

The funeral train—ten Pullman cars filled with senators, congressmen, several White House aides, 4,000 floral arrangements, and the casket with the body of Joe Robinson—departed Union Station at ten o'clock that night. Instantly, every compartment and corridor became a caucus room, holding meetings of two, three, or more men. Factions in the Court fight and the leadership fight eyed each other warily. Farley, along for the ride, was struck by the bitterness of those on board. "They are saying unkind words about one another, and are getting rather petty," he noted in his diary. Yet he still held out hope for some kind of compromise. Keenan and his counterpart Charlie West were walking the aisles, canvassing opinions, but Wheeler flatly rejected every alternative.

Farther they sped, through the next day. Small crowds appeared along the tracks—some to pay respects to Robinson, removing their hats as the train passed by; others to see the locomotive itself, the first diesel engine ever to pass through the Midwest. At every stop along the way, newspapers were collected on the platform and senators scoured them for comment. As ever, most midwestern papers were harshly critical of FDR. Opponents handed these around the train, discussing them eagerly. Even geography now appeared to conspire against Roosevelt. One administration official grumbled: "We should have routed this train through the South"—where public support for the Court bill was stronger.

The train pulled into Little Rock early in the morning of July 18. John Nance Garner greeted them there. Three weeks earlier, he had written Robinson that only two people could compel him to cut short his vacation: "one of them is you, and the other is the 'Chief.'" The "Chief," in fact, had tried and failed—"Frankly, I honestly think you ought to be coming back pretty soon," FDR had written him on July 7, "timing it so that it would not be said that you were rushing back to save the amended Court Bill. . . . I want to tell you again how I miss you. . . . Do come back very soon and make me and a whole lot of others very happy." Robinson's death had done it. The vice president's appearance on the platform brought relief to the faces of the traveling senators—who embraced him, reporters observed, "like a long-lost father."

Garner joined the procession to the Arkansas Capitol, where Robinson was to lie in state, and then to the Little Rock Country Club, where senators sought respite from the rising heat by taking a naked swim in the pool—requiring the few women present to turn and look out the building's back windows. Then, as dark clouds gathered, the men showered, put on linen suits, and all the while kept up a stream of invective about FDR, the Court bill, and one another, pausing only during the hour-long church service.

They carried the casket to Roselawn Cemetery. And finally, just as Joe Robinson's body was committed to the grave, the storm broke—bolts of lighting, claps of thunder, sheets of rain. Two thousand mourners remained and were soaked. When they finally dispersed, the clouds did as well, revealing a rainbow.

The rolling caucus resumed. Boarding the special train in Little Rock, Garner entered his private car, which one day before had borne the coffin. He removed his coat. Then he removed his shirt and called for the porter. "Boy, bring me some branch water," Garner yelled—drinking water, in Garner's vernacular. Farley, joining him in the compartment, found the vice president "in a happy frame of mind," eager to get back to Washington "to clear up the impression that was created when he left."

Except that Garner, during the long ride home, could see that there was little if anything he could do on Roosevelt's behalf. The opposition was unyielding. It also received aid from unlikely sources. When the train stopped in West Virginia, senators were told that New York governor Herbert Lehman—who had been FDR's lieutenant governor, whom Roosevelt had called his "strong right arm"—had written a public letter to Senator Robert Wagner opposing the bill. The letter had a galvanizing effect in the train. "All that remains to be done," one senator said, "is to call the coroner."

Events were moving quickly now. As the train traveled eastward, Roosevelt convened his advisers at the White House. They were incensed by Lehman's letter. "A stab in the back," said an aide. Roosevelt knew there was a lot more than the Court bill at issue for Lehman—frustrated ambitions, for example, and perceived (and real) slights—but none of that lessened the humiliation that Lehman had dealt him. Lehman's opposition could not be dismissed as personal pique—as, say, Wheeler's was. Lehman was not a volatile man; neither was he an iconoclast. He was a quiet, efficient, reform-minded liberal. This heightened the impact of his letter. There was little time, though, to dwell on this. The senators were due back in Washington around midnight, and the fate of the bill—if not already determined—would be settled shortly upon their return.

For three hours that afternoon, Roosevelt met with Hugo Black, Cummings, Corcoran, Cohen, and Keenan—who had flown back from Little Rock to report on his discussions. As Cummings recorded in his diary, Keenan told the group that "the situation was not as desperate as some people thought and we ought not go too far, just at present at least, in the matter of compromise. . . . Apparently some Senators, who are opposed to the plan, are still afraid of defeating the President even if they could. After all he is the greatest asset the Democratic Party has." Black, though, was pessimistic. He saw no reason for hope if the opposition indeed had the votes to recommit. In the event that Wheeler was bluffing, Roosevelt's men decided to "send out feelers" to see whether any kind of compromise stood a chance. At the very least, that might buy some time.

The next morning, July 20, Garner came to see Roosevelt. "Do you want it with the bark on or the bark off?" Garner asked. Roosevelt did not know what that meant, so Garner explained that it was a Texas expression: "bark" was the gloss, the sugarcoating, on a painful truth. The president laughed. "Bark off," he said.

And so, mincing no words, Garner declared that the fight to expand the Supreme Court was lost. FDR did not protest. Whatever question remained about the precise number of senators on either side, he knew that his vice president was, in effect, the acting majority leader. There was no higher authority in the Senate. So when Garner asked Roosevelt's permission to go back to the Capitol and see whether the bill's other provisions—its lower court reforms—could be salvaged, Roosevelt agreed, seeing no choice.

Later that day, at lunch with Ickes, Roosevelt professed to be optimistic, insisting that he had the votes to pass the bill. Of course he knew better. But even in the worst circumstances, it was Roosevelt's nature to keep up a brave face. This time, however, it failed to convince. Ickes had never seen him "looking so tired and nervous." Roosevelt was unable to contain his irritation: at a misquotation by the press, at an unflattering column, at the mere mention of his vice president.

The following morning, Democratic senators met to choose their new leader. It was Barkley. He won the secret ballot by a single vote—a vote acquired, in no small part, by White House intervention. Roosevelt, while surprised by the closeness of the vote, was delighted. In his view, he had won a referendum on his presidency.

And then within hours he had lost one, too. Having made, at best, a perfunctory effort to sell opponents on a compromise, Garner gave up. "Go ahead and write your own ticket," he told Wheeler. "But for God's sake and the sake of the party, be reasonable." But even this rang hollow. Moments later, before an audience of Wheeler, Ashurst, Barkley, and a few others, Garner pronounced the Court plan a plague upon the country, the Senate, and the Democratic Party. He asked Henry Ashurst, as chairman of the Judiciary Committee, to "act as undertaker." Ashurst laughed and then, in his thespian manner, bowed to his colleagues. "Gentlemen, I am at your service."

The final act began at 10 a.m. on July 22. Garner stood before the members of the committee, which was augmented, this morning, by Wheeler and Barkley. "There is no use kidding yourselves," Garner lectured the bill's most stubborn supporters. "Everybody with any sense knows that all proposals with reference to the Supreme Court are out of the window."

He turned to the victors. "We must not give the president any kicks in the face which we can avoid," the vice president cautioned. "He is still head of the party."

Barkley proposed that the existing bill, the Robinson version, be left on the Senate calendar until the committee had drafted a substitute limited to the lower courts. This was a symbolic gesture—allowing the president, if he wished, to claim that the Senate had not actually rejected his plan but had merely set it aside. This semantic, technical distinction was not likely to convince anyone, but Barkley could not see the harm in it. Opposition senators, however, exploded at the suggestion, calling it a Roosevelt trick to keep the Court plan alive. They wanted the bill dead and buried. They demanded a motion to recommit.

For more than an hour the group bickered—until the bill's defenders, like a retreating army that had spent its last round, exhausted themselves and went quiet. Finally, on a Senate notepad, Joseph O'Mahoney drafted the terms of surrender: "No change in S.C.," it began. Yet by general agreement, this crucial fact was not to be acknowledged on the Senate floor. Not even the words "Supreme Court" were to be spoken. This was as far as Wheeler would go to let Roosevelt save face; but in truth, as Rex Tugwell reflected, Roosevelt "had no face left to save."

Two hours later, on the Senate floor, Marvel Logan rose wearily to his feet. The opposition had selected Logan (after Barkley said no) to kill the substitute bill he had helped to draft. Now he called for "unanimous consent" on his motion to recommit the bill. This, too, had been part of the accord between the warring Democratic factions. Unanimous consent meant no speeches, no debate, no public "kicks to the face"—just acquiescence.

Republicans, though, had a different idea. Having deferred to, taken orders from, and hidden behind Wheeler for more than five months, G.O.P. senators now made clear that he and other Democratic rebels had served their purpose; agreements made by Democrats would no longer bind the opposing party. Thus Charles McNary, the Senate Republican leader, stood and objected to the motion for unanimous consent. Now a roll-call vote on recommittal was required, and Democrats had to face the awful choice between backing a dead and discredited bill—or voting, on the record, against their president.

This was not all. For a few minutes more, the Republicans toyed with Logan—baiting him to utter the forbidden words, to make clear what the Senate was doing. "Reform of the judiciary"—what does that mean? one of them asked, feigning confusion. Logan did his best to finesse the question, but the Republicans had him cornered now. Old Hiram Johnson delivered the final blow. He pushed his heavy frame up out of his chair. "I desire to know what the judicial reform refers to," he bellowed. "Does it," he asked, knowing full well the answer, "refer to the Supreme Court or to the inferior courts?" Logan foundered for a moment. Then, finally, he gave up. "Judicial reform," he conceded, "did not refer to the Supreme Court."

"The Supreme Court is out of the way?"

"The Supreme Court is out of the way."

"Glory be to God!" Johnson erupted, his arms outstretched, his eyes looking upward to the galleries, which obliged him with laughter and wild applause.

The roll-call vote followed. As the Senate clerk ran through the list, some of the diehards, Hugo Black and others, boomed "no!" to the motion to recommit. But when Ashurst and Barkley voted yes, signaling that there would be no pointless, defiant last stand, most of Roosevelt's supporters got the message. As the roll call continued, each weak, almost inaudible "aye" provoked a new round of laughter above. When Sherman Minton half-whispered his assent, the galleries grew so raucous that Garner had to bang his gavel for order.

The final tally was 70 to 20. The bill was dead. But what exactly the victors had won, and what Franklin Roosevelt had lost, was not as yet remotely clear.

Epilogue

WE HAVE ONLY JUST BEGUN TO FIGHT

"I MAY NOT KNOW much law," Theodore Roosevelt once said, "but I do know that one can put the fear of God in judges."

A generation later, reflecting on the defeat of his plan to pack the Court, Theodore's distant cousin Franklin took a similar view. On July 23, 1937, the day after the Senate rejected the Court bill, FDR held his weekly press conference in the Oval Office and considered the similarities, as he saw them, between his own struggle and earlier crusades against the Court. The president was cheerful this morning, utterly at ease. He betrayed no ill will toward the Senate, no sense of disappointment, and, apparently, no regrets.

"There was a lot of feeling back in T.R.'s time about the need for judicial reform," he mused, "and it took the form, in the 1912 campaign, of the Progressive Party asking for all kinds of things like recall of judges and overriding of decisions by popular vote. Well, the interesting thing was that for about fifteen or twenty years, that demand on the part of a very large group of Americans had an enormous effect on the courts, as you all know." He added that in 1924, "the La Follette–Wheeler ticket . . . demanded all kinds of drastic things. And during those years when there was agitation for judicial reform, there were some pretty effective results. The courts listened and they legislated—" Reporters laughed at the slip. "I mean they decided," Roosevelt smiled.

Then, lest anyone miss his point, he stated it plainly: "The same thing had to be done again this year." Here, for the first time, FDR implied that his aim all along had not been to pack the Court, but rather to compel it, by the application of pressure, to assume a more liberal outlook.

And this, he declared, the Court had done. He found it "rather interesting," he said, that in the months since his launch of the Court plan, the Court majority had adopted a more flexible brand of jurisprudence. Here Roosevelt glanced at two lists he had just dictated. The first, "Before the Court Bill," itemized the Court's anti–New Deal decisions prior to February 5, 1937. The second, "After the Court Bill," cited the minimum-wage, labor, and Social Security decisions as evidence that his fundamental goal "has already been obtained, temporarily. I say, 'temporarily,' but I hope permanently." The public, he added, wanted assurance that the liberal trend would continue. "We are getting somewhere," Roosevelt concluded, "but we have a long ways to go."

The correspondents, eager for some kind of explosion, went away disappointed. (The only drama came when a few reporters mistakenly believed that Roosevelt had called the justices "morons." The transcript, alas, revealed that he had said the justices' "decisions were *more on* legislative lines than judicial.") Over lunch that day with Jim Farley, Roosevelt expressed satisfaction with his performance at the press conference. As his advisers had urged, he had refused to show even the slightest trace of disappointment in the Senate's rejection of the bill; instead he "accept[ed] it as a good fellow," as Farley observed. Still, as Farley recorded in his diary, Roosevelt made clear to his aides that "he isn't going to take his defeat lying down. . . . He has been double-crossed and let down by people who should have been loyal supporters."

Chief among them, in Roosevelt's mind, was his vice president. At a cabinet meeting that afternoon, FDR gave Garner a terse lecture about the responsibility of Congress to get moving on the rest of the presidential agenda. He spoke so harshly that he expressed regrets afterward. Even so, as Harold Ickes observed the following week, the president could not contain himself. "He doesn't overlook any chance to send a pointed barb, albeit with a laugh, in the direction of the Vice President."

It could not have helped that Garner was now getting the best press of his vice presidency; newspaper profiles hailed him as "the man of the hour," who "knows to the last hair the ancient technique of face-saving." To the contrary, Roosevelt had concluded that Garner, not anyone or anything else, had cost him a deal. Most of the president's circle agreed. A White House aide, speaking anonymously to the press, put it bluntly: "Garner was told to compromise, and he did so by surrendering."

Garner was not, however, the only scapegoat. As presidential advisers issued private postmortems, the list of villains grew long. In a single memo, Felix Frankfurter cited Henry Ashurst (for "incompetence"), Farley (for "incredible gaucheries that offended Senators' feelings of self-respect"), Hughes (for his "strategic retreat," which "cut [the] President's concrete grievances from under" him), Hatton Sumners, Herbert Lehman, sit-down strikers, and, not least, Joe Robinson (for his "dramatic death").

Some members of the administration took a more philosophical view. They agreed with Dean Alfange, a liberal commentator on the Court, who wrote that the plan "was defeated by a combination of imponderables which sprang from emotionalism, mysticism, and fear." The American people, he argued, regarded the Court with something like religious veneration, believing deeply in the myth of judicial divinity and recoiling at portrayals of the justices as mere mortals. In this sense, as Robert Jackson observed, "the court reform bill was like throwing a stone through a cathedral window. It isn't the damage that's done, it's the spirit of the thing that stirs up all the passion."

The degree of public veneration for the Court could be questioned (and was). It was far from clear that most Americans—after decades of controversial Court rulings and recent "self-inflicted wounds" like *Tipaldo*—really believed that justices were impartial oracles of law and truth. The intensity of the opposition to Roosevelt's plan may have had less to do with esteem for the Court than with fear of FDR, the New Deal, the centralization of power, the threat of an American dictatorship, or all of these. Reverence and revulsion were two sides of the same coin.

Still, it was natural, and somehow more satisfying, to pin blame on individuals instead of imponderables. Aides began a vigorous, and decades-long, campaign of finger-pointing: Tom Corcoran charged

Farley's men at the DNC with disloyalty; Farley accused Corcoran of the same; and everybody blamed Homer Cummings for conceiving the plan in the first place.

Corcoran, Cohen, Frankfurter, Rosenman—most of the "conspirators," as Cummings had labeled them (and himself)—went to some lengths to deny their roles in developing or promoting the plan. They concocted elaborate alibis, affected innocence, and painted themselves, with varying degrees of truth, as having dissented from the start or having seen the handwriting on the wall all along. Corcoran and Cohen—both of whom had participated in meetings and written memos supporting the plan in the weeks before its launch—now maintained that they had known nothing about it until it was too late. In a letter to Brandeis, Cohen insisted that "neither Tom nor I was consulted in the formulation of the Court proposals." For the rest of his life, Cohen told even his dearest friends that he had learned about the plan by glancing at a newspaper in Penn Station on February 5 and that he had, of course, been horrified by it. They fed these accounts to friendly journalists, who reported them as fact. One newspaper claimed that Frankfurter had not spoken with FDR for the past several months—that is, since February 1937. This was not surmise; it was misinformation, eagerly provided by Frankfurter himself and confirmed by Corcoran.

Of those present at the creation, only Warner Gardner—the twenty-seven-year-old Justice Department lawyer who had helped draft the bill—owned up to his involvement. This was out of an excess, perhaps, of scruples. A former clerk to Justice Stone, Gardner felt that "I owed Stone a confession, and called on him in order to admit authorship of the bill." Stone chuckled paternally. "After all," he said, "you *were* very young."

But Gardner was only an underling. It was Cummings, of course, who had been the plan's chief architect. In August, looking back at the debacle, the attorney general was ruminative—not regretful, exactly, but ruminative. One Sunday evening, he filled pages of his diary with a recounting of misjudgments, surprises, and examples of bad luck that, in his view, had conspired to kill the Court bill. The administration's allies in Congress had been ineffectual, Cummings wrote; its enemies had been better organized and had unleashed a wave of "tremendous propaganda"; the Court, of course, had switched to "apparent liberalism"; and the political climate, from the labor unrest to the rise in prosperity, had diminished the public's appetite for reform of any kind.

Cummings conceded that the administration had made a fundamental, strategic error—which he attributed to presidential advisers he did not name. He alleged that these men unwisely shifted "the accent of the fight . . . from general judicial reform to a mere matter of membership on the Supreme Court. The opposition," he continued, "naturally selected this as the most vulnerable point. . . . As a matter of fact we were conducting a fight on a broad front and should not have permitted the issue to be narrowed. . . . It threw the whole fight out of perspective and led to a completely false impression as to what the proposition was." And, for the record: "I protested against it."

It was a remarkable claim. After all that had happened over the past six months, Cummings actually believed that if the White House had stuck with the premise of the February 5 message—its focus on efficiency, its apparent unconcern with ideology—then the bill would have passed. Of course, this strategy—Cummings's own—had indeed been tried, and maintained for weeks, at a terrible cost to Roosevelt's credibility. The plan's patently false front enabled the president's opponents to cast doubt on his sincerity and speculate darkly about his motives. As Sam Rosenman recalled, "the bill started with a black eye because it was based on a phony reason." The attorney general's idea that an effort to pack the Court with as many as six new justices could have been concealed behind a scrim of procedural reforms, however urgently needed or earnestly sought, was—and had always been—pure fantasy.

Still, Cummings peddled this story for the rest of his days. It became something of an obsession. In the summer of 1938, he hosted a dinner party for a few friends, including Ray Clapper. Afterward, the columnist noted in his diary that the attorney general "kept coming back to [the] court thing . . . trying hard to vindicate himself because, as he said at the table, 'everybody knows by now that this was my plan.' " The following year, having returned to private practice, Cummings sat in his law office on K Street, just north of the White House, and dictated a hopeful, if wistful, note to Robert Jackson, who had become Solicitor General. "When the history of the court fight is finally written and projected against the background of constitutional history . . . ," Cummings insisted, "we shall all come off well."

• • •

The missing element in these accounts was Roosevelt himself.

Even in the safe haven of their diaries and memos marked "confidential," the president's men were loath to commit their true feelings to paper. In private conversation they were less circumspect—Corcoran, perhaps, least of all. He complained bitterly to Harold Ickes and others that "the Skipper" had been terribly stubborn throughout the fight, had rejected good advice (namely, Corcoran's), and turned down every chance to compromise until it was too late. He and others said the same thing—off the record—to the reporting tandem of Joseph Alsop and Turner Catledge, who, in the fall of 1937, published a two-part recap of the Court fight for the *Saturday Evening Post*. In expanded form, the article would be released the next year as a book called *The 168 Days*. White House aides provided the reporters with a wealth of details—many accurate, some either misremembered or invented—about Roosevelt's actions and motivations.

The portrait that the reporters painted of Roosevelt was devastating. The thrust of their narrative was captured by one of the chapter titles: "A Gay Commander and a Desperate Staff." The president, they argued, "turned his back on the battle. . . . He simply would not listen to pessimistic reports from the front." Instead, he "smiled, puffed at his cigarette and changed the subject"—vacantly repeating, like a mantra, "The people are with me." When congressional leaders urged him to change course, he "laughed in their faces." All the while his beleaguered staff members, having made "every effort to open [his] eyes," found that "he was living almost in a dream world." And so, wearily, his soldiers had returned to battle:

> They worked very hard and very faithfully, this little group of men. . . . They sensed their responsibility, and they did their best to live up to it. Their only difficulty, which most of them loyally failed even to formulate in their minds, was simply that the President did nothing to unify or give direction to their efforts.

Roosevelt, here, is a character in a Greek tragedy. Its theme, as the authors make explicit, is the old, familiar one of "hubris . . . of pride and the fall that comes after." In this account, Roosevelt, blinded by arrogance after his landslide reelection, comes unmoored from all constraints and seeks vengeance against the Court, the last bastion of resistance to his supreme power. It is folly; it is an affront to the gods (in this case, the nation's founders); it is doomed from the start; and everyone can see this but Roosevelt himself.

This is, of course, a caricature. Like all effective caricatures, it has power because it reflects aspects of reality—which helps explain why, during the decades since, it has achieved a certain permanence. Alsop and Catledge's account has become part of the received wisdom about FDR. It provides a neat, pat, unambiguous answer to otherwise vexing questions. *Why would Roosevelt embrace an idea as preposterous as packing the Court?* Hubris. *What made him think he could get away with it?* Hubris. *Why did he refuse to listen to reason?* Hubris. *Why did he keep fighting when he had already lost (or won)?* Hubris. Not only does this response satisfy the conventions of the genre—making the tale worthy of Aeschylus or Sophocles—but it allows us to reconcile the Roosevelt of the Court fight with the more skillful, more estimable Roosevelt of the Hundred Days or the Second World War. Answering "hubris" permits us, in effect, to explain this troublesome episode away—to dismiss it as an aberration, the political equivalent of a fever, a delirium, that set in suddenly and violently in November 1936, and cleared only after Roosevelt had been badly beaten.

He was hubristic. This cannot be denied. Well before his reelection, Roosevelt was, as Rex Tugwell described him, "a man with fewer doubts than anyone I had ever known." Another former aide, Stanley High, perceived "an almost mystical quality" to FDR's faith in himself, his destiny, the rightness of his actions and the certainty of his success. "The stars," High wrote mockingly, "have taken counsel together and written it." More than any other trait, this certainty of success defined the man. "With most people," Frankfurter wrote to Stone in 1936, "optimism is an evasion or an anodyne; with F.D.R. it is an energy, a driving force for overcoming the obstructions and difficulties of life. It is that energy in him, I think, which explains his triumph over [polio]." It also explained his ability to transmit hope amid so much suffering, and to dispel, as if by the sheer force of his personality, "fear itself." All this had been true long before November 1936.

Yet Alsop and Catledge were right that something did shift after the election. It did not cause a sea change in FDR's personality; he did not become a different man; but some of the qualities he had always possessed in abundance were now found in excess. Before the landslide, his self-confidence had usually (if not always) been tempered by his eagerness for consensus and conciliation; by his ability to remain a bit detached from his own decisions, in case he might need to alter or abandon them; and by his willingness to "force himself," as Frances Perkins had long observed, "to face the most dreary and discouraging facts." These strengths of Roosevelt's—so badly needed in 1937—went into eclipse. Confidence gave way to overconfidence, boldness to recklessness, urgency to impatience, tolerance to vengefulness, persuasion to coercion.

Even so, "hubris" alone is an insufficient answer to the question of what went wrong. It fails to account, first of all, for the quiet diligence with which Roosevelt and his advisers, over the course of more than two years, formulated their plans and considered the obstacles and objections to court reform. It overlooks the extensive surveys of legal history; the binders thick with every conceivable amendment to the Constitution; the correspondence with scholars, judges, journalists, and sundry reformers. The "project," as Cummings called it, was a serious one, an earnest one, and, for an extended period, a collective endeavor. An impressively wide range of approaches were scrutinized, debated, drafted, floated, and ultimately discarded before Roosevelt and Cummings, in late 1936, finally closed the discussion. And though the decision to pack the Court was made, to be sure, in a state of high political intoxication, it was not a choice that Roosevelt made impulsively. It may have been driven—to a dangerous degree—by ego and emotion, but it was also the product of reason. It may have been wrong, but it was not rash.

Neither was it made in a vacuum. By the time of Roosevelt's second inauguration, there was a growing national consensus that something had to be done about the Court—that either Congress or, more likely, the president would have to act to end the impasse. An embattled minority disputed this, but many Americans seemed to accept Roosevelt's argument that "to stand still was to invite disaster." If democracy could not be made to function, if the three branches of government could not work together toward the betterment of the "forgotten man at the bottom," as FDR had put it in 1932, then there was a very real risk of total social and industrial collapse, of wide-scale disorder of the sort being seen on the shop floors of General Motors—the very conditions that in other nations, had hastened the slide into tyranny. The wave of popular discontentment with the Supreme Court—which crested in 1936, with an outpouring of elite commentary, popular songs, pamphlets, and proposals in Congress to curb the Court—had developed without much exertion by Roosevelt, who had said little publicly on the subject. While it was unwise for FDR not to consult Congress or prepare the public in the months before launching his plan, it was not irrational for him to expect that both, in the end, would support it.

Finally, "hubris" is said to explain Roosevelt's conduct during the fight for the bill. Here the case is quite strong. Without question, Roosevelt acted imperiously, compounding his crucial, initial failure to consult congressional leaders by refusing to heed them for months thereafter, and treating them instead with a loose contempt. "It took him an unconscionable time to discover his weakness," Tugwell reflected. "This must be charged mostly to overconfidence." Still, "hubris" falls short of fully accounting for his behavior. Clearly Roosevelt's political instincts, so acute in the past, went awry. But they did not escape him altogether. Roosevelt did not, on election night, or at any point thereafter, become a fool. If he trusted his intuition over what the newspapers, the opinion polls, his outraged opponents, and even some of his allies told him—and he did—he was reflecting the experience of the 1936 election, when so many had grossly underestimated his strength.

In 1937, just as in the previous year, Roosevelt found reason to disregard the alarmists. In 1937, just as in 1936, he received a steady stream of upbeat reports from the field—from governors and political operatives and friendly journalists in every part of the country—proving, in his view, that his opponents were misreading the national mood. "As you know," FDR wrote to his ambassador to Spain, "all the fat-cat newspapers—85% of the whole—have been utterly opposed to everything the Administration is seeking, and the best way to describe the situation is that the campaign of . . . 1936 is continuing actively throughout the year 1937. However," he hastened to add, "the voters are with us today just as they were last fall."

Some of them were; too many, however, were not—at least, with respect to the Court plan. The assessments he received were overly optimistic. He should have questioned them. Still, they were not, on their face, implausible. A reasonable man might well have believed them. Especially if that reasonable man was usually right in his assumptions.

None of this is to exculpate Roosevelt, but rather to try to understand him better. The Court fight does read like a Greek tragedy, right down to the deus ex machina of Joe Robinson's death. But the parable that endeavors to explain these events—the neat pairing of cause (pride) and effect (fall)—is, it turns out, no more accurate or instructive than the myth it displaced, that of FDR as "the greatest politician ever to be placed within a human skin," as one magazine put it at the time. The Court plan was not necessarily doomed to fail. Pride does not always result in a fall. If the Court plan was the product of hubris, then so, in a real sense, was the entire New Deal.

He was not unaffected by his defeat. Though outwardly merry, full as ever of bravado, Roosevelt showed signs of strain. The burdens of the past four years seemed to have finally caught up with him. Just after the Senate vote on the Court plan, Harold Ickes joined him for a weekend fishing trip on the *Potomac*. "As I watched the President," Ickes noted a few days later, "it was clear to me that he has paid a heavy toll. . . . His face is heavily lined and inclined to be gaunt as compared with what it was . . . in 1933, and he is distinctly more nervous. He is punch drunk from the punishment that he has suffered recently." Roosevelt confided to Cummings just how badly he needed a rest; he recalled the heart problems that had plagued and eventually killed his father, and said that had it not been for his own affliction—he meant his polio—he would have overexerted himself and burned out long ago.

Still, no laments were heard in the Oval Office. Roosevelt was not, as a rule, inclined toward remorse or self-reproach. Over lunch on August 2, Cummings asked him whether he had, at any point, regretted starting the Court fight. No, Roosevelt replied; it had been inevitable. It was just one of those things that had to be done. And that, it appeared, was the extent of Roosevelt's reflection on what had been the most consuming conflict—and biggest setback—of his four and a half years as president. Eleanor Roosevelt described his temperament: "You made up your mind to do a thing and you did it to the best of your ability. If it went sour, why then you started in all over again and did something else, but you never spent time repining."

Especially not when the fight was ongoing. As far as Roosevelt and many of his advisers were concerned, "the party isn't over yet by a darned sight," as Corcoran put it in late July. "We're in for a long war." Frankfurter urged Roosevelt to remember the dictum of Charles W. Eliot, president of Harvard when FDR had been an undergraduate: "For a real fighter, after a battle has miscarried, the question is, 'when will the fighting be renewed?' " Sam Rosenman, similarly, wrote a heartfelt letter reminding the president of his own words (or, more accurately, his paraphrasing of John Paul Jones) from the final speech of the fall campaign. "I know," Rosenman wrote,

> that the phrase of Madison Square Garden is still a living thing for you: "We have only just begun to fight." The objectives of your Second Inaugural cannot be stopped by such reverses as this, I know. Before the next session of the Congress, it will be made clear whether the attainment of those objectives will require a renewed Court fight or whether the threat of it will make the present Court willing to do its share in making "democracy work."

"Dear Sammy," Roosevelt replied, "The things you say are quite true and we know that the fight for our objectives has only just begun!"

Roosevelt was not alone in this belief. Few on either side of the argument saw any great likelihood that the Court's "shotgun liberalism" marked a permanent shift. "After Roberts switched, there was hope—but only hope," recalled David Ginsburg, a young lawyer in the administration. He and many of his colleagues still viewed upcoming New Deal cases with "frantic concern." If Roberts and Hughes reunited with the three remaining hard-line conservatives now that the political storm had passed, the group would again constitute a majority, irrespective of whom FDR appointed to fill Van Devanter's seat.

The larger struggle, therefore, had neither been won nor lost; it was merely in "recess," as *The Nation* observed. With this, many conservatives agreed. A friend of McReynolds's, while hailing the defeat of the

Court bill as "the greatest victory since the Declaration of Independence was signed," cautioned the justice that "the fight has really just begun. The foes of Constitutional Government, motivated by Moscow, will continue their attack. . . . I want you to stay on that bench. Don't yield a point. Never resign. Live a hundred years, and fight more vigorously than ever."

The Court bill's foes readied themselves for the next round. "If opposition is relaxed," Frank Gannett warned supporters of his National Committee to Uphold Constitutional Government, "the President will succeed in his continuing efforts to control the Supreme Court." Gannett raised the specter of presidential reprisals against senators who led the fight against the bill. These brave men, he said, were sure to face "the most concentrated attack the administration can make. Taxpayers' millions will be used for propaganda and unlimited patronage, and the power of the presidential office will be turned against them." The loss of three or four of them from the Senate would be enough, he claimed, to permit Roosevelt to pack the Court. In August 1937, Herbert Hoover sent an open letter to the head of the League for Supreme Court Independence, urging that such groups "should not be dissolved" and should instead prepare to defend any Republican or Democrat who had "actively attacked" the Court plan. Wheeler, himself a presumed target, discussed plans to send a "flying squadron" of orators to any state where an opponent of the Court plan was in political jeopardy.

In a speech on August 4, Jim Farley scoffed at the notion of a presidential vendetta as well as press portrayals of "an unbridgeable gulf and an incurable rift" in the Democratic Party. "Moonshine," said Farley. Court reform was merely "one item" on the president's agenda, and Democrats agreed on most other issues. Besides, the administration was "in the building business, not the wrecking business." This, however, did little to dispel the poison in the atmosphere, or to assuage the Democrats who now felt like marked (or martyred) men. "Hardly a day passes," Arthur Krock reported in the *New York Times*, "that threatening words do not come from Democrats about other Democrats."

Not least from the president himself. Eleanor urged Franklin repeatedly not to indulge his feelings of resentment, but the bitterness ran too deep. Privately, the president expressed disbelief, verging on contempt, at the inability of party rebels to appreciate how fully they depended on his popularity. "It was a bitter pill for him," Rosenman said later, "so soon after the glorious victory of the re-election."

But Roosevelt was less interested in exacting revenge than in reasserting control. Alf Landon, watching with a certain satisfaction from Topeka, concluded that his rival had little choice in the matter: "I have felt from the start," the governor wrote to Ray Clapper, "that Mr. Roosevelt would bury the knife into . . . senators instead of burying the hatchet with them," adding that "I could not see how he could do otherwise if he were to retain any control" over Congress. "The natural human instinct of a crowd," Landon observed, was to prey on weakness.

Roosevelt's men agreed. In August, Rex Tugwell advised him that "your real problem" now was Congress, "which must be humbled"; the Court issue, he said, was "secondary." Roosevelt took Tugwell's point about Congress, but did not see the two issues as distinct. They were, in fact, entangled. FDR could not regain the upper hand on Capitol Hill until he had forced Congress to reverse itself on judicial reform—just as the Court had reversed itself.

He would, therefore, keep up the fight. "He is just as determined as ever . . . ," Farley observed that summer. "He will probably bide his time and bring it out again at the proper moment." Indeed, within days of the bill's defeat, Homer Cummings was back on Capitol Hill, canvassing congressmen about the possibility of reconsidering the Supreme Court provisions of the original bill sometime later that year ("probably inadvisable," was the tactful response of at least one member). Meanwhile, as senators prepared what some called the "baby Court bill," covering the lower courts, the president himself worked up a list of poison-pill amendments—each, on its face, unacceptable to the Senate—including, most obnoxiously, an amendment to add two justices to the Supreme Court. FDR told Cummings he did not mind being voted down; he just wanted to put senators on the spot as the midterm elections approached. Alternatively, as Roosevelt cheerily announced to the cabinet, he could just veto the lower-court bill. He said he intended to have a great deal of fun in the months ahead, and it was time for the country to laugh again.

• • •

On August 12, in much the same spirit, the president announced his choice to fill the vacant seat on the Supreme Court: Senator Hugo Black of Alabama. In an echo of the Court plan, Roosevelt had not told a single member of his staff about his decision and looked forward, with delight, to their reactions. (That morning, in fact, Steve Early had briefed reporters that Roosevelt might not fill the seat for months.) Black was, indeed, a startling choice. Privately, Roosevelt conceded that Black was not as able a lawyer as some of the others he had considered—namely, Solicitor General Reed—and Frankfurter had warned him that Black lacked the technical knowledge to "beat the C.J. [Hughes] in some of his shenanigans." Also, Black had the very opposite of a judicial temperament; he had the bearing of a prosecutor, and was best known as the relentless leader of Senate investigations.

At the same time, there was much to recommend him, in Roosevelt's view. Black, at fifty-one, was young; he came from a judicial circuit that was underrepresented on the Court; and, more important, he was a real fighting liberal, an "evangelic progressive," as one colleague described him. FDR often said privately that the New Deal would not have been the same without Black. Indeed, Black's identification with wages-and-hours legislation in particular was causing him so much trouble back home in Alabama that he was at risk of losing his bid for reelection in 1938. Roosevelt figured it would be easier to put Black on the Court than to keep him in Congress, for if nominated, Black would benefit from "senatorial courtesy," the tradition by which the Senate took care of its own. Despite Black's unpopularity among his colleagues, his confirmation was a given.

"They'll have to take him," Roosevelt told Farley, with evident glee. And here was the heart of it. Senators would feel compelled to confirm a man most of them despised—and, even more perversely, to put the judicial robes on one of the Court's fiercest critics. Black had been unrestrained in his enthusiasm for packing the Court. In February he had proclaimed on the radio that "if ninety-six judges were needed . . . , I would unhesitatingly favor ninety-six judges." Black, in short, was the perfect choice for a president who wished to antagonize rather than assuage his opponents. "Father was very angry at the Senate—hopping mad, almost," James Roosevelt later recalled. "He wanted to get back at them, stick it to them."

The Black nomination, delivered to the Senate in a sealed envelope—the symbolism of which was lost on no one—had its intended effect. When Black's name was revealed, gasps were heard in the chamber. FDR "certainly succeeded in stirring up the animals," Ickes observed with satisfaction. Senators churned with rage and revulsion. So did some of their constituents. A woman wired Borah that "the President should be impeached for the mere suggestion." Another voter wrote him that "when our SC bench is filled with . . . spineless political puppets, it is time to advocate the use of 'bullets instead of ballots.' " Liberals, meanwhile, were overjoyed. *The Nation* called the Black nomination the "most courageous" since Woodrow Wilson had appointed Brandeis, and others relished the joke FDR had played on his Senate opponents. "What a swell nomination!" Irving Brant wrote Corcoran. "It must have made [Edward] Burke see green."

Black's detractors were unable to summon sufficient numbers to overcome the Senate's "immemorial custom" of courtesy. They did, however, manage to drag out the discussion for a few days, during which it was publicly revealed, to FDR's dismay and discredit, that during the 1920s Black had been a member of the Ku Klux Klan—an affiliation that Roosevelt seems not to have known about, even though it was, in Catledge's view, "almost a known fact." On August 17, the Senate confirmed Black anyway, 63–16.

Refusing to let tempers cool, Roosevelt celebrated his victory the next day with a belligerent speech at Roanoke Island, North Carolina, in which he attacked what he called "American Lord Macaulays"—after the nineteenth-century British Whig who had been skeptical of American democracy and favored, in his own words, the vesting of "supreme power" in the hands of a "select . . . educated class . . . deeply interested in the security of property." Roosevelt quoted these lines with a sarcastic smile.

By now Roosevelt's sense of grievance went well beyond the Court issue. After killing the Court-packing bill, conservative Democrats in Congress conducted an "audacious rout of [FDR's] whole program," as a columnist put it. Over three busy weeks, they indulged in an orgy of obstruction that denied Roosevelt even the smallest symbolic victories. "Something has happened," declared the *Wall Street Journal*. "Congress knows that it can disregard orders from the White House. . . . President Roosevelt knows this, too; and knows that Congress knows it." The New Deal was stalled, and FDR, to use his own term, had lost his whip hand.

The congressional session, which had begun with such high expectations, now expired in a spasm of recriminations and name-calling. After a meeting with FDR, Senator Joseph Guffey went on the radio to attack Wheeler, Burke, and other Democratic "ingrates" by name, predicting that voters would soon "bury [them] in the oblivion of defeat." This turned the final day of the session, August 21, into a squall, as Guffey's targets returned fire. Then, as Vice President Garner readied his gavel to bang the session into welcome oblivion, the clerk read aloud a letter from FDR, thanking senators for their service and offering best wishes—to the sound of snickering in the galleries and, indeed, on the Senate floor.

On that fitting note, members of Congress finally fled Washington. One of the few pieces of legislation they did pass before adjourning was the lower-court reform act. While a far cry from what Roosevelt had originally proposed, it took meaningful steps toward curbing some of the abuses he had identified. Among other things, it enabled the government to intervene in cases between private parties any time constitutional questions were raised; expedited the appeal of such cases to the Supreme Court; limited the ability of lower courts to issue injunctions against acts of Congress; and allowed a senior circuit judge to temporarily reassign judges from one district to another, to help clear congested dockets. *The New Republic* called the act "a minor victory that, in other circumstances, might be regarded as major."

Still, it was hard for Roosevelt or his allies to embrace this half (or quarter) measure. Their humiliation at the hands of the rebels was too fresh. Roosevelt pressed the Senate leadership for "a real show-down on the measure," as Cummings noted, but his allies told him flatly to forget it; "the sooner the matter was over with the better," they said. Garner then gaveled the bill through to passage with such ruthless dispatch that the diehards were unable to blurt their objections until it was too late.

Even this did not settle the matter, for Roosevelt could still veto the bill. He spent the next few weeks entertaining the possibility. A veto would bring a certain psychological satisfaction, but Cummings, who had ardently sought these reforms, saw nothing outright objectionable in the bill, and recommended that the president sign it. FDR could do so in one of two ways: silently, signaling acquiescence, or grudgingly, conveying disapproval. The latter suited him. At the end of August, he signed the bill—"with bad grace," as Rex Tugwell recalled. In a statement, Roosevelt called the act a "limited advance" that would serve mostly as a reminder of unfinished business. He went on, at some length, to list the act's sins of omission, beginning with its failure to relieve "the burden now imposed on the Supreme Court" or to provide a "flow of new blood to any of the federal benches." This resort to old, ridiculed refrains left commentators incredulous.

The last word—for the time being, at least—came on Constitution Day.

September 17, 1937, was the 150th anniversary of the signing of the Constitution. Roosevelt marked the occasion by first traveling to Antietam, Maryland, to watch a reenactment of the bloodiest one-day battle of the Civil War. Then, that evening, he stood at the base of the floodlit Washington Monument and addressed a crowd of 65,000 that was sprawled across the grounds. It was a fighting speech, no less so than any he had delivered over the course of the Court fight. Frankfurter had supplied a lengthy draft, Corcoran and Rosenman had rewritten it, but Roosevelt dictated much of the final product himself. It was, in effect, his closing argument in the case for a liberal interpretation of the Constitution.

The Constitution, as Roosevelt described it, was "a layman's document, not a lawyer's contract." Its adaptability, he said, had well served the nation. Yet its ambiguities had also engendered "an unending struggle between those who would preserve this original broad concept of the Constitution" and those who "cry 'unconstitutional' at every effort to better the condition of our people. Such cries," he said, "have always been with us; and ultimately, they have always been overruled."

Roosevelt cited examples from the early days of the republic; but the ones with sting—with "the right poison," as Frankfurter wired him after the speech—were more recent. "Less than two years ago,"

Roosevelt said, "fifty-eight of the highest priced lawyers in the land gave . . . a solemn and formal opinion that the Wagner Labor Relations Act was unconstitutional. And in a few months, first a national election and later the Supreme Court overruled them. For twenty years the Odd Man on the Supreme Court"—the man who cast the deciding vote in a 5–4 opinion—"refused to admit that state minimum wage laws for women were constitutional. A few months ago, after my message to the Congress on the rejuvenation of the judiciary, the Odd Man admitted that the Court had been wrong—for all those twenty years—and overruled himself!" The people's will, he said, would always prevail; and in their insistence that the three branches work together, Americans saw "nothing *more* sacred about that branch furthest removed from the people than about either of the others, which are nearest to the people."

"It takes time to adjust government to the needs of society," Roosevelt acknowledged. Yet he ended on an urgent note. With "dictatorships displac[ing] democracies" overseas, with calls for either "plutocratic" or "proletarian" rule being heard in the United States, time was short; the nation could not afford to "sacrifice each generation in turn while the law catches up with life." And so, "on this solemn anniversary," he asked the American people to have faith in their Constitution—but, at the same time, to "justify that faith by making it work now rather than twenty years from now."

This was the Constitution as Roosevelt saw it—worthy of reverence "not because it is old, but because it is ever new."

"I agree with you . . . ," Hughes wrote to Stone in August, from his summer retreat in Alberta, Canada. "We have not seen the end of the discussion about the Court. There are those who are determined to change our form of government." By this he meant not only the size of the Court but the meaning of the Constitution. Of course he was right. In the coming months and years, what FDR had called the "unending struggle" went on without respite; for the Constitution remained, as it has always been, contested ground. Roosevelt's (and Marshall's and Hamilton's) notion of a broad and flexible national charter—one designed to empower and not frustrate the federal government—would always have its detractors.

Yet fewer of those detractors were to be found on the Court when it reconvened in October 1937. This was due, most apparently, to Hugo Black's arrival on the bench, replacing Willis Van Devanter; but also, more importantly, to the continuing presence of Hughes and Roberts among the liberal majority, through each succeeding New Deal case. They did not, as so many had feared, return to the right. Solicitor General Stanley Reed found himself winning even cases he expected to lose; the New Deal, again and again, marched to victory in the Court, prompting the administration's lawyers to press harder and further, to sweep down the constitutional barriers that remained in their path.

"American constitutional law," Edward Corwin observed at the time, "has . . . undergone a number of revolutions, but none so radical, so swift, so altogether dramatic" as the one the Supreme Court completed during those few months of 1937. This assessment was premature—but only slightly. Just as the revolution took some time to set in motion—the first shots, with hindsight, appear to have been cases like *Nebbia* and *Blaisdell* (both in 1934), or even their antecedents—it took some time to complete. The 1936–37 term was the watershed, but several years would pass before *Jones & Laughlin* and other liberal triumphs had the ring of finality.

It is unlikely that the transformation in the Court's outlook would have been either sweeping or enduring without a concurrent transformation in its personnel. Hughes and Roberts soon parted company with the Court's true liberals, though not in every case and not quite to the degree that Roosevelt had feared. After 1937, the two swing justices were more inclined than before to sustain economic regulations but were less deferential toward the other branches than their newer brethren were. By 1942, Roosevelt—who had completed his entire first term as president without naming a single justice—had appointed all the justices of the Supreme Court but two: Stone, whom FDR elevated to chief justice when Hughes retired in 1941, and Roberts. This new Court, which included Felix Frankfurter and Robert Jackson, effectively settled the argument that had dominated Roosevelt's first term as well as the preceding three decades—the judicial and political debate over the constitutionality of economic reform. Congressional power to regulate commerce, the majority now ruled, was virtually without limit. The increasingly nebulous distinction between "direct" and "indirect" commerce was finally discarded. In a 1938 case, *Carolene Products*, the Court signaled its near-total retreat from the realm of economic policy; from that point forward it would apply higher standards of judicial scrutiny to legislation that might tend to affect political participation, discriminate against minorities, or interfere with rights explicitly conferred in the Constitution. Decisions grounded in the unloved doctrinal legacies of laissez-faire—the due process clause, the contracts clause—were overturned in short succession, leaving no major area of constitutional law unaltered. The Court, at long last, had reconciled itself to the twentieth century.

Had it taken too long? Roosevelt, of course, certainly thought so. "Things were happening," he wrote in his *Public Papers*. "NOW!" (The capital letters were his own.) But there is another way of looking at the lag between his signing of New Deal laws and the Court's endorsement of them. "In a democracy," his former aide Stanley High wrote, "people have to have time to catch their breath." And the Constitution, as James Bryce observed years earlier, "secures time for deliberation. It forces the people to think seriously before they alter it or pardon a transgression of it."

Without question, much of what was said in defense of the Court and Constitution was irrational, extreme, and, at times, dishonest. As one writer put it in 1936: "A good many of the people who talk about the menace to our liberties really believe that Roosevelt's reelection will mean the suppression of Republican newspapers and the hustling off of dissenters to a concentration camp; but quite as many are worried only about the menace to the liberty of a rich man to do anything he can get away with." Yet whatever the motives of Roosevelt's critics, it must be acknowledged that they provoked a debate about the constitutional principles of the New Deal—a debate that arguably needed to take place and that the congressional opposition was too enfeebled to lead.

The belief in strict limitations on governmental power, having held sway in courtrooms for decades, deserved to be heard one more time by the bench, the public, and the president himself. Not to be heeded, necessarily, but at least to be heard. Beginning with the first New Deal cases, the Court required FDR to answer a serious and sustained constitutional critique. In the end, his position prevailed; and his reforms, most people agreed, stood on more solid ground.

It is an abiding irony that so much of this constitutional revolution, as well as the crisis that instigated it, occurred during the tenure of Charles Evans Hughes. Decades earlier, he had been known as a reformer, but never a revolutionary. He placed his faith, above all, in reason—in rational, gradual progress, the slow unfolding and maturing of ideas. On the Court he was not particularly an innovator. He did not see this as the judge's role. At the same time, he was less willing than some of his brethren to adhere blindly to legal precedent without regard to human welfare. Through the 1935–36 term this left him uncomfortably—and untenably—caught between the Court's two camps. At the height of the constitutional crisis, a dance company performed an interpretation of the Supreme Court. The three liberals danced on one side, the five conservatives (including Roberts) on the other, and Hughes flitted back and forth between them. This once godlike man had become a tragic, or tragicomic, figure.

If a middle ground existed on that bitterly divided Court, the Chief Justice never found it. Instead, like Roberts, Hughes swung back and forth as if he believed that the mere fact of his oscillation, his refusal to alight for long in either camp, established some kind of balance. In fact, it did the opposite. It accentuated the imbalance. It confirmed many Americans' sense of the Court as a political institution. It dealt the Court one of those "self-inflicted wounds" that Hughes had once described.

To his critics he was King Canute, foolishly trying to reverse the tide. This was unfair. Hughes was not trying to hold the law or the nation back; rather, he seemed to believe that he could advance the interpretation of the Constitution by minute degrees, by fine shadings, by cleverly distinguishing away precedents instead of boldly overruling them. Of course, he was a judge, no longer an elected politician, and the judicial process is most often an incremental one. Still, there are times when progress—in law and policy—must be made by bold strokes and clean breaks, if the government is not to fall dangerously out of step with social and economic realities. The 1930s was one of those times.

"Looking back," Roberts reflected years later, "it is difficult to see how the Court could have resisted the popular urge . . . for what in effect was a unified economy." Like Roberts, Hughes recognized this—too late to prevent some of the worst excesses of the 1935–36 term, but soon enough to undermine the Court bill and then to lead a steady, purposeful march toward a more flexible interpretation of the Constitution. Whether the Chief Justice saw himself as responding to the dictates of the cases at hand, or was acting to save the Court or country, can never be known; but it must be said that eventually, as *The Nation* observed, "Hughes had the acumen to recognize the inevitable." Whatever his motivation, Hughes kept faith with the "fighting governor" he had been at the turn of the century—the man who, on the eve of his first appointment to the Supreme Court in 1910, advised a group of Yale students that "whether you like it or not, the majority will rule. . . . I believe you will come to put your trust, as I do, in the common sense of the people of this country, and in the verdicts they give."

"We lost the battle," Roosevelt said many times, "but we won the war."

In the introduction to the 1937 volume of his *Public Papers*, published in 1941, FDR declared "a clear-cut victory . . . for the objectives of the fight. The Court yielded. The Court changed. The Court began to interpret the Constitution instead of torturing it. It was still the same Court, with the same justices. No new appointments had been made. And yet, beginning shortly after the message of February 5, 1937, what a change!" That, he added, was why he regarded the launch of his Court plan as "a turning point in our modern history." Roosevelt had no patience for those who questioned this account of the Court's conversion. "It would be a little naïve," he wrote, "to refuse to recognize some connection between these 1937 decisions and the Supreme Court fight."

Few, in his own time, failed to see that connection. To most who had witnessed the fight (and many who had not), it seemed self-evident that the Court had bent before the storm. Decades later, however, a number of historians, legal scholars, and others would question the claim. Some, like Chief Justice William Rehnquist, agreed that Roosevelt won the war, but believe that "he won it the way the Constitution envisions such wars being won—by the gradual process of changing the federal judiciary through the appointment process." Others place greater weight on the doctrinal changes that preceded the Court fight and doubt that the events of 1936 and 1937 had much (or anything) to do with the shift in doctrine. At its core, this is not a debate about the timing of the transformation. It is an argument about the nature of the judicial process, and what makes judges decide as they do.

Hughes objected violently to the idea that any decision of the period was "influenced in the slightest degree by the President's attitude, or his proposal to reorganize the Court." The claim, he insisted, was "utterly baseless." Yet the Court is not a vacuum. After the *Parrish* decision, *The New Yorker* ridiculed the notion that "the Supreme Court's about-face was not due to outside clamor. It seems that the new building has a soundproof room, to which the Justices retire to change their minds." Still, the myth of the Court as a "vehicle of revealed truth" (as one scholar put it, sardonically), incapable of doing that which the law and the facts did not require, had and still has resilience. To acknowledge that external events play a role in decisions is frightening to many, for it suggests that the judicial system is, in the end, not one of laws but of men—and thus vulnerable to the prejudices and whims and base instincts of men.

But this is a false dichotomy—that a nation is governed either by law or by men, rather than a dialectic between the two. It is one of many unhelpful antitheses that prevailed at the time and persist to this day, among them the idea that the Court is either a purely legal institution or a political body; that the framers' intentions are either easily discernible or always ambiguous (or even irrelevant); that legal doctrines are either preordained by the Constitution or are artificial constructs; and that justices are either impervious to social, political, and cultural influences or utterly at their mercy. The reality, in each case, is more complex.

Like all judges, the Nine Old Men were imbued with an ethic of impartiality. They were constrained by precedent, procedure, doctrine, and the particular cases in front of them, all of which limited their range of maneuver. Yet they were not merely judges; they were men—politically minded and socially aware men. All, to varying degrees, were attuned to changes in the climate of opinion and mindful of the level of public esteem for their institution and themselves as individuals. They were neither oblivious to life outside their chambers nor immune to feelings of pride, shame, vanity, rage, regret—all evident in decisions of this period (and every other). They were capable of change: growth, regression, and inconsistency. They were, again to different degrees, open to influence by legal briefs, oral arguments, pressure from their peers, and, not least, national events.

Too often, the Hughes Court's internal conflict has been portrayed as one between liberal justices who were responsive to the national emergency and conservative justices who were indifferent to it. In truth, both sides responded to the emergency as they themselves defined it: the liberals by giving the other branches of government greater room to relieve human suffering through new experiments; the conservatives by waging a last stand for "individual initiative, self-reliance, and other cardinal virtues which I was always taught were necessary to develop a real democracy," as George Sutherland wrote a friend in 1937.

It is, in the end, impossible to know what sways a judge. Even the judges themselves do not always know whether their decisions are driven, in the main, by doctrine or emotion, by the dictates of law or politics or conscience. "Who knows what causes a judge to decide as he does?" Roberts once shrugged, reflecting on *Parrish*. "Maybe," he joked, "the breakfast he had has something to do with it."

If Roosevelt won this war, he was, at the same time, losing another.

He was locked in combat with a substantial bloc of conservative Democrats. For all the predictions after the Court fight that "the recalcitrant Senators will want to get back into the fold," as Hiram Johnson put it, they showed no eagerness to do so. The battle lines of spring and summer 1937 had hardened considerably by the fall. Conservative Democrats in Congress resolved to fill the role the Court seemed to have abandoned: as the obstacle in Roosevelt's path. When they returned to Washington after the recess, they rendered the special congressional session a bust. The New Deal never recovered its lost momentum. Roosevelt never regained his squandered mandate.

Conservative Democrats were further emboldened by the economy's sharp, sudden contraction in late 1937; industrial production dropped by a third, stocks slumped, and two million more Americans lost their jobs. Taking the offensive, Josiah Bailey, the North Carolina senator, issued a "manifesto" demanding tax cuts and a balanced budget, and heralding private enterprise and states' rights. Bailey hoped to reenergize the bipartisan coalition that had beaten the Court plan and, ultimately, to spark a political realignment. Though the manifesto failed in this, it would come, over time, to serve as something of a mission statement for modern conservatism.

In retrospect it seems clear that the Democratic coalition, after the electoral triumph of 1936, had become unmanageably large and diverse. Each of its rival factions was intent on having its way. By the start of Roosevelt's second term, liberals were more impatient than ever for fundamental reform, while conservatives were more insistent than ever on a "breathing spell." The president could not possibly satisfy one side without inflaming the other. Increasingly, he threw his lot in with the liberals, which assured the antagonism of his party's southerners and westerners. While these divisions were more pronounced in Washington than in the country as a whole, Democratic voters had never been as enamored of the New Deal as they were of FDR himself.

The Court-packing plan, then, did not create these fissures in the party. Rather, it wrenched them wide open. It was not the cause, but the catalyst that helped fracture the New Deal coalition; reawaken the GOP; unite conservatives across party lines; and shatter the myth of Roosevelt's omnipotence. "He commands support," one observer remarked after the Court fight, "but not the old awe, reverence and idolatry." In early 1938, Roosevelt suffered further setbacks at the hands of congressional conservatives, and he began to grow unnerved by the fierce resistance to his leadership. The president, Ickes noted that spring, "does not seem to me to be the same man. Unless he does buck up, these next two or three years are going to be rather dreary ones, I am afraid."

Roosevelt, however, had some fight left in him. By the summer of 1938 he had been sufficiently provoked by advisers like Ickes and Corcoran, who had urged him, in the words of a federal judge, to "fill the sky with thunderbolts" and give "the betrayers in the Senate who come up for election . . . a taste of war." In a fireside chat that June, FDR announced his intention to support true liberals and oppose phony ones during the coming primary elections. He had reasons other than vengeance. He was deeply concerned that conservative Democrats, wrapping themselves in liberal clothing, were blocking essential reforms and weakening the nation just as it was about to confront major challenges overseas. Still, there was no question, as Sam Rosenman reflected, that Roosevelt's lingering bitterness about the Court fight "blinded [him] to the great dangers to his own standing and prestige" that would come of intervening in local politics.

The "purge," as it became known, was a disaster. Roosevelt had hoped to drive the "reactionaries" out of the Democratic party. Instead he strengthened them. Not only did he fail to oust a single senator who had opposed the Court plan, but nearly all the Democrats who lost their seats in the midterm elections that fall were liberals. The real victor in this internecine struggle was the Republican Party, which made great gains in both houses of Congress.

The Court fight and the purge did indeed touch off a partisan realignment, though it would not be apparent for some time yet, and did not unfold quite as Roosevelt had imagined it. Over the next four or five decades, the slow exodus of conservatives would weaken the Democratic party, for it would not be offset by an influx of progressives. The conservative coalition, born largely of expediency during the Court fight, became a permanent fixture of American political life and even, in time, a majority. But that did not happen until Lyndon Johnson, the young Texan elected to Congress in 1937 on a platform of Court-packing, had fulfilled FDR's prediction and become president of the United States. Johnson's embrace of civil rights for black Americans was what finally prompted southern, conservative Democrats, in massive numbers, to abandon the party of Franklin Roosevelt and complete their migration to, and capture of, the GOP.

"There is a mysterious cycle to human events," Roosevelt said in 1936, accepting his party's nomination for another term as president. "To some generations much is given. Of other generations much is expected. This generation of Americans has a rendezvous with destiny." Across the world, he said, nations had "yielded their democracy," people had "grown too weary to carry on the fight" for freedom. He wanted them to know that "here in America we are waging a great and successful war . . . a war for the survival of democracy. We are fighting to save a great and precious form of government for ourselves and for the world."

Three years later, as another election approached, it seemed that in many ways the rendezvous with destiny had been missed. True, the economy continued to improve, democratic institutions had withstood the worst of the Depression, and the Supreme Court had become a partner to the other branches of government. The Republican party showed no interest in reviving the constitutional battles of the past. Roosevelt himself remained highly popular with the public. All the same, by 1939, his second term appeared more likely to be remembered for lost opportunities than landmark achievements. At home, his political opponents had rendered the "great and successful war" a stalemate, while overseas, a war of an altogether different sort had begun.

On the morning of March 4, 1939—six years to the day after Roosevelt's first inauguration, and exactly two years after his "fighting speech" about the Supreme Court—the special presidential train pulled into Union Station and FDR came down the ramp. He was returning from a two-week cruise in the Caribbean. This had been a working vacation, far more than any he had taken in previous years. Aboard the flagship *Houston*, Roosevelt had passed the majority of each day at his desk; when he emerged to spend half a day in the sun, it was to inspect naval war maneuvers—a test of American security against a transatlantic invasion. The former assistant secretary of the Navy, charts and binoculars in hand, took his role as observer very seriously.

He rushed back to Washington on March 4 to celebrate an anniversary: not his own, which, by tradition, he marked quietly by praying for guidance at St. John's Episcopal Church, but the 150th anniversary of the first Congress of the United States. That night, he would honor the occasion by addressing a joint session of Congress. His would not be the only notable speech. The other would be delivered by the Chief Justice, Charles Evans Hughes.

The two rivals had never spoken on the same platform. They had not even stood on the same dais since January 20, 1937, when they faced one another across the width of Roosevelt's family Bible and

Hughes had administered the oath of office. Now, as the black-robed Hughes stepped to the rostrum, the previously solemn crowd of senators, congressmen, and other officials burst into wild cheering and whistling. Roosevelt's appearance sparked a similar reaction, the most exuberant he had received in that chamber in at least two years, before the Court fight.

The speeches that followed, according to *The Washington Post*, "took on the color of a debate." That, at least, had been the expectation. In reality, the points of disagreement were limited to one. Each speaker took just a moment to address—perhaps to lecture—the other about the proper pace of reform in a democracy. "If our checks and balances sometimes prevent the speedy action which is thought desirable," Hughes declared, "they also assure in the long run a more deliberate judgment. And what the people really want they generally get."

Roosevelt, as ever, expressed a greater degree of urgency, and a lesser tolerance for impediments to action. Grounding his views in American history, he used a once familiar expression. "You have heard the phrase the 'horse and buggy age,'" he said. Indeed they had. "We use it not in derogation of the men who had to spend weeks on the rough highways before they could establish a quorum of the Congress . . . ," he clarified. "We use it rather to explain the tedious delays and the local antagonisms and jealousies which beset our early paths. We use it perhaps to remind our citizens of today that the automobile, the railroad, the airplane, the electrical impulse over the wire and through the ether leave to no citizen of the United States an excuse for sectionalism, for delay in the execution of the public business or for a failure to maintain a full understanding of the acceleration of the processes of civilization."

Here, barely cloaked, were the only words that appeared to be aimed, pointedly if indirectly, at the white-bearded justice and his brethren who now sat beneath Roosevelt and vigorously applauded his remarks. Roosevelt was not chiding those who had failed to "develop" this important understanding, but, rather, those who failed to "maintain" it. Implicitly, he seemed to be warning Hughes—and Owen Roberts, also present—against forgetting what they had learned and returning to the right.

Thus concluded the "debate." More than these differences, what was striking about the two speeches was just how similar they were. With an eye to events abroad—to "a world in turmoil," as the Chief Justice put it—both Hughes and Roosevelt served notice that the freedoms that America's founders had enshrined in the Bill of Rights were fundamental, the birthright of men and women everywhere. Hughes denounced "glory in power." FDR condemned other nations' "reversions to personal rule" and to "the so-called 'justice' of the dark ages." Taken together, the speeches were a powerful one-two punch. "Roosevelt and Hughes Hit Dictators," cheered the next day's *Washington Post*.

Facing a common enemy, both men stressed their unity of purpose. "Our fathers," the president said, "rightly believed that this government which they set up would seek as a whole to act as a whole for the governing good of the nation." The Chief Justice struck a similar note: The Supreme Court, he declared, was "a separate but not an independent arm of government. . . . In the great enterprise of making democracy workable"—this a direct echo of FDR's signature line—"we are all partners."

Truly, the battlefield had shifted. By the time of Roosevelt's reelection the following November, the Nazis had occupied France, among other countries, Luftwaffe bombers had killed more than 10,000 Londoners, and Germany, Italy, and Japan had signed the Tripartite Pact, establishing the Axis alliance. "What would have happened to the political fortunes of Franklin D. Roosevelt," asked a historian in the late 1940s, "if the war had not created a new theater for his leadership?" It is impossible, of course, to know the answer. World events intervened—creating not only an opportunity but also, as most Americans saw it, an imperative for Roosevelt to remain in office.

"I am enlisted," he had said in 1936, "for the duration of the war." He meant the war at home. But it soon became clear that America's struggle for the survival of democracy would be waged on foreign shores, and that its rendezvous with destiny, so long deferred, would now be met—in Normandy, in the Ardennes, on the shores of Okinawa.

ACKNOWLEDGMENTS

THE ORDERLINESS OF a finished book is always a little misleading. For the sake of full disclosure, these pages should probably carry annotations indicating who planted the seed of an idea; the margins should probably retain comments scribbled by all who took time away from busy lives to improve the manuscript. The endnotes are heavy on citations but silent on sources of inspiration. Here, then, is a brief—if inadequate—attempt to set the record straight.

This book began, as many books do, with a slow-rolling recognition that there was more to a seemingly familiar story. My curiosity about the Court-packing fight began when Michael Waldman, my former boss in the Clinton White House, pointed me to Joseph Alsop and Turner Catledge's as-it-happened account, *The 168 Days*—one of the lost classics of political literature—and drew me into the ongoing argument about the events of 1937 and their causes. If not for Michael, I wouldn't have written this book.

Not long after that, a conversation with Arthur M. Schlesinger, Jr., and William vanden Heuvel sharpened my sense that the old, pat explanations of Roosevelt's actions were insufficient. Like so many other historians, I feel Arthur's absence—and can only hope my work proves worthy of his influence.

My introduction to the issues at the center of this book was provided some years ago by a pair of remarkable Brown University professors:

James T. Patterson, who continues to be a mentor, friend, and goad, and the late Edward Beiser, who reminded the students in his course on the politics of the legal system that we were not only studying the law but "examining some of the most fundamental questions in life."

I am thankful that three remarkable men were willing to share their personal recollections of the Supreme Court in the 1930s. Bennett Boskey clerked for Justices Harlan Fiske Stone and Stanley Reed and offered insights on both. Graciously, he also gave me access to the papers and unpublished memoir of Warner W. Gardner. David Ginsburg—sent by Felix Frankfurter to Washington seventy-five years ago to serve as aide-de-camp to Ben Cohen and Tom Corcoran—told me thrilling stories about the first days after the launch of the Court plan. (He also described speechwriting sessions with FDR, who would reach across his desk to hand Ginsburg and Sam Rosenman scraps of paper bearing sentence fragments.) And the late Austin Cunningham—who, as a young Supreme Court page, used to deliver documents to Justice Holmes—became my liaison to Washington as it existed before and during the New Deal. If I had written this book only as a pretext to solicit their stories, it would have been reason enough.

During a summer spent in the Manuscript Reading Room of the Library of Congress, I was lucky to have the guidance of Jeff Flannery and his colleagues. My stint there was more productive for the fact that Thomas G. Corcoran, Jr., generously gave me the key to the closed portions of his father's invaluable papers. At the Franklin D. Roosevelt Library in Hyde Park, Robert Clark helped me dig beneath the rich topsoil of material to find previously undiscovered or unexamined documents. In that effort, I was exceedingly fortunate to rely on the advice, encouragement, discerning eye, and relentless energy of Mike Hill. To appropriate what Frankfurter once said about Chief Justice Hughes, watching Mike at work in an archive is "like watching Toscanini lead an orchestra." I also want to thank Anna Evans, Adam Frankel, and Ben Reed for investing many hours in their fruitful search for material.

I am grateful for the hospitality of friends. Peter Orszag and Meeghan Prunty-Edelstein provided space at the Brookings Institution for me to develop a blueprint for this book. Later, when I was ready to write, Josh Gottheimer gave me and my materials what must, after a year and a half, have come to seem like a permanent home down the hall from his office. I am thankful for the patience and generosity shown by my partners at West Wing Writers—Paul Orzulak, Tom Rosshirt, Jeff Nussbaum, and Vinca LaFleur—throughout my extended absence. Paul and Tom also read large portions of the manuscript, offering valuable ideas and much-needed encouragement.

I have benefited greatly from the insights of others. From the beginning, John Q. Barrett offered his perspective on personalities, legal complexities, and the inner workings of various archives; later, he also gave my manuscript a careful look, all of which puts me deeply in his debt. My friends David Greenberg and Len Stark were also incredibly close readers, providing comments on everything from fundamentals to footnotes. In addition to reading the text and generating great ideas, Matt Dallek acted as a one-man lending library (with a very lenient late-return policy). West Wing Writers alums Nat Jackson and Megan Rooney, too, were kind to suggest improvements, large and small.

For their help in ways too varied to recount, I also want to thank Doug Band, Ralph Brenner, Robert Dallek, Brian Floca, Doris Kearns Goodwin, David Grove, Faye Haskins, Megan Jacobs, Michael Janeway, William Leuchtenburg, Carolyn McGoldrick, Lauren Morrell, Roger Newman, Steve Petteway, and Jeffrey Toobin.

To use precisely the kind of cliché that he would strike from the text, Starling Lawrence, my editor at W. W. Norton, has a remarkable ability to keep forest and trees in focus at the same time. Star edits in sweeping, graceful gestures, with the seeming effortlessness of a master. I have now been honored to work with him on two books, and my trust in his judgment only deepens with time. Nydia Parries, Rachel Salzman, and the rest of the team at W. W. Norton offered all the support—intellectual and logistical—that I needed in ample doses. And I humbly offer two decades' worth of gratitude to the indispensable Rafe Sagalyn, my literary agent and friend. All agents pitch books; Rafe provokes arguments, ideas, and far better work from his authors.

My family, as ever, lifted me throughout this long process. My parents, Susan and Barry, have given me unconditional support and, at the same time, constructive advice whenever I sought it (as I so often did). My in-laws, Bea and Stephen Epstein, helped sustain me with their warm enthusiasm when my own was flagging.

For more than a year, every night over dinner, my son, Jonah, now six, earnestly asked how many words I'd written. Even when my answer was "less than a hundred," Jonah would reply, genuinely, "Good job, Dad." As deadlines approached, my editors found an ally in my daughter, Anna, age three, who recently handed me a toy plastic envelope and said she had written me a letter. "Dear Daddy," it began. "I love you." She paused, then looked up. "If you finish your book I will write you another letter."

I find that I've exhausted the thesaurus entry for "gratitude" before coming to the person who deserves it most of all: my wife, Rebecca Epstein. But then, no word or words, however well selected, could begin to describe how indebted I feel to you, Rebecca. You are the lawyer in our family, the one who actually works on behalf of the "forgotten" man and woman, inspiring awe in those of us who only read (or write) about it in books. Every page of this book—no exaggeration—bears the imprint of your intellect. Month after month (after month), you also did the heavy lifting to create space in our household for this book to get done—a book that took up every inch of space we gave to it (and then some). Rebecca, I know I'll never be able to thank you fully for that—or for everything else that has nothing to do with this book but is all that is most important in life.

NOTES

ABBREVIATIONS USED IN NOTES

CDT	*Chicago Daily Tribune*
DOJ	U.S. Department of Justice
FDR	Franklin D. Roosevelt
FDRL	Franklin D. Roosevelt Presidential Library, Hyde Park, New York
FF	Felix Frankfurter
HSC	Homer S. Cummings
LOC	Library of Congress, Washington, D.C.
NYT	*New York Times*
OF	Office File, Franklin D. Roosevelt Papers
OH	Oral History
PPA	*Public Papers and Addresses of Franklin D. Roosevelt*, Random House, New York
PPF	President's Personal File, Franklin D. Roosevelt Papers
PSF	President's Secretary's Files, Franklin D. Roosevelt Papers
TGC	Thomas G. Corcoran
WP	*Washington Post*
WSJ	*Wall Street Journal*
UVA	University of Virginia, Charlottesville, Virginia
WVD	Willis Van Devanter

INTRODUCTION

1 **The cocktails were typically strong:** Rosenman, *Working with Roosevelt*, 152–53.

1 **"apparently the least worried man in the country":** Anne O'Hare McCormick, quoted in Schlesinger, *Coming of the New Deal*, 585; Rosenman, *Working with Roosevelt*, 153.

2 **Franklin Roosevelt stood at the pinnacle of power:** Patterson, *Congressional Conservatism*, 80–81; Schlesinger, *Politics of Upheaval*, 642–43.

2 **the Supreme Court—in a series of devastating rulings:** Jackson, *Struggle*, 40–41; Mason, *Supreme Court from Taft to Burger*, 98fn; Stone to FF, May 27, 1935, Stone Papers, Box 13, LOC.

3 **a "'no-man's-land' where no government . . . can function":** *PPA*, 1936, 191.

3 **"judicial tyranny":** Ickes, Jan. 24, 1936, *Secret Diary*, Vol. I, 524.

3 **"nine old men in kimonos":** Rogers quoted in *NYT Sunday Magazine*, Nov. 3, 1935: 4; Leuchtenburg, *Supreme Court Reborn*, 121; Alsop and Catledge, *168 Days*, 33; McKenna, *Franklin Roosevelt and the Great Constitutional War*, 269.

4 **"aloof from all reality":** Pearson and Allen, *The Nine Old Men*, 15.

4 **All were astounded:** Leuchtenburg, *Supreme Court Reborn*, 125; Alsop and Catledge, *168 Days*, 49, 58–59.

4 **"whether to take only one cocktail":** Richberg, *My Hero*, 222.

4 **The Judiciary Dinner:** Alsop and Catledge, *168 Days*, 63; *WP*, Feb. 3, 1937; *NYT*, Feb. 3, 1937, Feb. 2, 1883, Feb. 15, 1884; "Dinner at the White House," Feb. 2, 1937, Office of Social Entertainments, Box 42, FDRL; Henry F. Pringle, "Profiles: The President—II," *The New Yorker*, June 23, 1934, 23.

5 **Hughes, as ever, was a commanding presence:** Schlesinger, *Politics of Upheaval*, 465.

5 **the Hughes Court was at war:** Ibid., 466–67, 471, 482.

5 **Standing in the East Room:** Rosenman, *Working with Roosevelt*, 153; Alsop and Catledge, *168 Days*, 63; Hellman, *Benjamin N. Cardozo*, 220, 248; Pearson and Allen, *Nine Old Men at the Crossroads*, 19 (McReynolds quoted at 2).

6 **Senator William Borah:** *WP*, Feb. 3, 1937; Leuchtenburg, *Supreme Court Reborn*, 127, 129; "The Supreme Court," Address by Hon. William E. Borah, Feb. 1, 1937, 6–7, in Borah Papers, Box 783, LOC.

6 **Hughes strode across the room:** *CDT*, Feb. 2, 6, 1937.

6 **Cummings slid next to Sam Rosenman:** Rosenman, *Working with Roosevelt*, 154.

7 **Roosevelt, though, was savoring the moment:** Ibid., 154; Alsop and Catledge, *168 Days*, 64; Richberg, *My Hero*, 223; Davis, *FDR: Into the Storm*, 62–63.

CHAPTER ONE: COMPLETE CONTROL

8 **The Armory, by now:** *Baltimore Sun*, Oct. 26, 1932.

9 **"I am waging a war":** *PPA*, 1929–32, 831–42; *WP*, Oct. 26, 1932; *NYT*, Oct. 26, 1932.

9 **"Let's see who is responsible":** *PPA*, 1929–32, 837; *Time*, Nov. 7, 1932.

9 **"And now, a word as to beer":** *Baltimore Sun*, Oct. 26, 1932; *NYT*, Oct. 26, 1932.

10 **the answer to a fervent prayer:** *NYT*, Oct. 28, 1932.

10 **Republicans seized it with relish . . . The Roosevelt "slur":** *Time*, Nov. 7, 1932; *NYT*, Oct. 27, 1932; *WP*, Oct. 27, 1932.

11 **the other arbiters of opinion shrugged it off:** *WP*, Oct. 28, 1932; *Baltimore Sun*, Oct. 28, 1932; *NYT*, Oct. 27, 1932; *Baltimore Sun*, Nov. 1, 1932.

11 **Still, Roosevelt was not taking any chances:** *NYT*, Oct. 29, Nov. 1, 1932; Michelson, *The Ghost Talks*, 165; *Baltimore Sun*, Nov. 1, 1932.

12 **"What I said last night":** Leuchtenburg, *Supreme Court Reborn*, 83.

12 **the Depression continued to exact its heavy human toll:** Manchester, *The Glory and the Dream*, 37, 40–42; Kennedy, *Freedom from Fear*, 163–64; Chandler, *America's Greatest Depression*, 5–11, 31–32, 127–28; Bordo et al., *Defining Moment*, 7–9.

13 **He met with his advisers and made plans:** Schlesinger, *Crisis of the Old Order*, 456, 476–77, 467; Davis, *FDR: The New York Years*, 419–22.

14 **"future campaigns and victories together":** FDR to HSC, Jan. 19, 1917, HSC Papers, Box 169, UVA.

14 **Roosevelt and Cummings:** *Encyclopedia of Biography*, Vol. XV, 1924: 291–93, accessed at www.kichline.com/carrie/ICFA/homer.htm; *Time*, Jan. 9, 1939; TGC interview, Jul. 10, 1980, TGC Papers, Box 596, LOC; Pearson and Allen, *The Nine Old Men*, 239; *The Nation*, July 3, 1935, 14; *NYT*, Sept. 11, 1956; Shogan, *Backlash*, 64; Cummings, "The State vs. Harold Israel," 406–34; McKenna, *Franklin Roosevelt and the Great Constitutional War*, 8–9.

14 **At the 1920 Democratic Convention:** *Encyclopedia of Biography*, Vol. XV, 1924: 291–93; *NYT*, Jun. 29, 1920; Schlesinger, *Crisis of the Old Order*, 45; TGC interview, Jul. 10, 1980, TGC Papers, Box 596, LOC; *NYT*, Aug. 10, 1920; *WP*, Aug. 10, 1920; HSC Diary, June 11, 1937, 66.

15 **Cummings was back in the business:** Freidel, *FDR: The Triumph*, 242–43, 370; Farley,

Behind the Ballots, 94; Neal, *Happy Days Are Here Again*, 178; Shogan, *Backlash*, 66; Robert Jackson to FDR, May 31, 1932, courtesy of John Q. Barrett, who notes that this is Robert Jackson of New Hampshire, not Robert H. Jackson of New York, who figures prominently in later chapters of this book.

15 **"The spirit that died with Wilson":** HSC Diary, Jan. 27, 1933, 114, Dec. 8–11, 1932, 64–65, UVA.

16 **"the possibility of changing the law":** Ibid., Jan. 17, 1933, 101–2, UVA.

16 **FDR called Cummings to offer him a position:** Ibid., Feb. 3, 23, Mar. 5–Apr. 1, 1933, 121–22, 138, 159, UVA.

16 **FDR had selected Thomas Walsh . . . Walsh was dead:** Freidel, *FDR: Launching the New Deal*, 143–44, 150–51; Davis, *FDR: The New York Years*, 425; *Time*, Mar. 6, 13, 1933.

17 **"perhaps Homer Cummings":** McKenna, *Franklin Roosevelt and the Great Constitutional War*, 3–4; HSC Diary, Mar. 1–3, 1933, 148–50; Mar. 3–4, 1933, 151–53, UVA.

17 ***Time* magazine thought the appointment:** *Time*, Mar. 13, 1933.

17 **The inaugural platform:** Davis, *FDR: The New Deal Years*, 29; Schlesinger, *Coming of the New Deal*, 1.

18 **the site of the new Supreme Court Building:** Barbara A. Perry and Henry J. Abraham, "Franklin Roosevelt and the Supreme Court: A New Deal and a New Image," in Shaw et al., *FDR and the Transformation of the Supreme Court*, 13; Pearson and Allen, *The Nine Old Men*, 3.

19 **an American *Führer*:** Davis, *FDR: The New Deal Years*, 15; Landon and Smith quoted in Schlesinger, *Coming of the New Deal*, 3; *Barron's* quoted in Leuchtenburg, *FDR and the New Deal*, 30.

19 **"People are looking to you":** Leuchtenburg, *FDR and the New Deal*, 1.

19 **Roosevelt's power was manifest:** See Schlesinger, *Coming of the New Deal*, 20–23; Davis, *FDR: The New Deal Years*, 201–5.

20 **No president had attempted:** Schlesinger, *Coming of the New Deal*, 20–21; Chandler, *America's Greatest Depression*, 134; Bordo et al., *Defining Moment*, 10–11; Smith, Jean Edward, *FDR*, 316–17, 327; Hofstadter, *American Political Tradition*, 327; *PPA*, 1933, 17, 139.

20 **"To preserve . . . we had to reform":** FDR was paraphrasing Thomas Babington Macaulay, the nineteenth-century British Whig politician and historian. Felix Frankfurter had passed along the quotation: "You must reform in order to preserve" (FF to FDR, Feb. 14, 1934, in Freedman, *Roosevelt and Frankfurter*, 192). Also see Burns, *Roosevelt: The Lion and the Fox*, 235.

21 **"Roosevelt took the status quo":** Perkins, *The Roosevelt I Knew*, 328; Keynes in Schlesinger, *Coming of the New Deal*, foreword to the Mariner edition, viii.

21 **Roosevelt resisted calls:** *PPA*, 1933, 3, 7; *NYT Book Review*, Mar. 3, 1957, and Jan. 4, 1959.

21 **Still, there could be no understating:** *PPA*, 1928–1932, 752; Sidney M. Milkis and Jerome M. Mileur, "Introduction: The New Deal, Then and Now," in Milkis and Mileur, eds., *The New Deal and the Triumph of Liberalism*, 3–4. Senator Thomas Gore in Leuchtenburg, FDR and the New Deal, 61; also see 33, 336.

22 **"broad Executive power":** *PPA*, 1933, 14–15.

22 **"behind the façade of fear and need":** Ashurst Diary, Jun. 16, 1933, in Sparks, *A Many-Colored Toga*, 334; Irons, *New Deal Lawyers*, 116–17.

CHAPTER TWO: STORM CENTER

24 **"Mr. Hughes was the bull's eye":** *Time*, Feb. 24, 1930.

24 **the Supreme Court had defended:** *The American Mercury*, Vol. 15, No. 57, Sept. 1928: 51.

24 **a "carnival of unconstitutionality":** Mason, *Supreme Court from Taft to Burger*, 70; O'Brien, *Storm Center*, 43.

25 **Even so, Hughes had expected:** Pusey, *Charles Evans Hughes*, Vol. II, 652.

25 **its chief judge, Benjamin Cardozo:** Elman, *Of Law and Men*, 145.

26 **At Columbia Law School . . . his score:** Pusey, *Charles Evans Hughes*, Vol. I, 16–21, 24, 43; *The New Yorker*, July 6, 1935: 18–20.

26 **"His is the best mind":** Gilbert, *Mirrors of Washington*, 69.

26 **the downward sweep:** *New York Review of Books*, May 30, 1974; Alsop, *"I've Seen the Best of It": Memoirs*, 116; Danelski and Tulchin, eds., *Autobiographical Notes*, xxviii; Louchheim, *The Making of the New Deal*, 71; FF quoted in Lash, *From the Diaries of Felix Frankfurter*, 274–75.

26 **He had this effect on everyone:** Pusey, *Charles Evans Hughes*, Vol. I, 146–47, 166, 336; *Time*, Feb. 17, 1930; Danelski and Tulchin, eds., *Autobiographical Notes*, xvii, xxii–xxiv; *New York Review of Books*, May 30, 1974; Ross, *The Chief Justiceship of Charles Evans Hughes*, 3; Hamilton Holt, quoted in Hughes, *Addresses and Papers*, 1908, i.

27 **Hughes's sanctimony was leavened:** *The North American Review*, May 1916, 659; *NYT*, Apr. 19, 1920; *New York Review of Books*, May 30, 1974; *The New Yorker*, July 6, 1935, 18; Gilbert, *Mirrors of Washington*, 79–80.

27 **His guiding philosophy:** Irons, *A People's History*, 295; On Hughes's liberal record as associate justice, see Hendel, *Charles Evans Hughes and the Supreme Court*, 64–67; Leuchtenburg, "Charles Evans Hughes," 1188; Paul A. Freund, "Charles Evans Hughes as Chief Justice," 9; Pusey, *Charles Evans Hughes*, Vol. II, 661; and Ross, *The Chief Justiceship of Charles Evans Hughes*, xii, 4–5, 7.

27 **Hughes's liberalism seemed consigned:** Freund, 7fn; "Lawyer's Lawyer," *Time*, Feb. 17, 1930.

28 **"a conservatism less cheerful":** *Time*, Feb. 10, 1930.

28 **"subjected him to continued":** *The New Republic*, July 1, 1936; *The New Yorker*, July 1, 1936, 21.

28 **Hughes's apologists:** "McReynolds, Roberts and Hughes," *The New Republic*, July 1, 1936, 233; Murphy, Paul L., *The Constitution in Crisis Times*, 106–7.

28 **"the pure white flame of Liberalism":** *Time*, Feb. 17, 1930.

28 **an ugly confirmation fight:** Little, "The Omnipotent Nine," 57; *The Forum*, June 1930; *Time*, Feb. 24, 1930; *New York World*, Feb. 14, 1930.

28 **"no man in public life":** Mason, *Harlan Fiske Stone*, 297–98.

28 **"The Supreme Court is not only":** Ibid., 299.

28 **Another senator warned that:** Ibid.

28 **Their aim was not really to derail Hughes's nomination:** Ross, *The Chief Justiceship of Charles Evans Hughes*, 12, 15; FF, "The Supreme Court and the Public," 334; *Time*, Feb. 24, 1930; also see Mason, *Supreme Court: Vehicle*, 12–15.

29 **"Let us face the fact":** FF, "The Supreme Court and the Public."

29 **Owen J. Roberts:** Ross, *A Muted Fury*, 291, 293–94; Mason, *Harlan Fiske Stone*, 299–300; *Time*, Feb. 24, 1930, *The New Republic*, July 1, 1936.

29 **"As you well know":** Pusey, *Charles Evans Hughes*, Vol. II, 667.

29 **Hughes entered a Court long split:** Freund, "Charles Evans Hughes as Chief Justice," 8.

29 **The principal weapon:** Bertram Benedict, "The Guaranty of Due Process," *Editorial Research Reports*, Vol. 1, No. 19, May 20, 1937, 370–75, in Clapper Papers, Box 234, LOC.

30 **railroad lawyers, monopolists, and conservative thinkers:** Ibid., 376–78, 381; James W. Ely, Jr., "Property Rights and Democracy in the American Constitutional Order," in Hall and McGuire, eds., *The Judicial Branch*, 499–500; Irons, *A People's History*, 236–37.

30 **"substantive due process":** Ely, "Property Rights and Democracy in the American Constitutional Order," 500–502; Fallon, *The Dynamic Constitution*, 84; Benedict, "The Guaranty of Due Process," 367.

30 **radical and reform movements sprang up:** Irons, *A People's History*, 254; Beard quoted in Fred Rodell, *Nine Men*, 150.

31 **"bulwark of American individualism":** Maine quoted in Winchester, "The Judiciary—Its Growing Power and Influence," 812–13.

31 **"delusive exactness":** *Truax v. Corrigan*, 257 U.S. 312 (1921): 342, 344.

31 **the issue, as Holmes saw it:** *New State Ice Co. v. Liebmann*, 285 U.S. 262 (1932): 311; Harlan in *Lochner v. People of State of New York*, 198 U.S. 45 (1905): 68.

31 **By 1930, when Hughes returned:** Mason, *Supreme Court from Taft to Burger*, 60–61; author interview, Austin Cunningham, Dec. 6, 2005; *Time*, Feb. 24, 1930; Leuchtenburg, "Charles Evans Hughes," 1187; Sutherland, address at the Utah State Bar Association, 1895, in Paschal, *Mr. Justice Sutherland*, 27–28.

32 **"Liberals Have It":** *Time*, June 1, 1931.

32 **It was the triumph:** Paul L., Murphy, *The Constitution in Crisis Times*, 121fn.

32 **"abruptly dethroned":** *The New Republic*, Sept. 2, 1931.

33 **Many scholars agreed:** Mason, *Harlan Fiske Stone*, 314–15; Leonard, *A Search for a Judicial Philosophy*, 21; Corwin, "Social Planning Under the Constitution," 25, 27.

33 **despite initial impressions:** Ross, *The Chief Justiceship of Charles Evans Hughes*, 29, 41.

33 **Benjamin Cardozo of New York:** Mason, *Harlan Fiske Stone*, 310, 318, 323, 347–48.

34 **The schism could be:** Leonard, *A Search for a Judicial Philosophy*, 18.

34 **"The Supreme Court is above":** *NYT*, Oct. 27, 1932.

34 **Some of the justices:** Levinson, *Constitutional Faith*, 16; Kammen, *A Machine That Would Go of Itself*, 3; Ross, *The Chief Justiceship of Charles Evans Hughes*, 226.

34 **"black-robed gods":** *WP*, Feb. 16, 1936; *NYT*, Nov. 10, 1929. Also see Max Lerner's classic critique of the "fetishism" of the Court and Constitution (Lerner, "Constitution and Court as Symbols," 1290–1319).

35 **"a life of judicial piety":** Lawrence, *Nine Honest Men*, 6.

35 **"In their private hours":** *NYT*, Sept. 6, 1922.

35 **Brandeis . . . frequently discussed the campaign:** Brandeis to FF, July 2, 1932, in Urofsky, *"Half Brother,"* 492; Lash, *Dealers and Dreamers*, 82–83; Stone quoted in Ross, *The Chief Justiceship of Charles Evans Hughes*, 46; Stone to FF, Sept. 30, 1932, Stone Papers, Box 13, LOC.

36 **Willis Van Devanter . . . complained:** WVD to Mrs. John W. Lacey, Oct. 7 and 26, 1932, and to Dennis T. Flynn, Oct. 3, 1932, WVD Papers, LOC. It is unlikely that Hughes held FDR in such low esteem. As governors of New York—one bond between them—both had been heirs to the same reformist tradition of Theodore Roosevelt (Ross, *The Chief Justiceship of Charles Evans Hughes*, 46).

36 **Van Devanter followed every major speech:** Ibid.; also, WVD to Flynn, Oct. 21, 1932, WVD Papers, Box 3, LOC.

37 **"I was not expecting":** WVD to Flynn, Oct. 21, 1932, and to Montgomery Webster, Nov. 12, 1932, WVD Papers, LOC.

37 **"I cannot see in Roosevelt":** Stone to Lauson and Marshall Stone, Nov. 9, 1932, Stone Papers, Box 3, LOC.

37 **FDR "did most of the talking":** Brandeis to FF, Nov. 9, 1932, in Urofsky, *"Half Brother,"* 503; Lash, *Dealers and Dreamers*, 99.

37 **watched Lincoln's funeral procession:** WVD to D.C. Bond, Apr. 10, 1934, WVD Papers, LOC.

37 **Hughes, who as a college student:** Danelski and Tulchin, eds., *Autobiographical Notes*, 37–38.

38 **"due, in large measure":** Brandeis, address to the Chicago Bar Association, Jan. 3, 1916, reprinted in Brandeis, "The Living Law," 463–64.

38 **in a speech at Milton Academy:** Roosevelt, *Whither Bound?*, 12–13.

38 **Van Devanter had "rather definitely":** WVD to Mrs. John W. Lacey, Oct. 26, 1932, and to L. R. Gillette, Mar. 14, 1933, WVD Papers, LOC.

39 **To look at Van Devanter:** *WP*, Feb. 16, 1936; Schlesinger, *Politics of Upheaval*, 456; WVD to Mary White, Apr. 22, 1937, WVD Papers, LOC; Pearson and Allen, *The Nine Old Men*, 188–89.

39 **Van Devanter rose rapidly:** *The New Republic*, June 17, 1936.

39 **Van Devanter's vote:** *NYT*, Feb. 9, 1941; Wechsler in Louchheim, *The Making of the New Deal*, 53; Pusey, *Charles Evans Hughes*, Vol. II, 667–68.

40 **when Congress . . . slashed the pensions:** WVD to Mrs. John W. Lacey, Jan. 11, 1933, WVD Papers, LOC; Brandeis to FF, Jan. 10, 1933, in Urofsky, *"Half Brother,"* 507, 507fn, 508fn.

40 **"CONFIDENTIAL!!":** Stone to FF, Dec. 9, 1932, and FF to Stone, Dec. 13, 1932, Stone Papers, Box 13, LOC.

40 **"I do not like the idea":** Danelski and Tulchin, eds., *Autobiographical Notes*, 302–3; WVD to Mrs. John W. Lacey, Oct. 26, 1932, WVD Papers, LOC.

40 **"When the Court convened in the fall":** WVD to Mrs. John W. Lacey, Jan. 11, 1933, WVD Papers, LOC.

41 **"before long, you are likely":** FF memo on visit with FDR, March 8, 1933, in Freedman, *Roosevelt and Frankfurter*, 113; Nelson, "The President and the Court," 290.

41 **"was notice to all the Justices":** Danelski and Tulchin, eds., *Autobiographical Notes*, 302–3.

41 **"There is no assurance":** WVD to Mrs. John W. Lacey, May 3, 1933, WVD Papers, LOC.

41 **to "change in personnel":** Sullivan, "The Supreme Court as It Is Today," 298.

CHAPTER THREE: SHORTCUTS

42 **"Have I a legal right to do this?":** *The New Yorker*, June 16, 1934.

42 **Far more pressing was the question:** HSC Diary, Mar. 3–5, 1933, 151, 153–54, UVA; Perkins, *The Roosevelt I Knew*, 194; Schlesinger, *Coming of the New Deal*, 95.

42 **The first phase of the New Deal:** Sparks, *A Many Colored Toga*, 333.

43 **"I went about with my pockets bulging":** HSC Diary, Mar. 5–Apr. 1, 1933, 155–56, UVA.

43 **"Homer is a great fellow":** FDR comment to Ickes, quoted in ibid., Nov. 16, 1933, 125.

43 **the administration readied a series of reforms:** Schlesinger, *Coming of the New Deal*, 41–42, 200–201.

43 **"The matter had progressed":** HSC Diary, Apr. 21, 1933, 11–12, UVA.

43 **Agricultural Adjustment Act:** Irons, *New Deal Lawyers*, 23–24; Lash, *Dealers and Dreamers*, 122–23.

44 **"The whole project is very ambitious":** HSC Diary, June 16, 1933, UVA. The lawyer is Blackwell Smith of the NRA, quoted in Irons, *New Deal Lawyers*, 56.

44 **"the president had a tendency":** Jackson, *That Man*, 74.

45 **more a matter of temperament:** Davis, *FDR: The Beckoning of Destiny, 1882–1928*, 208; Ward, *Before the Trumpet*, 335; Ward, *A First-Class Temperament*, 61–62 (emphasis in original).

45 **In 1907, when he passed the bar:** Ward, *A First-Class Temperament*, 63–64.

45 **Carter, Ledyard & Milburn:** Ibid., 71–72, 76.

45 **"I don't think he liked":** Eleanor Roosevelt quoted in Ward, *A First-Class Temperament*, 72–73; FDR to Edwin De T. Bechtel, Nov. 10, 1932, in Elliott Roosevelt, ed., *FDR: His Personal Letters, 1928–1945*, Vol. 1, 305–6.

46 **he was good with clients:** Ward, *A First-Class Temperament*, 75, 77; Davis, *FDR: The Beckoning of Destiny, 1882–1928*, 213. The clerk was Grenville Clark. Cousins and Clifford, eds., *Memoirs of a Man: Grenville Clark*, 16.

46 **"While he began [his professional] life":** Jackson, *That Man*, 50; Ward, *A First-Class Temperament*, 562, 656; FDR quoted in *NYT*, June 16, 1931.

46 **"a barrier to progress":** White quoted in *Time*, Oct. 15, 1934; FF to Cohen, Sept. 18, 1934, Cohen Papers, Box 13, LOC; *PPA* 1928–32, 570.

47 **"Society . . . must obey the laws of life":** Kammen, *A Machine That Would Go of Itself,* 19–20; *NYT*, Dec. 16, 1900.

47 **The shift was more than semantic:** Ibid.; G. Edward White, *The Constitution and the New Deal*, 168, 207–9, 217; Purcell, *The Crisis of Democratic Theory*, 74–75; Paul R. Brace and Melinda Gann Hall, "Is Judicial Federalism Essential to Democracy? State Courts in the Federal System," in Hall and McGuire, eds., *The Judicial Branch*, 179. This was a very old argument. In the middle of the fourteenth century, English judges bickered with one another over whether they were ruling according to the dictates of reason or merely their own will ("Notes and Comment: The President and the Court," 63).

48 **In his landmark study:** Purcell, *The Crisis of Democratic Theory*, 75–77.

48 **The apostles of "organic law":** McBain, *The Living Constitution*, 2, 272; Keller, *In Defense of Yesterday*, 157; Mason, *Supreme Court: Vehicle of Revealed Truth or Power Group*: 4–5; FF to Stone, Sept. 28, 1933, Stone Papers, Box 13, LOC; Mason, *Harlan Fiske Stone*, 356.

48 **Yet by the 1930s it was getting harder:** See FF and Landis, *The Business of the Supreme Court*, 308, 310; Schlesinger, *Politics of Upheaval*, 486–87; Purcell, *The Crisis of Democratic Theory*, 77, 81; Frank quoted in Purcell, *The Crisis of Democratic Theory*, 84.

49 **"a concept of the greatest generality":** Cardozo, *The Nature of the Judicial Process*, 71, 76–77, 124.

49 **deep believers in democratic government:** Purcell, *The Crisis of Democratic Theory*, 88–94; Kalman, *Legal Realism at Yale*, 11, 14, 17.

49 **traditionalists like James M. Beck:** Keller, *In Defense of Yesterday*, 157; Beck quoted in Irons, *New Deal Lawyers*, 116–17.

50 **what Roosevelt sought:** See Freidel, *FDR: The Triumph*, 47–52, 94–95.

50 **"As I have told you":** FDR to Cardozo, Dec. 9, 1932, in Elliott Roosevelt, ed., *F.D.R.: His Personal Letters, 1928–1945*, Vol. I, 307.

50 **"Roosevelt didn't see as clearly":** Robert H. Jackson OH, 456–57.

50 **Neither did he feel as bound:** Bickel, *The Least Dangerous Branch*, 113–14.

51 **"being associated with you":** Pusey, *Charles Evans Hughes*, Vol. II, 733; Hughes to FDR, Feb. 28, 1933, FDRL.

51 **"As things come up from time to time":** FF to Stone, Sept. 28, 1933; Memo, OF 41A, Box 49, FDRL.

51 **If anyone was ideally suited:** Matthew Josephson, "Profiles: Jurist–I," *The New Yorker*, Nov. 30, 1940, 24–25, and "Profiles: Jurist–II," *The New Yorker*, Dec. 7, 1934, 36–37; *NYT Magazine*, Sept. 30, 1934; Clapper, "Felix Frankfurter's Young Men," *Review of Reviews*, Vol. 93, Jan. 1936, in TGC Papers, Box 638, LOC.

52 **Frankfurter's covert role:** Lash, *From the Diaries of Felix Frankfurter*, 44–47, 53; FF, *Felix Frankfurter Reminisces*, 236–37; Josephson, "Profiles: Jurist–I," *The New Yorker*, Nov. 30, 1940, 24.

52 **"technical legal doctrine":** *NYT Magazine*, Sept. 30, 1934.

52 **"an emergency more serious than war":** *Time*, Aug. 28, 1933.

53 **"aid in relieving a depressed industry":** *New State Ice Co. v. Liebmann*, 285 U.S. 262 (1932): 306.

53 **in a commencement address at Deerfield Academy:** *Time*, Mar. 27, 1933; Pusey, *Charles Evans Hughes*, Vol. II, 733.

53 **"not unresponsive to the shifting economic thought":** *Time*, Jan. 23, 1933.

53 **Historically, the Court:** Lasser, *Limits*, 120–21; Schlesinger, *Politics of Upheaval*, 451; Mason, *Harlan Fiske Stone*, 385–86; Mason, *Supreme Court: Vehicle*, 19.

53 **"In dealing with given cases":** "'Modern Tendencies and the Law,' an Address by the Honorable Homer S. Cummings, Attorney General of the United States, Delivered at a Meeting of the American Bar Association at Grand Rapids, Michigan," Aug. 31, 1933, OF 10, DOJ, Box 1, FDRL.

54 **An impression spread:** Mason, *Supreme Court: Vehicle*, 22; Schlesinger, *Politics of Upheaval*, 252. As a useful contrast, see Irons, *New Deal Lawyers*, 254–71, on the administration's shrewd and successful "master plan" to test the constitutionality of the National Labor Relations Act, beginning in 1935.

54 **an "open secret in Washington":** Quoted in Irons, *New Deal Lawyers*, 69.

54 **Others (Stone included) complained:** FF to FDR, July 10, 1933, in Freedman, *Roosevelt and Frankfurter*, 139; Stone to Marshall Stone, Dec. 13, 1934, Stone Papers, Box 2, LOC; Pearson and Allen, "The Men Around the President," 271.

54 **the administration was simply distracted:** Schlesinger, *Politics of Upheaval*, 252; Beard, *America in Midpassage*, 257.

55 **"Our good fortune still holds":** HSC to FDR, and Biggs to HSC, Apr. 30, 1934, OF 10, DOJ, Box 2, FDRL; Irons, *New Deal Lawyers*, 68–69.

55 **"Why are you so anxious":** Freedman, *Roosevelt and Frankfurter*, 132; Mason, *Supreme Court: Vehicle*, 21.

55 **"Supreme Court decisions . . . may unmake us":** FF to Josephine Goldmark, Jan. 10, 1933, Cohen Papers, Box 11, LOC.

55 **General Hugh Johnson:** Davis, *FDR: The New Deal Years*, 76.

55 **Johnson had demanded and received:** Ibid., 244–45; Schlesinger, *Coming of the New Deal*108; *Time*, Oct. 8, 1934.

55 **From the start, then, the NRA was something of a bluff:** Schlesinger, *Coming of the New Deal*, 114–15.

56 **It spawned songs:** *Saturday Evening Post*, Oct. 28, 1933: 68–69, 72.

56 **Roosevelt was approving codes:** Davis, *FDR: The New Deal Years*, 246–50, 253; Mason, *Supreme Court: Vehicle*, 21.

57 **"the political alignments now existing":** HSC to FDR, Nov. 8, 1933, OF 41, Box 48, FDRL.

57 **derided the Court as "powerless":** *The Nation*, Oct. 18, 1933, 428, 430.

57 **the number of justices was not sacrosanct:** Wilson, *Congressional Government*, 38; Bryce, *The American Commonwealth*, Vol. 1, 275.

58 **Up and down the number went:** Hall, *The Oxford Companion to the Supreme Court*, 472–75; Warren, *The Supreme Court in United States History*, Vol. II, 39, 380, 422–23, 446–47.

58 **Yet it loomed:** Bryce, *The American Commonwealth*, 276; Warren, *The Supreme Court in United States History*, Vol. II, 501.

59 **a precinct committeeman:** John P. Byrne to FDR, Apr. 18, 1933, OF 41a, Box 49, FDRL; Louis Howe to Byrne, May 1, 1933, OF 41a, Box 49, FDRL; Leuchtenburg, *Supreme Court Reborn*, 85; *Congressional Digest*, Dec. 1933, 297.

CHAPTER FOUR: THE DYING OF THE LIGHT

60 **"This afternoon Mother and I go":** Stone to Lauson and Marshall Stone, Mar. 16, 1933, Stone Papers, Box 3, LOC.

60 **"much pleased":** WVD to Mrs. John W. Lacey, Mar. 14, 1933, WVD Papers, Box 17, LOC.

60 **"Some of the subsequent measures":** WVD to Dennis T. Flynn, Apr. 6, 1933, WVD Papers, Box 17, LOC.

60 **"the new President has gotten":** James McReynolds to Robert McReynolds, Mar. 20, 1933, and Aug. 19, 1933, McReynolds Papers, Box 1, UVA.

61 **Brandeis looked more favorably:** *The New Republic*, Nov. 18, 1931, 4–6; Schlesinger, *Crisis of the Old Order*, 29; Mason, *Brandeis*, 245, 250; *Muller v. Oregon*: 208 U.S. 412 (1908); *The New Republic*, Feb. 5, 1916.

61 **Brandeis stood above reproach:** *The New Republic*, Mar. 25, 1916, 202; Robert L. Stern in Louchheim, *The Making of the New Deal*, 83; Ickes, Mar. 12, 1933, *Secret Diary*, Vol. I, 6; Mason, *Brandeis*, 582–83; *Time*, Oct. 13, 1941.

62 **Brandeis was uneasy about important aspects:** Rexford Tugwell, "Revised Diary," in Namorato, ed., *Diary of Rexford G. Tugwell*, 295–97, 337fn, 338fn; Mason, *Brandeis*, 613–15.

62 **"promise in many specific undertakings":** Brandeis to FF, June 13, Aug. 3 and 14, and Oct. 24, 1933, and Feb. 27, 1934, in Urofsky, *"Half Brother,"* 523, 526, 528, 532, 541.

63 **Bigness, Brandeis warned:** Mason, *Brandeis*, 554–55, 557–58, 560, 574, 578; Schlesinger, *Crisis of the Old Order*, 30–31; *The New Republic*, Nov. 12, 1956, 16–17; Apr. 15, 1933, in Namorato, ed., *Diary of Rexford G. Tugwell*, 338.

63 **"It was a terrible thing":** Brandeis to FF, Aug. 3, Nov. 9, 16, 1933, in Urofsky, *"Half Brother,"* 526, 534–35.

63 **"if the Lord":** Brandeis to Elizabeth Brandeis Raushenbush, Nov. 19, 1933, in Urofsky and Levy, *Family Letters of Louis D. Brandeis*, 533.

63 **"You are, I am sure":** FF to FDR, Apr. 17, 1933, TGC Papers, Box 588, LOC.

63 **Son of a Chesterfield, New Hampshire, farmer:** *Time*, June 23, 1941; Mason, *Harlan Fiske Stone*, 306, 322, 351; Gardner, "Mr. Chief Justice Stone," 1205.

63 **in the company of the Court's conservatives:** *Saturday Evening Post*, Sept. 20, 1941, 15; Mason, *Harlan Fiske Stone*, 252–54, 261–62, 306; Mason, *Brandeis*, 606.

64 **McReynolds, trying clumsily to draw Stone:** Gardner, "Harlan Fiske Stone," 9; Mason, *Harlan Fiske Stone*, 258, 351, 380; McReynolds to Stone, n.d., Stone Papers, Box 76, LOC.

64 **"Perhaps the most astonishing":** Stone to FF, Feb. 17, 1933, Stone Papers, Box 13, LOC.

64 **"The issues . . . cannot be settled":** Stone to Hoover, May 2, 1933, Stone Papers, Box 17, LOC; Gardner, "Harlan Fiske Stone," 11.

64 **"I certainly wish him well":** Stone to Lauson and Marshall Stone, Mar. 16, 1933, Stone Papers, Box 3, LOC.

64 **Dispirited by the New Deal:** Mason, *Harlan Fiske Stone*, 344–45, 347–48, 359–60, 370–71, 373.

65 **But Stone was resilient:** Ibid., 357–58.

65 **"We live from day to day":** Stone to Lauson and Marshall Stone, Jan. 18, 1934, Stone Papers, Box 3, LOC.

65 **"the first of the 'New Deal' cases":** Ibid., Nov. 9, 1933, Stone Papers, Box 3, LOC.

65 **a Minnesota state law:** Irons, *A People's History*, 297–98; Paul L. Murphy, *The Constitution in Crisis Times*, 110fn; Mason, *Harlan Fiske Stone*, 360–61.

65 **Hughes had gone farther:** See Hendel, *Charles Evans Hughes and the Supreme Court*, 36–45; Dawson, "The Supreme Court and the New Deal," 648–49.

66 **After the *Blaisdell* decision:** *Home Building & Loan Association v. Blaisdell*, 290 U.S. 398 (1934): 442.

66 **Hughes described the Constitution:** Ibid., 425–26, 447; Hendel, *Charles Evans Hughes and the Supreme Court*, 174, 178; Leuchtenburg, "Charles Evans Hughes," 1190; Hughes, *The Supreme Court of the United States*, 222–23.

67 **"We find no warrant":** 290 U.S. 398 (1934): 443–44.

67 **Sutherland wrote the dissent:** *WP*, Feb. 16, 1936; Pearson and Allen, *The Nine Old Men*, 199; Paschal, *Mr. Justice Sutherland*, 3–4, 7–8 , 56–57, 62–63, 76; Arkes, *The Return of George Sutherland*, 4–6, 10; *Rocky Mountain News*, Jan. 6, 1938: 5, in Sutherland Papers, Box 8, LOC; *NYT*, Sept. 10, 1922.

67 **his dissent in *Blaisdell*:** 290 U.S. 398 (1934): 448–49, 451, 453, 472–74, 483; Arkes, *The Return of George Sutherland* 42–43, 246–47; Paschal, *Mr. Justice Sutherland*, 27–28, 79.

68 **"one of the great opinions":** Brandeis quoted in Friedman, "Switching Time," 1915.

68 **The Depression . . . was "nothing new":** 290 U.S. 398 (1934): 454, 471–72.

68 **here was the verdict of Justice Sutherland:** Paschal, *Mr. Justice Sutherland*, 9, 15, 28–29, 173fn; Steven Shapin, "Man with a Plan," *The New Yorker*, Aug. 13, 2007, 75, 77; Twiss, *Lawyers and the Constitution*, 16–17, 258, 264.

69 **the "mercy of severity":** Paschal, *Mr. Justice Sutherland*, 10–12; Spencer, *Social Statics*, 149–52, 238, 363 (emphasis in original).

69 **"A red-letter day":** HSC Diary, Jan. 8, 1934, 9–10, UVA.

70 **On the basis of the *Blaisdell* decision:** *NYT*, Jan. 9, 10, 1934; *Collier's*, Feb. 17, 1934.

70 ***Nebbia v. New York:*** *NYT*, Mar. 6, 1934; Mason, *Harlan Fiske Stone*, 365–66; Irons, *A People's History*, 298; 291 U.S. 502 (1934): 523, 531; Cushman, *Rethinking the New Deal Court*, 79.

71 **Roberts's abandonment of the restrictive "public interest":** Leonard, *A Search for a Judicial Philosophy*, 84–86; Ross, *The Chief Justiceship of Charles Evans Hughes*, 52; Friedman, "Switching Time," 1921–22; Cushman, *Rethinking the New Deal Court*, 79; Pusey, *Charles Evans Hughes*, Vol. II, 700; 291 U.S. 502 (1934): 525, 536, 538–39.

71 **Arthur Krock:** *NYT*, Mar. 6, 1934.

71 **"Facile disregard of the Constitution":** 291 U.S. 502 (1934): 545–46, 548, 558–59.

72 **liberals were overjoyed by a decision:** *NYT*, Mar. 6, 1934; Mason, *Brandeis*, 617; Corwin, *The Twilight of the Supreme Court*, xvi, 44–45, 99; Mason, *Harlan Fiske Stone*, 367; Lasser, *Limits*, 123.

72 **"leaves a trail a mile wide":** Dennis T. Flynn to WVD, Mar. 23, 1934, WVD Papers, Box 37, LOC.

72 **Stone perceived *Nebbia*:** Mason, *Harlan Fiske Stone*, 368–69.

72 **"Has the Supreme Court abdicated?":** Mason, "Has the Supreme Court Abdicated?," 360.

CHAPTER FIVE: HEAVY BOMBARDMENT

74 **gathering of the Gridiron Club:** WVD to Mrs. John W. Lacey, Apr. 18, 1934, WVD Papers, Box 18, LOC; Tompkins, "Princes of the Press," 171–73; Brayman, *The President Speaks*, 2–3; Essary, *Covering Washington*, 234, 236.

75 **The evening's entertainment:** WVD to Lacey, Apr. 18, 1934, WVD Papers, Box 18, LOC; Brayman, *The President Speaks*, 245–46.

75 **Senator Reed stiffly sang:** WVD to Lacey, Apr. 18, 1934, WVD Papers, Box 18, LOC; Brayman, *The President Speaks*, 248. Clearly, Reed now took a different view of constitutional democracy than the one he had expressed in 1933, when he said, "If ever this country needed a Mussolini, it needs one now." (Quoted in Alter, *The Defining Moment*, 6.)

76 **"Are you wanting the President":** WVD to Lacey, Apr. 18, 1934, WVD Papers, Box 18, LOC; Brayman, *The President Speaks*, 248–49.

76 **A few moments later:** Brayman, *The President Speaks*, 249; "Reading Copy," Gridiron Club Remarks, Spring 1934, Speech Files #87, FDRL; WVD to Lacey, Apr. 18, 1934, WVD Papers, Box 18, LOC.

77 **Van Devanter . . . found the speech "ingenious":** WVD to Lacey, Apr. 18, 1934, WVD Papers, Box 18, LOC.

77 **"under very heavy bombardment":** FDR to FF, Mar. 24, 1934, in Freedman, *Roosevelt and Frankfurter*, 210.

77 **"The honeymoon is over":** Stone quoted in Schlesinger, *Coming of the New Deal*, 471.

78 **"private fulminations":** *Time* quoted in ibid.

78 **"As soon as the businessman":** Connally quoted in Wolfskill and Hudson, *All but the People*, 144.

78 **the spirit of shared sacrifice:** Chandler, *America's Greatest Depression*, 3, 129; Wolfskill and Hudson, *All but the People*, 145–46; Schlesinger, *Coming of the New Deal*, 471–74; Leuchtenburg, *FDR and the New Deal*, 91.

78 **"It is perfectly apparent":** Snell quoted in Brant, *Storm over the Constitution*, 39; Schlesinger, *Coming of the New Deal*, 480.

78 **portrayed the New Deal as totalitarian:** Wolfskill and Hudson, *All but the People*, 148–49, 152.

79 **"an all-powerful central government":** Ogden Mills quoted in Schlesinger, *Coming of the New Deal*, 473.
79 **"post-depression psychosis":** Richberg quoted in ibid., 495.
79 **Roosevelt . . . began to express:** Ibid., 496–97; Davis, *FDR: The New Deal Years*, 372–73.
79 **He used his first fireside chat:** *PPA* 1934, 314–15, 317, 373.
80 **"The fundamental trouble":** FDR to Adolph Berle, quoted in Davis, *FDR: The New Deal Years*, 373.
80 **"We're far stronger than ever":** TGC and Cohen to FF, Apr. 22, 1934, TGC Papers, Box 638, LOC.
80 **The principal trouble:** *Time*, June 25, 1934, and Oct. 8, 1934.
81 **"Administrative mistakes":** TGC and Cohen to FF, Apr. 22, 1934, TGC Papers, Box 638, LOC.
81 **The NRA was tilted:** Chandler, *America's Greatest Depression*, 231; Schlesinger, *Coming of the New Deal*, 120–21, 126; Davis, *FDR: The New Deal Years*, 243, 260.
81 **"a bird of prey":** Nye quoted in Davis, *FDR: The New Deal Years*, 315; Schlesinger, *Coming of the New Deal*, 161.
82 **Workers appealed to the NRA:** Watkins, *The Great Depression*, 168–71; Schlesinger, *Coming of the New Deal*, 144–47, 149–51; *Time*, Oct. 15, 1934.
82 **"The NRA was headed hell-bent":** Creel, *Rebel at Large*, 276.
83 **"the great bulk of complaint":** *PPA*, 1934, 125–27.
83 **"*You* have set up":** Ibid., 126, 129, emphasis added.
83 **"If the business features . . . are defective":** Cohen quoted in Lash, *Dealers and Dreamers*, 234.
83 **"purely as an emergency agency":** Perkins, *The Roosevelt I Knew*, 211; Richberg, *My Hero*, 185, 188.
83 **Roosevelt himself remained enormously popular:** Fletcher, Farley, and FDR quoted in Lasser, *Limits*, 118–19; also see Schlesinger, *Coming of the New Deal*, 480–81, 505; Ickes, Sept. 27, 1934, *Secret Diary*, Vol. I, 198–99; Davis, *FDR: The New Deal Years*, 416–19.
84 **The November results:** *NYT*, Nov. 7, 1934; *Time*, Jan. 7, 1935, Nov. 8, 1934.
85 **"opposition is fading":** *PPA*, 1934, 462.
85 **"Mr. Justice Holmes had":** FF to FDR, Nov. 21, 1934, and FDR to FF, Oct. 4, 1934, in Freedman, *Roosevelt and Frankfurter*, 242, 237.
85 **"dogged determination":** Nov. 26, 1934, in Namorato, ed., *Diary of Rexford G. Tugwell*, 152.

CHAPTER SIX: THE GOLDEN RULING

87 **The New Deal was already on trial:** *Time*, Feb. 12, 1934, Oct. 15, 1934, Nov. 26, 1934; Jackson, *Struggle*, 115.
88 **"I would like to have":** HSC to J. Crawford Biggs, Oct. 10, 1934, and Biggs to HSC, Oct. 11, 1934, HSC Papers, Box 177, UVA.
88 **concerned "hot oil":** Stern, "The Commerce Clause and the National Economy," 654–55; Pearson and Allen, *The Nine Old Men*, 244–46; Jackson, *Struggle*, 87–89; Schlesinger, *Coming of the New Deal*, 89.
89 **Cummings reported to Roosevelt:** DOJ Press Release, Oct. 20, 1934, OF 10, Box 2, FDRL; Cummings to FDR, Nov. 5, 1934, UVA.
89 **"in the hip pocket":** *Time*, Dec. 24, 1934; Stern, "The Commerce Clause and the National Economy," 656–57.
89 **"It is a rather extraordinary":** H. F. Stone to Lauson Stone, Jan. 8, 1935, Stone Papers, Box 1, LOC.
89 **"sunlight is the best disinfectant":** Mason, *Brandeis*, 618.

90 **the delegation of power by Congress:** Irons, *New Deal Lawyers*, 70; G. Edward White, *The Constitution and the New Deal*, 108; "The Decision in the NIRA Cases," 284–88.

90 **"the old doctrine prohibiting":** G. Edward White, *The Constitution and the New Deal*, 108; "The Decision in the NIRA Cases," 288.

90 **"several of the others":** Lash, *Dealers and Dreamers*, 187.

91 **overturned the hot oil provision:** *NYT*, Jan. 8, 1935; *CDT*, Feb. 19, 1935; *Panama Refining Co. v. Ryan*, 293 U.S. 388 (1935): 430.

91 **Cardozo, the lone dissenter:** 293 U.S. 388 (1935): 434, 443.

91 **"The Supreme Court went Republican":** *NYT*, Jan. 9, 1935; Leuchtenburg, *Supreme Court Reborn*, 86; *CDT*, Jan. 8, 9, 1935.

91 **The administration was inclined:** *Time*, Jan. 14, 21, 1935, *WP*, Jan. 8, 1935; *NYT*, Jan. 8, 1935.

92 **"The anxiety . . . was profound":** Jackson, *Struggle*, 94–95.

92 **but left little clue where:** *NYT*, Jan. 9, 1935.

92 **"There was less delegation":** *The Nation*, Jan. 23, 1935.

92 **Even "the wildest New Dealer":** *CDT*, Jan. 9, 1935.

92 **a small "stag dinner":** Ickes, Jan. 11, 1935, *Secret Diary*, Vol. I, 273.

93 **FDR, ever since his first day:** Chandler, *America's Greatest Depression*, 135, 161, 164, 166; Blum, *From the Morgenthau Diaries*, 62–63; *NYT*, Mar. 6, 1933, Mar. 10, 1933, Oct. 23, 1933, Jan. 31, 1934.

93 **The "gold clause":** Chandler, *America's Greatest Depression*, 166; Jackson, *Struggle*, 98–99.

93 **"The action on the gold clause":** Brandeis to FF, June 13, 1933, and Oct. 30, 1933, in Urofsky, *"Half Brother,"* 523, 533.

94 **Stone was so appalled:** Mason, *Harlan Fiske Stone*, 391.

94 **"the difficulty is that most people":** Kaufman, *Cardozo*, 514.

94 **Was the cancellation of the gold clauses constitutional?:** George W. Whiteside to HSC, Jan. 5, 1935, OF 10, DOJ, Box 2, FDRL; DOJ Memorandum [most likely by Angus MacLean], Nov. 23, 1934, HSC Papers, Box 197, UVA.

94 **"to feel a bit like King Midas":** HSC to LeHand, Jan. 8, 1935, and *Advocate*, Jan. 17, 1935, attached to HSC to FDR, Jan. 28, 1935, both in OF 10, Box 2, FDRL.

94 **Cummings sat serenely:** *Time*, Jan. 21, 1935; Swisher, *Selected Papers of Homer Cummings*, 116–20; *NYT*, Jan. 9, 1935; Ickes, Jan. 11, 1935, *Secret Diary*, Vol. I, 273.

95 **"All is not gold":** FDR to Homer and Cecelia Cummings, Feb. 4, 1935, HSC Papers, Box 170, UVA.

96 **"outright defiance":** Jackson OH, 430–31.

96 **Jackson mentioned an article:** Ibid.; Ratner, "Was the Supreme Court Packed by President Grant?", 343–58.

96 **"I told him":** Ickes, Jan. 11, 1935, *Secret Diary*, Vol. I, 273.

96 **to nameless presidential advisers:** For examples of leaks, see *Time*, Jan. 21, 1935, and previous chapters; *The Nation*, Jan. 23, 1935, 85.

97 **readied a range of constitutional amendments:** *NYT*, May 30, 1935; Costigan to FDR, May 29, 1935, and FDR to McIntyre, June 11, 1935, OF 466, Box 11, FDRL; George W. Kretzinger, Jr., Assistant Attorney, NRA, "Suggestion Concerning Constitutional Amendment," and Jack Garrett Scott, Acting General Counsel, NRA, to TGC, Sept. 9, 1935, TGC Papers, Box 270, LOC; "Constitutional Amendment," unsigned memorandum, Office of the Attorney General, Jan. 21, 1935, PPF 1055, FDRL; Kyvig, "The Road Not Taken," 470–71; *Time*, Jan. 21, 1935.

97 **Henry Wallace, the Secretary of Agriculture:** *NYT*, Jan. 25, 26, 1935.

97 **as Robert Jackson advised FDR:** Jackson OH, 430–31; Robert H. Jackson to FDR, the Secretary of the Treasury [Henry Morgenthau, Jr.], the General Counsel of the Treasury [Herman Oliphant], and George D. Haas, Jan. 12, 1935, memo courtesy of John Q. Barrett; for draft legislation, see PPF 1055, FDRL.

98 **At a dinner at the vice president's home:** Blum, *From the Morgenthau Diaries*, 127–29; Schlesinger, *Politics of Upheaval*, 257.

98 **Weeks passed without a ruling:** *Time*, Jan. 21, 1935; HSC to FDR, Feb. 4, 1935, PSF Justice, Box 56, FDRL; Ickes, Feb. 10, 1935, *Secret Diary*, Vol. I, 294; HSC Diary, Feb. 1, 9, 1935, 4, 6, UVA.

99 **Roosevelt called Cummings and Donald Richberg:** FDR, draft remarks, HSC Papers, Box 170, UVA; a revised later draft is found in PSF 165, FDRL.

100 **Pearson's, a small Washington:** *The New Yorker*, June 29, 1935; *NYT*, Feb. 18, 19, 1935.

100 **"We are all reasonably confident":** HSC Diary, Feb. 16, 1935, 10, UVA.

100 **At 12 p.m. the justices:** *Time*, Feb. 25, 1935; *U.S. v. Bankers' Trust Co.*, 294 U.S. 240 (1935): 307–8, 311, 316; *Perry v. United States*, 294 U.S. 330 (1935): 348, 350, 354–55.

101 **McReynolds had a personality:** Childs OH, 71; Sen. George Wharton Pepper in "Proceedings Before the Supreme Court of the United States, March 31, 1948, in Memory of James Clark McReynolds," McReynolds Papers, Box 7, UVA: 26; Pearson and Allen, *The Nine Old Men*, 224, 231; FF, *Felix Frankfurter Reminisces*, 101; *Time*, Dec. 4, 1939; John Knox to Donald McPherson, Jan. 19, 1937, Knox Papers, University of Chicago.

102 **Unlike his conservative brethren:** *NYT*, Aug. 19, 1914; *The New Republic*, July 1, 1936, 234; Ross, *A Muted Fury*, 91; Creel, *Rebel at Large*, 244.

102 **From the bench:** Little, "The Omnipotent Nine," 51; Joseph Percival Pollard, "Four New Dissenters," *The New Republic*, Sept. 2, 1931, 63; Fletcher, "Mr. Justice McReynolds," 35–36; McReynolds quoted in *Time*, Nov. 1, 1926, and Rodell, *Nine Men*, 201–2; W. G. Brantley to WVD, Aug. 29, 1934, WVD Papers, Box 37, LOC.

102 **"We would have been much better off":** James McReynolds to Robert McReynolds, Feb. 23, 1935, McReynolds Papers, Box 1, UVA; on the Sutherland memo, see Paschal, *Mr. Justice Sutherland*, 181–82, 255–58.

103 **On decision day:** *CDT*, Feb. 19, 1935; *NYT*, Feb. 19, 1935.

103 **"It is impossible":** McReynolds quoted in *NYT*, Feb. 19, 1935, and in Walter F. Murphy, *Congress and the Court*, 54fn. There is no exact transcript of McReynolds's extemporaneous dissent, but most versions are similar; Murphy believes the most accurate rendering is McReynolds's hand-corrected version of what appeared in the *Wall Street Journal*.

103 **"the last roar of an old lion":** Childs OH, 64–65.

103 **"took a good deal out of me":** James McReynolds to Robert McReynolds, Feb. 23, 1935, McReynolds Papers, Box 1, UVA.

103 **"as a disquieting reminder":** *The Nation*, Feb. 27, 1935.

104 **"The President is gratified":** *CDT*, Feb. 19, 1935.

104 **exhilaration in the White House:** Tully, *F.D.R.: My Boss*, 157–59.

104 **for a handful of appreciative aides:** The group included Tugwell and Moley. Tugwell Diary, Feb. 19, 1935, in Namorato, ed., *Diary of Rexford G. Tugwell*, 222.

104 **"Everybody was smiling":** HSC Diary, Feb. 18, 1935, 11–12, UVA.

104 **in a memo to Kennedy:** Tully, *F.D.R.: My Boss*, 160.

105 **"it would have marked the most":** *NYT*, Feb. 21, 24, 1935.

105 **Raymond Moley:** Namorato, ed., *Diary of Rexford G. Tugwell*, 222.

105 **"golden ruling":** *NYT*, Feb. 24, 1935.

105 **"in spite of our rejoicing":** FDR to MacLean, Feb. 21, 1935, OF 10F, Box 29, FDRL.

105 **the "curious language":** HSC Diary, Feb. 19, 1935, 14; HSC to FDR, June 15, 1935, HSC Papers, Box 174, UVA.

105 **"A great diversity":** HSC Diary, Feb. 19, 1935, UVA; Pusey, *Charles Evans Hughes*, Vol. II, 737; Cardozo quoted by Hughes in Danelski and Tulchin, eds., *Autobiographical Notes*, 301.

105 **"seemed to face both ways":** Stone to Lauson and Marshall Stone, Mar. 1, 1935, Stone

Papers, Box 3, UVA. In his concurring opinion, Stone scorned the government's repudiation of its own "solemn promise," but refused to agree with Hughes that the gold clause in U.S. bonds carried a greater obligation than in corporate bonds. Learned Hand wrote to Stone that he was "the only one who intellectually 'comes clean.'" (See 294 U.S. 330 [1935]: 359; Hand quoted in Mason, *Harlan Fiske Stone*, 391.)

105 **Wall Street bankers, too, saw a "straddle":** *WP*, Feb. 20, 1935.

106 **"few more baffling pronouncements":** Hart, "The Gold Clause in United States Bonds," 1057.

106 **"followed the command of a simple":** Gardner, *Pebbles*, 57.

CHAPTER SEVEN: THE LAST THIN LINE

107 **"People can't eat the Constitution":** *Time*, Nov. 19, 1934.

107 **the American Liberty League:** *NYT*, Aug. 23, 24, 1934.

107 **Raskob wrote to an associate:** Raskob quoted in *NYT*, Dec. 21, 1934; and in Schlesinger, *Coming of the New Deal*, 485.

108 **"a moral or an emotional issue":** Stayton quoted in Wolfskill, *The Revolt of the Conservatives*, 111–12.

108 **This rescue mission:** Keller, *In Defense of Yesterday*, 127–29, 257–61; Kammen, *A Machine That Would Go of Itself*, 219–25, 231–33; Schudson, *The Good Citizen*, 202–4.

109 **The Liberty League, therefore, tapped into:** Kyvig, "The Road Not Taken," 469; Schlesinger, *Coming of the New Deal*, 484.

109 **The League was also heir to the "Stop Roosevelt" movement:** Neal, *Happy Days Are Here Again*, 110–15, 238–39; Wolfskill, *The Revolt of the Conservatives*, 103–6; Kyvig, *Repealing National Prohibition*, 158; Schlesinger, *Politics of Upheaval*, 518–19.

109 **the American Liberty League filled its coffers:** *NYT*, Aug. 24, 1934; *Time*, Sept. 3, 1934.

110 **a Kansas City lawyer named Jouett Shouse:** *NYT*, May 12, 1929; *Time*, Nov. 10, 1930.

110 **"I want my fellow Democrats":** *NYT*, May 12, 1929; *Time*, Nov. 10, 1930.

110 **Victim of a press leak:** *Time*, Sept. 3, 1934.

111 **The very structure of the League:** Ickes, *New Democracy*, 45, 47; *NYT*, Nov. 10, Sept. 7, Aug. 23, 29, 1934.

111 **Alfred P. Sloan:** *NYT*, Aug. 31, 1934. On GM, see Shogan, *Backlash*, 44.

111 **"gold dollar men":** Thomas quoted in *Time*, Sept. 3, 1934.

111 **In December 1934, a Gridiron skit:** *NYT*, Dec. 9, 1934; Brayman, *The President Speaks*, 258.

111 **Roosevelt himself gleefully jumped in:** *Time*, Sept. 3, 1934; *NYT*, Aug. 25, 1934.

112 **Its leaders . . . still commanded a certain respect:** *NYT*, Aug. 23, 26, 29, 1934.

112 **"Who is going to be the other party now?":** *Time*, Nov. 19, 1934.

112 **"That's fine!":** *Time*, Sept. 3, 1934 (ellipses in original). FDR had a certain ambivalence about his role as party leader—sometimes embracing the party, other times distancing himself from it, but always intending to redefine it over time. The Democratic party, long controlled by the states and Congress, had traditionally been an obstacle to a strong executive; so to fulfill his pledge of a New Deal, FDR took steps to seize control of the machinery and, beginning in 1936, effected a shift from the old brand of patronage, based on partisanship, to one based on ideological affinity—on loyalty to program, principles, and the president more than to party. See Milkis, *The President and the Parties*, 53–54, 57–58.

112 **The American Liberty League roared:** *NYT*, Jan. 15, 21, 1935.

113 **Across the landscape they roamed:** See *NYT*, Jan. 28, Feb. 4, 5, 11, Apr. 15, 22, May 20, 1935; Wolfskill, *The Revolt of the Conservatives*, 127.

113 **the "last thin line":** Wolfskill, *The Revolt of the Conservatives*, 114; *NYT*, Aug. 27, 1934.

113 **the New Deal had not gone far enough:** *WP*, Mar. 3, 1935; also see Schlesinger, *Politics of Upheaval*, 16, 96–98, 158–61.

113 **Credible leaders emerged across the nation:** Schlesinger, *Politics of Upheaval*, 98–107, 111–23; *Time*, July 27, 1936.

114 **a duo of demagogues:** Brinkley, *Voices of Protest*, 71, 114, 169, 179, 207–8, 212–15; *NYT*, May 26, 1935; Holli, *The Wizard of Washington*, 66.

114 **a motley collection of aging radicals . . . "Prima donnas":** Schlesinger, *Politics of Upheaval*, 134–35; Tugwell in Namorato, ed., *Diary of Rexford G. Tugwell*, 416–17; Ross, *A Muted Fury*, 303.

115 **these progressives had been unhappy with the New Deal:** Schlesinger, *Politics of Upheaval*, 134–35; Milkis and Mileur, "Introduction," and Morton Keller, "The New Deal and Progressivism: A Fresh Look," in Milkis and Mileur, eds., *The New Deal and the Triumph of Liberalism*, 7–8, 315–16; Hofstadter, *Age of Reform*, 302–4, 306–7, 310–11; Ross, *A Muted Fury*, 296–97, 303–4.

115 **feared its centralization of power . . . Wheeler declared:** Ross, *A Muted Fury*, 303–5; Burton K. Wheeler, "Issues Before America," Apr. 8, 1935, in TGC Papers, Box 234, LOC.

115 **On the evening of May 14:** Ickes, May 15, 1935, *Secret Diary*, Vol. I, 363.

115 **"going to go into the stride":** FF to FDR, May 16, 1935, in Freedman, *Roosevelt and Frankfurter*, 271.

115 **"tired, harassed and supersensitive":** HSC Diary, Mar. 2, 1935, 21, UVA.

115 **"growing confusion among plain citizens":** *Time*, May 6, 1935.

116 **the overall picture was bleak:** *NYT*, May 26, 1935; *WP*, Mar. 3, 1935; Schlesinger, *Politics of Upheaval*, 2–3, 11, 211–13.

116 **the Railroad Retirement Act:** Leuchtenburg, *Supreme Court Reborn*, 28–32; "Pensions Out," *Time*, Nov. 5, 1934; Donald Richberg, "Memorandum Concerning Railroad Retirement Act," Aug. 17, 1937, Richberg Papers, Box 47, LOC.

116 **the railroad companies . . . filed suit:** Leuchtenburg, *Supreme Court Reborn*, 31–33; *Time*, Nov. 5, 1934; HSC to FDR, Mar. 16, 1935, and attached letter, Harold M. Stephens to HSC, Mar. 15, 1935, OF 10, Justice Department, Box 2, FDRL.

117 **This it did, in dramatic fashion:** *NYT*, May 7, 1935; *CDT*, May 7, 1935; *WP*, Feb. 16, 1936; Griswold, "Owen J. Roberts as a Judge," 336; *Railroad Retirement Board v. Alton R. Co.*, 295 U.S. 330 (1935): 349, 351, 368, 371; Leonard, *A Search for a Judicial Philosophy*, 61–62; Hendel, *Charles Evans Hughes and the Supreme Court*, 231–32.

118 **Hughes had written the dissent:** *NYT*, May 7, 1935; 295 U.S. 330 (1935): 374–75, 377, 379–80.

118 **"I perceive no constitutional ground":** Cardozo to Hughes, Apr. 19, 1935, Stone Papers, Box 61, LOC; 295 U.S. 330 (1935): 384, 391–92.

119 **"the boldest, frankest . . . opinion of his career":** "The Court Rules Out Security," unsigned article by Thurman Arnold, *The Nation*, May 22, 1935, 588.

119 **"I am prepared to believe":** FF to Stone, Stone Papers, Box 13, LOC.

119 **"the worst performance of the Court":** Stone to FF, May 9, 1935, Stone Papers, Box 13, LOC.

119 **"was not a very good bill":** Stone to Lauson and Marshall Stone, May 9, 1935, Stone Papers, Box 3, LOC.

119 **"reinforced, as nothing else could":** FF and Hart in Leuchtenburg, *Supreme Court Reborn*, 45–46; *The Nation*, May 22, 1935.

119 **"SOCIAL PROGRAM IN PERIL":** *NYT*, May 7, 1935.

119 **The *Alton* decision . . . was "rotten":** FDR quoted in Leonard, *A Search for a Judicial Philosophy*, 62; *WP*, May 7, 1935: *NYT*, May 7, 8, 9, 1935; *The Nation*, May 22, 1935.

120 **The NRA . . . was now doomed:** FDR view described in Tugwell Diary, May 9, 1935, in Namorato, ed., *Diary of Rexford G. Tugwell*, 247–48, and Leuchtenburg, *Supreme Court Reborn*, 50; HSC to FDR, May 7, 1935, HSC Papers, Box 170, UVA.

120 **Within twenty-four hours:** *NYT*, May 7, 8, 1935; Leuchtenburg, *Supreme Court Reborn*, 49–50.

120 **"There seems to be no way out":** Tugwell Diary, May 9, 1935, in Namorato, ed., *Diary of Rexford G. Tugwell*, 247–48.
121 **Cummings, on May 11:** Leuchtenburg, *Supreme Court Reborn*, 51.
121 **On Sunday, May 12:** Harry Hopkins Diary, May 12, 1935, Hopkins Papers, Box 6, FDRL; *NYT*, Feb. 18, 1935.
122 **"inflict injury" . . . "a new era":** *Nebbia v. People of State of New York*, 291 U.S. 502 (1934): 539. The newspaper is the *New York World-Telegram*, quoted in Lasser, *Limits*, 123.
122 **Who was Owen Roberts?:** *WP*, Feb. 16, 1936; *NYT*, May 18, 1955, May 10, 1930.
122 **he confounded nearly all:** See *The New Republic*, July 1, 1936, 235; *Time*, Nov. 26, 1934; Childs OH, 70; *NYT*, May 10, 1930; Leuchtenburg, *Supreme Court Reborn*, 45; *WP*, Feb. 16, 1936; *Time*, May 13, 1935; *WSJ*, May 7, 1935; author interview, Austin Cunningham, Dec. 6, 2005.
123 **Roberts shuttled back and forth:** Leonard, *A Search for a Judicial Philosophy*, 8–9; *Time*, May 19, 1930; *NYT*, May 10, 1930, May 18, 1955; Griswold, "Owen J. Roberts as a Judge," 333, 336–37; McCracken, "Owen J. Roberts—Master Advocate," 329; *The New Republic*, July 1, 1936, 235.
123 **Philadelphia, in the 1920s:** Weigley, *Philadelphia*, n535; Pearson and Allen, *The Nine Old Men*, 154–55.
123 **"Are we prepared":** *NYT*, Feb. 16, 1923.
124 **when President Hoover nominated:** *NYT*, May 10, 1930; Leonard, *A Search for a Judicial Philosophy*, 8, 10–12.
125 **Stone . . . had written:** Mason, *Harlan Fiske Stone*, 300fn, 310, 368, 429.
125 **Roberts . . . emitted enough mixed signals:** *Harper's Magazine*, Vol. 167, Nov. 1933, 648; FF to HFS, Jan. 9, 1935, Stone Papers, Box 13, LOC. The case is *Dimick v. Schiedt*, 293 U.S. 474 (1935). According to Roberts's clerk of many years, the justice was fundamentally a pragmatist (Leonard, *A Search for a Judicial Philosophy*, 12).
125 **"I was particularly delighted":** Robert H. Kelley to WVD, May 9, 1935, WVD Papers, Box 37, LOC.
126 **"Justice Roberts is a young man":** Louchheim, *The Making of the New Deal*, 99.

CHAPTER EIGHT: BLACK MONDAY

127 **Daniel Oren Hastings:** *Time*, Mar. 18, 1935.
127 **Donald Richberg . . . "pep talk":** Ibid., May 27, 1935.
127 **The Recovery Act . . . was due:** Ibid., Apr. 29, 1935.
128 **The NRA was not entirely devoid of support:** Ibid., June 3, 1935.
128 **even ardent New Dealers:** Lash, *Dealers and Dreamers*, 250.
128 **"throwing-up of the presidential hands":** Moley, *After Seven Years*, 304.
128 **The Senate . . . passed a resolution:** *Time*, May 27, 1935.
128 **The NRA was waging a war:** Ibid., Mar. 18, 1935; Irons, *New Deal Lawyers*, 46, 54–56.
128 **Most of these cases concerned:** Schlesinger, *Coming of the New Deal*, 161; Irons, *New Deal Lawyers*, 55–57.
129 **the pool of potential test cases:** *Time*, Apr. 8, 1935; Lash, *Dealers and Dreamers*, 250–51.
129 **"You're pretty unconstitutional":** Perkins, *The Roosevelt I Knew*, 249.
130 **It was unlikely, however, that one appointment:** *Time*, Apr. 8, 1935; Irons, *New Deal Lawyers*, 76–80.
130 **"I have not defended":** Memo, Mar. 7, 1935, HSC Papers, Box 78, UVA.
130 **Richberg had reluctantly agreed to go forward:** Richberg, *The Rainbow*, 215–16.
130 **"the President was not particularly enthusiastic":** HSC to Stephens, Feb. 8, 1935, HSC Papers, Box 78, HSC Diary, Feb. 8, 1935, 5, UVA.
130 **Neither was Stanley Reed:** Reed, "Memorandum Re Supreme Court Review of BELCHER

Case," n.d. [March 1935], and Paul A. Freund to G. Stanleigh Arnold, Mar. 14, 1935, 1, 8–10, HSC Papers, Box 78, UVA; Irons, *New Deal Lawyers*, 80–82.

130 **G. Stanleigh Arnold . . . made a strong, eleventh-hour pitch:** G. Stanleigh Arnold to HSC, Mar. 18, 1935, HSC Papers, Box 78, UVA.

131 **On March 25, with oral arguments:** HSC to Stephens, Feb. 8, 1935, HSC Papers, Box 78, HSC Diary, Feb. 8, 1935, 5, UVA.

131 **"The White House . . . was afraid to go":** *Time*, Apr. 15, 1935; Lash, *Dealers and Dreamers*, 252.

131 **"I knew the NRA":** *Time*, Apr. 15, 1935.

131 **There were in fact few industries:** Frank Freidel, "The Sick Chicken Case," in Garraty, *Quarrels*, 191–92, 200–201; Irons, *New Deal Lawyers*, 86–87; Schlesinger, *Politics of Upheaval*, 277.

132 **"a strong favorable decision":** *Time*, Apr. 15, May 13, 1935; Second Circuit opinion at 11–12, in McJimsey, *Documentary History*, Vol. 22, 162–63; Richberg, *The Rainbow*, 217–19; Schlesinger, *Politics of Upheaval*, 278; Lash, *Dealers and Dreamers*, 251.

132 **The message touched off:** Hopkins, "A statement to me by Thomas Corcoran giving his recollection of the genesis of the Supreme Court fight between the President and the U.S. Senate, Warm Springs, Georgia, April 3, 1939," Hopkins Papers, Sherwood Collection, Box 299, Folder 7, FDRL.

133 **"I assume that you have been kept":** TGC to FDR, Apr. 4, 1935, in Freedman, *Roosevelt and Frankfurter*, 260; Lash, *Dealers and Dreamers*, 252; *Time*, Apr. 15, 1935; Abe Feller to FF, Apr. 17, 1935, TGC Papers, Box 198, LOC.

133 **Representing the Schechters:** Richberg, *My Hero*, 193–94; Irons, *New Deal Lawyers*, 95–100; Freund in Louchheim, *The Making of the New Deal*, 103; *The Nation*, June 12, 1935, 669–70; Freidel in Garraty, *Quarrels*, 203; *Time*, May 13, 1935.

134 **The justices made quick work:** *NYT*, May 28, 1935; *Time*, June 3, 1935.

134 **Sutherland's opinion:** Leuchtenburg, *Supreme Court Reborn* 70; *Humphrey's Executor v. United States*, 295 U.S. 602 (1935); *Louisville Joint Stock Land Bank v. Radford*, 295 U.S. 555 (1935); *NYT*, May 28, 1935.

134 **When the Chief Justice began:** *Time*, June 3, 1935.

135 **"The poultry . . . had come to a permanent rest":** *NYT*, May 28, 1935; *A.L.A. Schechter Poultry Corporation v. United States*, 295 U.S. 495 (1935): 542–43, 546, 548–49.

135 **Hughes did not invent the doctrine:** Stern, "The Commerce Clause and the National Economy," 649–52; Mason, *Harlan Fiske Stone*, 396; "The Decision in the NIRA Cases," 290; Louchheim, *The Making of the New Deal*, 98; Jackson, *Struggle*, 114.

136 **Stone had long distrusted:** Mason, *Harlan Fiske Stone*, 395; Kaufman, *Cardozo*, 513; Corwin, "The Schechter Case," 169; 295 U.S. 495 (1935): 554; Stone quoted in Schlesinger, *Politics of Upheaval*, 282, and in Lasser, *Limits*, 133; Hendel, *Charles Evans Hughes and the Supreme Court*, 237.

136 **Donald Richberg . . . now slumped in his seat:** *Time*, June 3, 1935; *NYT*, May 28, 1935; *WP*, May 28, 1935.

136 **Corcoran expressed concern:** Cohen memorandum ("Given me by B.V.C. in Washington on Tuesday, May 28, 1935. FF"), Lash Papers, Box 68, FDRL; Lash, *Dealers and Dreamers*, 254–55; Schlesinger, *Politics of Upheaval*, 280; McKenna, *Franklin Roosevelt and the Great Constitutional War*, 104.

137 **"Where was Old Isaiah?":** Jackson OH, 428–29; Jackson *That Man*, 66.

137 **he seemed to be taking it all rather well:** Davis, *FDR: The New Deal Years*, 516; Clapper Diary, Feb. 24, 1937, Clapper Papers, Box 8, LOC.

137 **Later that evening:** High Diary, Mar. 28, 1936, Box 1, FDRL.

138 **"Today . . . was a bad day":** HSC Diary, May 27, 1935, 64–66, UVA; *NYT*, May 28, 1935.

138 **"The Constitution . . . has survived":** *WSJ*, May 28, 1935.

138 **The morning papers howled:** *Time*, June 10, 1935; *NYT*, May 28, 1935; *WP*, May 28, 1935; *CDT*, May 29, 31, 1935.

138 **In Washington, D.C., outside the town house:** *WP*, May 30, 1935; *NYT*, May 28, 29, 30, 1935.

139 **"We won't listen to the Supreme Court":** Hillman quoted in Fraser, *Labor Will Rule*, 324; *NYT*, June 8, 9, 1935.

139 **"Nine old men, nine old men":** "Let's Sing," Education Department, International Ladies' Garment Workers' Union, n.d. [1935], collection of author.

139 **"The Supreme Court, which places property rights":** *NYT*, June 9, 1935.

140 **"Well my Dear Sir":** F. L. Evans to FDR, May 28, 1935, OF 466, NRA Misc., Box 11, FDRL.

140 **But many businessmen:** *WP*, May 30, 1935; Fraser, *Labor Will Rule*, 325; *NYT*, May 29, 1935; A. F. Hinrichs to Frances Perkins, June 15, 1935, in McJimsey, *Documentary History*, Vol. 22, 613–23; United States Department of Commerce, *Statistical Abstract*, 322.

140 **Prices . . . dropped immediately:** *NYT*, May 29, 30, June 2, 1935, 29; *Time*, June 10, 1935.

141 **Congress watched it all:** *NYT*, May 30, 1935; HSC Diary, May 27, 1935, 66; May 28, 1935, 69, UVA; Charles Wyzanski, "What the Schechter Case Does and Does Not Decide with Respect to Congressional Power over Commerce," second draft, July 27, 1935, OF 466, NRA Misc., Box 12, FDRL; Richberg, *The Rainbow*, 221.

141 **"Hardly a single major act":** *NYT*, May 28, 29, 30, June 1, 2, 1935; *WP*, May 29, 1935.

141 **Conservative Democrats who had never liked:** Hiram W. Johnson to Hiram W. Johnson, Jr., June 2, 1935, in Burke, *Diary Letters*; *NYT*, May 29, 1935.

142 **"It has been an awful headache":** Perkins, *The Roosevelt I Knew*, 252–53.

142 **Roosevelt had not determined:** *NYT*, May 29, 30, 1935; *Time*, June 10, 1935; Perkins, *The Roosevelt I Knew*, 252; Cummings quoted in Schlesinger, *Politics of Upheaval*, 288–89.

142 **"We have to meet this issue":** Ickes, June 1, 1935, *Secret Diary*, Vol. I, 372; May 30, 1935, in Namorato, ed., *Diary of Rexford G. Tugwell*, 252.

143 **Roosevelt did not drop any hints:** Press Conference #208 May 29, 1935, in FDR, *Complete Presidential Press Conferences*, Vol. 5, 302, 304–5; *NYT*, May 30, 1935.

143 **"I suppose that we have had":** Press Conference #208, May 29, 1935, in FDR, *Complete Presidential Press Conferences*, Vol. 5, 302, 304–5, 306–7.

143 **Privately, he seethed:** *NYT*, May 30, 1935, 16; Corwin, "The Schechter Case," 189; Hendel, *Charles Evans Hughes and the Supreme Court*, 239; Charles Wyzanski, "What the Schechter Case Does and Does Not Decide with Respect to Congressional Power over Commerce," second draft, July 27, 1935, OF 466, NRA Misc., Box 12, FDRL, 10–11, 15, 20; Richberg, *The Rainbow*, 221.

143 **"That damn little case":** Jackson OH, 431–32; Jackson also quoted in Leuchtenburg, *Supreme Court Reborn*, 79.

143 **The case concerned William E. Humphrey:** Leuchtenburg, *Supreme Court Reborn*, 53–54, 58–62, 68; Jackson OH, 431–32; *Time*, Sept. 25, 1933; *NYT*, June 2, 1935.

144 **"couldn't be lost":** Reed quoted in Leuchtenburg, *Supreme Court Reborn*, 64; "The President's 'Right to Fire,' " *The Literary Digest*, Nov. 6, 1926, 5–6; *Myers v. United States*, 272 U.S. 52 (1926).

144 **Sutherland neatly dispensed:** 295 U.S. 602 (1935): 627–29; Fallon, *The Dynamic Constitution*, 185–87; Jackson, *Struggle*, 109.

144 **"They cannot tell the Executive":** May 30, 1935, in Namorato, ed., *Diary of Rexford G. Tugwell*, 253.

145 **"the throwback force":** *NYT*, May 30, 1935.

145 **the *New York Times* printed a guide:** *NYT*, May 30, June 9, 1935.

145 **"Respectfully suggest you urge":** Charles Ide Kahn to FDR, May 28, 1935, OF 466, NRA Misc., Box 11, FDRL.

145 **A group of four House members:** *NYT*, May 29, 30, 1935.
145 **On May 29, in a letter to Roosevelt:** FF to FDR, May 29, 1935, HSC Papers, Box 170, UVA.
146 **"going to lie down":** May 31, 1935, in Namorato, ed., *Diary of Rexford G. Tugwell*, 256–57.

CHAPTER NINE: OPENING GUN

147 **"George says that those boys":** Rosenman, *Working with Roosevelt*, 111; Schlesinger, *Politics of Upheaval*, 284–85; *NYT*, May 28, 1935.
147 **As the press filed in:** *WP*, June 2, 1935; *Time*, June 10, 1935; *NYT*, June 1, 1935.
148 **Roosevelt began as he almost always did:** Press Conference #209, May 31, 1935, in FDR, *Complete Presidential Press Conferences*, Vol. 5, 309.
148 **He lifted the first telegram:** Ibid., 309–12, 314–15.
148 **"The implications of this decision":** *WP*, June 2, 1935.
149 **he dissected the opinion:** Press Conference #209, May 31, 1935, in FDR, *Complete Presidential Press Conferences*, 318, 320–22. FDR used the phrase in his 1933 book, *Looking Forward*: "Sometimes we hear the past referred to as the 'horse and buggy age'" (73). And as Arthur M. Schlesinger, Jr., noted (*Politics of Upheaval*, 285), Woodrow Wilson, in *Constitutional Government in the United States* (1908), used a variant in precisely the same context as Roosevelt later did: "*The Constitution was not meant to hold the government back to the time of horses and wagons*. . . . The United States have clearly from generation to generation been taking on more the characteristics of a community; more and more have their economic interests come to seem common interests; *and the courts have rightly endeavored to make the Constitution a suitable instrument of the national life*" (169–70, emphasis added).
149 **"does bring us up rather squarely":** Press Conference #209, May 31, 1935, in FDR, *Complete Presidential Press Conferences*, 325, 329, 334.
149 **"every other nation":** Ibid., 333, 335–36.
150 **"You made a reference":** Ibid., 336–37.
150 **"Horse-and-buggy" touched off a firestorm:** *WP*, June 2, 1935; *NYT*, June 1, 1935; *Time*, June 10, 1935, *WSJ*, June 1, 1935; *CDT*, June 1, 1935.
151 **"definitely turned his back":** *WP*, June 1, 1935; Patterson, *Congressional Conservatism*, 42–43; *CDT*, June 2, 1935.
152 **What had happened overnight?:** *NYT*, May 31, June 2, 1935.
152 **"a marked change of front":** Ibid., June 1, 2, 1935.
152 **"you . . . have got the wrong idea":** FDR to James T. Soutter, June 10, 1935, PPF 2585, FDRL.
152 **"stop, look and listen":** Henry L. Stimson to FDR, June 4, 1935, PPF, 20, FDRL.
153 **"somewhere between your thought":** FDR to Stimson, June 10, 1935, PPF 20, FDRL.
153 **"we would have our hands full":** HSC Diary, June 20, 1935, 82–83, UVA.
153 **"If it [the Court] had split":** Robert H. Kelley to WVD, May 30, 1935, WVD Papers, Box 37, LOC.
153 **"talk of blackjacking":** *WP*, May 29, 1935.
153 **Roosevelt . . . had backed amendments:** *Pollock v. Farmers' Loan and Trust Co.*, 158 U.S. 601 (1895); *Hammer v. Dagenhart*, 247 U.S. 251 (1918): 276.
154 **it was "very dangerous":** *The Nation*, July 10, 1935, 41; Kyvig, *Repealing National Prohibition*, 478–79.
154 **"simple and practical":** *PPA*, 1933, 14–15; Kyvig, *Repealing National Prohibition*, 467–68; FDR quoted in Schlesinger, *Politics of Upheaval*, 453 (emphasis in original). The official is Charles Wyzanski.
155 **"It is common sense":** *PPA*, 1929–1932, 646.
155 **he began to forward:** FDR to HSC and Reed, June 8, 1935, OF 10, DOJ, Box 2; FDR to

HSC, July 5, 1935, and FF to FDR, Aug. 23, 1935, OF 10F, Box 29; Sen. Edward P. Costigan to FDR, May 29, 1935, and FDR to McIntyre, June 11, 1935, OF 466, NRA Misc., Box 11; Charlton Ogburn to FDR, Aug. 7, 1935, OF 41A, Box 49, FDRL; Leuchtenburg, *Supreme Court Reborn*, 93; FDR to J. Hamilton Lewis, June 28, 1935, PPF 1707, FDRL.

155 **he decided to send up a trial balloon:** *Collier's*, Sept. 7, 1935: 7–8, 45–46; Davis, *FDR: The Beckoning of Destiny*, 505–6, 512–13; Creel, *Rebel at Large*, 289–91.

155 **Creel and Roosevelt's latest collaboration:** *Collier's*, Sept. 7, 1935, 7–8.

156 **"Fire that":** Ibid., 8; Creel, *Rebel at Large*, 291–92.

156 **"Nothing . . . was more plain":** Creel, *Rebel at Large*; Gallup, *The Gallup Poll*, 2.

157 **"a fighting chance":** Jack Garrett Scott to TGC, Sept. 9, 1935, TGC Papers, Box 270, LOC.

CHAPTER TEN: VIGILANTES

158 **"The Roosevelt tidal wave":** *Time*, Aug. 12, 1935; Holli, *The Wizard of Washington*, 65–66.

158 **"a good deal talkier":** Moley, *After Seven Years*, 302; Wolfskill, *The Revolt of the Conservatives*, 116.

158 **Despite predictions by the Liberty League:** *NYT*, Aug. 18, 1935; McNary quoted in Patterson, *Congressional Conservatism*, 36.

159 **Every step now seemed a stumble:** HSC Diary, May 28, 1935, 68, UVA.

159 **"like Joe Robinson":** FF memorandum, July 10, 1935, in Freedman, *Roosevelt and Frankfurter*, 282–83.

159 **"exhausted, irritable":** *NYT*, July 14, 1935.

159 **to "steal [Huey] Long's thunder":** FDR quoted in Moley, *After Seven Years*, 308, 310, 315–17; Schlesinger, *Politics of Upheaval*, 325–28, 333–34; Leuchtenburg, *FDR and the New Deal*, 152–54.

160 **"so tired that I would have enjoyed":** Schlesinger, *Politics of Upheaval*, 337, 499; Leuchtenburg, *FDR and the New Deal*, 162.

160 **"facing 1936 with their chins":** *NYT*, Aug. 18, 1935.

160 **"Can Roosevelt be beaten?":** *Time*, Aug. 12, 1935; *WP*, June 3, 1935.

160 **"manna from heaven":** *WP*, May 31, 1935.

160 **Edith Roosevelt . . . implored:** *NYT*, Sept. 17, 1935; *Time*, Aug. 12, 1935; Schlesinger, *Politics of Upheaval*, 526–27; Keller, *In Defense of Yesterday*, 26.

161 **These were signs of life:** *The New Republic*, Jan. 22, 1936, 312; Schlesinger, *Politics of Upheaval*, 518, 524–25; *NYT*, June 15, May 31, 1935.

161 **The League also showed a new breadth of vision:** *NYT*, July 10, 11, 12, 13, 18, 21, 1935; *WP*, July 12, 1935.

161 **The press lavished attention on the League:** *NYT*, Oct. 28, Nov. 2, 11, Dec. 26, 1935; *NYT Sunday Magazine*, Dec. 8, 1935, 23.

162 **For all the League's ambitions:** Keller, *In Defense of Yesterday*, 252, 267–68; *WP*, May 31, 1935; *NYT*, Sept. 7, 1934, Sept. 22, 1935; *Time*, Dec. 30, 1946.

162 **The Constitution had no shortage:** *NYT*, Sept. 10, 1934, June 6, 1898, Mar. 17, 1937, Oct. 5, 1934, Jan. 9, 1935; *Time*, Mar. 29, 1937; R. P. Hobson to Donaldson Brown, Aug. 21, 1935, and Hobson to Andrew W. Mellon, Sept. 30, 1935, Hobson Papers, Box 47, CDA, LOC; Hobson to H. H. Timken, Oct. 7, 1935, Hobson Papers, Box 52, LOC; Hobson to W. J. Cameron, Sept. 9, 1935, Hobson Papers, Box 50, LOC; A. J. Lepine to Hobson, Oct. 16, 1935, and Hobson to Lepine, Dec. 30, 1935, Hobson Papers, Box 50, LOC.

163 **the Lawyers' Vigilance Committee:** Kyvig, *Repealing National Prohibition*, 127–29, 172–74.

163 **Now, under the auspices of the Liberty League:** *NYT*, Aug. 22, 1935; Wolfskill, *The Revolt of the Conservatives*, 70–71; *The Nation*, June 12, 1935, 669–70.

164 **"58 Lawyers Hold Labor Act Invalid":** *NYT*, Sept. 19, 1935; Reed quoted in Wolfskill, *The Revolt of the Conservatives*, 72–74.

164 **"When a lawyer tells":** Wolfskill, *The Revolt of the Conservatives.*
164 **This sparked a cry of protest:** Ibid.; *NYT*, Sept. 20, 1935.
164 **At Roosevelt's prompting:** FF, unsigned editorial, Sept. 1935, in Freedman, *Roosevelt and Frankfurter*, 285–86.
164 **the American Bar Association (ABA) weighed:** *NYT*, Sept. 21, Oct. 17, 20, Nov. 1, 18, 1935.
165 **None of the committee's subsequent reports:** *NYT*, Dec. 30, 1935, 2; Wolfskill, *The Revolt of the Conservatives*, 77; Freedman, *Roosevelt and Frankfurter*, 292.
165 **"The legal profession certainly seems bent":** Stone to FF, Oct. 28, 1935, Stone Papers, Box 13, LOC.
165 **"Roosevelt's friends":** Rosenman quoted in Wolfskill, *The Revolt of the Conservatives*, 163.
165 **Roosevelt knew he was vulnerable:** *NYT*, Dec. 9, 1935.
165 **"A great many people":** Press Conference #210, in FDR, *Complete Presidential Press Conferences*, Vol. 5, June 4, 1935, 350.
166 **"I could not give them much comfort":** HSC Diary, July 5, 1935, 86–87, UVA.
166 **conditions in the coal industry:** *NYT*, Sept. 22, 1935; *Time*, April 8, 1935; Schlesinger, *Politics of Upheaval*, 334–35.
166 **"I understand that questions":** FDR to Samuel B. Hill, July 5, 1935, OF 41a, FDRL; Cummings draft of same, July 2, 1935, HSC Papers, Box 109, UVA.
167 **"President Roosevelt has come perilously close":** Snell quoted in Schlesinger, *Politics of Upheaval*, 336; *WP*, May 31, 1935.
167 **lawmakers were taking increasing care:** Schlesinger, *Politics of Upheaval*, 395; Mason, *Harlan Fiske Stone*, 395; *Time*, July 1, 15, 1935.
167 **Constitution Day:** "Patriots to Mark Constitution Day," *NYT*, Sept. 15, 1935.
167 **"A great holiday":** *New York Post*, Sept. 17, 1935, in PPF 1820, Box 9, FDRL.
168 **he was "more tranquil":** Moley quoted in Davis, *FDR: The Beckoning of Destiny*, 572; Holli, *The Wizard of Washington*, 66; Schlesinger, *Politics of Upheaval*, 338–41, 499; *Time*, Nov. 11, 1935.
168 **"disturbances loomed":** *Time*, Nov. 11, 1935.
168 **"I'm walking a tight rope":** FDR quoted in Davis, *FDR: The New Deal Years*, 590; Schlesinger, *Politics of Upheaval*, 500–502.
168 **"'hell broke loose' in the lower courts":** Jackson, *Struggle*, 115–16; *Time*, July 15, 1935.
169 **"At no time in the country's history":** FF and Fisher. "The Business of the Supreme Court," 611.
169 **the "alphabetical combinations":** Cardozo quoted in Hellman, *Benjamin N. Cardozo*, 295; *NYT*, Nov. 13, 1935.
169 **"Then" . . . FDR "said that":** Ickes, Nov. 13, 1935, *Secret Diary*, Vol. I, 467–68; Wills, *Explaining America*, 151–52.
170 **the justices "get away with":** *Washington Daily News*, Jan. 7, 1936, in Clapper Papers, Box 15, LOC.
170 **The charge, in fact, was nearly as old:** Fallon, *The Dynamic Constitution*, 6, 9; Wills, *Explaining America*, 131, 135, 150, 155, 161; Warren, *The Supreme Court in United States History*, Vol. I, 7–8, and Vol. II, 702–3; William E. Nelson, "The Historical Foundations of the American Judiciary," and Kermit L. Hall, "Judicial Independence and the Majoritarian Difficulty," in Hall and McGuire, eds., *The Judicial Branch*, 20–23, 62–63; Warren, "The Origin of Its Power," *The Nation*, May 7, 1924, 526–28; La Follette quoted in Ross, *A Muted Fury*, 193; Warren, *The Supreme Court in United States History*, Vol. I, 266 (emphasis in original).
171 **This was likely true of Roosevelt:** Jackson, *Struggle*, 323.
171 **"It is but a decent respect":** Bushrod Washington quoted in Schlesinger, *Politics of Upheaval*, 450.
171 **"This presumption of constitutionality":** *PPA*, 1935, 4.
171 **"The President's mind":** Ickes, Nov. 13, 1935, *Secret Diary*, Vol. I, 467–68.

172 **He was somewhat misremembering:** Manchester, *The Last Lion*, 408–13.
172 **what he emphasized to Ickes:** Ickes, Dec. 27, 1935, *Secret Diary*, Vol. I, 494–95; *WP*, May 29, 1935, 2.
172 **Roosevelt's view of the problem:** FDR to Reed, Oct. 24, 1935, OF 41, Box 48, FDRL; HSC Diary, Nov. 15, 1935, 130, UVA; Irons, *New Deal Lawyers*, 249; Pusey, *Charles Evans Hughes*, Vol. I, 204.
172 **"We are under a Constitution":** On the general tendency, then and since, to take Hughes's statement out of context, and Hughes's aggravation at that, see Chapter 22, pp. 395–96.

CHAPTER ELEVEN: SLOW POISON

173 **On the afternoon of November 20:** HSC Diary, Nov. 20, 1935, 137, UVA; *Time*, Dec. 2, 1935.
173 **Roosevelt "seemed strong and happy":** FF to FDR, Nov. 23, 1935, and FDR to FF, Dec. 1, 1935, in Freedman, *Roosevelt and Frankfurter*, 295–96.
174 **The Agricultural Adjustment Act had been one of the proudest:** Bordo, *Defining Moment*, introduction, 12; Gary D. Libecap, "The Great Depression and the Regulating State: Federal Government Regulation of Agriculture, 1884–1970," pp. 181–224, in Bordo, ibid., 185–86, 189–90; Chandler, *America's Greatest Depression*, 53–56.
175 **The public's view remained:** Chandler, *America's Greatest Depression*, 217, 219; Schlesinger, *Coming of the New Deal*, 82; *NYT*, Jan. 7, 8, 1936; Gallup, *The Gallup Poll*, 9; Watkins, *The Great Depression*, 160, 193–94; Alexander Farmer, "The Good Giant and the A.A.A.," *The New Republic*, July 17, 1935, 272–73.
175 **Meanwhile, the AAA was under assault:** Schlesinger, *Politics of Upheaval*, 470; *Time*, July 15, 1935; Irons, *New Deal Lawyers*, 182–83; Schlesinger, *Coming of the New Deal*, 82.
176 **lawyers for the Hoosac Cotton Mills:** Irons, *New Deal Lawyers*, 185–86.
176 **A long dormant debate:** Fallon, *The Dynamic Constitution*, 171; Irons, *New Deal Lawyers*, 188–89.
176 **the first argument of consequence:** Perry and Abraham in Shaw et al., *FDR and the Transformation of the Supreme Court*, 18–21; Pearson and Allen, *The Nine Old Men*, 14–15.
177 **After seventy-five years:** *NYT*, Nov. 10, 1929; Martin, *CCB: The Life and Century*, 128–29.
177 **"I fear I shall never be reconciled":** Stone to FF, Oct. 18, 1935, Stone Papers, Box 13, LOC; Pearson and Allen, *The Nine Old Men*, 9.
177 **from "an artistic standpoint":** McReynolds to Robert McReynolds, Oct. 24, 1935, McReynolds Papers, Box 1, UVA.
177 **The gilded ceiling:** Stone to Helen Stone Willard, Nov. 15, 1935, Stone Papers, Box 4, LOC; *Time*, Dec. 16, 1935, Feb. 17, 1936; *WP*, Feb. 16, 1936.
177 **"I like to think":** *PPA*, 1935, 384–85; Irons, *New Deal Lawyers*, 189–90; HSC Diary, Dec. 9, 1935, 140, UVA.
178 **the Home Owners' Loan Act:** *NYT*, Dec. 10, 1935.
178 **Thus the oral defense of the AAA:** HSC Diary, Dec. 9, 1935, 140, UVA; Stone to Lauson and Marshall Stone, Dec. 13, 1935, Stone Papers, Box 3, LOC; Irons, *New Deal Lawyers*, 192–93.
178 **Reed was no match:** Irons, *New Deal Lawyers*, 182–83, 193–94; Pearson and Allen, *The Nine Old Men*, 283–84; Leonard, *Search for a Judicial Philosophy*, 7–9.
179 **Pepper built toward a crescendo:** Irons, *New Deal Lawyers*, 193–94; *Time*, Dec. 16, 1935; Jackson, *Struggle*, 132; Pearson and Allen, *The Nine Old Men*, 285.
179 **At the Gridiron Dinner:** Menu, "Schechter Skit," and "Supreme Court Skit," Clapper Papers, Box 28, LOC ; Brayman, *The President Speaks*, 279–80; Pearson and Allen, *The Nine Old Men*, 22; Ickes, Dec. 15, 1935, *Secret Diary*, Vol. I, 485.
180 **"I am not one of those":** Reading copy, Gridiron speech, Dec. 14, 1935, pp. 1, 7, in Speech Files, Box 87, FDRL.

180 **his closing argument in the AAA case:** Pearson and Allen, *The Nine Old Men*, 24; McReynolds to Robert McReynolds, Dec. 16, 1935, McReynolds Papers, Box 1, UVA.

181 **There had been no conversion:** Stone, "Memorandum No. 8," Feb. 4, 1936, Stone Papers, Box 62, LOC; *Colgate v. Harvey*, 296 U.S. 404 (1935): 445–46; Fallon, *The Dynamic Constitution*, 228–29; Amar, *America's Constitution*, 254; Schlesinger, *Politics of Upheaval*, 468–69.

181 **Then Stone fired back:** "Memorandum No. 8," Feb. 4, 1936, Stone Papers, Box 62, LOC; Stone to Lauson and Marshall Stone, Dec. 6, 1935, Stone Papers, Box 3, LOC; Paschal, *Mr. Justice Sutherland*, 176; 296 U.S. 404 (1935): 426, 441, 443; Stone to Lauson and Marshall Stone, Dec. 20, 1935, Stone Papers, Box 3, LOC.

181 **The *Colgate* decision drew little comment:** *NYT*, Dec. 17, 1935; Powell quoted in Schlesinger, *Politics of Upheaval*, 469.

181 **"Gosh it is unbelievable":** FF to Stone, Dec. 18, 19, 1935, Stone Papers, Box 13, LOC.

182 **"The tendency to press":** Stone to FF, Dec. 16, 20, 23, 1935, Stone Papers, Box 13, LOC; Wechsler in Louchheim, *The Making of the New Deal*, 54; Childs OH, 92.

182 **The bloc of three dissenters was secure:** Mason, *Supreme Court from Taft to Burger*, 70; Schlesinger, *Politics of Upheaval*, 468; Kaufman, *Cardozo*, 478.

182 **the justices had little to do:** Gardner, *Pebbles*, 47, 48fn; Kaufman, *Cardozo*, 477–80; Mason, *Brandeis*, 537–39; Pusey, *Charles Evans Hughes*, Vol. II, 670.

183 **"The mastiffs have been":** Brandeis to FF, Apr. 10, 1932, in Urofsky, *"Half Brother,"* 484, 484fn; Hellman, *Benjamin N. Cardozo*, 220, 248.

183 **In mid-December, the Court announced:** *NYT*, Dec. 17, 1935.

183 **The cabinet met on . . . December 27:** HSC Diary, Dec. 27, 1935, 151, UVA; description of Oval Room based on pictures at www.whitehousemuseum.org/floor2/yellow-oval-room .htm (accessed May 27, 2008).

183 **FDR . . . was in an expansive mood:** Ickes, Dec. 27, 1935, *Secret Diary*, Vol. I, 494–96.

184 **Roberts . . . opinion in *United States v. Butler*:** *NYT*, Jan. 7, 1936; *CDT*, Jan. 7, 1936; Schlesinger, *Politics of Upheaval*, 471.

184 **Roberts began by affirming:** Leonard, *A Search for a Judicial Philosophy*, 48; *U.S. v. Butler*, 297 U.S. 1 (1936): 61, 64; *Time*, Jan. 13, 1936; 297 U.S. 1 (1936): 62–63.

185 **The "broader construction":** 297 U.S. 1 (1936): 63–68, 70, 75, 77–78.

185 **Stone answered sharply:** Mason, *Supreme Court: Vehicle*, 28; Mason, *Harlan Fiske Stone*, 408, 408fn.

186 **a "hot dissent":** *NYT*, Jan. 7, 1936; *WP*, Jan. 7, 1936; Jackson, *Struggle*, 134–35.

186 **The dissent, joined by Brandeis and Cardozo:** 297 U.S. 1 (1936): 81, 83, 85; Mason, *Harlan Fiske Stone*, 408–9.

186 **called the "slot machine" theory:** Pound quoted in Leonard, *A Search for a Judicial Philosophy*, 53; 297 U.S. 1 (1936): 78–79, 87.

186 **"it is the business of courts":** 297 U.S. 1 (1936): 87–88.

187 **He seemed wholly unsurprised:** *NYT*, Jan. 7, 1936.

187 **Word filtered quickly:** Irons, *New Deal Lawyers*, 197.

187 **Cummings read it aloud:** HSC Diary, Jan. 6, 1936, 4–5, UVA.

187 **"Never before":** Jackson, *Struggle*, 136–37; Brant, *Storm over the Constitution*, 139.

187 **"so sweeping":** *NYT*, Jan. 7, 1936.

187 **Conservatives were overjoyed:** *NYT*, Jan. 7, 1936; *CDT*, Jan. 7, 8, 1936.

187 **"The lawyers and business men":** R. H. Kelley to WVD, Jan. 6, 1936, WVD Papers, Box 38, LOC.

188 **"The forces who control":** McReynolds to Robert McReynolds, Jan. 10, 17, 1936, McReynolds Papers, Box 1, UVA.

188 **Republicans grew more restrained:** *NYT*, Jan. 7, 8, 1936; *Time*, Jan. 20, 1936; Stone to Franklin W. Fort, Jan. 11, 1936, Stone Papers, Box 82, LOC.

188 **"The tongues of politicians":** *Time*, Jan. 20, 1936.

188 **"bureaucrats masquerading":** Basil Brewer to Roy W. Howard, Jan. 11, 1936, Clapper Papers, Box 48, LOC.
188 **the justices who had struck down the AAA:** *NYT*, Jan. 7, 8, 1936.
188 **a consensus quickly took hold:** Mason, *Harlan Fiske Stone*, 413; *NYT*, Jan. 8, 1936.
189 **"The Constitution is the Lord":** *The New Republic*, Jan. 15, 1936, 269.
189 **"mowed down":** Clapper, "Clapper Sees AAA Ruling as Blow at Democratic Government," *Washington Daily News*, Jan. 7, 1936, in Clapper Papers, Box 15, LOC. This particular column got Clapper dropped from at least one paper: the editor of the *Standard-Times Morning Mercury* in New Bedford, Massachusetts, considered it "contempt of court" and "distinctly subversive in tone, purpose, and results, if any" (Basil Brewer to Roy W. Howard, Jan. 11, 1936, Clapper Papers, Box 48, LOC).
189 **when he held a press conference:** *Time*, Jan. 20, 1936; *NYT*, Jan. 8, 9, 1936; *CDT*, Jan. 8, 1936.
190 **"History repeats":** *NYT*, Jan. 9, 1936; *PPA*, 1936, 39–41, 43–44.
190 **a dinner of Young Democrats:** *NYT*, Jan. 9, 1936; Lora and Longton, *The Conservative Press*, 121, 127 (ellipses in original).
190 **the annual judicial reception:** *Time*, Jan. 20, 1936; Pearson and Allen, *The Nine Old Men*, 24; HSC Diary, Jan. 13, 1936, 17, UVA.
191 **"Your dissenting opinion":** HSC to Stone, Jan. 8, 1936, Stone Papers, Box 10, LOC (emphasis in original); HSC Diary, Jan. 10, 1936, 12, UVA.
191 **"The joke of it":** Stone to Lauson and Marshall Stone, Jan. 9, 1936, Stone Papers, Box 3, LOC.
191 **"But the Constitution":** Stone to Judge Moore, July 15, 1937, Stone Papers, Box 82, LOC; Stone to C. C. Burlingham, Jan. 9, 1936, Stone Papers, Box 7, LOC.
191 **Stone wrote a letter:** Stone to Hoover, Jan. 22, 1936, Stone Papers, Box 17, LOC; Mason, *Harlan Fiske Stone*, 417.
192 **"Frankly . . . I do question the motives":** McBain exchange quoted in Mason, *Harlan Fiske Stone*, 411–12; *Time*, Jan. 13, 1936.
192 **"What bothers me most":** FF to Stone, Feb. 14, 1936, Stone Papers, Box 13, LOC.
192 **"I don't know that I shall ever":** Stone to FF, Feb. 17, 1936, Stone Papers, Box 13, LOC.
193 **Hughes had recommended:** Rodell, *Nine Men*, 238; Stone, "Memorandum Re: No. 401," Feb. 4, 1936, Stone Papers, Box 62, LOC; Freund, "Charles Evans Hughes as Chief Justice," 34; Leuchtenburg, "Charles Evans Hughes," 1194; Danelski and Tulchin, eds., *Autobiographical Notes*, 309–10; Roberts quoted in Ariens, "A Thrice-Told Tale," 648–49fn.
193 **"My how they do push":** Helen Stone Willard to Stone, Jan. 16, 1936, Stone Papers, Box 4, LOC.
194 **"Keep up the good work":** Howard Westwood to Stone, Jan. 14, 1936, Stone Papers, Box 82, LOC.
194 **a constitutional test of the Bankhead Act:** *Moor v. Texas & N.O.R. Co.*, 297 U.S. 101 (1936); *NYT*, Jan. 14, 1936; Wallace quoted in Schlesinger, *Politics of Upheaval*, 505.
194 **"puzzled . . . and disturbed":** HSC Diary, Jan. 13, 1936, 13–18, UVA.
195 **In the press, the conflict was usually:** Nichols, *Congress or the Supreme Court*, 1.
195 **Congress was not without tools:** Wills, *Explaining America*, 135.
195 **The proposals came in a cascade:** A. E. McCullough to Farley, n.d. [Jan. 1936], and Farley to FDR, Jan. 17, 1936, OF 41a, Box 49, FDRL; *NYT*, Jan. 7, 18, 1936; Leuchtenburg, "Origins," 373; Fite and Rubinstein, "Curbing the Supreme Court," 765; Joseph O'Mahoney to FDR, Jan. 10, 1936, PPF 1191–1211, Folder 1200, FDRL.
196 **All three Senate proposals:** *NYT*, Jan. 7, 17, 1936; "The Supreme Court Rules!" *The New Republic*, Jan. 15, 1936, 270.
196 **"Knowing some of the members":** Hiram W. Johnson to Hiram W. Johnson, Jr., Jan. 11, 1936, in Burke, *Diary Letters*; *The New Republic*, Jan. 29, 1936, 328–30.
197 **Roosevelt did not disagree:** Kenneth S. Davis, "FDR as a Biographer's Problem," 104–8.
197 **Still, the pressure to act:** *Washington Daily News*, Jan. 7, 1936; *WSJ*, Jan. 9, 1936.

197 **"the position taken by Lincoln":** Dickinson quoted in Irons, *New Deal Lawyers*, 198; Ickes, Jan. 17, 1936, *Secret Diary*, Vol. I, 514–15.
197 **Roosevelt told the cabinet:** Ickes, Jan. 24, 1936, *Secret Diary*, Vol. I, 524; Cantril, ed., *Public Opinion*, 148, 344; Lash, *Dealers and Dreamers*, 267.
198 **"It is plain to see":** Ickes, Jan. 24, 1936, *Secret Diary*, Vol. I, 524.

CHAPTER TWELVE: A PROJECT OF GREAT IMPORTANCE

199 **the night of the banquet:** *NYT*, Jan. 18, 24, 26, 29, 1936.
199 **the group's campaign against Roosevelt:** *NYT*, Jan. 19, 1936; Holli, *The Wizard of Washington*, 67; Cantril, ed., *Public Opinion*, 978.
200 **The League had been girding itself:** *NYT*, Jan. 26, 1936.
200 **the League had something to prove:** Cantril, ed., *Public Opinion*, 678; Gallup, *The Gallup Poll*, 5.
200 **Smith . . . would give it his all:** *NYT*, Jan. 24, 26, 1936; Wolfskill, *The Revolt of the Conservatives*, 151–52.
201 **The next day:** *NYT*, Jan. 26, 27, Feb. 1, 1936; Wolfskill, *The Revolt of the Conservatives*, 160–61;
201 **Smith "would have pleased me":** McReynolds to Robert McReynolds, Jan. 26, 1936, McReynolds Papers, Box 1, UVA.
201 **Democrats expressed bitterness:** *NYT*, Jan. 26, 27, 1936; HSC Diary, Jan. 28, 1936, 35–36, UVA.
202 **Joseph Robinson . . . delivered a rebuttal:** HSC Diary, Jan. 28, 1936, 35–36, UVA; *NYT*, Jan. 29, 1936.
202 **Eugene Talmadge:** *NYT*, Feb. 2, 1936: Schlesinger, *Politics of Upheaval*, 522–23.
203 **the president publicly blessed a proposal:** *NYT*, Feb. 1, 1936.
203 **Washington . . . constitutional convention:** Charles A. Beard, "What About the Constitution?" *The Nation*, Apr. 1, 1936, 405; *Time*, Feb. 24, 1936; Ernst, *Ultimate Power*, 318.
203 **For the past year, Cummings:** Irons, *A People's History*, 312; HSC to John Dickinson, Dec. 28, 1935, in HSC, *Selected Papers*, 147–48; McKenna, *Franklin Roosevelt and the Great Constitutional War*, 158–59; Clapper Diary, June 12, 1938, Clapper Papers, Box 8, LOC.
203 **"What was the McArdle [*sic*] case . . . ?":** FDR to HSC, Jan. 14, 1936, HSC to FDR, Jan. 16, 1936, and Alexander Holtzoff to HSC, Jan. 16, 1936, in PSF Box 165, FDRL; *Ex parte McCardle*, 74 U.S. 506 (1868). For contrasting views on whether Congress had actually subdued the Court, see Kutler, "*Ex parte McCardle*: Judicial Impotency," 835–51, and Murphy, Walter F., *Congress and the Court*, 37–40; Warner W. Gardner to Reed, Jan. 14, 1936, J. T. Fowler to Golden W. Bell, Jan. 23, 1936, and Reed to HSC, Feb. 6, 1936, HSC Papers, Box 88, UVA.
204 **the "project" was still in its infancy:** Lasser, *Limits*, 148–50; Ickes, Jan. 24, 1936, *Secret Diary*, Vol. I, 524; FF quoted in Lash, *Dealers and Dreamers*, 267.
204 **Roosevelt's instincts:** Charles A. Beard, "What About the Constitution?" *The Nation*, Apr. 1, 1936, 406; Brant, *Storm over the Constitution*, 243; Kyvig, *Repealing National Prohibition*, 200; La Follette quoted in Ross, *A Muted Fury*, 195.
205 **the pragmatic bent of the New Deal:** Ackerman, *We the People: Transformations*, 347–48.
205 **Roosevelt was prepared to defy the Court:** Ickes, Jan. 29, 1936, *Secret Diary*, Vol. I, 527–30. According to Charles Warren, Andrew Jackson never asserted a right to ignore a Court ruling; rather, he said that when a president was weighing whether to veto a bill, he could make up his own mind as to its constitutionality (Warren, *The Supreme Court in United States History*, Vol. I, 761–64). Henry J. Abraham says the quote was probably apocryphal (Abraham, *The Judicial Process*, 355).
206 **"It will have to be fought":** Ickes, Jan. 29, 1936, *Secret Diary*, Vol. I, 527–30.
206 **"The real difficulty":** HSC to FDR, Jan. 29, 1936 (received Jan. 30), PPF 1820, FDRL (emphasis in original).

206 **"It will fall to your lot":** Ashurst quoted in Baker, *Back to Back*, 8; Schlesinger, *Politics of Upheaval*, 493; HSC to FDR, Jan. 29, 1936 (received Jan. 30), PPF 1820, FDRL.
207 **"some serious thought":** HSC to FDR, Jan. 29, 1936 (received Jan. 30), PPF 1820, FDRL.
207 **Now McAdoo's proposal reemerged:** HSC Diary, Jan. 17, 1933, 101–2, UVA.
207 **"a relic of the past":** *New York Herald* quoted in Borah Papers, Box 809, LOC; Robert W. Welch, "Old Men Rulers of the Nation," *NYT Sunday Magazine*, May 25, 1902, 5.
207 **when the Court was not composed . . . of venerable men:** Ross, *A Muted Fury*, 1; *NYT*, Dec. 30, 1932, Feb. 15, 19, 1936; Stone to Charles C. Burlingham, Oct. 4, 1935, Stone Papers, Box 7, LOC.
208 **in his speech at Milton Academy:** FDR, *Whither Bound?*, 12–13.
208 **Even Brandeis . . . was losing sight:** Ickes, Nov. 13, 1935, *Secret Diary*, Vol. I, 467.
208 **"That they are behind":** Leuchtenburg, "Origins," 366.
208 **such as Robert Jackson, felt the problem:** Jackson, *Struggle*, 187, 315; FDR to Clarence Ousley, Feb. 12, 1936, OF 41, Box 48, FDRL.
208 **Life tenure had long been a focus:** Ross, *A Muted Fury*, 93–95; Charles Fairman, "The Retirement of Federal Judges," *Harvard Law Review*, Vol. 51, No. 3, Jan. 1938: 430–31; B. F. Welty to FDR, Aug. 30, 1935, OF 41, Box 48, FDRL.
208 **"the imaginary danger":** Hamilton, *Federalist No. 79*, in Lodge, ed., *The Federalist*, 494.
209 **"Probably the faults of the system":** Krock, "Nine Judges—and Nine Men, Too," *NYT Sunday Magazine*, Mar. 29, 1936, 15.
209 **"I am glad that you found":** Hughes to Krock, Mar. 21, 1936, Hughes Papers, Reel 5, LOC; Hughes, *The Supreme Court of the United States*, 74–77.
209 **the Justice Department began:** Holtzoff to HSC, Jan. 29, 1936, HSC Papers, Box 147; "Report of the Royal Commission on the Despatch of Business at Common Law, 1934–6, Presented by the Secretary of State for the Home Department to Parliament by Command of His Majesty January 1936," pp. 90–91, in TGC Papers, Box 272, LOC; Memo, "Retirement of Judges in England," HSC Papers, Box 206, "Research Material, Aged English Judges," UVA.
210 **"they have lost vigor":** Taft quoted in HSC to FDR, Feb. 7, 1936, HSC Papers, Box 170, UVA. The passage was oddly prophetic: at the age of seventy-two, his health badly failing, Taft clung to his seat as Chief Justice. "I am older and slower and less acute and more confused," he wrote to his brother in November 1929, "however . . . I must stay on the Court in order to prevent the Bolsheviki from getting control." In February 1930, Taft finally bowed to the inevitable and resigned; he died a month later. (Taft letter quoted in Schlesinger, *Politics of Upheaval*, 455.)
210 **The idea of an age limit:** FDR to Henry F. Ashurst, Feb. 15, 1936; FDR to Hatton Sumners, Feb. 13, 1936; Ashurst to FDR, Feb. 19, 1936, FDRL.
210 **"Will you speak to me":** FDR to HSC, Feb. 24, 1936, in OF 41, Box 48 and PPF 195, FDRL.
210 **On February 17:** *Ashwander v. Tennessee Valley Authority*, 297 U.S. 288 (1936); *NYT*, Feb. 18, 1936; *Time*, Feb. 24, 1936.
210 **"It was naturally a day":** HSC Diary, Feb. 17, 1936, 53–55, UVA.
211 **"the popular impression":** Stone to Lauson and Marshall Stone, Feb. 21, 1936, Stone Papers, Box 3, LOC.
211 **Hughes had confined his opinion:** Jackson, *Struggle*, 145–46; Hendel, *Charles Evans Hughes and the Supreme Court*, 207–9; Mason, *Brandeis*, 629; Mason, *Harlan Fiske Stone*, 418; Leuchtenburg, *FDR and the New Deal*, 164–65.
211 **"The Court . . . narrowed the opinion":** Clapper to Marshall McNeil, Feb. 21, 1936, Clapper Papers, Box 231, LOC.
211 **"most carefully and definitely limited":** Frederick F. Faville to WVD, Feb. 26, 1936, WVD Papers, Box 38, LOC.
211 **"Not the least of [the] excellences":** *NYT*, Feb. 18, 1936; *The Nation*, Feb. 26, 1936, 236–37.

211 ***Jones v. Securities*:** *Time*, Apr. 13, 1936; Paschal, *Mr. Justice Sutherland*, 190–91; *Jones v. Securities and Exchange Commission*, 298 U.S. 1 (1936): 12–14, 23, 28; Jackson, *Struggle*, 152–53; *The Nation*, Apr. 15, 1936, 465.

212 **"Sutherland writes as though":** FF to Stone, Apr. 7, 1936, Stone Papers, Box 13, LOC.

212 **"It was written for morons":** Stone to FF, Apr. 7, 9, 1936, Stone Papers, Box 13, LOC.

212 **"I am happy to report":** *NYT*, May 8, 1936; FF to Stone, May 18, 1936, Stone Papers, Box 13, LOC.

212 **On May 18, in *Carter*:** Schlesinger, *Politics of Upheaval*, 476–77; Stern, "The Commerce Clause and the National Economy," 671, 672; Hendel, *Charles Evans Hughes and the Supreme Court*, 223; Leonard, *A Search for Judicial Philosophy*, 73; *Carter v. Carter Coal Co.*, 298 U.S. 238 (1936): 307–8, 311–16.

213 **Cardozo thought this absurd:** 298 U.S. 238: 317–41; Hendel, *Charles Evans Hughes and the Supreme Court*, 243–44; Freund, "Charles Evans Hughes as Chief Justice," 33.

214 **"Perhaps when you have read":** Stone to FF, May 18, 1936, Stone Papers, Box 13, LOC; *The Nation*, May 27, 1936, 664.

214 **"He is deeply unhappy":** Friedman, "Switching Time," 1962–63.

214 **Stanley High:** Stanley High Diary, May 18, 1936, High Papers, Box 1, FDRL; HSC Diary, May 19, 1936, 106–12, UVA.

215 **"no political justification":** HSC Diary, May 19, 1936, 106–12, UVA.

215 **"President Will Dodge":** *CDT*, May 20, 1936;

215 **"till after the campaign":** Gov. James M. Curley to FDR, Jan. 9, 1936, OF 41A, Box 49, FDRL; Leuchtenburg, "Origins," 379.

215 **Even Ickes . . . had cooled:** Ickes, May 22, 1936, *Secret Diary*, Vol. I, 602–3.

215 **Roosevelt was doing just fine:** Holli, *The Wizard of Washington*, 67; *NYT*, Mar. 22, 1936.

216 **Republicans were squandering:** *NYT*, Mar. 22, 1936.

216 **The League, by the late spring:** Ibid., Mar. 7, 11, Apr. 11, 15, 1936.

216 **the Senate Lobby Investigating Committee:** Ibid., Mar. 22, Apr. 17, 18, 1936.

217 **In April, in another blow to the League:** Ibid., Mar. 7, Apr. 13, 20, 1936.

217 **"The more they work":** Ibid., Apr. 14, 1936.

CHAPTER THIRTEEN: NO-MAN'S-LAND

218 **the Municipal Bankruptcy Act:** *NYT*, May 26, 27, 1936, 22; Schlesinger, *Politics of Upheaval*, 478.

218 **"a form of indecent exposure":** Stone to FF, May 30, 1936, Stone Papers, Box 13, LOC.

219 ***Morehead v. Tipaldo*:** Chambers, "The Big Switch," 48–49; *NYT*, June 2, 1936.

219 ***Adkins v. Children's Hospital*:** *Adkins v. Children's Hospital of District of Columbia*, 261 U.S. 525 (1923); Perkins, *The Roosevelt I Knew*, 250; FF to Mary ("Molly") Dewson, Dec. 7, 10, 1928, Cohen Papers, Box 11, LOC. Frankfurter and Cohen sought to distinguish New York's statute from D.C.'s by requiring that the minimum wage reflect the reasonable value of the service rendered; D.C. had attached its minimum wage to the cost of living for women workers (*Morehead v. People of State of New York ex rel. Tipaldo*, 298 U.S. 587 [1936]: 623; Chambers, "The Big Switch," 65–66).

220 **Hughes was prepared to differentiate:** FF and Fisher, 634, 634fn; Cushman, *Rethinking the New Deal Court*, 101. Hughes's ambiguous treatment of the *Adkins* precedent in his *Tipaldo* dissent has led, almost inevitably, to wildly divergent interpretations about his intentions. Alpheus Thomas Mason, a critic of Hughes, argued that Hughes "tried desperately to keep alive the *Adkins* precedent" in order to leave himself an avenue for a possible retreat in a future case. Richard Friedman, on the other hand, perceives in Hughes's dissent his "deep disdain" for *Adkins*; Hughes, he writes, "abruptly cast it aside." The truth, which must remain elusive, probably lies somewhere in between: the Chief Justice indirectly expresses discomfort with *Adkins*, casting an oblique shadow of

doubt on its validity not only in *Tipaldo* but in general; but at the same time, he accords *Adkins* enough respect to explain why it is not "a precise authority" in this case. His measured tone suggests that he is not shoving the case aside so much as holding it at arm's length. (See Mason, "Charles Evans Hughes," 7–8; Friedman, "Switching Time," 1937.)

220 **"sad business":** Stone to Burlingham, June 12, 1936, Stone Papers, Box 7; Stone to FF, June 3, 1936, Stone Papers, Box 13, LOC; Schlesinger, *Politics of Upheaval*, 479–80; Brown, *The Social and Economic Philosophy of Pierce Butler*, 68–69; Chambers, "The Big Switch," 52–53, 53fn; 298 U.S. 587 (1936).

221 **"has no more embedded":** 298 U.S. 587 (1936): 633, 636; Rodell, *Nine Men*, 241–42.

221 **the final act of a Shakespearean tragedy:** Clapper, *Washington Daily News*, June 1, 1936, in Clapper Papers, Box 230, LOC.

221 **"in many ways one of the most disastrous":** Stone to Helen Stone Willard, June 2, 1936, Stone Papers, Box 4, LOC.

221 **"the climax to this course":** *PPA*, 1937, lvii; Ross, *The Chief Justiceship of Charles Evans Hughes*, 58–59, 84.

221 **"history . . . may well refer":** *PPA*, 1935, 13.

221 **"Positively medieval":** Ickes, June 2, 1936, *Secret Diary*, Vol. I, 614.

222 **condemnation . . . was well near universal:** Rodell, *Nine Men*, 241–42; *The New Republic*, July 15, 1936, 290; *WP*, June 2, 1936. The oft-cited statistics on the conservative press come from *The New Republic*.

222 **"the liberty of contract":** *The New Republic*, June 10, 1936.

222 **"Increase number of jurists":** E. Larkin to FDR, June. 4, 1936, OF 41a, Box 49, FDRL; *WP*, June 2, 1936.

223 **"more than any previous decision":** High to FDR, June 2, 1936, PSF 165, FDRL.

223 **"Have you any comment":** H. G. Lea to FDR, June 3, 1936, HSC Papers, Box 179, UVA; Press Conference #300, June 2, 1936, in FDR, *Complete Presidential Press Conferences*, Vol. 7, 280–81; *NYT*, June 3, 1936. In 1910, Theodore Roosevelt had used a similar phrase in a similar context, charging that certain Supreme Court decisions risked creating "a neutral ground in which neither State nor Nation can exercise authority, and which would become a place of refuge . . . for the very rich men who wish to act against the interests of the community as a whole." (TR in Denver, Aug. 29, 1910, quoted in *NYT*, Aug. 30, 1910.)

223 **"The issue . . . is packed":** *The Nation*, June 3, 1936.

223 **Historically, election-year attacks:** Stephenson, *Campaigns and the Court*, 125, 128–32; Winchester, "The Judiciary," 807; Ross, *A Muted Fury*, 35–38, 133–37, 148–50, 263, 266–67; *NYT*, Oct. 5, 25, 1924.

224 **In 1936, Senator Burt Wheeler:** Ross, *A Muted Fury*, 270–71, 279; Ben Cohen to FF, July 9, 1937, Lash Papers, Box 68, FDRL.

224 **the "No. 1 political issue":** *Washington Daily News*, June 1, 1936, in Clapper Papers, Box 230, LOC; John L. Lewis in Pearson and Allen, *Nine Old Men at the Crossroads*, 1; Senator George Norris in *The Nation*, June 3, 1936.

224 **that idea would have been laughable:** *NYT*, June 3, 7, 1936.

224 **"Don't let the Republicans":** H. G. Lea to FDR, June 3, 1936, HSC Papers, Box 179, UVA.

224 **Republicans were in a panic:** Lasser, *Limits*, 142.

224 **"landed on the front steps":** *NYT*, June 5, 1936.

224 ***Tipaldo* had put two planks:** *Boston Herald*, June 9, 1936, in Stone Papers, Box 13, LOC; White quoted in *Time*, June 15, 1936; Schlesinger, *Politics of Upheaval*, 539; *NYT*, June 9, 1935; *The New Republic*, June 24, 1936, 195; George Soule, "Back to States' Rights," 485–86, 488; Irving Brant, *Storm over the Constitution*, 180.

225 **In the convention hall:** *Time*, June 15, 1936; Schlesinger, *Politics of Upheaval*, 535–36, 539, 542; Landon quoted in ibid., 540.

226 ***Tipaldo* had made this position:** Clapper Diary, July 29, 1936, Clapper Papers, Box 8, LOC.
226 **"Slow on Amendments, Please!":** *Boston Herald*, June 9, 1936.
226 **"a hasty surrender":** *NYT*, June 9, 1935; Schlesinger, *Politics of Upheaval*, 542–43.
226 **"bitter-enders":** Landon to Clapper, Aug. 7, 1935, Clapper Papers, Box 48, LOC.
226 **Into this contentious mix:** *NYT*, June 8, 9, 11, 1936.
227 **Roosevelt began by talking:** Ibid., June 11, 1936; *PPA*, 1936, 195–96, 200–202.
227 **"with growing intensity":** *PPA*, 1936, 200–201.
228 **"Totally unexpected":** *NYT*, June 11, 12, 1936; Schlesinger, *Politics of Upheaval*, 542–43.
228 **"The American people":** Hoover, *Addresses upon the American Road*, 174–75, 181; *The New Republic*, June 24, 1936, 194–95; Schlesinger, *Politics of Upheaval*, 544–45.
228 **delegates stood on their seats:** *NYT*, June 12, 1936; Wolfskill and Hudson, *All but the People*, 206.
229 **Landon's men had managed:** Lasser, *Limits*, 143; Schlesinger, *Politics of Upheaval*, 543; *NYT*, June 12, 1936; *The New Republic*, June 24, 1936, 195; *The Oregonian* quoted in *NYT*, June 13, 1936.
229 **"I think we should be more than human":** Cardozo quoted in Hellman, *Benjamin N. Cardozo*, 230.
229 **"The reception given":** Brandeis to Stone, June 22, 1936, Box 73, LOC.
229 **"amusing":** Stone to Brandeis, June 23, 1936, Stone Papers, Box 73; Stone to Sterling Carr, June 26, 1936, Stone Papers, Box 8, LOC.
229 **"My dear Pierce":** WVD to Butler, June 11, 1936, WVD Papers, Box 19, Letterbook #52, LOC.
230 **After *Tipaldo*:** Brant, *Storm over the Constitution*, xiv, 254.
230 **"I am delighted":** Stone to Brant, July 19, 1936, Stone Papers, Box 7, LOC.
230 **"wish [that] the fairies":** Brandeis to Stone, Aug. 5, 1936, Stone Papers, Box 73, LOC.
230 **a "substantial 'native son' vote":** *NYT*, May 30, 1936.
230 **"some of the bankers":** Sterling Carr to Stone, June 4, 1936, Stone Papers, Box 8, LOC.
231 **The Roberts boomlet:** *Time*, May 20, 1935; *NYT*, May 26, 1935; Pearson and Allen, *The Nine Old Men*, 161–62; *NYT*, July 9, 1935.
231 **a "subtle" inducement:** Borah quoted in "Supreme Court Justices as Presidential Candidates," 396–97.
231 **"I never had the notion":** Roberts quoted in Nelson, "The President and the Court," 292, citing "Composition and Jurisdiction of the Supreme Court," Hearings before a Subcommittee of the Committee on the Judiciary, US Senate, 83 Cong., 2 Sess. (Washington, D.C.: U.S. GPO, 1954): 8–9; Pearson and Allen, *The Nine Old Men*, 161–62; *NYT*, June 5, 1936.
231 **"too anxious for worldly approval":** Childs OH, 70–71.
232 **This was also true:** Mason, *Harlan Fiske Stone*, 413.
232 **"You hit him hard":** Burlingham to Stone, June 11, 1936, Stone Papers, Box 7, LOC.
232 **"They walked up and down":** Elizabeth Roberts confided these memories to an old school friend—Labor Secretary Frances Perkins. Perkins OH, 71–74, quoted in Leuchtenburg, "Charles Evans Hughes," 1199.
233 **letters flooded the White House:** A. Raymond Cornwall to FDR, June 20, 1936, D. McDonald to FDR, June 3, 1936, Roger Telis to FDR, June 18, 1936, Daniel L. Smith to FDR, June 22, 1936, Rep. Kent Keller to FDR, June 22, 1936, Frank J. Burns to FDR, June 18, 1936, all in OF 1871a, DNC, Box 2, FDRL.
233 **a "growing conviction":** HSC to FDR, June 20, 1936, HSC Papers, Box 170, UVA.
233 **Rosenman was there to work:** Rosenman, *Working with Roosevelt*, 100–102.
234 **"Most pressing":** Ibid., 102–3; Richberg, *My Hero*, 204.
234 **Richberg's language:** Richberg to McIntyre, June 16, 1936, and Richberg to FDR, June 16, 1936, PSF Box 165, FDRL; Richberg, *My Hero*, 204; Rosenman, *Working with Roosevelt*, 103; Moley, *After Seven Years*, 346–47.

234 **"The Democratic party":** *NYT*, June 24, 1936.

235 **Convention speakers reinforced:** *NYT*, June 24, 1936; Schlesinger, *Politics of Upheaval*, 580.

235 **On June 27:** *PPA*, 1936, 230–36, FDRL; *NYT*, June 28, 1936.

235 **"We had everything set":** Landon to Clapper, Aug. 26, 1937, Clapper Papers, Box 48, LOC.

235 **Colonel Frank Knox:** White to Clapper, Aug. 19, 1936, Clapper Papers, Box 48, LOC; Schlesinger, *Politics of Upheaval*, 528–29, 541, 604, 606.

236 **"leading us toward Moscow":** Knox and Hamilton quoted in Schlesinger, *Politics of Upheaval*, 606–7; *NYT*, June 24, July 1,1936.

236 **"The political liability":** *NYT*, Aug. 7, 1936.

236 **When Landon finally emerged:** Schlesinger, *Politics of Upheaval*, 613–15.

236 **"The governor's campaign":** Clapper to White, Oct. 23, 1936, Clapper Papers, Box 48, LOC.

237 **"The answer . . . is no one can be sure":** *NYT*, Oct. 8, 29, 30, 1936.

237 **"conspiracy of silence":** *The Nation*, June 3, 1936.

237 **"frequently returns to a discussion":** High Diary, Oct. 28, 1936, and Feb. 10, 1937, FDRL.

237 **"There's one issue in this campaign":** FDR quoted in Schlesinger, *Politics of Upheaval*, 577–78, also 586, 639–40; Gallup, *The Gallup Poll*, 31, 38–39.

238 **"There seems a growing feeling":** McReynolds to Robert McReynolds, July 3, 1936, McReynolds Papers, Box 1, UVA.

238 **"the consensus of newspaper opinion":** WVD to Dennis T. Flynn, Oct. 19, 1936, to E. J. Hunt, Oct. 31, 1936, and to Mrs. John W. Lacey, Nov. 2, 1936, WVD Papers, Box 19, LOC.

238 **"Jesus":** High Diary, n.d. [Nov. 1936], FDRL.

CHAPTER FOURTEEN: PLANS AND PURPOSES

239 **"It is very difficult":** *NYT*, Nov. 5, 1936; Schlesinger, *Politics of Upheaval*, 643.

239 **"I am at [an] absolute loss":** Bankhead to Farley, Nov. 5, 1936, Farley Papers, Box 5, LOC; Patterson, *Congressional Conservatism*, 81; Cora B. Howe to Landon, Nov. 4, 1936, Clapper Papers, Box 48, LOC; *NYT*, Nov. 8, 1936.

239 **The landslide brought the nation closer:** Patterson, *Congressional Conservatism*, 81; Kennedy, *Freedom from Fear*, 286.

240 **"is not dead":** *NYT*, Nov. 8, 1936.

240 **"I agree with you":** Mills quoted in Weed, *The Nemesis of Reform*, 115.

240 **Roosevelt had lifted, forcibly:** Kennedy, *Freedom from Fear*, 284–85; *NYT*, Nov. 5, 1936.

240 **"And now will come the test":** Hiram W. Johnson to Hiram W. Johnson, Jr., Nov. 10, 15, 1936, in Burke, *Diary Letters*.

240 **the nation's editorial pages were filled:** Editorials quoted in *NYT*, Nov. 5, 1936.

241 **at the first post-election meeting:** Ickes, Nov. 7, 1936, *Secret Diary*, Vol. I, 703; FDR and Early quoted in Clapper Diary, Nov. 16, 1936, Clapper Papers, Box 8, LOC; Alfange, *The Supreme Court and the National Will*, 230.

241 **Visitors to the White House:** Davis, *FDR: Into the Storm*, 25, 28; Schlesinger, *Coming of the New Deal*, 3, 5.

241 **"Now he stands as victor":** *NYT*, Nov. 5, 1936.

241 **"the reactionary element":** FDR to Josephus Daniels, Nov. 9, 1936, Elliott Roosevelt, ed., *F.D.R.: His Personal Letters, 1928–1945*, Vol. I, 626; Richard Norton Smith, *The Colonel*, 352.

242 **Roosevelt saw an opportunity:** Davis, *FDR: The New Deal Years*, 663; Kennedy, *Freedom from Fear*, 324–25; Chandler, *America's Greatest Depression*, 129; *PPA*, 1936, 572.

242 **"Today there is war":** *PPA*, 1936, 572; Kennedy, *Freedom from Fear*, 398–99; Davis, *FDR: Into the Storm*, 13.

242 **"Mr. Roosevelt is likely to break":** Clapper Diary, Nov. 16, 1936, LOC.

243 **Stanley Reed . . . told the president:** Reed to HSC, Nov. 6, 1936, HSC Papers, Box 146, UVA; Mason, *Harlan Fiske Stone*, 440; Ickes, Nov. 7, 1936, *Secret Diary*, Vol. I, 705.

243 **"The President . . . is getting ready":** Ickes, Nov. 7, 1936, *Secret Diary*, Vol. I, 705.

243 **"there may be growing changes":** Reed to McIntyre, Nov. 5, 1936, OF 10F, Box 29, FDRL.

243 **"Now that we see":** Clapper, "Supreme Court All That's Needed to Make Victory Unanimous," *Washington Daily News*, Nov. 6, 1936, in Clapper Papers, Box 230, LOC.

243 **"Either the election":** Jackson, *Struggle*, 321.

243 **"squinted sideways":** The dean is Wiley Rutledge of the University of Iowa (quoted in Ross, *The Chief Justiceship of Charles Evans Hughes*, 247). Rutledge, in 1943, became the last of FDR's appointees to the Supreme Court.

244 **"The result is encouraging":** HSC Diary, Nov. 15, 1936, 166, UVA; *Time*, Nov. 30, 1936; *NYT*, Nov. 24, 1936; Cummings quoted in Lasser, *Limits*, 146.

244 **other "halting steps":** Jackson, *Struggle*, 197–99; *NYT*, Dec. 8, 13, 1936.

245 **A confidential Justice Department memo:** Memorandum, "Litigation Involving New Deal Measures," Dec. 17, 1936, in McJimsey, *Documentary History*, Vol. 1, 66–68.

245 **"certain that President Roosevelt":** Clapper Diary, Nov. 16, 1936, LOC; Clapper, "What's Ahead in Washington?" *Review of Reviews*, Dec. 1936, Clapper Papers, Box 210, LOC; *Time*, Nov. 16, 1936.

245 **"a stupor":** *NYT*, Jan. 17, 1937; Leuchtenburg, "Origins," 383.

246 **Gallup polls presented:** Gallup, *The Gallup Poll*, 43, 47; Cantril, ed., *Public Opinion*, 148.

246 **In denying ammunition:** Jackson, *Struggle*, 177.

246 **a "tremendous debate":** Oswald Garrison Villard, "Issues and Men," *The Nation*, Nov. 7, 1936, 547.

246 **"Now that the election is over":** Quoted in McKenna, *Franklin Roosevelt and the Great Constitutional War*, 243.

246 **"gone off on a protracted bender":** HSC Diary, Nov. 15, 1936, 164, UVA.

246 **Cummings brought up a topic:** Ibid., 165; Frederick, *Rugged Justice*, 177–81; "Denman Is Known as Liberal," *San Francisco Examiner*, July 26, 1937, in TGC Papers, Box 195, LOC; *Time*, Aug. 10, 1942; Bailey Millard, *History of the San Francisco Bay Region*, Vol. 3, Chicago, 1924: 395–97, accessed at http://freepages.genealogy.rootsweb.ancestry.com/~npmelton/sfbdenm.htm; Burlingham to Stone, Jan. 5, 1938, Stone Papers, Box 7, LOC. Stone replied: "I agree with all you say about Judge D[enman] and could add to it. If he has ability, it is not judicial. When he has found time to stay at home and do the work of his circuit his performance has been terrible" (Stone to Burlingham, Jan. 6, 1938, Stone Papers, Box 7, LOC.).

247 **Denman began lobbying FDR:** Frederick, *Rugged Justice*, 221; Denman to HSC, Aug. 19, 1935, OF 209h–209i, and Denman to FDR, Mar. 16, 1936, PPF 1820, Box 13, FDRL.

247 **"If he would stay home":** Sterling Carr to Stone, Apr. 17, 1937, Stone Papers, Box 8, LOC.

247 **"The New Deal needs":** Denman quoted in Frederick, *Rugged Justice*, 223.

247 **Roosevelt was increasingly drawn:** Freidel, *FDR: The Triumph*, 53; Moley, *Our Criminal Courts*, 228; FDR, *Looking Forward*, 195–96; FDR to HSC, Feb. 26, 1934, OF 41, Box 48, FDRL; Leuchtenburg, *Supreme Court Reborn*, 112–14.

248 **"Do you think that many":** HSC Diary, Nov. 15, 1936, 164, UVA.

248 **Roosevelt embarked on the USS *Indianapolis*:** Davis, *FDR: The New Deal Years*, 655–56; FDR to Sarah Roosevelt, Nov. 20, 1936, in Elliott Roosevelt, ed., *F.D.R.: His Personal Letters, 1928–1945*, Vol. I, 631; Pringle, "Profiles: The President—III," *The New Yorker*, June 30, 1934, 20.

248 **When the ship docked:** Davis, *FDR: The New Deal Years*, 656–57.

249 **after opening the conference in Buenos Aires:** Ibid., 657–60.

249 **"The tragedy of poor Gus":** FDR to Eleanor Roosevelt, Dec. 3, 1936, in Elliott Roosevelt, ed., *F.D.R.: His Personal Letters, 1928–1945*, Vol. I, 635.

249 **Louis Howe:** Tully, *F.D.R.: My Boss*, 135–37; Farley, *Behind the Ballots*, 67, 351; Rosenman, *Working with Roosevelt*, 24–25.

249 **"a kind of religion":** Howe quoted in Davis, *FDR: Into the Storm*, 6.

249 **He deeply trusted Howe's political judgment:** Davis, ibid.

250 **"My job is to supply":** Davis, *FDR: The New Deal Years*, 600.

250 **"no one quite filled the void":** Eleanor Roosevelt quoted in Davis, ibid., 603.

250 **Momentum was building:** Kyvig, "The Road Not Taken," 475; "Clarifying the Constitution by Amendment," National Consumers' League, Dec. 15, 1936, 8–9, in Cohen Papers, Box 7, LOC.

250 **Cummings grew concerned:** Cohen to FF, Nov. 23, 1936, and to Henry Shulman, Nov. 23, 1936, both in Cohen Papers, Box 7, LOC. For the contention that Cummings kept Cohen, Corcoran, and Frankfurter out of the loop because he resented their influence and possibly their superior intellects, see Moley, *After Seven Years*, 358, and Lash, *Dealers and Dreamers*, 292–93. For the notion that Reed was "uninformed of what was going on in his own department," see McKenna, *Franklin Roosevelt and the Great Constitutional War*, 248. For evidence to the contrary—on Corcoran and Cohen's knowledge, Reed's involvement, and Cummings's evolving views, see Gardner, *Pebbles*, 75–77; Edwin S. Corwin to HSC, Dec. 16, 1936, and HSC to Corwin, Dec. 17, 1936, HSC Papers, Box 88, UVA; and HSC Diary, Dec. 24, 1936, 180–81, UVA.

251 **Cohen immediately dashed off a series:** Cohen to FF, Nov. 23, 1936, to Shulman, Nov. 23, 1936, and to Charles E. Clark, Dec. 26, 1936, all in Cohen Papers, Box 7, LOC; FF quoted in Irons, *New Deal Lawyers*, 274. Irons argues on the basis of this letter that Frankfurter "favored the constitutional amendment route" (274). There is, I think, considerable evidence that suggests otherwise, including Frankfurter's repeated insistence, in letters to Stone and FDR over the preceding two years (see, for example, Chapters 7, 11, 12, pp. 119, 181–82, 204), that the problem was the Court's wrongful interpretation of the Constitution; also, his statement, cited above, that "if we are to have amending . . ." appears equivocal—hardly the kind of assertive advocacy one would expect from Frankfurter.

251 **that Cohen had any interest in an amendment:** Lasser, *Benjamin V. Cohen*, 165; Cohen to Clark, Dec. 26, 1936, Cohen Papers, Box 7, LOC; Clark to Cohen, Dec. 28, 1936, ibid.

251 **Warner W. Gardner:** Gardner, *Pebbles*, 75–76; Gardner, "Memories," 13. In *Pebbles*, Gardner says the meeting took place in early October; in "Memories," he places it in late September.

252 **Gardner had raised a long list of objections:** See Leuchtenburg, *Supreme Court Reborn*, 93; Gardner, unpublished draft of "Memories," June 1, 1999, 12fn (copy provided by Bennett Boskey).

252 **a remarkable 65-page memorandum:** Gardner, "Memorandum for the Solicitor General: Congressional Control of Judicial Power to Invalidate Legislation," Dec. 10, 1936, Cohen Papers, Box 7, LOC, esp. pp. 1–2, 14, 29–30, 55–59, 65.

253 **Cummings saw in Gardner's memo:** Gardner, "Memories," 14.

253 **the bill's "central provision":** HSC and McFarland, *Federal Justice*, 531; HSC Diary, Dec. 31, 1936, 200, UVA; Leuchtenburg, *Supreme Court Reborn*, 200. The exact timing of the McReynolds revelation cannot be determined, but it can be said with some confidence that it occurred (or was presented) to Cummings sometime between his reply to Corwin on December 17 and his note to FDR five days later. Leuchtenburg (ibid., 119–21) argues, on the basis of considerable circumstantial evidence (e.g., the imminent publication of *Federal Justice*, and Gardner's possible awareness of the precedent in late December, well before Cummings first mentioned it to FDR on January 17—see Gardner, *Pebbles*, 77fn), that the plan Cummings outlined for FDR on December 26 could not have taken the precise shape it did if Cummings were not yet aware of McReynolds's recommendation. My discovery of the early draft of Cohen and Corcoran's memo (see Chapter 15, pp. 263–64)

makes it absolutely plain that those two men knew about it (after all, they quote from it) before reworking and then submitting their memo on January 7—again, weeks before Cummings told FDR on January 17.

254 **Roosevelt sent up another trial balloon:** Creel, *Rebel at Large*, 292–94; Gardner, "Memorandum for the Solicitor General: Congressional Control of Judicial Power to Invalidate Legislation," Dec. 10, 1936, Cohen Papers, Box 7, LOC, 3–14.

255 **"Roosevelt's Plans and Purposes":** *Collier's*, Dec. 26, 1936. The issue appeared on stands, per industry practice, about a week before this date.

255 **Stanley Reed, meanwhile:** Gardner, "Memories," 14.

256 **Cummings asked that Gardner broaden:** Ibid.

256 **The letter came from Edward Corwin:** HSC to FDR, Feb. 3, 1936, PPF 1820; HSC to Corwin, Feb. 3, 1936, HSC Papers, Box 88, UVA; Mark O'Brien, "Curbing the Court," *Princeton Alumni Weekly*, Mar. 8, 2006, accessed at www.princeton.edu/~paw/archive_new/PAW05-06/09-0308/features_court.html; Corwin, *Commerce Power*, 265.

256 **Corwin was on record:** Corwin, *Commerce Power*; *New York Post*, Dec. 3, 1936, in Borah Papers, Box 809, LOC; Leuchtenburg, *Supreme Court Reborn*, 116.

257 **"What would you say":** Holcombe quoted in Leuchtenburg, *Supreme Court Reborn*, 117.

257 **"*most* ingenious, devilishly so":** Corwin to HSC, Dec. 16, 1936, HSC Papers, Box 88, UVA.

257 **linking Holcombe's proposal:** On the mystery of Cohen and Corcoran's court-packing proposal—a copy of which has never materialized—see Lash, *Dealers and Dreamers*, 268, 292; Lasser, *Benjamin V. Cohen*, 170–72; McKean, *Tommy the Cork*, 88; Wheeler, *Yankee from the West*, 320; and Cohen to FF, July 9, 1937, Lash Papers, Box 68, FDRL. Lash asserts—largely on the basis of interviews, decades later, with Cohen and Corcoran—that their plan would have provided an additional appointment for every justice over seventy, until a majority of the Court was below that age. Lash also repeats Corcoran's assertion that the plan was seen by FDR and Cummings (though Corcoran refers to the bill, incongruously, as an "amendment"—Lash, *Dealers and Dreamers*, 292). Wheeler, whose hostility to the "two young men" is on vivid display in Chapter 22, pp. 392–93, later alleged that Corcoran gave him a bill to expand the Court by three, which roughly aligns with Lash's description of the bill (Wheeler, 320).

257 **"Of course . . . I realize that":** HSC to Corwin, Dec. 17, 1936, HSC Papers, Box 88. UVA.

258 **"I am 'bursting' with ideas":** HSC to FDR, Dec. 22, 1936, HSC Papers, Box 170, FDRL.

CHAPTER FIFTEEN: WARNING BELL

259 **On Saturday, December 26, 1936:** HSC Diary, Dec. 26, 1936, 182–86, UVA.

259 **Tell me what you have in mind:** Ibid., 186.

260 **"nothing the matter with it":** Ibid., 186–88.

260 **Roosevelt interrupted to pass along a rumor:** Ibid., 188–89.

261 **Denman's concern about overloaded dockets:** Ibid., 190.

261 **"could be put through quickly":** Ibid., 191–92.

262 **"try it and see how it worked out":** Ibid., 192–93.

262 **"Do you really want me to stay":** Ibid., 193–95.

262 **"Your hunches":** Ibid., 195–96.

263 **"our circle of court-packers":** Gardner, "Memories," 14–15.

263 **"were in strong support":** Ibid., 14; Gardner, *Pebbles*, 77.

263 **Cohen, with Corcoran's help:** Cohen and TGC, "Memorandum," n.d., 19–20, Lash Papers, Box 68, FDRL.

263 **"Not a single appointment":** Gardner, "Memories," 21.

263 **an echo of a Brandeis dissent:** Brandeis, in a celebrated dissent, had referred to the depression as "an emergency more serious than war." *New State Ice Co. v. Liebmann*, 285 U.S. 262 (1932): 306.

264 **Cohen and Corcoran seemed unsure:** "Memorandum," n.d., 19–20, Lash Papers, Box 68, FDRL.

264 **the Court had issued a series of opinions:** Jackson, *Struggle*, 201–5.

264 **"a Psalmist lauding the Almighty":** *Time*, Jan. 4, 1937; *NYT*, Jan. 5, 1937.

265 **rejected the arguments of a Liberty League lawyer:** "Horse Collars," *Time*, Jan. 11, 1937.

265 **the Court sustained a federal tax on speculation in silver:** "Silver Tax Upheld by Supreme Court," *NYT*, Jan. 12, 1937.

265 **"Is the Court Shifting?":** *Washington Daily News*, Jan. 5, 1937, in TGC Papers, Box 210, LOC.

265 **the New Deal's worst critics:** Moley, *After Seven Years*, 356; *NYT*, Jan. 9, 1937.

265 **"I asked him":** FF to FDR, Dec. 17, 1936, in Freedman, *Roosevelt and Frankfurter*, 366.

265 **"the country can use the rest":** *NYT*, Jan. 1, 1937.

265 **Of course, the peace that prevailed:** *NYT*, Jan. 3, 5, 10, 17, 1937.

266 **would "goose-step along":** *NYT*, Jan. 10, 1937.

266 **"would provoke much debate":** *NYT*, Jan. 3, 5, 1937.

267 **The conservative *New York Herald Tribune*:** Hugh S. Johnson, "General Johnson Defends Plan for Two-Thirds Vote as Curb on Supreme Court," Nov. 24, 1936, in Borah Papers, Box 809, LOC; *New York Herald Tribune*, Dec. 28, 1936, in Clapper Papers, Box 230, LOC; *NYT*, Jan. 5, 1937.

268 **A late draft of the speech:** Rosenman, *Working with Roosevelt*, 141; "First Draft," n.d., 8–9, "Second Draft," n.d., 7–8, and "Third Draft Amended," n.d., 9–10, 14, and Insert A, Master Speech File, Box 31, Dec. 2, 1936–Feb. 5, 1937, File 1028, "F.D.R. Message Delivered to Congress—Jan. 6, 1937"; "Fourth Draft," TGC Papers, Box 226, LOC.

268 **a "subtle speech":** HSC Diary, Jan. 5, 1937, 2, UVA; Ickes, Jan. 10, 1937, *Secret Diary*, Vol. II, 31.

268 **Democrats leapt to their feet:** *Time*, Jan. 18, 1937; *NYT*, Jan. 7, 1937; *PPA*, 1936, 639.

268 **Roosevelt continued:** *PPA*, 1936, 639–41.

269 **the "warning bell":** Rosenman, *Working with Roosevelt*, 142.

269 **"appeared in complete control":** *NYT*, Jan. 7, 1937.

269 **Roosevelt suspected that someone had shown:** Ickes, Jan. 10, 1937, *Secret Diary*, Vol. II, 31; HSC Diary, Jan. 6, 1937, 4, UVA.

269 **"at least read the remarks":** FDR to Claude Bowers, Jan. 15, 1937, in Elliott Roosevelt, ed., *F.D.R.: His Personal Letters, 1928–1945*, Vol. I, 651.

270 **Roosevelt's words were ambiguous enough:** "Points Made by Roosevelt," and Catledge, "Basic Law Upheld," *NYT*, Jan. 7, 1937.

270 **a "conservative approach":** Krock, "Roosevelt Puts Court on Trial before Nation," *NYT*, Jan. 10, 1937; Krock, "In Washington," *NYT*, Jan. 7, 1937; *Time*, Jan. 18, 1937; *NYT*, Jan. 7, 1937.

270 **Roosevelt was just playing for time:** *NYT*, Jan. 7, 8, 1937.

270 **members proposed nearly fifty amendments:** Copies of bills and resolutions are in Cohen Papers, Box 14, LOC; Ross, *A Muted Fury*, 301; article (newspaper unknown), Jan. 18, 1937, in Clapper Papers, Box 230, LOC.

270 **Emanuel Celler of New York:** "Celler in Warning to Supreme Court," *NYT*, Jan. 11, 1937.

270 **Constitutional reform groups . . . began to proliferate:** *NYT*, Jan. 8, 10, 14, 24, 1937; press release, National Conference on Constitutional Amendment, Feb. 8, 1937, in TGC Papers, Box 271, LOC; Morris L. Ernst to FDR, Jan. 18, 1937, in McJimsey, *Documentary History*, Vol. 1, 208.

271 **he brought Democratic leaders to the White House:** Davis, *FDR: Into the Storm*, 32–35.

272 **Though FDR did not acknowledge:** Schlesinger, *Coming of the New Deal*, 554–56 (FDR quoted at 555); Pearson and Allen, "How the President Works," 8–9.

272 **Roosevelt loved discussion:** Pringle, "Profiles: The President—III," *The New Yorker*, June 30, 1934, 20.

272 **"Huddles and 'bull sessions'":** Creel, *Rebel at Large*, 333.
272 **Roosevelt knew that a small circle:** Anne O'Hare McCormick, "As Mr. Roosevelt Sees His Role," *NYT*, Jan. 17, 1937; Schlesinger, *Coming of the New Deal*, 542–44.
273 **"This precipitate action":** Pearson and Allen, "How the President Works," 9; on the tax bill, also see Chapter 10, p. 159.
273 **"of the dramatic and climactic":** Rosenman, *Working with Roosevelt*, 468.
273 **He delighted in surprises:** Pringle, "Profiles: The President—III," *The New Yorker*, June 30, 1934; High Diary, May 22, 1936, Box 1, FDRL; Burns, *Roosevelt: The Lion and the Fox*, 297; Davis, *FDR: Into the Storm*, 61.
273 **"clever, cunning and quick":** Johnson quoted in Schlesinger, *Coming of the New Deal*, 531.
273 **Secrecy, at times, became an end:** Tugwell, *Democratic Roosevelt*, 398; Davis, "FDR as a Biographer's Problem," 101–2.
273 **"He loved mystery":** Rosenman, *Working with Roosevelt*, 468.
274 **"Never let your left hand":** FDR and Morgenthau quoted in Schlesinger, *Coming of the New Deal*, 583.
274 **"Sometimes . . . I thought it was because":** Rosenman, *Working with Roosevelt*, 468.
274 **It could be worse:** Schlesinger, *Politics of Upheaval*, 494.
274 **"How is your plan coming along":** HSC Diary, Dec. 18, 29, 1936, 174–75, 199, UVA.
274 **Roosevelt may have seen no need:** Burns, *Roosevelt: The Lion and the Fox*; Alsop and Catledge, *168 Days*, 28.

CHAPTER SIXTEEN: PRESERVE, PROTECT, DEFEND

276 **Warner Gardner was appalled:** Gardner, *Pebbles*, 78; Gardner, "Memories," 15.
277 **when Gardner made that discovery:** Gardner, *Pebbles*, 78; Gardner, "Memories," 15; "Draft No. 5," Jan. 5, 1937, 2–3fn, PSF 165, "Supreme Court: Jan.–July 1937, FDRL.
277 **Ben Cohen and Tom Corcoran . . . recoiled:** Cohen and TGC, "Memorandum," n.d., 19–20, Lash Papers, Box 68, FDRL; "Memorandum," Jan. 7, 1937, 18–22, Cohen Papers, Box 7, LOC.
277 **Old age, they now wrote:** "Memorandum," Jan. 7, 1937, Cohen Papers, Box 7, LOC, 12–17, 35–37, Ickes, Jan. 10, 1937, *Secret Diary*, Vol. II, 33–34.
278 **"a stimulant to buoy him up":** Anne O'Hare McCormick, "As Mr. Roosevelt Sees His Role," *NYT*, Jan. 17, 1937.
278 **"so little desirous of raising":** Ibid.
279 **"Very confidentially":** FDR to FF, Jan. 15, 1937, in Freedman, *Roosevelt and Frankfurter*, 377.
279 **the presidential inauguration:** *NYT*, Jan. 17, 1937; Davis, *FDR: Into the Storm*, 38; *NYT*, Jan. 21, 1937; Ickes, Jan. 24, 1937, *Secret Diary*, Vol. II, 51, 52; *Time*, Feb. 1, 1937. Knox, *The Forgotten Memoir of John Knox*, 165; Knox to "Folks," Jan. 21, 1937, Knox Letters, University of Chicago.
280 **"If they can take it":** *NYT*, Jan. 21, 1937.
280 **The oath:** Ibid.; *Time*, Jan. 21, 1937; Davis, *FDR: Into the Storm*, 40.
281 **"It was not what was said":** *NYT*, Jan. 21, 1937.
281 **Roosevelt's address:** Ibid.
281 **Still, those who remained:** *NYT*, Jan. 21, 1937; "FDR, First Draft," n.d., 6, Master Speech File, Box 31, FDRL; High Diary, n.d., "Inauguration—1937," FDRL; The Second Inaugural Address, Jan. 20, 1937, *PPA*, 1937, 1–3, 5; *NYT*, Jan. 21, 1937.
282 **"There was no doubt":** Rosenman, *Working with Roosevelt*, 144.
282 **"Yes, but it's the Constitution":** Ibid.
282 **"It has been a long time":** Henry L. Brant to Hughes, Jan. 21, 1937, Hughes Papers, Reel 87, LOC.
282 **"I have no comment":** Hughes to Brant, Jan. 27, 1937, Hughes Papers, Reel 87, LOC.

282 **"attitude . . . of watchful waiting":** *NYT*, Jan. 19, 1937; "The New Deal Versus the Old Courts," *The Literary Digest*, Feb. 13, 1937, 5; *NYT*, Jan. 24, 1937.
283 **they . . . had told Richberg more than that:** Richberg, *My Hero*, 220–21; HSC Diary, Jan. 7, 1937, 5, UVA.
283 **"Rvt has a number":** Clapper Diary, Jan. 20, 1937, Clapper Papers, Box 8, LOC.
283 **Clapper kept this scoop to himself:** Leuchtenburg, *Supreme Court Reborn*, 286fn–287fn; Clapper to Landon, Nov. 4, 1936, Clapper Papers, Box 48, LOC.
283 **The number of potential sources:** Leuchtenburg, *Supreme Court Reborn*, 127–28; HSC Diary, Jan. 24, 1937, 13, UVA; Shogan, *Backlash*, 87, 91; TGC Oral History, July 26, 1969, 18, TGC Papers, Box 602, LOC.
284 **"several senators have told me":** Brant to FDR, Jan. 24, 1937, Stone Papers, Box 7, LOC.
284 **heard the rumors from Brant:** Ibid.
284 **"The Justice has been tipped off":** Knox to "Folks," n.d. [between Jan. 31 and Feb. 4, 1937], Knox Letters, University of Chicago.
284 **The annual Judiciary Dinner:** Clapper Diary, Feb. 8, 1937, Clapper Papers, LOC; Rosenman, *Working with Roosevelt*, 148.
285 **Sam Rosenman traveled:** Rosenman, *Working with Roosevelt*, 145; *WP*, Jan. 30, 1937.
285 **The table in the Oval Room:** Rosenman, *Working with Roosevelt*, 146, 146–47.
285 **"Delay in the administration of justice":** Cummings to FDR, draft, Jan. 23, 1937, Master Speech File, Box 31 (1033), FDRL.
286 **The draft message to Congress:** "FDR Draft #1," n.d., Master Speech File, Box 31 (1033), FDRL.
286 **"hard to understand":** Rosenman, *Working with Roosevelt*, 147. Years later, most would accept Rosenman's claim that this luncheon was the first he had heard of the court-packing plan. What is more likely, given Gardner's recollection of briefing both FDR and Rosenman in the president's bedroom weeks earlier, is that this was the first he had heard of the plan's rationale.
286 **"appearance of deceptiveness":** Richberg, *My Hero*, 221–22; Reed to Early, Jan. 22, 1936, and Reed, "An Address Before the Judicial Section of the New York State Bar Association," Jan. 25, 1936, 1–3, OF 10F, Box 29, FDRL.
287 **Reed and Cummings had just submitted reports:** *NYT*, Feb. 8, 1937; *WP*, Feb. 8, 1937.
287 **a point of rare agreement:** The curtailment of the Court's jurisdiction was the product of a long, successful campaign by liberals and conservatives. The dockets of the federal courts, including the Supreme Court, had expanded through the nineteenth century to meet the needs of a growing nation. The Court struggled to keep up with its work. In 1891 and again in 1916, Congress tried to lighten the burden by reducing the kinds of cases the Court was required to hear. The Court was relieved of its jurisdiction over patents, bankruptcies, and disputes over land. Still, by the time Taft became Chief Justice in 1921, the Court was more than a year behind in its business. Taft pushed hard for judicial reform, and in 1925 his efforts yielded a bill that, in the words of Frankfurter and Jerome Landis, "cut the Supreme Court's jurisdiction to the bone." The justices never fell behind again. (Swisher, *American Constitutional Development*, 780–82; FF and Landis, *The Business of the Supreme Court*, 1–2, 299–302.)
287 **"the message in its present form":** Rosenman OH, 5; Rosenman, *Working with Roosevelt*, 146–48; HSC Diary, Jan. 30, 1937, 16–17, UVA.
287 **Rosenman went back to work:** Rosenman, *Working with Roosevelt*, 149; Davis, *FDR: Into the Storm*, 51–52.
288 **Roosevelt spent the better part:** Rosenman, *Working with Roosevelt*, 149–50; HSC Diary, Jan. 31, Feb. 1–2, 1937, 17–19, UVA; Hopkins, "A statement to me by Thomas Corcoran . . . April 3, 1939," Hopkins Papers, Sherwood Collection, Box 299, FDRL; *WP*, Feb. 2, 1937.
288 **Don Richberg rushed home to change:** Richberg, *My Hero*, 222–23.
288 **He considered it "very important":** HSC Diary, Feb. 3, 1937, 21, UVA.

288 **"The President . . . is terribly nervous":** Rosenman, *Working with Roosevelt*, 154–55; HSC Diary, Feb. 3, 1937, 18–19, UVA.
289 **On the afternoon of February 4:** HSC Diary, Feb. 4, 1937, 22, UVA; Rosenman, *Working with Roosevelt*, 155–56; Davis, *FDR: Into the Storm*, 63.
289 **on the evening of February 4:** Office of Social Entertainments, Box 43, FDRL.
289 **"All of us":** James Roosevelt Diary, Feb. 5, 1937, FDRL.
290 **He was, that night:** Rosenman, *Working with Roosevelt*, 156.
290 **"there will be big news":** *NYT*, Feb. 6, 1937.

CHAPTER SEVENTEEN: THE BEGINNING OF THE END OF EVERYTHING

291 **in the Cabinet Room:** Ashurst Diary, Feb. 5, 1937, in Sparks, *A Many-Colored Toga*, 366–67. James Roosevelt Diary, Feb. 5, 1937, FDRL.
292 **He then revealed contents of the papers:** Ickes, Feb. 6, 1937, *Secret Diary*, Vol. II, 64–66.
292 **Roosevelt presented his alternative:** Ashurst Diary, Feb. 5, 1937, in Sparks, *A Many-Colored Toga*, 367.
292 **Cummings eagerly scanned:** HSC Diary, Feb. 5, 1937, 23, 25, UVA.
292 **Ickes . . . keeping an eye on Garner:** Ickes, Feb. 6, 1937, *Secret Diary*, Vol. II, 66; Alsop and Catledge, *168 Days*, 66. HSC Diary, Feb. 5, 1937, 24; Ashurst Diary, Feb. 5, 1937 in Sparks, *A Many-Colored Toga*, 368; Alsop and Catledge, *168 Days*, 66–67; Patterson, *Congressional Conservatism*, 91–92.
293 **In the Oval Office, the correspondents were waiting:** *CDT*, Feb. 6, 1937; Michelson, *The Ghost Talks*, 166.
293 **Roosevelt took his place:** *CDT*, Feb. 6, 1937; FDR Press Conference #342, Feb. 5, 1937, in FDR, *Complete Presidential Press Conferences*, Vol. 9, 130–37; Early to FDR, Feb. 5, 1937, MSF Box 31 (1033), FDRL; Clapper Diary, Feb. 5, 1937, LOC.
294 **Sam Rosenman had carefully crafted:** *NYT*, Feb. 6, 1937; *WP*, Feb. 6, 1937; Alsop and Catledge, *168 Days*, 67; Clapper Diary, Feb. 5, 1937, LOC; Press Conference #342, Feb. 5, 1937, in FDR, *Complete Presidential Press Conferences*, Vol. 9, 138.
295 **a "partial solution":** Press Conference #342, Feb. 5, 1937, in FDR, *Complete Presidential Press Conferences*, Vol. 9, 138.
295 **Roosevelt's refusal to name Hughes:** "Draft #4," n.d., 5, MSF, Box 31 (1033), FDRL; HSC Diary, Feb. 3, 1937, 19, UVA; Press Conference #342, Feb. 5, 1937, in FDR, *Complete Presidential Press Conferences*, Vol. 9, 139; *Time*, Feb. 15, 1937.
295 **"Modern complexities":** Master Speech File, Box 31, Dec. 2, 1936–Feb. 5, 1937, File 1033, FDRL; *PPA*, 1937, 55.
296 **Then Roosevelt ran through the highlights:** Press Conference #342, Feb. 5, 1937, in FDR, *Complete Presidential Press Conferences*, Vol. 9, 141–47; Clapper Diary, Feb. 5, 1937, LOC; *CDT*, Feb. 6, 1937.
296 **"crashed the sacred robing room":** Rosenman, *Working with Roosevelt*, 156; TGC, Draft Autobiography, C/14–15, "Court Fight—1—3/5/79," 2, and "Court Fight Notes", all in TGC Papers, Box 593, LOC; Hopkins, "A statement to me by Thomas Corcoran . . . April 3, 1939," Hopkins Papers, Sherwood Collection, Box 299, FDRL.
297 **Corcoran caught a cab:** TGC, Draft Autobiography, C/15-16, and "Court Fight—1—3/5/79," both in TGC Papers, Box 593, LOC; Hopkins, "A statement to me by Thomas Corcoran . . . April 3, 1939," Hopkins Papers, Sherwood Collection, Box 299, FDRL.
297 **In the courtroom, a crowd had gathered:** Knox, *The Forgotten Memoir of John Knox*, 172.
297 **The justices' reaction:** *NYT*, Feb. 6, 1937; *Time*, Feb. 15, 1937.
298 **After the oral argument:** Knox, *The Forgotten Memoir of John Knox*, 171; *NYT*, Feb. 6, 1937.
298 **the Clerk of the House read aloud:** *NYT*, Feb. 6, 1937; *WP*, Feb. 6, 1937; *PPA*, 1936, 639–40; Burns, *Roosevelt: The Lion and the Fox*, 294.

299 **Discontent spread instantly:** *CDT*, Feb. 7, 1937; *NYT*, Feb. 6, 1937; Alsop and Catledge, *168 Days*, 69.

299 **Loyalty to FDR was strong:** *NYT*, Feb. 6, 1937; "The New Deal Versus the Old Courts," *The Literary Digest*, Feb. 13, 1937, 7.

300 **"the greatest legislative battle":** *CDT*, Feb. 7, 1937; *NYT*, Feb. 6, 1937; *WP*, Feb. 7, 1937.

300 **A "tentative survey":** *WSJ*, Feb. 6, 1937.

300 **"The situation looks promising":** HSC Diary, Feb. 5, 1937, 25, UVA.

301 **"Some good—some bad":** James Roosevelt Diary, Feb. 5, 6, 1937, FDRL.

301 **The press, by Roosevelt's estimate:** Graham J. White, *FDR and the Press*, 69, 73, 90; Alsop and Catledge, *168 Days*, 71.

301 **"banners flying and trumpets blowing":** *The New Yorker*, Mar. 13, 1937, 50.

301 **A survey taken:** Seldes, *Lord of the Press*, 340.

301 **"I do not recall":** Ickes, Feb. 16, 1937, *Secret Diary*, Vol. II, 74–75.

301 **Attacks came in such a rush:** The White House effort begins with "Arguments Against the President's Judiciary Bill," n.d., Cohen Papers, Box 14, LOC. Also see *NYT*, Feb. 7, 8, 1937; *WP*, Feb. 7, 1937.

302 **This might not have mattered:** *Time*, Feb. 15, 1937; *WP*, Feb. 6, 1937.

302 **the plan's great "cleverness":** *NYT*, Feb. 6, 1937; *WP*, Feb. 7, 1937.

303 **"This is a bloodless coup d'état":** Walter Lippmann, "The Seizure of the Court," *New York Herald Tribune*, Feb. 9, 1937, in Borah Papers, Box 778, LOC; *WP*, Feb. 7, 1937; *CDT*, Feb. 7, 1937.

303 **The plan, if enacted,"would end":** *CDT*, Feb. 6, 7, 1937; "Memorandum 2: Press Arguments on President's Judiciary Bill Feb. 10 to Feb. 13," Feb. 18, 1937, 3, TGC Papers, Box 272, LOC.

303 **Cartoonists portrayed the Court:** Cartoon is in the *WP*, Feb. 7, 1937.

304 **H. L. Mencken wrote that:** Mencken quoted in Patterson, *Congressional Conservatism*, 87.

304 **"know they must listen":** Lawrence, *Supreme Court or Political Puppets?*, 12; *NYT*, Feb. 7, 1937.

304 **"in time," as the White House memo put it:** "Memorandum 2, Press Arguments on President's Judiciary Bill Feb. 10 to Feb. 13," Feb. 18, 1937, 3, TGC Papers, Box 272, LOC.

304 **This criticism assumed that Roosevelt:** Pearson and Allen, *Nine Old Men at the Crossroads*, 3; *St. Louis Star-Times*, Feb. 8, 1937, in Stone Papers, Box 7, LOC.

304 **Still, most commentators accepted the idea:** *WP*, Feb. 6, 1937; Clapper, "Roosevelt Opponents on Courts Answered," *New York World-Telegram*, Feb. 11, 1937, in TGC Papers, Box 272, LOC; Clapper Diary, Feb. 8, 1937, LOC; "The New Deal Versus the Old Courts," *The Literary Digest*, Feb. 13, 1937, 6.

305 **Congressional offices . . . overwhelmed:** McKenna, *Franklin Roosevelt and the Great Constitutional War*, 303; Margaret Crowe to FDR, Feb. 6, 1937, OF 41, Box 48, FDRL; *CDT*, Feb. 7, 1937.

CHAPTER EIGHTEEN: THE FIRST WEDGE

307 **"What a grand fight":** FDR quoted in Burns, *Roosevelt: The Lion and the Fox*, 298.

307 **"[hold] his fire":** Clapper Diary, Feb. 8, 1937, 2, Clapper Papers, Box 8, LOC.

307 **"because he knew that hell":** Bankhead quoted in Patterson, *Congressional Conservatism*, 90–91.

308 **"shown up as clear out of step":** Clapper Diary, Feb. 5, 1937, LOC; James Farley Diary, Feb. 10, 11, 1937, Farley Papers, Box 41, LOC; Alsop and Catledge, *168 Days*, 48; Pusey, *The Supreme Court Crisis*, 16.

308 **"Their feelings":** James Roosevelt Diary, Feb. 6, 1937, FDRL.

308 **"One of the things that I am proud of":** FDR quoted in Leuchtenburg, *The White House Looks South*, 79. "It is the duty of the President to propose and it is the privilege of the

Congress to dispose," FDR said famously at a press conference late in the Court fight. (Press Conference #383, July 23, 1937, in FDR, *Complete Presidential Press Conferences*, Vol. 10, p. 61.)

309 **Robinson, though, was a special case:** Alsop and Catledge, *168 Days*, 156–57.

309 **He had never been shy:** Weller, *Joe T. Robinson*, 6–10; Alsop and Catledge, "Joe Robinson, the New Deal's Old Reliable," *Saturday Evening Post*, Sept. 26, 1936, 5, 7, 68, 74; *Time*, July 15, 1935.

310 **"Liberty League folded up":** Clapper Diary, Feb. 5, 1937, FDRL; *Time*, Mar. 1, 1937.

310 **"black beasts":** White quoted in Wolfskill, *The Revolt of the Conservatives*, 251; Kittelle to Hobson, Feb. 26, 1937, Hobson Papers, Box 55, LOC; *WP*, Feb. 9, 1937; "The Court and Fascism," *The Nation*, Feb. 20, 1937, 200.

310 **"let the boys across the aisle":** McNary and Vandenberg quoted in Patterson, *Congressional Conservatism*, 106–9.

310 **"If this is beaten":** Borah to Henry L. Stoddard, Feb. 20, 1937, Borah Papers, Box 483, LOC.

311 **Meanwhile, John Hamilton:** Alsop and Catledge, *168 Days*, 97.

311 **"sticking my foot in my mouth":** Landon quoted in High Diary, Feb. 14, 1937, FDRL. There are three or four variations of the Landon story. The most convincing is Wolfskill's, *The Revolt of the Conservatives*, 252, with additional details provided by Baker, *Back to Back*, 90–91. Alsop and Catledge's account in *168 Days*, 97–98, is slightly at odds with both.

311 **Not everyone was so easily persuaded:** *NYT*, Feb. 6, 1937; Alsop and Catledge, *168 Days*, 98–99; Leuchtenburg, "Franklin D. Roosevelt's Supreme Court 'Packing' Plan," in Hollingsworth and Holmes, *Essays on the New Deal*, 89; Patterson, *Congressional Conservatism*, 107; Hoover, *Addresses upon the American Road*, 235–36.

312 **"Do not be misled":** Robert M. La Follette, "Backing the President's Court Proposal," Feb. 13, 1937, *Vital Speeches of the Day*, n.d., 311, in TGC Papers, LOC.

312 **dissident Democrats . . . began to announce:** Bailey, Address to the New England Society of Charleston, SC, Dec. 21, 1935, in Borah Papers, Box 789, LOC; *WP*, Feb. 7, 1937; FDR quoted in Alsop, *"I've Seen the Best of It": Memoirs*, 105; Patterson, *Congressional Conservatism*, 20, 95–96.

312 **joined in insurgency by Thomas Connally:** Patterson, *Congressional Conservatism*, 111–12; Alsop, *"I've Seen the Best of It": Memoirs*, 100; Catledge to Alsop, Nov. 9, 1937, Alsop Papers, Box 2, LOC; *NYT*, Feb. 10, 1937; Pearson and Allen, *Nine Old Men at the Crossroads*, 34–39; *Dallas Morning News*, Mar. 4, 1937.

312 **"The issue of packing":** *WP*, Feb. 6, 1937; Jerome M. Mileur, "The 'Boss': Franklin Roosevelt, the Democratic Party, and the Reconstitution of American Politics," in Milkis and Mileur, eds., *The New Deal and the Triumph of Liberalism*, 88, 96. Leuchtenburg, *The White House Looks South*, 29–31, 35–38, 50–51, 53; Freidel, *F.D.R. and the South*, 35–36; Brinkley in Cobb and Namorato, eds., *The New Deal and the South*, 98–99; Davenport, "The Changing Character of Congress," 303. Davenport was a progressive Republican congressman from New York between 1925 and 1933.

313 **States' rights remained:** Soule, "Back to States' Rights," 484–85; Leuchtenburg, *The White House Looks South*, 119–21; Alsop, *"I've Seen the Best of It": Memoirs*, 102.

314 **"You have fed the poor":** Matthew C. Harrison to FDR, Mar. 13, 1937, in Levine and Levine, *The People and the President*, 180–81.

314 **to placate his southern base:** Milkis, *The President and the Parties*, 74, 76, 89–90.

314 **Fears of eclipse:** Mileur, "The 'Boss,'" 107–8. On the demise of the two-thirds rule, see Milkis, *The President and the Parties*, 69–71; Freidel, *F.D.R. and the South*, 72–73, 80, 97; Leuchtenburg, *The White House Looks South*, 75, 77–78; Brinkley in Cobb and Namorato, eds., *The New Deal and the South*, 113; *Time*, May 11, 1936.

315 **"is determined to get the Negro vote":** Bailey quoted in Patterson, *Congressional Conservatism*, 98–99.

315 **Senate progressives:** Ross, *A Muted Fury*, 188, 286, 297, 310.

316 **Yet their suspicion of judicial power:** Ross, *The Chief Justiceship of Charles Evans Hughes*, 109–11; Friedman, *The Will of the People*, 220–22; Jackson OH, 452–53.

316 **Progressives' wariness:** Alsop, *"I've Seen the Best of It": Memoirs*, 100; Ickes, Feb. 14, 1937, *Secret Diary*, Vol. II, 69–70; High Diary, May 22, 1936, Box 1, FDRL.

316 **"We're on the road to Fascism":** Hiram W. Johnson to Hiram W. Johnson, Jr., Feb. 6, 1937, in Burke, *Diary Letters*; Ickes, Feb. 14, 1937, *Secret Diary*, Vol. II, 70; Catledge, "Opposition Grows," *NYT*, Feb. 9, 1937.

317 **Johnson's defection:** "The New Deal Versus the Old Courts," *The Literary Digest*, Feb. 13, 1937, 8; *CDT*, Feb. 6, 1937; *NYT*, Feb. 12, 1937; *WP*, Feb. 12, 13, 1937; *Time*, Mar. 1, 1937; Alsop and Catledge, *168 Days*, 94–95; *The New Republic*, May 22, 1976; TGC interview, July 5, 1980, TGC Papers, Box 596, LOC.

317 **A heavier blow fell on February 13:** *NYT*, Feb. 13, 1937; Creel, "Man from Montana," *Collier's*, Aug. 10, 1935; *Time*, Apr. 15, 1940; Schlesinger, *Politics of Upheaval*, 142; *The Nation*, July 30, 1924, 111.

318 **Wheeler . . . was not a native:** *The Nation*, July 30, 1924, 111; *The Nation*, Nov. 22, 1922, 545; *The Nation*, Apr. 27, 1940, 532–33; Schlesinger, *Politics of Upheaval*, 136–37; Wheeler, *Yankee from the West*, 104, 165; *The New Republic*, May 22, 1976.

318 **The relationship had gone sour:** Freidel, *FDR: The Triumph*, 136–37, 294–95; FDR to Wheeler, June 3, 1930, in Elliott Roosevelt, ed., *F.D.R.: His Personal Letters, 1928–1945*, Vol. I, 129.

319 **While distrustful of FDR:** Freidel, *FDR: The Triumph*, 279; Wheeler, *Yankee from the West*, 298; Shogan, *Backlash*, 131; Farley, *Behind the Ballots*, 152; Neal, *Happy Days Are Here Again*, 7, 302.

320 **"I told the Governor":** HSC Diary, Dec. 8–11, 1932, 69–70, UVA; Wheeler, *Yankee from the West*, 298–99, 302; Colman, *Mrs. Wheeler Goes to Washington*, 140–41; Schlesinger, *Coming of the New Deal*, 248–49.

320 **Walsh's death:** Wheeler, *Yankee from the West*, 300–301; Colman, *Mrs. Wheeler Goes to Washington*, 162; Tugwell, *Democratic Roosevelt*, 402fn.

320 **Wheeler's list of grievances:** Childs, *Witness*, 35; Feb. 2, 1935, in Namorato, ed., *Diary of Rexford G. Tugwell*, 193, 197.

320 **What Wheeler resented most of all:** Burns, *Roosevelt: The Lion and the Fox*, 341–42.

321 **Roosevelt was cutting Wheeler out:** Wheeler, *Yankee from the West*, 302; Schlesinger, *Politics of Upheaval*, 139; Childs OH, 69; TGC to Rayburn, Sept. 19, 1936, TGC Papers, Box 210, LOC.

321 **"throw over their friends":** Wheeler to TGC, Aug. 16, 1936, TGC Papers, Box 215, LOC.

321 **By 1937, Wheeler's sense of duty:** Childs OH, 69; Wheeler, *Yankee from the West*, 313, 319; Patterson, *Congressional Conservatism*, 115–16; *NYT*, Jan. 17, 1936.

322 **Before Wheeler had publicly declared:** Lash, *Dealers and Dreamers*, 204–5; Wheeler to TGC, Sept. 12, 1935, TGC Papers, Box 215; Tape 4, TGC Draft Autobiography, TGC Papers, Box 595, LOC; Childs, *Witness*, 35.

322 **Corcoran sputtered about the Court:** Tape 4, TGC Draft Autobiography, TGC Papers, Box 595, LOC; Wheeler, *Yankee from the West*, 322; Alsop and Catledge, *168 Days*, 100.

323 **Corcoran returned to the White House:** Tape 4, TGC Draft Autobiography, TGC Papers, Box 595, LOC.

323 **"Charley . . . the President ought":** Michelson, *The Ghost Talks*, 177–78; Wheeler, *Yankee from the West*, 321; *NYT*, Feb. 1, 1937.

323 **No White House meeting followed:** Wheeler, *Yankee from the West*, 322–23; Patterson, *Congressional Conservatism*, 117.

324 **"Burt, we can't lick it":** Alsop and Catledge, *168 Days*, 103; Wheeler, *Yankee from the West*, 322.

324 **"I would judge":** James Roosevelt Diary, Feb. 8, 1937, FDRL; Burns, *Roosevelt: The Lion*

and the Fox, 300; Alsop and Catledge, *168 Days*, 84–85; *Time*, Nov. 5, 1928; *Time*, Sept. 11, 1933; *Time*, May 20, 1935; *NYT*, Jan. 7, 1937.

325 **The board he now led:** James Roosevelt Diary, Feb. 4, 8, 9, 10, 1937, FDRL; Burns, *Roosevelt: The Lion and the Fox*, 300; Alsop and Catledge, *168 Days*, 85–86; Catledge to Alsop, Nov. 9, 1937, Alsop Papers, Box 2, LOC; Tugwell, *Democratic Roosevelt*, 404; Michelson, *The Ghost Talks*, 169–70.

325 **Corcoran, though, was well suited:** Burns, *Roosevelt: The Lion and the Fox*, 300; *NYT*, Feb. 14, 1937; FDR to HSC, Feb. 6, 1937, PPF 1820, FDRL; Phelps to McIntyre, Feb. 18, 1937, and McIntyre to James Roosevelt, Mar. 1, 1937, TGC Papers, Box 269, LOC.

326 **Corcoran worked in tandem:** Lasser, *Benjamin V. Cohen*, 161–62; Lash, *Dealers and Dreamers*, 296–97. An example of their handiwork is seen in TGC to Keenan, Feb. 25, 1937, TGC Papers, Box 638, LOC. TGC interview, Mar. 12, 1980, TGC Papers, Box 596, LOC; Childs OH, 52; Michelson, *The Ghost Talks*, 60; James Roosevelt Diary, Feb. 16, 1937, FDRL.

326 **"As to the New Deal":** Michelson, *The Ghost Talks*, xi, 143, 176; *Time*, Nov. 10, 1930; Ickes, Jan. 18, 1936, *Secret Diary*, Vol. I, 518.

327 **The strategy board met in groups:** James Roosevelt to McIntyre, Feb. 12, 1937, OF 41, Box 48, FDRL; James Roosevelt Diary, Feb. 9, 10, 11, 13, 1937, FDRL; Alsop and Catledge, *168 Days*, 91; *NYT*, Feb. 11, 1937; *Time*, Feb. 22, 1937; *WP*, Feb. 12, 1937.

327 **Through most of February:** Alsop and Catledge, *168 Days*, 91; *NYT*, Feb. 18, 1937.

327 **"it looked almost as if":** *Time*, Feb. 22, 1937.

327 **Indeed, some sharpened their critiques:** Alsop and Catledge, *168 Days*, 94–96; Pearson and Allen, *Nine Old Men at the Crossroads*, 48.

328 **"It is things like that":** James Roosevelt Diary, Feb. 11, 1937, FDRL.

328 **Emerging from his meeting with FDR:** *CDT*, Feb. 6, 1937; *NYT*, Feb. 12, 1937; *WP*, Feb. 12, 1937.

328 **"Father outlined new plan":** James Roosevelt Diary, Feb. 14, 1937; FDRL; *NYT*, Feb. 16, 1937. The cartoon is by Bruce Bairnsfather.

328 **"Can you tell us":** Press Conference #344, Feb. 12, 1937, in FDR, *Complete Presidential Press Conferences*, Vol. 9, 162; *Time*, Feb. 22, 1937.

329 **Still, he was confident":** Reed to HSC, Feb. 19, 1937, HSC Papers, Box 146, UVA; *Time*, Feb. 15, 1937; *NYT*, Feb. 14, 1937; Hiram W. Johnson to Hiram W. Johnson, Jr., Feb. 14, 22, 1937, in Burke, *Diary Letters*.

329 **"It is becoming clearer":** *The Nation*, Feb. 27, 1937.

329 **It seemed to be the one thing:** Memo, Feb. 17, 1937, OF 41A, Box 49, FDRL; *NYT*, Feb. 19, 1937.

329 **"I am sure we will be asked":** James Roosevelt Diary, Feb. 16, 1937, FDRL.

329 **And farm groups:** *NYT*, Feb. 8, 9, 1937.

329 **"Roosevelt Will Win":** "Roosevelt Will Win," *The Nation*, Feb. 20, 1937, 202; *NYT*, Feb. 6, 1937; "The New Deal Versus the Old Courts," *The Literary Digest*, Feb. 13, 1937, 5.

329 **"I respectfully recommend":** Thomas J. Watson to FDR, Feb. 16, 1937, PSF 165, FDRL.

330 **This was all a bit premature:** FDR to Judge J. Warren Davis, Feb. 26, 1937, OF 41, Box 48, FDRL; Cantwell, "Public Opinion," 926; Gallup, *The Gallup Poll*, 50; Cantril, ed., *Public Opinion*, 149–50; *WP*, Feb. 20, 1937.

330 **"I believe it is due":** Brant to TGC, Feb. 18, 1937, TGC Papers, Box 190, LOC.

330 **"I fear that some of our representatives":** Dan Magill to Harllee Branch, Feb. 11, 1937, and Branch to McIntyre, Feb. 16, 1937, TGC Papers, Box 638, Folder 14, LOC.

330 **the tide of angry telegrams:** *NYT*, Feb. 18, 1937; Leuchtenburg in Hollingsworth and Holmes, *Essays on the New Deal*, 99.

331 **"It may be possible":** Royal Copeland to Mary Dewson, Feb. 27, 1937, in McJimsey, *Documentary History*, Vol. 1, 293.

331 **a "prudent silence":** *NYT*, Feb. 6, 7, 1937; Alsop and Catledge, *168 Days*, 92–93; *NYT*, Feb. 16, 1937.

331 **Homer Cummings was enjoying himself:** Alsop and Catledge, *168 Days*, 86–87.

331 **"What do you think":** HSC to Corwin, Feb. 11, 1937, HSC Papers, Box 88, UVA; Clapper Diary, Feb. 8, 1937, 11, LOC.

331 **another of the most distasteful aspects:** *WP*, Feb. 11, 1937. The public may not have been as outraged by the "age" argument as the editorialists were. In April 1937, a Gallup poll showed two-to-one support for a constitutional amendment requiring justices to retire at some age between seventy and seventy-five. This idea was far more popular than the Court plan and, for months, remained the most popular alternative (Cantril, ed., *Public Opinion*, 388).

332 **"I have been very much amused":** HSC Diary, Feb. 8, 1937, 27, UVA; James Roosevelt Diary, Feb. 10, 1937, FDRL.

332 **Cummings sat down with Ray Clapper:** Clapper Diary, Feb. 8, 1937, 3, LOC.

332 **Neither was Felix Frankfurter:** *WSJ*, Feb. 8, 1937.

332 **"There is no magic":** Encyclopedia entry quoted in Lash, *From the Diaries of Felix Frankfurter*, 59; FF and Landis, *The Business of the Supreme Court: A Study in the Federal Judicial System*, 187.

333 **In a sharply worded letter:** Raymond M. Remick to FF, June 24, 1935, and FF to Remick, June 26, 1935, FF Papers, Box 91, LOC, courtesy of John Q. Barrett.

333 **"a subtly instigated movement":** Cohen to Harold J. Laski, Feb. 7, 1937, Cohen Papers, Box 13, LOC.

333 **Roosevelt, too, had anticipated this:** Freedman, *Roosevelt and Frankfurter*, 372; Louchheim, *The Making of the New Deal*, 98.

333 **"You 'shocked' me":** FF to FDR, Feb. 7, 1937, PSF 135.

334 **he offered advice, encouragement:** On Frankfurter's intellectual and tactical contributions to the Court fight, see, for example, FF to TGC and BVC, n.d. [Feb. 1937], and FF to FDR, Feb. 18, 1937, both in TGC Papers, Box 198, LOC.

334 **His periodic neuritis:** Josephson, "Profiles: Jurist–III," *The New Yorker*, Dec. 14, 1934, 34; *St. Louis Post-Dispatch*, July 25, 1937, in Rauh Papers, Box 286, LOC; author interview, David Ginsburg, Jan. 7, 2005; Douglas, *Go East, Young Man*, 324.

334 **Frankfurter was tight-lipped:** Clark quoted in George Martin, *CCB: The Life and Century of Charles C. Burlingham, New York's First Citizen, 1858–1959*, 378; FF to Emory R. Buckner, May 10, 1937, FF Papers, Box 32, LOC.

334 **"My formula":** Freund, "Charles Evans Hughes as Chief Justice," 25; FF to FDR, Feb. 23, 1937, PSF 135, FDRL, and Mar. 6, 1937, TGC Papers, Box 210, LOC; Lash, *From the Diaries of Felix Frankfurter*, 59; Martin, *CCB*, 379.

335 **"The court debate now raging":** Rosenman to FDR, n.d. [Feb. 1937], PPF 64, FDRL.

335 **"We are . . . going to do":** James Roosevelt Diary, Feb. 15, 1937, FDRL.

CHAPTER NINETEEN: PUNCH DRUNK

336 **The clamor was unrelenting:** Alsop and Catledge, *168 Days*, 176–77; *The New Yorker*, Feb. 27, 1937, 11; Dewson to Royal S. Copeland, Feb. 23, 1937, in McJimsey, *Documentary History*, Vol. 1, 215.

336 **"deeper seclusion than ever":** *NYT*, Feb. 7, 1937.

336 **Henry Wallace held a small dinner party:** Clapper Diary, Feb. 7, 1937, LOC.

337 **John Knox . . . mentioning the president's plan:** Knox, *The Forgotten Memoir of John Knox*, 171–72.

337 **Outside the courtroom:** *WP*, Feb. 9, 1937; *NYT*, Feb. 9, 1937; Clapper Diary, Feb. 8, 1937, LOC.

337 **Other lapses in protocol followed:** *NYT*, Feb. 9, 1937; Clapper, Feb. 8, 1937, LOC.

338 **"'Off the record'":** Cardozo quoted in Hellman, *Benjamin N. Cardozo*, 253, and in Rauh, "A Personalized View of the Court-Packing Episode."

338 **"clever tricks":** Brandeis quoted in Baker, *Brandeis and Frankfurter*, 322, and in Leuchtenburg, "The Nine Justices Respond," 58.
338 **"The men of eighty":** *The New Yorker*, Feb. 20, 1937.
338 **"the Court has brought it all":** Stone to Helen Stone Willard, Feb. 25, 1937, Stone Papers, Box 4, LOC.
338 **"I know . . . that the present posture":** FF to Stone, Feb. 25, 1937, Stone Papers, Box 13, LOC; Mason, *Harlan Fiske Stone*, 444–45.
338 **"To see [the Court] become":** Stone to Brant, Feb. 6, 1937, Stone Papers, Box 7, LOC.
339 **"While it is couched":** Stone to Marshall Stone, Feb. 20, 25, 1937, Stone Papers, Box 2, LOC.
339 **"I do not think the country":** Ibid.
340 **Knox stopped giving McReynolds:** Knox, *The Forgotten Memoir of John Knox*, 173–74.
340 **"It is definite that McR. is not":** Knox to "Folks," Jan. 16, Feb. 21, 1937, and Knox to Frederic Burnham, Mar. 3, 1937, Knox Letters, University of Chicago; Leonard, *A Search for a Judicial Philosophy*, 154.
341 **The only other justice:** WVD to Dennis T. Flynn, Dec. 21, 1936; to Mrs. Arthur Ramsay, Feb. 17, 1937; to Isaac Van Devanter, Dec. 14, 1936; and to George G. Wharton, Feb. 17, 1937; all in WVD Papers, Box 19, LOC.
341 **None of the justices made:** Baker, *Back to Back*, 36–37; Shogan, *Backlash*, 167.
342 **"[A]fter Roosevelt launched":** Knox, *The Forgotten Memoir of John Knox*, xiii; *NYT*, Feb. 7, 1937. The senator was Frederick Van Nuys of Indiana.
342 **"might at any time be cut off":** Stone to Brant, Feb. 6, 1937, Stone Papers, Box 7, LOC.
342 **Roosevelt later tried to remedy:** Holtzoff to HSC, Jan. 29, 1936, HSC Papers, Box 147, LOC; *NYT*, Mar. 2, 7, 10, 1937.
343 **Sumners reintroduced the pensions bill:** HSC to FDR, Dec. 29, 1936, PSF Box 165; FDR to Archibald R. Watson, Feb. 9, 1937, OF 41, Box 48, FDRL.
343 **to "shove through":** *NYT*, Feb. 9, 10, 12, 1937.
343 **"to put his strength behind":** Ashurst Diary, Feb. 8, 1937, in Sparks, *A Many-Colored Toga*, 368–69.
343 **"*alone* at as early a moment":** Bankhead to FDR, Feb. 8, 1937, PSF 165, FDRL.
343 **"I do not like to have anybody":** FDR quoted in Schlesinger, *Coming of the New Deal*, 66.
344 **"savage in attack":** Early to FDR, Feb. 8, 1937, PSF 165, FDRL; *NYT*, Feb. 9, 1937.
344 **"needs to be straightened out":** James Roosevelt Diary, Feb. 10, 1937, FDRL; *NYT*, Feb. 11, 1937; *WP*, Feb. 6, 1937.
344 **"a bait and a lure":** Hiram W. Johnson to Hiram W. Johnson, Jr., Feb. 27, Mar. 7, 1937, in Burke, *Diary Letters*; *Time*, Mar. 1, 1937; Alsop and Catledge, *168 Days*, 88–89.
345 **At the time of James Roosevelt's meeting:** James Roosevelt Diary, Feb. 11, 13, 1937, FDRL; Alsop and Catledge, *168 Days*, 88–89.
345 **"more than the slightest chance":** *NYT*, Feb. 18, 1937.
345 **"Nothing new":** *NYT*, Feb. 21, 1937.
346 **And now it seemed:** Ickes, Feb. 6, 1937, *Secret Diary*, Vol. II, 64–65.
346 **But some on the left:** *The New Republic*, Feb. 17, 1937, 31–32, 44; *The Nation*, Feb. 13, 1937, 173–74; Jackson to Ernest Cawcroft, Feb. 25, 1937, Jackson Papers, Box 29, LOC.
346 **"To hell with their sincerity":** Heywood Broun, "Those Liberals Again," *The Nation*, Mar. 6, 1937, 269; Richberg to Clapper, Feb. 26, 1937, Richberg Papers, Box 2, LOC; *The Nation*, Feb. 13, 1937. For one example of the conservatives' sudden ardor for constitutional change, see Lawrence, *Supreme Court or Political Puppets?*, 42–43.
347 **Burlingham had been outspoken:** C. C. Burlingham to FDR, Feb. 19, 1937, PSF 165, FDRL.
348 **"I agree with Molly Dewson!":** FDR to Burlingham, Feb. 23, 1937, PSF 165, FDRL.
348 **Roosevelt made the same point:** Press Conferences #343 and #345, Feb. 9, 16, 1937, in FDR, *Complete Presidential Press Conferences*, Vol. 9, 159, 170.

CHAPTER TWENTY: THE REAL MISCHIEF

350 **The counteroffensive began on February 13:** *NYT*, Feb. 14, 1937; James Roosevelt Diary, Feb. 11, 1937, FDRL; La Follette, "Backing the President's Court Proposal," Feb. 13, 1937, *Vital Speeches of the Day*, n.d., 312, 314, in TGC Papers, LOC.

350 **Next in line, on February 14:** HSC to Reed, Feb. 14, 1937, HSC Papers, Box 195, UVA; *NYT*, Feb. 15, 1937; HSC, "The President's Proposals for Judicial Reorganization," Feb. 14, 1937, OF 10, Box 4, FDRL; HSC Diary, Feb. 15, 1937, UVA; Alsop and Catledge, *168 Days*, 107.

351 **The barrage continued:** Early to FDR, Feb. 8, 1937, PSF 165, FDRL; *WP*, Feb. 10, 11, 1937; *NYT*, Feb. 10, 12, 1937.

351 **Enter Ickes:** Ickes, Feb. 16, 20, 1937, *Secret Diary*, Vol. II, 75, 79–81.

352 **The contrast with Burt Wheeler:** *WP*, Feb. 20, 1937; *NYT*, Feb. 20, 1937; Solomon, *FDR v. The Constitution*, 121–22.

352 **The columnists Pearson and Allen:** Pearson and Allen, *Nine Old Men at the Crossroads*, 49.

353 **The air war continued without relent:** Burns, *Roosevelt: The Lion and the Fox*, 300.

353 **more direct forms of pressure:** Farley, *Jim Farley's Story*, 73–74; Ickes, Feb. 14, 1937, *Secret Diary*, Vol. II, 69; Pearson and Allen, "The President's Trigger Man," 394; James Roosevelt Diary, Feb. 8, 1937, FDRL; Farley Diary, July 20, 1937, LOC.

353 **a "straddling attitude":** Andrews's son quoted in Leuchtenburg, in Hollingsworth, *Essays on the New Deal*, 92; Keenan to TGC, Mar. 29, 1937, and Fred P. Cone to Charles O. Andrews, Mar. 27, 1937, both in TGC Papers, Box 202, LOC.

353 **Pressure could be exerted:** McKean, *Tommy the Cork*, 90–91; Baker, *Back to Back*, 57–59, 62–63; Burns, *Roosevelt: The Lion and the Fox*, 300.

354 **In a sense, the Court bill itself:** *NYT*, Feb. 7, 1937; *WSJ*, Feb. 8, 1937; Tugwell, *Democratic Roosevelt*, 388.

354 **"An attack on the Supreme Court":** Tugwell, *Democratic Roosevelt*; Alsop and Catledge, *168 Days*, 192.

355 **Roosevelt was not an especially good bully:** Baker, *Back to Back*, 68–69.

355 **"I never quite understood":** TGC interview, Mar. 11, 1980, p. 3, TGC Papers, Box 595, LOC.

355 **get their latest orders from Wheeler:** Wheeler, *Yankee From the West*, 322–23; Murphy, Walter F., *Congress and the Court*, 65; Pearson and Allen, *Nine Old Men at the Crossroads*, 34.

356 **"I never knew for certain":** Wheeler, *Yankee From the West*, 322–23.

356 **The old alignments were breaking down:** *CDT*, Aug. 11, 1935; *The Nation*, Apr. 27, 1940, 535; *CDT*, Feb. 23, 1937.

356 **Frank E. Gannett:** Alsop and Catledge, *168 Days*, 181; Seldes, *Lords of the Press*, 205–7; *Time*, Dec. 16, 1957; unsigned memo, Apr. 23, 1938, in TGC Papers, Box 270, LOC; Williamson, *Frank Gannett: A Biography*, 27, 228–29.

357 **That jab referred to Gannett's social:** Gannett to Borah, Mar. 7, 1936, Borah Papers, Box 440, LOC; Williamson, *Frank Gannett: A Biography*, 162–63, 169; *Time*, Mar. 5, 1934; High Diary, Sept. 17, 1936, Box 1, FDRL.

358 **"I am very busy":** Gannett to Borah, Feb. 4, Mar. 7, May 19, 1936, Borah Papers, Box 440, LOC; Williamson, *Frank Gannett: A Biography*, 165–68.

358 **Gannett won a seat:** *NYT*, Feb. 27, 1936; *Time*, May 25, 1936; Gannett to Borah, May 13, 1936, Borah Papers, Box 440, LOC; *NYT*, June 12, 1936.

358 **"We fought a good fight":** Gannett to Borah, June 16, 1936, Borah Papers, Box 440, LOC.

358 **The chance came sooner:** *WP*, Feb. 7, 1937; McKenna, *Franklin Roosevelt and the Great Constitutional War*, 305.

359 **The coming days brought fevered discussions:** *NYT*, Feb. 15, 16, 1937; Williamson, *Frank*

Gannett: A Biography, 177–78, 180; Richard Polenberg, "The National Committee," 583; Alsop and Catledge, *168 Days*, 181.

359 **Gannett's group settled into:** Description of the loft space and Rumely is in unsigned memo, Apr. 23, 1938, TGC Papers, Box 270, LOC; on Rumely and the Committee for the Nation, see Polenberg, "The National Committee," 582–84, and Schlesinger, *Coming of the New Deal*, 198–99.

360 **Dr. Rumely:** Unsigned memo, Apr. 23, 1938, TGC Papers, Box 270, LOC; *NYT*, Nov. 28, 1964, Dec. 19, 1920, and July 11, 1918.

360 **"There is a psychology":** Rumely quoted in Polenberg, "The National Committee," 592.

360 **Amos Pinchot:** Polenberg, ibid., 582; *NYT*, Feb. 19, 1944; Unsigned memo, Apr. 23, 1938, TGC Papers, Box 270, LOC.

360 **Gannett disliked the term "propaganda":** Williamson, *Frank Gannett: A Biography*, 183–85, 203–4;

361 **"covered completely the 700,000 individuals":** Rumely quoted in Polenberg, "The National Committee," 591.

361 **Robert Jackson received a letter:** NCUCG poster, Mar. 24, 1937, Gannett (form letter) to Jackson, Apr. 17, 1937, and to TGC, Apr. 19, 1937, all in TGC Papers, Box 270, LOC.

361 **"leadership individuals":** Polenberg, "The National Committee," 591; Williamson, *Frank Gannett: A Biography*, 184–85, 188; NCUCG poster, TGC Papers, Box 270, LOC.

362 **by further fund-raising appeals:** Envelope included in David Blackshear to TGC, Aug. 6, 1937, TGC Papers, Box 228, LOC.

362 **Gannett looked to amplify:** Baker, *Back to Back*, 76–77; Gannett (form letter) to the editor, *The Post*, Worcester, Mass., n.d., in TGC Papers, Box 270, LOC.

362 **These small-town papers were an important outlet:** Williamson, *Frank Gannett: A Biography*, 191–92; Alsop and Catledge, *168 Days*, 81; Evjue quoted in Seldes, *Lords of the Press*, 210, and in "A Reply to a Letter," Feb. 16, 1937, in TGC Papers, Box 269, LOC. Steve Early suggested to Corcoran that Evjue's letter be read into the *Congressional Record* by Bob La Follette, who did so on Feb. 19 (Early to TGC, Feb. 19, 1937, TGC Papers, Box 269, LOC).

363 **Gannett claimed with pride:** Williamson, *Frank Gannett: A Biography*, 207; Seldes, *Lords of the Press*, 207–8

363 **"too many publishers":** George Carlin to Clapper, Feb. 19, 25, 1937, LOC.

363 **"I am taking the only attitude":** Clapper to Carlin, Feb. 22, 26, 1937; Clapper to Robert Hall, Feb. 25, 1937, LOC.

363 **"Things look bright":** Carlin to Clapper, Mar. 23, 1937, Clapper Papers, Box 48, LOC.

364 **"the chief organized group so far":** *The New Republic*, Mar. 3, 1937.

364 **Critics pointed out:** Alsop and Catledge, *168 Days*, 181–82.

364 **an "international conspiracy":** Pinchot quoted in Polenberg, "The National Committee," 585; *NYT*, Aug. 3, 1918; unsigned memo, Apr. 23, 1938, TGC Papers, Box 270, LOC.

365 **"The fight will be won":** "Progress Report, Mar. 1–9, 1937," Hobson Papers, Box 50; Ernest Greenwood to Dean Chenoweth, Apr. 10, 1937, Hobson Papers, Box 54; Hobson correspondence with editors, Hobson Papers, Box 53, LOC.

365 **"Many of these . . . were formed":** E. C. Fielder to Sam L. Cunningham, Apr. 24, 1937, and "Memorandum on Local Committee Activities in Connection with the Supreme Court Issue," n.d., both in Hobson Papers, Box 54, LOC.

365 **"THIS IS HOW":** "An Aroused America Brings Back Town Hall Meetings," Hobson Papers, Box 54, LOC.

365 **Hobson had been cultivating relationships:** Hobson to Francis H. Kinnicutt, Feb. 23, 1937, and Theo. H. Millington to Hobson, Mar. 12, 1937, Hobson Papers, Box 45, LOC; L. M. Bailey to "Fellow American," Apr. 14, 1937, TGC Papers, Box 270, LOC; Helen Dortch Longstreet to Borah, Apr. 3, 1937, Borah Papers, Box 465, LOC; "Resolutions," Nov. 20, 1936, "Societies Cooperating with the American Coalition," "Constitution of the

American Coalition," "Call for Action," and Mrs. W. S. Walker to Fielder, May 8, 1937, all in Hobson Papers, Box 45, LOC.

366 **"militant godlessness":** Hobson to Victoria Booth Demarest, Oct. 1, 1936, and Demarest to Hobson, Oct. 5, 1936, Hobson Papers, Box 45, LOC.

366 **Gerald B. Winrod:** *NYT*, Aug. 21, 1990; Demarest, "Information concerning Associations fighting Communism from the religious point of view," n.d. [1936], Hobson Papers, Box 45, LOC; *Congressional Record*, No. 41, Mar. 1, 1937, 2079–82; *NYT*, Mar. 2, 1937.

366 **Pro-packing groups:** Massachusetts Progressive Committee form letter, n.d. [1937], TGC Papers, Box 271, LOC; "The Supreme Court and the General Welfare," National Popular Government League, July 19, 1937, TGC Papers, Box 270, LOC; *Dallas Morning News*, Mar. 25, 1937.

366 **The "wizard of public relations":** Alsop and Catledge, *168 Days*, 108, 182–83; *The New Republic*, Mar. 3, 1937.

367 **"In Jamestown . . . the people that":** Jackson OH, 436, 456; Jackson, *Struggle*, 189.

367 **"I have returned":** Jackson to FDR, Feb. 22, 1937, Jackson Papers, Box 79, LOC.

368 **On February 25, in a White House meeting:** Jackson, *That Man*, 51–52; Jackson OH, 438; *PPA*, 1937, lxv.

368 **"to dwell . . . on the reorganization":** FDR to FF, Feb. 9, 1937, PSF 135, FDRL.

369 **"waded into it":** Jackson, *That Man*, 52.

369 **"I told him I was afraid":** Jackson OH, 438.

369 **the White House reacted angrily:** *NYT*, Mar. 7, 1937; *Time*, Mar. 8, 1937.

369 **"Dare we reject it":** *NYT*, July 11, 1919.

369 **On February 26 . . . FDR held his Friday press conference:** *Time*, Mar. 8, 1937; Press Conference #348, Feb. 26, 1937, in FDR, *Complete Presidential Press Conferences*, Vol. 9, 186–88.

370 **gathering of Democrats at the Mayflower Hotel:** *NYT*, Mar. 5, 1937; James Roosevelt Diary, Feb. 23, 24, 1937, FDRL.

370 **"Looks like a working weekend":** James Roosevelt Diary, Feb. 26, 27, 1937, FDRL.

CHAPTER TWENTY-ONE: THIS NEW ROAR

371 **"Pa is both nervous and tired":** Eleanor Roosevelt quoted in Cook, *Eleanor Roosevelt*, 433, 438; James Roosevelt Diary, Feb. 27–28 and Mar. 1–3, 1937, FDRL.

371 **Tom Corcoran's original notes:** Notes for Victory Dinner Address, n.d. [Feb. 1937], MSF Box 32, File 1040, FDRL; "Victory Dinner Address . . ."; Notes, n.d. [Feb. 1937], TGC Papers, Box 227, LOC.

371 **"a fighting speech":** HSC Diary, Mar. 4, 1937, 29, UVA.

372 **"as meek as skimmed milk":** Ickes, Mar. 15, 1937, *Secret Diary*, Vol. II, 93.

372 **Joe Robinson had given a speech:** *Congressional Record*, No. 41, Mar. 1, 1937, 2079–82.

372 **the "dark and dismal period":** Connally quoted in Baker, *Back to Back*, 83, and *Dallas Morning News*, Mar. 3, 1937.

372 **"trench warfare":** Alsop and Catledge, *168 Days*, 106; Cantwell, "Public Opinion," 926; Jackson to Ernest Cawcroft, Mar. 3, 1937, Jackson Papers, Box 79, LOC; "Progress Report, Mar. 1–9, 1937," Hobson Papers, Box 50, LOC.

372 **At the Mayflower:** *NYT*, Mar. 5, 1937; *Time*, Mar. 15, 1937; "Democratic Victory Dinner" Program, Mar. 4, 1937, in Clapper Papers, Box 17, LOC.

373 **Roosevelt and the 1,300 Democrats:** "Democratic Victory Dinner," Program, Mar. 4, 1937, in Clapper Papers, Box 17, LOC; *PPA*, 1937, 113.

373 **"we faced and met":** *PPA*, 1937, 113–14; Draft #14, Victory Dinner Address, p. 4, MSF Box 32, File 1040, FDRL.

374 **an unprecedented third term:** That night, FDR told Farley that he had no interest in a third term. Farley, though, had his doubts. As he noted in his diary, foreign events might make it

"compulsory for [FDR] to carry on" as president; at the very least, it was clear that FDR expected to have a big say in who would succeed him (Scroop, *Mr. Democrat*, 157).

374 **"I could feel just what horrid":** *PPA*, 1937, 114–15.

374 **Roosevelt had delighted in dictating:** Rosenman, *Working with Roosevelt*, 157–58; PPA, 1937, 115–16; Solomon, *FDR v. The Constitution*, 128–31.

374 **The Democrats whistled:** *PPA*, 1937, 117–21; *NYT*, Mar. 7, 1937.

375 **"Here is one-third of a nation":** *PPA*, 1937, 121; Solomon, *FDR v. The Constitution*, 128–31. The peroration—particularly its refrain of "now!"—had been borrowed from an unpublished letter to the *New York Times* that had been circulating among the president's advisers since mid-February. The author was an economist named Stuart Chase. "What would happen . . . ," FDR asked Frankfurter on February 18, "if I were to go on the air and talk to America along the lines of Chase's article [*sic*] to the *Times*?" Frankfurter replied: "The American people would get some enlightenment." Chase gave Corcoran his assent to use his ideas; in the end, he may have regretted this. After the Victory Dinner, Senator La Follette made the dubious decision to read Chase's letter into the *Congressional Record* and send 100,000 copies across the country. Newspapers ran stories on the similarity between the letter and the speech, leaving Chase "distressed," as he wrote Corcoran in late March. (Stuart Chase to the Editor, *NYT*, Feb. 15, 1937, in Chase Papers, Box 5, LOC; FDR to FF, Feb. 18, 1937, and FF to FDR, Feb. 23, 1937, PSF 135, FDRL; Rosenman note, n.d., in Master Speech File, Box 32, File 1040, "Victory Dinner Address, Mar. 4, 1937," FDRL; Chase to TGC, Mar. 25, 1937, Chase Papers, Box 5, LOC.

376 **A "fighting speech" indeed:** HSC Diary, Mar. 4, 1937, UVA; *Time*, Mar. 15, 1937; *NYT*, Mar. 5, 1937; *The New Republic*, Mar. 17, 1937, 153; *Philadelphia Record*, Mar. 6, 1937, in TGC Papers, Box 272, LOC.

376 **"If the country now faces":** *NYT*, Mar. 6, 1937; *The New Yorker*, Mar. 13, 1937; *Time*, Mar. 22, 1937.

376 **For Democrats opposing the Court plan:** *Time*, Mar. 22, 1937; *NYT*, Mar. 5, 1937; *WP*, Mar. 8, 1937.

377 **"refused to listen":** "Roosevelt on the Radio," *The Nation*, Mar. 13, 1937, 284; *Time*, Mar. 22, 1937; *NYT*, Mar. 5, 1937.

377 **"Mr. President . . . is that your fan mail?":** Press Conference #350, Mar. 5, 1937, in FDR, *Complete Presidential Press Conferences*, Vol. 9, 199.

377 **"in the final analysis":** Sumner E. W. Kittelle to Laurence S. Adams, Mar. 8, 1937, Hobson Papers, Box 55, LOC.

377 **"never seen the President":** James Farley Diary, Mar. 4, 7, 1937; Farley Papers, Box 41, LOC.

378 **"in a bad way":** Ickes, Mar. 15, 1937, *Secret Diary*, Vol. II, 95.

378 **"the silly stage":** Tully, *F.D.R.: My Boss*, 96; Draft #2 and Draft #4, MSF Box 32, "White House Broadcast (1041)," 18, 20, FDRL.

378 **Roosevelt had made his peace with the draft:** Rosenman, *Working with Roosevelt*, 93; Tully, *F.D.R.: My Boss*, 92, 98; Schlesinger, *Coming of the New Deal*, 560.

379 **Roosevelt entered about 10:20 p.m.:** Rosenman, *Working with Roosevelt*, 93; Tully, *F.D.R.: My Boss*, 100.

379 **"He was perfectly aware":** TGC interview, Jan. 14, 1980, TGC Papers, Box 595, LOC.

379 **He was the master of his medium:** *NYT*, July 20, 1924; Perkins, *The Roosevelt I Knew*, 72; Rosenman, *Working with Roosevelt*, 93; Buhite and Levy, *FDR's Fireside Chats*, xvii–xviii.

379 **Roosevelt was preceded on the NBC Red network:** *NYT*, Mar. 7, 1937; Solomon, *FDR v. The Constitution*, 136; Rosenman, *Working with Roosevelt*, 93.

380 **"its constitutionality was upheld":** *PPA*, 1937, 122. Points of emphasis and slight corrections to the official transcript are based on a recording of the speech, accessed at www.presidency.ucsb.edu/ws/index.php?pid=15381&st=&st1=#.

380 **"The Court . . . has been acting":** *PPA*, 1937, 126.
380 **"plan will save our national Constitution":** Ibid., 128.
380 **But this time he was angry:** Ibid., 128–29.
381 **"Our difficulty with the Court today":** Ibid., 130.
381 **Roosevelt turned to the question:** Cantril, ed., *Public Opinion*, 345; Michelson, *The Ghost Talks*, 172.
382 **"an amendment, like the rest of the Constitution":** *PPA*, 1937, 131–32.
382 **the "newspaper publishers":** Ibid., 132.
382 **"tipped out of balance":** Ibid., 133.
382 **The radio engineer signaled:** Rosenman, *Working with Roosevelt*, 93–94; Cook, *Eleanor Roosevelt*, 435.
383 **Most of his supporters agreed:** *NYT*, Mar. 10, 1937; Cantril, ed., *Public Opinion*, 149; Esther Eldred to M. L. Williamson, Mar. 13, 1937, Hobson Papers, Box 55, LOC.
383 **"The news reel displayed":** Stone to Lauson and Marshall Stone, Mar. 12, 1937, Stone Papers, Box 3, LOC.
383 **the "best ammunition":** Stone quoted in Mason, *Harlan Fiske Stone*, 447.
383 **"No haste, no heat":** Ashurst Diary, Feb. 14, 26, Mar. 10, 1937, in Sparks, *A Many-Colored Toga*, 369, 371–72; James Roosevelt Diary, Feb. 16, 1937, FDRL; *WP*, Feb. 22, 1937; *Time*, Sept. 23, 1940; *Time*, June 8, 1962.
384 **"the prelude to tyranny":** Ashurst Diary, Feb. 5, 1937, in Sparks, *A Many-Colored Toga*, 368; on his sympathy with Hoover's views, see ibid., Nov. 11, 1932, and Aug. 31, 1935, at pp. 323 and 355. Ashurst quoted in Patterson, *Congressional Conservatism*, 90; *NYT*, Feb. 7, 1937; *Time*, June 8, 1962; and Pearson and Allen, *Nine Old Men at the Crossroads*, 44.
384 **On March 10 . . . the eighteen members:** Ashurst Diary, Mar. 10, 1937, in Sparks, *A Many-Colored Toga*; Eldred to Williamson, Mar. 10, 1937, Hobson Papers, Box 55, LOC; *Reorganization of the Federal Judiciary*, 2.
384 **Homer Cummings was the first witness:** Eldred to Williamson, Mar. 10, 1937, Hobson Papers, Box 55, LOC; *Reorganization of the Federal Judiciary*, 4–13, Cummings at 11–12.
385 **his "appearance of suavity":** *NYT*, Mar. 11, 1937; *Time*, June 8, 1962; *Reorganization of the Federal Judiciary*, 15, 17–19, 23–24.
385 **"there might be some difference":** Jackson OH, 437–38; *Time*, June 8, 1962; *NYT*, Mar. 12, 1937; *Reorganization of the Federal Judiciary*, 38, 43–44, 47.
385 **"Hearty congratulations":** Ashurst to Jackson, Mar. 11, 1937, Jackson Papers, Box 79, LOC; "The Shape of Things," *The Nation*, Mar. 20, 1937, 309.
385 **"a powerful exposition":** Stone to Lauson and Marshall Stone, Mar. 12, 1937, Stone Papers, Box 3, LOC.
386 **Roosevelt boarded a special train:** *NYT*, Mar. 12, 21, 1937; Ickes, Mar. 26, 1937, *Secret Diary*, Vol. II, 103.
386 **For the first time:** Ickes, Mar. 20, 1937, *Secret Diary*, Vol. II, 98; Cantril, ed., *Public Opinion*, 149–50; Cantwell, "Public Opinion," 927–28; Gallup, *The Gallup Poll*, 53–54; Caldeira, "Public Opinion," 1147; *WP*, Mar. 28, 1937; *NYT*, Mar. 13, 14, 1937; Hiram W. Johnson to Hiram W. Johnson, Jr., Mar. 15, 1937, in Burke, *Diary Letters*; Eldred to Williamson, Mar. 13, 1937, Hobson Papers, Box 55, LOC.
386 **"they are picking off":** Hiram W. Johnson to Hiram W. Johnson, Jr., Mar. 15, 1937, in Burke, *Diary Letters*; *NYT*, Feb. 23, Mar. 13, 1937; Jackson to Ernest Cawcroft, Mar. 16, 1937, Jackson Papers, Box 79, LOC.
386 **While the president rested:** *NYT*, Mar. 8, 13, 14, 25, 1937; *WP*, Mar. 25, 1937; *Dallas Morning News*, Feb. 23, 1937; Caldeira, "FDR's Court-Packing Plan," 13, 16.
387 **Momentum was building:** Shogan, *Backlash*, 45, 49, 91–104, 138; *NYT*, Feb. 2, 1937.
387 **"Something is seething":** *NYT*, Mar. 12, 1937.
388 **By the time of Roosevelt's trip:** *NYT*, Mar. 25, 1937.

388 **"That . . . shows why":** Press Conference #354, Mar. 24, 1937, in FDR, *Complete Presidential Press Conferences*, Vol. 9, 217.
388 **"an insuperable, impossible obstacle":** Black quoted in Shogan, *Backlash*, 151; *NYT*, Mar. 25, 1937; "Steel Victory—and After," *The Nation*, Mar. 13, 1937, 286.
388 **"It seems to me":** Ickes, Mar. 26, 1937, *Secret Diary*, Vol. II, 102.
388 **Roosevelt's opponents . . . kept fighting:** *NYT*, Mar. 11, 13, 1937.
389 **James McReynolds broke the justices' silence:** *NYT*, Mar. 17, 1937.
389 **McReynolds had believed his comments:** *Time*, Mar. 29, 1937. The editor is George Fort Milton of the *Chattanooga News*, quoted in McKenna, *Franklin Roosevelt and the Great Constitutional War*, 366. "'Congress, the Court and the Constitution,' Radio Address by Hon. Joseph T. Robinson, Mar. 30, 1937," in TGC Papers, Box 224, LOC.
390 **Chevy Chase Country Club:** McReynolds's offense was repeatedly refusing to move off the tee and let other club members play through while his caddy searched fruitlessly for a lost ball. Pearson and Allen, *Nine Old Men*, 226; *Time*, June 30, 1924, and Aug. 11, 1924.
390 **"There seems to be a breakdown":** Jackson to Judge Wilber Clark, Mar. 15, 1937, and to Ernest Cawcroft, Mar. 16, 1937, Jackson Papers, Box 79, LOC.
390 **"the psychology has changed":** HSC to McIntyre, Mar. 15, 1937, HSC Papers, Box 174, UVA.
390 **"Of course you are going to win":** Dewson to FDR, Mar. 19, 1937, PSF Box 165, FDRL.
390 **"cracking up":** Farley to Bowers, Mar. 6, 1937, Farley Papers, Box 5, LOC; Farley Diary, Mar. 21, 1937, Farley Papers, Box 41, LOC.
390 **Field reports . . . described:** Memoranda, Mar. 9, 16, 1937, TGC Papers, Box 270, LOC.
390 **"somewhat confused":** FDR to Key Pittman, Mar. 17, 1937, in Elliott Roosevelt, ed., *F.D.R.: His Personal Letters, 1928–1945*, Vol. I, 668.
391 **these stalling tactics suggested:** Jackson, *That Man*, 53; Alsop and Catledge, *168 Days*, 123–24; Davis, *FDR: Into the Storm*, 76; *Reorganization of the Federal Judiciary*, Part 1, 101, and Part 2, 168, 381–82; Eldred to Williamson, Mar. 13, 1937, Hobson Papers, Box 55, LOC.

CHAPTER TWENTY-TWO: THE YIELDING

392 **"There will be widespread regret":** *WP*, Mar. 22, 1937.
392 **Henry Ashurst called the committee to order:** *NYT*, Mar. 23, 1937; *Reorganization of the Federal Judiciary*, Part 3, 485–86.
393 **"these young men":** *Reorganization of the Federal Judiciary*, Part 3, 485–86. As Corcoran recalled it, he had gone to see Wheeler in early 1936 about a pending New Deal bill and found the senator in a rage about the Supreme Court—possibly in reaction to its recent AAA decision, which Wheeler had publicly attacked. According to Corcoran, Wheeler asked him what could be done about it. Corcoran answered that he could not think of anything but packing the Court. "Well," Wheeler reportedly replied, "let us pack the Court, then." He asked Corcoran to prepare a speech on increasing the number of justices. Corcoran and Cohen went to work on a draft, but by the time they finished it, Wheeler had lost interest in the idea. Corcoran later denied that he or Cohen had prepared a bill to pack or otherwise curb the Court, but Corcoran's and Cohen's biographers believe that the two "young men" may well have done so in the spring of 1936, either with or without FDR's knowledge. (HSC Diary, July 10, 1937, 81, UVA; Cohen to FF, July 9, 1937, Lash Papers, Box 68, FDRL; Lasser, *Benjamin V. Cohen*, 172–73; Lash, *Dealers and Dreamers*, 268, 292; McKean, *Tommy the Cork*, 88.)
393 **"Shocked and surprised":** *Reorganization of the Federal Judiciary*, Part 3, 486–87.
393 **The letter began on a coolly defiant note:** *NYT*, Mar. 23, 1937; *WP*, Mar. 23, 1937; *Reorganization of the Federal Judiciary*, Part 3, 488–91.
393 **Hughes turned the tables on Roosevelt:** *Reorganization of the Federal Judiciary*, Part 3, 491–92.

394 **The letter was explosive:** *WP*, Mar. 23, 1937.

394 **"Please be assured":** L. James to Hughes, Feb. 8, 1937, Hughes Papers, Reel 5, LOC.

394 **"the central, if silent, figure":** *Time*, Mar. 1, 1937.

394 **Or so he intended it to appear:** Merlo J. Pusey to FF, July 23, 1959, FF Papers, Box 91, LOC, courtesy of John Q. Barrett; *WP*, Feb. 7, 12, 1937.

395 **"We are under a Constitution":** Hughes quote is from a speech before the Elmira Chamber of Commerce, May 3, 1907, in Hughes, *Addresses and Papers*, 185–87; Danelski and Tulchin, eds., *Autobiographical Notes*, xxvii; 297 U.S. 1 (1936): 62–63.

395 **In March, he sought help from Ogden Reid:** Ogden Reid to Hughes, Mar. 29, 1937, and Hughes to Reid, Apr. 5, 1937, Hughes Papers, Reel 5, LOC.

396 **It is unlikely that Wheeler knew:** Brandeis to FF, May 28, 1924, in Urofsky, *"Half Brother,"* 168fn, 169; Colman, *Mrs. Wheeler Goes to Washington*, 165–66; Mason, *Brandeis*, 626.

396 **Wheeler went to see Brandeis:** Mason, *Brandeis*, 626.

396 **On Thursday, March 18:** Danelski and Tulchin, eds., *Autobiographical Notes*, 304–5; Pusey, *Charles Evans Hughes*, Vol. II, 667.

397 **In the morning Hughes placed calls:** "Memorandum of telephone conversation of Chief Justice Hughes with Senator William H. King," and "Telephone conversation of Chief Justice Hughes with Senator Burton K. Wheeler," Mar. 19, 1937, Hughes Papers, Reel 5, LOC.

397 **"This gave me very limited time":** Danelski and Tulchin, eds., *Autobiographical Notes*, 305; Wheeler, *Yankee from the West*, 329. Wheeler's version of these events is unreliable, and inconsistent with Hughes's transcripts. According to Wheeler, after Hughes handed him the letter he asked Wheeler to sit down and talk for a bit, whereupon Hughes attacked FDR and Cummings at length—a lively account that makes Hughes sound suspiciously like Wheeler himself (327–30).

397 **"Bull's Eye!":** Cartoon by Carmack in the *Christian Science Monitor*, Mar. 23, 1937, in McKenna, *Franklin Roosevelt and the Great Constitutional War*, 371; *NYT*, Mar. 23, 1937.

397 **Roosevelt spent the morning:** *CDT*, Mar. 23, 1937; Ickes, Mar. 26, 1937, *Secret Diary*, Vol. II, 102–4; HSC Diary, Mar. 22, 23, 1937, 33, UVA; *NYT*, Mar. 25, 1937.

398 **much attention was paid to Hughes's statement:** Hughes, *The Supreme Court of the United States*, 30–31; Warren, *The Supreme Court in United States History,* Vol. I, 595–96; *The New Republic*, Apr. 7, 1937; Thurman Arnold to Robert H. Jackson, Mar. 23, 1937, Jackson Papers, Box 79, LOC; *NYT*, Mar. 24, 1937.

398 **Hughes had given himself license:** Mason, "Charles Evans Hughes," 11–12; Rauh in Louchheim, *The Making of the New Deal*, 60.

399 **"I simply cannot believe":** FF to Stone, Apr. 8, 1937, and Stone to FF, Apr. 8, 1937, Stone Papers, Box 13, LOC.

399 **"You are right!":** FF to Stone, Apr. 8, 1937, and Stone to FF, Apr. 8, 1937, Stone Papers, Box 13, LOC.

399 **"The intimate conference":** Stone to Brant, Feb. 26, 1937, Stone Papers, Box 7, LOC; Mason, *Harlan Fiske Stone*, 447–50, 453–54. On the morning of March 21, the day that Hughes delivered his letter to Wheeler, a young man named Alfred Lief came to call on Stone, who knew Lief a bit and thought it was a social call. Lief asked whether Stone would, as a theoretical matter, sign a letter against the court-packing plan. Stone said no, it was inappropriate to get involved in a political controversy. Only the next morning, when Wheeler revealed the Hughes letter, did Stone realize what Lief was after and who had sent him: Wheeler. The senator later denied it; if anyone sent Lief for that purpose, Wheeler said, it must have been Hughes (Mason, *Harlan Fiske Stone*, 453).

399 **"Brandeis had up to that time":** TGC Interview, Mar. 31, 1980, TGC Papers, Box 595, LOC; Lash, *Dealers and Dreamers*, 305; Leuchtenburg, "The Nine Justices Respond," 64.

399 **"*That* was a characteristic":** FF to FDR, Mar. 30, 1937, PSF 135, FDRL.

400 **his feelings about both justices:** Jackson OH, 451–52; Douglas, *Go East, Young Man*, 327.

400 **"at the very first opportunity":** Danelski and Tulchin, eds., *Autobiographical Notes*, 305fn. For a somewhat exculpatory view of the Hughes letter, see Friedman, "Chief Justice Hughes' Letter on Court-Packing," 76–86.

400 **"so conclusively refuted":** Tugwell, *Democratic Roosevelt*, 405.

400 **"pretty much turned the tide":** Jackson OH, 441.

401 **"there is no question":** Jackson to John P. Devaney, Mar. 29, 1937, Jackson Papers, Box 29, LOC; Ickes, Mar. 26, 1937, *Secret Diary*, Vol. II, 103–4. By one measure (Cantwell, "Public Opinion," 928), it was Wheeler's appearance that began the opposition's rebound in the polls; but most others locate the shift at least a week later, after the *Parrish* decision. Friedman notes that the Hughes letter earned the opposition no converts in the Senate (Friedman, "Chief Justice Hughes' Letter on Court-Packing," 83).

401 **FDR was working on a surprise:** *NYT*, Sept. 10, 1922, Mar. 23, 1937; Ross, *A Muted Fury*, 208, 208fn;

401 **"I have been counting on":** Wilson quoted in Jackson, *Struggle*, 186–87.

402 **Urgent interventions followed:** *Time*, Nov. 9, 1936; James Roosevelt Diary, Mar. 12, 1937, FDRL; Creel to Ralph E. Jenney, Mar. 11, 1937, TGC Papers, Box 638, Folder 14, LOC.

402 **Clarke went on the radio:** James Roosevelt to Jenney, Mar. 15, 1937, James Roosevelt Papers, Box 13, FDRL; *NYT*, Mar. 23, 1937.

402 **"Apparently . . . he was under the misapprehension":** *WP*, Mar. 24, 1937; Leuchtenburg, "The Nine Justices Respond," 67.

402 **"Had I interpreted":** John H. Clarke to FDR, Mar. 29, 1937, TGC Papers, Box 210, LOC.

402 **the annual Easter Egg Roll:** *Time*, Apr. 5, 1937; *WP*, Mar. 30, 1937.

403 **Roosevelt was well rested:** *NYT*, Mar. 27, 1937.

403 ***West Coast Hotel Co. v. Parrish*:** *Time*, Apr. 5, 1937; *West Coast Hotel Co. v. Parrish*, 300 U.S. 379 (1937): 388.

404 **the *Parrish* case:** FF, "Mr. Justice Roberts," 315; *NYT*, Dec. 17, 1936; "The Court, Politics and Minimum Wage Legislation," n.d. [Mar. 1937], TGC Papers, Box 270, LOC.

404 **On March 29:** *Time*, Apr. 5, 1937; Knox, *The Forgotten Memoir of John Knox*, 194; Jackson, *Struggle*, 207, 212–13; *Virginian Railway Co. v. System Federation No. 40 et al.*, 300 U.S. 515 (1937); *Sonzinsky v. United States*, 300 U.S. 506 (1937); *Wright v. Vinton Branch*, 300 U.S. 440 (1937); Knox, *The Forgotten Memoir of John Knox*,196–98; *NYT*, Mar. 30, 1937.

405 **The spectators were beginning to flag:** *CDT*, Mar. 30, 1937.

405 **"This case . . . presents":** Knox, *The Forgotten Memoir of John Knox*, 198–99.

405 **Hughes had been in the minority:** 298 U.S. 587: 604–5; Mason, *Harlan Fiske Stone*, 423–24.

406 **At the heart of both previous minimum-wage cases:** 298 U.S. 587: 628; 300 U.S. 379: 391; Knox, *The Forgotten Memoir of John Knox*, 201.

406 **Was a minimum wage for women reasonable?:** 300 U.S. 379: 398–400; G. Edward White, *The Constitution and the New Deal*, 222–23, 227.

406 **Hughes was now ready:** 300 U.S. 379: 389–90, 397–98, 400; *amicus* brief quoted in Cushman, *Rethinking the New Deal Court*, 85; on *Nebbia*, see Cushman, ibid., 85–87, 105.

407 **George Sutherland now leaned forward:** Knox, *The Forgotten Memoir of John Knox*, 201; *WP*, Mar. 30, 1937.

409 **For "a more complete discussion":** 300 U.S. 379: 401–4, 414; *WP*, Mar. 30, 1937.

409 **"What a day!":** Jackson, *Struggle*, 213.

409 **Joe Robinson . . . roared his approval:** *NYT*, Mar. 30, 1937; *WP*, Mar. 30, 1937.

409 **Wheeler had never put much faith:** Washington state's minimum wage was not, in fact, a New Deal law, but Waltman well captured the contradictions in Robinson's thinking. *WP*, Apr. 1, 1937.

410 ***Parrish* had scrambled the pieces:** *CDT*, Mar. 30, 1937; Jackson, *Struggle*, 211; *NYT*, Mar. 30, 1937; Borah to T. W. Rainey, Mar. 30, 1937, Borah Papers, Box 484, LOC.

410 **"Even government victories":** *Reorganization of the Federal Judiciary*, Part 1, 48.

410 **"Only by the shift of the vote":** Swisher, *Selected Papers of Homer Cummings*, 155–56. Swisher omits the last line of the statement, which appears in *CDT*, Apr. 1, 1937.

411 **The problem, in the view of:** "Is the Supreme Court Going Liberal?" *The Nation*, Apr. 3, 1937, 367–68.

411 **"the hard-boiled four":** Ickes, Mar. 30, 1937, *Secret Diary*, Vol. II, 106;

411 **"fear . . . that the dissent":** Stone to Lauson and Marshall Stone, Apr. 1, 1937, Stone Papers, Box 2, LOC.

411 **Not even the unanimous decisions:** Swisher, *American Constitutional Development*, 948.

411 **"Shotgun liberalism":** *The Nation*, Apr. 3, 1937; *NYT*, Mar. 30, 1937.

411 **"I don't think there is any news":** Press Conference #356, Mar. 30, 1937, in FDR, *Complete Presidential Press Conferences*, Vol. 9, 225–26, 231–32.

412 **"Just to think that silly Roberts":** Dewson quoted in Chambers, "The Big Switch," 63; *NYT*, Mar. 30, Apr. 1, 1937.

412 **Felix Frankfurter . . . shared Dewson's enthusiasm:** FF quoted in Lash, *Dealers and Dreamers*, 305–6; FF to Stone, Mar. 30, 1937, Stone Papers, Box 13, LOC; Swisher, *American Constitutional Development*, 946.

412 **"with the shift by Roberts":** FF to FDR, Mar. 30, 1937, PSF 135, FDRL; *Philadelphia Record* quoted in Leonard, *A Search for a Judicial Philosophy*, 128; *CDT*, Apr. 1, 1937.

412 **For Roberts, this must have been a painful period:** Mason, *Harlan Fiske Stone*, 449–50. On the *Tipaldo* furor and its effect on Roberts, see Chapter 13, pp. 230–33.

413 **In a three-page memorandum:** The memo appears in FF, "Mr. Justice Roberts," 314–15. Roberts wrote the memo at Frankfurter's urging in late 1945. By then, Frankfurter was an associate justice, having been appointed by FDR in 1939 to fill the vacancy created by Cardozo's death. Frankfurter and Roberts, improbably, had become friends—due less to a shared legal philosophy than to shared antagonisms on a Court that, during Stone's tenure as chief justice (1941–46), seethed with internecine conflict. Frankfurter, having come, by this point, to regard Roberts as a man of integrity, principle, and humility, and having come to regret his role in the chorus of critics that had attacked Roberts in the 1930s, persuaded him to set the record straight about the minimum-wage cases. Roberts entrusted the memo to Frankfurter, who kept it under lock and key for the next decade and published it in 1955 (see FF, "Mr. Justice Roberts," 312, 317). Michael Ariens has charged that Frankfurter, for complex reasons having less to do with defending Roberts than with defending the Court at the time of *Brown v. Board of Education*, forged the Roberts memo after Roberts's death. The claim has been authoritatively debunked by Richard D. Friedman. See Ariens, "A Thrice-Told Tale," 620–76; and Friedman, "A Reaffirmation," 1985–95.

413 **In its *Tipaldo* petition:** Chambers, "The Big Switch," 64–65fn; Kaufman, *Cardozo*, 692fn; Freedman, *Roosevelt and Frankfurter*, 392–93; FF, "Mr. Justice Roberts," 315. Roberts has his facts slightly wrong (see Friedman, "Switching Time," 1949), but his line of argument is clear. According to Paul Freund, Roberts's irritation with New York's "disingenuous" approach—and its effect on his decision—was "entirely in keeping with Roberts's character, which led him to react violently against what he thought was intellectual slipperiness and sometimes to decide cases on a seemingly impressionistic, ad hoc basis" (Freund, "Charles Evans Hughes as Chief Justice," 30).

413 **"If counsel for the parties":** Griswold, "Owen J. Roberts as a Judge," 341.

414 **"I know of no rule":** 298 U.S. 587, at 636. As traditionally applied, the rule helps ensure that both the Court and the parties in a case have adequate notice of the legal issues at stake. To suggest—as both the majority opinion in *Tipaldo* and, later, the Roberts memo did—that this rule denied the Court the ability to consider the soundness of *Adkins* was,

as Frankfurter put it, a "self-created disability" (FF and Adrian S. Fisher. "The Business of the Supreme Court," 634, 634fn; FF to Stone, Mar. 30, 1937, Stone Papers, Box 13, LOC). The majority had to know—indeed, the sweep of their opinion made clear—that the legal issue in this case was not merely whether the New York and D.C. statutes could be distinguished, but the more fundamental question of whether a state minimum-wage law so restricted the liberty of contract that it violated the constitutional guarantee of due process. This implicated *Adkins* directly and, one would think, inescapably.

414 **Moreover, Roberts's recollections were wrong:** Chambers, "The Big Switch," 56, 65–66; FF and Fisher, "The Business of the Supreme Court," 634fn; Leonard, *A Search for a Judicial Philosophy*, 91. In October 1936, when Roberts voted in conference to hear the *Parrish* case, neither Washington State's nor the chambermaid's lawyers had, as Roberts later claimed, "assailed" *Adkins*; neither, in fact, had so much as submitted a statement to the Court. (The appeal, rather, had come from Elsie Parrish's employer.) And when Washington State finally filed its brief, it asked the justices to distinguish the statutes—making the same "disingenuous" argument that Roberts insisted had driven him, in *Tipaldo*, into the company of the conservatives. See Friedman, "Switching Time," 1951.

414 **"My proper course":** FF, "Mr. Justice Roberts," 315. Roberts's failure to concur in the result or "on narrow ground" may have had something to do with his discomfort with standing alone: during his eleven years on the Hughes Court, he never once wrote a separate, concurring opinion. See Friedman, "Switching Time," 1944–46.

414 **The timing of the Court's reversal:** FF, "Mr. Justice Roberts," 315.

415 **Hughes withheld his announcement:** Ibid.; Danelski and Tulchin, eds., *Autobiographical Notes*, 311–13. The justices' work on the Wagner Act decisions may also have contributed to the delay (Irons, *A People's History*, 324).

415 **But even though the *Parrish* decision:** Danelski and Tulchin, eds., *Autobiographical Notes*, 311–13. The range of external pressures on the Court are outlined by Leuchtenburg in "Comment on Laura Kalman's Article," 1089–91.

415 **"Few speculations . . . are more treacherous":** FF quote is in FF, "Mr. Justice Roberts," 317; Pusey, "Justice Roberts' 1937 Turnaround," 106; Pusey, *Charles Evans Hughes*, Vol. II, 757.

CHAPTER TWENTY-THREE: BLOOD OR INK

416 **Carter Glass was helped from his sickbed:** *CDT*, Mar. 30, 1937; *WP*, Mar. 30, 31, 1937; Glass radio address, Mar. 29, 1937, 2, copy in TGC Papers, Box 271, LOC.

417 **On April 1, at lunch:** Farley, *Jim Farley's Story*, 79; Farley Diary, Apr. 1, 1937, Farley Papers, Box 41, LOC.

417 **That same day, FDR sent a message:** *NYT*, Apr. 2, 1937.

417 **"The opposition is putting on a great show":** Farley to Bowers, Apr. 8, 1937, Farley Papers, Box 5, LOC; *WP*, Mar. 28, 1937, B4; TGC to Robert Cushman, May 14, 1937, TGC Papers, Box 269, LOC; *Time*, Apr. 12, 1937.

418 **Typical testimony:** William Alfred Eddy in *Reorganization of the Federal Judiciary*, Part 6, 1665–66.

418 **"an admirer and a friend":** Burlingham in *Reorganization of the Federal Judiciary*, Part 5, 1044.

418 **"The modern coup d'état":** Dorothy Thompson in *Reorganization of the Federal Judiciary*, Part 4, 864; Dodds in ibid., Part 3, 619–20; *NYT*, Mar. 25, 1937.

418 **Across the country, despite the economic recovery:** *Time*, Apr. 12, 1937; *Reorganization of the Federal Judiciary*, Part 3, 591.

419 **William McDowell . . . provided senators:** McDowell in *Reorganization of the Federal Judiciary*, Part 4, 994–95; *NYT*, Mar. 24, 1937; *WP*, Mar. 24, 1937.

419 **the hearings were heavy with portents:** Siegfried F. Hartman in *Reorganization of the Fed-*

eral Judiciary, Part 5, 1201–2; Griswold quoted in *Time*, Apr. 12, 1937; *Dallas Morning News*, Apr. 25, 1937.

420 **Still, there were lighter moments:** L. L. James in *Reorganization of the Federal Judiciary*, Part 5, 1363, 1366; Burlingham in ibid., 1061; Senators Burke and King during the testimony of Cathrine Curtis in ibid., Part 6, 1789–90.

420 **On the whole, the hearings:** TGC to Corwin, Apr. 7, 1937, TGC Papers, Box 269, LOC.

420 **"steady barrages of oratory":** Alsop and Catledge, *168 Days*, 106–7.

421 **Corcoran . . . still talked big about "breaking":** TGC to Leon Green, Apr. 10, 1937, TGC Papers, Box 269, LOC; McKean, *Tommy the Cork*, 92; TGC interview, Mar. 31, 1980, TGC Papers, Box 595, LOC; *WP*, Mar. 28, 31, 1937; *NYT*, Apr. 7, 1937.

421 **"we are carrying out":** FDR to FF, Apr. 5, 1937, PSF 135, FDRL.

421 **"Nine men will decide":** Ernst, *Ultimate Power*, 291.

421 **to rest on the fate of the National Labor Relations Act:** Robert Wagner to HSC, Jan. 1937, OF 10, DOJ, Box 4, FDRL; Irons, *New Deal Lawyers*, 226–33; Lash, *Dealers and Dreamers*, 428; HSC Diary, June 20, 1935, 82–83, UVA.

422 **Though Senator Wagner and the bill's drafters:** M. S. Huberman to Judge Stephens, June 4, 1935, McFarland Papers, Box 1, UVA; Irons, *New Deal Lawyers*, 229–32.

422 **To liberals, this seemed obvious:** Turning the doctrine of substantive due process on its head, the Wagner Act's drafters also argued that the "inequality of bargaining power" between management and labor impaired workers' liberty of contract—and that this, too, impeded interstate commerce. Irons, *New Deal Lawyers*, 230. Preamble quoted in Irons, *A People's History*, 319; Charles Horsky quoted in Louchheim, *The Making of the New Deal*, 85.

422 **The NLRB's lawyers knew:** "The Wagner Decisions," *The Nation*, Apr. 17, 1937; on the Liberty League lawyers' committee ruling, see Chapter 10, p. 164; Irons, *New Deal Lawyers*, 242–43; Lash, *Dealers and Dreamers*, 430; Irons, *A People's History*, 320–21.

423 **"the matter now rests":** HSC to FDR, Feb. 11, 1937, OF 41A, Box 49, FDRL.

423 **"The sit-down . . . has reached":** "The Sitdown Hysteria," *The Nation*, Apr. 3, 1937; *WSJ*, Mar. 31, 1937; *Time*, Apr. 12, 1937.

424 **"This is a case . . . where the president":** Shogan, *Backlash*, 181–83 (Johnson quoted at 182), 239.

424 **These were assertions:** *NYT*, Apr. 4, 1937; *Time*, Apr. 12, 19, 1937.

424 **Unions generally . . . were making:** K. A. McRae to James Roosevelt, Feb. 25, 1937, TGC Papers, Box 638, LOC; Daniel J. Tobin to James Roosevelt, Mar. 1, 1937, McJimsey, *Documentary History*, Vol. 1, 259.

425 **"to rise and support":** Alsop and Catledge, *168 Days*, 164–74; Shogan, *Backlash*, 211; Address by George L. Berry, Mar. 8, 1937, in McJimsey, *Documentary History*, Vol. 1, 303.

425 **leaders of the warring factions:** Alsop and Catledge, *168 Days*.

425 **Administration spokesmen . . . tried to draw labor:** *NYT*, Mar. 25, 1937; Jackson, Address at Carnegie Hall, Mar. 24, 1937, TGC Papers, Box 220, LOC; Lewis E. Myers, "Report on Organization and Activities," Apr. 13, 1937, TGC Papers, Box 269, LOC; *CDT*, Apr. 11, 1937; Radio Address by Harold L. Ickes, Apr. 10, 1937, 1–2, in TGC Papers, Box 220, LOC.

426 **The implicit invitation:** By the time Labor's Non-Partisan League got around to holding mass meetings—in twenty-six cities on a single day—it was April 19, 1937, one week after the Court upheld the National Labor Relations Act. Beyond attacking Roberts for inconsistency, senators who spoke at the rallies seemed at a loss for words. "Even the Supreme Court is beginning to see the light," Joseph Guffey had to concede. Newspapers virtually ignored these non-events ("Supreme Court Calendar of Labor's Non-Partisan League," Apr. 1, 1937, in Clapper Papers, Box 232, LOC; *NYT*, Apr. 19, 20, 1937).

426 **"How is your Court fight coming along?":** HSC Diary, Apr. 8, 1937, 36, UVA.

426 **If there was an edge:** *Reorganization of the Federal Judiciary*, Part 5, 1045; *Baltimore Sun*, Mar. 28, 1937, attached to HSC to FDR, Apr. 3, 1937, PSF 165, FDRL.

427 **at the Gridiron Dinner on April 10:** Clapper Papers, Box 29, LOC; Pearson and Allen, *Nine Old Men at the Crossroads*, 22–23.

427 **"a long and very intimate conversation":** HSC Diary, Apr. 10, 1937, 40–42, UVA.

428 **Late in the evening:** Clapper Papers, Box 29, LOC; Pearson and Allen, *Nine Old Men at the Crossroads*, 22–23; Brayman, *The President Speaks*, 308.

428 **"My dearest and my gallant":** Antoinette Carter Hughes to C. E. Hughes, Apr. 11, 1937, Hughes Papers, Reel 5, LOC.

428 **"the only calendar":** C. E. Hughes to Samuel Winslow, Apr. 13, 1937, Hughes Papers, Reel 5, LOC.

CHAPTER TWENTY-FOUR: THE SWITCH IN TIME

429 ***Associated Press v. National Labor Relations Board:*** *WP*, Apr. 13, 1937; *Time*, Apr. 19, 1937. *Associated Press v. N.L.R.B*, 301 U.S. 103 (1937); *Washington, Maryland & Virginia Coach Co. v. N.L.R.B.*, 301 U.S. 142 (1937).

430 **"an overtone of infallibility":** Alsop and Catledge, *168 Days*, 146.

430 **as if "the law had always been":** NLRB lawyer, Tom Emerson, quoted in Irons, *A People's History*, 322; Kaufman, *Cardozo*, 526; *N.L.R.B. v. Jones & Laughlin Steel Corp.*, 301 U.S. 1 (1937): 33, 37, 40–42; Pusey, *Hughes*, Vol. 2, 759.

431 **"We are asked to shut our eyes":** 301 U.S. 1: 41–42.

431 **"as if [he] had been through hell":** Clapper Diary, Apr. 12, 1937, Clapper Papers, Box 8, LOC; HSC Diary, Apr. 9, 1937, 39, UVA.

431 **"rather ominously silent":** Wyzanski quoted in Lash, *Dealers and Dreamers*, 431. Wyzanski, among New Deal lawyers the great hero of the Wagner cases, was so appalled by the Court plan that he had nearly resigned in February when FDR announced it (Louchheim, *The Making of the New Deal*, 87).

431 **the two men had traveled different roads:** Hendel, *Charles Evans Hughes and the Supreme Court*, 48, 61–62, 237, 241–42, 244, 265; Danelski and Tulchin, eds., *Autobiographical Notes*, 312–13; Friedman, "Switching Time," 1962–65; Cushman, *Rethinking the New Deal Court*, 168–69.

432 **Roberts, by contrast:** Friedman, "Switching Time," 1967–70; Robert L. Stern, "The Court-Packing Plan and the Commerce Clause," *Supreme Court Historical Society Yearbook* (1988); Leonard, *A Search for a Judicial Philosophy*, 137–39; Griswold, "Owen J. Roberts as a Judge," 345, 348.

432 **Roberts had joined the liberals before:** Knox, *The Forgotten Memoir of John Knox*, 189–91.

432 **Sutherland's dissent in the AP case:** *Associated Press v. N.L.R.B.*, 301 U.S. 103 (1937): 141.

433 **Sutherland's "homily":** HSC Diary, Apr. 12, 1937, 43, UVA.

433 **McReynolds's dissent:** Irons, *New Deal Lawyers*, 288; Knox, *The Forgotten Memoir of John Knox*, 212–15; *WP*, Apr. 13, 1937; *CDT*, Apr. 13, 1937; McKenna, *Franklin Roosevelt and the Great Constitutional War*, 429.

433 **He spoke calmly:** HSC Diary, Apr. 12, 1937, 44, UVA.

433 **If one followed the majority's reasoning:** *WP*, Apr. 13, 1937; *CDT*, Apr. 13, 1937.

433 **"I think . . . he has saved":** *WP*, Apr. 13, 1937.

433 **FDR "in fine humor":** Alsop and Catledge, *168 Days*, 153, depict FDR as having "an old-fashioned fit of temper," but all evidence suggests the opposite. HSC Diary, Apr. 12, 1937, 44, UVA; Farley Diary, Apr. 12, 1937, Farley Papers, Box 41, LOC.

434 **"Nothing short of a miracle":** "The Wagner Decisions," *The Nation*, Apr. 17, 1937, 423–24; Paul L. Murphy, *The Constitution in Crisis Times*, 158; *WP*, Apr. 13, 1937.

434 **"these decisions":** Clapper Diary, Apr. 12, 1937, LOC; Cushman, *Rethinking the New*

Deal Court, 175; Friedman, "Switching Time," 1982; Cardozo quoted in Kaufman, *Cardozo*, 526.

434 **In a quip that made the rounds:** The origin of the phrase—"a switch in time saved nine"—remains unclear. The first recorded use appears to be a May 19, 1937, letter from Corwin to Cummings, in which the professor asked whether the attorney general had heard the witticism. Cummings had not. Abe Fortas—then a Yale Law School professor, later a Supreme Court justice—is sometimes credited with the coinage, but it was not until June 1937 that he told a group of labor representatives that "Mr. Justice Roberts's theory must be a switch in time serves nine." Also in June, Donald Richberg told Ray Clapper that he had first heard the phrase "in February at the White House," intimating that FDR had said it—though of course, at that point, no justice had switched. (Corwin to HSC, May 19, 1937, and HSC to Corwin, May 24, 1937, HSC Papers, Box 88, UVA; *NYT*, June 15, 1937; Clapper Diary, June 1937, Clapper Papers, Box 8, LOC.)

434 **"R[oosevelt] proposal forced this change":** Clapper Diary, Apr. 12, 1937, Clapper Papers, Box 8, LOC; Ernst to FDR, Apr. 13, 1937, TGC Papers, Box 197, LOC; *The New Republic*, Apr. 28, 1937; *The Nation*, Apr. 17, 24, 1937.

434 **"This would not have happened":** Hiram W. Johnson to Hiram W. Johnson, Jr., Apr. 16, 1937, in Burke, *Diary Letters*.

434 **"rather adroit piece of work":** HSC Diary, Apr. 12, 1937, 43, UVA.

435 **"After today . . . I feel like":** HSC Diary, Apr. 12, 1937, 43, UVA; FF to FDR, Apr. 12, 1937, PSF 135, FDRL.

435 **"The Court bill is dead":** *WP*, Apr. 13, 15, 1937.

435 **The moment was ripe:** *WSJ*, Apr. 2, 1937.

435 **Robinson summoned Joseph Keenan:** Alsop and Catledge, *168 Days*, 152–53.

436 **Roosevelt, who was hearing similar advice:** Clapper Diary, Apr. 12, 1937, LOC; Leuchtenburg, "Nine Justices Respond," 60; Corwin to HSC, Apr. 9, 10, 1937, HSC Papers, Box 88, UVA; Brant to Stone, Apr. 15, 1937, Stone Papers, Box 7, LOC.

436 **But those who counseled compromise:** Borah to J. T. Adams, May 22, 1937, Borah Papers, Box 484, LOC; Burke to J. G. Phelps Stokes, May 14, 1937, Hobson Papers, Box 54, LOC; Pearson, "The President-Elect," 263; Farley Diary, Apr. 12, 1937, LOC; HSC Diary, Apr. 12, 1937, UVA.

436 **At a press conference the next day:** Press Conference #360, Apr. 13, 1937, in FDR, *Complete Presidential Press Conferences*, Vol. 9, 259–62. Press Conference #360-A, Apr. 15, 1937, in ibid., 271; "After the Wagner Act," n.d., Cohen Papers, Box 14, "Supreme Court—BVC's Drafts"; "After the Wagner Act," n.d., TGC Papers, Box 270, LOC; Jackson OH, 450–51.

438 **Analyses by Justice Department lawyers:** Holtzoff to HSC, May 12, 1937, HSC Papers, Box 121, UVA; W. L. Pope memorandum, Apr. 19, 1937, HSC Papers, Box 195, UVA; Cushman, *Rethinking the New Deal Court*, 175, 177, 179–80; Friedman, "Switching Time," 1982; Press Conference #360, Apr. 13, 1937, in FDR, *Complete Presidential Press Conferences*, Vol. 9, 263.

438 **"Our national destiny":** *The Nation*, Apr. 24, 1937; *WP*, Apr. 13, 1937.

438 **"a reactionary court":** HSC Diary, Apr. 12, 1937, UVA; Swisher, *Selected Papers of Homer Cummings*, 159.

439 **At a press conference on April 16:** Press Conference #361, Apr. 16, 1937, in FDR, *Complete Presidential Press Conferences*, Vol. 9, 319–20; *Time*, Apr. 26, 1937; Ickes, Apr. 25 and May 2, 1937, *Secret Diary*, Vol. II, 125–26;

439 **"I flew out . . . on wings":** FF to FDR, Apr. 21, 1937, in Freedman, *Roosevelt and Frankfurter*, 398.

439 **On April 28, Roosevelt sped:** *NYT*, Apr. 29, May 1, 2, 1937.

439 **His yield was poor:** *NYT*, May 10, 11, 1937; Caro, *The Path to Power*, 446.

439 **One of them was the congressman-elect:** Caro, *The Path to Power*, 395–96.

440 **Johnson came out swinging:** Dallek, *Lone Star Rising*, 148, 150; *Reorganization of the Federal Judiciary*, Part 6, 1561; Caro, *The Path to Power*, 417, 436, 445; *Dallas Morning News*, Mar. 1, Apr. 5, 9, 1937; Thomas B. Love to FDR, Apr. 11, 1937, OF 41, Box 48, FDRL.

440 **Roosevelt got the message:** Dallek, *Lone Star Rising*, 150.

440 **"elated by this victory":** TGC interview, July 10, 1980, TGC Papers, Box 596, LOC; Gallup, *The Gallup Poll*, 55, 57 (these polls have been subject to widely varying interpretations. See Cantwell, "Public Opinion," 929–30, and, by contrast, Caldeira, "Public Opinion," 1148–49); Caro, *The Path to Power*, 446.

441 **Johnson's first reward:** Caro, *The Path to Power*, 446–49; TGC interview, July 10, 1980, TGC Papers, Box 596, LOC.

441 **Johnson's election was soon transformed:** Caro, *The Path to Power*, 448, 546; *Reorganization of the Federal Judiciary*, Part 6, 1561; TGC interview, July 10, 1980, TGC Papers, Box 596, LOC. Back in Washington, in the Senate hearings, witnesses made competing claims about the meaning of Johnson's victory. An Austin attorney testified on April 12 that the vote had nothing at all to do with the Court. Four days later, Tom Miller, the mayor of Austin, appeared at LBJ's insistence to refute that idea, displaying, as proof, local newspaper headlines and multiple statements LBJ had made about the Court during the campaign. Connally wrapped up the session by saying that irrespective of the Court issue, "so far as Lyndon Johnson is personally concerned, he is a very admirable young man with a very attractive personality. . . . I am sure he will make a very admirable congressman." (*Reorganization of the Federal Judiciary*, Part 6, 1545, 1559–63, 1568, 1570.)

441 **Corcoran was back in Washington:** Ickes, Apr. 25, 1937, *Secret Diary*, Vol. II, 125–26; Alsop and Catledge, *168 Days*, 201–3.

442 **"There is a good deal of defeatist":** HSC Diary, May 4, 1937, 58–59, UVA; Alsop and Catledge, *168 Days*, 203–4.

442 **FDR called reporters into his dining car:** *NYT*, May 14, 1937.

442 **Jim Farley joined the traveling party:** Ibid.; Press Conference # 366, May 13, 1937, in FDR, *Complete Presidential Press Conferences*, Vol. 9, 363; Ickes, May 15, 1937, *Secret Diary*, Vol. II, 141–42. Farley, after his eventual break with Roosevelt, described these events quite differently than when he relayed them to Ickes a day or two after the fact. In his memoir *Jim Farley's Story* (1948), he writes that he warned FDR against further dividing the Democratic Party, and that FDR made a thinly veiled reference to running for a third term (82). Ickes's contemporaneous account is more credible.

443 **the president promptly summoned Robinson:** *NYT*, May 15, 18, 1937; Alsop and Catledge, *168 Days*, 204–5; FDR to Paul V. McNutt, May 17, 1937, in Elliott Roosevelt, ed., *F.D.R.: His Personal Letters, 1928–1945*, Vol. I, 679–80.

443 **but he did not seem to be bluffing now:** *NYT*, May 18, 1937; Alsop and Catledge, *168 Days*; *Time*, May 24, 1937; *NYT*, May 15, 1937.

CHAPTER TWENTY-FIVE: CONSENT

444 **"There was only one story":** *NYT*, May 23, 1937.

444 **WATCH FOR COURT RETIREMENTS:** *NYT*, May 16, 1937; *The New Republic*, Apr. 28, May 19, 1937.

445 **"Brandeis is going to resign":** Keenan to McIntyre, Apr. 19, 1937, OF 41, Box 48, Folder 2, FDRL. The former senator was Smith W. Brookhart, a progressive Republican from Iowa.

445 **Many conservatives, too, were alarmed:** Mary P. Welker to WVD, Apr. 18, 1936, Helen and William H. Ford to WVD, Jan. 17, 1936, Mason B. Starring, Jr., to WVD, Apr. 18, 1936, Edward H. Ellis to WVD, Mar. 12, 1937, Rachel Van Devanter to WVD, Mar. 6, 1937, and D. Walter Bell to WVD, Feb. 12, 1937, all in WVD Papers, Box 38, LOC; Martha

Young et al. to Sutherland, Mar. 1937, Sutherland Papers, Box 6, LOC; Bertha Harwood-Arrowood to Stone, Mar. 5, 1937, Stone Papers, Box 80, LOC; McReynolds to Mrs. Walter A. Watson, Mar. 13, 1937, Knox Letters, University of Chicago.

446 **"What I really wanted to see you about":** *NYT*, May 19, 23, 1937; *CDT*, May 19, 1937; WVD to FDR, May 18, 1937, WVD Papers, Box 44, LOC; *Time*, May 31, 1937.

446 **"My dear Mr. Justice Van Devanter":** FDR to WVD, May 18, 1937, WVD Papers, Box 44, LOC.

446 **The members of the Judiciary Committee:** *Time*, May 31, 1937; *NYT*, May 19, 1937.

446 **The timing of these two developments:** *NYT*, May 20, 1937; Childs OH, 65, 67–69; Alsop and Catledge, *168 Days*, 206; Pusey, *Charles Evans Hughes*, Vol. II, 761; Borah to A. A. Lewis, Aug. 11, 1937, Borah Papers, Box 484, LOC.

447 **"You have done a most courageous thing":** Sumners to WVD, May 19, 1937, WVD Papers, Box 44, LOC.

447 **"perhaps fortunate":** Hiram W. Johnson to Hiram W. Johnson, Jr., May 21, 1937, in Burke, *Diary Letters*.

447 **Van Devanter himself confessed:** WVD to A. C. Whidden, June 10, 1937, and to Clara B. Fleming, June 5, 1937, WVD Papers, Box 20, LOC; WVD to Thomas Doran, May 10, 1937, Box 19, LOC.

447 **A cartoon in *The Washington Post*:** *WP* cartoon appears in *NYT*, May 23, 1937; *NYT*, May 19, 20, 1937.

448 **"Mr. Roosevelt is 'on the spot' ":** *Boston Transcript* quoted in *WP*, May 23, 1937.

448 **"to kid him about":** Farley Diary, May 18, 1937, Farley Papers, Box 41, LOC.

448 **"I don't think there is any news":** Press Conference #367, May 18, 1937, in FDR, *Complete Presidential Press Conferences*, Vol. 9, 375, 377.

448 **Roosevelt wasn't fooling anyone:** *NYT*, May 19, 1937; Alsop and Catledge, *168 Days*, 156–57, 209–10.

448 **Within hours of Van Devanter's announcement:** Alsop and Catledge, *168 Days*, 210–11; Farley Diary, May 18, 1937, LOC; *NYT*, May 23, 1937; *Time*, May 31, 1937; Clapper Diary, May 20, 1937, Clapper Papers, Box 8, LOC.

448 **A promise, of course, had been made:** Ickes, May 22, 1937, *Secret Diary*, Vol. II, 144–45; *NYT*, May 20, 1937; Lash, *Dealers and Dreamers*, 304; Weller, *Joe T. Robinson*, xii–xiii; Bertram Benedict, "The Pre-New Deal Record of Senator Robinson," Editorial Research Reports, May 20, 1937, in Clapper Papers, Box 209, LOC; *Time*, May 31, 1937.

449 **"Robinson Will Not Do!":** *The Nation*, May 29, 1937, 607–8; Cook, *Eleanor Roosevelt*, 460, 636fn; A. Philip Randolph et al. to FDR, June 19, 1937, in Clapper Papers, Box 209, LOC.

450 **"For the last two years":** Brant to TGC, June 12, 1937, TGC Papers, Box 190, LOC.

450 **Roosevelt had begun looking:** Archibald R. Watson to FDR, Mar. 10, 1937, TGC Papers, Box 269, LOC; *NYT*, May 20, 1937; HSC Diary, May 21, 1937, 60–61, UVA.

450 **Roosevelt was in a terrible bind:** *Time*, May 31, 1937; *CDT*, May 21, 1937; Baker, *Back to Back*, 250.

450 **The situation was replete with ironies:** Childs, "'I've Got This Thing Simplified,'" *American Heritage*, Apr. 1957, Vol. 8, No. 3; Alsop and Catledge, *168 Days*, 211–12.

451 **"Do you intend to confirm":** Press Conference # 368, May 21, 1937, in FDR, *Complete Presidential Press Conferences*, Vol. 9, 380.

451 **Robinson made no secret:** Farley, *Behind the Ballots*, 332; Farley, *Jim Farley's Story*, 86; Farley Diary, July 18, 1937, Farley Papers, Box 41, LOC; Alsop and Catledge, *168 Days*, 213.

451 **Presidential aides scrambled to determine:** Alsop and Catledge, *168 Days*; Michelson, *The Ghost Talks*, 172–73, 175–76, 182–83; Farley, *Jim Farley's Story*, 80; Tugwell, *Democratic Roosevelt*, 404; Burns, *Roosevelt: The Lion and the Fox*, 300–301; Farley Diary, Apr. 1, 1937, Farley Papers, Box 41, LOC.

452 **FDR "never actually took charge":** TGC interview, Aug. 11, 1980, TGC Papers, Box 595, LOC.

452 **"the whole thing had been badly handled":** Clapper Diary, Apr. 28 and May 20, 1937, Clapper Papers, Box 8, LOC.

452 **Even Farley . . . had swaggered:** *NYT*, May 15, 1937; Farley Diary, May 20, 1937, LOC. The public, in mid-May, strongly opposed the idea of a two-judge compromise; it was perhaps the one thing on which both sides could agree (Gallup, *The Gallup Poll*, 59).

453 **Farley felt the brunt:** Scroop, *Mr. Democrat*, 13, 134; Pearson and Allen, "The President's Trigger Man," 385–86, 388.

453 **On May 24, in a trio of decisions:** Jackson, *Struggle*, 229; Leuchtenburg, "Charles Evans Hughes," 1201.

453 **"I was arguing to a one-man court":** Clapper Diary, May 6, 1937, LOC; *St. Louis Star-Times*, n.d., in Stone Papers, Box 7, LOC.

453 **Apparently, the strategy worked brilliantly:** *Steward Machine Co. v. Davis*, 301 U.S. 548 (1937); *Helvering v. Davis*, 301 U.S. 619 (1937); Friedman, "Switching Time," 1956; Kaufman, *Cardozo*, 527; Jackson, *Struggle*, 234; *NYT*, May 25, 1937.

454 **"went out of [his] way to salve":** Clapper Diary, May 24, 1937, LOC.

454 **It was a fitting end to a term:** *Time*, June 7, 1937; *WP*, May 25, 1937; *NYT*, May 26, 1937; Stone to Sterling Carr, June 2, 1937, Stone Papers, Box 8, LOC. Three weeks after the Wagner decisions, the Court showed its increasing solicitude for presidential power in the realm of foreign affairs, upholding FDR's right to award diplomatic recognition to the Soviet Union in 1933 (Ross, *The Chief Justiceship of Charles Evans Hughes*, 127).

454 **"one of the most exciting ones":** Stone to Lauson and Marshall Stone, Apr. 29, 1937, Stone Papers, Box 3, LOC. On June 1, 1937, the last day of the term, Stone paid a visit to Homer Cummings's conference room at the Department of Justice to view a mural by his friend Leon Kroll. The painter had spent all of 1936 at work on two massive panels representing the defeat and triumph of justice. In February 1936, his sketch of "The Triumph of Justice," already approved by the attorney general, got around Washington; all could see that the image of a black-gowned judge leading people out of the misery of a factory to the promised land was obviously Stone. On viewing it, Stone declared that he quite liked the painting (*Time*, Oct. 26, 1936; *NYT*, Feb. 25, 1936, June 2, 1937).

455 **"I have not much faith":** Stone to FF, May 20, 28, 1937, Stone Papers, Box 13, LOC.

455 **felt "pretty low":** FF to Stone, May 25, June 2, 1937, Stone Papers, Box 13, LOC; *NYT*, May 7, 1937.

455 **Frankfurter overstated the case:** "The Wagner Decisions," *The Nation*, Apr. 17, 1937, 423–24; Robert S. Allen, "Hughes Checkmates the President," *The Nation*, May 29, 1937.

456 **"I think more than ever":** Brant to FDR, June 12, 1937, TGC Papers, Box 190; Brant, "How Liberal Is Justice Hughes?" *The New Republic*, July 21, 1937, 295–98, and July 28, 1937, 329–32; Ickes, May 22, 1937, *Secret Diary*, Vol. II, 145.

456 **"That is just what I expected":** Clapper Diary, May 24, 1937, LOC.

456 **At a press conference the following afternoon:** Press Conference, #369, May 25, 1937, in FDR, *Complete Presidential Press Conferences*, Vol. 9, 391–92; *PPA*, 1937, 220.

456 **In drafting the bill:** *WP*, May 25, 1937; HSC Diary, Apr. 15, 1937, 46, and Aug. 1, 1937, 118, UVA; Hall, *The Oxford Companion to the Supreme Court,* 359–60; *PPA*, 1937, 210–14.

456 **"is filling the Congress":** Hiram W. Johnson to Hiram W. Johnson, Jr., May 29, 1937, in Burke, *Diary Letters*.

457 **Yet here again, he miscalculated:** *CDT*, May 28, 1937; *WP*, May 27, 1937.

457 **"To ask them simultaneously":** *The New Republic*, May 19, 1937, 44.

457 **an "era of ill-feeling":** *NYT*, May 2, 1937; "Will the Democrats Divide?" *The New Republic*, May 26, 1937, 60–61; *NYT*, June 6, 1937; *NYT*, Mar. 14, 1937.

458 **"Apparently . . . he would rather":** Clapper Diary, May 25, 1937, LOC.

458 **It had been an astonishing . . . period:** Clapper Diary, June 4, 1937, LOC; Caldeira, "Public Opinion," 1148; Cantwell, "Public Opinion," 930–31; *Time*, May 31, 1937; Alsop and Catledge, *168 Days*, 214.
459 **"I pointed out to him":** Jackson, *That Man*, 53; "Possible Statement in Anticipation of Winning Social Security Decision," n.d., McJimsey, *Documentary History*, Vol. 1, 563–65.
459 **Roosevelt leaned against shelving the plan:** Alsop and Catledge, *168 Days*, 214.
459 **"If you're going to pack a Court":** TGC to James Rowe et al., May 6, 1937, TGC Papers, Box 270, LOC.
460 **A few hours later at the White House:** Alsop and Catledge, *168 Days*, 214–16; Ickes, June 17, 1937, *Secret Diary*, Vol. II, 153.
460 **On his way out, the senator encountered a group:** *NYT*, June 4, 6, 1937.

CHAPTER TWENTY-SIX: STRIKING A BLOW FOR LIBERTY

461 **"Tell us about your conversation":** Press Conference #371, June 4, 1937, in FDR, *Complete Presidential Press Conferences*, Vol. 9, 407–12; *Time*, June 14, 1937.
462 **Joe Robinson, having emerged from purgatory:** *Time*, June 14, 1937; *NYT*, June 6, 1937; Alsop and Catledge, *168 Days*, 222.
462 **Two compromise measures:** Alsop and Catledge, *168 Days*, 223; HSC Diary, June 18, 1937, 68, UVA. For reasons he failed to specify, FDR told Robinson the Andrews plan was "clearly unconstitutional" (FDR to Robinson, June 11, 1937, OF 41A, Box 49, FDRL).
462 **Roosevelt was inclined toward a second alternative:** Alsop and Catledge, *168 Days*, 223; *NYT*, June 5, 1937; HSC Diary, June 18, 1937, 68, UVA.
463 **Robinson asked Logan:** Alsop and Catledge, *168 Days*, 223–24, 227; HSC Diary, June 8, 17, 1937, 65, 67, UVA.
463 **It was on onerous task:** Alsop and Catledge, *168 Days*, 226; *NYT*, June 5, 27, 1937.
464 **Compromise . . . had appealed to both sides:** Cantril, ed., *Public Opinion*, 150, 388; *The New Republic*, June 16, 1937, 156–57; *NYT*, June 5, 1937.
464 **There was . . . a nervousness:** Alsop and Catledge, *168 Days*, 227–28, 240–41.
464 **On June 11, after a cabinet meeting:** *NYT*, June 13, 1937, and Nov. 8, 1967; Schlesinger, *Crisis of the Old Order*, 227–28; *The Nation*, Mar. 2, 1940, 299–301; Childs, *Witness*, 17–18; Milburn, "The Statesmanship of Mr. Garner," 669–70, 674; *NYT*, Jan. 22, 1937; Alsop and Catledge, *168 Days*, 129; Alsop and Catledge, "Joe Robinson, the New Deal's Old Reliable," *Saturday Evening Post*, Sept. 26, 1936, 6; *NYT*, Nov. 8, 1967; *Time*, June 21, 1937; *NYT*, June 19, 1937; HSC Diary, June 11, 1937, 65, UVA; *WSJ*, June 15, 1937.
466 **The huff . . . had only partly to do with the Court plan:** Farley Diary, Mar. 7, 1937, LOC; Ickes, May 15, 1937, *Secret Diary*, Vol. II, 140; Alsop and Catledge, *168 Days*, 236–37; Garner to Farley, July 1, 1937, Farley Papers, Box 5, LOC; Schlesinger, *Crisis of the Old Order*, 228. Roosevelt, for his part, thought it impossible for a man of Garner's generation or background to comprehend the social and economic challenges facing the country (Ickes, July 21, 1937, *Secret Diary*, Vol. II, 166).
466 **By the spring of 1937:** Pearson and Allen, *Nine Old Men at the Crossroads*, 42–43; Alsop and Catledge, *168 Days*, 130–32; Ickes Diary, Apr. 3, May 15, 22, 1937, *Secret Diary*, Vol. II, 108, 140–41, 143–44.
467 **"He selected the right psychological":** *The Nation*, June 26, 1937, 722–23; Clapper Diary, June 15, 1937, Clapper Papers, Box 8, LOC.
467 **On June 13, Garner got in his . . . car:** McKenna, *Franklin Roosevelt and the Great Constitutional War*, 480–81. The ten signatories of the report included three Republicans (Borah, Warren R. Austin of Vermont, and Frederick Steiwer of Oregon) and seven Democrats (Edward R. Burke of Nebraska, Tom Connally of Texas, Carl A. Hatch of New

Mexico, Patrick McCarran of Nevada, William H. King of Utah, Joseph C. O'Mahoney of Wyoming, and Frederick Van Nuys of Indiana). *Adverse Report of the Committee on the Judiciary*, 1.

467 **McCarran and Joseph O'Mahoney:** McKenna, *Franklin Roosevelt and the Great Constitutional War*, 481; Alsop and Catledge, *168 Days*, 229–30; Catledge to Alsop, Nov. 9, 1937, Alsop Papers, Box 2, LOC.

467 **The Court bill, they declared:** *Adverse Report of the Committee on the Judiciary*, 9–10, 16, 19, 21, 27, 44, 45–46; *WSJ*, May 27, 1937.

469 **"Bitter document":** Clapper Diary, June 14, 1937, LOC; Ickes, June 17, 1937, *Secret Diary*, Vol. II, 152.

469 **Liberal journals . . . launched a counterattack:** *The New Republic*, June 23, 1937, 169–70; *The Nation*, June 19, 1937, 689.

469 **The GOP, of course, was beside itself:** Wolfskill, *The Revolt of the Conservatives*, 252–53; *NYT*, June 16, 1937; Williamson, *Frank Gannett: A Biography*, 194; *CDT*, June 16, 1937; Leuchtenburg, "FDR's Court-Packing Plan," 676–77.

470 **At the very least:** Tugwell, *Democratic Roosevelt*, 406; Alsop and Catledge, *168 Days*, 234–35; Press Conference #374, June 15, 1937, in FDR, *Complete Presidential Press Conferences*, Vol. 9, 430, 433.

470 **Privately, of course, he was enraged:** *NYT*, June 16, 1937; Landon to Clapper, June 14, 1937, Clapper Papers, Box 48, LOC; Clapper Diary, June 10, 14, 1937, LOC.

471 **"Will the Democrats Divide?":** *The Nation*, May 26, 1937, 60–61; HSC Diary, June 11, 1937, 66, UVA.

471 **On June 16, only two days:** Alsop and Catledge, *168 Days*, 241–42; Leuchtenburg, "FDR's Court-Packing Plan," 677; *NYT*, June 28, 1937; Ickes, June 23, 1937, *Secret Diary*, Vol. II, 155; *NYT*, June 18, 1937; *WP*, June 22, 1937.

472 **"Everything very depressing":** Clapper Diary, June 23, 25, 1937, LOC; *WP*, June 19, 22, 1937.

472 **"The arch enemies of society":** Hughes quoted in Pusey, *Charles Evans Hughes*, Vol. II, 762, 764.

472 **All this weighed heavily on Roosevelt:** Farley Diary, June 18, 1937, LOC; Clapper Diary, June 20, 1937, LOC.

472 **The Jefferson Island retreat:** *Time*, July 22, 1935; *NYT*, June 26, 1937; *CDT*, June 27, 1937; *Time*, June 28, 1937; *NYT*, June 26, 1937; *WP*, June 15, 17, 26, 28, 1937; HSC Diary, June 25, 1937, 71, UVA; *WSJ*, June 26, 1937; Lindsay quoted in Leuchtenburg, "FDR's Court-Packing Plan," 679; *NYT*, June 29, 1937. On June 29, FDR told Ickes that the retreat had strengthened party unity (Ickes, July 1, 1937, *Secret Diary*, Vol. II, 156).

474 **"Nobody got religion":** *WP*, June 26, 29, 1937; Leuchtenburg, "FDR's Court-Packing Plan," 681.

474 **"You know what that means":** Hiram W. Johnson to Hiram W. Johnson, Jr., June 12, 1937, in Burke, *Diary Letters*.

474 **This now seemed inevitable:** *NYT*, June 6, 1937; *Time*, Mar. 14, 1927; *WP*, June 13, 29, 1937; *CDT*, June 27, 1937.

475 **There were other time-worn tactics:** Alsop and Catledge, *168 Days*, 248–50.

475 **Before the Jefferson Island picnic:** *NYT*, July 4, 6, 1937.

476 **"I know how men tire":** Hiram W. Johnson to Hiram W. Johnson, Jr., July 10, 1937, in Burke, *Diary Letters*.

476 **"public opinion will select the victor":** *NYT*, July 6, 1937; Cantril, ed., *Public Opinion*, 150; Leuchtenburg, "FDR's Court-Packing Plan," 681–82; *The Nation*, July 10, 1937, 29.

476 **Neither, one imagined, was their tolerance:** *Time*, Mar. 14, 1927, Jan. 30, 1933, June 24, 1935.

476 **By July 3, union members:** *NYT*, July 4, 6, 1937.

477 **"We . . . had very little difficulty":** HSC Diary, June 22, 28–30, July 1–2, 1937, 69, 72–77, UVA.
477 **Yet, for Roosevelt, it constituted a retreat:** *NYT*, July 2, 3, 1937.

CHAPTER TWENTY-SEVEN: TO FIGHT AGAINST GOD

479 **The heat built up over the Great Plains:** *NYT*, July 9, 10, 1937; *WP*, July 10, 1937.
479 **The residents of Washington:** Leuchtenburg, "FDR's Court-Packing Plan," 682–84; *NYT*, July 15, 1937.
480 **Debate on the substitute bill:** *Time*, July 19, 1937; *Washington, City and Capital,* 231–32.
480 **For the moment, the leader of the opposition:** Alsop and Catledge, *168 Days*, 251–53; Wheeler, *Yankee from the West*, 334–36; *NYT*, July 7, 1937. Wheeler's accounts of the meeting cannot, of course, be taken at face value. I have limited my account to points on which Wheeler's version is in agreement with Alsop and Catledge's.
481 **Joe Robinson entered the green-carpeted:** Alsop and Catledge, *168 Days*, 254–56; *NYT*, July 15, 1937; *Time*, July 7, 8, 11, 19, 1937; *Congressional Record*, Part 6, 6791, 6793–96.
481 **His speech was long:** *Congressional Record*, Part 6, 6796–98; *Time*, July 19, 26, 1937; *WP*, July 15, 1937.
483 **The next two days unfolded:** *Congressional Record*, Part 6, 6879; *NYT*, July 8, 1937.
483 **Then the hostilities resumed:** *NYT*, July 9, 1937; *CDT*, July 9, 1937; *NYT*, July 11, 1937; *Time*, July 19, 1937; *Congressional Record*, Part 6, 6896–97, 6900.
483 **Shedding their self-restraint:** *Congressional Record*, Part 6, 6877, 6982, 6986–87.
484 **Mostly, however, the senators attacked:** *NYT*, July 8, 1937; *Congressional Record*, Part 6, 6800, 6895, 6982.
484 **The bill's supporters also laid:** *NYT*, July 6, 8, 9, 1937; *The Nation*, July 10, 1937, 35; *Congressional Record*, Part 6, 6882–84, 6905–6.
484 **Still, amid this kind of talk:** *Congressional Record*, Part 6, 6889–90, 6920.
485 **During the first few days:** *NYT*, July 10, 1937; *CDT*, July 10, 1937; *Congressional Record*, Part 6, 6966–68, 6972, 6974.
485 **On Friday, Saturday, and . . . Monday:** *Congressional Record*, Part 6, 7022–23, 7054–55.
486 **They were gaining ground:** Alsop and Catledge, *168 Days*, 262; *NYT*, July 11, 14, 1937; Ickes, July 11, 1937, *Secret Diary*, Vol. II, 160.
486 **Before the noon session:** Alsop and Catledge, *168 Days*, 260–63; *NYT*, July 13, 15, 1937; *Time*, July 26, 1937; Ashurst Diary, July 12, 1937, in Sparks, *A Many-Colored Toga*, 376.
487 **He crossed the street:** *NYT*, July 15, 1937; Ashurst Diary, July 14, 1937, in Sparks, *A Many-Colored Toga*, 377.
487 **The rest seemed to do him some good:** *NYT*, July 15, 1937.
488 **"Henry, when will you speak?":** Ashurst Diary, July 13, 1937, in Sparks, *A Many-Colored Toga*, 376.
488 **Robinson, in fact, had no intention:** *Congressional Record*, Part 6, 7141–44; *NYT*, July 14, 15, 1937; *WP*, July 15, 1937; *Time*, July 26, 1937; Alsop and Catledge, *168 Days*, 265–67.
489 **Half an hour later:** *NYT*, July 15, 1937; Ickes, July 16, 1937, *Secret Diary*, Vol. II, 161–62.
489 **At noon, Senator Hattie Caraway:** *Congressional Record*, Part 7, 7153–55 (the statement belongs to Copeland); Borah, press statement, July 14, 1937, Borah Papers, Box 783, LOC; Clapper to O'Mahoney, July 15, 1937, Clapper Papers, Box 230, LOC; *NYT*, July 15, 1937.
490 **A few blamed his opponents:** Charlotte Evans Shaw to Borah, Aug. 14, 1937, Borah Papers, Box 754, LOC; *NYT*, July 15, 1937.
490 **"Finish trip":** Cloyd Laporte to Grenville Clark, in Cousins and Clifford, eds., *Memoirs of a Man*, 25; *WP*, July 15, 1937; Ickes, July 16, 1937, *Secret Diary*, Vol. II, 162; Farley

Diary, July 14, 1937, Farley Papers, Box 41, LOC; *The Nation*, July 24, 1937, 85; *The Nation*, July 10, 1937, 36.

490 **For many of Roosevelt's Democratic opponents:** *NYT*, July 16, 1937; Alsop and Catledge, *168 Days*, 269–70.

491 **There, another fight was brewing:** *NYT*, July 15, 16, 1937; Michelson, *The Ghost Talks*, 182; Leuchtenburg, *The White House Looks South*, 79–82 (Broun quoted at 81–82); Ickes, July 16, 1937, *Secret Diary*, Vol. II, 164.

492 **"My dear Alben":** FDR to Barkley, July 15, 1937, TGC Papers, Box 588, LOC.

493 **"I have no doubt":** HSC Diary, July 15, 1937, 88, UVA; *NYT*, July 16, 17, 1937.

493 **"What the president":** Borah to M. S. Sherman, July 19, 1937, Borah Papers, Box 484, LOC; Farley Diary, July 16, 1937, Farley Papers, Box 41, LOC; Clapper Diary, Aug. 4, 1937, Clapper Papers, Box 8, LOC.

493 **the state funeral of Joe Robinson:** *Time*, July 26, 1937; *NYT*, July 16, 17, 1937; *WP*, July 17, 1937; Alsop and Catledge, *168 Days*, 272–74.

494 **Despite his increasingly dire predicament:** Farley Diary, July 16, 1937, LOC; HSC Diary, July 15, 1937, 86, UVA; Alsop and Catledge, *168 Days*, 273–75; *NYT*, July 17, 1937.

494 **The funeral train:** "Arrangements for the Funeral of the Late Senator Joseph T. Robinson," July 16, 1937, Farley Papers, Box 41, LOC; Farley Diary, July 18, 1937, LOC; *NYT*, July 18, 1937; *Time*, July 26, 1937; *WP*, July 18, 1937.

495 **The train pulled into Little Rock:** Garner quoted in Weller, *Joe T. Robinson*, 167; FDR to Garner, July 7, 1937, in Elliott Roosevelt, ed., *F.D.R.: His Personal Letters, 1928–1945*, Vol. I, 692–93; Alsop and Catledge, *168 Days*, 277–78; *Time*, July 26, 1937; *NYT*, July 19, 1937.

496 **The rolling caucus resumed:** *WP*, July 23, 1937; Farley Diary, July 18, 1937, LOC; Alsop and Catledge, *168 Days*, 279; *NYT*, July 20, 25, 1937.

496 **Events were moving quickly now:** Rosenman OH, 9–10; Ickes, July 21, 1937, *Secret Diary*, Vol. II, 167–68; High Diary, Feb. 9, 1937, FDRL; FDR to FF, July 22, 1937, PSF 135, FDRL; *NYT*, Nov. 9, 1938.

497 **For three hours that afternoon:** *NYT*, July 20, 1937; HSC Diary, July 19, 20, 1937, 89–90, 92, UVA.

497 **The next morning, July 20:** *WP*, July 21, 1937; Alsop and Catledge, *168 Days*, 279–80; *NYT*, July 21, 1937; *The Nation*, July 31, 1937, 124. According to Ickes (July 25, 1937, *Secret Diary*, Vol. II, 171), Garner told FDR at a meeting on July 20 that he could still get a Court of eleven—if FDR would agree to Garner's terms on labor and relief policy. By this account—which Ickes heard secondhand from a source he does not identify—FDR refused to cut a deal, prompting Garner to retaliate by allowing a vote to recommit the bill. While possible, this kind of raw, artless horse-trading seems unlikely, especially given the presence in the meeting of loyal Roosevelt men and New Dealers like Barkley and Pittman.

497 **"looking so tired and nervous":** Ickes, July 21, 1937, *Secret Diary*, Vol. II, 165–66, 168–69.

497 **The following morning:** Ickes, July 25, 1937, *Secret Diary*, Vol. II, 171; Farley Diary, July 21, 1937, LOC.

498 **And then within hours:** Wheeler, *Yankee from the West*, 338; Ashurst Diary, July 21, 1937, in Sparks, *A Many-Colored Toga*, 377–78; Alsop and Catledge, *168 Days*, 282–88.

498 **The final act began at 10 a.m.:** Ashurst Diary, July 22, 1937, in Sparks, *A Many-Colored Toga*, 378–79; Alsop and Catledge, *168 Days*, 288–91; *CDT*, July 23, 1937; *Time*, Aug. 2, 1937; Leuchtenburg, "FDR's Court-Packing Plan," 688; Tugwell, *Democratic Roosevelt*, 405.

499 **Two hours later, on the Senate floor:** *Congressional Record*, Part 7, 7375–76, 7381; Baker, *Back to Back*, 271–73; Alsop and Catledge, *168 Days*, 291–94; *WP*, July 23, 1937; Leuchtenburg, "FDR's Court-Packing Plan," 689.

EPILOGUE: WE HAVE ONLY JUST BEGUN TO FIGHT

501 **"I may not know much law":** Theodore Roosevelt quoted in Mason, *Supreme Court from Taft to Burger*, 30.

501 **FDR held his weekly press conference:** Press Conference #383, July 23, 1937, in FDR, *Complete Presidential Press Conferences*, Vol. 10, 58–62; *NYT*, July 24, 1937; Ross, *A Muted Fury*, 20, 155–60, 285–90; Mason, *Supreme Court from Taft to Burger*, 61–64; FDR, Memorandum, n.d. [July 1937], PSF 165, FDRL; Elliott Roosevelt, ed., *F.D.R.: His Personal Letters, 1928–1945*, Vol. I, 686. FDR overstated the case, as he may have been aware. Though state and federal courts did take a more lenient view of reform at the end of the Progressive era, the gains were tentative and the cause unclear. But the 1924 La Follette campaign brought, if anything, a counterreaction in the Supreme Court: the 1920s, after all, were the years of "Holmes, Brandeis and Stone, dissenting."

502 **The correspondents, eager for some kind of explosion:** *Time*, Aug. 2, 1937; Farley to Bowers, July 30, 1937, Farley Papers, Box 5, LOC; Farley Diary, July 23, 1937, LOC.

502 **Chief among them, in Roosevelt's mind:** Ickes, July 25, 1937, *Secret Diary*, Vol. II, 173–74; *NYT*, Aug. 1, 1937; HSC Diary, July 22–23, 1937, 98–99, 101, UVA; Thomas P. Corcoran to TGC, July 25, 1937, TGC Papers, Box 210, LOC; Clapper Diary, Aug. 3, 1937, Clapper Papers, Box 8, LOC; *The Nation*, July 31, 1937, 124.

503 **Felix Frankfurter cited:** FF, Memorandum, n.d. [July–Aug. 1937], in Cohen Papers, Box 13, LOC.

503 **"a combination of imponderables":** Alfange, "The Supreme Court Battle in Retrospect," 497, 500; Jackson OH, 445.

503 **campaign of finger-pointing:** Farley, *Jim Farley's Story*, 80.

504 **Corcoran, Cohen, Frankfurter, Rosenman:** Rosenman, *Working with Roosevelt*, 154; author interviews, David Ginsburg, Jan. 7, 2005, and June 12, 2006; Ickes, July 27, 1937, *Secret Diary*, Vol. II, 177; TGC, draft autobiography, pp. C2, C12, TGC Papers, Box 593, LOC; Hopkins, "A statement to me by Thomas Corcoran . . . , April 3, 1939," Hopkins Papers, Sherwood Collection, Box 299, FDRL; Lasser, *Benjamin V. Cohen*, 168–69. Gardner alone disputed the claims of his two friends Cohen and Corcoran. "My memory," he wrote late in his life, "is entirely clear" that he and the attorney general had met with the pair before the 1937 inauguration to reveal the plan. He even remembered where each man sat—Cummings at his desk, Gardner in a chair in front of it, and Cohen and Corcoran on a sofa to the right. But it would be Gardner's word against theirs, and he showed no interest in pressing his case. (Gardner, "Memories of the 1937 Constitutional Revolution," 14–15; Gardner, *Pebbles*, 77fn; Rauh, "A Personalized View of the Court-Packing Episode"; author interview, David Ginsburg, June 12, 2006.)

504 **One newspaper claimed:** Stokes, "Roosevelt Drops Prof. Frankfurter," *St. Louis Post-Dispatch*, Sept. 21, 1937; Stokes to TGC, Oct. 4, 1937, Stokes to FF, Oct. 6, 1937, and FF to Stokes, Oct. 7, 1937, in TGC Papers, Box 198, LOC; Freedman, *Roosevelt and Frankfurter*, 14, 372.

504 **Of those present at the creation:** Gardner, *Pebbles*, 81.

504 **In August, looking back:** HSC Diary, Aug. 1, 1937, 111–16, UVA.

505 **"the bill started with a black eye":** Rosenman OH, 11–12.

505 **"kept coming back to [the] court thing":** Clapper Diary, June 12, 1938, Clapper Papers, Box 8, LOC; Ickes, Dec. 3, 1938, *Secret Diary*, Vol. II, 511;

505 **"When the history of the court fight":** HSC to Jackson, Nov. 28, 1939, Jackson Papers, Box 11, LOC.

506 **The missing element:** Ickes, July 27, 1937, *Secret Diary*, Vol. II, 175–76; Alsop and Catledge, "The 168 Days," *Saturday Evening Post*, Sept. 18 and Oct. 16, 1937; Cohen to Jane Harris, Sept. 22, 1937, Lash Papers, Box 68, FDRL. Corcoran's hand in this effort is revealed by the extent to which *The 168 Days* parrots, down to the level of the most

minute detail, Corcoran's own account of the fight. Alsop and Corcoran were also friends and dinner party companions; in 1939, Alsop and another collaborator, Robert Kintner, created a similarly heroic portrait of Corcoran in a book called *Men around the President.*

506 **The portrait that the reporters:** Alsop and Catledge, *168 Days*, 10, 74, 78, 109, 185–86.

507 **"a man with fewer doubts than anyone":** Tugwell quoted in Schlesinger, *Coming of the New Deal*, 586; High, "Mr. Roosevelt and the Future," 345; FF to Stone, Feb. 3, 1936, Stone Papers, Box 13, LOC.

507 **Yet Alsop and Catledge were right:** Lash, *Dealers and Dreamers*, 7; Farley, *Behind the Ballots*, 352; Perkins, *The Roosevelt I Knew*, 164.

508 **"to stand still":** *PPA*, 1936, lix–lx.

508 **"forgotten man at the bottom":** *PPA*, 1928–32, 625.

509 **"It took him an unconscionable time":** Tugwell, *Democratic Roosevelt*, 404.

509 **Roosevelt found reason:** High, "Mr. Roosevelt and the Future," 345; FDR to Claude Bowers, Aug. 3, 1937, in Elliott Roosevelt, ed., *F.D.R.: His Personal Letters, 1928–1945*, Vol. I, 704.

510 **He was not unaffected:** Ickes, Aug. 4, 1937, *Secret Diary*, Vol. II, 181–82; HSC Diary, Aug. 12, 1937, 144, UVA.

510 **Over lunch on August 2, Cummings asked him:** HSC Diary, Aug. 2, 1937, 123, UVA; Eleanor Roosevelt quoted in Schlesinger, *Coming of the New Deal*, 586.

511 **Especially not when the fight was ongoing:** TGC to Brant, July 28, 1937, TGC Papers, Box 190, LOC; TGC to Rosenman, July 26, 1937, TGC Papers, Box 211, LOC; FF to FDR, Aug. 9, 1937, TGC Papers, Box 210, LOC; Rosenman to FDR, July 23, 1937, and FDR to Rosenman, Aug. 4, 1937, PPF 64, FDRL.

511 **Roosevelt was not alone in this belief:** Author interview, David Ginsburg, June 12, 2006; "Memorandum on Features of Proposed Plan," n.d. [July 1937], PSF 165, FDRL; "Court Reform: A Recess," *The Nation*, Aug. 14, 1937, 163–64; M. A. Matthews to McReynolds, July 23, 1937, McReynolds Papers, Box 2, UVA.

512 **"If opposition is relaxed":** Gannett to V. C. Dwyer, Sept. 17, 1937, and to John J. Watson, Sept. 29, 1937, Gannett Papers, Box 1, Cornell; *NYT*, Aug. 5, 6, 1937.

512 **"Moonshine":** Farley, Address in Akron, Ohio, Aug. 4, 1937, Farley Papers, Box 62, LOC; *NYT*, Aug. 6, 1937.

512 **Not least from the president:** Lash, *Dealers and Dreamers*, 353; TGC interview, Mar. 12, 1980, TGC Papers, Box 596, LOC; Rosenman OH, 161–62.

513 **"I have felt from the start":** Landon to Clapper, Aug. 26, 1937, Clapper Papers, Box 48, LOC.

513 **"your real problem":** Tugwell and Charles W. Taussig to FDR, July 21, 1937, Tugwell Papers, Box 41, FDRL; Tugwell to FDR, Aug. 26, 1937, in McJimsey, *Documentary History*, Vol. 1, 708.

513 **"He is just as determined":** Farley to Bowers, July 30, 1937, Farley Papers, Box 5, LOC; HSC, Memorandum, July 26, 1937, PSF Justice, Box 56, FDRL; HSC Diary, July 26, 30, 1937, 105–6, 109, UVA.

514 **the president announced his choice:** HSC Diary, Aug. 6, 11, 12, 1937, 126–27, 134, 138–39, UVA; *NYT*, Aug. 13, 1937; Ickes, Aug. 4, 15, 1937; *Secret Diary*, Vol. II, 182–83, 190–91; FF quoted in TGC notes, TGC Papers, Box 270, LOC.

514 **Black, at fifty-one:** Newman, *Hugo Black*, 228, 230, 236; Leuchtenburg, *The White House Looks South*, 84; *WSJ*, Aug. 23, 1937.

514 **"They'll have to take him":** Farley, *Jim Farley's Story*, 98; Michelson, *The Ghost Talks*, 184; "America's Town Meeting of the Air," Feb. 11, 1937, Series 2, No. 13, p. 41, in TGC Papers, Box 272, LOC; Alsop and Catledge, *168 Days*, 299; James Roosevelt quoted in Newman, *Hugo Black*, 236.

515 **The Black nomination, delivered:** *NYT*, Aug. 13, 1937; Newman, *Hugo Black*, 238; Ickes, Aug. 15, 1937, *Secret Diary*, Vol. II, 190; Hiram W. Johnson to Hiram W. Johnson,

Jr., Aug. 14, 1937, in Burke, *Diary Letters*; Nina Gade to Borah, Aug. 13, 1937, and H. M. Weldon to Borah, n.d. [Aug. 1937], Borah Papers, Box 754, LOC; "Salute to Justice Black," *The Nation*, Aug. 21, 1937, 183–84; Brant to TGC, Aug. 13, 1937, TGC Papers, Box 190, LOC.

515 **Black's detractors:** Alsop and Catledge, *168 Days*, 302–3, 311; Catledge to Alsop, Nov. 9, 1937, Alsop Papers, Box 2, LOC; Newman, *Hugo Black*, 239, 244. Newman has found no evidence that FDR knew of Black's membership in the KKK prior to these press reports. On the nature of Black's ties to the Klan, see Newman, 89–100.

515 **"American Lord Macaulays":** *PPA*, 1937, 330–32; *NYT*, Aug. 19, 1937; *WP*, Aug. 19, 1937.

515 **After killing the Court-packing bill:** Among other things, conservative Democrats "chewed [the wages and hours bill] all up with amendments," as Ben Cohen complained, gutted its child labor provision, and then tied the whole thing up in committee; they crippled the housing bill at the urging of private builders; passed a sugar quota act that FDR had promised to veto; and refused to act on "must" legislation to limit crop production, reorganize the executive branch, or set up "little" TVAs across the nation. *The Nation*, Aug. 21, 1937, 187–88; *The New Republic*, Aug. 18, 1937, 32; Cohen to Jane Harris, Aug. 15, 1937, Lash Papers, Box 68, FDRL; *The New Republic*, Sept. 1, 1937, 90; *Time*, Aug. 30, 1937; *WSJ*, July 23, 1937.

516 **The congressional session, which had begun:** *WP*, Aug. 21, 22, 1937; *CDT*, Aug. 22, 1937.

516 **On that fitting note:** Beard, *America in Midpassage*, 368–69; *The New Republic*, Aug. 4, 1937, 348.

516 **"a real show-down":** HSC to FDR, Aug. 17, 1937, HSC Papers, Box 170, UVA; *Time*, Aug. 16, 1937.

517 **Roosevelt could still veto the bill:** FDR to Judge J. Warren Davis, Aug. 11, 1937, PSF 165, FDRL; HSC Diary, Aug. 7, 24, 1937, 129–30, 159–60, UVA; *PPA*, 1937, 338–40; Tugwell, *Democratic Roosevelt*, 407; *WP*, Aug. 26, 1937.

517 **September 17, 1937:** *Time*, Sept. 27, 1937; Freedman, *Roosevelt and Frankfurter*, 409–16; Rosenman, *Working with Roosevelt*, 163–64.

517 **"a layman's document":** FDR, Reading Copy, Address on Constitution Day, Sept. 17, 1937, 2, 5–6, 8–17, Speech Files, Box 33, FDRL; FF to FDR, Sept. 17, 1937, in Freedman, *Roosevelt and Frankfurter*, 417.

518 **"nothing *more* sacred about that branch":** This stinging line—"that branch furthest removed from the people"—was added in pencil by FDR between the typed lines of text; for this reason, perhaps, it does not appear in the "official" version in the *PPA*. FDR, Reading Copy, Address on Constitution Day, Sept. 17, 1937, 13, Speech Files, Box 33, FDRL.

518 **"I agree with you . . .":** Hughes to Stone, Aug. 10, 1937, Stone Papers, Box 75, LOC.

519 **Yet fewer of those detractors:** Ickes, Apr. 10, 1938, *Secret Diary*, Vol. II, 365; Irons, *New Deal Lawyers*, 290–91.

519 **"American constitutional law":** Corwin, "The Court Sees a New Light," *The New Republic*, Aug. 4, 1937, 354; G. Edward White, *The Constitution and the New Deal*, 4, 165, 202, 310–11; Cushman, *Rethinking the New Deal Court*, 41, 43; Friedman, "Switching Time," 1979–81; Ross, *The Chief Justiceship of Charles Evans Hughes*, 134, 142, 146, 167, 249; Irons, *New Deal Lawyers*, 292–94; Paul L. Murphy, *The Constitution in Crisis Times*, 160–61, 169; Rosen, *The Most Democratic Branch*, 42; Ackerman, *We the People: Transformations*, 368–69, 373.

520 **"Things were happening":** *PPA*, 1937, lxii; High, "Roosevelt: Democratic or Dictatorial?", 484–86; Bryce, *The American Commonwealth*, Vol. I, 406–7.

520 **"A good many of the people":** Davis, "Post-Convention Reflections," 417; Ackerman, *We the People: Transformations*, 291, 305, 312, 380.

521 **It is an abiding irony:** Steamer, *Chief Justice*, 74–75; Pearson and Allen, *The Nine Old Men*, 89, 96–97; Hughes, *Supreme Court*, 50; Hendel, *Charles Evans Hughes and the Supreme Court of the United States*, 279.

522 **"Looking back," Roberts reflected:** Roberts, *The Court and the Constitution*, 61; Mason, "Charles Evans Hughes," 6fn, 17; Hughes, *Conditions of Progress*, 30.

522 **"We lost the battle":** Quoted, for example, in Richberg, *My Hero*, 226.

522 **"a clear-cut victory":** *PPA*, 1937, lxvi, lxix. FDR also attributed the Court's change to the 1936 election results (*PPA*, 1935, 14).

522 **bent before the storm:** See Friedman, *The Will of the People*, especially 370–85.

522 **Some, like Chief Justice William Rehnquist:** William Rehnquist, "2004 Year-End Report on the Federal Judiciary," 8, accessed at www.supremecourtus.gov/publicinfo/2004year-endreport.pdf.

523 **Hughes objected violently:** Danelski and Tulchin, eds., *Autobiographical Notes*, 311–13; *The New Yorker*, Apr. 10, 1937; Mason, *Supreme Court: Vehicle*.

523 **But this is a false dichotomy:** The strongest argument for collapsing these false categories has been made by Kalman, "The Constitution, the Supreme Court, and the New Deal," especially 1073–79, and by Brinkley, "Introduction," 1049–50. For contrasting views, see Leuchtenburg, "Comment on Laura Kalman's Article," 1081–92; and White, "Constitutional Change and the New Deal," especially 1114–15. Also see Ackerman, *We the People: Transformations*, 291.

524 **"individual initiative, self-reliance":** Sutherland to Henry M. Bates, Apr. 21, 1937, Sutherland Papers, Box 6, LOC.

524 **"Who knows what causes":** Roberts quoted in Pusey, "Justice Roberts' 1937 Turnaround," 106.

524 **"the recalcitrant Senators will want":** Hiram W. Johnson to Hiram W. Johnson, Jr., July 24, 1937, in Burke, *Diary Letters*; Farley, *Behind the Ballots*, 95–96.

524 **The New Deal never recovered:** Brinkley, *The End of Reform*, 3, 20.

524 **Conservative Democrats were further emboldened:** Chandler, *America's Greatest Depression*, 130; Patterson, *Congressional Conservatism*, 188–90, 202–6; Kennedy, *Freedom from Fear*, 340, 350–51.

525 **In retrospect it seems clear:** Brinkley, *The End of Reform*, 6–17; Patterson, *Congressional Conservatism*, 127, 162–63; Ickes, Mar. 30, 1938, *Secret Diary*, Vol. II, 350.

525 **Roosevelt . . . had some fight left:** Rosenman, *Working with Roosevelt*, 175–77; Seth Thomas to Henry Wallace, July 23, 1937, PSF 165, FDRL; *PPA*, 1938, 391–440; Milkis, *The President and the Parties*, 77, 83–87; Patterson, *Congressional Conservatism*, 288–90. Robert Caro points out that even had FDR succeeded in ousting every one of the men he campaigned against, it would not have substantially altered the composition of the Senate (Caro, *Master of the Senate*, 64).

526 **"There is a mysterious cycle":** *PPA*, 1936, 235–36; Kennedy, *Freedom from Fear*, 454–55, 464; Ackerman, *We the People: Transformations*, 357–58.

527 **On the morning of March 4, 1939:** *NYT*, Mar. 1, 3, 5, 1939.

527 **The two rivals:** *NYT*, Mar. 5, 1939; *WP*, Mar. 5, 1939.

528 **"took on the color":** *WP*, Mar. 5, 1939.

528 **"If our checks and balances":** *NYT*, Mar. 5, 1939.

528 **"You have heard the phrase":** *PPA*, 1939, 149.

529 **"a world in turmoil":** *NYT*, Mar. 5, 1939; *PPA*, 1939, 152–53; *WP*, Mar. 5, 1939.

529 **Facing a common enemy:** *PPA*, 1939, 153; *NYT*, Mar. 5, 1939.

529 **"What would have happened":** Hofstadter, *American Political Tradition*, 338.

BIBLIOGRAPHY

MANUSCRIPT COLLECTIONS AND PERSONAL PAPERS

Joseph Alsop Papers, Library of Congress, Washington, D.C.
William Edgar Borah Papers, Library of Congress, Washington, D.C.
Stuart Chase Papers, Library of Congress, Washington, D.C.
Raymond Clapper Papers, Library of Congress, Washington, D.C.
Benjamin V. Cohen Papers, Library of Congress, Washington, D.C.
Thomas G. Corcoran Papers, Library of Congress, Washington, D.C.
Homer S. Cummings Papers, University of Virginia, Charlottesville, Virginia
James Farley Papers, Library of Congress, Washington, D.C.
Felix Frankfurter Papers, Library of Congress, Washington, D.C.
Frank E. Gannett Papers, Cornell University, Ithaca, New York
Stanley High Papers, Franklin D. Roosevelt Presidential Library, Hyde Park, New York
Richmond P. Hobson Papers, Library of Congress, Washington, D.C.
Harry Hopkins Papers, Franklin D. Roosevelt Presidential Library, Hyde Park, New York
Charles Evans Hughes Papers, Library of Congress, Washington, D.C.
Robert H. Jackson Papers, Library of Congress, Washington, D.C.
John Knox Papers, University of Chicago, Chicago, Illinois
Joseph Lash Papers, Franklin D. Roosevelt Presidential Library, Hyde Park, New York
Carl McFarland Papers, University of Virginia School of Law, Charlottesville, Virginia
James Clark McReynolds Papers, University of Virginia School of Law, Charlottesville, Virginia
Joseph L. Raugh, Jr. Papers, Library of Congress, Washington, D.C.
Donald Richberg Papers, Library of Congress, Washington, D.C.
Franklin D. Roosevelt Papers, Presidential Library, Hyde Park, New York
James Roosevelt Papers, Franklin D. Roosevelt Presidential Library, Hyde Park, New York
Harlan Fiske Stone Papers, Library of Congress, Washington, D.C.
George Sutherland Papers, Library of Congress, Washington, D.C.
Willis Van Devanter Papers, Library of Congress, Washington, D.C.
Burton K. Wheeler Papers, Montana Historical Society, Helena, Montana

PERSONAL INTERVIEWS

Bennett Boskey, Washington, D.C., August 18, 2005
Ralph Brenner, telephone interview, October 16, 2006
Austin Cunningham, telephone interview, December 6, 2005
David Ginsburg, Washington, D.C., January 7, 2005, and June 12, 2006

ORAL HISTORY TRANSCRIPTS

Columbia University, New York
Marquis Childs
Robert H. Jackson
Frances Perkins
Samuel Rosenman

BOOKS

Abraham, Henry J. *The Judicial Process*. 5th ed. New York: Oxford University Press, 1986.
Ackerman, Bruce. *We the People: Foundations*. Cambridge, MA: Harvard University Press, 1991.
———. *We the People: Transformations*. Cambridge, MA: Harvard University Press, 1998.
Adverse Report of the Committee on the Judiciary on a Bill to Reorganize the Judicial Branch of the Government. Stamford, CT: Overbrook Press, 1937.
Alfange, Dean. *The Supreme Court and the National Will*. Garden City, NY: Doubleday, Doran & Co., 1937.
Alsop, Joseph. *FDR: A Centenary Remembrance*. New York: Viking, 1982.
———, with Adam Platt. *"I've Seen the Best of It": Memoirs*. New York: W. W. Norton, 1992.
———, and Robert Kintner. *Men around the President*. New York: Doubleday, Doran & Co., 1939.
———, and Turner Catledge. *The 168 Days*. Garden City, NY: Doubleday, Doran & Co., 1938.
Alter, Jonathan. *The Defining Moment: FDR's Hundred Days and the Triumph of Hope*. New York: Simon & Schuster, 2006.
Amar, Akhil Reed. *America's Constitution: A Biography*. New York: Random House, 2005.
Arkes, Hadley. *The Return of George Sutherland: Restoring a Jurisprudence of Natural Rights*. Princeton, NJ: Princeton University Press, 1994.
Baker, Leonard. *Back to Back: The Duel between FDR and the Supreme Court*. New York: Macmillan, 1967.
———. *Brandeis and Frankfurter: A Dual Biography*. New York: Harper & Row, 1984.
Baker, Richard A., and Roger H. Davidson, eds. *First Among Equals: Outstanding Senate Leaders of the Twentieth Century*. Washington, DC: Congressional Quarterly, 1991.
Barnes, William R., and A.W. Littlefield, eds. *The Supreme Court Issue and the Constitution*. New York: Barnes & Noble, 1937.
Beard, Charles A., and Mary R. Beard. *America in Midpassage*. New York: Macmillan, 1939.
Bellush, Bernard. *Franklin D. Roosevelt as Governor of New York*. New York: Columbia University Press, 1955.
Bickel, Alexander M. *The Least Dangerous Branch: The Supreme Court at the Bar of Politics*. Indianapolis: Bobbs-Merrill, 1962.
Black, Conrad. *Franklin Delano Roosevelt: Champion of Freedom*. New York: Public Affairs, 2003.
The Blue Book of Washington, D.C., 1933 Spring Issue. Washington, DC: Blue Book Publishing Co., 1933.
Blum, John Morton. *From the Morgenthau Diaries: Years of Crisis, 1928–1938*. Boston: Houghton Mifflin, 1959.
———. *The Republican Roosevelt*. Cambridge, MA: Harvard University Press, 1954.
Bordo, Michael D., Claudia Goldin, and Eugene N. White, eds. *The Defining Moment: the Great Depression and the American Economy in the Twentieth Century*. Chicago: University of Chicago, 1998.
Boskey, Bennett. *Some Joys of Lawyering: Selected Writings, 1946–2007*. Washington, DC: Green Bag, 2007.

Brant, Irving. *Storm over the Constitution.* Indianapolis: Bobbs-Merrill, 1936.

Brayman, Harold. *The President Speaks Off-the-Record.* Princeton, NJ: Dow Jones, 1976.

Brinkley, Alan. *The End of Reform: New Deal Liberalism in Recession and War.* New York: Knopf, 1995.

———. *Voices of Protest: Huey Long, Father Coughlin, and the Great Depression.* New York: Knopf, 1982.

Brown, Francis Joseph. *The Social and Economic Philosophy of Pierce Butler.* Diss., Catholic University of America. Washington, DC: Catholic University of America Press, 1945.

Bruce, Philip Alexander. *The Virginia Plutarch.* Two vols. Chapel Hill: University of North Carolina, 1929.

Bryce, James. *The American Commonwealth,* Vols. 1 and 2. 3rd ed. New York: Macmillan, 1909.

Buhite, Russell D., and David W. Levy, eds. *FDR's Fireside Chats.* Norman: University of Oklahoma Press, 1992.

Burke, Robert E., ed. *The Diary Letters of Hiram Johnson,* Vol. 6, *1934–1938.* New York: Garland, 1983.

Burns, James MacGregor. *Roosevelt: The Lion and the Fox.* New York: Harcourt, Brace and Co., 1956.

Cantril, Hadley, ed. *Public Opinion, 1935–1946.* Princeton, NJ: Princeton University Press, 1951.

Cardozo, Benjamin N. *The Nature of the Judicial Process.* New Haven, CT: Yale University Press, 1921.

Caro, Robert A. *The Years of Lyndon Johnson: The Path to Power.* New York: Knopf, 1983.

———. *The Years of Lyndon Johnson: Master of the Senate.* New York: Knopf, 2002.

Chandler, Lester V. *America's Greatest Depression, 1929–1941.* New York: Harper & Row, 1970.

Childs, Marquis W. *They Hate Roosevelt!* New York: Harper & Brothers, 1936.

———. *Witness to Power.* New York: McGraw-Hill, 1975.

Cobb, James C., and Michael V. Namorato, eds. *The New Deal and the South.* Jackson, MS: University Press of Mississippi, 1984.

Cohen, Adam. *Nothing to Fear: FDR's Inner Circle and the Hundred Days That Created Modern America.* New York: Penguin, 2009.

Colman, Elizabeth Wheeler. *Mrs. Wheeler Goes to Washington.* Helena, MT: Falcon Press, 1989.

Congressional Record, 75th Cong., 1st Sess., Vol. 81, Parts 6 and 7. Washington, DC: U.S. Government Printing Office, 1937.

Cook, Blanche Wiesen. *Eleanor Roosevelt,* Vol. 2, *1933–1938.* New York: Viking, 1999.

Cope, Alfred Haines, and Fred Krinsky, eds. *Franklin D. Roosevelt and the Supreme Court.* Boston: D.C. Heath, 1952.

Corwin, Edward S. *The Commerce Power Versus States Rights: "Back to the Constitution."* Princeton, NJ: Princeton University, 1936.

———. *Constitutional Revolution, Ltd.* Claremont, CA: Claremont Colleges, 1941.

———. *The President: Office and Powers, 1787–1957.* 4th ed. New York: New York University, 1957.

———. *The Twilight of the Supreme Court.* New Haven, CT: Yale University Press, 1934.

Cousins, Norman, and J. Garry Clifford, eds. *Memoirs of a Man: Grenville Clark. Collected by Mary Clark Dimond.* New York: W. W. Norton, 1975.

Creel, George. *Rebel at Large: Recollections of Fifty Crowded Years.* New York: G.P. Putnam's Sons, 1947.

Cummings, Homer. *Modern Tendencies and the Law.* Washington, DC: U.S. Government Printing Office, 1933.

———, and Carl McFarland. *Federal Justice.* New York: Macmillan, 1937.

Cushman, Barry. *Rethinking the New Deal Court: The Structure of a Constitutional Revolution.* New York: Oxford University Press, 1998.

Dallek, Robert. *Lone Star Rising: Lyndon Johnson and His Times, 1908–1960*. New York: Oxford University Press, 1991.

Danelski, David J., and Joseph S. Tulchin, eds. *The Autobiographical Notes of Charles Evans Hughes*. Cambridge, MA: Harvard University Press, 1973.

Davis, Kenneth S. *FDR: The Beckoning of Destiny, 1882–1928*. New York: G.P. Putnam's Sons, 1972.

———. *FDR: The New York Years, 1928–1933*. New York: Random House, 1985.

———. *FDR: The New Deal Years, 1933–1937*. New York: Random House, 1986.

———. *FDR: Into the Storm, 1937–1940*. New York: Random House, 1993.

Douglas, William O. *Go East, Young Man: The Early Years*. New York: Random House, 1974.

Elman, Philip, ed. *Of Law and Men: Papers and Addresses of Felix Frankfurter, 1939–1956*. New York: Harcourt, Brace and Co., 1956.

Ernst, Morris L. *The Ultimate Power*. Garden City, NY: Doubleday, Doran & Co., 1937.

Essary, J. Frederick. *Covering Washington*. Boston: Houghton Mifflin, 1927.

Fallon, Richard H., Jr. *The Dynamic Constitution*. New York: Cambridge University Press, 2004.

Farley, James A. *Behind the Ballots: The Personal History of a Politician*. New York: Harcourt, Brace, 1938.

———. *Jim Farley's Story: The Roosevelt Years*. New York: Whittlesey House, 1948.

Feinstein, Isidor (I. F. Stone). *The Court Disposes*. New York: Covici, Friede, 1937.

Frankfurter, Felix, recorded in talks with Harlan B. Phillips. *Felix Frankfurter Reminisces*. New York: Reynal & Company, 1960.

———, and James M. Landis. *The Business of the Supreme Court: A Study in the Federal Judicial System*. New York: Macmillan, 1927.

Fraser, Steven. *Labor Will Rule: Sidney Hillman and the Rise of American Labor*. New York: The Free Press, 1991.

Frederick, David C. *Rugged Justice: The Ninth Circuit Court of Appeals and the American West, 1891–1941*. Berkeley: University of California Press, 1994.

Freedman, Max, ed. *Roosevelt and Frankfurter: Their Correspondence, 1928–1945*. Boston: Little, Brown, 1967.

Freidel, Frank. *F.D.R. and the South*. Baton Rouge: Louisiana State University, 1965.

———. *Franklin D. Roosevelt: The Triumph*. Boston: Little, Brown, 1956.

———. *Franklin D. Roosevelt: Launching the New Deal*. Boston: Little, Brown, 1973.

Friedman, Barry. *The Will of the People: How Public Opinion Has Influenced the Supreme Court and Shaped the Meaning of the Constitution*. New York: Farrar, Straus and Giroux, 2009.

Gallup, George H. *The Gallup Poll: Public Opinion, 1935–1971*, Vol. 1, *1935–1948*. New York: Random House, 1972.

Gardner, Warner W. *Pebbles from the Paths Behind: The Public Path, 1909–1947*. Warner W. Gardner, 1989.

Garraty, John A., ed. *Quarrels That Have Shaped the Constitution*. New York: Harper & Row, 1964.

Garry, Patrick M. *An Entrenched Legacy: How the New Deal Constitutional Revolution Continues to Shape the Role of the Supreme Court*. University Park, PA: Pennsylvania State University Press, 2008.

Gilbert, Clinton W. *The Mirrors of Washington*. New York: G.P. Putnam's Sons, 1921.

Hall, Kermit L., ed. *The Least Dangerous Branch: Separation of Powers and Court-Packing. The Supreme Court in American Society*, Vol. 5. New York: Garland, 2000.

———, ed. *The Oxford Companion to the Supreme Court of the United States*. New York: Oxford University Press, 1992.

———, and Kevin T. McGuire, eds. *The Judicial Branch*. New York: Oxford University Press, 2005.

Hamby, Alonzo L. *For the Survival of Democracy: Franklin Roosevelt and the World Crisis of the 1930s*. New York: Free Press, 2004.

Hellman, George S. *Benjamin N. Cardozo: American Judge*. New York: Russell & Russell, 1940.

Hendel, Samuel. *Charles Evans Hughes and the Supreme Court*. New York: King's Crown Press, Columbia University: 1951.

Henry, John M. *Nine Above the Law: Our Supreme Court*. Pittsburgh: R.T. Lewis, 1936.

Hoar, George F. *The Charge Against President Grant and Attorney General Hoar of Packing the Supreme Court of the United States, to Secure the Reversal of the Legal Tender Decision, by the Appointment of Judges Bradley and Strong, Refuted. Letter to the Boston Herald*. Worcester, MA: Charles Hamilton, 1896.

Hofstadter, Richard. *The Age of Reform*. New York: Knopf, 1955.

———. *The American Political Tradition and the Men Who Made It*. New York: Knopf, 1948.

Holli, Melvin G. *The Wizard of Washington: Emil Hurja, Franklin Roosevelt, and the Birth of Public Opinion Polling*. New York: Palgrave, 2002.

Hollingsworth, Harold M., and William F. Holmes, eds. *Essays on the New Deal*. Austin: University of Texas Press, 1969.

Hoover, Herbert. *Addresses upon the American Road, 1933–1938*. New York: Charles Scribner's Sons, 1938.

Hughes, Charles Evans. *Addresses and Papers of Charles Evans Hughes, Governor of New York, 1906–1908*. New York: G.P. Putnam's Sons, 1908.

———. *Conditions of Progress in Democratic Government*. New Haven, CT: Yale University Press, 1910.

———. *The Supreme Court of the United States*. New York: Columbia University Press, 1928.

Ickes, Harold L. *The New Democracy*. New York: W. W. Norton, 1934.

———. *The Secret Diary of Harold L. Ickes: Vol. I, The First Thousand Days, 1933–1936*. New York: Simon and Schuster, 1953.

———. *The Secret Diary of Harold L. Ickes: Vol. II, The Inside Struggle, 1936–1939*. New York: Simon & Schuster, 1954.

Irons, Peter H. *The New Deal Lawyers*. Princeton, NJ: Princeton University Press, 1982.

———. *A People's History of the Supreme Court*. New York: Viking, 1999.

Jackson, Robert H. *The Struggle for Judicial Supremacy: A Study of a Crisis in American Power Politics*. New York: Knopf, 1941.

———. *That Man: An Insider's Portrait of Franklin D. Roosevelt*. Edited by John Q. Barrett. New York: Oxford University Press, 2003.

Janeway, Michael. *The Fall of the House of Roosevelt: Brokers of Ideas and Power from FDR to LBJ*. New York: Columbia University Press, 2004.

Jenkins, Roy. *Franklin Delano Roosevelt*. New York: Times Books/Henry Holt, 2003.

Johnsen, Julia E., ed. *Limitation of Power of Supreme Court to Declare Acts of Congress Unconstitutional. The Reference Shelf, Vol. 10, No. 6*. New York: H.W. Wilson, 1935.

Johnson, Claudius O. *Borah of Idaho*. New York: Longmans, Green and Co., 1936.

Kalman, Laura. *Legal Realism at Yale, 1927–1960*. Chapel Hill: University of North Carolina Press, 1986.

Kammen, Michael. *A Machine That Would Go of Itself: The Constitution in American Culture*. New York: Knopf, 1986.

Kaufman, Andrew L. *Cardozo*. Cambridge, MA: Harvard University Press, 1998.

Kaufman, George S., and Morrie Ryskind, with music by George Gershwin and lyrics by Ira Gershwin. *Of Thee I Sing*. New York: A. A. Knopf, 1932.

Keller, Morton. *In Defense of Yesterday: James M. Beck and the Politics of Conservatism, 1861–1936*. New York: Coward-McCann, 1958.

Kennedy, David M. *Freedom from Fear: The American People in Depression and War, 1929–1945*. New York: Oxford University Press, 1999.

Knox, John. *The Forgotten Memoir of John Knox: A Year in the Life of a Supreme Court Clerk in FDR's Washington*. Edited by David J. Garrow and Dennis J. Hutchinson. Chicago: University of Chicago Press, 2002.

Kyvig, David E. *Repealing National Prohibition*. 2nd ed. Kent, OH: Kent State University Press, 2000.

Lash, Joseph P. *Dealers and Dreamers: A New Look at the New Deal*. New York: Doubleday, 1988.

———. *From the Diaries of Felix Frankfurter*. New York: W. W. Norton, 1975.

Lasser, William. *Benjamin V. Cohen: Architect of the New Deal*. New Haven, CT: Yale University Press, 2002.

———. *The Limits of Judicial Power: The Supreme Court in American Politics*. Chapel Hill, NC: University of North Carolina Press, 1988.

Lawrence, David. *Nine Honest Men*. New York: D. Appleton-Century, 1936.

———. *Supreme Court or Political Puppets? Shall the Supreme Court be Free or Controlled by a Supreme Executive?* New York: D. Appleton-Century, 1937.

Leonard, Charles A. *A Search for a Judicial Philosophy: Mr. Justice Roberts and the Constitutional Revolution of 1937*. Port Washington, NY: Kennikat Press National University Publications, 1971.

Leuchtenburg, William E. *Franklin D. Roosevelt and the New Deal*. New York: Harper & Row, 1963.

———. *The Supreme Court Reborn: The Constitutional Revolution in the Age of Roosevelt*. New York: Oxford University Press, 1995.

———. *The White House Looks South: Franklin D. Roosevelt, Harry S. Truman, Lyndon B. Johnson*. Baton Rouge: Louisiana State University Press, 2005.

Levine, Lawrence W., and Cornelia R. Levine. *The People and the President: America's Conversation with FDR*. Boston: Beacon Press, 2002.

Levinson, Sanford. *Constitutional Faith*. Princeton, NJ: Princeton University Press, 1988.

Lodge, Henry Cabot, ed. *The Federalist*. New York: G.P. Putnam's Sons, 1889.

Lora, Ronald, and William Henry Longton, eds. *The Conservative Press in Twentieth-Century America*. Westport, CT: Greenwood Press, 1999.

Louchheim, Katie, ed. *The Making of the New Deal: The Insiders Speak*. Cambridge, MA: Harvard University Press, 1983.

Manchester, William. *The Glory and the Dream: A Narrative History of America, 1932–1972*. Boston: Little, Brown, 1974.

———. *The Last Lion: Winston Spencer Churchill, Visions of Glory: 1874–1932*. Boston: Little, Brown, 1983.

Martin, George. *CCB: The Life and Century of Charles C. Burlingham, New York's First Citizen, 1858–1959*. New York: Hill and Wang, 2005.

Mason, Alpheus Thomas. *Brandeis: A Free Man's Life*. New York: Viking, 1946.

———. *Harlan Fiske Stone: Pillar of the Law*. New York: Viking, 1956.

———. *The Supreme Court from Taft to Burger*. 3rd ed. Baton Rouge: Louisiana State University Press, 1979.

———. *The Supreme Court: Vehicle of Revealed Truth or Power Group, 1930–1937*. Boston: Boston University Press, 1953.

McBain, Howard Lee. *The Living Constitution*. New York: Macmillan, 1928.

McCullough, David. *Truman*. New York: Simon & Schuster, 1992.

McJimsey, George, general ed. *Documentary History of the Franklin D. Roosevelt Presidency. Vol. 1, "Packing" the Supreme Court and the Judicial Reorganization Bill, January–July 1937*. University Publications of America, 2001.

———. *Documentary History of the Franklin D. Roosevelt Presidency. Vol. 22, Schechter Case and Unconstitutionality of the NRA, 1935*. LexisNexis, 2004.

McKean, David. *Tommy the Cork: Washington's Ultimate Insider from Roosevelt to Reagan*. Hanover, NH: Steerforth Press, 2004.

McKenna, Marian C. *Borah*. Ann Arbor: University of Michigan Press, 1961.

———. *Franklin Roosevelt and the Great Constitutional War: The Court-Packing Crisis of 1937*. New York: Fordham University Press, 2002.

Michelson, Charles. *The Ghost Talks*. New York: G.P. Putnam's Sons, 1944.

Milkis, Sidney M. *Political Parties and Constitutional Government: Remaking American Democracy*. Baltimore: Johns Hopkins University Press, 1999.

———. *The President and the Parties: The Transformation of the American Party System since the New Deal*. New York: Oxford University Press, 1993.

———, and Jerome M. Mileur, eds. *The New Deal and the Triumph of Liberalism*. Boston: University of Massachusetts Press, 2002.

Moley, Raymond. *After Seven Years*. New York: Harper & Brothers, 1939.

———. *Our Criminal Courts*. New York: Minton, Balch & Co., 1930.

Morgan, Ted. *FDR: A Biography*. New York: Simon and Schuster, 1985.

Murphy, Paul L. *The Constitution in Crisis Times, 1918–1969*. New York: Harper & Row, 1972.

Murphy, Walter F. *Congress and the Court*. Chicago: University of Chicago Press, 1962.

Namorato, Michael Vincent, ed. *The Diary of Rexford G. Tugwell: The New Deal, 1932–1935*. Westport, CT: Greenwood Press, 1992.

Nash, Gerald D., ed. *Franklin Delano Roosevelt*. Englewood Cliffs, NJ: Prentice-Hall, 1967.

Neal, Steve. *Happy Days Are Here Again*. New York: William Morrow, 2004.

Newman, Roger K. *Hugo Black: A Biography*. New York: Pantheon, 1994.

Nichols, Egbert Ray, ed. *Congress or the Supreme Court: Which Shall Rule America? The University Debaters' Help Book*, Vol. II. New York: Noble and Noble, 1935.

O'Brien, David M. *Storm Center: The Supreme Court in American Politics*. New York: W. W. Norton, 1986.

Paschal, Joel Francis. *Mr. Justice Sutherland: A Man Against the State*. Princeton, NJ: Princeton University Press, 1951.

Patterson, James T. *Congressional Conservatism and the New Deal: The Growth of the Conservative Coalition in Congress, 1933–1939*. Lexington, KY: University of Kentucky Press, 1967.

Pearson, Drew, and Robert S. Allen. *The Nine Old Men*. Garden City, NY: Doubleday, Doran & Co., 1937.

———. *Nine Old Men at the Crossroads*. Garden City, NY: Doubleday, Doran & Co., 1937.

Perkins, Frances. *The Roosevelt I Knew*. New York: Viking, 1946.

Post, Charles Gordon, Jr. *The Supreme Court and Political Questions. The Johns Hopkins University Studies in Historical and Political Science, Series LIV, No. 4*. Baltimore: Johns Hopkins Press, 1936.

Pritchett, C. Herman. *The Roosevelt Court*. New York: Macmillan, 1948.

Pusey, Merlo J. *Charles Evans Hughes*, Vols. I and II. New York: Macmillan, 1951.

———. *The Supreme Court Crisis*. New York: Macmillan, 1937.

Purcell, Edward A., Jr. *The Crisis of Democratic Theory: Scientific Naturalism and the Problem of Value*. Lexington: University Press of Kentucky, 1973.

Reorganization of the Federal Judiciary: Hearings Before the Committee on the Judiciary, United States Senate, 75th Cong., 1st Sess., on S. 1392, A Bill to Reorganize the Judicial Branch of the Government. Parts 1–6. Washington, DC: U.S. Government Printing Office, 1937.

Richberg, Donald. *My Hero*. New York: G.P. Putnam's Sons, 1954.

———. *The Rainbow*. Garden City, NY: Doubleday, Doran, 1936.

Roberts, Owen J. *The Court and the Constitution: The Oliver Wendell Holmes Lectures*. Cambridge, MA: Harvard University Press, 1951.

Rodell, Fred. *Nine Men: A Political History of the Supreme Court from 1790 to 1955*. New York: Random House, 1955.

Roosevelt, Elliott, ed. *F.D.R.: His Personal Letters, 1905–1928*. New York: Duell, Sloan and Pearce, 1948.

———. *F.D.R.: His Personal Letters, 1928–1945,* Vols. I and II. New York: Duell, Sloan and Pearce, 1950.

Roosevelt, Franklin D. *Complete Presidential Press Conferences of Franklin D. Roosevelt.* Introduction by Jonathan Daniels. New York: Da Capo Press, 1972.

———. *Looking Forward.* New York: John Day, 1933.

———. *Public Papers and Addresses of Franklin D. Roosevelt,* Vols. 1–5. Compiled and with an introduction by Samuel I. Rosenman. New York: Random House, 1938.

———. *Public Papers and Addresses of Franklin D. Roosevelt,* Vols. 6–8. Compiled and with a foreword by Samuel I. Rosenman. New York: Macmillan, 1941.

———. *Whither Bound?* Boston: Houghton Mifflin, 1926.

Rosen, Jeffrey. *The Most Democratic Branch: How the Courts Serve America.* New York: Oxford, 2006.

Rosenman, Samuel I. *Working with Roosevelt.* New York: Harper, 1952.

Ross, William G. *A Muted Fury: Populists, Progressives, and Labor Unions Confront the Courts, 1890–1937.* Princeton, NJ: Princeton University Press, 1994.

———. *The Chief Justiceship of Charles Evans Hughes, 1930–1941.* Columbia: University of South Carolina Press, 2007.

Schlesinger, Arthur M., Jr. *The Age of Roosevelt: The Crisis of the Old Order, 1919–1933.* Boston: Houghton Mifflin Co., 1957.

———. *The Age of Roosevelt: The Coming of the New Deal.* Boston: Houghton Mifflin Co., 1959.

———. *The Age of Roosevelt: The Politics of Upheaval.* Boston: Houghton Mifflin Co., 1960.

Schudson, Michael. *The Good Citizen: A History of American Civic Life.* New York: The Free Press, 1998.

Scroop, Daniel. *Mr. Democrat: Jim Farley, the New Deal, and the Making of Modern American Politics.* Ann Arbor: University of Michigan Press, 2006.

Seldes, George. *Lords of the Press.* New York: Julian Messner, 1938.

Shaw, Stephen K., William D. Pederson, and Frank J. Williams, eds. *Franklin D. Roosevelt and the Transformation of the Supreme Court.* Armonk, NY: M.E. Sharpe, 2004.

Sherwood, Robert E. *Abe Lincoln in Illinois.* New York: Charles Scribner's Sons, 1937.

———. *Roosevelt and Hopkins: An Intimate History.* New York: Harper, 1948.

Shlaes, Amity. *The Forgotten Man: A New History of the Great Depression.* New York: HarperCollins, 2007.

Shogan, Robert. *Backlash: The Killing of the New Deal.* Chicago: Ivan R. Dee, 2006.

Smith, Jean Edward. *FDR.* New York: Random House, 2007.

Smith, Richard Norton. *The Colonel: The Life and Legend of Robert R. McCormick, 1880–1955.* Boston: Houghton Mifflin, 1997.

Solomon, Burt. *FDR v. The Constitution: The Court-Packing Fight and the Triumph of Democracy.* New York: Walker & Company, 2009.

Sparks, George F., ed. *A Many-Colored Toga: The Diary of Henry Fountain Ashurst.* Tucson: University of Arizona Press, 1962.

Spencer, Herbert. *Social Statics, Abridged and Revised; Together with Man Versus the State.* New York: D. Appleton, 1892.

Steamer, Robert J. *Chief Justice: Leadership and the Supreme Court.* Columbia: University of South Carolina, 1986.

Stephenson, Donald Grier, Jr. *Campaigns and the Court: The U.S. Supreme Court in Presidential Elections.* New York: Columbia University Press, 1999.

Swisher, Carl Brent. *American Constitutional Development.* 2nd ed. Cambridge, MA: Riverside Press, 1954.

———, ed. *Selected Papers of Homer Cummings, Attorney General of the United States, 1933–1939.* Washington, DC: Scribner's, 1939.

Talese, Gay. *The Kingdom and the Power.* New York: World Publication Co., 1969.

Tugwell, Rexford G. *The Democratic Roosevelt*. Garden City, NY: Doubleday & Co., 1957.

———. *Roosevelt's Revolution: The First Year—A Personal Perspective*. New York: Macmillan, 1977.

Tully, Grace. *F.D.R.: My Boss*. New York: Scribner's, 1949.

Twiss, Benjamin R. *Lawyers and the Constitution: How Laissez Faire Came to the Supreme Court*. Princeton, NJ: Princeton University Press, 1942.

United States Department of Commerce, Bureau of Foreign and Domestic Commerce. *Statistical Abstract of the United States 1936*. 58th number. Washington, DC: Government Printing Office, 1936.

Urofsky, Melvin I., and David W. Levy, eds. *The Family Letters of Louis D. Brandeis*. Norman: University of Oklahoma Press, 2002.

———. *"Half Brother, Half Son": The Letters of Louis D. Brandeis to Felix Frankfurter*. Norman: University of Oklahoma Press, 1991.

———. *Letters of Louis D. Brandeis. Vol. V (1921–1941): Elder Statesman*. Albany: State University of New York Press, 1978.

Wallace, William Kay. *Our Obsolete Constitution*. New York: John Day, 1932.

Warburg, James P. *Hell Bent for Election*. Garden City, NY: Doubleday, Doran & Co., 1936.

Ward, Geoffrey C. *Before the Trumpet: Young Franklin Roosevelt, 1882–1905*. New York: Harper & Row, 1985.

———. *A First-Class Temperament: The Emergence of Franklin Roosevelt*. New York: Harper & Row, 1989.

Warren, Charles. *Congress, The Constitution and the Supreme Court*. Boston: Little, Brown, 1925.

———. *The Supreme Court in United States History. Vol. I, 1789–1835; Vol. II, 1836–1918*. Revised ed. Boston: Little, Brown, 1926.

Washington, City and Capital: Federal Writers' Project, Works Progress Administration (American Guide Series). Washington, DC: Government Printing Office, 1937.

Watkins, T. H. *The Great Depression: America in the 1930s*. Boston: Little, Brown, 1993.

———. *Righteous Pilgrim: The Life and Times of Harold L. Ickes, 1874–1952*. New York: Henry Holt, 1990.

Weed, Clyde P. *The Nemesis of Reform: The Republican Party During the New Deal*. New York: Columbia University, 1994.

Weigley, Russell F., ed. *Philadelphia: A 300-Year History*. New York: W. W. Norton, 1982.

Weller, Cecil Edward, Jr. *Joe T. Robinson: Always a Loyal Democrat*. Fayetteville: University of Arkansas Press, 1998.

Wheeler, Burton K., with Paul F. Healy. *Yankee from the West*. Garden City, NY: Doubleday & Co., 1962.

White, G. Edward. *The Constitution and the New Deal*. Cambridge, MA: Harvard University Press, 2000.

White, Graham J. *FDR and the Press*. Chicago: University of Chicago Press, 1979.

Williamson, Samuel T. *Frank Gannett: A Biography*. New York: Duell, Sloan and Pierce, 1940.

Wills, Garry. *Explaining America: The Federalist*. New York: Doubleday, 1981.

Wilson, Woodrow. *Congressional Government: A Study in American Politics*. Boston: Houghton Mifflin, 1885.

———. *Constitutional Government in the United States*. New York: Columbia University Press, 1908.

Wolf, Thomas P., William D. Pederson, and Byron W. Daynes, eds. *Franklin D. Roosevelt and Congress: The New Deal and Its Aftermath*. Armonk, NY: M.E. Sharpe, 2001.

Wolfskill, George. *The Revolt of the Conservatives: A History of the American Liberty League, 1934–1940*. Boston: Houghton Mifflin, 1962.

———, and John A. Hudson, *All but the People: Franklin D. Roosevelt and His Critics, 1933–39*. New York: Macmillan, 1969.

ARTICLES

Acheson, Dean G. "Mr. Justice Cardozo and Problems of Government," *Michigan Law Review*, Vol. 37, No. 4, February 1939: 513–39.

Alfange, Dean. "The Supreme Court Battle in Retrospect," *United States Law Review*, Vol. 71, 1937: 497–502.

Alton, Stephen R. "Loyal Lieutenant, Able Advocate: The Role of Robert H. Jackson in Franklin D. Roosevelt's Battle with the Supreme Court," *William & Mary Bill of Rights Journal*, Vol. 5, No. 2, 1997: 527–618.

Ariens, Michael. "A Thrice-Told Tale, or Felix the Cat," *Harvard Law Review*, Vol. 107, 1994: 620–76.

Brabner-Smith, John W. "Congress vs. Supreme Court—A Constitutional Amendment?" *Virginia Law Review*, Vol. 22, 1935–1936: 665–75.

Brandeis, Louis D. "The Living Law," *Illinois Law Review*, Vol. 10, No. 7, February 1916: 461–71.

Brinkley, Alan. "Introduction," in "AHR Forum: The Debate over the Constitutional Revolution of 1937," *American Historical Review*, Vol. 110, Issue 4, October 2005: 1046–50.

Caldeira, Gregory A. "FDR's Court-Packing Plan in the Court of Public Opinion," Paper prepared for delivery at the 1999 Annual Meeting of the American Political Science Association, Atlanta, GA, September 1–5, 1999.

———. "Public Opinion and the U.S. Supreme Court: FDR's Court-Packing Plan," *The American Political Science Review*, Vol. 81, No. 4, December 1987: 1139–53.

Cantwell, Frank V. "Public Opinion and the Legislative Process," *The American Political Science Review*, Vol. 40, No. 5, October 1946: 924–35.

Carpenter, Charles E. "The President and the Court," *United States Law Review*, Vol. 71, 1937: 139–49.

Carson, Jamie L., and Benjamin A. Kleinerman, "A Switch in Time Saves Nine: Institutions, Strategic Actors, and FDR's Court-Packing Plan," *Public Choice*, Vol. 113, December 2002: 301–24.

Chambers, John W. "The Big Switch: Justice Roberts and the Minimum-Wage Cases," *Labor History*, Vol. 10, No. 1, Winter 1969: 44–73.

"Charles Evans Hughes," *The North American Review*, Vol. 203, No. 726, May 1916: 657–61.

Corwin, Edward S. "The Schechter Case—Landmark, or What?" *New York University Law Quarterly Review*, Vol. 13, No. 2, January 1936: 151–90.

———. "Social Planning under the Constitution—A Study in Perspectives," *The American Political Science Review*, Vol. 26, No. 1, February 1932: 1–27.

Cummings, Homer S. "The State vs. Harold Israel," *Journal of the American Institute of Criminal Law and Criminology*, Vol. 15, May 1924–February 1925: 406–34.

Cushman, Barry. "The Secret Lives of the Four Horsemen," *Virginia Law Review*, Vol. 83, 1997: 559–645.

Davenport, Frederick M. "The Changing Character of Congress," *Boston University Law Review*, Vol. 14, 1934: 299–312.

Davis, Elmer. "Post-Convention Reflections," *Harper's Magazine*, Vol. 173, September 1936: 412–20.

Davis, Kenneth S. "FDR as a Biographer's Problem," *The American Scholar*, Vol. 53, Winter 1983–84: 100–108.

Dawson, Mitchell. "The Supreme Court and the New Deal," *Harper's Magazine*, Vol. 167, November 1933: 641–52.

"The Decision in the NIRA Cases," *United States Law Review*, Vol. 69, No. 6, June 1935: 281–92.

Feinberg, Wilfred. "Constraining 'The Least Dangerous Branch': The Tradition of Attacks on Judicial Power," *New York University Law Review*, Vol. 59, May 1984: 252–76.

Fite, Katherine B., and Louis Baruch Rubinstein, "Curbing the Supreme Court—State Experiences and Federal Proposals," *Michigan Law Review*, Vol. 35, 1936–1937: 762–87.

Fletcher, R.V. "Mr. Justice McReynolds—An Appreciation," *Vanderbilt Law Review*, Vol. 2, 1948: 35–46.

Fraenkel, Osmond K. "What Can Be Done about the Constitution and the Supreme Court?" *Columbia Law Review*, Vol. 37, No. 2, February 1937: 212–26.

Frankfurter, Felix. "Chief Justices I Have Known," *Virginia Law Review*, Vol. 39, No. 7, November 1953: 883–905.

———. "Mr. Justice Roberts," *University of Pennsylvania Law Review*, Vol. 104, No. 3, December 1955: 311–17.

———. "The Supreme Court and the Public," *The Forum*, June 1930: 329–34.

———, and Adrian S. Fisher. "The Business of the Supreme Court at the October Terms, 1935 and 1936," *Harvard Law Review*, Vol. 51, No. 4, February 1938: 577–637.

Freund, Paul A. "Charles Evans Hughes as Chief Justice," *Harvard Law Review*, Vol. 81, No. 4, 1967: 4–43.

Friedman, Richard D. "Chief Justice Hughes' Letter on Court-Packing," *Journal of Supreme Court History*, Vol. 1, 1997: 76–86.

———. "A Reaffirmation: The Authenticity of the Roberts Memorandum, or Felix the Non-Forger," *University of Pennsylvania Law Review*, Vol. 142, June 1994: 1985–95.

———. "Switching Time and Other Thought Experiments: The Hughes Court and Constitutional Transformation," *University of Pennsylvania Law Review*, Vol. 142, June 1994: 1891–1984.

Gardbaum, Stephen. "New Deal Constitutionalism and the Unshackling of the States," *University of Chicago Law Review*, Vol. 64, 1997: 483–566.

Gardner, Warner W. "Harlan Fiske Stone: The View from Below," *The Supreme Court Historical Society Quarterly*, Vol. 22, No. 2, 2001: 1, 8–12.

———. "Memories of the 1937 Constitutional Revolution," *The Supreme Court Historical Society Quarterly*, Vol. 20, No. 1, 1999: 1, 10–18.

———. "Mr. Chief Justice Stone," *Harvard Law Review*, Vol. 59, 1946: 1203–9.

Griswold, Erwin N. "Owen J. Roberts as a Judge," *University of Pennsylvania Law Review*, Vol. 104, 1955–1956: 332–49.

Hart, Henry M., Jr. "The Gold Clause in United States Bonds," *Harvard Law Review*, Vol. 48, No. 7, May 1935: 1057–99.

High, Stanley. "Roosevelt: Democratic or Dictatorial?" *Harper's Magazine*, Vol. 175, October 1937: 480–87.

"Introducing the Youngest Justice of the U.S. Supreme Court," *Current Opinion*, February 1, 1923: 156.

Johnson, Wallace H. "Willis Van Devanter—A 'Re-examination,'" *Wyoming Law Review*, Vol. 1, 2001: 403–12.

Kalman, Laura. "The Constitution, the Supreme Court, and the New Deal," in "AHR Forum: The Debate over the Constitutional Revolution of 1937," *American Historical Review*, Vol. 110, Issue 4, October 2005: 1052–79.

Kutler, Stanley I. "*Ex parte McCardle*: Judicial Impotency? The Supreme Court and Reconstruction Reconsidered," *The American Historical Review*, Vol. 72, No. 3, April 1967: 835–51.

Kyvig, David E. "The Road Not Taken: FDR, the Supreme Court, and Constitutional Amendment," *Political Science Quarterly*, Vol. 104, No. 3, Autumn 1989: 463–81.

Lerner, Max. "Constitution and Court as Symbols," *Yale Law Journal*, Vol. 46, 1937: 1290–1319.

Leuchtenburg, William E. "Charles Evans Hughes: The Center Holds," *North Carolina Law Review*, Vol. 83, June 2005: 1187–1203.

———. "Comment on Laura Kalman's Article," in "AHR Forum: The Debate over the Constitutional Revolution of 1937," *American Historical Review*, Vol. 110, Issue 4, October 2005: 1081–92.

———. "FDR's Court-Packing Plan: A Second Life, a Second Death," *Duke Law Journal*, 1985: 673–89.

———. "The Nine Justices Respond to the 1937 Crisis," *Journal of Supreme Court History*, Vol. 1, 1997: 55–75.

———. "The Origins of Franklin D. Roosevelt's 'Court-Packing' Plan," *The Supreme Court Review*, 1966: 347–400.

Little, Herbert. "The Omnipotent Nine," *The American Mercury*, Vol. 15, No. 57, September 1928: 48–57.

Mason, Alpheus T. "Charles Evans Hughes: An Appeal to the Bar of History," *Vanderbilt Law Review*, Vol. 6, No. 1, December 1952: 1–19.

———. "Has the Supreme Court Abdicated?" *The North American Review*, Vol. 238, No. 4, October 1934: 353–60.

———. "Labor, the Courts, and Section 7(A)," *The American Political Science Review*, Vol. 28, No. 6, December 1934: 999–1015.

McCracken, Robert T. "Owen J. Roberts—Master Advocate," *University of Pennsylvania Law Review*, Vol. 104, 1955: 322–31.

Milburn, George. "The Statesmanship of Mr. Garner," *Harper's Magazine*, Vol. 165, November 1932: 669–82.

Nelson, Michael. "The President and the Court: Reinterpreting the Court-packing Episode of 1937," *Political Science Quarterly*, Vol. 103, No. 2, Summer, 1988: 267–293.

"Notes and Comment: The President and the Court," *United States Law Review*, Vol. 71, 1937: 61–73.

"Party Issues in the Supreme Court," *United States Law Review*, Vol. 69, No. 3, March 1935: 123–32.

Pearson, Drew. "The President-Elect," *Harper's Magazine*, Vol. 166, February 1933: 257–64.

———, and Robert S. Allen. "How the President Works," *Harper's Magazine*, Vol. 173, June 1936: 1–14.

———. "The Men Around the President," *Harper's Magazine*, Vol. 168, February 1934: 267–77.

———. "The President's Trigger Man," *Harper's Magazine*, Vol. 170, March 1935: 385–94.

Polenberg, Richard, "The National Committee to Uphold Constitutional Government, 1937–1941," *The Journal of American History*, Vol. 52, No. 3, December 1965: 582–98.

Powell, Thomas Reed. "The Constitution and Social Security," *Annals of the American Academy of Political and Social Science*, Vol. 181, September 1935: 149–58.

Pusey, Merlo J. "Justice Roberts' 1937 Turnaround," *Supreme Court Historical Society Yearbook 1983*: 102–7.

Ratner, Sidney. "Was the Supreme Court Packed by President Grant?" *Political Science Quarterly*, Vol. 50, No. 3, September 1935: 343–58.

Rauh, Joseph L., Jr. "A Personalized View of the Court-Packing Episode," *Supreme Court Historical Society Yearbook*, 1990.

Soule, George. "Back to States' Rights," *Harper's Magazine*, Vol. 171, September 1935: 484–91.

Stern, Robert L. "The Commerce Clause and the National Economy, 1933–1946," *Harvard Law Review*, Vol. 59, No. 5, May 1946: 645–93.

"Suggested Constitutional Amendments," *United States Law Review*, Vol. 69, No. 8, August 1935: 393–96.

Sullivan, Mark. "The Supreme Court as It Is Today," *Congressional Digest*, December 1933: 296–98.

"Supreme Court Justices as Presidential Candidates," *United States Law Review*, Vol. 69, No. 8, August 1935: 396–408.

Sutherland, William A. "Politics and the Supreme Court," *American Law Review*, Vol. 48, 1914: 390–402.

Tompkins, Raymond S. "Princes of the Press," *The American Mercury*, Vol. 12, No. 45, October 1927: 171–77.

Warren, Charles. "The Progressiveness of the United States Supreme Court," *Columbia Law Review*, Vol. 13, 1913: 294–313.

White, G. Edward. "Constitutional Change and the New Deal: The Internalist/Externalist Debate," in "AHR Forum: The Debate over the Constitutional Revolution of 1937," *American Historical Review*, Vol. 110, Issue 4, October 2005: 1094–115.

Winchester, Boyd. "The Judiciary—Its Growing Power and Influence," *The American Law Review*, Vol. 32, November–December 1898: 801–13.

Wormser, I. Maurice. "The Development of the Law," *American Law Review*, Vol. 58, 1924: 296–316.

INDEX